THE COLLECTED POEMS OF
ROBERT LOUIS STEVENSON

Robert Louis Stevenson by Girolamo, Count Nerli

The Collected Works of Robert Louis Stevenson

General Editor: Catherine Kerrigan

THE COLLECTED POEMS OF ROBERT LOUIS STEVENSON

Edited by

Roger C. Lewis

EDINBURGH UNIVERSITY PRESS

Arrangement and editorial matter © Roger C. Lewis, 2003

Edinburgh University Press Ltd
22 George Square, Edinburgh

Typeset in Goudy by
Norman Tilley Graphics, and
printed and bound in Great Britain by
Antony Rowe Ltd, Chippenham, Wilts

A CIP record for this book is available from the British Library

ISBN 0 7486 1557 1 (hardback)
ISBN 0 7486 1624 1 (paperback)

The right of Roger C. Lewis to be identified as author of this work has been asserted in accordance with the Copyright, Designs and Patents Act 1988.

The publisher acknowledges subsidy from the Scottish Arts Council towards the publication of this volume.

Scottish
Arts Council

Contents

Analytical Table of Contents

UNDERWOODS

Preface by the General Editor

Since his death in 1894, Robert Louis Stevenson's works have continued to find a global audience. His novels, poems, short stories, travel books, essays, criticism, journalism and letters have given countless readers many hours of entertainment and intellectual engagement. Yet the perception of Stevenson as a popular author has often obscured his contribution to world literature. Too often, Stevenson has been dismissed as simply a writer of stories and verses for children when in fact he was one of the most innovative writers of the late nineteenth century. His ideas on literature, language and their social relations are set out in a number of essays which chart his understanding of both the technicalities of his craft and the cultural currents of his day.

While many of Stevenson's works have remained in print, it has become increasingly apparent that these works are corrupted texts which impair the reader's full appreciation of the writer. The purpose of the Centenary Edition is to remedy this situation by producing the first authoritative editions of Stevenson's works. The new editions return to Stevenson's manuscripts, proofs and related materials to examine what the author actually wrote; they will correct long-standing errors and, on occasion, introduce material which Stevenson intended to include but which, for various reasons, was omitted from first editions. In accuracy, authority and authenticity the Centenary Edition improves on all previous editions of Stevenson's works.

No one understood better than Stevenson himself that a literary work does not exist in a cultural vacuum. His comments on copyright, censorship, commercial forces, printing innovations and relations between publishers and authors indicate that he was all too familiar with how such factors could affect the writing and reception of a work. Where appropriate, some account of these factors and their effects will be given so that the reader will have a sense of Stevenson's literary milieu and cultural constituency.

The new editions are clear texts, free from any editorial signals. An editorial commentary and explanatory notes accompany each edition and are designed to enhance the reader's understanding of the various stages of the work from its conception in Stevenson's mind (as recorded in his letters, notes and drafts) through to its production in manuscript and printed form, and on to the work's critical and public reception.

Stevenson began writing as a child in Edinburgh and his first literary efforts were about the domestic and the local. From his birthplace, he travelled to many familiar and unfamiliar parts of the world and chronicled what he saw in factual and fictional forms. His great strength was that he never reduced the particular to the general, but struggled to articulate human circumstance in all its variety and contradiction.

In keeping with the spirit of Stevenson, the Centenary Edition is edited by a group of international scholars whose goal is to recapture the freshness of Stevenson's complex imagination, so that those familiar with his works may discover new pleasures, and those new to them may experience all the excitement of a first encounter with this most enduring 'teller of tales'.

Catherine Kerrigan
University of Guelph

Acknowledgements

A work such as the present edition requires the sympathetic co-operation of both institutions and individuals. Since undertaking this project in 1995, I have had plenty of each kind of help. To the late William E. Fredeman, a true master of scholarly editing, I owe the greatest debt, though regrettably Dick's keen eye never scanned the final MS. The most important part of my research was carried out at the Beinecke Rare Book and Manuscript Library at Yale University, which houses the finest Stevenson collection anywhere; it was originally formed by Edwin J. Beinecke, for whom this great library is named. I am grateful to its Director, Ralph W. Franklin, and his associates, for awarding me a Beinecke Visiting Fellowship in 1997. Vincent Giroud, curator in charge of these vast Stevenson holdings, guided me around the collection and answered my questions tirelessly: his generosity and expertise were invaluable. The Beinecke staff was unfailingly courteous and efficient; I especially wish to thank Stephen Jones and Alfred Mueller.

The Henry E. Huntington Library, Art Collections and Botanical Gardens in San Marino, CA, possesses a superb collection of Stevenson poetry MSS and a setting of unparalleled beauty. I am most grateful to Sara Hodson, Gayle Barkley and the other staff in Literary Manuscripts who accommodated my wife and I in our researches there. At the Huntington I had an opportunity, much to my benefit, to confer with noted Stevensonian Barry Menikoff. Further north at St Helena, CA, there is the unique Silverado Museum, devoted to the life and works of Stevenson. I especially wish to thank curator Ed Reynolds for going well beyond the call of duty in giving me access to MSS, and Trustee John Ritchie for his enthusiastic support of this edition. The academic adviser to Silverado is Roger Swearingen, whose lifelong work as a Stevenson scholar has resulted in numerous important publications which will soon be augmented by a new biography. My consultations with Roger led to the avoidance of several blunders and to some major improvements in the edition.

The Pierpont Morgan Library in New York City was most generous in allowing me to examine and copy their Stevenson MSS. Special thanks are owed to Christine Nelson and Marilyn Palmeri. The New York Public Library staff fetched many MSS and rare books from the Berg Collection for me to examine. Other North American repositories which must be thanked are as follows: the Firestone Library, Princeton University; the Houghton Library, Harvard University; Special Collections, University of British Columbia Library; Special Collections, Haverford College Library (Elisabeth P. Brown); The Rosenbach Museum and Library (Najia Khan); Boston Public Library; Gonzaga University Library.

The National Library of Scotland looked out and copied poetry MSS in their increasingly important Stevenson collection. Dr Iain G. Brown, Principal Curator of the NLS Manuscripts Division, made helpful suggestions and drew some new acquisitions to my attention. Elaine Greig, Curator of the Writers' Museum in Edinburgh, made copies of numerous important documents available to me, provided me with valuable information and hunted for untraced MSS. I wish to thank the staff of the Mitchell Library in Glasgow for their assistance with the Scottish poems. The British Library provided me with unique materials from their Department of Manuscripts and their archive of periodicals.

This edition began with a suggestion made by Wendy Katz, editor of *Treasure Island* in this series, who followed up her original idea with assistance as the work progressed. My General Editor Catherine Kerrigan, who conceived and executed the plan for this series of authoritative editions of Stevenson, guided me throughout; I have depended on her skilled advice in research matters, professional contacts and editing procedures. Catherine also helped me to avoid hazards and deal patiently with setbacks, and she put in many hours of hard work tracking down sources and editing copy. I also wish to thank my Editors at Edinburgh University Press, especially Nicola Carr.

Acadia University offered solid support of my research throughout, in the form of leaves, grants and administrative services: my colleagues there who must be thanked by name are Richard Davies, Gwen Davies, Ralph Stewart and Beert Verstraete. Finally, I must acknowledge the immeasurable assistance of my wife Nancy, who acted as my research assistant both on the road and at home, transcribing and collating texts, examining MSS, writing descriptive and analytic bibliography and proofreading: she is a comma hunter *par excellence*.

Roger C. Lewis
Silverton, British Columbia
26 June 2002

Abbreviations and Symbols

RLS   Robert Louis Stevenson
CP   *Collected Poems of RLS*
JAS   Janet Adam Smith (editor of *CP*, 1950, revd edn 1971)
CGV   *A Child's Garden of Verses*
PW   *Penny Whistles*
UW   *Underwoods*
BAL   *Ballads*
ST   *Songs of Travel*
EDIN   Edinburgh Edition of RLS's *Works*
VAIL   Vailima Edition of RLS's *Works*
TUS   Tusitala Edition of RLS's *Works*
NP   *New Poems* (*TUS*, Vol. XXIII)
BBS I–III   *Poems Hitherto Unpublished*, the Boston Bibliophile Society, I and II in 1916, III in 1921
BRBML   Beinecke Rare Book and Manuscript Library, Yale University
B   all numbered citations preceded by 'B' identify RLS items in Beinecke
HL   Henry E. Huntington Library and Art Gallery, San Marino, CA
H   All numbered citations preceded by H identify RLS items in Huntington
NYPL   Berg Collection in the New York Public Library, New York City, NY
NLS   National Library of Scotland
BL   British Library
LETBM   *The Letters of Robert Louis Stevenson* (1994–5), ed. Booth and Mehew
McKay   *A Stevenson Library: Catalogue of a Collection of Writings By and About Robert Louis Stevenson* (1951–64), compiler George L. McKay

EDITORIAL SYMBOLS

< >   deletion in manuscript or proofsheet
≪ ≫   deletion within a deleted passage
∧ ∧   insertion in manuscript or proofsheet
{ }   insertion by editor
[ ]   conjecture by editor concerning words or date
~   reading agrees with copy-text

Chronology

1850	Robert Louis Stevenson is born 13 November at 8 Howard Place, Edinburgh, the only child of Margaret Isabella Balfour and Thomas Stevenson of the famous family of engineers.
1853	The family moves to 1 Inverleith Terrace.
1857	The family moves to 17 Heriot Row.
1857–67	A sickly child, he first attends school in September 1857. By 1864 his health has improved and in 1867 he is admitted to Edinburgh University, where he studies engineering and becomes a student of Professor Fleeming Jenkin.
1869	Tours the Orkney and Shetland islands on board the steamboat of the Commissioners of Northern Lights.
1871	Decides to abandon engineering and study law.
1873–4	Goes to Suffolk and stays with a Balfour cousin, Maud Babington, and her husband. Contributes to the *Cornhill Magazine*. At the end of the year he goes to Mentone, in the south of France, to spend the winter.
1875	Meets Henley in Edinburgh Royal Infirmary. RLS is called to the Scottish Bar but does not practise law. Joins his cousin Bob Stevenson in France.
1876–7	Takes the canoe trip around the canals of northern France with Sir Walter Simpson recorded in *An Inland Voyage*. Meets Mrs Fanny Van de Grift Osbourne at Paris and Grez. Spends the winter in Edinburgh.
1878	Fanny Osbourne returns to America. RLS goes travelling in the Cevennes with a donkey called Modestine. *An Inland Voyage* *Edinburgh: Picturesque Notes*
1879	Spends time in Edinburgh, London and France.
1880	RLS, Fanny and Lloyd spend the winter of 1880–1 in Davos.
1881	At Pitlochry writes 'The Merry Men' and 'Thrawn Janet'. At Braemar develops the plot of *Treasure Island*.
1882	Returns from Davos to Scotland. Returns to France and moves to Hyères.
1883	*The Silverado Squatters* *Treasure Island*
1884	Returns to Hyères and in May has a major haemorrhage. After a brief visit to Royat returns to England. *Admiral Guinea* *Beau Austin* (both with W. E. Henley)
1885	RLS and Fanny settle at Bournemouth in Skerryvore, the house bought by Thomas Stevenson for Fanny. Henry James (among others) is a frequent visitor. *A Child's Garden of Verses*

Prince Otto
More New Arabian Nights and
The Dynamiter (both with Fanny)
Macaire (with W. E. Henley)

1886   *Strange Case of Dr Jekyll and Mr Hyde*
        Kidnapped

1887   Thomas Stevenson dies in May. RLS, his mother, Fanny and Lloyd sail for
        America.
        The Misadventures of John Nicholson
        The Merry Men and other Tales and Fables
        Memories and Portraits
        Underwoods

1888   *Memoir of Fleeming Jenkin*
        The Black Arrow
        RLS plans a voyage on the *Casco* to the Marquesas, the Paumotus, Tahiti and
        Hawaii. The American publisher S. S. McClure agrees to syndicate the South Sea
        letters.

1889   The *Casco* arrives in Hawaii. Mrs Stevenson returns to Scotland, RLS, Fanny
        and Lloyd remain. RLS visits Father Damien's leper colony at Molokai, sails on
        the schooner *Equator* to the Gilbert Islands and Samoa, where he buys an estate,
        Vailima, at Upolu.
        The Wrong Box (with Lloyd Osbourne)
        The Master of Ballantrae

1890   Sails on the *Janet Nicoll* to the Eastern and Western Pacific. Has a lung haemor-
        rhage. For health reasons decides to live permanently in Samoa.
        The South Seas
        Ballads
        Father Damien

1891   Becomes involved in Samoan politics and writes letters to *The Times*.

1892   *A Footnote to History*
        Across the Plains
        The Wrecker (with Lloyd Osbourne)

1893   RLS is served with The Sedition (Samoa) Regulation 1892.
        Island Nights' Entertainments
        Catriona

1894   Civil order is restored in Samoa. The supporters of Mataafa build 'The Road of
        Loving Hearts' in honour of RLS's help to them during the war.
        The Ebb-Tide (with Lloyd Osbourne)
        On 3 December, after working all morning on *Weir of Hermiston*, RLS collapses
        and dies of a brain haemorrhage. He is buried in Samoa.

1896   *Weir of Hermiston*
1897   *St Ives*

List of Illustrations

The Collected Works of Robert Louis Stevenson

Weir of Hermiston
Edited by Catherine Kerrigan

The Ebb-Tide
Edited by Peter Hinchcliffe and Catherine Kerrigan

Treasure Island
Edited by Wendy Katz

Strange Case of Dr Jekyll and Mr Hyde
Edited by Richard Dury

The Master of Ballantrae
Edited by Ian Duncan

For my son
Simon
1971–1998

'Do thou the deeds I die too young to do.'
Matthew Arnold, *Sohrab and Rustum*

Introduction

I

For much of the twentieth century Stevenson shared with Housman the reputation of a poet popular with adolescents but whom one outgrows. The easy charm of *Requiem*, with its imagery of noble death following heroic exploits 'under the wide and starry sky', or the happy wanderer who introduces *Songs of Travel* were dismissed by the ruling suggestion-givers of modern taste in favour of ironists and iconoclasts. But a growing consensus among readers of late Victorian verse now holds that Stevenson's poetry has been underrated, that the limpid artlessness of his most memorable poems has been confused with slightness. It is arguable that his best verse is as good as his best fiction, and better than much other eighties and nineties poetry with a higher reputation. In the polished lyrics of *Underwoods* he sometimes achieved the classical elegance of his models for occasional verse, Martial and Horace. Lightheartedly disavowing the Horatian imperative to erect a literary monument more lasting than bronze, the poet concluded *Underwoods* by observing that since his family of civil engineers had built so many permanent structures of iron and granite, he could 'play at home with paper like a child'.

Nothing bedevils discussion of Stevenson's achievement as a poet so much as his perverse insistence that he was not a poet. On the publication of his most famous book of poems, *A Child's Garden of Verses*, he wrote to Edmund Gosse, 12 March 1885:

> I have now published on 101 small pages *The Complete Proof of Mr R L Stevenson's Incapacity to Write Verse: in a Series of Graduated Examples with Table of Contents*. I think I shall issue a companion volume of exercises: 'Analyse this poem. Collect and comminate the ugly words.' ... They look ghastly in the cold light of print. (*LETBM*, Vol. V, No. 1403, p. 85)

There is no comparable ambiguity about his abortive career as a playwright: he tried dramatic writing, failed at it and abandoned it. But he wrote and revised poems all his life, planning various collections which he never stopped readying for publication. While still in his teens and early twenties he assembled his verses under such titles as *Little Odes* and *Recruiting Songs*, arranging fair copies in numbered sequence with a title page, although his first volume, *A Child's Garden of Verses*, was not published until he was thirty-six. Following on from the success of this poetic debut, he issued *Underwoods* two years later and planned a third volume, *Ballads and Verses*, for 1890. However, only *Ballads* was issued that year; it was a failure. Before his death in 1894 he had nearly completed *Underwoods Book III*, which came out post-humously as *Songs of Travel*. He packed his unpublished MS poetry with him on his transcontinental travels, leading his stepson Lloyd Osbourne to assert, speciously, that he meant for it all to be published after his death. Osbourne's attitude was shared by the Boston Bibliophile Society; their printings of *Poems Hitherto Unpublished* (1916, 1921), a poorly edited travesty, seemed to many readers to support Stevenson's oft-repeated assertion that he had no poetic talent.

What did Stevenson mean by denying that he was a poet? He obviously sought recognition as one and privately admired what he considered to be his best poems while off-handedly referring to himself as Poetaster and Prosator. This question needs to be looked at in various contexts. In general, we may note that diffidence is not uncommon in poets, even in those regarded as great: Virgil tried to destroy the *Aeneid*, Keats chose for his epitaph, 'Here lies one whose name was writ in water' and Tennyson kept mislaying the unpublished *In Memoriam*. Self-deprecation was a habitual pose with Stevenson, but his nervousness about entering the poetic lists at age thirty-six was no affectation and was shared by his literary circle of Henley, Colvin, Baxter, Gosse *et al*. In fragile health and precarious finances, he had finally begun to succeed as a writer of *belles-lettres*, travel literature and fiction by the mid-1880s; his protective 'set' did not want to risk catastrophe by exposing their dolphin to the critical sharks. In April 1879, after Henley had harshly criticised Stevenson's Arnoldian poem *Our Lady of the Snows*, the wounded poet replied:

> I am a weak brother in verse. You ask me to rewrite things that I have already managed just to write with the skin of my teeth. If I don't rewrite them, it's because I don't see how to write them better, not because I don't think they should be. (*LETBM*, Vol. II, No. 607, p. 310)

While he was working in 1883 on *Penny Whistles*, the forerunner to *A Child's Garden*, he struck this note again, telling Henley:

> I shall try to do the Whistle as suggested; but I can usually do whistles only by giving my whole mind to it: to produce even such limping verse demanding the whole forces of my untuneful soul. (*LETBM*, Vol. IV, No. 1178, pp. 202–3)

In 1884 he joked to Henley that he was 'a kind of prose Herrick, divested of the gift of verse' (*LETBM*, Vol. IV, No. 1246, p. 267).

Reviews of his second volume proved for the most part that the fears of Stevenson and his circle were not groundless. Joseph Knight in the *Athenaeum* (10 September 1887) and William Sharp in the *Academy* (1 October 1887) adjudged *Underwoods* to be derivative, contrived and prosaic. The poet responded defensively on 21 November to his friend J. A. Symonds (a critic who had not reviewed *Underwoods*):

> I wonder if you saw my book of verses? It went into a second edition, because of my name, I suppose, and its *prose* merits. I do not set up to be a poet. Only an all round

literary man: a man who talks, not one who sings. But I believe the very fact that it was only speech served the book with the public. Horace is much a speaker, and see how popular! Most of Martial is only speech, . . . most of Burns also . . . Excuse this little apology for my muse; but I don't like to come before people who have a note of song, and let it be supposed I do not know the difference. (*LETBM*, Vol. VI, No. 1950, p. 65)

When he wrote these words Stevenson was no longer so penurious as he had been while agonising over what the public's judgement might be on *Penny Whistles*, for he had tasted large-scale success with *A Child's Garden*, *Treasure Island* and *Dr Jekyll and Mr Hyde*. Diffidence is still apparent here but when he draws attention to the prose merits of his verse, noting that it talks rather than sings, he is not confessing incompetence but indicating intention. His choice of models and his preference for 'verse' over 'poetry' to describe his metrical composition suggest that he saw himself as more an occasional poet than a lofty oracle. His favoured genres are elegy, the familiar epistle, *vers de société*, homely narrative in dialect, elegant presentations or compliments to friends, and intricate forms like the sonnet and the rondel. If this seems dilettantish it should be remembered that Stevenson 'set up' as a professional essayist, just as Rossetti 'set up' as a painter and Housman as a professor: for these men, poetry was a pleasant diversion rather than a career, all the more enjoyable for being untainted by commercial imperatives. For Stevenson, writing poems was often a sickbed activity when he was too ill to work at his fiction.

The lyrics of his last phase, which make up most of *Songs of Travel*, represent an important advance, being to his earlier lyrics what *Weir of Hermiston* is to his earlier novels. Much as he revered the great Romantics and their high Victorian successors, Stevenson did not write poetry that seemed, like theirs, an outcome of nature and inspiration, lines that came as easily as leaves to a tree; his verse seems more an outcome of culture and diligence. He often began with a prose sketch, turning it into rhyming octosyllabics or blank verse only after roughing out what he wanted to say, usually reducing the word count to one-eighth or less of the original draft. The first version of the superb elegy 'In Memoriam F.A.S.', a sixteen-line poem which appears as *Underwoods* XXVII, consists in the poet's Notebook 'C' (Beinecke Library) of a tortured, sprawling draft of sixty-three lines. The original form of *Requiem*, as the poet scribbled it on the train from New York to San Francisco, is barely recognisable as a draft of his most famous lines, being six times longer and poetically undistinguished (see the Textual Notes on these poems). Before he could achieve what he wanted in verse, Stevenson had to apply what Rossetti called the 'fundamental brainwork' of revision; frequently the enterprise had to be abandoned in any case. Stevenson's more than seventy notebooks and abundant leaves of MS contain hundreds of unfinished poems.

As the self-styled 'sedulous ape' he wrote experimentally in the manners of, among others, Chaucer, Jonson, Herrick, Marvell, Dryden, Pope, Burns, Wordsworth, Baudelaire, Heine, Shelley, Arnold, Swinburne, Morris and Whitman. Yet insofar as his best verse resembles that of other poets, they tend to be symbolists, aesthetes and decadents such as Rossetti and Dowson. The *Songs of Travel* talk more than they sing. Nature was not his teacher, and he found no sermons in stones: his worst mode is the didactic-heroic, the brassy heartiness that he seems to have picked up from Arnold without recognising that it is Arnold's worst mode too. Stevenson the lyricist at his best looks ahead to the Georgians more than he looks back to anyone, influencing A. E. Housman and Rupert Brooke. Like his fellow novelist-poets Meredith and Hardy, he turned his back on eloquent poetic diction. In his finest lyrics, 'In the highlands, in the country places', or 'Blows the wind today', the effect he achieves is not so much prosaic as paratactic:

> Be it granted me to behold you again in dying,
> Hills of home! And to hear again the call;
> Hear about the graves of the martyrs the peewees crying,
> And hear no more at all.
>
> (*Songs of Travel* XLV)

II

It has often been remarked upon that Stevenson wrote poetry when he was too ill to write prose but it is equally true that he wrote poetry when he was supposed to be taking notes on a law lecture or solving a trigonometry problem. Several of his academic exercise books intersperse verse scribbling with dutifully recorded lore from his studies. In the so-called Geometry Notebook (at Haverford College), sandwiched between observations on Ontological Utilitarianism and Pascal's Hexagon are two six-page drafts, 'Hail, childish slaves of social rules' and 'Motley I count the only wear' (later titled *A Valentine's Song*), both fervent outpourings of youthful rebellion against the 'unco guid' of Edinburgh, the whited sepulchres of middle-class respectability that generated as much passionate versifying as young Louis' hopes and disappointments in love. Some of these efforts were revised and copied into other notebooks with a view to preservation, if not publication, but most of the student notebook verse from the 1860s and 1870s remained there, unprinted and unimproved, but not uninteresting to the biographer or to anyone wishing to study the process by which the young poet was teaching himself to write verse.

Imitation of models and experimentation with various genres and techniques was at the heart of this process, which Stevenson described in 'A College Magazine', *Memories and Portraits* (1887):

> All through my boyhood and youth I was known and pointed out for the pattern of an idler; and yet I was always busy on my own private end, which was to learn to write. I kept always two books in my pocket, one to read, one to write in. As I walked, my mind was busy fitting what I saw with appropriate words; when I sat by the roadside, I would either read, or a pencil and a penny-version book would be in my hand, to note down the features of the scene or commemorate some halting stanzas. Thus I lived with words.

To set a standard of achievement for himself he needed models:

> Whenever I read a book or passage that particularly pleased me, in which a thing was
> said or an effect rendered with propriety, ... I must sit down at once and set myself
> to ape that quality. ... I have thus played the sedulous ape to Hazlitt, to Lamb,
> to Wordsworth, to Sir Thomas Browne, to Defoe, to Hawthorne, to Montaigne, to
> Baudelaire, and to *Obermann*. ... *Cain*, an epic, was (save the mark!) an imitation of
> *Sordello*; *Robin Hood*, a tale in verse, took an eclectic middle course among the fields
> of Keats, Chaucer and Morris; in *Monmouth*, a tragedy, I reclined on the bosom of Mr
> Swinburne; in my innumerable gouty-footed lyrics, I followed many masters ... It is the
> great point of these imitations that there still shines, beyond the student's reach, his
> inimitable model. Let him try as he please, he is still sure of failure; and it is an old and
> a very true saying that failure is the only highroad to success.

Stevenson jokingly called himself The Minor Poet but the tag is nevertheless
accurate. Of the major poet's attributes – abundance, variety and complete com-
petence, as T. S. Eliot puts it in speaking of Tennyson – he has none; on the
contrary, his range is narrow, his output of first-rate work small and his technique
limited. But some much admired poets belong to this category one thinks of
Arnold and Housman – and the period (1885–94) in which Stevenson flourished as
a writer of verse was not a golden, but a silver age of minor poetry. Among his
contemporary bards, only Yeats arose to become a major poet. Stevenson's small
number of characteristic themes and images emerge early – the elegiac, the pastoral,
the hortatory, friendship, songs, familiar epistles, epigrams, satire, Edinburgh and
other Scots subjects, addresses to places or houses and the travel motif – the
vagabond on road or river, the emigrant on train or ship. Some of his favourite
modes are his least successful: few poems of noble aspiration, religious questioning,
social criticism or philosophical speculation get beyond commonplace rhetoric, and
his love lyrics seem for the most part flat and derivative. Among the verse he chose
for publication the only love poems are a Polynesian ballad and a few lyrics in
the first part of *Songs of Travel*. Indeed, his judgement in selecting his finest work
was acute – the editor searches the remainder in vain for diamonds among the
zircons.

III

A Child's Garden of Verses may have begun as a money-making scheme, when the
struggling writer heard that one of Kate Greenaway's children's books had sold
150,000 copies, but it ended as a *tour de force*, a unique achievement for the poet
that, wisely, he never tried to revisit. Romantic poetry and philosophy and, more
particularly, German psychology had created a new awareness of children in the
nineteenth century – one might almost say they created the modern child. Wordsworth's child, who was father to the man ('My Heart Leaps Up'), was very different
from the youngster for whom the Rev. Isaac Watts wrote his *Divine Songs for Children*
(1715). Saint Augustine had taught that it was quite proper for unbaptised babies

to be damned eternally because, without the Church's sacraments, they were creatures of evil. But the innocent child envisioned by the Romantics enters this world trailing clouds of glory, able to remember the radiant garden whence he came and, for a time, able to perceive the vestigial splendour in his new world – a vision that gets lost as he grows up. Germans, such as Fichte, explained in purely rational and sometimes empirical terms how infants learned and developed but poets adopted these new models. Tennyson's 'baby new to earth and sky' (*In Memoriam* XLV) begins with a consciousness of itself as identical with its mother's breast: as it explores its surroundings, it gradually becomes a separate identity but never forgets that blissful oneness with its parent. Christina Rossetti in *Sing-Song* and Swinburne in *Poems and Ballads* wrote poems not only about babies but also from their point of view. Dickens brilliantly articulated the child's perspective and narrative voice. When, late in his life, Sigmund Freud was credited with inventing the concept of adult behaviour being driven by the desires and memories of the inner child, he denied having done any more than formulate methods of studying what in fact had been invented by imaginative writers.

Stevenson's happy garden of childhood is contemporary with the *Kindergarten* movement that had spread to Europe and America from Germany, where the term was coined around 1837 by children's education specialist Friedrich Froebel (1782–1852). Great importance was attached by the new sciences of paediatrics and pedagogy to encouraging free, creative play and self-expression among small children. That Stevenson was interested in these new ideas is demonstrated in two of his early essays, 'Notes on the Movements of Young Children' (1874, rpt *Edin.*, Vol. XXI, pp. 124–31) and 'Child's Play' (1878, rpt *Edin.*, Vol. III, pp. 157–71). He mentioned to his cousin Henrietta Milne that the latter paper contained references to experiences that she, as his childhood playmate, would recognise. Despite his chronic sickliness, perhaps even because of it, he had had the kind of childhood that the new theories were promoting. The only child of monied, educated parents, he was surrounded by storybooks, toys and a pastoral environment in Colinton and Swanston, always watched over by his doting mother, Margaret, who encouraged his imaginative play and helped him write stories and make books as well as read them. His father Thomas loved to play with his little 'Smout' and made up stories to tell him. Especially when residing in the country, he had a host of aunts, cousins and friends who indulged his fantastic whims. Then there was his nurse, Alison Cunningham, to whom *A Child's Garden of Verses* is dedicated and with whom he maintained an affectionate correspondence throughout his life. Although Cummy's terrifying evocations of the hell and damnation that awaited the wicked were no part of a progressive *Kindergarten* environment, her rousing stories of Covenanters, bible figures and Scottish folklore stimulated the imagination of her 'laddie' and remained vivid in his memory.

Although very much a book, and filled with the imagery of book-reading, *A Child's Garden of Verses* is also supremely auditory and visual. The reader hears chants, nursery rhymes, hymns and jingles, the sounds of stormy nights and farm-yard days. One is never far from song and music with Stevenson the lyricist; many of these pieces were set to music with the poet's blessing. Wonderfully graphic in their appeal to the imagination, these poems conjure up so many objects and scenes that the poet's insistence upon an illustrator seems odd – how clearly we see the whistle, the lead soldier, four little blue eggs in a bird's nest. This intensity is often ascribed to the poet's remarkable ability to remember even his earliest childhood days. The extensively revised MSS and other documentary sources described below in the textual notes demonstrate beyond question that these poems did spring from Stevenson's own childhood experiences and perceptions. No 'sedulous ape' is evident here, although influences are duly acknowledged, such as Isaac Watts. Certainly the pastoral imagery and simple diction suggest Watts, as they do Blake, but these rhymes are didactic only in a childish way, as when the speaker, sometimes rather priggishly, recites the moral teachings or exhibits the correct manners that he has just learned from adults. Even though he considered calling them *New Songs of Innocence*, these verses are not very Blakian – religious or spiritual references are strikingly absent. Any resemblance to *Sing-Song* or Christina Rossetti's other poetry for children also seems slight because of this point: Stevenson has no hidden moral, political or religious agenda. Indeed, the virtual absence of God, church, school, flags and the like make it difficult for the modern reader to identify these as Victorian children's poems. Even strict fidelity to the facts of the poet's childhood experiences is not enforced: explaining to his nurse that he has not told the truth about one of their shared adventures, recorded in *My Treasures*, he informed Cummy, 'rhyme is a very great monarch and goes before honesty' (p. 381). These apparently simple poems were often crafted with much labour: *Block City* was drafted several times in different parts of Huntington Library's Notebook 'D', seventy lines in all which were reduced to twenty-four. The poem that follows it, *The Land of Story-books*, was painstakingly rendered into verse from what began as a prose passage in Stevenson's reminiscences of childhood (p. 379).

It is true that some literary sophistication and resonance occurs in the later sections, mostly written just before publication to bulk the volume up to 100 pages and, as Stevenson said of the *Envoys*, to 'hedge in the Garden', to impose form and structure on this collection, which had begun in such a delightfully anarchic manner, roaming easily among disparate childish fancies. *The Child Alone* section has a common theme, *Garden Days* a common place. The final poem before the concluding *Envoys*, *Historical Associations*, imports a new level of diction that belongs to an older child and to the tales of romance mentioned there rather than to picture-books and block cities. The six *Envoys* bring us into the main stream of Stevenson's verse – witty and charming addresses to friends and family, clever allusions to a wide range of reading, and a strong sense of something that had remained suspended until now in this sequence of poems – the reality of Scotland. The final envoy, *To Any Reader*, is laden with intertextual reference in its first draft, but Stevenson stripped most of that away to emphasise, almost cruelly, his point that the child in this garden is now an illusion, 'a child of air'. Earlier, rejecting

Colvin's suggestion that the pail by the wall in *Escape at Bedtime* should have 'twinkled half full of water and stars' instead of 'would be half full of water and stars', he said '"twinkled" is just the error; to the child the stars appear to be there; any word that suggests illusion is a horror' (p. 360). But now, even though children hate to have their illusions shattered, the story has to end, the child in the garden must grow up, go away. One thinks of Kipling's heart-rending end to *The Jungle Books* – 'And that is the last of the Mowgli stories'.

IV

Underwoods begins with a confession of plagiarism: the poet tells us that he stole his title from 'a better man', Ben Jonson. This tip of the hat no doubt indicates what kind of poetry we may expect in these pages – occasional verse following classical models – and what relation it bears to the author's more substantial prose accomplishments. Explaining why he chose this title, Jonson described his lyrics and other occasional pieces as lesser poems of later growth, underbrush dwarfed by the 'Forest' of his formal verse which is itself overshadowed by the 'Timber' of his plays. In adapting this sylvan metaphor, Stevenson implies that his poetry is the underwoods in the forest of his professional writing but not without value in the *opera* of the 'all round literary man' which both Jonson and Stevenson 'set up' to be: the first English writer to publish his own *Works*, Jonson wrote, besides tragedies and comedies, formal epigrams and odes, much light verse in the manner of Horace and Martial (both favourites of RLS) and a small body of literary criticism.

Nevertheless, some reviewers of *Underwoods* rejected Stevenson's implicit claim to be a late Victorian 'son of Ben', arguing that he would have done better to appropriate Robert Herrick's collective title for his lyrics, *Hesperides*. Stevenson sometimes did attempt to emulate Herrick: one of the *New Poems* published after his death, 'Gather ye roses while ye may', is very close to being a plagiarised version of *To the Virgins, To Make Much of Time*. He is also indebted to Marvell, especially in his poems about houses and gardens and his use of rhyming octosyllabics. But there is a point to the comparison with Jonson, who has been called an Annandale Scot. The seventeenth- and nineteenth-century collections called *Underwoods* have genres, modes, subjects and images in common, especially the seeking after elegant conceits, graceful eulogies and poignant epitaphs. Stevenson, who wrote so well on the death of a child (see his *Underwoods* XXVII), must have been moved by Jonson's laments for the child-actor Salathiel Pavy, and for his own son, who died aged seven:

> For why
> Will man lament the state he should envie?
> To have so soone scap'd worlds, and fleshes rage,
> And, if no other miserie, yet age?
> Rest in soft peace, and, ask'd, say here doth lye

BEN: JONSON his best piece of *poetrie*.
For whose sake, hence-forth, all his vows be such,
As what he loves may never like too much.
(*On My First Sonne*)

Jonson's life and personality must have attracted Stevenson as well. Both had a gift
for coining allegorical names – one can imagine Sir Epicure Mammon from *The
Alchemist* meeting Stevenson's epistolary alias Sir Indecision Contentment, and the
Scottish writer embraced the Jonsonian name Mr Fastidious Brisk appropriated for
him by Henley from *Every Man in his Humour*. Jonson's literary erudition co-existed
with a sort of Lothian Road roustabout's crude masculinity. As both a soldier and a
duellist he fought men in single combat. He was a pugnacious sybarite but also a rare
aesthete and charming courtier. J. A. Symonds dismissed his lyrics because 'Jonson
could not sing', yet his *To Celia* – 'Drink to me only with thine eyes' – remains one
of the famous songs of the world. Many critics of Stevenson's verse have denied that
he could sing, but William Sharp, pointing to the lyrical achievement of *Requiem*,
predicted that it would outlast all Stevenson's poetry and all his prose too. What
these two poems share is that they cost their authors dearly in laborious revision
they did not come of their own accord but had to be summoned.

Inspiration and originality of the sort celebrated by Wordsworth and Coleridge
are not much in evidence in Stevenson's *Underwoods*; the reader will more likely
think of Pope's famous dictum in Part 2 of his *Essay on Criticism*, which Stevenson
paraphrased more than once in his letters:

True wit is Nature to advantage dressed,
What oft was thought, but ne'er so well expressed.

Unity in this collection is neither narrative nor thematic but tonal and formal. The
poems are all built around occasions, places and friendship, with a limited number
of poetic modes being employed, usually more than once: the predominant mode
is rhyming octosyllabics, but there are seven blank verse lyrics. The occasions are
mostly conventional: courtship in the spring, a birthday, a death, a class reunion.
Seventeen of the poems are addressed to or written for family and friends, some
familiar and conversational, others solemn. The places, often depicted minutely
and always realised vividly, are easily identified: the garden at Hyères (VII);
Skerryvore, the Stevensons' home in Bournemouth from 1885 to 1887 and its
eponymous lighthouse (V, XVII, XVIII, XXXIV–XXXVIII); Edinburgh and
surrounding countryside, the setting for most of the Scots poems and four of the
English ones (IV, IX, XXVI, XXVIII); northern California (X, XXIV, XXIX); Davos
(XIII, XXI, XXVII); Barbizon, Grez-sur-Loing and the other French meccas for
artists where Louis met Fanny (I, XI, XII) and the roads, trails, canals and rivers of
rural France (II, III, XXIII, XXXII, XXXIII).

V

While there can be no argument against the fact that Stevenson, even in exile, had a passionate, lifelong involvement with his native Scotland, there is little agreement about the value or significance of his poetry written in Scots. Some have dismissed it as fake, a game of 'crambo-clink' (doggerel with rules), or scorned it as an exercise in 'Bonnie Scotland' sentimentality that belongs in the Victorian 'Whistle-Binkie' anthologies.[1] Others condemn these poems as mechanical imitations of Burns written in 'Standard Habbie', a stanza popularised by Burns, employing an *ersatz* Scots language which derives neither from the old poetic 'Makars' nor from any living, spoken tongue. One English critic, Joseph Knight, reviewing *Underwoods* in the *Athenaeum* for 10 September 1887, condescended to mention the Scots poems very briefly at the end of his review, noting that they were derivative from Burns but admiring their quaint and uncouth vigour, which he contrasted with 'the chaster Southern muse'. On the other hand, a more sympathetic critic wrote that '*The Scotsman's Return from Abroad* (and *Embro Hie Kirk* approaches it very close) is the finest national satire written since Burns and seems likely to remain so [these poems are *Underwoods* Book II, XI and XII]. The *déraciné* post-war Nationalist, attempting to make Scots the medium for expression of an outlook the less Scottish as it may be more emancipated, will never produce anything as wholly satisfying and delightful' (Dalglish 1937: 60). In critical comment on the Scottish Renaissance of the early twentieth century, it is not unusual to find praise for Stevenson as a pioneer in the modern revival of Scots poetry, a promoter and practitioner of the great Scottish tradition during the barren Victorian period when the highest achievement of Scots verse outside of Book II of *Underwoods* was *Wee Willie Winkie*. In his 'Modern Poetry in Scots Before MacDiarmid', Colin Milton identifies Stevenson as 'the country's major writer of the second half of the nineteenth century' and sees him, not as a mere Burns imitator, but as one who was 'able to tap the energy and inventiveness of spoken Scots by bringing the language of poetry into closer relationship with the living vernacular'. Stevenson's Scots verse is not 'literary' but a written representation of contemporary popular speech in his Lothian region; as such, it 'was to lead to the remarkable flowering of vernacular verse which preceeded – and in many ways provided the foundation and impetus for – MacDiarmid's "renaissance" achievements of the 1920s and 1930s' (Craig 1987–8: IV, 11–12). The most balanced and penetrating analysis of this complex aspect of the poet is found in David Daiches' essay, 'Stevenson and Scotland' (Calder 1981: 11–32).

We may dismiss out of hand the allegation that Stevenson was not a true Scot because he had been assimilated or colonised by imperial English culture, an inhabitant not of Scotland but of 'North Britain'. It is true that, hating Edinburgh winters and certain other aspects of his homeland, he chose to live abroad and, finally, in exile from 'the blessed, beastly place' (see below p. 512). It is also true that he could have contributed little to the Nationalist movement because he saw little that was homogeneous about Scotland, as the following passage from 'The Scot Abroad' in *The Silverado Squatters* makes clear:

> Scotland is indefinable; it has no unity except upon the map. Two languages, many dialects, innumerable forms of piety, and countless local patriotisms and prejudices, part us among ourselves more widely than the extreme east and west of that great continent of America. When I am at home, I feel a man from Glasgow to be something like a rival, a man from Barra to be more than half a foreigner. Yet let us meet in some far country, and, whether we hail from the braes of Manor or the braes of Mar, some ready-made affection joins us on the instant. It is not race. Look at us. One is Norse, one Celtic, and another Saxon. It is not community of tongue. We have it not among ourselves; and we have it, almost to perfection, with English, or Irish, or American. It is no tie of faith, for we detest each other's errors. And yet somewhere, deep down in the heart of each one of us, something yearns for the old land and the old kindly people. (Hart 1966a: 210–11)

Fifteen years after writing these words in northern California, as his exile lengthened in the South Seas and he accepted that he would never see the hills of home again, he came at last to view his Scottishness as a matter of race. Many letters of 1893–4 reveal this, as do his extensive genealogical inquiries at that time into the Stevenson roots, but he gives it poetic expression in the lines dedicating *Weir of Hermiston* to his wife: 'And here afar, Intent on my own *race* and place, I wrote'.

The question of language is addressed directly, though not without ambiguity, in the Note about the Scots poems in *Underwoods*. Whether or not he knew he was following the latest German theories in comparative philology, he rejected the notion of a pure, fixed language – or any dialect thereof – in favour of the malleable, living speech he grew up listening to in the Lothians. Not only his narratives, settings and characters are drawn from his local environment of Edinburgh and the Pentlands but so also is his vocabulary and diction. As a poet he feels kinship with Sir Walter Scott and Robert Fergusson because they were Edinburgh men, whereas Burns was a 'foreigner' from Ayrshire. He avoids cliché and sentiment because of his originality. John Adam, Clerk of Court, is not the stock drunkard of Scots burlesque humour but a man that Stevenson and Baxter knew during their time as Edinburgh law students. The zealous hostility of Niven and Begg in *Embro Hie Kirk* against the Popery of installing a pipe organ in St Giles's Cathedral is not a quaint anecdote from Covenanting days but is drawn from a contemporary controversy, informed though it may be with passions that date back to the Reformation. The poet's note to *A Lowden Sabbath Morn*, a poem which doubtless owes a good deal to Fergusson, states that the details therein are drawn from his own observation of local parishes and clergymen in the Lothians.

At the end of his Note and in the first poem of *Underwoods* Book II, *The Maker to Posterity*, Stevenson raises the question of whether or not Scots will survive as a poetic language. In the Note he resigns himself to its disappearance, hoping before that gloomy day comes 'to have my hour as a native Maker, and be read by my own countryfolk in our own dying language' (p. 76). In the poem, however, this defeatist tone modulates into defiance. Addressing some future reader who will sneeringly disregard his Lallan verse as written in a dead language, as incomprehensible as runes on standing stones among the heather, the poet imagines an almost comic apocalypse in which the world of the future, and its new culture of which it is so proud, disintegrates like the earth struck by a comet or a railway car in a train wreck. The forces of evolution, rapid technological change and scientific relativism have created a world in which nothing is or ever again will be stable. Perhaps this poem opening Book II is a witty variation on or continuation of *Underwoods* XXXVIII, the lyric ending Book I, suggesting that to write for posterity, to attempt a monument more lasting than bronze, is futile – the poet is primarily the creator of beauty, however ephemeral or transitory. Certainly Book II continues the light conversational tone established in Book I, repeating many earlier motifs. Friendship is again emphasised, especially in the concluding poem. The strong sense of occasion is there too: friends walking home together after a night of revelry, Sabbath morn in the country, verses presented to Dr John Brown in grateful appreciation of a wedding present. The classical pastoral note is struck again in II and III: the beloved cottage at Swanston is compared implicitly to Horace's villa or Catullus' Sirmio. In Book II the concrete apprehension of specific time and place is more marked than in the earlier poems because here the poet is less self-consciously neo-classical: the Scots poems draw on the vitality of Stevenson's ethnic heritage – religious attack and counter-attack, the love of good whisky, Scotland's unique landscape and weather, the humbug of the 'unco guid' and some moral legacies of Calvinism, such as a guilty conscience or invincible self-righteousness.

The view that the Scots poems are just a game, on a level with the juvenile silliness evident in Stevenson's Thomson-Johnstone letters and the Scots doggerel he addressed to Baxter and other friends, overlooks the fundamental seriousness with which Stevenson viewed himself as a Scottish 'maker'. For all his diffidence as a poet, he did not shrink from identifying himself with Burns and Fergusson as one of Scotland's 'three Rabbies'. He included his Scots poems in *Underwoods* partly to exploit his own international popularity as a means of promoting Scottish poetry and Lallans, 'that dark, oracular medium' as he described it to a dubious Henry James. He enjoyed baffling Americans by addressing letters or poems to them written in Scots, and by making exaggerated claims on behalf of Scottish literature (see his verses *To C. W. Stoddard*, p. 278). Anyone who thinks that his sense of identity with Robert Fergusson is a joke or a pose should read his letter of May 1894 to Baxter in which he first considers dedicating the *Edinburgh Edition* to him, then wonders if he may not, as Burns did, make a contribution and addition to Fergusson's gravestone in the Canongate; Fergusson had experienced the disastrous life and early demise that Stevenson thought would be his destiny, dying at twenty-four in an Edinburgh madhouse. Although nothing came of the project, because Baxter eventually discovered that Fergusson's grave was quite well-maintained, Stevenson in this letter proposed the following inscription:

This stone originally erected by Robert Burns, has been repaired at the charges of Robert Louis Stevenson and is by him re-dedicated to the Memory of Robert Fergusson as the gift of one Edinburgh lad to another. (*LETBM*, Vol. VIII, No. 2734, p. 291)

VI

The death of Stevenson's father in May 1887 was one of the three major turning points in his life, the others being his 1871 decision to abandon engineering for writing and his 1880 marriage to Fanny. Always close to his parents, even when quarrelling over religion with them, he had become increasingly desperate during his father's long descent into sickness and insanity. Knowing that he could not under these circumstances abandon the elder Stevensons to live abroad (as he believed his health required), he languished in Skerryvore, the home they had given Fanny and him, describing his life there as that of 'a weevil in a biscuit'. But with the long horror done and Thomas Stevenson finally at peace, Louis and Fanny left Britain (forever, as it turned out), making their escape into a new life, his mother Maggie gamely willing to accompany them. Upon his arrival in New York, the author discovered that he was a celebrity there, and soon parlayed this status into a larger income than he had ever received. With royalty revenues augmented by regular journalism for Scribner's, plus a considerable legacy from his father, he was now able to go anywhere he liked as long as his health bore up. First, he wintered in New York's salubrious Adirondack Mountains, then chartered a yacht and headed for the South Seas. While he continued to suffer some lapses into sickness (occurring usually when he was in a city), he enjoyed better health and strength for the last six and a half years of his life than he had known for most of it.

He composed his first ballad, *Ticonderoga*, in Edinburgh immediately after his father died. It offers an uncanny foreshadowing of the rest of his life, telling of a Scot who is forced to go abroad and who encounters his doom in the wilderness of the New World. Stevenson's local Adirondack city, where he got supplies for his cabin at Saranac Lake during the winter of 1887–8, was Plattsburgh, New York, just a few miles up Lake Champlain from Fort Ticonderoga. Thereafter, when he had made a home in the even more remote wilderness of Samoa, Stevenson was increasingly haunted by his Scottish destiny, the wrenching fear that he would never again see Scotland or even be returned for burial there, and premonitions of impending death. The poetic fruits of this period are the *Ballads*, *Songs of Travel* and the verses on his Vailima family.

Stevenson's literary heritage included many ballads – the old anonymous ones, border ballads and the popular compositions in this genre by Sir Walter Scott. As a boy he was spellbound by Swinburne's *Poems and Ballads*. In the 1880s there was a ballad-mania which the poet hoped to exploit. Tennyson's *Ballads and Other Poems* (1880) enjoyed great success with the public; Rossetti's last volume, *Ballads and Sonnets* (1881), went through four editions, Swinburne continued to publish ballads and Morris' long verse narratives, *The Earthly Paradise* and his Nordic sagas, were eagerly devoured by Stevenson. He remarked to Henley that his main models for *Ticonderoga* were Thomas Macaulay and 'the old ones' (p. 546). Excited by his discovery of the South Seas poetic culture and by the challenge of experimenting with an unfamiliar genre, he was greatly absorbed at first. He gathered abundant material in Tahiti and Hawaii, and consulted with local bards and scholars before embarking on his own creations. The first two, *The Tale of Rahéro* and *The Feast of Famine*, were completed rapidly. Then, he seems to have become less interested in writing the many South Seas ballads he had projected than in studying Polynesian folklore and prosody. To the horror of the sensible Fanny, he began to spend less time on his fiction and poetry than on gathering lore for a book which she recognised would be mostly a work of scholarship. Observing that he had neither the training nor the talent for such work, she also pointed out that it does not pay. This project was never completed, although some material intended for it was issued posthumously by Chatto and Windus as *In The South Seas* (1900). Research not only sidetracked him while he was writing the ballads, it also got loaded into them in the form of sociology and politics, the whole further weighed down by an antiqued diction that seems to have come all too easily to him, for the MSS show that he rarely cancelled a line. Edmund Gosse, who, like Sidney Colvin, was concerned that RLS had 'gone native', commented privately that 'the effort to become a Polynesian Walter Scott is a little too obvious, the inspiration a little too mechanical. And ... the versification is atrocious' (Maixner 1981: 375).

Harsh criticism of *Ballads* such as the foregoing appeared in reviews, and, combined with poor sales of the volume, inhibited further schemes to publish verse until in 1894 the poet sent Colvin the collection of poems that became *Songs of Travel* for inclusion in the poetry volume of the *Edinburgh Edition*. He had continued to write verse in his notebooks, sporadically as always. At first glance his chosen title of *Underwoods Book III* seems appropriate, for the new compilation, while offering no Scots poems this time, repeats the most successful aspects of the first *Underwoods*: friendships are celebrated, occasions are marked, places are unerringly apprehended, musicality and conciseness are evident. However, the pattern is repeated in altogether darker colours. Remembering friends now prompts homesick yearning and gloomy presentiment. Most of the occasions at which the poet presents his verses are not familiar but formal and exotic, taking place in Tahiti, Hawaii or Molokai. Delight in new places is sometimes subverted by terror: in *The Woodman*, the underside of the Cook's Tour tropical paradise is discovered to be a Darwinian struggle for existence in which Stevenson's customary cheerful optimism surrenders to the nihilism of survival at any cost; *Tropic Rain* is a fierce pagan affirmation of the oneness of beauty and terror during what seems to be a hurricane, done with true Swinburnian gusto, but a similar passage in the unfinished *To My Wife* breaks off at the height of a storm at sea that seems about to send *The Equator* to the bottom. These darker colours result from an overall apprehension of the South Seas, which Stevenson summarises for Colvin as follows:

By the time I am done with this cruise I shall have the material for a very singular book of travels: masses of strange stories and characters, cannibals, pirates, ancient legends, old Polynesian poetry; never was so generous a farrago ... The Pacific is a strange place, the nineteenth century only exists there in spots; all round, it is a no man's land of the ages, a stir-about of epochs and races, barbarisms and civilisations, virtues and crimes. (*LETBM*, Vol. VI, No. 2176, p. 312)

There is much light lyricism here too, wedded to actual music and sometimes accompanied in MS by music written out with the words. Nos I, XII, XIII, XVII and XLIV are set to well-known airs or tunes; other song-like lyrics are Nos VII, VIII, XI and XV. He wrote new words to two old Scottish songs, 'Wandering Willie' and 'Over the Sea to Skye'. A Paterian aspiration towards the condition of music, evident in certain lyrics (e.g. XVI, XXXV, XXXVI, XLV), makes him a not-so-distant relative of the Aesthetic and Decadent poets. To identify the Stevenson of *Songs of Travel* as an 1890s poet may seem a critical (though not a chronological) error, if only because he is characteristically neither perverse nor pessimistic. As an intimate and a collaborator of Henley, he might even be more properly associated with that poet's 'Counter-Decadence' movement. Vagabonds, soldiers and other such hearty *personae* who want to be 'up and doing' are not usually grouped with decadents. However, Stevenson also loved to pose as Baudelairean dandy and Byronic Fatal Man, resembling, with his large, luminous eyes and velvet jacket, no-one so much as Poe's Roderick Usher. He was recognised as an aesthetic poet, and a hierophant of the cult of style, by no less an aesthete than Gleeson White,[2] for his rondeaux, his homage to Villon and his 1885 article, 'On Style in Literature'.

In this essay Stevenson announced his discovery of 'PVF', patterns of consonance in prose and verse, which he explained as a melic mode of writing, 'an arrangement of according letters, which is altogether arabesque and sensual'. Metaphorically identifying verbal with musical composition, he treats lines of poetry and metric feet as musical phrases and bars while individual letters are notes. Passages from Milton and Shakespeare are analysed to discover counterpointed harmonies of PVF. In an imaginary letter to Stevenson, Gleeson White writes,

You started the search for the buried P.V.F. ... If ... we heard the ancient liturgy of the Church, it was no longer a sequence of stately cadences but a rich deposit of buried P.V.F.; if we tried to read or listen to Shakespeare, the '*purple*, perfumed sails' set us tracking syllables, running after the sound and letting the sense take care of itself. (White 1892: 52)

Ernest Dowson's *Coronal* has the repeated lines 'Violets and leaves of vine/ We gather and entwine', which Linda Dowling sees as expressive of the PVF ideal (Dowling 1986: 208). By the 1890s, Stevenson himself was no longer quite so intrigued as he had been by the artifice and elegance of aesthetic connoisseurs, but he still sought to create quintessential poetry purged of what Verlaine called 'éloquence' and 'littérature' to leave only 'la musique'. Some of the *Songs of Travel* seem almost autistic in their stark, introverted simplicity: in XLV, he takes the words of S. R. Crockett's dedication of his book to Stevenson, 'where about the graves of the martyrs the whaups are crying – his heart remembers how', and (in his own words written to Crockett with the poem), 'extend[s] your beautiful phrase of prose into three indifferent stanzas' (see Textual Note on this poem). The picturesque landscape which is the context here is sharply restricted, to emphasise the 'beautiful phrase' and its music – wind, sun, rain, heather, stones, the cries of birds, then nothing. The last fifteen lines of *To My Old Familiars* (XXXVI) produce a similar effect in blank verse, a dying fall composed of negative words tumbling slowly towards entropy. The next poem (XXXVII), another expression of longing for Scotland written at the same time at Apemama, is a variation on this theme: the verbal music modulates through degrees of indifference towards extinction in the final phrase, 'city of the dead'. In these last lyrics there is much that anticipates the modernist idiom. A poem from Notebook B6022 at Yale, 'Is it a dream?', considered for inclusion in *Songs of Travel* but never finished, has this stanza which anticipates Eliot's *The Hollow Men*:

> Ghosts in the street
> Empty falling of feet
> The empty eyes that I meet
> And the hollow faces
> Here in the Empty Country
> Here in the pallid place.

VII

During the first half of the twentieth century Stevenson's poetry was prized by collectors, enjoyed by ordinary readers but disregarded by critics. He was not spared in the post-Great War onslaught on all Victorian writers, which continued during the ascendancy of modernism and the Bloomsbury set in London: Robert Graves and Virginia Woolf led the sneering. Revaluation of his poetry did not begin until the centenary of his birth in 1950, with Janet Adam Smith's groundbreaking *Collected Poems of Robert Louis Stevenson*; in 1951, J. C. Furnas' biography, *Voyage to Windward*, cleared away much error and confusion about his life and work. Smith's book reversed a tradition of indifferent editing that began with Sidney Colvin's bowdlerising and was continued by the poet's stepson Lloyd Osbourne and the egregious George S. Hellman of the Boston Bibliophile Society; she stated that poor editing of Stevenson's MSS and texts was to blame for the neglect of his poetry. Unfortunately this neglect has persisted despite her notable achievement of 1950 (revised in 1971), because there seems to be some analogue of Gresham's Law in operation by which bad editions drive out good ones.

The value of Stevenson's books and MSS to collectors is another story. In 1903 Thomas J. Wise, by then a powerful arbiter of taste in book-collecting, advised his wealthy Chicago client J. H. Wrenn not to acquire any more Stevenson items because the boom following his death was over. During the rest of the Edwardian period RLS prices were low. In 1914 Fanny Stevenson died in California, leaving an enormous collection of her husband's original MS poetry, mostly in notebooks, to her daughter Belle, who had acted as the poet's amanuensis during the Vailima years. The Isobel Strong Sale, held in three sessions during 1914–16 in New York, broke all existing records for Stevenson, some items going for more than $1,000.00. Dusting off long-forgotten RLS proofsheets and private printings in his collection for this new boom, Wise now recycled them at a handsome profit. In the Red Cross Sale at Christies in 1918, Stevenson prices went higher still, and continued to rise until the stock market crashed in 1929.

During and immediately after the Strong Sale, G. S. Hellman, F. S. Peabody and other members of a group called the Boston Bibliophile Society managed to acquire most of Stevenson's unpublished MS poetry – more than fifty notebooks plus many loose sheets. They issued three privately-printed volumes comprising two limited editions (1916, 1921) 'for members only', of *Poems Hitherto Unpublished*, claiming to have added more than one hundred 'new poems' to the Stevenson canon. While they contained some finished poems printed from fair copies, these expensively-produced volumes printed MS verse that was for the most part not so much unpublished as unfinished, incoherent or fragmentary, 'stray leavings' as Colvin called them. Mistranscriptions abounded. Hellman, the principal editor of these books, spiced them up with lurid but mostly inaccurate 'revelations' about Stevenson's sex life, illustrated by poems which a jealous Fanny had 'suppressed'. Hellman concocted an elaborate sexual mystery story around 'Claire', the poet's secret love, that J. C. Furnas debunked in 1951 by showing that 'Claire' was one of many names by which the young RLS addressed his *dame lointaine*, Fanny Sitwell, later Lady Colvin. Numerous other Hellman allegations were derived from his readings of these 'suppressed' poems: the poet seduced the family maid, Valentine Roch, he chased after young female staff in hotels, he had an affair with a Samoan girl. But the worst of it is what Hellman did to several notebooks after he acquired them and published their contents. In order to make factitious rarities for sale to wealthy collectors, he disbound notebooks and mutilated MSS, distributing the leaves to make many slim volumes bound in morocco with silk end leaves, stamped in gilt on side and back and placed inside expensively-tooled slipcases. These volumes typically contained only three or four leaves of actual Stevenson MS, padded out with a hand-lettered title-page, a typescript (often inaccurate) of the poetry, handwritten annotations, a reproduced portrait of the poet, an 'association' photograph of one of his homes and several thick, blank pages to facilitate binding. Smith records in her Introduction to the *Collected Poems* that she examined these pretentious volumes before they were sold at Sothebys in 1949. I can record seeing dozens of them, distributed as they now are around repositories that have Stevenson MS holdings. It is a nearly impossible task to reconstruct the contents of these mutilated notebooks (see Appendix One).

Even though Stevenson's heirs had agreed to sell their copyright as well as the actual MSS, they demanded, soon after the two 1916 volumes appeared, the right to republish these poems 'in the interest of literature'.[3] Chatto and Windus, who had published many Stevenson titles, worked with Lloyd Osbourne to get the Bibliophile Society's permission to allow the publication of *New Poems and Variant Readings* (London, 1918), consisting of the poems (without notes) from the 1916 volumes with a foreword by Osbourne. In 1922, a consortium of publishers led by Scribner's brought out the Vailima Edition of Stevenson's complete works in twenty-six volumes. Volume VIII contained only poetry, all that had been published in the poet's lifetime and in the Edinburgh Edition of his Works as well as – under the heading 'New Poems' – all the poems from the three Bibliophile Society volumes, plus 'Additional Poems' printed for the first time in the Pentland Edition (1907) and a grab-bag of unpublished verse in Volume XXVI (1923) under the heading of 'Sonnets and The Light-keeper'. In the fall of 1923 Scribner's published, on their own and without acknowledging the Bibliophile Society, *The Complete Poems of Robert Louis Stevenson*: under 'New Poems' they included everything listed in this paragraph, claiming to have doubled the poet's output. The main problem with all this reissuing and reshuffling is that it was nothing more than that: shorn of the introductions, dates, notes and chronological ordering provided in the bibliophile volumes, the Vailima and Scribner's *Complete Poems* editions are, as Smith noted, 'nothing but a fine higgledy-piggledy'. Stevenson's family, who, like the Boston Bibliophiles, were less interested in literary than financial outcomes, explicitly authorised these reckless publications; Lloyd Osbourne made this claim in a 1918 foreword: 'That Stevenson should have preserved these poems through all the vicissitudes of his wandering life shows how dearly he must have valued them; and shows too, I think, beyond any contradiction, that he meant they should be ultimately published.' There is abundant evidence, in the MSS themselves and in his letters, that he meant no such thing: he selected rigorously from his unpublished verse, abandoning ten MS poems for every one sent to his agents and publishers.

The corrupt texts printed by the Boston Bibliophile Society were transmitted, complete with most of the howlers and groaners, untouched by the hand of a scholarly editor, through all these editions to Heinemann's Tusitala Edition (1923–4), which became the standard *Works* of Stevenson: 'New Poems' in Volume XXIII, in spite of Smith's laborious correcting of its texts in her edition by reference to MSS and authorised printings, continues to mislead readers to this day. Nevertheless, I have selected some of the 'New Poems' for inclusion in this edition, but only if I could provide a sound copy-text (usually from MS) and a context (a date, reference in a letter or other source). 'God gave to me a child in part' (p. 329) is such a poem, expressing as it apparently does Stevenson's reaction to the prospect of being a father when he thought his wife Fanny might be pregnant.

VIII

The opposite extreme from publishing every versicle that an editor's research has unearthed for an edition such as this one is to include nothing that the poet did not explicitly select for presentation to the public. That would mean omitting the

Vailima family poems (he envisaged printing them for private circulation but did not), the Davos-Platz printings and all the verse in his letters; on the other hand, this criterion would require the editor to include every piece of verse sent off for cash to magazines or contributed to gift books, even though some of these were not included in his collected volumes. Between these extremes are many options: Stevenson's thirty best unpublished poems; selections already familiar to readers from anthologies, memoirs or biographies; pieces that add to our understanding of Stevenson as a person or as a poet; all verse that was sent with or as part of a letter. Being aware of no existing protocols that guide the editor in these circumstances, I exercised my discretion, with the following result.

There are few poems included here that have never been printed in any form. As I said earlier, Stevenson had a good eye for selecting his best work: I read thousands of pages of MS poetry, in notebooks and on loose leaves, and left most of it in file folders as what Tennyson once called 'chips of the poet's workshop'. All the productions of Samuel Lloyd Osbourne and Company that contain original poetry by Stevenson have been included. He became intensely involved with his stepson's printing and engraving, although his first contributions were little more than poetic pranks. He was irritated when Colvin refused to include *Moral Emblems* in the Edinburgh Edition of his *Works* (see pp. 478, 534). It may be that these and the *Moral Tales* display the Scotsman's love of black humour, for the poker-faced moralist of these poems is edifying the young with some very queer *exempla*: for example, avoid murder because it may spoil your dinner. Some of the bitter ironies found more often in Stevenson's prose than in his poetry are evident in the *Moral Tales*, which suggest, for instance, that the outwardly respectable hypocrite is a baser villain than any pirate.

I wanted to offer a sample of the youthful (mostly love) poetry but instead of individual selections I have chosen two cycles of Stevenson's own devising, *Songs* and *Little Odes*. In *Poems* (1869–70), another unit assembled in MS, he departs from his usual forms to experiment with free verse in the manner of Arnold (in *The Strayed Reveller*) and Whitman in order to express his rebellious bohemianism in its Edinburgh context. In this group *The Daughter of Herodias* stands out as the only Victorian treatment of Salome as a comic figure. The sonnets and rondeaux, selected from many experiments in these intricate forms, represent an aspect of Stevenson's versecraft which he shared with the Savile Club connoisseurs Dobson, Lang and Henley, and poets like Frederick Locker-Lampson. *Poems* (1879–80) belong to the same period as the famous *Requiem*, when he pursued Fanny to America, married her there and brought her back to Edinburgh. *More Poems in Scots* brings together dialect poems from various times and places; some of these will be new to most readers. The Vailima family poems, copied out in a numbered sequence for the printer but not published until Belle Strong's private issue *Teuila* (1899), were properly edited for the first time by Smith in 1950. There is a particularly rich context for these poems in the series of long autobiographical letters Stevenson wrote to Sidney Colvin during 1890–4 (not published in full until Volumes VII and

VIII of the Yale *Letters* appeared in 1995); they depict daily life on the Vailima plantation which the poet ruled as the tribal chief *Tusitala*, a far cry from the effete invalid of the 1880s.

The 'Occasional' and 'Miscellaneous' sections that conclude this edition may be less full than some readers would wish; some of the poems in Smith's edition and in the Yale *Letters* and many of the *New Poems* in Vol. XXIII of the Tusitala Edition are not included here. I have omitted all translations and experiments in classical meters (except the Epistle *To H. F. Brown*) in order to concentrate attention on Stevenson's original verse. Few unfinished poems, however promising, were selected. I have not followed Smith in setting up a 'Light Verse' category because much of what would belong there derives from letters. Removed from that context, Stevenson's epistolary verse may seem trivial, even silly; some of it is just doggerel in any case. However, read as part of a letter to Henley or Charles Baxter, high-spirited nonsense can be enjoyed for what it was intended to be. As Stevenson is one of the most admired letter-writers in English, the integrity of his correspondence combining verse and prose should be preserved. Unlike Smith's *Collected Poems*, *Letters* is not an out-of-print rare book but readily available, also in a one-volume *Selected Letters*. Some exceptions to this principle were made: a few Scots poems not previously collected are printed from letters; and, taken from RLS's letters to Baxter, the Brasheana sonnet sequence appears in its complete form for the first time in this edition, arranged in the order suggested by the poet.

The poems published as leaflets or in newspapers, periodicals, sale catalogues and books have been exhaustively catalogued in Volumes 1 and 2 of George McKay's *A Stevenson Library*. Principal editions of Stevenson's *Works* that include poems are listed in Appendix Two. Appendix Three describes the main repositories in which MSS of the poems are held. Appendix One attempts to shed light on the complex matter of Stevenson's notebooks. The textual notes give places and dates of composition and publication, important printed texts and location and description of MSS. These notes also record drafts, alternate versions and variants. Relevant passages from the poet's letters, journals, notebooks and other writings are cited, and reference is made to biography and criticism.

Notes

1. The title of a popular poetic anthology, first published in 1832 and frequently revised and reprinted. In the 1878 edition a whistle-binkie is defined as 'one who, in his attendance upon weddings and other convivial occasions, rendered himself so agreeable to the company by his skill in whistling, that he was allowed to sit at the Bink or board, and partake of the good things free of all expense' (*Whistle-Binkie, or, The Piper of the Party*, Vol. 1, pp. 71–2).
2. Artist, art historian and book designer associated with Beardsley and *The Studio*, which he edited. He dedicated his 1887 anthology *Ballades and Rondeaus* to RLS, there crediting him with introducing François Villon to English readers in his 1877 essay, 'Villon: Student, Poet and Housebreaker'. By the late 1880s Villon, whose poetry had been introduced to English readers in the 1860s through translations by Rossetti and Swinburne, had become a decadent archetype, the artist as criminal.
3. For more detail on these matters see Smith's Introduction to her *Collected Poems*, pp. 32–53, and Appendix Two, *Editions of Stevenson's Poems*, pp. 612–13.

A CHILD'S GARDEN OF VERSES

To Alison Cunningham
From her boy

For the long nights you lay awake
And watched for my unworthy sake:
For your most comfortable hand
That led me through the uneven land:
For all the story-books you read:
For all the pains you comforted:
For all you pitied, all you bore,
In sad and happy days of yore: –
My second Mother, my first Wife,
The angel of my infant life –
From the sick child, now well and old,
Take, nurse, the little book you hold!

And grant it, Heaven, that all who read
May find as dear a nurse at need,
And every child who lists my rhyme,
In the bright, fireside, nursery clime,
May hear it in as kind a voice
As made my childish days rejoice!

R.L.S.

I

Bed in Summer

In winter I get up at night
And dress by yellow candle-light.
In summer, quite the other way,
I have to go to bed by day.

I have to go to bed and see
The birds still hopping on the tree,
Or hear the grown-up people's feet
Still going past me in the street.

And does it not seem hard to you,
When all the sky is clear and blue,
And I should like so much to play,
To have to go to bed by day?

At the Sea-side

II

A Thought

It is very nice to think
The world is full of meat and drink,
With little children saying grace
In every Christian kind of place.

III

At the Sea-side

When I was down beside the sea
A wooden spade they gave to me
    To dig the sandy shore.
My holes were empty like a cup,
In every hole the sea came up,
    Till it could come no more.

IV

Young Night Thought

All night long and every night,
When my mamma puts out the light,
I see the people marching by,
As plain as day, before my eye.

Armies and emperors and kings,
All carrying different kinds of things,
And marching in so grand a way,
You never saw the like by day.

So fine a show was never seen,
At the great circus on the green;
For every kind of beast and man
Is marching in that caravan.

At first they move a little slow,
But still the faster on they go,
And still beside them close I keep
Until we reach the town of Sleep.

V

Whole Duty of Children

A child should always say what's true
And speak when he is spoken to,
And behave mannerly at table:
At least as far as he is able.

VI

Rain

The rain is raining all around,
It falls on field and tree,
It rains on the umbrellas here,
And on the ships at sea.

VII

Pirate Story

Three of us afloat in the meadow by the swing,
   Three of us aboard in the basket on the lea.
Winds are in the air, they are blowing in the spring,
   And waves are on the meadow like the waves there are at sea.

Where shall we adventure, today that we're afloat,
   Wary of the weather and steering by a star?
Shall it be to Africa, a-steering of the boat,
   To Providence, or Babylon, or off to Malabar?

Hi! but here's a squadron a-rowing on the sea –
   Cattle on the meadow a-charging with a roar!
Quick, and we'll escape them, they're as mad as they can be,
   The wicket is the harbour and the garden is the shore.

VIII

Foreign Lands

Up into the cherry tree
Who should climb but little me?
I held the trunk with both my hands
And looked abroad on foreign lands.

I saw the next door garden lie,
Adorned with flowers, before my eye,
And many pleasant places more
That I had never seen before.

I saw the dimpling river pass
And be the sky's blue looking-glass;
The dusty roads go up and down
With people tramping in to town.

If I could find a higher tree
Farther and farther I should see,
To where the grown-up river slips
Into the sea among the ships,

To where the roads on either hand
Lead onward into fairy land,
Where all the children dine at five,
And all the playthings come alive.

IX

Windy Nights

Whenever the moon and stars are set,
    Whenever the wind is high,
All night long in the dark and wet,
    A man goes riding by.
Late in the night when the fires are out,
Why does he gallop and gallop about?

Whenever the trees are crying aloud,
    And ships are tossed at sea,
By, on the highway, low and loud,
    By at the gallop goes he.
By at the gallop he goes, and then
By he comes back at the gallop again.

X

Travel

I should like to rise and go
Where the golden apples grow; –
Where below another sky
Parrot islands anchored lie,

And, watched by cockatoos and goats,
Lonely Crusoes building boats; –
Where in sunshine reaching out
Eastern cities, miles about,
Are with mosque and minaret
Among sandy gardens set,
And the rich goods from near and far
Hang for sale in the bazaar; –
Where the Great Wall round China goes,
And on one side the desert blows,
And with bell and voice and drum,
Cities on the other hum; –
Where are forests, hot as fire,
Wide as England, tall as a spire,
Full of apes and cocoa-nuts
And the negro hunter's huts; –
Where the knotty crocodile
Lies and blinks in the Nile,
And the red flamingo flies
Hunting fish before his eyes; –
Where in jungles, near and far,
Man-devouring tigers are,
Lying close and giving ear
Lest the hunt be drawing near,
Or a comer-by be seen
Swinging in a palanquin; –
Where among the desert sands
Some deserted city stands,
All its children, sweep and prince,
Grown to manhood ages since,
Not a foot in street or house,
Not a stir of child or mouse,
And when kindly falls the night,
In all the town no spark of light.
There I'll come when I'm a man
With a camel caravan;
Light a fire in the gloom
Of some dusty dining-room;
See the pictures on the walls,
Heroes, fights and festivals;
And in a corner find the toys
Of the old Egyptian boys.

XI

Singing

Of speckled eggs the birdie sings
    And nests among the trees;
The sailor sings of ropes and things
    In ships upon the seas.

The children sing in far Japan,
    The children sing in Spain;
The organ with the organ man
    Is singing in the rain.

XII

Looking Forward

When I am grown to man's estate
I shall be very proud and great,
And tell the other girls and boys
Not to meddle with my toys.

XIII

A Good Play

We built a ship upon the stairs
All made of the back-bedroom chairs,
And filled it full of sofa pillows
To go a-sailing on the billows.

We took a saw and several nails,
And water in the nursery pails;
And Tom said, 'Let us also take
An apple and a slice of cake;' –
Which was enough for Tom and me
To go a-sailing on, till tea.

We sailed along for days and days,
And had the very best of plays;
But Tom fell out and hurt his knee,
So there was no one left but me.

XIV

Where Go the Boats?

Dark brown is the river,
    Golden is the sand.
It flows along for ever,
    With trees on either hand.

Green leaves a-floating,
    Castles of the foam,
Boats of mine a-boating –
    Where will all come home?

On goes the river
    And out past the mill,
Away down the valley,
    Away down the hill.

Away down the river,
    A hundred miles or more,
Other little children
    Shall bring my boats ashore.

XV

Auntie's Skirts

Whenever Auntie moves around,
Her dresses make a curious sound;
They trail behind her up the floor,
And trundle after through the door.

XVI

The Land of Counterpane

When I was sick and lay a-bed
I had two pillows at my head,
And all my toys beside me lay
To keep me happy all the day.

And sometimes for an hour or so
I watched my leaden soldiers go,
With different uniforms and drills,
Among the bed-clothes, through the hills;

The Land of Counterpane

And sometimes sent my ships in fleets
All up and down among the sheets;
Or brought my trees and houses out,
And planted cities all about.

I was the giant great and still
That sits upon the pillow-hill,
And sees before him, dale and plain,
The pleasant land of counterpane.

XVII

The Land of Nod

From breakfast on through all the day
At home among my friends I stay;
But every night I go abroad
Afar into the land of Nod.

All by myself I have to go,
With none to tell me what to do –
All alone beside the streams
And up the mountain-sides of dreams.

The strangest things are there for me,
Both things to eat and things to see,
And many frightening sights abroad
Till morning in the land of Nod.

Try as I like to find the way,
I never can get back by day,
Nor can remember plain and clear
The curious music that I hear.

XVIII

My Shadow

I have a little shadow that goes in and out with me,
And what can be the use of him is more than I can see.
He is very, very like me from the heels up to the head;
And I see him jump before me, when I jump into my bed.

The funniest thing about him is the way he likes to grow –
Not at all like proper children, which is always very slow;
For he sometimes shoots up taller like an india-rubber ball,
And he sometimes gets so little that there's none of him at all.

My Shadow

He hasn't got a notion of how children ought to play,
And can only make a fool of me in every sort of way.
He stays so close beside me, he's a coward you can see;
I'd think shame to stick to nursie as that shadow sticks to me!

One morning, very early, before the sun was up,
I rose and found the shining dew on every buttercup;
But my lazy little shadow, like an arrant sleepy-head,
Had stayed at home behind me and was fast asleep in bed.

XIX

System

Every night my prayers I say,
And get my dinner every day;
And every day that I've been good,
I get an orange after food.

The child that is not clean and neat,
With lots of toys and things to eat,
He is a naughty child, I'm sure –
Or else his dear papa is poor.

XX

A Good Boy

I woke before the morning, I was happy all the day,
I never said an ugly word, but smiled and stuck to play.

And now at last the sun is going down behind the wood,
And I am very happy, for I know that I've been good.

My bed is waiting cool and fresh, with linen smooth and fair,
And I must off to sleepsin-by, and not forget my prayer.

I know that, till tomorrow I shall see the sun arise,
No ugly dream shall fright my mind, no ugly sight my eyes.

But slumber hold me tightly till I waken in the dawn,
And hear the thrushes singing in the lilacs round the lawn.

XXI

Escape at Bedtime

The lights from the parlour and kitchen shone out
  Through the blinds and the windows and bars;
And high overhead and all moving about,
  There were thousands of millions of stars.
There ne'er were such thousands of leaves on a tree,
  Nor of people in church or the Park,
As the crowds of the stars that looked down upon me,
  And that glittered and winked in the dark.

The Dog, and the Plough, and the Hunter, and all,
  And the star of the sailor, and Mars,
These shone in the sky, and the pail by the wall
  Would be half full of water and stars.
They saw me at last, and they chased me with cries,
  And they soon had me packed into bed;
But the glory kept shining and bright in my eyes,
  And the stars going round in my head.

XXII

Marching Song

Bring the comb and play upon it!
  Marching, here we come!
Willie cocks his highland bonnet,
  Johnnie beats the drum.

Mary Jane commands the party,
  Peter leads the rear;
Feet in time, alert and hearty,
  Each a Grenadier!

All in the most martial manner
  Marching double-quick;
While the napkin like a banner
  Waves upon the stick!

Here's enough of fame and pillage,
  Great commander Jane!
Now that we've been round the village,
  Let's go home again.

XXIII

The Cow

The friendly cow all red and white,
  I love with all my heart:
She gives me cream with all her might,
  To eat with apple-tart.

She wanders lowing here and there,
  And yet she cannot stray,
All in the pleasant open air,
  The pleasant light of day;

And blown by all the winds that pass
  And wet with all the showers,
She walks among the meadow grass
  And eats the meadow flowers.

XXIV

Happy Thought

The world is so full of a number of things,
I'm sure we should all be as happy as kings.

XXV

The Wind

I saw you toss the kites on high
And blow the birds about the sky;
And all around I heard you pass,
Like ladies' skirts across the grass –
  O wind, a-blowing all day long,
  O wind, that sings so loud a song!

I saw the different things you did,
But always you yourself you hid.
I felt you push, I heard you call,
I could not see yourself at all –
  O wind, a-blowing all day long,
  O wind, that sings so loud a song!

O you that are so strong and cold,
O blower, are you young or old?
Are you a beast of field and tree,
Or just a stronger child than me?

O wind, a-blowing all day long,
O wind, that sings so loud a song!

XXVI

Keepsake Mill

Over the borders, a sin without pardon,
   Breaking the branches and crawling below,
Out through the breach in the wall of the garden,
   Down by the banks of the river, we go.

Here is the mill with the humming of thunder,
   Here is the weir with the wonder of foam,
Here is the sluice with the race running under –
   Marvellous places, though handy to home!

Sounds of the village grow stiller and stiller,
   Stiller the note of the birds on the hill;
Dusty and dim are the eyes of the miller,
   Deaf are his ears with the moil of the mill.

Years may go by, and the wheel in the river
   Wheel as it wheels for us, children, today,
Wheel and keep roaring and foaming for ever
   Long after all of the boys are away.

Home from the Indies and home from the ocean,
   Heroes and soldiers we all shall come home;
Still we shall find the old mill wheel in motion,
   Turning and churning that river to foam.

You with the bean that I gave when we quarrelled,
   I with your marble of Saturday last,
Honoured and old and all gaily apparelled,
   Here we shall meet and remember the past.

XXVII

Good and Bad Children

Children, you are very little,
And your bones are very brittle;
If you would grow great and stately,
You must try to walk sedately.

You must still be bright and quiet,
And content with simple diet;
And remain, through all bewild'ring,
Innocent and honest children.

Happy hearts and happy faces,
Happy play in grassy places –
That was how, in ancient ages,
Children grew to kings and sages.

But the unkind and the unruly,
And the sort who eat unduly,
They must never hope for glory –
Theirs is quite a different story!

Cruel children, crying babies,
All grow up as geese and gabies,
Hated, as their age increases,
By their nephews and their nieces.

XXVIII

Foreign Children

Little Indian, Sioux or Crow,
Little frosty Eskimo,
Little Turk or Japanee,
O! don't you wish that you were me?

You have seen the scarlet trees
And the lions over seas;
You have eaten ostrich eggs,
And turned the turtles off their legs.

Such a life is very fine,
But it's not so nice as mine:
You must often, as you trod,
Have wearied *not* to be abroad.

You have curious things to eat,
I am fed on proper meat;
You must dwell beyond the foam,
But I am safe and live at home.

   Little Indian, Sioux or Crow,
   Little frosty Eskimo,
   Little Turk or Japanee,
O! don't you wish that you were me?

XXIX

The Sun's Travels

The sun is not a-bed, when I
At night upon my pillow lie;
Still round the earth his way he takes,
And morning after morning makes.

While here at home, in shining day,
We round the sunny garden play,
Each little Indian sleepy-head
Is being kissed and put to bed.

And when at eve I rise from tea,
Day dawns beyond the Atlantic Sea;
And all the children in the West
Are getting up and being dressed.

XXX

The Lamplighter

My tea is nearly ready and the sun has left the sky;
It's time to take the window to see Leerie going by;
For every night at teatime and before you take your seat,
With lantern and with ladder he comes posting up the street.

Now Tom would be a driver and Maria go to sea,
And my papa's a banker and as rich as he can be;
But I, when I am stronger and can choose what I'm to do,
O Leerie, I'll go round at night and light the lamps with you!

For we are very lucky, with a lamp before the door,
And Leerie stops to light it as he lights so many more;
And O! before you hurry by with ladder and with light,
O Leerie, see a little child and nod to him tonight!

XXXI

My Bed is a Boat

My bed is like a little boat;
  Nurse helps me in when I embark;
She girds me in my sailor's coat
  And starts me in the dark.

My Bed is a Boat

At night, I go on board and say
   Good-night to all my friends on shore;
I shut my eyes and sail away
   And see and hear no more.

And sometimes things to bed I take,
   As prudent sailors have to do;
Perhaps a slice of wedding-cake,
   Perhaps a toy or two.

All night across the dark we steer;
   But when the day returns at last,
Safe in my room, beside the pier,
   I find my vessel fast.

XXXII

The Moon

The moon has a face like the clock in the hall;
She shines on thieves on the garden wall,
On streets and fields and harbour quays,
And birdies asleep in the forks of the trees.

The squalling cat and the squeaking mouse,
The howling dog by the door of the house,
The bat that lies in bed at noon,
All love to be out by the light of the moon.

But all of the things that belong to the day
Cuddle to sleep to be out of her way;
And flowers and children close their eyes
Till up in the morning the sun shall arise.

XXXIII

The Swing

How do you like to go up in a swing,
   Up in the air so blue?
Oh, I do think it the pleasantest thing
   Ever a child can do!

Up in the air and over the wall,
   Till I can see so wide,
Rivers and trees and cattle and all
   Over the countryside –

The Swing

Till I look down on the garden green,
Down on the roof so brown –
Up in the air I go flying again,
Up in the air and down!

XXXIV

Time to Rise

A birdie with a yellow bill
Hopped upon the window sill,
Cocked his shining eye and said:
'Ain't you 'shamed, you sleepy-head?'

XXXV

Looking-glass River

Smooth it slides upon its travel,
　Here a wimple, there a gleam –
　　O the clean gravel!
　　O the smooth stream!

Sailing blossoms, silver fishes,
　Paven pools as clear as air –
　　How a child wishes
　　To live down there!

We can see our coloured faces
　Floating on the shaken pool
　　Down in cool places,
　　Dim and very cool;

Till a wind or water wrinkle,
　Dipping marten, plumping trout,
　　Spreads in a twinkle
　　And blots all out.

See the rings pursue each other;
　All below grows black as night,
　　Just as if mother
　　Had blown out the light!

Patience, children, just a minute –
　See the spreading circles die;
　　The stream and all in it
　　Will clear by-and-by.

XXXVI

Fairy Bread

Come up here, O dusty feet!
    Here is fairy bread to eat.
Here in my retiring room,
    Children, you may dine
On the golden smell of broom
    And the shade of pine;
And when you have eaten well,
Fairy stories hear and tell.

XXXVII

From a Railway Carriage

Faster than fairies, faster than witches,
Bridges and houses, hedges and ditches;
And charging along like troops in a battle,
All through the meadows the horses and cattle:
All of the sights of the hill and the plain
Fly as thick as driving rain;
And ever again, in the wink of an eye,
Painted stations whistle by.

Here is a child who clambers and scrambles,
All by himself and gathering brambles;
Here is a tramp who stands and gazes;
And there is the green for stringing the daisies!
Here is a cart run away in the road
Lumping along with man and load;
And here is a mill and there is a river:
Each a glimpse and gone for ever!

XXXVIII

Winter-time

Late lies the wintry sun a-bed,
A frosty, fiery sleepy-head;
Blinks but an hour or two; and then,
A blood-red orange, sets again.

Before the stars have left the skies,
At morning in the dark I rise;
And shivering in my nakedness,
By the cold candle, bathe and dress.

Close by the jolly fire I sit
To warm my frozen bones a bit;
Or with a reindeer-sled, explore
The colder countries round the door.

When to go out, my nurse doth wrap
Me in my comforter and cap:
The cold wind burns my face, and blows
Its frosty pepper up my nose.

Black are my steps on silver sod;
Thick blows my frosty breath abroad;
And tree and house, and hill and lake,
Are frosted like a wedding-cake.

XXXIX

The Hayloft

Through all the pleasant meadow-side
    The grass grew shoulder-high,
Till the shining scythes went far and wide
    And cut it down to dry.

These green and sweetly smelling crops
    They led in waggons home;
And they piled them here in mountain tops
    For mountaineers to roam.

Here is Mount Clear, Mount Rusty-Nail,
    Mount Eagle and Mount High; –
The mice that in these mountains dwell,
    No happier are than I!

O what a joy to clamber there,
    O what a place for play,
With the sweet, the dim, the dusty air,
    The happy hills of hay!

XL

Farewell to the Farm

The coach is at the door at last;
The eager children, mounting fast
And kissing hands, in chorus sing:
Good-bye, good-bye, to everything!

To house and garden, field and lawn,
The meadow-gates we swang upon,
To pump and stable, tree and swing,
Good-bye, good-bye, to everything!

And fare you well for evermore,
O ladder at the hayloft door,
O hayloft where the cobwebs cling,
Good-bye, good-bye, to everything!

Crack goes the whip, and off we go;
The trees and houses smaller grow;
Last, round the woody turn we swing:
Good-bye, good-bye, to everything!

XLI

North-West Passage

1. Good Night

When the bright lamp is carried in,
The sunless hours again begin;
O'er all without, in field and lane,
The haunted night returns again.

Now we behold the embers flee
About the firelit hearth; and see
Our faces painted as we pass,
Like pictures, on the window-glass.

Must we to bed indeed? Well then,
Let us arise and go like men,
And face with an undaunted tread
The long black passage up to bed.

Farewell, O brother, sister, sire!
O pleasant party round the fire!
The songs you sing, the tales you tell,
Till far tomorrow, fare ye well!

2. Shadow March

All round the house is the jet-black night;
  It stares through the window-pane;
It crawls in the corners, hiding from the light,
  And it moves with the moving flame.

Now my little heart goes a-beating like a drum,
   With the breath of the Bogie in my hair;
And all round the candle the crooked shadows come
   And go marching along up the stair.

The shadow of the balusters, the shadow of the lamp,
   The shadow of the child that goes to bed –
All the wicked shadows coming, tramp, tramp, tramp,
   With the black night overhead.

3. In Port

Last, to the chamber where I lie
My fearful footsteps patter nigh,
And come from out the cold and gloom
Into my warm and cheerful room.

There, safe arrived, we turn about
To keep the coming shadows out,
And close the happy door at last
On all the perils that we passed.

Then, when mamma goes by to bed,
She shall come in with tip-toe tread,
And see me lying warm and fast
And in the Land of Nod at last.

The Child Alone

I

The Unseen Playmate

When children are playing alone on the green,
In comes the playmate that never was seen.
When children are happy and lonely and good,
The Friend of the Children comes out of the wood.

Nobody heard him and nobody saw,
His is a picture you never could draw,
But he's sure to be present, abroad or at home,
When children are happy and playing alone.

He lies in the laurels, he runs on the grass,
He sings when you tinkle the musical glass;
Whene'er you are happy and cannot tell why,
The Friend of the Children is sure to be by!

He loves to be little, he hates to be big,
'Tis he that inhabits the caves that you dig;
'Tis he when you play with your soldiers of tin
That sides with the Frenchmen and never can win.

'Tis he, when at night you go off to your bed,
Bids you go to your sleep and not trouble your head;
For wherever they're lying, in cupboard or shelf,
'Tis he will take care of your playthings himself!

II

My Ship and I

O it's I that am the captain of a tidy little ship,
   Of a ship that goes a-sailing on the pond;
And my ship it keeps a-turning all around and all about;
But when I'm a little older, I shall find the secret out
   How to send my vessel sailing on beyond.

For I mean to grow as little as the dolly at the helm,
   And the dolly I intend to come alive;
And with him beside to help me, it's a-sailing I shall go,
It's a-sailing on the water, when the jolly breezes blow
   And the vessel goes a divie-divie-dive.

O it's then you'll see me sailing through the rushes and the reeds,
   And you'll hear the water singing at the prow;
For beside the dolly sailor, I'm to voyage and explore,
To land upon the island where no dolly was before,
   And to fire the penny cannon in the bow.

III

My Kingdom

Down by a shining water well
I found a very little dell,
   No higher than my head.
The heather and the gorse about
In summer bloom were coming out,
   Some yellow and some red.

I called the little pool a sea;
The little hills were big to me;
   For I am very small.
I made a boat, I made a town,

I searched the caverns up and down,
And named them one and all.

And all about was mine, I said,
The little sparrows overhead,
The little minnows too.
This was the world and I was king;
For me the bees came by to sing,
For me the swallows flew.

I played there were no deeper seas,
Nor any wider plains than these,
Nor other kings than me.
At last I heard my mother call
Out from the house at evenfall,
To call me home to tea.

And I must rise and leave my dell,
And leave my dimpled water well,
And leave my heather blooms.
Alas! and as my home I neared,
How very big my nurse appeared,
How great and cool the rooms!

IV

Picture-books in Winter

Summer fading, winter comes –
Frosty mornings, tingling thumbs,
Window robins, winter rooks,
And the picture story-books.

Water now is turned to stone
Nurse and I can walk upon;
Still we find the flowing brooks
In the picture story-books.

All the pretty things put by,
Wait upon the children's eye,
Sheep and shepherds, trees and crooks,
In the picture story-books.

We may see how all things are,
Seas and cities, near and far,
And the flying fairies' looks,
In the picture story-books.

How am I to sing your praise,
Happy chimney-corner days,
Sitting safe in nursery nooks,
Reading picture story-books?

V

My Treasures

These nuts, that I keep in the back of the nest
Where all my lead soldiers are lying at rest,
Were gathered in autumn by nursie and me
In a wood with a well by the side of the sea.

This whistle we made (and how clearly it sounds!)
By the side of a field at the end of the grounds.
Of a branch of a plane, with a knife of my own,
It was nursie who made it, and nursie alone!

The stone, with the white and the yellow and gray,
We discovered I cannot tell *how* far away;
And I carried it back although weary and cold,
For though father denies it, I'm sure it is gold.

But of all my treasures the last is the king,
For there's very few children possess such a thing;
And that is a chisel, both handle and blade,
Which a man who was really a carpenter made.

VI

Block City

What are you able to build with your blocks?
Castles and palaces, temples and docks.
Rain may keep raining, and others go roam,
But I can be happy and building at home.

Let the sofa be mountains, the carpet be sea,
There I'll establish a city for me:
A kirk and a mill and a palace beside,
And a harbour as well where my vessels may ride.

Great is the palace with pillar and wall,
A sort of a tower on the top of it all,
And steps coming down in an orderly way
To where my toy vessels lie safe in the bay.

This one is sailing and that one is moored:
Hark to the song of the sailors on board!
And see on the steps of my palace, the kings
Coming and going with presents and things!

Now I have done with it, down let it go!
All in a moment the town is laid low.
Block upon block lying scattered and free,
What is there left of my town by the sea?

Yet as I saw it, I see it again,
The kirk and the palace, the ships and the men,
And as long as I live and where'er I may be,
I'll always remember my town by the sea.

VII

The Land of Story-books

At evening when the lamp is lit,
Around the fire my parents sit;
They sit at home and talk and sing,
And do not play at anything.

Now, with my little gun, I crawl
All in the dark along the wall,
And follow round the forest track
Away behind the sofa back.

There, in the night, where none can spy,
All in my hunter's camp I lie,
And play at books that I have read
Till it is time to go to bed.

These are the hills, these are the woods,
These are my starry solitudes;
And there the river by whose brink
The roaring lions come to drink.

I see the others far away
As if in firelit camp they lay,
And I, like an Indian scout,
Around their party prowled about.

So, when my nurse comes in for me,
Home I return across the sea,
And go to bed with backward looks
At my dear land of Story-books.

The Land of Story-books

VIII

Armies in the Fire

The lamps now glitter down the street;
Faintly sound the falling feet;
And the blue even slowly falls
About the garden trees and walls.

Now in the falling of the gloom
The red fire paints the empty room:
And warmly on the roof it looks,
And flickers on the backs of books.

Armies march by tower and spire
Of cities blazing, in the fire; –
Till as I gaze with staring eyes,
The armies fade, the lustre dies.

Then once again the glow returns;
Again the phantom city burns;
And down the red-hot valley, lo!
The phantom armies marching go!

Blinking embers, tell me true
Where are those armies marching to,
And what the burning city is
That crumbles in your furnaces!

IX

The Little Land

When at home alone I sit
And am very tired of it,
I have just to shut my eyes
To go sailing through the skies –
To go sailing far away
To the pleasant Land of Play;
To the fairy-land afar
Where the Little People are;
Where the clover-tops are trees,
And the rainpools are the seas,
And the leaves like little ships
Sail about on tiny trips;
And above the daisy tree
    Through the grasses,
High o'erhead the Bumble Bee
    Hums and passes.

In that forest to and fro
I can wander, I can go;
See the spider and the fly,
And the ants go marching by
Carrying parcels with their feet
Down the green and grassy street.
I can in the sorrel sit
Where the ladybird alit.
I can climb the jointed grass;
    And on high
See the greater swallows pass
     In the sky,
And the round sun rolling by
Heeding no such things as I.

Through that forest I can pass
Till, as in a looking-glass,
Humming fly and daisy tree
And my tiny self I see,
Painted very clear and neat
On the rainpool at my feet.
Should a leaflet come to land
Drifting near to where I stand,
Straight I'll board that tiny boat
Round the rainpool sea to float.

Little thoughtful creatures sit
On the grassy coasts of it;
Little things with lovely eyes
See me sailing with surprise.
Some are clad in armour green –
(These have sure to battle been!) –
Some are pied with ev'ry hue,
Black and crimson, gold and blue;
Some have wings and swift are gone; –
But they all look kindly on.

When my eyes I once again
Open, and see all things plain:
High bare walls, great bare floor;
Great big knobs on drawer and door;
Great big people perched on chairs,
Stitching tucks and mending tears,
Each a hill that I could climb,
And talking nonsense all the time –
    O dear me,
     That I could be

A sailor on that rainpool sea,
A climber in the clover tree,
And just come back, a sleepy head,
Late at night to go to bed.

Garden Days

I

Night and Day

When the golden day is done,
  Through the closing portal,
Child and garden, flower and sun,
  Vanish all things mortal.

As the blinding shadows fall,
  As the rays diminish,
Under evening's cloak, they all
  Roll away and vanish.

Garden darkened, daisy shut,
  Child in bed, they slumber –
Glow-worm in the highway rut,
  Mice among the lumber.

In the darkness houses shine,
  Parents move with candles;
Till on all, the night divine
  Turns the bedroom handles.

Till at last the day begins
  In the east a-breaking,
In the hedges and the whins
  Sleeping birds a-waking.

In the darkness shapes of things,
  Houses, trees and hedges,
Clearer grow; and sparrow's wings
  Beat on window ledges.

These shall wake the yawning maid;
  She the door shall open –
Finding dew on garden glade
  And the morning broken.

There my garden grows again
   Green and rosy painted,
As at eve behind the pane
   From my eyes it fainted.

Just as it was shut away,
   Toy-like, in the even,
Here I see it glow with day
   Under glowing heaven.

Every path and every plot,
   Every bush of roses,
Every blue forget-me-not
   Where the dew reposes,

'Up!' they cry, 'the day is come
   On the smiling valleys:
We have beat the morning drum;
   Playmate, join your allies!'

II

Nest Eggs

Birds all the sunny day
   Flutter and quarrel
Here in the arbour-like
   Tent of the laurel.

Here in the fork
   The brown nest is seated;
Four little blue eggs
   The mother keeps heated.

While we stand watching her,
   Staring like gabies,
Safe in each egg are the
   Bird's little babies.

Soon the frail eggs they shall
   Chip, and upspringing
Make all the April woods
   Merry with singing.

Younger than we are,
   O children, and frailer,
Soon in blue air they'll be,
   Singer and sailor.

We, so much older,
    Taller and stronger,
We shall look down on the
    Birdies no longer.

They shall go flying
    With musical speeches
High overhead in the
    Tops of the beeches.

In spite of our wisdom
    And sensible talking,
We on our feet must go
    Plodding and walking.

III

The Flowers

All the names I know from nurse:
Gardener's garters, Shepherd's purse,
Bachelor's buttons, Lady's smock,
And the Lady Hollyhock.

Fairy places, fairy things,
Fairy woods where the wild bee wings,
Tiny trees for tiny dames –
These must all be fairy names!

Tiny woods below whose boughs
Shady fairies weave a house;
Tiny tree-tops, rose or thyme,
Where the braver fairies climb!

Fair are grown-up people's trees,
But the fairest woods are these;
Where if I were not so tall,
I should live for good and all.

IV

Summer Sun

Great is the sun, and wide he goes
Through empty heaven without repose;
And in the blue and glowing days
More thick than rain he showers his rays.

Though closer still the blinds we pull
To keep the shady parlour cool,
Yet he will find a chink or two
To slip his golden fingers through.

The dusty attic spider-clad
He, through the keyhole, maketh glad;
And through the broken edge of tiles,
Into the laddered hay-loft smiles.

Meantime his golden face around
He bears to all the garden ground,
And sheds a warm and glittering look
Among the ivy's inmost nook.

Above the hills, along the blue,
Round the bright air with footing true,
To please the child, to paint the rose,
The gardener of the World, he goes.

V

The Dumb Soldier

When the grass was closely mown,
Walking on the lawn alone,
In the turf a hole I found
And hid a soldier underground.

Spring and daisies came apace;
Grasses hid my hiding place;
Grasses run like a green sea
O'er the lawn up to my knee.

Under grass alone he lies,
Looking up with leaden eyes,
Scarlet coat and pointed gun,
To the stars and to the sun.

When the grass is ripe like grain,
When the scythe is stoned again,
When the lawn is shaven clear,
Then my hole shall reappear.

I shall find him, never fear,
I shall find my grenadier;
But for all that's gone and come,
I shall find my soldier dumb.

He has lived, a little thing,
In the grassy woods of spring;
Done, if he could tell me true,
Just as I should like to do.

He has seen the starry hours
And the springing of the flowers;
And the fairy things that pass
In the forests of the grass.

In the silence he has heard
Talking bee and ladybird,
And the butterfly has flown
O'er him as he lay alone.

Not a word will he disclose,
Not a word of all he knows.
I must lay him on the shelf,
And make up the tale myself.

VI

Autumn Fires

In the other gardens
    And all up the vale,
From the autumn bonfires
    See the smoke trail!

Pleasant summer over
    And all the summer flowers,
The red fire blazes,
    The gray smoke towers.

Sing a song of seasons!
    Something bright in all!
Flowers in the summer,
    Fires in the fall!

VII

The Gardener

The gardener does not love to talk,
He makes me keep the gravel walk;
And when he puts his tools away,
He locks the door and takes the key.

Away behind the currant row
Where no one else but cook may go,
Far in the plots, I see him dig
Old and serious, brown and big.

He digs the flowers, green, red, and blue,
Nor wishes to be spoken to.
He digs the flowers and cuts the hay,
And never seems to want to play.

Silly gardener! summer goes,
And winter comes with pinching toes,
When in the garden bare and brown
You must lay your barrow down.

Well now, and while the summer stays,
To profit by these garden days
O how much wiser you would be
To play at Indian wars with me!

VIII

Historical Associations

Dear Uncle Jim, this garden ground
That now you smoke your pipe around,
Has seen immortal actions done
And valiant battles lost and won.

Here we had best on tip-toe tread,
While I for safety march ahead,
For this is that enchanted ground
Where all who loiter slumber sound.

Here is the sea, here is the sand,
Here is simple Shepherd's Land,
Here are the fairy hollyhocks,
And there are Ali Baba's rocks.

But yonder, see! apart and high,
Frozen Siberia lies; where I,
With Robert Bruce and William Tell,
Was bound by an enchanter's spell.

There, then, awhile in chains we lay,
In wintry dungeons, far from day;
But ris'n at length, with might and main,
Our iron fetters burst in twain.

Then all the horns were blown in town;
And to the ramparts clanging down,
All the giants leaped to horse
And charged behind us through the gorse.

On we rode, the others and I,
Over the mountains blue, and by
The Silver River, the sounding sea
And the robber woods of Tartary.

A thousand miles we galloped fast,
And down the witches' lane we passed,
And rode amain, with brandished sword,
Up to the middle, through the ford.

Last we drew rein – a weary three –
Upon the lawn, in time for tea,
And from our steeds alighted down
Before the gates of Babylon.

Envoys

I

To Willie and Henrietta

If two may read aright
These rhymes of old delight
And house and garden play,
You two, my cousins, and you only, may.

You in a garden green
With me were king and queen,
Were hunter, soldier, tar,
And all the thousand things that children are.

Now in the elders' seat
We rest with quiet feet,
And from the window-bay
We watch the children, our successors, play.

'Time was,' the golden head
Irrevocably said;
But time which none can bind,
While flowing fast away, leaves love behind.

II

To My Mother

You too, my mother, read my rhymes
For love of unforgotten times,
And you may chance to hear once more
The little feet along the floor.

III

To Auntie

Chief of our aunts – not only I,
But all your dozen of nurslings cry –
What did the other children do?
And what were childhood, wanting you?

IV

To Minnie

The red room with the giant bed
Where none but elders laid their head;
The little room where you and I
Did for awhile together lie
And, simple suitor, I your hand
In decent marriage did demand;
The great day nursery, best of all,
With pictures pasted on the wall
And leaves upon the blind –
A pleasant room wherein to wake
And hear the leafy garden shake
And rustle in the wind –
And pleasant there to lie in bed
And see the pictures overhead –
The wars about Sebastopol,
The grinning guns along the wall,
The daring escalade,
The plunging ships, the bleating sheep,
The happy children ankle-deep
And laughing as they wade:
All these are vanished clean away,
And the old manse is changed today;
It wears an altered face
And shields a stranger race.
The river, on from mill to mill,
Flows past our childhood's garden still;

But ah! we children never more
Shall watch it from the water-door!
Below the yew   it still is there
Our phantom voices haunt the air
As we were still at play,
And I can hear them call and say:
'How far is it to Babylon?'

Ah, far enough, my dear,
Far, far enough from here –
Yet you have farther gone!
'Can I get there by candlelight?'
So goes the old refrain.
I do not know – perchance you might –
But only, children, hear it right,
Ah, never to return again!
The eternal dawn, beyond a doubt,
Shall break on hill and plain,
And put all stars and candles out
Ere we be young again.
To you in distant India, these
I send across the seas,
Nor count it far across.
For which of us forgets
The Indian cabinets,
The bones of antelope, the wings of albatross,
The pied and painted birds and beans,
The junks and bangles, beads and screens,
The gods and sacred bells,
And the loud-humming, twisted shells?
The level of the parlour floor
Was honest, homely, Scottish shore;
But when we climbed upon a chair,
Behold the gorgeous East was there!
Be this a fable; and behold
Me in the parlour as of old,
And Minnie just above me set
In the quaint Indian cabinet!
Smiling and kind, you grace a shelf
Too high for me to reach myself.
Reach down a hand, my dear, and take
These rhymes for old acquaintance' sake!

V

To My Name-child

1

Some day soon this rhyming volume, if you learn with proper speed,
Little Louis Sanchez, will be given you to read.
Then shall you discover, that your name was printed down
By the English printers, long before, in London town.

In the great and busy city where the East and West are met,
All the little letters did the English printer set;
While you thought of nothing, and were still too young to play,
Foreign people thought of you in places far away.

Ay, and while you slept, a baby, over all the English lands
Other little children took the volume in their hands;
Other children questioned, in their homes across the seas:
Who was little Louis, won't you tell us, mother, please?

2

Now that you have spelt your lesson, lay it down and go and play,
Seeking shells and seaweed on the sands of Monterey,
Watching all the mighty whalebones, lying buried by the breeze,
Tiny sandy-pipers, and the huge Pacific seas.

And remember in your playing, as the sea-fog rolls to you,
Long ere you could read it, how I told you what to do;
And that while you thought of no one, nearly half the world away
Some one thought of Louis on the beach of Monterey!

VI

To Any Reader

As from the house your mother sees
You playing round the garden trees,
So you may see, if you will look
Through the windows of this book,
Another child, far, far away,
And in another garden, play.
But do not think you can at all,
By knocking on the window, call
That child to hear you. He intent
Is all on his play-business bent.
He does not hear; he will not look,
Nor yet be lured out of this book.
For, long ago, the truth to say,
He has grown up and gone away,
And it is but a child of air
That lingers in the garden there.

UNDERWOODS

Of all my verse, like not a single line;
But like my title, for it is not mine.
That title from a better man I stole:
Ah, how much better, had I stol'n the whole!

Dedication

There are men and classes of men that stand above the common herd: the soldier, the sailor and the shepherd not unfrequently; the artist rarely; rarelier still, the clergyman; the physician almost as a rule. He is the flower (such as it is) of our civilisation; and when that stage of man is done with, and only remembered to be marvelled at in history, he will be thought to have shared as little as any in the defects of the period, and most notably exhibited the virtues of the race. Generosity he has, such as is possible to those who practise an art, never to those who drive a trade; discretion, tested by a hundred secrets; tact, tried in a thousand embarrassments; and what are more important, Heraclean cheerfulness and courage. So it is that he brings air and cheer into the sickroom, and often enough, though not so often as he wishes, brings healing.

Gratitude is but a lame sentiment; thanks, when they are expressed, are often more embarrassing than welcome; and yet I must set forth mine to a few out of many doctors who have brought me comfort and help: to Dr Willey of San Francisco, whose kindness to a stranger it must be as grateful to him, as it is touching to me, to remember; to Dr Karl Ruedi of Davos, the good genius of the English in his frosty mountains; to Dr Herbert of Paris, whom I knew only for a week, and to Dr Caissot of Montpellier, whom I only knew for ten days, and who have yet written their names deeply in my memory; to Dr Brandt of Royat; to Dr Wakefield of Nice; to Dr Chepmell, whose visits make it a pleasure to be ill; to Dr Horace Dobell, so wise in counsel; to Sir Andrew Clark, so unwearied in kindness; and to that wise youth, my uncle, Dr Balfour.

I forget as many as I remember; and I ask both to pardon me, these for silence, those for inadequate speech. But one name I have kept on purpose to the last, because it is a household word with me, and because if I had not received favours from so many hands and in so many quarters of the world, it should have stood upon this page alone: that of my friend Thomas Bodley Scott of Bournemouth. Will he accept this, although shared among so many, for a dedication to himself? and when next my ill-fortune (which has thus its pleasant side) brings him hurrying to me when he would fain sit down to meat or lie down to rest, will he care to remember that he takes this trouble for one who is not fool enough to be ungrateful?

R.L.S.

Skerryvore, Bournemouth

Note

The human conscience has fled of late the troublesome domain of conduct for what I should have supposed to be the less congenial field of art: there she may now be said to rage, and with special severity in all that touches dialect; so that in every novel the letters of the alphabet are tortured, and the reader wearied, to commemorate shades of mispronunciation. Now spelling is an art of great difficulty in my eyes, and I am inclined to lean upon the printer, even in common practice, rather than to venture abroad on new quests. And the Scots tongue has an orthography of its own, lacking neither 'authority nor author.' Yet the temptation is great to lend a little guidance to the bewildered Englishman. Some simple phonetic artifice might defend your verses from barbarous mishandling, and yet not injure any vested interest. So it seems at first; but there are rocks ahead. Thus, if I wish the diphthong *ou* to have its proper value, I may write *oor* instead of *our*; many have done so and lived, and the pillars of the universe remain unshaken. But if I did so, and came presently to *doun*, which is the classical Scots spelling of the English *down*, I should begin to feel uneasy; and if I went on a little farther, and came to a classical Scots word like *stour* or *dour* or *clour*, I should know precisely where I was – that is to say, that I was out of sight of land on those high seas of spelling reform in which so many strong swimmers have toiled vainly. To some the situation is exhilarating; as for me, I give one bubbling cry and sink. The compromise at which I have arrived is indefensible, and I have no thought of trying to defend it. As I have stuck for the most part to proper spelling, I append a table of some common vowel sounds which no one need consult; and just to prove that I belong to my age and have in me the stuff of a reformer, I have used modification marks throughout. Thus I can tell myself, not without pride, that I have added a fresh stumbling-block for English readers, and to a page of print in my native tongue, have lent a new uncouthness. *Sed non nobis.*

I note again, that among our new dialecticians, the local habitat of every dialect is given to the square mile. I could not emulate this nicety if I desired; for I simply wrote my Scots as well as I was able, not caring if it hailed from Lauderdale or Angus, from the Mearns or Galloway; if I had ever heard a good word, I used it without shame; and when Scots was lacking, or the rhyme jibbed, I was glad (like my betters) to fall back on English. For all that, I own to a friendly feeling for the tongue of Fergusson and of Sir Walter, both Edinburgh men; and I confess that Burns has always sounded in my ear like something partly foreign. And indeed I am from the Lothians myself; it is there I heard the language spoken about my childhood; and it is in the drawling Lothian voice that I repeat it to myself. Let the precisians call my speech that of the Lothians. And if it be not pure, alas! what matters it? The day draws near when this illustrious and malleable tongue shall be quite forgotten; and Burns's Ayrshire, and Dr Macdonald's Aberdeen-awa', and

Scott's brave, metropolitan utterance will be all equally the ghosts of speech. Till then I would love to have my hour as a native Maker, and be read by my own countryfolk in our own dying language: an ambition surely rather of the heart than of the head, so restricted as it is in prospect of endurance, so parochial in bounds of space.

Book I – *In English*

I

Envoy

Go, little book, and wish to all
Flowers in the garden, meat in the hall,
A bin of wine, a spice of wit,
A house with lawns enclosing it,
A living river by the door,
A nightingale in the sycamore!

II

A Song of the Road

The gauger walked with willing foot,
And aye the gauger played the flute;
And what should Master Gauger play
But *Over the hills and far away?*

Whene'er I buckle on my pack
And foot it gaily in the track,
O pleasant gauger, long since dead,
I hear you fluting on ahead.

You go with me the self-same way –
The self-same air for me you play;
For I do think and so do you
It is the tune to travel to.

For who would gravely set his face
To go to this or t'other place?
There's nothing under Heav'n so blue
That's fairly worth the travelling to.

On every hand the roads begin,
And people walk with zeal therein;
But whereso'er the highways tend,
Be sure there's nothing at the end.

Then follow you, wherever hie
The travelling mountains of the sky.
Or let the streams in civil mode
Direct your choice upon a road;

For one and all, or high or low,
Will lead you where you wish to go;
And one and all go night and day
Over the hills and far away!

Forest of Montargis, 1878.

III

The Canoe Speaks

On the great streams the ships may go
About men's business to and fro.
But I, the egg-shell pinnace, sleep
On crystal waters ankle-deep:
I, whose diminutive design,
Of sweeter cedar, pithier pine,
Is fashioned on so frail a mould,
A hand may launch, a hand withhold:
I, rather, with the leaping trout
Wind, among lilies, in and out;
I, the unnamed, inviolate,
Green, rustic rivers, navigate;
My dipping paddle scarcely shakes
The berry in the bramble-brakes;
Still forth on my green way I wend
Beside the cottage garden-end;
And by the nested angler fare,
And take the lovers unaware.
By willow wood and water-wheel
Speedily fleets my touching keel;
By all retired and shady spots
Where prosper dim forget-me-nots;
By meadows where at afternoon
The growing maidens troop in June
To loose their girdles on the grass.
Ah! speedier than before the glass
The backward toilet goes; and swift
As swallows quiver, robe and shift
And the rough country stockings lie
Around each young divinity.
When, following the recondite brook,
Sudden upon this scene I look,
And light with unfamiliar face
On chaste Diana's bathing-place,
Loud ring the hills about and all
The shallows are abandoned …

IV

It is the season now to go
About the country high and low,
Among the lilacs hand in hand,
And two by two in fairy land.

The brooding boy, the sighing maid,
Wholly fain and half afraid,
Now meet along the hazel'd brook
To pass and linger, pause and look.

A year ago, and blithely paired,
Their rough-and-tumble play they shared;
They kissed and quarrelled, laughed and cried,
A year ago at Eastertide.

With bursting heart, with fiery face,
She strove against him in the race;
He unabashed her garter saw,
That now would touch her skirts with awe.

Now by the stile ablaze she stops,
And his demurer eyes he drops;
Now they exchange averted sighs
Or stand and marry silent eyes.

And he to her a hero is
And sweeter she than primroses;
Their common silence dearer far
Than nightingale and mavis are.

Now when they sever wedded hands,
Joy trembles in their bosom-strands,
And lovely laughter leaps and falls
Upon their lips in madrigals.

V

The House Beautiful

A naked house, a naked moor,
A shivering pool before the door,
A garden bare of flowers and fruit
And poplars at the garden foot:
Such is the place that I live in,
Bleak without and bare within.

Yet shall your ragged moor receive
The incomparable pomp of eve,
And the old glories of the dawn
Behind your shivering trees be drawn;
And when the wind from place to place
Doth the unmoored cloud-galleons chase,
Your garden gloom and gleam again,
With leaping sun, with glancing rain.
Here shall the wizard moon ascend
The heavens, in the crimson end
Of day's declining splendour; here
The army of the stars appear.
The neighbour hollows dry or wet,
Spring shall with tender flowers beset;
And oft the morning muser see
Larks rising from the broomy lea,
And every fairy wheel and thread
Of cobweb dew-bediamonded.
When daisies go, shall winter time
Silver the simple grass with rime;
Autumnal frosts enchant the pool
And make the cart-ruts beautiful;
And when snow-bright the moor expands,
How shall your children clap their hands!
To make this earth our hermitage,
A cheerful and a changeful page,
God's bright and intricate device
Of days and seasons doth suffice.

VI

A Visit from the Sea

Far from the loud sea beaches
    Where he goes fishing and crying,
Here in the inland garden
    Why is the sea-gull flying?

Here are no fish to dive for;
    Here is the corn and lea;
Here are the green trees rustling.
    Hie away home to sea!

Fresh is the river water
    And quiet among the rushes;
This is no home for the sea-gull
    But for the rooks and thrushes.

Pity the bird that has wandered!
Pity the sailor ashore!
Hurry him home to the ocean,
Let him come here no more!

High on the sea-cliff ledges
The white gulls are trooping and crying,
Here among rooks and roses,
Why is the sea-gull flying!

VII

To a Gardener

Friend, in my mountain-side demesne,
My plain-beholding, rosy, green
And linnet-haunted garden-ground,
Let still the esculents abound.
Let first the onion flourish there,
Rose among roots, the maiden-fair,
Wine-scented and poetic soul
Of the capacious salad bowl.
Let thyme the mountaineer (to dress
The tinier birds) and wading cress,
The lover of the shallow brook,
From all my plots and borders look.
Nor crisp and ruddy radish, nor
Pease-cods for the child's pinafore
Be lacking; nor of salad clan
The last and least that ever ran
About great nature's garden-beds.
Nor thence be missed the speary heads
Of artichoke; nor thence the bean
That gathered innocent and green
Outsavours the belauded pea.

These tend, I prithee; and for me,
Thy most long-suffering master, bring
In April, when the linnets sing
And the days lengthen more and more,
At sundown to the garden door.
And I, being provided thus,
Shall, with superb asparagus,
A book, a taper, and a cup
Of country wine, divinely sup.

La Solitude, Hyères.

VIII

To Minnie

(*With a hand-glass*)

A picture-frame for you to fill,
    A paltry setting for your face,
A thing that has no worth until
    You lend it something of your grace,

I send (unhappy I that sing
    Laid by awhile upon the shelf)
Because I would not send a thing
    Less charming than you are yourself.

And happier than I, alas!
    (Dumb thing, I envy its delight)
'Twill wish you well, the looking-glass,
    And look you in the face tonight.

1869

IX

To K. de M.

A lover of the moorland bare
And honest country winds, you were;
The silver-skimming rain you took;
And loved the floodings of the brook,
Dew, frost and mountains, fire and seas,
Tumultuary silences,
Winds that in darkness fifed a tune,
And the high-riding, virgin moon.

And as the berry, pale and sharp,
Springs on some ditch's counterscarp
In our ungenial, native north –
You put your frosted wildings forth,
And on the heath, afar from man,
A strong and bitter virgin ran.

The berry ripened keeps the rude
And racy flavour of the wood.
And you that loved the empty plain
All redolent of wind and rain,
Around you still the curlew sings –
The freshness of the weather clings –

The maiden jewels of the rain
Sit in your dabbled locks again.

X

To N.V. de G.S.

The unfathomable sea, and time, and tears,
The deeds of heroes and the crimes of kings
Dispart us; and the river of events
Has, for an age of years, to east and west
More widely borne our cradles. Thou to me
Art foreign, as when seamen at the dawn
Descry a land far off and know not which.
So I approach uncertain; so I cruise
Round thy mysterious islet, and behold
Surf and great mountains and loud river-bars,
And from the shore hear inland voices call
Strange is the seaman's heart; he hopes, he fears;
Draws closer and sweeps wider from that coast;
Last, his rent sail refits, and to the deep
His shattered prow uncomforted puts back.
Yet as he goes he ponders at the helm
Of that bright island; where he feared to touch,
His spirit rëadventures; and for years,
Where by his wife he slumbers safe at home,
Thoughts of that land revisit him; he sees
The eternal mountains beckon, and awakes
Yearning for that far home that might have been.

XI

To Will. H. Low

Youth now flees on feathered foot,
Faint and fainter sounds the flute,
Rarer songs of gods; and still
Somewhere on the sunny hill,
Or along the winding stream,
Through the willows, flits a dream;
Flits but shows a smiling face,
Flees but with so quaint a grace,
None can choose to stay at home,
All must follow, all must roam.

This is unborn beauty: she
Now in air floats high and free,

Takes the sun and breaks the blue; –
Late with stooping pinion flew
Raking hedgerow trees, and wet
Her wing in silver streams, and set
Shining foot on temple roof:
Now again she flies aloof,
Coasting mountain clouds and kiss't
By the evening's amethyst.

In wet wood and miry lane,
Still we pant and pound in vain;
Still with leaden foot we chase
Waning pinion, fainting face;
Still with gray hair we stumble on,
Till, behold, the vision gone!
Where hath fleeting beauty led?
To the doorway of the dead.
Life is over, life was gay:
We have come the primrose way.

XII

To Mrs Will. H. Low

Even in the bluest noonday of July,
There could not run the smallest breath of wind
But all the quarter sounded like a wood;
And in the chequered silence and above
The hum of city cabs that sought the Bois,
Suburban ashes shivered into song.
A patter and a chatter and a chirp
And a long dying hiss – it was as though
Starched old brocaded dames through all the house
Had trailed a strident skirt, or the whole sky
Even in a wink had over-brimmed in rain.
Hark, in these shady parlours, how it talks
Of the near Autumn, how the smitten ash
Trembles and augurs floods! O not too long
In these inconstant latitudes delay,
O not too late from the unbeloved north
Trim your escape! For soon shall this low roof
Resound indeed with rain, soon shall your eyes
Search the foul garden, search the darkened rooms,
Nor find one jewel but the blazing log.

12 Rue Vernier, Paris.

XIII

To H. F. Brown
(*Written during a dangerous sickness.*)

I sit and wait a pair of oars
On cis-Elysian river-shores.
Where the immortal dead have sate,
'Tis mine to sit and meditate;
To re-ascend life's rivulet,
Without remorse, without regret;
And sing my *Alma Genetrix*
Among the willows of the Styx.

And lo, as my serener soul
Did these unhappy shores patrol,
And wait with an attentive ear
The coming of the gondolier,
Your fire-surviving roll I took,
Your spirited and happy book;[1]
Whereon, despite my frowning fate,
It did my soul so recreate
That all my fancies fled away
On a Venetian holiday.

Now, thanks to your triumphant care,
Your pages clear as April air,
The sails, the bells, the birds, I know,
And the far-off Friulan snow;
The land and sea, the sun and shade,
And the blue even lamp-inlaid.
For this, for these, for all, O friend,
For your whole book from end to end –
For Paron Piero's muttonham –
I your defaulting debtor am.

Perchance, reviving, yet may I
To your sea-paven city hie,
And in a *felze*, some day yet
Light at your pipe my cigarette.

---

1. *Life on the Lagoons*, by H. F. Brown, originally burned in the fire at Messrs. Kegan Paul, Trench, and Co.'s

XIV

To Andrew Lang

Dear Andrew, with the brindled hair,
Who glory to have thrown in air,
High over arm, the trembling reed,
By Ale and Kail, by Till and Tweed:
An equal craft of hand you show
The pen to guide, the fly to throw:
I count you happy starred; for God
When He with inkpot and with rod
Endowed you, bade your fortune lead
Forever by the crooks of Tweed,
Forever by the woods of song
And lands that to the Muse belong;
Or if in peopled streets, or in
The abhorred pedantic sanhedrin,
It should be yours to wander, still
Airs of the morn, airs of the hill,
The plovery Forest and the seas
That break about the Hebrides,
Should follow over field and plain
And find you at the window pane;
And you again see hill and peel,
And the bright springs gush at your heel.
So went the fiat forth, and so
Garrulous like a brook you go,
With sound of happy mirth and sheen
Of daylight – whether by the green
You fare that moment, or the gray;
Whether you dwell in March or May;
Or whether treat of reels and rods
Or of the old unhappy gods:
Still like a brook your page has shone,
And your ink sings of Helicon.

XV

Et Tu in Arcadia Vixisti
(To R.A.M.S.)

In ancient tales, O friend, thy spirit dwelt;
There, from of old, thy childhood passed; and there
High expectation, high delights and deeds,
Thy fluttering heart with hope and terror moved.
And thou hast heard of yore the Blatant Beast,

And Roland's horn, and that war-scattering shout
Of all-unarmed Achilles, aegis-crowned.
And perilous lands thou sawest, sounding shores
And seas and forests drear, island and dale
And mountain dark. For thou with Tristram rod'st
Or Bedevere, in farthest Lyonesse.
Thou hadst a booth in Samarcand, whereat
Side-looking Magians trafficked; thence, by night,
An Afreet snatched thee, and with wings upbore
Beyond the Aral mount; or, hoping gain,
Thou, with a jar of money, didst embark,
For Balsorah, by sea. But chiefly thou
In that clear air took'st life; in Arcady
The haunted, land of song; and by the wells
Where most the gods frequent. There Chiron old,
In the Pelethronian antre, taught thee lore:
The plants, he taught, and by the shining stars
In forests dim to steer. There hast thou seen
Immortal Pan dance secret in a glade,
And, dancing, roll his eyes; these, where they fell,
Shed glee, and through the congregated oaks
A flying horror winged; while all the earth
To the god's pregnant footing thrilled within.
Or whiles, beside the sobbing stream, he breathed,
In his clutched pipe, unformed and wizard strains,
Divine yet brutal; which the forest heard,
And thou, with awe; and far upon the plain
The unthinking ploughman started and gave ear.

Now things there are that, upon him who sees,
A strong vocation lay; and strains there are
That whoso hears shall hear for evermore.
For evermore thou hear'st immortal Pan
And those melodious godheads, ever young
And ever quiring, on the mountains old.

What was this earth, child of the gods, to thee?
Forth from thy dreamland thou, a dreamer cam'st,
And in thine ears the olden music rang,
And in thy mind the doings of the dead,
And those heroic ages long forgot.
To a so fallen earth, alas! too late,
Alas! in evil days, thy steps return,
To list at noon for nightingales, to grow
A dweller on the beach till Argo come
That came long since, a lingerer by the pool
Where that desirèd angel bathes no more.

As when the Indian to Dakota comes,
Or farthest Idaho, and where he dwelt,
He with his clan, a humming city finds;
Thereon awhile, amazed, he stares, and then
To right and leftward, like a questing dog,
Seeks first the ancestral altars, then the hearth
Long cold with rains, and where old terror lodged,
And where the dead. So thee undying Hope,
With all her pack, hunts screaming through the years:
Here, there, thou fleeëst; but nor here nor there
The pleasant gods abide, the glory dwells.

That, that was not Apollo, not the god.
This was not Venus, though she Venus seemed
A moment. And though fair yon river move,
She, all the way, from disenchanted fount
To seas unhallowed runs; the gods forsook
Long since her trembling rushes; from her plains
Disconsolate, long since adventure fled;
And now although the inviting river flows,
And every poplared cape, and every bend
Or willowy islet, win upon thy soul
And to thy hopeful shallop whisper speed;
Yet hope not thou at all; hope is no more;
And O, long since the golden groves are dead,
The faery cities vanished from the land!

XVI

To W. E. Henley

The year runs through her phases; rain and sun,
Springtime and summer pass; winter succeeds;
But one pale season rules the house of death.
Cold falls the imprisoned daylight; fell disease
By each lean pallet squats, and pain and sleep
Toss gaping on the pillows.

                              But O thou!
Uprise and take thy pipe. Bid music flow,
Strains by good thoughts attended, like the spring
The swallows follow over land and sea.
Pain sleeps at once; at once, with open eyes,
Dozing despair awakes. The shepherd sees
His flock come bleating home; the seaman hears
Once more the cordage rattle. Airs of home!
Youth, love and roses blossom; the gaunt ward

Dislimns and disappears, and, opening out,
Shows brooks and forests, and the blue beyond
Of mountains.

        Small the pipe; but O! do thou,
Peak-faced and suffering piper, blow therein
The dirge of heroes dead; and to these sick,
These dying, sound the triumph over death.
Behold! each greatly breathes; each tastes a joy
Unknown before, in dying; for each knows
A hero dies with him – though unfulfilled,
Yet conquering truly – and not dies in vain.

So is pain cheered, death comforted; the house
Of sorrow smiles to listen. Once again –
O thou, Orpheus and Heracles, the bard
And the deliverer, touch the stops again!

XVII

Henry James

Who comes tonight? We ope the doors in vain.
Who comes? My bursting walls, can you contain
The presences that now together throng
Your narrow entry, as with flowers and song,
As with the air of life, the breath of talk?
Lo, how these fair immaculate women walk
Behind their jocund maker; and we see
Slighted *De Mauves*, and that far different she,
Gressie, the trivial sphynx; and to our feast
Daisy and *Barb* and *Chancellor* (she not least!)
With all their silken, all their airy kin,
Do like unbidden angels enter in.
But he, attended by these shining names,
Comes (best of all) himself – our welcome James.

XVIII

The Mirror Speaks

Where the bells peal far at sea
Cunning fingers fashioned me.
There on palace walls I hung
While that Consuelo sung;
But I heard, though I listened well,
Never a note, never a trill,

Never a beat of the chiming bell.
There I hung and looked, and there
In my gray face, faces fair
Shone from under shining hair.
Well I saw the poising head,
But the lips moved and nothing said;
And when lights were in the hall,
Silent moved the dancers all.

So awhile I glowed, and then
Fell on dusty days and men;
Long I slumbered packed in straw,
Long I none but dealers saw;
Till before my silent eye
One that sees came passing by.

Now with an outlandish grace,
To the sparkling fire I face
In the blue room at Skerryvore;
Where I wait until the door
Open, and the Prince of Men,
Henry James, shall come again.

XIX

Katharine

We see you as we see a face
That trembles in a forest place
Upon the mirror of a pool
Forever quiet, clear and cool;
And in the wayward glass, appears
To hover between smiles and tears,
Elfin and human, airy and true,
And backed by the reflected blue.

XX

To F.J.S.

I read, dear friend, in your dear face
Your life's tale told with perfect grace;
The river of your life, I trace
Up the sun-chequered, devious bed
To the far-distant fountain-head.

XXXII   Requiem.

Under the wide and starry sky,
Dig the grave and let me lie.
Glad did I live and gladly die
    And I laid me down with a will.

Here may the winds about me blow;
Here the clouds may come and go;
Here shall be rest for evermo,
    And the heart for aye shall be still

This be the verse you grave for me:
Here he lies where he longed to be;
Home is the sailor, home from sea,
    And the hunter home from the hill

Original MS of three-stanza version of *Requiem*

Not one quick beat of your warm heart,
Nor thought that came to you apart,
Pleasure nor pity, love nor pain
Nor sorrow, has gone by in vain;

But as some lone, wood-wandering child
Brings home with him at evening mild
The thorns and flowers of all the wild,
From your whole life, O fair and true
Your flowers and thorns you bring with you!

XXI

Requiem

Under the wide and starry sky,
Dig the grave and let me lie.
Glad did I live and gladly die,
    And I laid me down with a will.

This be the verse you grave for me:
Here he lies where he longed to be;
Home is the sailor, home from sea,
    And the hunter home from the hill.

XXII

The Celestial Surgeon

If I have faltered more or less
In my great task of happiness;
If I have moved among my race
And shown no glorious morning face;
If beams from happy human eyes
Have moved me not; if morning skies,
Books, and my food, and summer rain
Knocked on my sullen heart in vain: –
Lord, thy most pointed pleasure take
And stab my spirit broad awake;
Or, Lord, if too obdurate I,
Choose thou, before that spirit die,
A piercing pain, a killing sin,
And to my dead heart run them in!

XXIII

Our Lady of the Snows

Out of the sun, out of the blast,
Out of the world, alone I passed
Across the moor and through the wood
To where the monastery stood.
There neither lute nor breathing fife,
Nor rumour of the world of life,
Nor confidences low and dear,
Shall strike the meditative ear.
Aloof, unhelpful, and unkind,
The prisoners of the iron mind,
Where nothing speaks except the bell
The unfraternal brothers dwell.
Poor passionate men, still clothed afresh
With agonising folds of flesh;
Whom the clear eyes solicit still
To some bold output of the will,
While fairy Fancy far before
And musing Memory-Hold-the door
Now to heroic death invite
And now uncurtain fresh delight:
O, little boots it thus to dwell
On the remote unneighboured hill!

O to be up and doing, O
Unfearing and unshamed to go
In all the uproar and the press
About my human business!
My undissuaded heart I hear
Whisper courage in my ear.
With voiceless calls, the ancient earth
Summons me to a daily birth.
Thou, O my love, ye, O my friends –
The gist of life, the end of ends –
To laugh, to love, to live, to die,
Ye call me by the ear and eye!

Forth from the casemate, on the plain
Where honour has the world to gain,
Pour forth and bravely do your part,
O knights of the unshielded heart!
Forth and forever forward! – out
From prudent turret and redoubt,
And in the mellay charge amain,
To fall but yet to rise again!

Captive? ah, still, to honour bright,
A captive soldier of the right!
Of free and fighting, good with ill?
Unconquering but unconquered still!

And ye, O brethren, what if God,
When from Heav'n's top he spies abroad,
And sees on this tormented stage
The noble war of mankind rage:
What if his vivifying eye,
O monks, should pass your corner by?
For still the Lord is Lord of might;
In deeds, in deeds, he takes delight;
The plough, the spear, the laden barks,
The field, the founded city, marks;
He marks the smiler of the streets,
The singer upon garden seats;
He sees the climber in the rocks;
To him, the shepherd folds his flocks.
For those he loves that underprop
With daily virtues Heaven's top,
And bear the falling sky with ease,
Unfrowning caryatides.
Those he approves that ply the trade,
That rock the child, that wed the maid,
That with weak virtues, weaker hands,
Sow gladness on the peopled lands,
And still with laughter, song and shout,
Spin the great wheel of earth about.

But ye? – O ye who linger still
Here in your fortress on the hill,
With placid face, with tranquil breath,
The unsought volunteers of death,
Our cheerful General on high
With careless looks may pass you by.

XXIV

Not yet, my soul, these friendly fields desert,
Where thou with grass, and rivers, and the breeze,
And the bright face of day, thy dalliance hadst;
Where to thine ear first sang the enraptured birds;
Where love and thou that lasting bargain made.
The ship rides trimmed, and from the eternal shore
Thou hearest airy voices; but not yet
Depart, my soul, not yet awhile depart.

Freedom is far, rest far. Thou art with life
Too closely woven, nerve with nerve intwined;
Service still craving service, love for love,
Love for dear love, still suppliant with tears.
Alas, not yet thy human task is done!
A bond at birth is forged; a debt doth lie
Immortal on mortality. It grows –
By vast rebound it grows, unceasing growth;
Gift upon gift, alms upon alms, upreared,
From man, from God, from nature, till the soul
At that so huge indulgence stands amazed.

Leave not, my soul, the unfoughten field, nor leave
Thy debts dishonoured, nor thy place desert
Without due service rendered. For thy life,
Up, spirit, and defend that fort of clay,
Thy body, now beleaguered; whether soon
Or late she fall; whether today thy friends
Bewail thee dead, or, after years, a man
Grown old in honour and the friend of peace.
Contend, my soul, for moments and for hours;
Each is with service pregnant; each reclaimed
Is as a kingdom conquered, where to reign.
As when a captain rallies to the fight
His scattered legions, and beats ruin back,
He, on the field, encamps, well pleased in mind.
Yet surely him shall fortune overtake,
Him smite in turn, headlong his ensigns drive;
And that dear land, now safe, tomorrow fall.
But he, unthinking, in the present good
Solely delights, and all the camps rejoice.

XXV

It is not yours, O mother, to complain,
Not, mother, yours to weep,
Though nevermore your son again
Shall to your bosom creep,
Though nevermore again you watch your baby sleep.

Though in the greener paths of earth,
Mother and child, no more
We wander; and no more the birth
Of me whom once you bore,
Seems still the brave reward that once it seemed of yore;

Though as all passes, day and night,
The seasons and the years,
From you, O mother, this delight,
This also disappears –
Some profit yet survives of all your pangs and tears.

The child, the seed, the grain of corn,
The acorn on the hill,
Each for some separate end is born
In season fit, and still
Each must in strength arise to work the almighty will.

So from the hearth the children flee,
By that almighty hand
Austerely led; so one by sea
Goes forth, and one by land;
Nor aught of all man's sons escapes from that command.

So from the sally each obeys
The unseen almighty nod;
So till the ending all their ways
Blindfolded loth have trod:
Nor knew their task at all, but were the tools of God.

And as the fervent smith of yore
Beat out the glowing blade,
Nor wielded in the front of war
The weapons that he made,
But in the tower at home still plied his ringing trade;

So like a sword the son shall roam
On nobler missions sent;
And as the smith remained at home
In peaceful turret pent,
So sits the while at home the mother well content.

XXVI

The Sick Child

Child.   O mother, lay your hand on my brow!
          O mother, mother, where am I now?
          Why is the room so gaunt and great?
          Why am I lying awake so late?

Mother.   Fear not at all: the night is still.
          Nothing is here that means you ill –

Nothing but lamps the whole town through,
And never a child awake but you.

Child. Mother, mother, speak low in my ear,
Some of the things are so great and near,
Some are so small and far away,
I have a fear that I cannot say.
What have I done, and what do I fear,
And why are you crying, mother dear?

Mother. Out in the city, sounds begin
Thank the kind God, the carts come in!
An hour or two more, and God is so kind,
The day shall be blue in the window-blind,
Then shall my child go sweetly asleep,
And dream of the birds and the hills of sheep.

XXVII

In Memoriam F.A.S.

Yet, O stricken heart, remember, O remember
  How of human days he lived the better part.
April came to bloom and never dim December
  Breathed its killing chills upon the head or heart.

Doomed to know not Winter, only Spring, a being
  Trod the flowery April blithely for a while,
Took his fill of music, joy of thought and seeing,
  Came and stayed and went, nor ever ceased to smile.

Came and stayed and went, and now when all is finished,
  You alone have crossed the melancholy stream,
Yours the pang, but his, O his, the undiminished
  Undecaying gladness, undeparted dream.

All that life contains of torture, toil, and treason,
  Shame, dishonour, death, to him were but a name.
Here, a boy, he dwelt through all the singing season
  And ere the day of sorrow departed as he came.

Davos, 1881.

XXVIII

To My Father

Peace and her huge invasion to these shores
Puts daily home; innumerable sails
Dawn on the far horizon and draw near;
Innumerable loves, uncounted hopes
To our wild coasts, not darkling now, approach:
Not now obscure, since thou and thine are there,
And bright on the lone isle, the foundered reef,
The long, resounding foreland, Pharos stands.

These are thy works, O father, these thy crown;
Whether on high the air be pure, they shine
Along the yellowing sunset, and all night
Among the unnumbered stars of God they shine;
Or whether fogs arise and far and wide
The low sea-level drown – each finds a tongue
And all night long the tolling bell resounds:
So shine, so toll, till night be overpast,
Till the stars vanish, till the sun return,
And in the haven rides the fleet secure.

In the first hour, the seaman in his skiff
Moves through the unmoving bay, to where the town
Its earliest smoke into the air upbreathes
And the rough hazels climb along the beach.
To the tugg'd oar the distant echo speaks.
The ship lies resting, where by reef and roost
Thou and thy lights have led her like a child.

This hast thou done, and I – can I be base?
I must arise, O father, and to port
Some lost, complaining seaman pilot home.

XXIX

In the States

With half a heart I wander here
    As from an age gone by
A brother – yet though young in years,
    An elder brother, I.

You speak another tongue than mine,
    Though both were English born.
I towards the night of time decline,
    You mount into the morn.

Youth shall grow great and strong and free,
    But age must still decay:
Tomorrow for the States – for me,
    England and Yesterday.

San Francisco.

XXX

A Portrait

I am a kind of farthing dip,
    Unfriendly to the nose and eyes;
A blue-behinded ape, I skip
    Upon the trees of Paradise.

At mankind's feast, I take my place
    In solemn, sanctimonious state,
And have the air of saying grace
    While I defile the dinner plate.

I am 'the smiler with the knife,'
    The battener upon garbage, I –
Dear Heaven, with such a rancid life,
    Were it not better far to die?

Yet still, about the human pale,
    I love to scamper, love to race,
To swing by my irreverent tail
    All over the most holy place;

And when at length, some golden day,
    The unfailing sportsman, aiming at,
Shall bag, me – all the world shall say:
    Thank God, and there's an end of that!

XXXI

Sing clearlier, Muse, or evermore be still,
Sing truer or no longer sing!
No more the voice of melancholy Jacques
To wake a weeping echo in the hill;
But as the boy, the pirate of the spring,
From the green elm a living linnet takes,
One natural verse recapture – then be still.

XXXII

A Camp[1]

The bed was made, the room was fit,
By punctual eve the stars were lit;
The air was still, the water ran,
No need was there for maid or man,
When we put up, my ass and I,
At God's green caravanserai.

XXXIII

The Country of the Camisards[2]

We travelled in the print of olden wars,
    Yet all the land was green,
    And love we found, and peace,
    Where fire and war had been.

They pass and smile, the children of the sword –
    No more the sword they wield;
    And O, how deep the corn
    Along the battlefield!

XXXIV

Skerryvore

For love of lovely words, and for the sake
Of those, my kinsmen and my countrymen,
Who early and late in the windy ocean toiled
To plant a star for seamen, where was then
The surfy haunt of seals and cormorants:
I, on the lintel of this cot, inscribe
The name of a strong tower.

XXXV

Skerryvore: The Parallel

Here all is sunny, and when the truant gull
Skims the green level of the lawn, his wing
Dispetals roses; here the house is framed

1. From *Travels with a Donkey*.
2. From *Travels with a Donkey*.

Of kneaded brick and the plumed mountain pine,
Such clay as artists fashion and such wood
As the tree-climbing urchin breaks. But there
Eternal granite hewn from the living isle
And dowelled with brute iron, rears a tower
That from its wet foundation to its crown
Of glittering glass, stands, in the sweep of winds,
Immovable, immortal, eminent.

XXXVI

My house, I say. But hark to the sunny doves
That make my roof the arena of their loves,
That gyre about the gable all day long
And fill the chimneys with their murmurous song:
Our house, they say; and *mine*, the cat declares
And spreads his golden fleece upon the chairs;
And *mine* the dog, and rises stiff with wrath
If any alien foot profane the path.
So too the buck that trimmed my terraces,
Our whilome gardener, called the garden his;
Who now, deposed, surveys my plain abode
And his late kingdom, only from the road.

XXXVII

My body which my dungeon is,
And yet my parks and palaces: –
    Which is so great that there I go
All the day long to and fro,
And when the night begins to fall
Throw down my bed and sleep, while all
The building hums with wakefulness –
Even as a child of savages
When evening takes her on her way,
(She having roamed a summer's day
Along the mountain-sides and scalp)
Sleeps in an antre of that alp: –
    Which is so broad and high that there,
As in the topless fields of air,
My fancy soars like to a kite.
And faints in the blue infinite: –
    Which is so strong, my strongest throes
And the rough world's besieging blows
Not break it, and so weak withal,
Death ebbs and flows in its loose wall

As the green sea in fishers' nets,
And tops its topmost parapets: –
   Which is so wholly mine that I
Can wield its whole artillery,
And mine so little, that my soul
Dwells in perpetual control,
And I but speak and think and do
As my dead fathers move me to: –
   If this born body of my bones
The beggared soul so barely owns,
What money passed from hand to hand,
What creeping custom of the land,
What deed of author or assign,
Can make a house a thing of mine?

XXXVIII

Say not of me that weakly I declined
The labours of my sires, and fled the sea,
The towers we founded and the lamps we lit,
To play at home with paper like a child.
But rather say: *In the afternoon of time*
A strenuous family dusted from its hands
The sand of granite, and beholding far
Along the sounding coasts its pyramids
And tall memorials catch the dying sun,
Smiled well content, and to this childish task
Around the fire addressed its evening hours.

Book II – *In Scots*

Table of Common Scottish Vowel Sounds

ae
ai } open A as in rare.

a'
au } Aw as in law.
aw

ea = open E as in mere, but this with exceptions, as heather = heather, wean = wain, lear = lair.

ee
ei } open E as in mere.
ie

oa = open O as in more.

ou = doubled O as in poor.

ow = OW as in bower.

u= doubled O as in poor.

ui or ü before R = (say roughly) open A as in rare.

ui or ü before any other consonant = (say roughly) close I as in grin.

y = open I as in kite.

i = pretty nearly what you please, much as in English. Heaven guide the reader through that labyrinth! But in Scots it dodges usually from the short I, as in grin, to the open E, as in mere. Find and blind, I may remark, are pronounced to rhyme with the preterite of grin.

I

The Maker to Posterity

Far 'yont amang the years to be
When a' we think, an' a' we see,
An' a' we luve, 's been dung ajee
        By time's rouch shouther,
An' what was richt and wrang for me
        Lies mangled throu'ther,

It's possible – it's hardly mair –
That some ane, ripin' after lear –
Some auld professor or young heir,
        If still there's either –
May find an' read me, an' be sair
        Perplexed, puir brither!

'What tongue does your auld bookie speak?'
He'll spier; an' I, his mou to steik:
'No bein' fit to write in Greek,
      I wrote in Lallan,
Dear to my heart as the peat reek,
      Auld as Tantallon.

'Few spak it than, an' noo there's nane.
My puir auld sangs lie a' their lane,
Their sense, that aince was braw an' plain,
      Tint a'thegether,
Like runes upon a standin' stane
      Amang the heather.

'But think not you the brae to speel;
You, tae, maun chow the bitter peel;
For a' your lear, for a' your skeel,
      Ye're nane sae lucky;
An' things are mebbe waur than weel
      For you, my buckie.

'The hale concern (baith hens an' eggs,
Baith books an' writers, stars an' clegs)
Noo stachers upon lowsent legs
      An' wears awa';
The tack o' mankind, near the dregs,
      Rins unco law.

'Your book, that in some braw new tongue,
Ye wrote or prentit, preached or sung,
Will still be just a bairn, an' young
      In fame an' years,
Whan the hale planet's guts are dung
      About your ears;

'An' you, sair gruppin' to a spar
Or whammled wi' some bleezin' star,
Cryin' to ken whaur deil ye are,
      Hame, France, or Flanders –
Whang sindry like a railway car
      An' flie in danders.'

II

Ille Terrarum

Frae nirly, nippin', Eas'lan breeze,
Frae Norlan' snaw, an' haar o' seas,
Weel happit in your gairden trees,
    A bonny bit,
Atween the muckle Pentland's knees,
    Secure ye sit.

Beeches an' aiks entwine their theek,
An' firs, a stench, auld-farrant clique.
A' simmer day, your chimleys reek,
    Couthy and bien;
An' here an' there your windies keek
    Amang the green.

A pickle plats an' paths an' posies,
A wheen auld gillyflowers an' roses:
A ring o' wa's the hale encloses
    Frae sheep or men;
An' there the auld housie beeks an' dozes,
    A' by her lane.

The gairdner crooks his weary back
A' day in the pitaty-track,
Or mebbe stops awhile to crack
    Wi' Jane the cook,
Or at some buss, worm-eaten black,
    To gie a look.

Frae the high hills the curlew ca's;
The sheep gang baaing by the wa's;
Or whiles a clan o' roosty craws
    Cangle thegether;
The wild bees seek the gairden raws,
    Weariet wi' heather.

Or in the gloamin' douce an' gray
The sweet-throat mavis tunes her lay;
The herd comes linkin' doun the brae;
    An' by degrees
The muckle siller müne maks way
    Amang the trees.

Here aft hae I, wi' sober heart,
For meditation sat apairt,

When orra loves or kittle art
        Perplexed my mind;
Here socht a balm for ilka smart
        O' humankind.

Here aft, weel neukit by my lane,
Wi' Horace, or perhaps Montaigne,
The mornin' hours hae come an' gane
        Abüne my heid –
I wadnae gi'en a chucky-stane
        For a' I'd read.

But noo the auld city, street by street,
An' winter fu' o' snaw an' sleet,
Awhile shut in my gangrel feet
        An' goavin' mettle;
Noo is the soopit ingle sweet,
        An' liltin' kettle.

An' noo the winter winds complain;
Cauld lies the glaur in ilka lane;
On draigled hizzie, tautit wean
        An' drucken lads,
In the mirk nicht, the winter rain
        Dribbles an' blads.

Whan bugles frae the Castle rock,
An' beaten drums wi' dowie shock,
Wauken, at cauld-rife sax o'clock,
        My chitterin' frame,
I mind me on the kintry cock,
        The kintry hame.

I mind me on yon bonny bield;
An' Fancy traivels far afield
To gaither a' that gairdens yield
        O' sun an' Simmer:
To hearten up a dowie chield,
        Fancy's the limmer!

III

When aince Aprile has fairly come,
An' birds may bigg in winter's lum,
An' pleisure's spreid for a' and some
        O' whatna state,

Love, wi' her auld recruitin' drum,
　　Than taks the gate.

The heart plays dunt wi' main an' micht;
The lasses' een are a' sae bricht,
Their dresses are sae braw an' ticht,
　　The bonny birdies! –
Puir winter virtue at the sicht
　　Gangs heels ower hurdies.

An' aye as love frae land to land
Tirls the drum wi' eident hand,
A' men collect at her command,
　　Toun-bred or land'art,
An' follow in a denty band
　　Her gaucy standart.

An' I, wha sang o' rain an' snaw,
An' weary winter weel awa',
Noo busk me in a jacket braw,
　　An' tak my place
I' the ram-stam, harum-scarum raw,
　　Wi' smilin' face.

IV

A Mile an' a Bittock

A mile an' a bittock, a mile or twa,
Abüne the burn, ayont the law,
Davie an' Donal' an' Cherlie an' a',
　　An' the müne was shinin' clearly!

Ane went hame wi' the ither, an' then
The ither went hame wi' the ither twa men,
An' baith wad return him the service again,
　　An' the müne was shinin' clearly!

The clocks were chappin' in house an' ha',
Eleeven, twal an' ane an' twa;
An' the guidman's face was turnt to the wa',
　　An' the müne was shinin' clearly!

A wind got up frae affa the sea,
It blew the stars as clear's could be,
It blew in the een of a' o' the three,
　　An' the müne was shinin' clearly!

Noo, Davie was first to get sleep in his head,
'The best o' frien's maun twine,' he said;
'I'm weariet, an' here I'm awa' to my bed.'
    An' the müne was shinin' clearly!

Twa o' them walkin' an' crackin' their lane,
The mornin' licht cam gray an' plain,
An' the birds they yammert on stick an' stane,
    An' the müne was shinin' clearly!

O years ayont, O years awa',
My lads, ye'll mind whate'er befa' –
My lads, ye'll mind on the bield o' the law,
    When the müne was shinin' clearly.

V

A Lowden Sabbath Morn

The clinkum-clank o' Sabbath bells
Noo to the hoastin' rookery swells,
Noo faintin' laigh in shady dells,
    Sounds far an' near,
An' through the simmer kintry tells
    Its tale o' cheer.

An' noo, to that melodious play,
A' deidly awn the quiet sway –
A' ken their solemn holiday,
    Bestial an' human,
The singin' lintie on the brae,
    The restin' plou'man.

He, mair than a' the lave o' men,
His week completit joys to ken;
Half-dressed, he daunders out an' in,
    Perplext wi' leisure;
An' his raxt limbs he'll rax again
    Wi' painfü' pleesure.

The steerin' mither strang afit
Noo shoos the bairnies but a bit;
Noo cries them ben, their Sinday shüit
    To scart upon them,
Or sweeties in their pouch to pit,
    Wi' blessin's on them.

The lasses, clean frae tap to taes,
Are busked in crunklin' underclaes;
The gartened hose, the weel-filled stays,
    The nakit shift,
A' bleached on bonny greens for days,
    An' white's the drift.

An' noo to face the kirkward mile:
The guidman's hat o' dacent style,
The blackit shoon, we noo maun fyle
    As white's the miller:
A waefü' peety tae, to spile
    The warth o' siller.

Our Marg'et, aye sae keen to crack,
Douce-stappin' in the stoury track,
Her emeralt goun a' kiltit back
    Frae snawy coats,
White-ankled, leads the kirkward pack
    Wi' Dauvit Groats.

A thocht ahint, in runkled breeks,
A' spiled wi' lyin' by for weeks,
The guidman follows closs, an' cleiks
    The sonsie missis;
His sarious face at aince bespeaks
    The day that this is.

And aye an' while we nearer draw
To whaur the kirkton lies alaw,
Mair neebours, comin' saft an' slaw
    Frae here an' there,
The thicker thrang the gate an' caw
    The stour in air.

But hark! the bells frae nearer clang;
To rowst the slaw, their sides they bang;
An' see! black coats a'ready thrang
    The green kirkyaird;
And at the yett, the chestnuts spang
    That brocht the laird.

The solemn elders at the plate
Stand drinkin' deep the pride o' state:
The practised hands as gash an' great
    As Lords o' Session;
The later named, a wee thing blate
    In their expression.

The prentit stanes that mark the deid,
Wi' lengthened lip, the sarious read;
Syne wag a moraleesin' heid,
          An' then an' there
Their hirplin' practice an' their creed
          Try hard to square.

It's here our Merren lang has lain,
A wee bewast the table-stane;
An' yon's the grave o' Sandy Blane;
          An' further ower,
The mither's brithers, dacent men!
          Lie a' the fower.

Here the guidman sall bide awee
To dwall amang the deid; to see
Auld faces clear in fancy's e'e;
          Belike to hear
Auld voices fa'in saft an' slee
          On fancy's ear.

Thus, on the day o' solemn things,
The bell that in the steeple swings
To fauld a scaittered faim'ly rings
          Its walcome screed;
An' just a wee thing nearer brings
          The quick an' deid.

But noo the bell is ringin' in;
To tak their places, folk begin;
The minister himsel' will shüne
          Be up the gate,
Filled fu' wi' clavers about sin
          An' man's estate.

The tünes are up – *French*, to be shüre,
The faithfü' *French*, an' twa-three mair;
The auld prezentor, hoastin' sair,
          Wales out the portions,
An' yirks the tüne into the air
          Wi' queer contortions.

Follows the prayer, the readin' next,
An' than the fisslin' for the text –
The twa-three last to find it, vext
          But kind o' proud;
An' than the peppermints are raxed,
          An' southernwood.

For noo's the time whan pows are seen
Nid-noddin' like a mandareen;
When tenty mithers stap a preen
    In sleepin' weans;
An' nearly half the parochine
    Forget their pains.

There's just a waukrif' twa or three:
Thrawn commentautors sweer to 'gree,
Weans glowrin' at the bumlin' bee
    On windie-glasses,
Or lads that tak a keek a-glee
    At sonsie lasses.

Himsel', meanwhile, frae whaur he cocks
An' bobs belaw the soundin'-box,
The treesures of his words unlocks
    Wi' prodigality,
An' deals some unco dingin' knocks
    To infidality.

Wi' sappy unction, hoo he burkes
The hopes o' men that trust in works,
Expounds the fau'ts o' ither kirks,
    An' shaws the best o' them
No muckle better than mere Turks,
    When a's confessed o' them.

Bethankit! what a bonny creed!
What mair would ony Christian need? –
The braw words rumm'le ower his heid,
    Nor steer the sleeper;
An' in their restin' graves, the deid
    Sleep aye the deeper.

[*R.L.S.'s Note* – It may be guessed by some that I had a certain parish in my eye, and this makes it proper I should add a word of disclamation. In my time there have been two ministers in that parish. Of the first I have a special reason to speak well, even had there been any to think ill. The second I have often met in private and long (in the due phrase) 'sat under' in his church, and neither here nor there have I heard an unkind or ugly word upon his lips. The preacher of the text had thus no original in that particular parish; but when I was a boy, he might have been observed in many others; he was then (like the schoolmaster) abroad; and by recent advices, it would seem he has not yet entirely disappeared.]

VI

The Spaewife

O, I wad like to ken – to the beggar-wife says I –
Why chops are guid to brander and nane sae guid to fry.
An' siller, that's sae braw to keep, is brawer still to gi'e.
– *It's gey an' easy spierin'*, says the beggar-wife to me.

O, I wad like to ken – to the beggar-wife says I –
Hoo a' things come to be whaur we find them when we try,
The lasses in their claes an' the fishes in the sea.
– *It's gey an' easy spierin'*, says the beggar-wife to me.

O, I wad like to ken – to the beggar-wife says I –
Why lads are a' to sell an' lasses a' to buy;
An' naebody for dacency but barely twa or three.
– *It's gey an' easy spierin'*, says the beggar-wife to me.

O, I wad like to ken – to the beggar-wife says I –
Gin death's as shüre to men as killin' is to kye,
Why God has filled the yearth sae fu' o' tasty things to pree.
– *It's gey an' easy spierin'*, says the beggar-wife to me.

O, I wad like to ken – to the beggar-wife says I –
The reason o' the cause an' the wherefore o' the why,
Wi' mony anither riddle brings the tear into my e'e.
– *It's gey an'easy spierin'*, says the beggar-wife to me.

VII

The Blast – 1875

It's rainin'. Weet's the gairden sod,
Weet the lang roads whaur gangrels plod –
A maist unceevil thing o' God
          In mid July –
If ye'll just curse the sneckdraw, dod!
          An' sae wull I!

He's a braw place in Heev'n, ye ken,
An' lea's us puir, forjaskit men
Clamjamfried in the but and ben
          He ca's the earth –
A wee bit inconvenient den
          No muckle worth;

An' whiles, at orra times, keeks out,
Sees what puir mankind are about;
An' if He can, I've little doubt,
    Upsets their plans;
He hates a' mankind, brainch and root,
    An a' that's man's.

An' whiles, whan they tak heart again,
An' life i' the sun looks braw an' plain,
Doun comes a jaw o' droukin' rain
    Upon their honours –
God sends a spate outower the plain,
    Or mebbe thun'ers.

Lord safe us, life's an unco thing!
Simmer an' Winter, Yule an' Spring,
The damned, dour-heartit seasons bring
    A feck o' trouble.
I wadnae try't to be a king –
    No, nor for double.

But since we're in it, willy-nilly,
We maun be watchfü', wise an' skilly,
An' no mind ony ither billy,
    Lassie nor God.
But drink – that's my best counsel till 'e:
    Sae tak the nod.

VIII

The Counterblast – 1886

My bonny man, the warld, it's true,
Was made for neither me nor you;
It's just a place to warstle through,
    As Job confessed o't;
And aye the best that we'll can do
    Is mak the best o't.

There's rowth o' wrang, I'm free to say:
The simmer brunt, the winter blae,
The face of earth a' fyled wi' clay
    An' dour wi' chuckies,
An' life a rough an' land'art play
    For country buckies.

An' food's anither name for clart;
An' beasts an' brambles bite an' scart;
An' what would WE be like, my heart!
        If bared o' claethin'?
– Aweel, I cannae mend your cart:
        It's that or naethin'.

A feck o' folk frae first to last
Have through this queer experience passed;
Twa-three, I ken, just damn an' blast
        The hale transaction;
But twa-three ithers, east an' wast,
        Fand satisfaction.

Whaur braid the briery muirs expand,
A waefü' an' a weary land,
The bumblebees, a gowden band,
        Are blithely hingin';
An' there the canty wanderer fand
        The laverock singin'.

Trout in the burn grow great as herr'n;
The simple sheep can find their fair'n;
The wind blaws clean about the cairn
        Wi' caller air;
The muircock an' the barefit bairn
        Are happy there.

Sic-like the howes o' life to some:
Green loans whaur they ne'er fash their thumb,
But mark the muckle winds that come,
        Soopin' an' cool,
Or hear the powrin' burnie drum
        In the shilfa's pool.

The evil wi' the guid they tak;
They ca' a gray thing gray, no black;
To a steigh brae, a stubborn back
        Addressin' daily;
An' up the rude, unbieldy track
        O' life, gang gaily.

What you would like's a palace ha',
Or Sinday parlour dink an' braw
Wi' a' things ordered in a raw
        By denty leddies.
Weel, than, ye cannae hae't: that's a'
        That to be said is.

An' since at life ye've taen the grue,
An' winnae blithely hirsle through,
Ye've fund the very thing to do –
     That's to drink speerit;
An' shüne we'll hear the last o' you –
     An' blithe to hear it!

The shoon ye coft, the life ye lead,
Ithers will heir when aince ye're deid;
They'll heir your tasteless bite o' breid,
     An' find it sappy;
They'll to your dulefü' house succeed,
     An' there be happy.

As whan a glum an' fractious wean
Has sat an' sullened by his lane
Till, wi' a rowstin' skelp, he's taen
     An' shoo'd to bed –
The ither bairns a' fa' to play'n',
     As gleg's a gled.

IX

The Counterblast Ironical

It's strange that God should fash to frame
    The yearth and lift sae hie,
An' clean forget to explain the same
    To a gentleman like me.

They gutsy, donnered ither folk,
    Their weird they weel may dree;
But why present a pig in a poke
    To a gentleman like me?

They ither folk their parritch eat
    An' sup their sugared tea;
But the mind is no to be wyled wi' meat
    Wi' a gentleman like me.

They ither folk, they court their joes
    At gloamin' on the lea;
But they're made of a commoner clay, I suppose,
    Than a gentleman like me.

They ither folk, for richt or wrang,
    They suffer, bleed, or dee;

But a' thir things are an emp'y sang
   To a gentleman like me.

It's a different thing that I demand,
   Tho' humble as can be –
A statement fair in my Maker's hand
   To a gentleman like me:

A clear account writ fair an' broad,
   An' a plain apologie;
Or the deevil a ceevil word to God
   From a gentleman like me.

X

Their Laureate to an Academy Class Dinner Club

Dear Thamson class, whauer'er I gang
It aye comes ower me wi' a spang:
'Lordsake! they Thamson lads – (deil hang
      Or else Lord mend them!) –
An' that wanchancy annual sang
      I ne'er can send them!'

Straucht, at the name, a trusty tyke,
My conscience girrs ahint the dyke;
Straucht on my hinderlands I fyke
      To find a rhyme t' ye;
Pleased – although mebbe no pleased-like –
      To gie my time t' ye.

'Weel' an' says you, wi' heavin' breist,
'Sae far, sae guid, but what's the neist?
Yearly we gaither to the feast,
      A' hopefü' men –
Yearly we skelloch "Hang the beast –
      Nae sang again!"'

My lads, an' what am I to say?
Ye shürely ken the Muse's way:
Yestreen, as gleg's a tyke – the day,
      Thrawn like a cuddy:
Her conduc', that to her's a play,
      Deith to a body.

Aft whan I sat an' made my mane,
Aft whan I laboured burd-alane,

Fishin' for rhymes an' findin' nane,
       Or nane were fit for ye –
Ye judged me cauld's a chucky stane –
       No car'n' a bit for ye!

But saw ye ne'er some pingein' bairn
As weak as a pitaty-par'n' –
Less üsed wi' guidin' horse-shoe airn
       Than steerin' crowdie –
Packed aff his lane, by moss an' cairn,
       To ca' the howdie.

Wae's me, for the puir callant than!
He wambles like a poke o' bran,
An' the lowse rein, as hard's he can,
       Pu's, trem'lin' handit;
Till, blaff! upon his hinderlan'
       Behauld him landit.

Sic-like – I awn the weary fac' –
Whan on my muse the gate I tak,
An' see her gleed e'e raxin' back
       To keek ahint her; –
To me, the brig o' Heev'n gangs black
       As blackest winter.

'Lordsake! we're aff,' thinks I, 'but whaur?
On what abhorred an' whinny scaur,
Or whammled in what sea o' glaur,
       Will she desert me?
An' will she just disgrace? Or waur –
       Will she no hurt me?'

Kittle the quaere! But at least
The day I've backed the fashious beast,
While she, wi' mony a spang an' reist,
       Flang heels ower bonnet;
An' a' triumphant – for your feast,
       Hae! there's your sonnet!

XI

Embro Hie Kirk

The Lord Himsel' in former days
Waled out the proper tünes for praise
An' named the proper kind o' claes

For folk to preach in:
Preceese and in the chief o' ways
        Important teachin'.

He ordered a' things late and air';
He ordered folk to stand at prayer.
(Although I cannae just mind where
        He gave the warnin'.)
An' pit pomatum on their hair
        On Sabbath mornin'.

The hale o' life by His commands
Was ordered to a body's hands;
But see! this *corpus juris* stands
        By a' forgotten;
An' God's religion in a' lands
        Is deid an' rotten.

While thus the lave o' mankind's lost,
O' Scotland still God maks His boast –
Puir Scotland, on whase barren coast
        A score or twa
Auld wives wi' mutches an' a hoast
        Still keep His law.

In Scotland, a wheen canty, plain,
Douce, kintry-leevin' folk retain
The Truth – or did so aince – alane
        Of a' men leevin';
An' noo just twa o' them remain –
        Just Begg an' Niven.

For noo, unfaithfü' to the Lord
Auld Scotland joins the rebel horde;
Her human hymn-books on the board
        She noo displays:
An' Embro Hie Kirk's been restored
        In popish ways.

O *punctum temporis* for action
To a' o' the reformin' faction,
If yet, by ony act or paction,
        Thocht, word, or sermon,
This dark an' damnable transaction
        Micht yet determine!

For see – as Doctor Begg explains –
Hoo easy 't's düne! a pickle weans,
Wha in the Hie Street gaither stanes
    By his instruction,
The uncovenantit, pentit panes
    Ding to destruction.

Up, Niven, or ower late – an' dash
Laigh in the glaur that carnal hash;
Let spires and pews wi' gran' stramash
    Thegether fa';
The rumlin' kist o' whustles smash
    In pieces sma'.

Noo choose ye out a walie hammer;
About the knottit buttress clam'er;
Alang the steep roof stoyt an' stammer,
    A gate mis-chancy;
On the aul' spire, the bells' hie cha'mer,
    Dance your bit dancie.

Ding, devel, dunt, destroy, an' ruin,
Wi' carnal stanes the square bestrewin',
Till your loud chaps frae Kyle to Fruin,
    Frae Hell to Heeven,
Tell the guid wark that baith are doin' –
    Baith Begg an' Niven.

XII

The Scotsman's Return from Abroad

In a letter from Mr Thomson to Mr Johnstone.

In mony a foreign pairt I've been,
An' mony an unco ferlie seen,
Since, Mr. Johnstone, you and I
Last walkit upon Cocklerye.
Wi' gleg, observant een, I pass't
By sea an' land, through East an' Wast,
And still in ilka age an' station
Saw naething but abomination.
In thir uncovenantit lands
The gangrel Scot uplifts his hands
At lack of a' sectarian füsh'n,
An' cauld religious destitütion.
He rins, puir man, frae place to place,

Tries a' their graceless means o' grace,
Preacher on preacher, kirk on kirk –
This yin a stot an' thon a stirk –
A bletherin' clan, no warth a preen,
As bad as Smith of Aiberdeen!

At last, across the weary faem,
Frae far, outlandish pairts I came.
On ilka side o' me I fand
Fresh tokens o' my native land.
Wi' whatna joy I hailed them a' –
The hilltaps standin' raw by raw,
The public house, the Hielan' birks,
And a' the bonny U.P. kirks!
But maistly thee, the bluid o' Scots,
Frae Maidenkirk to John o' Grots,
The king o' drinks, as I conceive it,
Talisker, Isla, or Glenlivet!

For after years wi' a pockmantie
Frae Zanzibar to Alicante,
In mony a fash and sair affliction
I gie't as my sincere conviction –
Of a' their foreign tricks an' pliskies,
I maist abominate their whiskies.
Nae doot, themsels, they ken it weel,
An' wi' a hash o'leemon peel,
And ice an' siccan filth, they ettle
The stawsome kind o' goo to settle;
Sic wersh apothecary's broos wi'
As Scotsmen scorn to fyle their moo's wi'.

An', man, I was a blithe hame-comer
Whan first I syndit out my rummer.
Ye should hae seen me then, wi' care
The less important pairts prepare;
Syne, weel contentit wi' it a',
Pour in the speerits wi' a jaw!
I didnae drink, I didnae speak, –
I only snowkit up the reek.
I was sae pleased therein to paidle,
I sat an' plowtered wi' my ladle.

An' blithe was I, the morrow's morn,
To daunder through the stookit corn,
An' after a' my strange mishanters,
Sit doun amang my ain dissenters.

An', man, it was a joy to me
The pu'pit an' the pews to see,
The pennies dirlin' in the plate,
The elders lookin' on in state;
An' 'mang the first, as it befell,
Wha should I see, sir, but yoursel'!

I was, and I will no deny it,
At the first gliff a hantle tryit
To see yoursel' in sic a station –
It seemed a doubtfü' dispensation.
The feelin' was a mere digression;
For shüne I understood the session,
An' mindin' Aiken an' M'Neil,
I wondered they had düne sae weel.
I saw I had mysel' to blame;
For had I but remained at hame,
Aiblins – though no ava' deservin' 't –
They micht hae named your humble servant.

The kirk was filled, the door was steeked;
Up to the pu'pit ance I keeked;
I was mair pleased than I can tell –
It was the minister himsel'!
Proud, proud was I to see his face,
After sae lang awa' frae grace.
Pleased as I was, I'm no denyin'
Some maitters were not edifyin';
For first I fand – an' here was news! –
Mere hymn-books cockin' in the pews –
A humanised abomination,
Unfit for ony congregation.
Syne, while I still was on the tenter,
I scunnered at the new prezentor;
I thocht him gesterin' an' cauld –
A sair declension frae the auld.
Syne, as though a' the faith was wreckit,
The prayer was not what I'd exspeckit.
Himsel', as it appeared to me,
Was no the man he üsed to be.
But just as I was growin' vext
He waled a maist judeecious text,
An', launchin' into his prelections,
Swoopt, wi' a skirl, on a' defections.

O what a gale was on my speerit
To hear the p'ints o' doctrine clearit,

And a' the horrors o' damnation
Set furth wi' faithfu' ministration!
Nae shauchlin' testimony here –
We were a' damned, an' that was clear.
I owned, wi' gratitude an' wonder,
He was a pleisure to sit under.

XIII

Late in the nicht in bed I lay,
The winds were at their weary play,
An' tirlin' wa's an' skirlin' wae
      Through Heev'n they battered; –
On-ding o' hail, on-blaff o' spray,
      The tempest blattered.

The masoned house it dinled through;
It dung the ship, it cowped the coo';
The rankit aiks it overthrew,
      Had braved a' weathers;
The strang sea-gleds it took an' blew
      Awa' like feathers.

The thrawes o' fear on a' were shed,
An' the hair rose, an' slumber fled,
An' lichts were lit an' prayers were said
      Through a' the kintry;
An' the cauld terror clum in bed
      Wi' a' an' sindry.

To hear in the pit-mirk on hie
The brangled collieshangie flie,
The warl', they thocht, wi' land an' sea,
      Itsel' wad cowpit;
An' for auld airn, the smashed debris
      By God be rowpit.

Meanwhile frae far Aldeboran,
To folks wi' talescopes in han',
O' ships that cowpit, winds that ran,
      Nae sign was seen,
But the wee warl' in sunshine span
      As bricht's a preen.

I, tae, by God's especial grace,
Dwall denty in a bieldy place,

Wi' hosened feet, wi' shaven face,
      Wi' dacent mainners:
A grand example to the race
      O' tautit sinners!

The wind may blaw, the heathen rage,
The deil may start on the rampage; –
The sick in bed, the thief in cage –
      What's a' to me?
Cosh in my house, a sober sage,
      I sit an' see.

An' whiles the bluid spangs to my bree,
To lie sae saft, to live sae free,
While better men maun do an' die
      In unco places.
'Whaur's God?' I cry, an' 'Whae is me
      To hae sic graces?'

I mind the fecht the sailors keep,
But fire or can'le, rest or sleep,
In darkness an' the muckle deep;
      An' mind beside
The herd that on the hills o' sheep
      Has wandered wide.

I mind me on the hoastin' weans –
The penny joes on causey stanes –
The auld folk wi' the crazy banes,
      Baith auld an' puir,
That aye maun thole the winds an' rains,
      An' labour sair.

An' whiles I'm kind o' pleased a blink,
An' kind o'fleyed forby, to think,
For a' my rowth o'meat an' drink
      An' waste o' crumb,
I'll mebbe have to thole wi' skink
      In Kingdom Come.

For God whan jowes the Judgment bell,
Wi' His ain Hand, His Leevin' Sel',
Sall ryve the guid (as Prophets tell)
      Frae them that had it;
And in the reamin' pat o' Hell,
      The rich be scaddit.

O Lord, if this indeed be sae,
Let daw that sair an' happy day!
Again' the warl', grawn auld an' gray,
    Up wi' your aixe!
An' let the puir enjoy their play –
    I'll thole my paiks.

XIV

My Conscience

Of a' the ills that flesh can fear,
The loss o' frien's, the lack o' gear,
A yowlin' tyke, a glandered mear,
    A lassie's nonsense –
There's just ae thing I cannae bear,
    An' that's my conscience.

Whan day (an' a' excüse) has gane,
An' wark is düne, and duty's plain,
An' to my chalmer a' my lane
    I creep apairt,
My conscience! hoo the yammerin' pain
    Stends to my heart!

A' day wi' various ends in view
The hairsts o' time I had to pu',
And made a hash wad staw a soo,
    Let be a man! –
My conscience! whan my han's were fu',
    Whaur were ye than?

An' there were a' the lures o' life,
There pleesure skirlin' on the fife,
There anger, wi' the hotchin' knife
    Ground shairp in Hell –
My conscience! – you that's like a wife! –
    Whaur was yoursel'?

I ken it fine: just waitin' here,
To gar the evil waur appear,
To clart the guid, confüse the clear,
    Mis-ca' the great,
My conscience! an' to raise a steer
    Whan a's ower late.

Sic-like, some tyke grawn auld and blind,
Whan thieves brok' through the gear to p'ind,
Has lain his dosened length an' grinned
            At the disaster;
An' the morn's mornin', wud's the wind,
            Yokes on his master.

XV

To Doctor John Brown

(Whan the dear doctor, dear to a',
Was still amang us here belaw,
I set my pipes his praise to blaw
            Wi' a' my speerit;
But noo, Dear Doctor! he's awa',
            An' ne'er can hear it.)

By Lyne and Tyne, by Thames and Tees,
By a' the various river-Dee's,
In Mars and Manors 'yont the seas
            Or here at hame,
Whaure'er there's kindly folk to please,
            They ken your name.

They ken your name, they ken your tyke,
They ken the honey from your byke;
But mebbe after a' your fyke,
            (The trüth to tell)
It's just your honest Rab they like,
            An' no yoursel'.

As at the gowff, some canny play'r
Should tee a common ba' wi' care –
Should flourish and deleever fair
            His souple shintie –
An' the ba' rise into the air,
            A leevin' lintie:

Sae in the game we writers play,
There comes to some a bonny day,
When a dear ferlie shall repay
            Their years o' strife,
An' like your Rab, their things o' clay,
            Spreid wings o' life.

Ye scarce deserved it, I'm afraid –
You that had never learned the trade,
But just some idle mornin' strayed
　　　　Into the schüle,
An' picked the fiddle up an' played
　　　　Like Niel himsel'.

Your e'e was gleg, your fingers dink;
You didnae fash yoursel' to think,
But wove, as fast as puss can link,
　　　　Your denty wab: –
Ye stapped your pen into the ink,
　　　　An' there was Rab!

Sinsyne, whaure'er your fortune lay
By dowie den, by canty brae,
Simmer an' winter, nicht an' day,
　　　　Rab was aye wi' ye;
An' a' the folk on a' the way
　　　　Were blithe to see ye.

O sir, the gods are kind indeed,
An' hauld ye for an honoured heid,
That for a wee bit clarkit screed
　　　　Sae weel reward ye,
An' lend – puir Rabbie bein' deid
　　　　His ghaist to guard ye.

For though, whaure'er yoursel' may be,
We've just to turn an' glisk a wee,
An' Rab at heel we're shüre to see
　　　　Wi' gladsome caper: –
The bogle of a bogle, he –
　　　　A ghaist o' paper!

And as the auld-farrand hero sees
In Hell a bogle Hercules,
Pit there the lesser deid to please,
　　　　While he himsel'
Dwalls wi' the muckle gods at ease
　　　　Far raised frae hell:

Sae the true Rabbie far has gane
On kindlier business o' his ain
Wi' aulder frien's; an' his breist-bane
　　　　An' stumpie tailie,
He birstles at a new hearth stane
　　　　By James and Ailie.

XVI

It's an owercome sooth for age an' youth
    And it brooks wi' nae denial,
That the dearest friends are the auldest friends
    And the young are just on trial.

There's a rival bauld wi' young an' auld
    And it's him that has bereft me,
For the sürest friends are the auldest friends
    And the maist o' mines hae left me.

There are kind hearts still, for friends to fill
    And fools to take and break them;
But the nearest friends are the auldest friends
    And the grave's the place to seek them.

BALLADS

The Song of Rahéro: A Legend of Tahiti

Dedication: To Ori a Ori

Ori, my brother in the island mode,
In every tongue and meaning much my friend,
This story of your country and your clan,
In your loved house, your too much honoured guest,
I made in English. Take it, being done;
And let me sign it with the name you gave.

Teriitera

The Song of Rahéro: A Legend of Tahiti
I The Slaying of Támatéa

It fell in the days of old, as the men of Taiárapu tell,
A youth went forth to the fishing, and fortune favoured him well.
Támatéa his name: gullible, simple, and kind,
Comely of countenance, nimble of body, empty of mind,
His mother ruled him and loved him beyond the wont of a wife,
Serving the lad for eyes and living herself in his life.

Alone from the sea and the fishing came Támatéa the fair,
Urging his boat to the beach, and the mother awaited him there,
– 'Long may you live!' said she. 'Your fishing has sped to a wish.
And now let us choose for the king the fairest of all your fish.   10
For fear inhabits the palace and grudging grows in the land,
Marked is the sluggardly foot and marked the niggardly hand,
The hours and the miles are counted, the tributes numbered and weighed,
And woe to him that comes short, and woe to him that delayed!'

So spoke on the beach the mother, and counselled the wiser thing,
For Rahéro stirred in the country and secretly mined the king.
Nor were the signals wanting of how the leaven wrought,
In the cords of obedience loosed and the tributes grudgingly brought.
And when last to the temple of Oro the boat with the victim sped,
And the priest uncovered the basket and looked on the face of the dead,   20
Trembling fell upon all at sight of an ominous thing,
For there was the aito¹ dead, and he of the house of the king.

So spake on the beach the mother, matter worthy of note,
And wattled a basket well, and chose a fish from the boat;
And Támatéa the pliable shouldered the basket and went,
And travelled, and sang as he travelled, a lad that was well content.
Still the way of his going was round by the roaring coast,
Where the ring of the reef is broke and the trades run riot the most.
On his left, with smoke as of battle, the billows battered the land;
Unscalable, turreted mountains rose on the inner hand.   30
And cape, and village, and river, and vale, and mountain above,
Each had a name in the land for men to remember and love;
And never the name of a place, but lo! a song in its praise:
Ancient and unforgotten, songs of the earlier days,
That the elders taught to the young, and at night, in the full of the moon,
Garlanded boys and maidens sang together in tune.
Támatéa the placable went with a lingering foot;
He sang as loud as a bird, he whistled hoarse as a flute;
He broiled in the sun, he breathed in the grateful shadow of trees,
In the icy stream of the rivers he waded over the knees;   40
And still in his empty mind crowded, a thousand-fold,
The deeds of the strong and the songs of the cunning heroes of old.

And now was he come to a place Taiárapu honoured the most,
Where a silent valley of woods debouched on the noisy coast,
Spewing a level river. There was a haunt of Pai.[2]
There, in his potent youth, when his parents drove him to die,
Honoura lived like a beast, lacking the lamp and the fire,
Washed by the rains of the trade and clotting his hair in the mire;
And there, so mighty his hands, he bent the tree to his foot –
So keen the spur of his hunger, he plucked it naked of fruit.   50
There, as she pondered the clouds for the shadow of coming ills,
Ahupu, the woman of song, walked on high on the hills.

Of these was Rahéro sprung, a man of godly race;
And inherited cunning of spirit and beauty of body and face.
Of yore in his youth, as an aito, Rahéro wandered the land,
Delighting maids with his tongue, smiting men with his hand.
Famous he was in his youth; but before the midst of his life
Paused, and fashioned a song of farewell to glory and strife.

> *House of mine (it went), house upon the sea,*
> *Belov'd of all my fathers, more belov'd by me!*   60
> *Vale of the strong Honoura, deep ravine of Pai,*
> *Again in your woody summits I hear the trade-wind cry.*

> *House of mine, in your walls, strong sounds the sea,*
> *Of all sounds on earth, dearest sound to me.*
> *I have heard the applause of men, I have heard it arise and die:*
> *Sweeter now in my house I hear the trade-wind cry.*

Thése were the words of his singing, other the thought of his heart;
For secret desire of glory vexed him, dwelling apart.
Lazy and crafty he was, and loved to lie in the sun,
And loved the cackle of talk and the true word uttered in fun;   70
Lazy he was, his roof was ragged, his table was lean,
And the fish swam safe in his sea, and he gathered the near and the green.
He sat in his house and laughed, but he loathed the king of the land,
And he uttered the grudging word under the covering hand.
Treason spread from his door; and he looked for a day to come,
A day of the crowding people, a day of the summoning drum,
When the vote should be taken, the king be driven forth in disgrace,
And Rahéro, the laughing and lazy, sit and rule in his place.

Here Támatéa came, and beheld the house on the brook;
And Rahéro was there by the way and covered an oven to cook.[3]   80
Naked he was to the loins, but the tattoo covered the lack,
And the sun and the shadow of palms dappled his muscular back.
Swiftly he lifted his head at the fall of the coming feet,

And the water sprang in his mouth with a sudden desire of meat;
For he marked the basket carried, covered from flies and the sun;[4]
And Rahéro buried his fire, but the meat in his house was done.

Forth he stepped; and took, and delayed the boy, by the hand;
And vaunted the joys of meat and the ancient ways of the land:
– 'Our sires of old in Taiárapu, they that created the race,
Ate ever with eager hand, nor regarded season or place,   90
Ate in the boat at the oar, on the way afoot; and at night
Arose in the midst of dreams to rummage the house for a bite.
It is good for the youth in his turn to follow the way of the sire;
And behold how fitting the time! for here do I cover my fire.'
– 'I see the fire for the cooking but never the meat to cook,'
Said Támatéa. – 'Tut!' said Rahéro. 'Here in the brook
And there in the tumbling sea, the fishes are thick as flies,
Hungry like healthy men, and like pigs for savour and size:
Crayfish crowding the river, sea-fish thronging the sea.'
– 'Well it may be,' says the other, 'and yet be nothing to me.   100
Fain would I eat, but alas! I have needful matter in hand,
Since I carry my tribute of fish to the jealous king of the land.'

Now at the word a light sprang in Rahéro's eyes.
'I will gain me a dinner,' thought he, 'and lend the king a surprise.'
And he took the lad by the arm, as they stood by the side of the track,
And smiled, and rallied, and flattered, and pushed him forward and back.
It was 'You that sing like a bird, I have never heard you sing,'
And 'The lads when I was a lad were none so feared of a king.
And of what account is an hour, when the heart is empty of guile?
But come, and sit in the house and laugh with the women awhile;   110
And I will but drop my hook, and behold! the dinner made.'

So Támatéa the pliable hung up his fish in the shade
On a tree by the side of the way; and Rahéro carried him in,
Smiling as smiles the fowler when flutters the bird to the gin,
And chose him a shining hook,[5] and viewed it with sedulous eye,
And breathed and burnished it well on the brawn of his naked thigh,
And set a mat for the gull, and bade him be merry and bide,
Like a man concerned for his guest, and the fishing, and nothing beside.

Now when Rahéro was forth, he paused and hearkened, and heard
The gull jest in the house and the women laugh at his word;   120
And stealthily crossed to the side of the way, to the shady place
Where the basket hung on a mango; and craft disfigured his face.
Deftly he opened the basket, and took of the fat of the fish,
The cut of kings and chieftains, enough for a goodly dish.
This he wrapped in a leaf, set on the fire to cook
And buried; and next the marred remains of the tribute he took,

And doubled and packed them well, and covered the basket close
– 'There is a buffet, my king,' quoth he, 'and a nauseous dose!' –
And hung the basket again in the shade, in a cloud of flies
– 'And there is a sauce to your dinner, king of the crafty eyes!'   130

Soon as the oven was open, the fish smelt excellent good.
In the shade by the house of Rahéro, down they sat to their food,
And cleared the leaves[6] in silence, or uttered a jest and laughed,
And raising the cocoanut bowls, buried their faces and quaffed.
But chiefly in silence they ate; and soon as the meal was done,
Rahéro feigned to remember and measured the hour by the sun,
And 'Támatéa,' quoth he, 'it is time to be jogging, my lad.'

So Támatéa arose, doing ever the thing he was bade,
And carelessly shouldered the basket, and kindly saluted his host;
And again the way of his going was round by the roaring coast.   140
Long he went; and at length was aware of a pleasant green,
And the stems and the shadows of palms, and roofs of lodges between.
There sate, in the door of his palace, the king on a kingly seat,
And aitos stood armed around, and the yottowas[7] sat at his feet.
But fear was a worm in his heart: fear darted his eyes;
And he probed men's faces for treasons and pondered their speech for lies.
To him came Támatéa, the basket slung in his hand,
And paid him the due obeisance standing as vassals stand.
In silence hearkened the king, and closed the eyes in his face,
Harbouring odious thoughts and the baseless fears of the base;   150
In silence accepted the gift and sent the giver away.
So Támatéa departed, turning his back on the day.

And lo! as the king sat brooding, a rumour rose in the crowd;
The yottowas nudged and whispered, the commons murmured aloud;
Tittering fell upon all at sight of the impudent thing,
At the sight of a gift unroyal flung in the face of a king.
And the face of the king turned white and red with anger and shame
In their midst; and the heart in his body was water and then was flame;
Till of a sudden, turning, he gripped an aito hard,
A youth that stood with his ómare,[8] one of the daily guard,   160
And spat in his ear a command, and pointed and uttered a name,
And hid in the shade of the house his impotent anger and shame.

Now Támatéa the fool was far on the homeward way,
The rising night in his face, behind him the dying day.
Rahéro saw him go by, and the heart of Rahéro was glad,
Devising shame to the king and nowise harm to the lad;
And all that dwelt by the way saw and saluted him well,
For he had the face of a friend and the news of the town to tell;
And pleased with the notice of folk, and pleased that his journey was done,

Támatéa drew homeward, turning his back to the sun.   170

And now was the hour of the bath in Taiárapu: far and near
The lovely laughter of bathers rose and delighted his ear.
Night massed in the valleys; the sun on the mountain coast
Struck, end-long; and above the clouds embattled their host,
And glowed and gloomed on the heights; and the heads of the palms were gems,
And far to the rising eve extended the shade of their stems;
And the shadow of Támatéa hovered already at home.

And sudden the sound of one coming and running light as the foam
Struck on his ear; and he turned, and lo! a man on his track,
Girded and armed with an ómare, following hard at his back.   180
At a bound the man was upon him; – and, or ever a word was said,
The loaded end of the ómare fell and laid him dead.

II The Venging of Támatéa

Thus was Rahéro's treason; thus and no further it sped.
The king sat safe in his place and a kindly fool was dead.

But the mother of Támatéa arose with death in her eyes.
All night long, and the next, Taiárapu rang with her cries.
As when a babe in the wood turns with a chill of doubt
And perceives nor home, nor friends, for the trees have closed her about,
The mountain rings and her breast is torn with the voice of despair:
So the lion-like woman idly wearied the air   190
For awhile, and pierced men's hearing in vain, and wounded their hearts.
But as when the weather changes at sea, in dangerous parts,
And sudden the hurricane wrack unrolls up the front of the sky,
At once the ship lies idle, the sails hang silent on high,
The breath of the wind that blew is blown out like the flame of a lamp,
And the silent armies of death draw near with inaudible tramp:
So sudden, the voice of her weeping ceased; in silence she rose
And passed from the house of her sorrow, a woman clothed with repose,
Carrying death in her breast and sharpening death with her hand.

Hither she went and thither in all the coasts of the land.   200
They tell that she feared not to slumber alone, in the dead of night,
In accursed places; beheld, unblenched, the ribbon of light[9]
Spin from temple to temple; guided the perilous skiff,
Abhorred not the paths of the mountain and trod the verge of the cliff;
From end to end of the island, thought not the distance long,
But forth from king to king carried the tale of her wrong.
To king after king, as they sat in the palace door, she came,
Claiming kinship, declaiming verses, naming her name
And the names of all her fathers; and still, with a heart on the rack,

Jested to capture a hearing and laughed when they jested back: 210
So would deceive them awhile, and change and return in a breath,
And on all the men of Vaiau imprecate instant death;
And tempt her kings – for Vaiau was a rich and prosperous land,
And flatter – for who would attempt it but warriors mighty of hand?
And change in a breath again and rise in a strain of song,
Invoking the beaten drums, beholding the fall of the strong,
Calling the fowls of the air to come and feast on the dead.
And they held the chin in silence, and heard her, and shook the head;
For they knew the men of Taiárapu famous in battle and feast,
Marvellous eaters and smiters: the men of Vaiau not least.   220

To the land of Námunu-úra,[10] to Paea, at length she came,
To men who were foes to the Tevas and hated their race and name.
There was she well received, and spoke with Hiopa the king.[11]
And Hiopa listened, and weighed, and wisely considered the thing.
'Here in the back of the isle we dwell in a sheltered place,'
Quoth he to the woman, 'in quiet, a weak and peaceable race.
But far in the teeth of the wind lofty Taiárapu lies;
Strong blows the wind of the trade on its seaward face, and cries
Aloud in the top of arduous mountains, and utters its song
In green continuous forests. Strong is the wind, and strong   230
And fruitful and hardy the race, famous in battle and feast,
Marvellous eaters and smiters: the men of Vaiau not least.
Now hearken to me, my daughter, and hear a word of the wise:
How a strength goes linked with a weakness, two by two, like the eyes.
They can wield the ómare well and cast the javelin far;
Yet are they greedy and weak as the swine and the children are.

Plant we, then, here at Paea, a garden of excellent fruits;
Plant we bananas and kava and taro, the king of roots;
Let the pigs in Paea be tapu[12] and no man fish for a year;
And of all the meat in Tahiti gather we threefold here.   240
So shall the fame of our plenty fill the island, and so,
At last, on the tongue of rumour, go where we wish it to go.
Then shall the pigs of Taiárapu raise their snouts in the air;
But we sit quiet and wait, as the fowler sits by the snare,
And tranquilly fold our hands, till the pigs come nosing the food:
But meanwhile build us a house of Trotéa, the stubborn wood,
Bind it with incombustible thongs, set a roof to the room,
Too strong for the hands of a man to dissever or fire to consume;
And there, when the pigs come trotting, there shall the feast be spread,
There shall the eye of the morn enlighten the feasters dead.   250
So be it done; for I have a heart that pities your state,
And Nateva and Námunu-úra are fire and water for hate.'

All was done as he said, and the gardens prospered; and now

The fame of their plenty went out, and word of it came to Vaiau,
For the men of Námunu-úra sailed, to the windward far,
Lay in the offing by south where the towns of the Tevas are,
And cast overboard of their plenty; and lo! at the Tevas' feet
The surf on all of the beaches tumbled treasures of meat.
In the salt of the sea, a harvest tossed with refluent foam;
And the children gleaned it in playing, and ate and carried it home;   260
And the elders stared and debated, and wondered and passed the jest,
But whenever a guest came by eagerly questioned the guest;
And little by little, from one to another, the word went round:
'In all the borders of Paea the victual rots on the ground,
And swine are plenty as rats. And now, when they fare to the sea,
The men of the Námunu-úra glean from under the tree
And load the canoe to the gunwale with all that is toothsome to eat;
And all day long on the sea the jaws are crushing the meat,
The steersman eats at the helm, the rowers munch at the oar,
And at length, when their bellies are full, overboard with the store!'   270
Now was the word made true, and as soon as the bait was bare,
All the pigs of Taiárapu raised their snouts in the air.
Songs were recited, and kinship was counted, and tales were told
How war had severed of late but peace had cemented of old
The clans of the island. 'To war,' said they, 'now set we an end,
And hie to the Námunu-úra even as a friend to a friend.'

So judged, and a day was named; and soon as the morning broke,
Canoes were thrust in the sea and the houses emptied of folk.
Strong blew the wind of the south, the wind that gathers the clan;
Along all the line of the reef the clamorous surges ran;   280
And the clouds were piled on the top of the island mountain-high,
A mountain throned on a mountain. The fleet of canoes swept by
In the midst, on the green lagoon, with a crew released from care,
Sailing an even water, breathing a summer air,
Cheered by a cloudless sun; and ever to left and right,
Bursting surge on the reef, drenching storms on the height.
So the folk of Vaiau sailed and were glad all day,
Coasting the palm-tree cape and crossing the populous bay
By all the towns of Tevas; and still as they bowled along,
Boat would answer to boat with jest and laughter and song,   290
And the people of all the towns trooped to the sides of the sea
And gazed from under the hand or sprang aloft on the tree,
Hailing and cheering. Time failed them for more to do;
The holiday village careened to the wind, and was gone from view
Swift as a passing bird; and ever as onward it bore,
Like the cry of the passing bird, bequeathed its song to the shore –
Desirable laughter of maids and the cry of delight of the child.
And the gazer, left behind, stared at the wake and smiled.

By all the towns of the Tevas they went, and Pápara last,
The home of the chief, the place of muster in war; and passed 300
The march of the lands of the clan, to the lands of an alien folk.
And there, from the dusk of the shore-side palms, a column of smoke
Mounted and wavered and died in the gold of the setting sun,
'Paea!' they cried. 'It is Paea.' And so was the voyage done.

In the early fall of the night, Hiopa came to the shore,
And beheld and counted the comers, and lo, they were forty score:
The pelting feet of the babes that ran already and played,
The clean-lipped smile of the boy, the slender breasts of the maid,
And mighty limbs of women, stalwart mothers of men.
The sires stood forth unabashed; but a little back from his ken 310
Clustered the scarcely nubile, the lads and maids, in a ring,
Fain of each other, afraid of themselves, aware of the king
And aping behaviour, but clinging together with hands and eyes,
With looks that were kind like kisses, and laughter tender as sighs.
There, too, the grandsire stood, raising his silver crest,
And the impotent hands of a suckling groped in his barren breast.
The childhood of love, the pair well-married, the innocent brood,
The tale of the generations repeated and ever renewed –
Hiopa beheld them together, all the ages of man,
And a moment shook in his purpose. 320

> But these were the foes of his clan,
And he trod upon pity, and came, and civilly greeted the king,
And gravely entreated Rahéro; and for all that could fight or sing,
And claimed a name in the land, had fitting phrases of praise;
But with all who were well-descended he spoke of the ancient days.
And ''Tis true,' said he, 'that in Paea the victual rots on the ground;
But, friends, your number is many; and pigs must be hunted and found,
And the lads troop to the mountains to bring the féis down,
And around the bowls of the kava cluster the maids of the town.

So, for tonight, sleep here; but king, common, and priest 330
Tomorrow, in order due, shall sit with me in the feast.'
Sleepless the live-long night, Hiopa's followers toiled.
The pigs screamed and were slaughtered; the spars of the guest-house oiled,
The leaves spread on the floor. In many a mountain glen
The moon drew shadows of trees on the naked bodies of men
Plucking and bearing fruits; and in all the bounds of the town
Red glowed the cocoanut fires, and were buried and trodden down.
Thus did seven of the yottowas toil with their tale of the clan,
But the eighth wrought with his lads, hid from the sight of man.
In the deeps of the woods they laboured, piling the fuel high 340
In fagots, the load of a man, fuel seasoned and dry,
Thirsty to seize upon fire and apt to blurt into flame.

And now was the day of the feast. The forests, as morning came,
Tossed in the wind, and the peaks quaked in the blaze of the day
And the cocoanuts showered on the ground, rebounding and rolling away:
A glorious morn for a feast, a famous wind for a fire.
To the hall of feasting Hiopa led them, mother and sire
And maid and babe in a tale, the whole of the holiday throng.
Smiling they came, garlanded green, not dreaming of wrong;
And for every three, a pig, tenderly cooked in the ground,   350
Waited; and féi, the staff of life, heaped in a mound
For each where he sat; – for each, bananas roasted and raw
Piled with bountiful hand, as for horses hay and straw
Are stacked in a stable; and fish, the food of desire,[13]
And plentiful vessels of sauce, and breadfruit gilt in the fire; –
And kava was common as water. Feasts have there been ere now,
And many, but never a feast like that of the folk of Vaiau.

All day long they ate with the resolute greed of brutes,
And turned from the pigs to the fish, and again from the fish to the fruits,
And emptied the vessels of sauce, and drank of the kava deep;   360
Till the young lay stupid as stones, and the strongest nodded to sleep.
Sleep that was mighty as death and blind as a moonless night
Tethered them hand and foot; and their souls were drowned, and the light
Was cloaked from their eyes. Senseless together, the old and the young,
The fighter deadly to smite and the prater cunning of tongue,
The woman wedded and fruitful, inured to the pangs of birth,
And the maid that knew not of kisses, blindly sprawled on the earth.

From the hall Hiopa the king and his chiefs came stealthily forth.
Already the sun hung low and enlightened the peaks of the north;
But the wind was stubborn to die and blew as it blows at morn,   370
Showering the nuts in the dusk, and e'en as a banner is torn,
High on the peaks of the island, shattered the mountain cloud.
And now at once, at a signal, a silent, emulous crowd
Sets hand to the work of death, hurrying to and fro,
Like ants, to furnish the fagots, building them broad and low,
And piling them high and higher around the walls of the hall.
Silence persisted within, for sleep lay heavy on all.
But the mother of Támatéa stood at Hiopa's side,
And shook for terror and joy like a girl that is a bride.
Night fell on the toilers, and first Hiopa the wise   380
Made the round of the house, visiting all with his eyes;
And all was piled to the eaves, and fuel blockaded the door;
And within, in the house beleaguered, slumbered the forty score.
Then was an aito dispatched and came with fire in his hand,
And Hiopa took it. – 'Within,' said he, 'is the life of a land;
And behold! I breathe on the coal, I breathe on the dales of the east,
And silence falls on forest and shore; the voice of the feast

Is quenched, and the smoke of cooking; the rooftree decays and falls
On the empty lodge, and the winds subvert deserted walls.'

Therewithal, to the fuel, he laid the glowing coal; 390
And the redness ran in the mass and burrowed within like a mole,
And copious smoke was conceived. But, as when a dam is to burst,
The water lips it and crosses in silver trickles at first,
And then, of a sudden, whelms and bears it away forthright:
So now, in a moment, the flame sprang and towered in the night,
And wrestled and roared in the wind, and high over house and tree,
Stood, like a streaming torch, enlightening land and sea.

But the mother of Támatéa threw her arms abroad,
'Pyre of my son,' she shouted, 'debited vengeance of God,
Late, late, I behold you, yet I behold you at last, 400
And glory, beholding! For now are the days of my agony past,
The lust that famished my soul now eats and drinks its desire,
And they that encompassed my son shrivel alive in the fire.
Tenfold precious the vengeance that comes after lingering years!
Ye quenched the voice of my singer? – hark, in your dying ears,
The song of the conflagration! Ye left me a widow alone?
– Behold, the whole of your race consumes, sinew and bone
And torturing flesh together: man, mother, and maid
Heaped in a common shambles; and already, borne by the trade,
The smoke of your dissolution darkens the stars of night.' 410

Thus she spoke, and her stature grew in the people's sight.

III Rahéro

Rahéro was there in the hall asleep: beside him his wife,
Comely, a mirthful woman, one that delighted in life;
And a girl that was ripe for marriage, shy and sly as a mouse;
And a boy, a climber of trees: all the hopes of his house.
Unwary, with open hands, he slept in the midst of his folk.
And dreamed that he heard a voice crying without, and awoke,
Leaping blindly afoot like one from a dream he fears.
A hellish glow and clouds were about him; – it roared in his ears
Like the sound of the cataract fall that plunges sudden and steep; 420
And Rahéro swayed as he stood, and his reason was still asleep.
Now the flame struck hard on the house, wind-wielded, a fracturing blow,
And the end of the roof was burst and fell on the sleepers below;
And the lofty hall, and the feast, and the prostrate bodies of folk,
Shone red in his eyes a moment, and then were swallowed of smoke.
In the mind of Rahéro clearness came; and he opened his throat;
And as when a squall comes sudden, the straining sail of a boat
Thunders aloud and bursts, so thundered the voice of the man.

– 'The wind and the rain!' he shouted, the mustering word of the clan,[14]
And 'up' and 'to arms, men of Vaiau!' But silence replied,   430
Or only the voice of the gusts of the fire, and nothing beside.

Rahéro stooped and groped. He handled his womankind,
But the fumes of the fire and the kava had quenched the life of their mind,
And they lay like pillars prone; and his hand encountered the boy,
And there sprang in the gloom of his soul a sudden lightning of joy.
'Him I can save!' he thought, 'if I were speedy enough.'
And he loosened the cloth from his loins, and swaddled the child in the stuff;
And about the strength of his neck he knotted the burden well.

There where the roof had fallen, it roared like the mouth of hell.
Thither Rahéro went, stumbling on senseless folk,   440
And grappled a post of the house, and began to climb in the smoke:
The last alive of Vaiau: and the son borne by the sire.
The post glowed in the grain with ulcers of eating fire,
And the fire bit to the blood and mangled his hands and thighs;
And the fumes sang in his head like wine and stung in his eyes;
And still he climbed, and came to the top, the place of proof,
And thrust a hand through the flame, and clambered alive on the roof.
But even as he did so, the wind, in a garment of flames and pain,
Wrapped him from head to heel; and the waistcloth parted in twain;
And the living fruit of his loins dropped in the fire below.   450

About the blazing feast-house clustered the eyes of the foe,
Watching, hand upon weapon, lest ever a soul should flee,
Shading the brow from the glare, straining the neck to see.
Only, to leeward, the flames in the wind swept far and wide,
And the forest sputtered on fire; and there might no man abide.
Thither Rahéro crept, and dropped from the burning eaves,
And crouching low to the ground, in a treble covert of leaves
And fire and volleying smoke, ran for the life of his soul
Unseen; and behind him under a furnace of ardent coal,
Cairned with a wonder of flame, and blotting the night with smoke,   460
Blazed and were smelted together the bones of all his folk.

He fled unguided at first; but hearing the breakers roar,
Thitherward shaped his way, and came at length to the shore.
Sound-limbed he was: dry-eyed; but smarted in every part;
And the mighty cage of his ribs heaved on his straining heart
With sorrow and rage. And 'Fools!' he cried, 'fools of Vaiau,
Heads of swine – gluttons – Alas! and where are they now?
Those that I played with, those that nursed me, those that I nursed?
God, and I outliving them! I, the least and the worst –
I, that thought myself crafty, snared by this herd of swine,   470
In the tortures of hell and desolate, stripped of all that was mine:

All! – my friends and my fathers – the silver heads of yore
That trooped to the council, the children that ran to the open door
Crying with innocent voices and clasping a father's knees!
And mine, my wife – my daughter – my sturdy climber of trees,
Ah, never to climb again!'

                Thus in the dusk of the night,
(For clouds rolled in the sky and the moon was swallowed from sight),
Pacing and gnawing his fists, Rahéro raged by the shore.
Vengeance: that must be his. But much was to do before;   480
And first a single life to be snatched from a deadly place,
A life, the root of revenge, surviving plant of the race:
And next the race to be raised anew, and the lands of the clan
Repeopled. So Rahéro designed, a prudent man
Even in wrath, and turned for the means of revenge and escape:
A boat to be seized by stealth, a wife to be taken by rape.

Still was the dark lagoon; beyond on the coral wall,
He saw the breakers shine, he heard them bellow and fall.
Alone, on the top of the reef, a man with a flaming brand
Walked, gazing and pausing, a fish-spear poised in his hand.   490
The foam boiled to his calf when the mightier breakers came,
And the torch shed in the wind scattering tufts of flame.
Afar on the dark lagoon a canoe lay idly at wait:
A figure dimly guiding it: surely the fisherman's mate.
Rahéro saw and he smiled. He straightened his mighty thews:
Naked, with never a weapon, and covered with scorch and bruise,
He straightened his arms, he filled the void of his body with breath,
And, strong as the wind in his manhood, doomed the fisher to death.

Silent he entered the water, and silently swam, and came
There where the fisher walked, holding on high the flame.   500
Loud on the pier of the reef volleyed the breach of the sea;
And hard at the back of the man, Rahéro crept to his knee
On the coral, and suddenly sprang and seized him, the elder hand
Clutching the joint of his throat, the other snatching the brand
Ere it had time to fall, and holding it steady and high.
Strong was the fisher, brave, and swift of mind and eye –
Strongly he threw in the clutch; but Rahéro resisted the strain,
And jerked, and the spine of life snapped with a crack in twain,
And the man came slack in his hands and tumbled a lump at his feet.

One moment: and there, on the reef, where the breakers whitened and beat,   510
Rahéro was standing alone, glowing and scorched and bare,
A victor unknown of any, raising the torch in the air.
But once he drank of his breath, and instantly set him to fish
Like a man intent upon supper at home and a savoury dish.

For what should the woman have seen? A man with a torch – and then
A moment's blur of the eyes – and a man with a torch again.
And the torch had scarcely been shaken. 'Ah, surely,' Rahéro said,
'She will deem it a trick of the eyes, a fancy born in the head;
But time must be given the fool to nourish a fool's belief.'
So for a while, a sedulous fisher, he walked the reef,   520
Pausing at times and gazing, striking at times with the spear:
– Lastly, uttered the call; and even as the boat drew near,
Like a man that was done with its use, tossed the torch in the sea.

Lightly he leaped on the boat beside the woman; and she
Lightly addressed him, and yielded the paddle and place to sit;
For now the torch was extinguished the night was black as the pit.
Rahéro set him to row, never a word he spoke,
And the boat sang in the water urged by his vigorous stroke.
– 'What ails you?' the woman asked, 'and why did you drop the brand?
We have only to kindle another as soon as we come to land.'   530
Never a word Rahéro replied, but urged the canoe.
And a chill fell on the woman. – 'Atta! speak! is it you?
Speak! Why are you silent? Why do you bend aside?
Wherefore steer to the seaward?' thus she panted and cried.
Never a word from the oarsman, toiling there in the dark;
But right for a gate of the reef he silently headed the bark,
And wielding the single paddle with passionate sweep on sweep,
Drove her, the little fitted, forth on the open deep.

And fear, there where she sat, froze the woman to stone:
Not fear of the crazy boat and the weltering deep alone;   540
But a keener fear of the night, the dark, and the ghostly hour,
And the thing that drove the canoe with more than a mortal's power
And more than a mortal's boldness. For much she knew of the dead
That haunt and fish upon reefs, toiling, like men, for bread,
And traffic with human fishers, or slay them and take their ware,
Till the hour when the star of the dead[15] goes down, and the morning air
Blows, and the cocks are singing on shore. And surely she knew
The speechless thing at her side belonged to the grave.

                                                  It blew
All night from the south; all night, Rahéro contended and kept
The prow to the cresting sea: and, silent as though she slept,   550
The woman huddled and quaked. And now was the peep of day.
High and long on their left the mountain island lay;
And over the peaks of Taiárapu arrows of sunlight struck.
On shore the birds were beginning to sing: the ghostly ruck
Of the buried had long ago returned to the covered grave;
And here on the sea, the woman, waxing suddenly brave,
Turned her swiftly about and looked in the face of the man.

And sure he was none that she knew, none of her country or clan:
A stranger, mother-naked, and marred with the marks of fire,
But comely and great of stature, a man to obey and admire.   560

And Rahéro regarded her also, fixed, with a frowning face,
Judging the woman's fitness to mother a warlike race.
Broad of shoulder, ample of girdle, long in the thigh,
Deep of bosom she was, and bravely supported his eye.

'Woman,' said he, 'last night the men of your folk –
Man, woman, and maid, smothered my race in smoke.
It was done like cowards; and I, a mighty man of my hands,
Escaped, a single life: and now to the empty lands
And smokeless hearths of my people, sail, with yourself, alone.
Before your mother was born, the die of today was thrown   570
And you selected: – your husband, vainly striving, to fall
Broken between these hands: – yourself to be severed from all,
The places, the people, you love – home, kindred, and clan –
And to dwell in a desert and bear the babes of a kinless man.'

The Feast of Famine: Marquesan Manners

I The Priest's Vigil

In all the land of the tribe was neither fish nor fruit,
And the deepest pit of popoi stood empty at the foot.[1]
The clans upon the left and the clans upon the right
Now oiled their carven maces and scoured their daggers bright;
They gat them to the thicket, to the deepest of the shade,
And lay with sleepless eyes in the deadly ambuscade.
And oft in the starry even the song of morning rose,
What time the oven smoked in the country of their foes;
For oft to loving hearts, and waiting ears and sight,
The lads that went to forage returned not with the night.   10
Now first the children sickened, and then the women paled,
And the great arms of the warrior no more for war availed.
Hushed was the deep drum, discarded was the dance;
And those that met the priest now glanced at him askance.
The priest was a man of years, his eyes were ruby-red,[2]
He neither feared the dark nor the terrors of the dead,
He knew the songs of races, the names of ancient date;
And the beard upon his bosom would have bought the chief's estate.
He dwelt in a high-built lodge, hard by the roaring shore,
Raised on a noble terrace and with tikis[3] at the door.   20
Within it was full of riches, for he served his nation well,
And full of the sound of breakers, like the hollow of a shell.
For weeks he let them perish, gave never a helping sign,
But sat on his oiled platform to commune with the divine,
But sat on his high terrace, with the tikis by his side,
And stared on the blue ocean, like a parrot, ruby-eyed.

Dawn as yellow as sulphur leaped on the mountain height:
Out on the round of the sea the gems of the morning light,
Up from the round of the sea the streamers of the sun; –
But down in the depths of the valley the day was not begun.   30
In the blue of the woody twilight burned red the cocoa-husk,
And the women and men of the clan went forth to bathe in the dusk.
A word that began to go round, a word, a whisper, a start:
Hope that leaped in the bosom, fear that knocked on the heart:
'See, the priest is not risen – look, for his door is fast!
He is going to name the victims; he is going to help us at last.'

Thrice rose the sun to noon; and ever, like one of the dead,
The priest lay still in his house with the roar of the sea in his head;
There was never a foot on the floor, there was never a whisper of speech;
Only the leering tikis stared on the blinding beach.   40
Again were the mountains fired, again the morning broke;
And all the houses lay still, but the house of the priest awoke.

Close in their covering roofs lay and trembled the clan,
But the agèd, red-eyed priest ran forth like a lunatic man;
And the village panted to see him in the jewels of death again,
In the silver beards of the old and the hair of women slain.
Frenzy shook in his limbs, frenzy shone in his eyes,
And still and again as he ran, the valley rang with his cries.
All day long in the land, by cliff and thicket and den,
He ran his lunatic rounds, and howled for the flesh of men;   50
All day long he ate not, nor ever drank of the brook;
And all day long in their houses the people listened and shook –
All day long in their houses they listened with bated breath,
And never a soul went forth, for the sight of the priest was death.

Three were the days of his running, as the gods appointed of yore,
Two the nights of his sleeping alone in the place of gore:
The drunken slumber of frenzy twice he drank to the lees,
On the sacred stones of the High-place under the sacred trees;
With a lamp at his ashen head he lay in the place of the feast,
And the sacred leaves of the banyan rustled around the priest.   60
Last, when the stated even fell upon terrace and tree,
And the shade of the lofty island lay leagues away to sea,
And all the valleys of verdure were heavy with manna and musk,
The wreck of the red-eyed priest came gasping home in the dusk.
He reeled across the village, he staggered along the shore,
And between the leering tikis crept groping through his door.

There went a stir through the lodges, the voice of speech awoke;
Once more from the builded platforms arose the evening smoke.
And those who were mighty in war, and those renowned for an art
Sat in their stated seats and talked of the morrow apart.   70

II *The Lovers*

Hark! away in the woods – for the ears of love are sharp –
Stealthily, quietly touched, the note of the one-stringed harp.[4]
In the lighted house of her father, why should Taheia start?
Taheia heavy of hair, Taheia tender of heart,
Taheia the well-descended, a bountiful dealer in love,
Nimble of foot like the deer, and kind of eye like the dove?
Sly and shy as a cat, with never a change of face,
Taheia slips to the door, like one that would breathe a space;
Saunters and pauses, and looks at the stars, and lists to the seas;
Then sudden and swift as a cat, she plunges under the trees.   80
Swift as a cat she runs, with her garment gathered high,
Leaping, nimble of foot, running, certain of eye;
And ever to guide her way over the smooth and the sharp,
Ever nearer and nearer the note of the one-stringed harp;

Till at length, in a glade of the wood, with a naked mountain above,
The sound of the harp thrown down, and she in the arms of her love.
'Rua!' – 'Taheia,' they cry – 'my heart, my soul, and my eyes,'
And clasp and sunder and kiss, with lovely laughter and sighs,
'Rua!' – 'Taheia, my love,' – 'Rua, star of my night,
Clasp me, hold me, and love me, single spring of delight.'   90

And Rua folded her close, he folded her near and long,
The living knit to the living, and sang the lover's song:

> Night, night it is, night upon the palms.
> Night, night it is, the land wind has blown.
> Starry, starry night, over deep and height;
> Love, love in the valley, love all alone.

'Taheia, heavy of hair, a foolish thing we have done,
To bind what gods have sundered unkindly into one.
Why should a lowly lover have touched Taheia's skirt,
Taheia the well-descended, and Rua child of the dirt?'   100

'– On high with the haka-ikis my father sits in state,
Ten times fifty kinsmen salute him in the gate;
Round all his martial body, and in bands across his face,
The marks of the tattooer proclaim his lofty place.
I too, in the hands of the cunning, in the sacred cabin of palm,⁵
Have shrunk like the mimosa, and bleated like the lamb;
Round half my tender body, that none shall clasp but you,
For a crest and a fair adornment go dainty lines of blue.
Love, love, beloved Rua, love levels all degrees,
And the well-tattooed Taheia clings panting to your knees.'   110

'– Taheia, song of the morning, how long is the longest love?
A cry, a clasp of the hands, a star that falls from above!
Ever at morn in the blue, and at night when all is black,
Ever it skulks and trembles with the hunter, Death, on its track.
Hear me, Taheia, death! For tomorrow the priest shall awake,
And the names be named of the victims to bleed for the nation's sake;
And first of the numbered many that shall be slain ere noon,
Rua the child of the dirt, Rua the kinless loon.
For him shall the drum be beat, for him be raised the song,
For him to the sacred High-place the chaunting people throng,   120
For him the oven smoke as for a speechless beast,
And the sire of my Taheia come greedy to the feast.'
'– Rua, be silent, spare me. Taheia closes her ears.
Pity my yearning heart, pity my girlish years!
Flee from the cruel hands, flee from the knife and coal,
Lie hid in the deeps of the woods, Rua, sire of my soul!'

'Whither to flee, Taheia, whither in all of the land?
The fires of the bloody kitchen are kindled on every hand;
On every hand in the isle a hungry whetting of teeth,
Eyes in the trees above, arms in the brush beneath.   130
Patience to lie in wait, cunning to follow the sleuth,
Abroad the foes I have fought, and at home the friends of my youth.'

'Love, love, beloved Rua, love has a clearer eye,
Hence from the arms of love you go not forth to die.
There, where the broken mountain drops sheer into the glen,
There shall you find a hold from the boldest hunter of men;
There, in the deep recess, where the sun falls only at noon,
And only once in the night enters the light of the moon,
Nor ever a sound but of birds, or the rain when it falls with a shout;
For death and the fear of death beleaguer the valley about.   140
Tapu it is, but the gods will surely pardon despair;
Tapu, but what of that? If Rua can only dare.
Tapu and tapu and tapu, I know they are every one right;
But the god of every tapu is not always quick to smite.
Lie secret there, my Rua, in the arms of awful gods,
Sleep in the shade of the trees on the couch of the kindly sods,
Sleep and dream of Taheia, Taheia will wake for you;
And whenever the land wind blows and the woods are heavy with dew,
Alone through the horror of night,[6] with food for the soul of her love,
Taheia the undissuaded will hurry as true as the dove.'   150

'Taheia, the pit of the night crawls with treacherous things,
Spirits of ultimate air and the evil souls of Kings;
The souls of the dead, the stranglers, that perch in the trees of the wood,
Waiters for all things human, haters of evil and good.'

'Rua, behold me, kiss me, look in my eyes and read;
Are these the eyes of a maid that would leave her lover in need?
Brave in the eye of day, my father ruled in the fight;
The child of his loins, Taheia, will play the man in the night.'

So it was spoken, and so agreed, and Taheia arose
And smiled in the stars and was gone, swift as the swallow goes;   160
And Rua stood on the hill, and sighed, and followed her flight,
And there were the lodges below, each with its door alight;
From folk that sat on the terrace and drew out the even long
Sudden crowings of laughter, monotonous drone of song;
The quiet passage of souls over his head in the trees;[7]
And from all around the haven the crumbling thunder of seas.
'Farewell, my home,' said Rua. 'Farewell, O quiet seat!
Tomorrow in all your valleys the drum of death shall beat.'

III The Feast

Dawn as yellow as sulphur leaped on the naked peak,
And all the village was stirring, for now was the priest to speak.   170
Forth on his terrace he came, and sat with the chief in talk;
His lips were blackened with fever, his cheeks were whiter than chalk;
Fever clutched at his hands, fever nodded his head,
But, quiet and steady and cruel, his eyes shone ruby-red.
In the earliest rays of the sun the chief rose up content;
Braves were summoned, and drummers; messengers came and went;
Braves ran to their lodges, weapons were snatched from the wall;
The commons herded together, and fear was over them all.
Festival dresses they wore, but the tongue was dry in their mouth,
And the blinking eyes in their faces skirted from north to south.   180

Now to the sacred enclosure gathered the greatest and least,
And from under the shade of the banyan arose the voice of the feast,
The frenzied roll of the drum, and a swift, monotonous song.
Higher the sun swam up; the trade wind level and strong
Awoke in the tops of the palms and rattled the fans aloud,
And over the garlanded heads and shining robes of the crowd
Tossed the spiders of shadow, scattered the jewels of sun.
Forty the tale of the drums, and the forty throbbed like one;
A thousand hearts in the crowd, and the even chorus of song,
Swift as the feet of the runner, trampled a thousand strong.   190
And the old men leered at the ovens and licked their lips for the food;
And the women stared at the lads, and laughed and looked to the wood.
As when the sweltering baker, at night, when the city is dead,
Alone in the trough of labour treads and fashions the bread;
So in the heat, and the reek, and the touch of woman and man,
The naked spirit of evil kneaded the hearts of the clan.

Now cold was at many a heart, and shaking in many a seat;
For there were the empty baskets, but who was to furnish the meat?
For here was the nation assembled, and there were the ovens anigh,
And out of a thousand singers nine were numbered to die.   200
Till, of a sudden, a shock, a mace in the air, a yell,
And, struck in the edge of the crowd, the first of the victims fell.[8]
Terror and horrible glee divided the shrinking clan,
Terror of what was to follow, glee for a diet of man.
Frenzy hurried the chaunt, frenzy rattled the drums;
The nobles, high on the terrace, greedily mouthed their thumbs;
And once and again and again in the ignorant crowd below,
Once and again and again descended the murderous blow.
Now smoked the oven, and now, with the cutting lip of a shell,
A butcher of ninety winters jointed the bodies well.   210
Unto the carven lodge, silent, in order due,

The grandees of the nation one after one withdrew;
And a line of laden bearers brought to the terrace foot,
On poles across their shoulders, the last reserve of fruit.
The victims bled for the nobles in the old appointed way;
The fruit was spread for the commons, for all should eat today.

And now was the kava brewed, and now the cocoa ran,
Now was the hour of the dance for child and woman and man;
And mirth was in every heart, and a garland on every head,
And all was well with the living and well with the eight who were dead.   220
Only the chiefs and the priest talked and consulted awhile:
'Tomorrow,' they said, and 'Tomorrow,' and nodded and seemed to smile:
'Rua the child of the dirt, the creature of common clay,
Rua must die tomorrow, since Rua is gone today.'

Out of the groves of the valley, where clear the blackbirds sang,
Sheer from the trees of the valley the face of the mountain sprang;
Sheer and bare it rose, unscalable barricade,
Beaten and blown against by the generous draught of the trade.
Dawn on its fluted brow painted rainbow light,
Close on its pinnacled crown trembled the stars at night.   230
Here and there in a cleft clustered contorted trees,
Or the silver beard of a stream hung and swung in the breeze.
High overhead, with a cry, the torrents leaped for the main,
And silently sprinkled below in thin perennial rain.
Dark in the staring noon, dark was Rua's ravine,
Damp and cold was the air, and the face of the cliffs was green.
Here in the rocky pit, accursed already of old,
On a stone in the midst of a river, Rua sat and was cold.

'Valley of mid-day shadows, valley of silent falls,'
Rua sang, and his voice went hollow about the walls,   240
'Valley of shadow and rock, a doleful prison to me,
What is the life you can give to a child of the sun and the sea?'

And Rua arose and came to the open mouth of the glen,
Whence he beheld the woods, and the sea, and the houses of men.
Wide blew the riotous trade, and smelt in his nostrils good;
It bowed the boats on the bay, and tore and divided the wood;
It smote and sundered the groves as Moses smote with the rod,
And the streamers of all of the trees blew like banners abroad;
And ever and on, in a lull, the trade wind brought him along
A far-off patter of drums and a far-off whisper of song.   250

Swift as the swallow's wings, the diligent hands on the drum
Fluttered and hurried and throbbed. 'Ah, woe that I hear you come,'
Rua cried in his grief, 'a sorrowful sound to me,

Mounting far and faint from the resonant shore of the sea!
Woe in the song! for the grave breathes in the singers' breath,
And I hear in the tramp of the drums the beat of the heart of death.
Home of my youth! no more, through all the length of the years,
No more to the place of the echoes of early laughter and tears,
No more shall Rua return; no more as the evening ends,
To crowded eyes of welcome, to the reaching hands of friends.'   260

All day long from the High-place the drums and the singing came,
And the even fell, and the sun went down, a wheel of flame;
And night came gleaning the shadows and hushing the sounds of the wood;
And silence slept on all, where Rua sorrowed and stood.
But still from the shore of the bay the sound of the festival rang,
And still the crowd in the High-place danced and shouted and sang.

Now over all the isle terror was breathed abroad
Of shadowy hands from the trees and shadowy snares in the sod;
And before the nostrils of night, the shuddering hunter of men
Hurried, with beard on shoulder, back to his lighted den.   270
'Taheia, here to my side!' – 'Rua, my Rua, you!'
And cold from the clutch of terror, cold with the damp of the dew,
Taheia, heavy of hair, leaped through the dark to his arms;
Taheia leaped to his clasp, and was folded in from alarms.

'Rua, beloved, here, see what your love has brought;
Coming – alas! returning – swift as the shuttle of thought;
Returning, alas! for tonight, with the beaten drum and the voice,
In the shine of many torches must the sleepless clan rejoice;
And Taheia the well-descended, the daughter of chief and priest,
Taheia must sit in her place in the crowded bench of the feast.'   280
So it was spoken; and she, girding her garment high,
Fled and was swallowed of woods, swift as the sight of an eye.

Night over isle and sea rolled her curtain of stars,
Then a trouble awoke in the air, the east was banded with bars;
Dawn as yellow as sulphur leaped on the mountain height;
Dawn, in the deepest glen, fell a wonder of light;
High and clear stood the palms in the eye of the brightening east,
And lo! from the sides of the sea the broken sound of the feast!
As, when in days of summer, through open windows, the fly
Swift as a breeze and loud as a trump goes by,   290
But when frosts in the field have pinched the wintering mouse,
Blindly noses and buzzes and hums in the firelit house:
So the sound of the feast gallantly trampled at night,
So it staggered and drooped, and droned in the morning light.

IV *The Raid*

It chanced as Rua sat in the valley of silent falls,
He heard a calling of doves from high on the cliffy walls.
Fire had fashioned of yore, and time had broken, the rocks;
There were rooting crannies for trees and nesting-places for flocks;
And he saw on the top of the cliffs, looking up from the pit of the shade,
A flicker of wings and sunshine, and trees that swung in the trade.   300
'The trees swing in the trade,' quoth Rua, doubtful of words,
'And the sun stares from the sky, but what should trouble the birds?'
Up from the shade he gazed, where high the parapet shone,
And he was aware of a ledge and of things that moved thereon.
'What manner of things are these? Are they spirits abroad by day?
Or the foes of my clan that are come, bringing death by a perilous way?'

The valley was gouged like a vessel, and round like the vessel's lip,
With a cape of the side of the hill thrust forth like the bows of a ship.
On the top of the face of the cape a volley of sun struck fair,
And the cape overhung like a chin a gulph of sunless air.   310
'Silence heart! What is that? – that, that flickered and shone,
Into the sun for an instant, and in an instant gone?
Was it a warrior's plume, a warrior's girdle of hair?
Swung in the loop of a rope, is he making a bridge of the air?'

Once and again Rua saw, in the trenchant edge of the sky,
The giddying conjuring done. And then, in the blink of an eye,
A scream caught in with the breath, a whirling packet of limbs,
A lump that dived in the gulph, more swift than a dolphin swims;
And there was the lump at his feet, and eyes were alive in the lump.
Sick was the soul of Rua, ambushed close in a clump;   320
Sick of soul he drew near, making his courage stout;
And he looked in the face of the thing, and the life of the thing went out.
And he gaze on the tattooed limbs, and, behold, he knew the man:
Hoka, a chief of the Vais, the truculent foe of his clan:
Hoka a moment since that stepped in the loop of the rope,
Filled with the lust of war, and alive with courage and hope.

Again to the giddy cornice Rua lifted his eyes,
And again beheld men passing in the armpit of the skies.
'Foes of my race!' cried Rua, 'the mouth of Rua is true:
Never a shark in the deep is nobler of soul than you.
There was never a nobler foray, never a bolder plan;   330
Never a dizzier path was trod by the children of man;
And Rua, your evil-dealer through all the days of his years,
Counts it honour to hate you, honour to fall by your spears.'

And Rua straightened his back. 'O Vais, a scheme for a scheme!'
Cried Rua and turned and descended the turbulent stair of the stream,
Leaping from rock to rock as the water-wagtail at home
Flits through resonant valleys and skims by boulder and foam.
And Rua burst from the glen and leaped on the shore of the brook,
And straight for the roofs of his clan his vigorous way he took.   340
Swift were the heels of his flight, and loud behind as he went
Rattled the leaping stones on the line of his long descent.
And ever he thought as he ran, and caught at his gasping breath,
'O the fool of a Rua, Rua that runs to his death!
But the right is the right,' thought Rua, and ran like the wind on the foam,
'The right is the right for ever, and home for ever home.
For what though the oven smoke? And what though I die ere morn?
There was I nourished and tended, and there was Taheia born.'
Noon was high on the High-place, the second noon of the feast;
And heat and shameful slumber weighed on people and priest;   350
And the heart drudged slow in bodies heavy with monstrous meals;
And the senseless limbs were scattered abroad like spokes of wheels;
And crapulous women sat and stared at the stones anigh
With a bestial droop of the lip and a swinish rheum in the eye.
As about the dome of the bees in the time for the drones to fall,
The dead and the maimed are scattered, and lie, and stagger, and crawl;
So on the grades of the terrace, in the ardent eye of the day,
The half-awake and the sleepers clustered and crawled and lay;
And loud as the dome of the bees, in the time of a swarming horde,
A horror of many insects hung in the air and roared.   360

Rua looked and wondered; he said to himself in his heart:
'Poor are the pleasures of life, and death is the better part.'
But lo! on the higher benches a cluster of tranquil folk
Sat by themselves, nor raised their serious eyes, nor spoke:
Women with robes unruffled and garlands duly arranged,
Gazing far from the feast with faces of people estranged;
And quiet amongst the quiet, and fairer than all the fair,
Taheia, the well-descended, Taheia, heavy of hair.
And the soul of Rua awoke, courage enlightened his eyes,
And he uttered a summoning shout, and called on the clan to rise.   370
Over against him at once, in the spotted shade of the trees,
Owlish and blinking creatures scrambled to hands and knees;
On the grades of the sacred terrace, the driveller woke to fear,
And the hand of the ham-drooped warrior brandished a wavering spear.
And Rua folded his arms, and scorn discovered his teeth;
Above the war-crowd gibbered, and Rua stood smiling beneath.
Thick, like leaves in the autumn, faint, like April sleet,
Missiles from tremulous hands quivered around his feet;
And Taheia leaped from her place; and the priest, the ruby-eyed,
Ran to the front of the terrace, and brandished his arms, and cried: 380

'Hold, O fools, he brings tidings!' and 'Hold, 't is the love of my heart!'
Till lo! in front of the terrace, Rua pierced with a dart.

Taheia cherished his head, and the aged priest stood by,
And gazed with eyes of ruby at Rua's darkening eye.
'Taheia, here is the end, I die a death for a man.
I have given the life of my soul to save an unsavable clan.
See them, the drooping of hams! behold me the blinking crew:
Fifty spears they cast, and one of fifty true!
And you, O priest, the foreteller, foretell for yourself if you can,
Foretell the hour of the day when the Vais shall burst on your clan!   390
By the head of the tapu cleft, with death and fire in their hand,
Thick and silent like ants, the warriors swarm in the land.'

And they tell that when next the sun had climbed to the noonday skies,
It shone on the smoke of feasting in the country of the Vais.

Ticonderoga: A Legend of the West Highlands

This is the tale of the man
    Who heard a word in the night
In the land of the heathery hills,
    In the days of the feud and the fight.
By the sides of the rainy sea,
    Where never a stranger came,
On the awful lips of the dead,
    He heard the outlandish name.
It sang in his sleeping ears,
    It hummed in his waking head: 10
The name – Ticonderoga,
    The utterance of the dead.

I The Saying of the Name

On the loch-sides of Appin,
    When the mists blew from the sea,
A Stewart stood with a Cameron:
    An angry man was he.
The blood beat in his ears,
    The blood ran hot to his head,
The mist blew from the sea,
    And there was the Cameron dead.   20
'O, what have I done to my friend,
    O, what have I done to mysel',
That he should be cold and dead,
    And I in the danger of all?
Nothing but danger about me,
    Danger behind and before,
Death at wait in the heather
    In Appin and Mamore,
Hate at all of the ferries
    And death at each of the fords,   30
Camerons priming gunlocks
    And Camerons sharpening swords.'

But this was a man of counsel,
    This was a man of score,
There dwelt no pawkier Stewart
    In Appin or Mamore.
He looked on the blowing mist,
    He looked on the awful dead,
And there came a smile on his face
    And there slipped a thought in his head.   40

Out over cairn and moss,
　　Out over scrog and scaur,
He ran as runs the clansman
　　That bears the cross of war.
His heart beat in his body,
　　His hair clove to his face,
When he came at last in the gloaming
　　To the dead man's brother's place.
The east was white with the moon,
　　The west with the sun was red,　　　　　　　　　50
　　And there, in the house-doorway,
Stood the brother of the dead.

'I have slain a man to my danger,
　　I have slain a man to my death.
I put my soul in your hands,'
　　The panting Stewart saith.
'I lay it bare in your hands,
　　For I know your hands are leal;
And be you my targe and bulwark
　　From the bullet and the steel.'　　　　　　　　60

Then up and spoke the Cameron,
　　And gave him his hand again:
'There shall never a man in Scotland
　　Set faith in me in vain;
And whatever man you have slaughtered,
　　Of whatever name or line,
By my sword and yonder mountain,
　　I make your quarrel mine.[1]
I bid you in to my fireside,
　　I share with you house and hall;　　　　　　　70
It stands upon my honour
　　To see you safe from all.'

It fell in the time of midnight,
　　When the fox barked in the den
And the plaids were over the faces
　　In all the houses of men,
That as the living Cameron
　　Lay sleepless on his bed,
Out of the night and the other world,
　　Came in to him the dead.　　　　　　　　　80

'My blood is on the heather,
　　My bones are on the hill;
There is joy in the home of ravens

That the young shall eat their fill.
My blood is poured in the dust,
    My soul is spilled in the air;
And the man that has undone me
    Sleeps in my brother's care.'

'I'm wae for your death, my brother,
    But if all of my house were dead,   90
I couldnae withdraw the plighted hand,
    Nor break the word once said.'

'O, what shall I say to our father,
    In the place to which I fare?
O, what shall I say to our mother,
    Who greets to see me there?
And to all the kindly Camerons
    That have lived and died long-syne –
Is this the word you send them,
    Fause-hearted brother mine?'   100

'It's neither fear nor duty,
    It's neither quick nor dead
Shall gar me withdraw the plighted hand,
    Or break the word once said.'

Thrice in the time of midnight,
    When the fox barked in the den,
And the plaids were over the faces
    In all the houses of men,
Thrice as the living Cameron
    Lay sleepless on his bed,   110
Out of the night and the other world
    Came in to him the dead,
And cried to him for vengeance
    On the man that laid him low;
And thrice the living Cameron
    Told the dead Cameron, no.

'Thrice have you seen me, brother,
    But now shall see me no more,
Till you meet your angry fathers
    Upon the farther shore.   120
Thrice have I spoken, and now,
    Before the cock be heard,
I take my leave for ever
    With the naming of a word.
It shall sing in your sleeping ears,

It shall hum in your waking head,
The name – Ticonderoga,
   And the warning of the dead.'

Now when the night was over
   And the time of people's fears,
The Cameron walked abroad,
   And the word was in his ears.   130
'Many a name I know,
   But never a name like this;
O, where shall I find a skilly man
Shall tell me what it is?'

With many a man he counselled
   Of high and low degree,
With the herdsmen on the mountains
   And the fishers of the sea.   140
And he came and went unweary,
   And read the books of yore,
And the runes that were written of old
   On stones upon the moor.
And many a name he was told,
   But never the name of his fears –
Never, in east or west,
   The name that rang in his ears:
Names of men and of clans,
   Names for the grass and the tree,   150
For the smallest tarn in the mountains,
   The smallest reef in the sea:
Names for the high and low,
   The names of the craig and the flat;
But in all the land of Scotland,
   Never a name like that.

II *The Seeking of the Name*

And now there was speech in the south,
   And a man of the south that was wise,
A periwig'd lord of London,[2]
   Called on the clans to rise.   160
And the riders rode, and the summons
   Came to the western shore,
To the land of the sea and the heather,
   To Appin and Mamore.
It called on all to gather
   From every scrog and scaur,
That loved their fathers' tartan

And the ancient game of war.
And down the watery valley
    And up the windy hill,   170
Once more, as in the olden time,
    The pipes were sounding shrill;
Again in highland sunshine
    The naked steel was bright;
And the lads, once more in tartan,
    Went forth again to fight.

'O, why should I dwell here
    With a weird upon my life,
When the clansmen shout for battle
    And the war-swords clash in strife?   180
I cannae joy at feast,
    I cannae sleep in bed,
For the wonder of the word
    And the warning of the dead.
It sings in my sleeping ears,
    It hums in my waking head,
The name – Ticonderoga,
    The utterance of the dead.
Then up, and with the fighting men
    To march away from here,   190
Till the cry of the great war-pipe
    Shall drown it in my ear!'

Where flew King George's ensign
    The plaided soldiers went:
They drew the sword in Germany,
    In Flanders pitched the tent.
The bells of foreign cities
    Rang far across the plain:
They passed the happy Rhine,
    They drank the rapid Main.   200
Through Asiatic jungles
    The Tartans filed their way,
And the neighing of the war-pipes
    Struck terror in Cathay.[3]
'Many a name I have heard,' he thought,
    'In all the tongues of men,
Full many a name both here and there,
    Full many both now and then.
When I was at home in my father's house
    In the land of the naked knee,   210
Between the eagles that fly in the lift
    And the herrings that swim in the sea,

And now that I am a captain-man
   With a braw cockade in my hat –
Many a name have I heard,' he thought,
   'But never a name like that.'

III *The Place of the Name*

There fell a war in a woody place,
   Lay far across the sea,
A war of the march in the mirk midnight
   And the shot from behind the tree,   220
The shaven head and the painted face,
   The silent foot in the wood,
In a land of a strange, outlandish tongue
   That was hard to be understood.

It fell about the gloaming
   The general stood with his staff,
He stood and he looked east and west
   With little mind to laugh.
'Far have I been and much have I seen,
   And kent both gain and loss,   230
But here we have woods on every hand
   And a kittle water to cross.
Far have I been and much have I seen,
   But never the beat of this;
And there's one must go down to that waterside
   To see how deep it is.'

It fell in the dusk of the night
   When unco things betide,
The skilly captain, the Cameron,
   Went down to that waterside.   240
Canny and soft the captain went;
   And a man of the woody land,
With the shaven head and the painted face,
   Went down at his right hand.
It fell in the quiet night,
   There was never a sound to ken;
But all of the woods to the right and the left
   Lay filled with the painted men.

'Far have I been and much have I seen,
   Both as a man and boy,   250
But never have I set forth a foot
   On so perilous an employ.'
It fell in the dusk of the night

When unco things betide,
That he was aware of a captain-man
    Drew near to the waterside.
He was aware of his coming
    Down in the gloaming alone;
And he looked in the face of the man
    And lo! the face was his own.   260

'This is my weird,' he said,
    'And now I ken the worst;
For many shall fall the morn,
    But I shall fall with the first.
O, you of the outland tongue,
    You of the painted face,
This is the place of my death;
    Can you tell me the name of the place?'

'Since the Frenchmen have been here
    They have called it Sault-Marie;   270
But that is a name for priests,
    And not for you and me.
It went by another word,'
    Quoth he of the shaven head:
'It was called Ticonderoga
    In the days of the great dead.'

And it fell on the morrow's morning,
    In the fiercest of the fight,
That the Cameron bit the dust
    As he foretold at night;   280
And far from the hills of heather,
    Far from the isles of the sea,
He sleeps in the place of the name
    As it was doomed to be.

Heather Ale: A Galloway Legend

From the bonny bells of heather
    They brewed a drink long-syne,
Was sweeter far than honey,
    Was stronger far than wine.
They brewed it and they drank it,
    And lay in a blessed swound
For days and days together
    In their dwellings underground.

There rose a king in Scotland,
    A fell man to his foes,   10
He smote the Picts in battle,
    He hunted them like roes.
Over miles of the red mountain
    He hunted as they fled,
And strewed the dwarfish bodies
    Of the dying and the dead.

Summer came in the country,
    Red was the heather bell;
But the manner of the brewing
    Was none alive to tell.   20
In graves that were like children's
    On many a mountain head,
The Brewsters of the Heather
    Lay numbered with the dead.

The king in the red moorland
    Rode on a summer's day;
And the bees hummed, and the curlews
    Cried beside the way.
The king rode, and was angry,
    Black was his brow and pale,   30
To rule in a land of heather
    And lack the Heather Ale.

It fortuned that his vassals,
    Riding free on the heath,
Came on a stone that was fallen
    And vermin hid beneath.
Rudely plucked from their hiding,
    Never a word they spoke:
A son and his aged father –
    Last of the dwarfish folk.   40

The king sat high on his charger,
    He looked on the little men;
And the dwarfish and swarthy couple
    Looked at the king again.
Down by the shore he had them;
    And there on the giddy brink –
'I will give you life, ye vermin,
    For the secret of the drink.'

There stood the son and father
    And they looked high and low;   50
The heather was red around them,
    The sea rumbled below.
And up and spoke the father,
    Shrill was his voice to hear:
'I have a word in private,
    A word for the royal ear.

Life is dear to the aged,
    And honour a little thing;
I would gladly sell the secret,'
    Quoth the Pict to the king.   60
His voice was as small as a sparrow's,
    And shrill and wonderful clear:
'I would gladly sell my secret,
    Only my son I fear.

For life is a little matter,
    And death is nought to the young;
And I dare not sell my honour
    Under the eye of my son.
Take *him*, O king and bind him,
    And cast him far in the deep;   70
And it's I will tell the secret
    That I have sworn to keep.'

They took the son and bound him,
    Neck and heels in a thong,
And a lad took him and swung him,
    And flung him far and strong,
And the sea swallowed his body,
    Like that of a child of ten; –
And there on the cliff stood his father,
    Last of the dwarfish men.   80

'True was the word I told you:
    Only my son I feared;

For I doubt the sapling courage
　　That goes without the beard.
But now in vain is the torture,
　　Fire shall never avail:
Here dies in my bosom
　　The secret of Heather Ale.'

Christmas at Sea

The sheets were frozen hard, and they cut the naked hand;
The decks were like a slide, where a seaman scarce could stand;
The wind was a nor'wester, blowing squally off the sea;
And cliffs and spouting breakers were the only things a-lee.

They heard the surf a-roaring before the break of day;
But 't was only with the peep of light we saw how ill we lay.
We tumbled every hand on deck instanter, with a shout,
And we gave her the maintops'l, and stood by to go about.

All day we tacked and tacked between the South Head and the North;
All day we hauled the frozen sheets, and got no further forth;   10
All day as cold as charity, in bitter pain and dread,
For very life and nature we tacked from head to head.

We gave the South a wider berth, for there the tide-race roared;
But every tack we made we brought the North Head close aboard:
So's we saw the cliffs and houses, and the breakers running high,
And the coastguard in his garden, with his glass against his eye.

The frost was on the village roofs as white as ocean foam;
The good red fires were burning bright in every 'longshore home;
The windows sparkled clear, and the chimneys volleyed out;
And I vow we sniffed the victuals as the vessel went about.   20

The bells upon the church were rung with a mighty jovial cheer;
For it's just that I should tell you how (of all days in the year)
This day of our adversity was blessèd Christmas morn,
And the house above the coastguard's was the house where I was born.

O well I saw the pleasant room, the pleasant faces there,
My mother's silver spectacles, my father's silver hair;
And well I saw the firelight, like a flight of homely elves,
Go dancing round the china-plates that stand upon the shelves.

And well I knew the talk they had, the talk that was of me,
Of the shadow on the household and the son that went to sea;   30
And O the wicked fool I seemed, in every kind of way,
To be here and hauling frozen ropes on blessèd Christmas Day.

They lit the high sea-light, and the dark began to fall.
'All hands to loose topgallant sails,' I heard the captain call.
'By the Lord, she'll never stand it,' our first mate, Jackson, cried.
… 'It's the one way or the other, Mr Jackson,' he replied.

She staggered to her bearings, but the sails were new and good,
And the ship smelt up to windward just as though she understood.
As the winter's day was ending, in the entry of the night,
We cleared the weary headland, and passed below the light.   40

And they heaved a mighty breath, every soul on board but me,
As they saw her nose again pointing handsome out to sea;
But all that I could think of, in the darkness and the cold,
Was just that I was leaving home and my folks were growing old.

Explanatory Notes to Ballads

{The following notes are Stevenson's own, prepared for the first edition:}

The Song of Rahéro

This tale, of which I have not consciously changed a single feature, I received from tradition. It is highly popular through all the country of the eight Tevas, the clan to which Rahéro belonged; and particularly in Táiarapu, the windward peninsula of Tahiti, where he lived. I have heard from end to end two versions; and as many as five different persons have helped me with details. There seems no reason why the tale should not be true.

1. line 22. 'The aito', quasi champion, or brave. One skilled in the use of some weapon, who wandered the country challenging distinguished rivals and taking part in local quarrels. It was in the natural course of his advancement to be at last employed by a chief, or king; and it would then be part of his duties to purvey the victim for sacrifice. One of the doomed families was indicated; the aito took his weapon and went forth alone; a little behind him bearers followed with the sacrificial basket. Sometimes the victim showed fight, sometimes prevailed; more often, without doubt, he fell. But whatever body was found, the bearers indifferently took up.

2. lines 45ff. 'Pai', 'Honoura' and 'Ahupu'. Legendary persons of Tahiti, all natives of Táiarapu. Of the two first, I have collected singular although imperfect legends, which I hope soon to lay before the public in another place. Of Ahupu, except in snatches of song, little memory seems to linger. She dwelt at least about Tepari – 'the sea cliffs' – the eastern fastness of the isle; walked by paths known only to herself upon the mountains; was courted by dangerous suitors who came swimming from adjacent islands, and defended and rescued (as I gather) by the loyalty of native fish. My anxiety to learn more of 'Ahupu Vehine' became (during my stay in Táiarapu) a cause of some diversion to that mirthful people, the inhabitants.

3. line 80. 'Covered an oven'. The cooking fire is made in a hole in the ground, and is then buried.

4. line 85. 'Flies'. This is perhaps an anachronism. Even speaking of today in Tahiti, the phrase would have to be understood as referring mainly to mosquitoes, and these only in watered valleys with close woods, such as I suppose to form the surroundings of Rahéro's homestead. Quarter of a mile away, where the air moves freely, you shall look in vain for one.

5. line 115. 'Hook' of mother-of-pearl. Bright-hook fishing, and that with the spear, appear to be the favourite native methods.

6. line 133. 'Leaves', the plates of Tahiti.

7. line 144. 'Yottowas', so spelt for convenience of pronunciation, quasi Tacksmen in the Scottish Highlands. The organisation of eight sub-districts, and eight yottawas to a division, which was in use (until yesterday) among the Tevas, I have attributed without authority to the next clan: see lines 341–2.

8. line 160. 'Ómare', pronounced as a dactyl. A loaded quarter-staff, one of the two favourite weapons of the Tahitian brave: the javelin, or casting spear, was the other.

9. line 202. 'The ribbon of light'. Still to be seen (and heard) spinning from one marae to another on Tahiti; or so I have it upon evidence that would rejoice the Psychical Society.

10. line 221. 'Námunu-úra'. The complete name is Namunu-ura te aropa. Why it should be

pronounced Námunu dactyllically, I cannot see, but so I have always heard it. This was the clan immediately beyond the Tevas on the south coast of the island. At the date of the tale the clan organisation must have been very weak. There is no particular mention of Támatéa's mother going to Papara, to the head chief of her own clan, which would appear her natural recourse. On the other hand, she seems to have visited various lesser chiefs among the Tevas, and these to have excused themselves solely on the danger of the enterprise. The broad distinction here drawn between Nateva and Námunu-úra is therefore not impossibly anachronistic.

11. line 223. 'Hiopa the king'. Hiopa was really the name of the king (chief) of Vaiau; but I could never learn that of the king of Paea – pronounce to rhyme with the Indian ayah – and I gave the name where it was most needed. This note must appear otiose indeed to readers who have never heard of either of these two gentlemen; and perhaps there is only one person in the world capable at once of reading my verses and spying the inaccuracy. For him, for Mr Tati Salmon, hereditary high chief of the Tevas, the note is solely written: a small attention from a clansman to his chief.

12. line 239. 'Let the pigs be tapu'. It is impossible to explain tapu in a note; we have it as an English word, taboo. Suffice it, that a thing which was tapu must not be touched, nor a place that was tapu visited.

13. line 354. 'Fish the food of desire'. There is a special word in the Tahitian language to signify hungering after fish. I may remark that here is one of my chief difficulties about the whole story. How did king, commons, women, and all come to eat together at this feast? But it troubled none of my numerous authorities; so there must certainly be some natural explanation.

14. line 429. 'The mustering word of the clan'. *Teva te ua, Teva te matai!*: Teva the wind, Teva the rain!

15. lines 546, 548. 'The star of the dead'. Venus as a morning star. I have collected much curious evidence as to this belief. The dead retain their taste for a fish diet, enter into copartnery with living fishers, and haunt the reef and the lagoon. The conclusion attributed to the nameless lady of the legend would be reached today, under the like circumstances, by ninety per cent of Polynesians and here I probably understate by one-tenth.

The Feast of Famine

In this ballad I have strung together some of the more striking particularities of the Marquesas. It rests upon no authority; it is in no sense, like 'Rahéro,' a native story; but a patchwork of details of manners and the impressions of a traveller. It may seem strange, when the scene is laid upon these profligate islands, to make the story hinge on love. But love is not less known in the Marquesas than elsewhere; nor is there any cause of suicide more common in the islands.

1. line 2. 'Pit of Popoi'. Where the bread fruit was stored for preservation.
2. line 15. 'Ruby-red'. The priest's eyes were probably red from the abuse of kava. His beard (line 18) is said to be worth an estate; for the beards of old men are the favourite head adornment of the Marquesas, as the hair of women formed their most costly girdle. The former, among this generally beardless and short-lived people, fetch today considerable sums.
3. line 20. 'Tikis'. The tiki is an ugly image hewn out wood or stone.

4. line 72. 'The one-stringed harp'. Usually employed for serenades.
5. line 105. 'The sacred cabin of palm'. Which, however, no woman could approach. I do not know where women were tattooed; probably in the common house, or in the bush, for a woman was a creature of small account. I must guard the reader against supposing Taheia was at all disfigured; the art of the Marquesan tattooer is extreme; and she would appear to be clothed in a web of lace, inimitably delicate, exquisite in pattern, and of a bluish hue that at once contrasts and harmonises with the warm pigment of the native skin. It would be hard to find a woman more becomingly adorned than ' a well tattooed' Marquesan.
6. line 149. 'The horror of night'. The Polynesian fear of ghosts and of the dark has been already referred to. Their life is beleaguered by the dead.
7. line 165. 'The quiet passage of souls'. So, I am told, the natives explain the sound of a little wind passing overhead unfelt.
8. line 202. 'The first of the victims fell'. Without doubt, this whole scene is untrue to fact. The victims were disposed of privately and some time before. And indeed I am far from claiming the credit of any high degree of accuracy for this ballad. Even in a time of famine, it is probable that Marquesan life went far more gaily than is here represented. But the melancholy of today lies on the writer's mind.

Ticonderoga

I first heard this legend of my own country from that friend of men of letters, Mr Alfred Nutt, 'there in roaring London's central stream'; and since the ballad first saw the light of day in *Scribner's Magazine*, Mr Nutt and Lord Archibald Campbell have been in public controversy on the facts. Two clans, the Camerons and the Campbells, lay claim to this bracing story; and they do well: the man who preferred his plighted troth to the commands and menaces of the dead is an ancestor worth disputing. But the Campbells must rest content: they have the broad lands and the broad page of history; this appanage must be denied them; for between the name of *Cameron* and that of *Campbell*, the muse will never hesitate.

1. line 68. Mr Nutt reminds me it was ' by my sword and Ben Cruachan' the Cameron swore.
2. line 159. 'A *periwig'd lord of London'*. The first Pitt.
3. line 204. 'Cathay'. There must be some omission in General Stewart's charming *History of the Highland Regiments*, a book that might well be republished and continued; or it scarce appears how our friend could have got to China.

Heather Ale

Among the curiosities of human nature, this legend claims a high place. It is needless to remind the reader that the Picts were never exterminated, and form to this day a large proportion of the folk of Scotland: occupying the eastern and central parts, from the Firth of Forth, or perhaps the Lammermoors, upon the south, to the Ord of Caithness on the north. That the blundering guess of a dull chronicler should have inspired men with imaginary loathing for their own ancestors is already strange: that it should have begotten this wild legend seems incredible. Is it possible the chronicler's error was merely nominal? that what he told, and what the people proved themselves so ready to receive, about the

Picts, was true or partly true of some anterior and perhaps Lappish savages, small of stature, black of hue, dwelling undergound – possibly also the distillers of some forgotten spirit? See Mr Campbell's *Tales of the West Highlands*.

SONGS OF TRAVEL

I

The Vagabond

(To an air of Schubert)

Give to me the life I love,
   Let the lave go by me,
Give the jolly heaven above
   And the byway nigh me.
Bed in the bush with stars to see,
   Bread I dip in the river –
There's the life for a man like me,
   There's the life for ever.

Let the blow fall soon or late,
   Let what will be o'er me;
Give the face of earth around
   And the road before me.
Wealth I seek not, hope nor love,
   Nor a friend to know me;
All I seek, the heaven above
   And the road below me.

Or let autumn fall on me
   Where afield I linger,
Silencing the bird on tree,
   Biting the blue finger.
White as meal the frosty field –
   Warm the fireside haven –
Not to autumn will I yield,
   Not to winter even!

Let the blow fall soon or late,
   Let what will be o'er me;
Give the face of earth around,
   And the road before me.
Wealth I ask not, hope nor love,
   Nor a friend to know me;
All I ask, the heaven above
   And the road below me.

II

Youth and Love – I

Once only by the garden gate
   Our lips we joined and parted.
I must fulfil an empty fate
   And travel the uncharted.

Hail and farewell! I must arise,
  Leave here the fatted cattle,
And paint on foreign lands and skies
  My Odyssey of battle.

The untented Kosmos my abode,
  I pass, a wilful stranger:
My mistress still the open road
  And the bright eyes of danger.

Come ill or well, the cross, the crown,
  The rainbow or the thunder,
I fling my soul and body down
  For God to plough them under.

III

Youth and Love – II

To the heart of youth the world is a highwayside
Passing for ever, he fares; and on either hand,
Deep in the gardens golden pavilions hide,
Nestle in orchard bloom, and far on the level land
Call him with lighted lamp in the eventide.

Thick as the stars at night when the moon is down,
Pleasures assail him. He to his nobler fate
Fares; and but waves a hand as he passes on,
Cries but a wayside word to her at the garden gate,
Sings but a boyish stave and his face is gone.

IV

In dreams, unhappy, I behold you stand
        As heretofore:
The unremembered tokens in your hand
        Avail no more.

No more the morning glow, no more the grace,
        Enshrines, endears.
Cold beats the light of time upon your face
        And shows your tears.

He came and went. Perchance you wept a while
        And then forgot.
Ah me! but he that left you with a smile
        Forgets you not.

V

She rested by the Broken Brook
   She drank of Weary Well,
She moved beyond my lingering look,
   Ah, whither none can tell!

She came, she went. In other lands,
   Perchance in fairer skies,
Her hands shall cling with other hands,
   Her eyes to other eyes.

She vanished. In the sounding town,
   Will she remember too?
Will she recall the eyes of brown
   As I recall the blue?

VI

The infinite shining heavens
   Rose and I saw in the night
Uncountable angel stars
   Showering sorrow and light.

I saw them distant as heaven,
   Dumb and shining and dead,
And the idle stars of the night
   Were dearer to me than bread.

Night after night in my sorrow
   The stars stood over the sea,
Till lo! I looked in the dusk
   And a star had come down to me.

VII

Madrigal

Plain as the glistering planets shine
   When winds have cleaned the skies,
Her love appeared, appealed for mine,
   And wantoned in her eyes.

Clear as the shining tapers burned
   On Cytherea's shrine,
Those brimming, lustrous beauties turned,
   And called and conquered mine.

The beacon-lamp that Hero lit
    No fairer shone on sea,
No plainlier summoned will and wit,
    Than hers encouraged me.

I thrilled to feel her influence near,
    I struck my flag at sight.
Her starry silence smote my ear
    Like sudden drums at night.

I ran as, at the cannon's roar,
    The troops the ramparts man –
As in the holy house of yore
    The willing Eli ran.

Here, lady, lo! that servant stands
    You picked from passing men,
And should you need nor heart nor hands
    He bows and goes again.

VIII

Dark Women

I must not cease from singing
    And leave their praise unsung,
The praise of swarthy women
    I have loved since I was young;
They shine like coloured pictures
    In the pale book of my life,
The gem of meditation,
    The dear reward of strife.

To you, let snow and roses
    And golden locks belong:
These are the world's enslavers,
    Let them delight the throng.
For her of duskier lustre
    Whose favour still I wear,
The snow be in her kirtle,
    The rose be in her hair!

The hue of highland rivers
    Careering, full and cool,
From sable on to golden,
    From rapid on to pool;
The hue of heather honey,

The hue of honey bees,
  Shall tinge her golden shoulder,
    Shall gild her tawny knees.

Dark as a wayside gypsy,
    Lithe as a hedgerow hare,
She moves, a glowing shadow,
    Through the sunshine of the fair.
Golden hue and orange,
    Bosom and hand and head,
She blooms, a tiger lily,
    In the snowdrift of the bed.

Tiger and tiger lily
    She plays a double part,
All woman in the body
    And all the man at heart.
She shall be brave and tender,
    She shall be soft and high,
She to lie in my bosom
    And *He* to fight and die.

There shines in her glowing favour
    A gem of darker look,
The eye of coal and topaz,
    The pool of the mountain brook;
And strands of brown and sunshine,
    Or threads of silver and snow,
In her dusky treasure of tresses
    Twinkle and shine and glow.

I have been young and am old,
    And trodden various ways,
Now I behold from a window
    The wonder of bygone days,
The mingling of many colours,
    The crossing of many threads,
The dear and smiling faces,
    The dark and graceful heads.

The defeats and the successes,
    The strife, the race, the goal; –
And the touch of a dusky woman
    Was fairly worth the whole.
And sun and moon and morning
    With glory I recall;
But the clasp of a dusky woman
    Outweighed them one and all.

IX

Let Beauty awake in the morn from beautiful dreams,
　　　　Beauty awake from rest!
　　　　Let Beauty awake
　　　　For Beauty's sake
In the hour when the birds awake in the brake
　　　　And the stars are bright in the west!

Let Beauty awake in the eve from the slumber of day,
　　　　Awake in the crimson eve!
　　　　In the day's dusk end
　　　　When the shades ascend,
Let her wake to the kiss of a tender friend
　　　　To render again and receive!

X

1
I know not how it is with you –
　　I love the first and last,
The whole field of the present view,
　　The whole flow of the past.

2
One tittle of the things that are,
　　Nor you should change nor I –
One pebble in our path – one star
　　In all our heaven of sky.

3
Our lives, and every day and hour,
　　One symphony appear:
One road, one garden – every flower
　　And every bramble dear.

XI

I will make you brooches and toys for your delight
Of bird-song at morning and star-shine at night.
I will make a palace fit for you and me
Of green days in forests and blue days at sea.

I will make my kitchen, and you shall keep your room,
Where white flows the river and bright blows the broom,
And you shall wash your linen and keep your body white
In rainfall at morning and dewfall at night.

And this shall be for music when no one else is near,
The fine song for singing, the rare song to hear!
That only I remember, that only you admire,
Of the broad road that stretches and the roadside fire.

XII

We Have Loved of Yore
(*To an air of Diabelli*)

Berried brake and reedy island,
   Heaven below, and only heaven above,
Through the sky's inverted azure
     Softly swam the boat that bore our love.
       Bright were your eyes as the day;
       Bright ran the stream,
       Bright hung the sky above.
Days of April, airs of Eden,
   How the glory died through golden hours,
And the shining moon arising,
     How the boat drew homeward filled with flowers!
       Bright were your eyes in the night:
       We have lived, my love –
       O, we have loved, my love.

Frost has bound our flowing river,
   Snow has whitened all our island brake,
And beside the winter fagot
     Joan and Darby doze and dream and wake.
       Still, in the river of dreams
       Swims the boat of love –
       Hark! chimes the falling oar!
And again in winter evens
   When on firelight dreaming fancy feeds,
In those ears of agèd lovers
     Love's own river warbles in the reeds.
       Love still the past, O my love!
       We have lived of yore
       O, we have loved of yore.

XIII

Ditty

(To an air from Bach)

The cock shall crow
    In the morning gray,
The bugles blow
    At the break of day:
The cock shall sing and the merry bugles ring,
And all the little brown birds sing upon the spray.

The thorn shall blow
    In the month of May,
And my love shall go
    In her holiday array:
But I shall lie in the kirkyard nigh
While all the little brown birds sing upon the spray.

XIV

Mater Triumphans

Son of my woman's body, you go, to the drum and fife,
To taste the colour of love and the other side of life –
From out of the dainty the rude, the strong from out of the frail,
Eternally through the ages from the female comes the male.

The ten fingers and toes, and the shell-like nail on each,
The eyes blind as gems and the tongue attempting speech;
Impotent hands in my bosom, and yet they shall wield the sword!
Drugged with slumber and milk, you wait the day of the Lord.

Infant bridegroom, uncrowned king, unanointed priest,
Soldier, lover, explorer, I see you nuzzle the breast.
You that grope in my bosom shall load the ladies with rings,
You, that came forth through the doors, shall burst the doors of kings.

XV

Bright is the ring of words
    When the right man rings them,
Fair the fall of songs
    When the singer sings them.
Still they carolled and said –
    On wings they are carried –
After the singer is dead
    And the maker buried.

Low as the singer lies
  In the field of heather,
Songs of his fashion bring
  The swains together.
And when the west is red
  With the sunset embers,
The lover lingers and sings
  And the maid remembers.

XVI

In the highlands, in the country places,
Where the old plain men have rosy faces,
And the young fair maidens
Quiet eyes;
Where essential silence cheers and blesses,
And for ever in the hill-recesses
Her more lovely music
Broods and dies.

O to mount again where erst I haunted;
Where the old red hills are bird-enchanted,
And the low green meadows
Bright with sward;
And when even dies, the million-tinted,
And the night has come, and planets glinted,
Lo, the valley hollow
Lamp-bestarred!

O to dream, O to awake and wander
There, and with delight to take and render,
Through the trance of silence,
Quiet breath;
Lo! for there, among the flowers and grasses,
Only the mightier movement sounds and passes;
Only winds and rivers,
Life and death.

XVII

(To the Tune of Wandering Willie)

Home no more home to me, whither must I wander?
  Hunger my driver, I go where I must.
Cold blows the winter wind over hill and heather;
  Thick drives the rain, and my roof is in the dust.

Loved of wise men was the shade of my roof-tree.
   The true word of welcome was spoken in the door –
Dear days of old, with the faces in the firelight,
   Kind folks of old, you come again no more.

Home was home then, my dear, full of kindly faces,
   Home was home then, my dear, happy for the child.
Fire and the windows bright glittered on the moorland;
   Song, tuneful song, built a palace in the wild.
Now, when day dawns on the brow of the moorland,
   Lone stands the house, and the chimney-stone is cold.
Lone let it stand, now the friends are all departed,
   The kind hearts, the true hearts, that loved the place of old.

Spring shall come, come again, calling up the moor-fowl,
   Spring shall bring the sun and rain, bring the bees and flowers;
Red shall the heather bloom over hill and valley,
   Soft flow the stream through the even-flowing hours;
Fair the day shine as it shone on my childhood –
   Fair shine the day on the house with open door;
Birds come and cry there and twitter in the chimney –
   But I go for ever and come again no more.

XVIII

Winter

   In rigorous hours, when down the iron lane
   The redbreast looks in vain
   For hips and haws,
   Lo, shining flowers upon my window pane
   The silver pencil of the winter draws.

   When all the snowy hill
   And the bare woods are still;
   When snipes are silent in the frozen bogs,
   And all the garden garth is whelmed in mire,
   Lo, by the hearth, the laughter of the logs–
   More fair than roses, lo, the flowers of fire!

   Saranac Lake

XIX

   The stormy evening closes now in vain,
   Loud wails the wind and beats the driving rain,

While here in sheltered house
With fire-ypainted walls,
I hear the wind abroad,
I hark the calling squalls –
'Blow, blow,' I cry, 'you burst your cheeks in vain!
Blow, blow,' I cry, 'my love is home again!'

Yon ship you chase perchance but yesternight
Bore still the precious freight of my delight,
That here in sheltered house
With fire-ypainted walls,
Now hears the wind abroad,
Now harks the calling squalls.
'Blow, blow,' I cry, 'in vain you rouse the sea,
My rescued sailor shares the fire with me!'

XX

To Dr Hake

(On receiving a copy of verses)

In the belovèd hour that ushers day,
In the pure dew, under the breaking gray,
One bird, ere yet the woodland quires awake,
With brief réveillé summons all the brake:
Chirp, chirp, it goes; nor waits an answer long;
And that small signal fills the grove with song.

Thus on my pipe I breathed a strain or two;
It scarce was music, but 'twas all I knew.
It was not music, for I lacked the art,
Yet what but frozen music filled my heart?
Chirp, chirp, I went, nor hoped a nobler strain;
But Heaven decreed I should not pipe in vain,
For, lo! not far from there, in secret dale,
All silent, sat an ancient nightingale.
My sparrow notes he heard; thereat awoke;
And with a tide of song his silence broke.

XXI

To –

I knew thee strong and quiet like the hills;
I knew thee apt to pity, brave to endure,
In peace or war a Roman full equipt;
And just I knew thee, like the fabled kings

Who by the loud sea-shore gave judgment forth,
From dawn to eve, bearded and few of words.
What, what, was I to honour thee? A child;
A youth in ardour but a child in strength,
Who after virtue's golden chariot-wheels
Runs ever panting, nor attains the goal.
So thought I, and was sorrowful at heart.

Since then my steps have visited that flood
Along whose shore the numerous footfalls cease,
The voices and the tears of life expire.
Thither the prints go down, the hero's way
Trod large upon the sand, the trembling maid's:
Nimrod that wound his trumpet in the wood,
And the poor, dreaming child, hunter of flowers,
That here his hunting closes with the great:
So one and all go down, nor aught returns.

For thee, for us, the sacred river waits,
For me, the unworthy, thee, the perfect friend;
There Blame desists, there his unfaltering dogs
He from the chase recalls, and homeward rides;
Yet Praise and Love pass over and go in.
So when, beside that margin, I discard
My more than mortal weakness, and with thee
Through that still land unfearing I advance:
If then at all we keep the touch of joy
Thou shalt rejoice to find me altered – I,
O Felix, to behold thee still unchanged.

XXII

The morning drum-call on my eager ear
Thrills unforgotten yet; the morning dew
Lies yet undried along my field of noon.
But now I pause at whiles in what I do,
And count the bell, and tremble lest I hear
(My work untrimmed) the sunset gun too soon.

XXIII

I have trod the upward and the downward slope;
I have endured and done in days before;
I have longed for all, and bid farewell to hope;
And I have lived and loved, and closed the door.

XXIV

He hears with gladdened heart the thunder
    Peal, and loves the falling dew;
He knows the earth above and under –
    Sits and is content to view.

He sits beside the dying ember,
    God for hope and man for friend,
Content to see, glad to remember,
    Expectant of the certain end.

XXV

Farewell, fair day and fading light!
The clay-born here, with westward sight,
Marks the huge sun now downward soar.
Farewell. We twain shall meet no more.

Farewell. I watch with bursting sigh
My late contemned occasion die.
I linger useless in my tent:
Farewell, fair day, so foully spent!

Farewell, fair day. If any God
At all consider this poor clod,
He who the fair occasion sent
Prepared and placed the impediment.

Let him diviner vengeance take –
Give me to sleep, give me to wake
Girded and shod, and bid me play
The hero in the coming day!

XXVI

If this were Faith

God, if this were enough,
That I see things bare to the buff
And up to the buttocks in mire;
That I ask nor hope nor hire,
Nut in the husk,
Nor dawn beyond the dusk,
Nor life beyond death:
God, if this were faith?

Having felt thy wind in my face
Spit sorrow and disgrace,
Having seen thine evil doom
In Golgotha and Khartoum,
And the brutes, the work of thine hands,
Fill with injustice lands
And stain with blood the sea:
If still in my veins the glee
Of the black night and the sun
And the lost battle, run:
If, an adept,
The iniquitous lists I still accept
With joy, and joy to endure and be withstood,
And still to battle and perish for a dream of good:
God, if that were enough?

If to feel, in the ink of the slough,
And the sink of the mire,
Veins of glory and fire
Run through and transpierce and transpire,
And a secret purpose of glory in every part,
And the answering glory of battle fill my heart;
To thrill with the joy of girded men
To go on forever and fail and go on again,
And be mauled to the earth and arise,
And contend for the shade of a word and a thing not seen with the eyes:
With the half of a broken hope for a pillow at night
That somehow the right is the right
And the smooth shall bloom from the rough:
Lord, if that were enough?

XXVII

My Wife

Trusty, dusky, vivid, true,
With eyes of gold and bramble-dew,
Steel-true and blade-straight,
The great artificer
Made my mate.

Honour, anger, valour, fire;
A love that life could never tire,
Death quench or evil stir,
The mighty master
Gave to her.

Teacher, tender, comrade, wife,
A fellow-farer true through life,
Heart whole and soul-free
The august father
Gave to me.

XXVIII

To the Muse

Resign the rhapsody, the dream,
   To men of larger reach;
Be ours the quest of a plain theme,
   The piety of speech.

As monkish scribes from morning break
   Toiled till the close of light,
Nor thought a day too long to make
   One line or letter bright:

We also with an ardent mind,
   Time, wealth, and fame forgot,
Our glory in our patience find
   And skim, and skim the pot:

Till last, when round the house we hear
   The evensong of birds,
One corner of blue heaven appear
   In our clear well of words.

Leave, leave it then, muse of my heart!
   Sans finish and sans frame,
Leave unadorned by needless art
   The picture as it came.

Apemama.

XXIX

To an Island Princess

Since long ago, a child at home,
I read and longed to rise and roam,
Where'er I went, whate'er I willed,
One promised land my fancy filled.
Hence the long roads my home I made;
Tossed much in ships: have often laid

Below the uncurtained sky my head,
Rain-deluged and wind-buffeted:
And many a thousand hills I crossed
And corners turned – Love's labour lost,
Till, Lady, to your isle of sun
I came, not hoping; and, like one
Snatched out of blindness, rubbed my eyes,
And hailed my promised land with cries.

Yes, Lady, here I was at last;
Here found I all I had forecast:
The long roll of the sapphire sea
That keeps the land's virginity;
The stalwart giants of the wood
Laden with toys and flowers and food;
The precious forest pouring out
To compass the whole town about;
The town itself with streets of lawn,
Loved of the moon, blessed by the dawn,
Where the brown children all the day
Keep up a ceaseless noise of play,
Play in the sun, play in the rain,
Nor ever quarrel or complain; –
And late at night, in the woods of fruit,
Hark! do you hear the passing flute?

I threw one look to either hand,
And knew I was in Fairyland.
And yet one point of being so,
I lacked. For, Lady (as you know),
Whoever by his might of hand
Won entrance into Fairyland,
Found always with admiring eyes
A Fairy princess kind and wise.
It was not long I waited; soon
Upon my threshold, in broad noon,
Gracious and helpful, wise and good,
The Fairy Princess Moë stood.[1]

Tautira, Tahiti, Nov. 5, 1888.

1. This is the same Princess Moë whose charms of person and disposition have been recorded by the
    late Lord Pembroke in *South Sea Bubbles*, and by M. Pierre Loti in the *Mariage de Loti*.

XXX

To Kalakua

(With a present of a pearl)

The Silver Ship, my King – that was her name
In the bright islands whence your fathers came – [1]
The Silver Ship, at rest from winds and tides,
Below your palace in your harbour rides:
And the seafarers, sitting safe on shore,
Like eager merchants count their treasures o'er.
One gift they find, one strange and lovely thing,
Now doubly precious since it pleased a king.

The right, my liege, is ancient as the lyre
For bards to give to kings what kings admire.
'Tis mine to offer for Apollo's sake;
And since the gift is fitting, yours to take.
To golden hands the golden pearl I bring:
The ocean jewel to the island king.

Honolulu, Feb. 3, 1889.

XXXI

To Princess Kaiulani

Forth from her land to mine she goes,
The island maid, the island rose,
Light of heart and bright of face:
The daughter of a double race.

Her islands here, in Southern sun,
Shall mourn their Kaiulani gone,
And I, in her dear banyan shade,
Look vainly for my little maid.

But our Scots islands far away
Shall glitter with unwonted day,
And cast for once their tempests by
To smile in Kaiulani's eye.

Honolulu, 1889.

1. The yacht *Casco* had been so called by the people of Fakarava in the Paumotus.

[Written in April to Kaiulani in the April of her age; and at Waikiki, within easy walk of Kaiulani's banyan! When she comes to my land and her father's, and the rain beats upon the window (as I fear it will) let her look at this page; it will be like a weed gathered and pressed at home; and she will remember her own islands, and the shadow of the mighty tree; and she will hear the peacocks screaming in the dusk and the wind blowing in the palms; and she will think of her father sitting there alone. – R.L.S.]

XXXII

To Mother Maryanne

To see the infinite pity of this place,
The mangled limb, the devastated face,
The innocent sufferer smiling at the rod –
A fool were tempted to deny his God.

He sees, he shrinks. But if he gaze again,
Lo, beauty springing from the breast of pain!
He marks the sisters on the mournful shores;
And even a fool is silent and adores.

Guest House, Kalawao, Molokai.

XXXIII

In Memoriam E.H.

I knew a silver head was bright beyond compare,
I knew a queen of toil with a crown of silver hair.
Garland of valour and sorrow, of beauty and renown,
Life, that honours the brave, crowned her himself with the crown.

The beauties of youth are frail, but this was a jewel of age.
Life, that delights in the brave, gave it himself for a gage.
Fair was the crown to behold, and beauty its poorest part –
At once the scar of the wound and the order pinned on the heart.

The beauties of man are frail, and the silver lies in the dust,
And the queen that we call to mind sleeps with the brave and the just;
Sleeps with the weary at length; but honoured and ever fair,
Shines in the eye of the mind the crown of the silver hair.

Honolulu.

XXXIV

To My Wife

(A fragment)

Long must elapse ere you behold again
Green forest frame the entry of the lane –
The wild lane with the bramble and the briar,
The year-old cart-tracks perfect in the mire,
The wayside smoke, perchance, the dwarfish huts,
And ramblers' donkey drinking from the ruts: –
Long ere you trace how deviously it leads,
Back from man's chimneys and the bleating meads
To the woodland shadow, to the silvan hush,
Where but the brooklet chuckles in the brush –
Back from the sun and bustle of the vale
To where the great voice of the nightingale
Fills all the forest like a single room,
And all the banks smell of the golden broom;
So wander on until the eve descends,
And back returning to your firelit friends,
You see the rosy sun, despoiled of light,
Hung, caught in the thickets, like a schoolboy's kite.

Here from the sea the unfruitful sun shall rise,
Bake the bare deck and blind the unshielded eyes;
The allotted hours aloft shall wheel in vain
And in the unpregnant ocean plunge again.
Assault of squalls that mock the watchful guard,
And pluck the bursting canvas from the yard,
And senseless clamour of the calm, at night
Must mar your slumbers. By the plunging light,
In beetle-haunted, most unwomanly bower
Of the wild-swerving cabin, hour by hour ...

Schooner 'Equator'.

XXXV

To My Old Familiars

Do you remember – can we e'er forget? –
How, in the coiled perplexities of youth,
In our wild climate, in our scowling town,
We gloomed and shivered, sorrowed, sobbed and feared?
The belching winter wind, the missile rain,
The rare and welcome silence of the snows,
The laggard morn, the haggard day, the night,

The grimy spell of the nocturnal town,
Do you remember? – Ah, could one forget!

As when the fevered sick that all night long
Listed the wind intone, and hear at last
The ever-welcome voice of chanticleer
Sing in the bitter hour before the dawn, –
With sudden ardour, these desire the day:
So sang in the gloom of youth the bird of hope;
So we, exulting, hearkened and desired.
For lo! as in the palace porch of life
We huddled with chimeras, from within –
How sweet to hear! – the music swelled and fell,
And through the breach of the revolving doors
What dreams of splendour blinded us and fled!

I have since then contended and rejoiced;
Amid the glories of the house of life
Profoundly entered, and the shrine beheld:
Yet when the lamp from my expiring eyes
Shall dwindle and recede, the voice of love
Fall insignificant on my closing ears,
What sound shall come but the old cry of the wind
In our inclement city? what return
But the image of the emptiness of youth,
Filled with the sound of footsteps and that voice
Of discontent and rapture and despair?
So, as in darkness, from the magic lamp,
The momentary pictures gleam and fade
And perish, and the night resurges – these
Shall I remember, and then all forget.

Apemama.

XXXVI

The tropics vanish, and meseems that I,
From Halkerside, from topmost Allermuir,
Or steep Caerketton, dreaming gaze again.
Far set in fields and woods, the town I see
Spring gallant from the shallows of her smoke,
Cragged, spired, and turreted, her virgin fort
Beflagged. About, on seaward-drooping hills,
New folds of city glitter. Last, the Forth
Wheels ample waters set with sacred isles,
And populous Fife smokes with a score of towns.

There, on the sunny frontage of a hill,
Hard by the house of kings, repose the dead,
My dead, the ready and the strong of word.
Their works, the salt-encrusted, still survive:
The sea bombards their founded towers, the night
Thrills pierced with their strong lamps. The artificers,
One after one, here in this grated cell,
Where the rain erases, and the rust consumes,
Fell upon lasting silence. Continents
And continental oceans intervene;
A sea uncharted, on a lampless isle,
Environs and confines their wandering child:
In vain. The voice of generations dead
Summons me, sitting distant, to arise,
My numerous footsteps nimbly to retrace,
And all mutation over, stretch me down
In that denoted city of the dead.

Apemama.

XXXVII

To S.C.

I heard the pulse of the besieging sea
Throb far away all night. I heard the wind
Fly crying and convulse tumultuous palms.
I rose and strolled. The isle was all bright sand,
And flailing fans and shadows of the palm;
The heaven all moon and wind and the blind vault;
The keenest planet slain, for Venus slept.
    The king, my neighbour, with his host of wives,
Slept in the precinct of the palisade;
Where single, in the wind, under the moon,
Among the slumbering cabins, blazed a fire,
Sole street-lamp and the only sentinel.
    To other lands and nights my fancy turned –
To London first, and chiefly to your house,
The many-pillared and the well-beloved.
There yearning fancy lighted; there again
In the upper room I lay, and heard far off
The unsleeping city murmur like a shell;
The muffled tramp of the Museum guard
Once more went by me; I beheld again
Lamps vainly brighten the dispeopled street;
Again I longed for the returning morn,
The awaking traffic, the bestirring birds,

The consentaneous trill of tiny song
That weaves round monumental cornices
A passing charm of beauty. Most of all,
For your light foot I wearied, and your knock
That was the glad réveillé of my day.
    Lo, now, when to your task in the great house
At morning through the portico you pass,
One moment glance, where by the pillared wall
Far-voyaging island gods, begrimed with smoke,
Sit now unworshipped, the rude monument
Of faiths forgot and races undivined:
Sit now disconsolate, remembering well
The priest, the victim, and the songful crowd,
The blaze of the blue noon, and that huge voice
Incessant, of the breakers on the shore.
As far as these from their ancestral shrine,
So far, so foreign, your divided friends
Wander, estranged in body, not in mind.

Apemama.

XXXVIII

The House of Tembinoka

[At my departure from the island of Apemama, for which you will look in vain in most atlases, the King and I agreed, since we both set up to be in the poetical way, that we should celebrate our separation in verse. Whether or not his Majesty has been true to his bargain, the laggard posts of the Pacific may perhaps inform me in six months, perhaps not before a year. The following lines represent my part of the contract, and it is hoped, by their pictures of strange manners, they may entertain a civilised audience. Nothing throughout has been invented or exaggerated; the lady herein referred to as the author's muse has confined herself to stringing into rhyme facts or legends that I saw or heard during two months residence upon the island. – R.L.S.]

Envoi

Let us, who part like brothers, part like bards;
And you in your tongue and measure, I in mine,
Our now division duly solemnise.
Unlike the strains, and yet the theme is one:
The strains unlike, and how unlike their fate!
You to the blinding palace-yard shall call
The prefect of the singers, and to him,
Listening devout, your valedictory verse
Deliver; he, his attribute fulfilled,
To the island chorus hand your measures on,
Wed now with harmony: so them, at last,

Night after night, in the open hall of dance,
Shall thirty matted men, to the clapped hand,
Intone and bray and bark. Unfortunate!
Paper and print alone shall honour mine.

The Song

Let now the King his ear arouse
And toss the bosky ringlets from his brows,
The while, our bond to implement,
My muse relates and praises his descent.

I

Bride of the shark, her valour first I sing
Who on the lone seas quickened of a King.
She, from the shore and puny homes of men,
Beyond the climber's sea-discerning ken,
Swam, led by omens; and devoid of fear,
Beheld her monstrous paramour draw near.
She gazed; all round her to the heavenly pale,
The simple sea was void of isle or sail –
Sole overhead the unsparing sun was reared –
When the deep bubbled and the brute appeared.
But she, secure in the decrees of fate,
Made strong her bosom and received the mate,
And, men declare, from that marine embrace
Conceived the virtues of a stronger race.

II

Her stern descendant next I praise,
Survivor of a thousand frays: –
In the hall of tongues who ruled the throng;
Led and was trusted by the strong;
And when spears were in the wood,
Like a tower of vantage stood: –
Whom, not till seventy years had sped,
Unscarred of breast, erect of head,
Still light of step, still bright of look,
The hunter, Death, had overtook.

III

His sons, the brothers twain, I sing,
Of whom the elder reigned a King.
No Childeric he, yet much declined
From his rude sire's imperious mind,
Until his day came when he died,
He lived, he reigned, he versified.

But chiefly him I celebrate
That was the pillar of the state,
Ruled, wise of word and bold of mien,
The peaceful and the warlike scene;
And played alike the leader's part
In lawful and unlawful art.
His soldiers with emboldened ears
Heard him laugh among the spears.
He could deduce from age to age
The web of island parentage;
Best lay the rhyme, best lead the dance,
For any festal circumstance:
And fitly fashion oar and boat,
A palace or an armour coat.
None more availed than he to raise
The strong, suffumigating blaze
Or knot the wizard leaf: none more,
Upon the untrodden windward shore
Of the isle, beside the beating main,
To cure the sickly and constrain,
With muttered words and waving rods,
The gibbering and the whistling gods.
But he, though thus with hand and head
He ruled, commanded, charmed, and led,
And thus in virtue and in might
Towered to contemporary sight –
Still in fraternal faith and love,
Remained below to reach above,
Gave and obeyed the apt command,
Pilot and vassal of the land.

IV

My Tembinok' from men like these
Inherited his palaces,
His right to rule, his powers of mind,
His cocoa-islands sea-enshrined.
Stern bearer of the sword and whip,
A master passed in mastership,
He learned, without the spur of need,
To write, to cipher, and to read;
From all that touch on his prone shore
Augments his treasury of lore,
Eager in age as erst in youth
To catch an art, to learn a truth,
To paint on the internal page

A clearer picture of the age.
His age, you say? But ah, not so!
In his lone isle of long ago,
A royal Lady of Shalott,
Sea-sundered, he beholds it not;
He only hears it far away.
The stress of equatorial day
He suffers; he records the while
The vapid annals of the isle;
Slaves bring him praise of his renown,
Or cackle of the palm-tree town;
The rarer ship and the rare boat
He marks; and only hears remote,
Where thrones and fortunes rise and reel,
The thunder of the turning wheel.

V

For the unexpected tears he shed
At my departing, may his lion head
Not whiten, his revolving years
No fresh occasion minister of tears;
At book or cards, at work or sport,
Him may the breeze across the palace court
For ever fan; and swelling near
For ever the loud song divert his ear.

Schooner 'Equator', at Sea.

XXXIX

The Woodman

In all the grove, nor stream nor bird
Nor aught beside my blows was heard,
And the woods wore their noonday dress –
The glory of their silentness.
From the island summit to the seas,
Trees mounted, and trees drooped, and trees
Groped upward in the gaps. The green
Inarboured talus and ravine
By fathoms. By the multitude,
The rugged columns of the wood
And bunches of the branches stood:
Thick as a mob, deep as a sea,
And silent as eternity.

With lowered axe, with backward head,
Late from this scene my labourer fled,
And with a ravelled tale to tell,
Returned. Some denizen of hell,
Dead man or disinvested god,
Had close behind him peered and trod,
And triumphed when he turned to flee.
How different fell the lines with me!
Whose eye explored the dim arcade
Impatient of the uncoming shade –
Shy elf, or dryad pale and cold,
Or mystic lingerer from of old:
Vainly. The fair and stately things,
Impassive as departed kings,
All still in the wood's stillness stood,
And dumb. The rooted multitude
Nodded and brooded, bloomed and dreamed,
Unmeaning, undivined. It seemed
No other art, no hope, they knew,
Than clutch the earth and seek the blue.

'Mid vegetable king and priest
And stripling, I (the only beast)
Was at the beast's work, killing; hewed
The stubborn roots across, bestrewed
The glebe with the dislustred leaves,
And bade the saplings fall in sheaves;
Bursting across the tangled math
A ruin that I called a path,
A Golgotha that, later on,
When rains had watered, and suns shone,
And seeds enriched the place, should bear
And be called garden. Here and there,
I spied and plucked by the green hair
A foe more resolute to live,
The toothed and killing sensitive.
He, semi-conscious, fled the attack;
He shrank and tucked his branches back;
And straining by his anchor strand,
Captured and scratched the rooting hand.
I saw him crouch, I felt him bite;
And straight my eyes were touched with sight.
I saw the wood for what it was:
The lost and the victorious cause,
The deadly battle pitched in line,
Saw silent weapons cross and shine:

Silent defeat, silent assault,
A battle and a burial vault.

Thick round me in the teeming mud
Briar and fern strove to the blood:
The hooked liana in his gin
Noosed his reluctant neighbours in:
There the green murderer throve and spread,
Upon his smothering victims fed,
And wantoned on his climbing coil.
Contending roots fought for the soil
Like frightened demons: with despair
Competing branches pushed for air.
Green conquerors from overhead
Bestrode the bodies of their dead:
The Caesars of the silvan field,
Unused to fail, foredoomed to yield:
For in the groins of branches, lo!
The cancers of the orchid grow.
Silent as in the listed ring
Two chartered wrestlers strain and cling,
Dumb as by yellow Hooghly's side
The suffocating captives died:
So hushed the woodland warfare goes
Unceasing; and the silent foes
Grapple and smother, strain and clasp
Without a cry, without a gasp.
Here also sound thy fans, O God,
Here too thy banners move abroad:
Forest and city, sea and shore,
And the whole earth, thy threshing-floor!
The drums of war, the drums of peace,
Roll through our cities without cease,
And all the iron halls of life
Ring with the unremitting strife.

The common lot we scarce perceive.
Crowds perish, we nor mark nor grieve:
The bugle calls – we mourn a few!
What corporal's guard at Waterloo?
What scanty hundreds more or less
In the man-devouring Wilderness?
What handful bled on Delhi ridge?
– See, rather, London, on thy bridge
The pale battalions trample by,
Resolved to slay, resigned to die.

Count, rather, all the maimed and dead
In the unbrotherly war of bread.
See, rather, under sultrier skies
What vegetable Londons rise,
And teem, and suffer without sound.
Or in your tranquil garden ground,
Contented, in the falling gloom,
Saunter and see the roses bloom.
That these might live, what thousands died!
All day the cruel hoe was plied;
The ambulance barrow rolled all day;
Your wife, the tender, kind, and gay,
Donned her long gauntlets, caught the spud
And bathed in vegetable blood;
And the long massacre now at end,
See! where the lazy coils ascend,
See, where the bonfire sputters red
At even, for the innocent dead.

Why prate of peace? when, warriors all,
We clank in harness into hall,
And ever bare upon the board
Lies the necessary sword.
In the green field or quiet street,
Besieged we sleep, beleaguered eat;
Labour by day and wake o' nights,
In war with rival appetites.
The rose on roses feeds; the lark
On larks. The sedentary clerk
All morning with a diligent pen
Murders the babes of other men;
And like the beasts of wood and park,
Protects his whelps, defends his den.

Unshamed the narrow aim I hold;
I feed my sheep, patrol my fold;
Breathe war on wolves and rival flocks,
A pious outlaw on the rocks
Of God and morning; and when time
Shall bow, or rivals break me, climb
Where no undubbed civilian dares,
In my war harness, the loud stairs
Of honour; and my conqueror
Hail me a warrior fallen in war.

Vailima.

XL

Tropic Rain

As the single pang of the blow, when the metal is mingled well,
Rings and lives and resounds in all the bounds of the bell:
So the thunder above spoke with a single tongue,
So in the heart of the mountain the sound of it rumbled and clung.

Sudden the thunder was drowned – quenched was the levin light –
And the angel-spirit of rain laughed out loud in the night.
Loud as the maddened river raves in the cloven glen,
Angel of rain! you laughed and leaped on the roofs of men;
And the sleepers sprang in their beds, and joyed and feared as you fell.

You struck, and my cabin quailed; the roof of it roared like a bell,
You spoke, and at once the mountain shouted and shook with brooks.
You ceased, and the day returned, rosy, with virgin looks.

And methought that beauty and terror are only one, not two;
And the world has room for love, and death, and thunder, and dew;
And all the sinews of hell slumber in summer air;
And the face of God is a rock, but the face of the rock is fair.

Beneficent streams of tears flow at the finger of pain;
And out of the cloud that smites, beneficent rivers of rain.

Vailima.

XLI

An End of Travel

Let now your soul in this substantial world
Some anchor strike. Be here the body moored; –
This spectacle immutably from now
The picture in your eye; and when time strikes,
And the green scene goes on the instant blind –
The ultimate helpers, where your horse today
Conveyed you dreaming, bear your body dead.

Vailima.

XLII

We uncommiserate pass into the night
From the loud banquet, and departing leave
A tremor in men's memories, faint and sweet
And frail as music. Features of our face,

The tones of the voice, the touch of the loved hand,
Perish and vanish, one by one, from earth:
Meanwhile, in the hall of song, the multitude
Applauds the new performer. One, perchance,
One ultimate survivor lingers on,
And smiles, and to his ancient heart recalls
The long forgotten. Ere the morrow die,
He too, returning, through the curtain comes,
And the new age forgets us and goes on.

XLIII

The Last Sight

Once more I saw him. In the lofty room,
Where oft with lights and company his tongue
Was trump to honest laughter, sate attired
A something in his likeness. – 'Look!' said one
Unkindly kind, 'look up, it is your boy!'
And the dread changeling gazed on me in vain.

XLIV

Sing me a song of a lad that is gone,
    Say, could that lad be I?
Merry of soul he sailed on a day
    Over the sea to Skye.

Mull was astern, Rum on the port,
    Eigg on the starboard bow;
Glory of youth glowed in his soul:
    Where is that glory now?

Sing me a song of a lad that is gone,
    Say, could that lad be I?
Merry of soul he sailed on a day
    Over the sea to Skye.

Give me again all that was there,
    Give me the sun that shone!
Give me the eyes, give me the soul,
    Give me the lad that's gone!

Sing me a song of a lad that is gone,
    Say, could that lad be I?
Merry of soul he sailed on a day
    Over the sea to Skye.

Billow and breeze, islands and seas,
    Mountains of rain and sun,
All that was good, all that was fair,
    All that was me is gone.

XLV

To S. R. Crockett

(On receiving a dedication)

Blows the wind today, and the sun and the rain are flying,
    Blows the wind on the moors today and now,
Where about the graves of the martyrs the whaups are crying,
    My heart remembers how!

Gray recumbent tombs of the dead in desert places,
    Standing Stones on the vacant wine-red moor,
Hills of sheep, and the howes of the silent vanished races,
    And winds, austere and pure!

Be it granted me to behold you again in dying,
    Hills of home! and to hear again the call;
Hear about the graves of the martyrs the peewees crying;
    And hear no more at all.

Vailima.

XLVI

Evensong

The embers of the day are red
Beyond the murky hill.
The kitchen smokes: the bed
In the darkling house is spread:
The great sky darkens overhead,
And the great woods are shrill.
So far have I been led,
Lord, by Thy will:
So far I have followed, Lord, and wondered still.

The breeze from the embalmèd land
Blows sudden toward the shore,
And claps my cottage door.
I hear the signal, Lord – I understand.
The night at Thy command
Comes. I will eat and sleep and will not question more.

Vailima.

THE PRIVATE PRINTINGS
OF S. L. OSBOURNE & CO.

A Martial Elegy for Some Lead Soldiers

For certain soldiers lately dead
Our reverent dirge shall here be said.
Them, when their martial leader called,
No dread preparative appalled;
But leaden hearted, leaden heeled,
I marked them steadfast in the field.
Death grimly sided with the foe,
And smote each leaden hero low.
Proudly they perished one by one:
The dread Pea-cannon's work was done!
O not for them the tears we shed,
Consigned to their congenial lead;
But while unmoved their sleep they take,
We mourn for their dear Captain's sake,
For their dear Captain, who shall smart
Both in his pocket and his heart,
Who saw his heroes shed their gore
And lacked a shilling to buy more!

Not I, and Other Poems

I

Not I

Some like drink
In a pint pot,
Some like to think;
    Some not.

Strong Dutch Cheese,
Old Kentucky Rye,
Some like these;
    Not I.

Some like Poe
And others like Scott,
Some like Mrs. Stowe;
    Some not.

Some like to laugh,
Some like to cry,
Some like chaff;
    Not I.

II

Here, perfect to a wish,
We offer, not a dish,
    But just the platter:
A book that's not a book,
A pamphlet in the look
    But not the matter.

I own in disarray;
As to the flowers of May
    The frosts of Winter,
To my poetic rage,
The smallness of the page
    And of the printer.

III

As seamen on the seas
With song and dance descry
Adown the morning breeze
An islet in the sky:
In Araby the dry,
As o'er the sandy plain
The panting camels cry
To smell the coming rain.

So all things over earth
A common law obey
And rarity and worth
Pass, arm in arm, away;
And even so, today,
The printer and the bard,
In pressless Davos, pray
Their sixpenny reward.

IV

The pamphlet here presented
Was planned and printed by
A printer unindented,
A bard whom all decry.

The author and the printer,
With various kinds of skill,
Concocted it in Winter
At Davos on the Hill.

They burned the nightly taper
But now the work is ripe –
Observe the costly paper,
Remark the perfect type!

Begun FEB. ended OCT. 1881

Moral Emblems I

A Collection of Cuts and Verses
By
ROBERT LOUIS STEVENSON
Author of
The Blue Scalper, Travels with a Donkey, Treasure Island, Not I etc.
Printers:
S. L. OSBOURNE & COMPANY.
Davos-Platz.

I

See how the children in the print
Bound on the book to see what's in't!
O, like these pretty babes, may you
Seize and *apply* this volume too!
And while your eye upon the cuts
With harmless ardour opes and shuts,
Reader, may your immortal mind
To their sage lessons not be blind.

II

Reader, your soul upraise to see,
In yon fair cut designed by me,
The pauper by the highwayside
Vainly soliciting from pride.
Mark how the Beau with easy air
Contemns the anxious rustic's prayer,
And casting a disdainful eye,
Goes gaily gallivanting by.
He from the poor averts his head ...
He will regret it when he's dead.

'See how the children ...'

'Reader, your soul upraise ...'

III

A Peak in Darien

Broad-gazing on untrodden lands,
See where adventurous Cortez stands;
While in the heavens above his head,
The Eagle seeks its daily bread.
How aptly fact to fact replies:
Heroes and Eagles, hills and skies.
Ye, who contemn the fatted slave,
Look on this emblem and be brave.

IV

See in the print, how moved by whim
Trumpeting Jumbo, great and grim,
Adjusts his trunk, like a cravat,
To noose that individual's hat.
The sacred Ibis in the distance
Joys to observe his bold resistance.

V

Mark, printed on the opposing page,
The unfortunate effects of rage.
A man (who might be you or me)
Hurls another into the sea.
Poor soul, his unreflecting act
His future joys will much contract;
And he will spoil his evening toddy
By dwelling on that mangled body.

A Peak in Darien

'See in the print …'

'Mark, printed on the opposing page …'

Moral Emblems II

A Second Collection of Cuts and Verses
By
ROBERT LOUIS STEVENSON
Author of *Latter-day Arabian Nights, Travels with a Donkey. Not I, &c.*
Printers:
S. L. OSBOURNE & COMPANY.
Davos-Platz.

I

With storms a-weather, rocks a-lee,
The dancing skiff puts forth to sea.
The lone dissenter in the blast
Recoils before the sight aghast.
But she, although the heavens be black,
Holds on upon the starboard tack.
For why? although today she sink
Still safe she sails in printer's ink,
And though today the seamen drown,
My cut shall hand their memory down.

II

The careful angler chose his nook
At morning by the lilied brook,
And all the noon his rod he plied
By that romantic riverside.
Soon as the evening hours decline
Tranquilly he'll return to dine,
And breathing forth a pious wish,
Will cram his belly full of fish.

III

The Abbot for a walk went out
A wealthy cleric, very stout,
And Robin has that Abbot stuck
As the red hunter spears the buck.
The djavel or the javelin
Has, you observe, gone bravely in,
And you may hear that weapon whack
Bang though the middle of his back.
Hence we may learn that abbots should
Never go walking in a wood.

'With storms a-weather …'

'The careful angler …'

'The Abbot for a walk …'

'The frozen peaks ...'

'Industrious pirate! ...'

Lord Nelson and the Tar

IV

The frozen peaks he once explored,
But now he's dead and by the board.
How better far at home to have stayed
Attended by the parlour maid,
And warmed his knees before the fire
Until the hour when folks retire!
So, if you would be spared to friends,
Do nothing but for business ends.

V

Industrious pirate! see him sweep
The lonely bosom of the deep,
And daily the horizon scan
From Hatteras or Matapan.
Be sure, before that pirate's old,
He will have made a pot of gold,
And will retire from all his labours
And be respected by his neighbours.
You also scan your life's horizon
For all that you can clap your eyes on.

VI

Lord Nelson and the Tar

'Fair is the sea,' Lord Nelson said,
'And fair yon vessel shears ahead.
But yet from all that I can learn
'Tis best to leave the sea astern.
If you and I, sea-faring Robin,
Were with yon harbour-buoy a-bobbin',
The thing is beyond reach of question,
All would be up with our digestion,
And I, rear admiral of the Blue,
Should have to strike my flag and spew.'
Thus spake Old England's naval glory,
And the old salt confirmed his story.
Hence we may learn that all is vanity,
Sea, shore and sky, and poor humanity.

The Graver and the Pen

Or, Scenes From Nature With Appropriate Verses

I

Proem

Unlike the common run of men,
    I wield a double power to please,
And use the GRAVER and the PEN
    With equal aptitude and ease.

I move with that illustrious crew,
    The ambidextrous Kings of Art;
And every mortal thing I do
    Brings ringing money in the mart.

Hence, in the morning hour, the mead,
    The forest and the stream perceive
Me wandering as the muses lead –
    Or back returning in the eve.

Two muses like two maiden aunts,
    The engravings and the singing muse,
Follow, through all my favorite haunts,
    My devious traces in the dews.

To guide and cheer me, each attends;
    Each speeds my rapid task along;
One to my cuts her ardour lends,
    One breathes her magic in my song.

II

The Precarious Mill

Alone above the stream it stands,
Above the iron hill,
The topsy-turvy, tumble-down,
Yet habitable mill.

Still as the ringing saws advance
To slice the humming deal,
All day the pallid miller hears
The thunder of the wheel.

The Precarious Mill

He hears the river plunge and roar
As roars the angry mob;
He feels the solid building quake,
The trusty timbers throb.

All night beside the fire he cowers:
He hears the rafters jar:
O why is he not in a proper house
As decent people are!

The floors are all aslant, he sees,
The doors are all a-jam;
And from the hook above his head
All crooked swings the ham.

'Alas,' he cries and shakes his head,
'I see by every sign,
There soon will be the deuce to pay,
With this estate of mine.'

III

The Disputatious Pines

The first pine to the second said:
'My leaves are black, my branches red;
I stand upon this moor of mine,
A hoar, unconquerable pine.'

The second sniffed and answered: 'Pooh,
I am as good a pine as you.'

'Discourteous tree' the first replied,
'The tempest in my boughs had cried,
The hunter slumbered in my shade,
A hundred years ere you were made.'

The second smiled as he returned:
'I shall be here when you are burned.'

So far dissension ruled the pair,
Each turned on each a frowning air,
When flickering from the bank anigh,
A flight of martens met their eye.
Some time their course they watched; and then
They nodded off to sleep again.

The Disputatious Pines

IV

The Tramps

Now long enough has day endured,
Or King Apollo Palinured,
Seaward he steers his panting team,
And casts on earth his latest gleam.

But see! the Tramps with jaded eye
Their destined provinces espy.
Long through the hills their way they took,
Long camped beside the mountain brook;
'Tis over; now with rising hope
They pause upon the downward slope.
And as their aching bones they rest,
Their anxious captain scans the west.

So paused Alaric on the Alps
And ciphered up the Roman scalps.

V

The Foolhardy Geographer

The howling desert miles around,
The tinkling brook the only sound –
Wearied with all his toils and feats,
The traveller dines on potted meats;
On potted meats and princely wines,
Not wisely but too well he dines.

The brindled Tiger loud may roar,
High may the hovering Vulture soar,
Alas! regardless of them all,
Soon shall the empurpled glutton sprawl –
Soon, in the desert's hushed repose,
Shall trumpet tidings through his nose!
Alack, unwise! that nasal song
Shall be the Ounce's dinner-gong!

A blemish in the cut appears;
Alas! it cost both blood and tears.
The glancing graver swerved aside,
Fast flowed the artist's vital tide!
And now the apologetic bard
Demands indulgence for his pard!

The Tramps

The Foolhardy Geographer

VI

The Angler and the Clown

The echoing bridge you here may see,
The pouring lynn, the waving tree,
The eager angler fresh from town –
Above, the contumelious clown.
The angler plies his line and rod,
The clodpole stands with many a nod, –
With many a nod and many a grin,
He sees him cast his engine in.

'What have you caught?' the peasant cries.

'Nothing as yet,' the Fool replies.

Moral Tales

I

Robin and Ben: Or, the Pirate and the Apothecary

Come lend me an attentive ear
A startling moral tale to hear,
Of Pirate Rob and Chemist Ben,
And different destinies of men.

Deep in the greenest of the vales
That nestle near the coast of Wales,
The heaving main but just in view,
Robin and Ben together grew,
Together worked and played the fool,
Together shunned the Sunday school,
And pulled each other's youthful noses
Around the cots, among the roses.

Together but unlike they grew.
Robin was rough, and through and through,
Bold, inconsiderate and manly,
Like some historic Bruce or Stanley.
Ben had a mean and servile soul.
He robbed not, though he often stole.
He sang on Sunday in the choir
And tamely capped the passing Squire.

At length, intolerant of trammels –
Wild as the wild Bithynian camels,

The Angler and the Clown

Robin and Ben: Scene the First

Wild as the wild sea-eagles – Bob
His widowed dam contrives to rob,
And thus with great originality
Effectuates his personality.
Thenceforth his terror-haunted flight
He follows through the starry night;
And with the early morning breeze,
Behold him on the azure seas.
The master of a trading dandy
Hires Robin for a go of brandy;
And all the happy hills of home
Vanish beyond the fields of foam.

Ben, meanwhile, like a tin reflector,
Attended on the worthy rector;
Opened his eyes and held his breath,
And flattered to the point of death;
And was at last, by that good fairy,
Apprenticed to the Apothecary.

So Ben, while Robin chose to roam,
A rising chemist was at home,
Tended his shop with learnèd air,
Watered his drugs and oiled his hair,
And gave advice to the unwary,
Like any sleek apothecary

Meanwhile upon the deep afar
Robin the brave was waging war,
With other tarry desperadoes
About the latitude of Barbadoes.
He knew no touch of craven fear;
His voice was thunder in the cheer;
First, from the main-to'-gallan' high,
The skulking merchantman to spy –
The first to bound upon the deck,
The last to leave the sinking wreck.
His hand was steel, his word was law,
His mates regarded him with awe.
No pirate in the whole profession
Held a more honourable position.

At length, from years of anxious toil,
Bold Robin seeks his native soil;
Wisely arranges his affairs
And to his native dale repairs.
The Bristol *Swallow* sets him down

Beside the well-remembered town.
He sighs, he spits, he marks the scene,
Proudly he treads the village green;
And free from pettiness and rancour,
Takes lodgings at the 'Crown and Anchor'.

Strange, when a man so great and good,
Once more in his home-country stood,
Strange that the sordid clowns should show
A dull desire to have him go.
His clinging breeks, his tarry hat,
The way he swore, the way he spat,
A certain quality of manner,
Alarming like the pirate's banner –
Something that did not seem to suit all –
Something, O call it bluff, not brutal –
Something at least, howe'er it's called,
Made Robin generally black-balled.

His soul was wounded; proud and glum,
Alone he sat and swigged his rum,
And took a great distaste to men
Till he encountered Chemist Ben.
Bright was the hour and bright the day,
That threw them in each other's way;
Glad were their mutual salutations,
Long their respective revelations.
Before the inn in sultry weather
They talked of this and that together;
Ben told the tale of his indentures,
And Rob narrated his adventures.
Last, as the point of greatest weight,
The pair contrasted their estate,
And Robin, like a boastful sailor,
Despised the other for a tailor.

'See,' he remarked, 'with envy, see
A man with such a fist as me!
Bearded and ringed, and big, and brown,
I sit and toss the stingo down.
Hear the gold jingle in my bag –
All won beneath the Jolly Flag!'

Ben moralised and shook his head:
'You wanderers earn and eat your bread.
The foe is found, beats or is beaten,
And either how, the wage is eaten;

Robin and Ben: Scene the Second

And after all your pully-hauly
Your proceeds look uncommonly small-ly.
You had done better here to tarry
Apprentice to the Apothecary.
The silent pirates of the shore
Eat and sleep soft, and pocket more
Than any red, robustious ranger
Who picks his farthings hot from danger.
You clank your guineas on the board;
Mine are with several bankers stored.
You reckon riches on your digits,
You dash in chase of Sals and Bridgets,
You drink and risk delirium tremens,
Your whole estate a common seaman's!
Regard your friend and school companion,
Soon to be wed to Miss Trevanion
(Smooth, honourable, fat and flowery,
With Lord knows how much land in dowry).
Look at me – am I in good case?
Look at my hands, look at my face;
Look at the cloth of my apparel;
Try me and test me, lock and barrel;
And own, to give the devil his due,
I have made more of life than you.
Yet I nor sought nor risked a life;
I shudder at an open knife;
The perilous seas I still avoided
And stuck to land whate'er betided.
I had no gold, no marble quarry,
I was a poor apothecary,
Yet here I stand at thirty-eight,
A man of an assured estate.'

'Well,' answered Robin – 'well, and how?'

The smiling chemist tapped his brow.
'Rob,' he replied, 'this throbbing brain
Still worked and hankered after gain.
By day and night, to work my will,
It pounded like a powder mill;
And marking how the world went round
A theory of theft it found.
Here is the key to right and wrong:
Steal little but steal all day long;
And this invaluable plan
Marks what is called the Honest Man.
When first I served with Doctor Pill,

Robin and Ben: Scene the Third

My hand was ever in the till.
Now that I am myself a master
My gains come softer still and faster.
As thus: on Wednesday, a maid
Came to me in the way of trade.
Her mother, an old farmer's wife,
Required a drug to save her life.
"At once, my dear, at once," I said,
Patted the child upon the head,
Bade her be still a loving daughter,
And filled the bottle up with water.'

'Well, and the mother?' Robin cried.

'O she!' said Ben, 'I think she died.'

'Battle and blood, death and disease,
Upon the tainted Tropic seas –
The attendant sharks that chew the cud –
The abhorred scuppers spouting blood –
The untended dead, the Tropic sun –
The thunder of the murderous gun –
The cut-throat crew – the Captain's curse –
The tempest blustering worse and worse –
These have I known and these can stand,
But you, I settle out of hand!'

Out flashed the cutlass, down went Ben
Dead and rotten, there and then.

II

The Builder's Doom

In eighteen twenty Deacon Thin
Feu'd the land and fenced it in,
And laid his broad foundations down
About a furlong out of town.

Early and late the work went on.
The carts were toiling ere the dawn;
The mason whistled, the hodman sang;
Early and late the trowels rang;
And Thin himself came day by day
To push the work in every way.
An artful builder, patent king
Of all the local building ring,

Who was there like him in the quarter
For mortifying brick and mortar,
Or pocketing the odd piastre
By substituting lath and plaster?
With plan and two-foot rule in hand,
He by the foreman took his stand,
With boisterous voice, with eagle glance
To stamp upon extravagance.
For thrift of bricks and greed of guilders,
He was the Buonaparte of Builders.

The foreman, a desponding creature,
Demurred to here and there a feature:
'For surely, sir – with your permeession –
Bricks here, sir, in the main parteetion …'
The builder goggled, gulped and stared,
The foreman's services were spared.
Thin would not count among his minions
A man of Wesleyan opinions.

'Money is money,' so he said.
'Crescents are crescents, trade is trade.
Pharaohs and emperors in their seasons
Built, I believe, for different reasons –
Charity, glory, piety, pride –
To pay the men, to please a bride,
To use their stone, to spite their neighbours,
Not for a profit on their labours.
They built to edify or bewilder;
I build because I am a builder.
Crescent and street and square I build,
Plaster and paint and carve and gild.
Around the city see them stand,
These triumphs of my shaping hand,
With bulging walls, with sinking floors,
With shut, impracticable doors,
Fickle and frail in every part,
And rotten to their inmost heart.
There shall the simple tenant find
Death in the falling window-blind,
Death in the pipe, death in the faucet,
Death in the deadly water-closet!
A day is set for all to die:
Caveat emptor! what care I?

As to Amphion's tuneful kit
Troy rose, with towers encircling it;

As to the Mage's brandished wand
A spiry palace clove the sand;
To Thin's indomitable financing,
That phantom crescent kept advancing.
When first the brazen bells of churches
Called clerk and parson to their perches,
The worshippers of every sect
Already viewed it with respect;
A second Sunday had not gone
Before the roof was rattled on:
And when the fourth was there, behold
The crescent finished, painted, sold!

The stars proceeded in their courses,
Nature with her subversive forces,
Time, too, the iron-toothed and sinewed,
And the edacious years continued.
Thrones rose and fell; and still the crescent,
Unsanative and now senescent,
A plastered skeleton of lath,
Looked forward to a day of wrath.
In the dead night, the groaning timber
Would jar upon the ear of slumber,
And like Dodona's talking oak,
Of oracles and judgments spoke.
When to the music fingered well
The feet of children lightly fell,
The sire, who dozed by the decanters,
Started and dreamed of misadventures.
The rotten brick decayed to dust;
The iron was consumed by rust;
Each tabid and perverted mansion
Hung in the article of declension.

So forty, fifty, sixty passed;
Until, when seventy came at last,
The occupant of number three
Called friends to hold a jubilee.
Wild was the night; the charging rack
Had forced the moon upon her back;
The wind piped up a naval ditty;
And the lamps winked through all the city.
Before that house where lights were shining,
Corpulent feeders, grossly dining,
And jolly clamour, hum and rattle
Fairly outvoiced the tempest's battle –
As still his moistened lip he fingered,

The envious policeman lingered;
While far the infernal tempest sped,
And shook the country folks in bed,
And tore the trees and tossed the ships,
He lingered and he licked his lips.
Lo, from within, a hush! the host
Briefly expressed the evening's toast;
And lo, before the lips were dry,
The Deacon rising to reply!
'Here in this house which once I built,
Papered and painted, carved and gilt,
And out of which, to my content,
I netted seventy-five per cent.;
Here at this board of jolly neighbours,
I reap the credit of my labours.
These were the days – I will say more –
These were the grand old days of yore!
The builder laboured day and night;
He watched that every brick was right;
The decent men their utmost did;
And the house rose – a pyramid!
These were the days, our provost knows,
When forty streets and crescents rose,
The fruits of my creative noddle,
All more or less upon a model,
Neat and commodious, cheap and dry,
A perfect pleasure to the eye!
I found this quite a country quarter;
I leave it solid lath and mortar.
In all, I was the single actor –
And am this city's benefactor!
Since then, alas! both thing and name,
Shoddy across the ocean came –
Shoddy that can the eye bewilder
And makes me blush to meet a builder!
Had this good house, in frame or fixture,
Been tempered by the least admixture
Of that discreditable shoddy,
Should we today compound our toddy,
Or gaily marry song and laughter
Below its sempiternal rafter?
Not so!' the Deacon cried.

                    The mansion
Had marked his fatuous expansion.
The years were full, the hour was fated,
The rotten structure crepitated!

A moment, and the silent guests
Sat pallid as their dinner vests.
A moment more, and root and branch,
That mansion fell in avalanche,
Story on story, floor on floor,
Roof, wall and window, joist and door,
Dead weight of damnable disaster,
A cataclysm of lath and plaster.

Siloam did not choose a sinner –
All were not builders at the dinner.

III

A Perfect Cure: Or, the Man of Habit

'Doctor,' the anxious patient said,
'I chew, I spit, I read in bed,
I whore and whittle, smoke and drink –
Pray can you cure me, do you think?'

The learned physician shook his head.
'Your case is very grave,' he said.
'Still by the lights of therapeutics,
I have uprooted one or two tricks;
The young, that crowd my helpful door,
Have but to pay and sin no more;
Ev'n from the old, that second fate
Called Habit, I deracinate;
And had you learned as many vices
As Mr Swinburne exercises,
And were you old as Albert Durer,
I would engage to be your curer.'

'Tis well,' the hopeful patient cried,
'Cure me of all!'

                    The Doctor tried;
With artfully concocted messes
Weaned him from all his naughtinesses;
And having duly charged and blessed him,
He from his doors at length dismissed him.

Forth into life the patient walked;
The wind with the green coppice talked;
The runnel babbled as it ran
To greet that renovated man.

In every valley, lads and maidens
Sang to the happy year in cadence;
The birds among the hawthorn branches
Shook blossoms down in avalanches;
And in the deep and daisied meadow
The wild bull bellowed from the shadow.
In all the fields, thus gaily neighboured,
The rook-escorted ploughman laboured;
And at each turn and come-again
Paused by the hedge the jug to drain.
High on the hill that April morning,
The tattered tramp, that awful warning,
Beside the milestone, bleared and sooty,
Stooped to ignite his sable cutty.
And all the country seemed to echo,
Love, laughter, liquor and tobacco.

The patient paused; he stood apart
And sounded all his empty heart;
In vain: no human ember glowed
In that untenanted abode;
Life might before him pour her treasure:
He was as bare as Nebuchadnezzar!
'Beggars,' he cried, 'are not so poor –
Great God, am I a perfect cure?'

Straightway, he turned and back he went
To that physician's tenement;
Where whistling like the happy hedger,
He sat and pored upon his ledger.
'My friend,' the smiling doctor cried:
'What – back again?'

                        The patient sighed.
'My case at first was fairly human;
I merely craved for wine and woman:
But you, alchemic transmuter,
Have changed me to a kind of tutor
And with my own insane complicity
Purged me of blood and electricity.
Now through the smiling earth I go,
A vain and ineffectual show;
I do not drink, I cannot smoke,
I am an egg without a yolk;
Advances of the fairer sex
Leave me as cold as a ship's decks.
And being wholly cured by you

I have not anything to do.
O let me not conjure in vain,
But haste and change me back again.'

'Too late,' the Doctor said. 'The cure
Is now pluperfect, granite sure.
I, in the exercise of art
Have wholly cleansed your every part,
And stealing forth your bone and gristle
Left you as empty as a whistle.
But do not hold that life is ended
Which may be measurably mended;
There still are harmless occupations
In which to drown your reluctations.
You may, like other similar martyrs,
Do crochet work for ladies' garters,
And thus to all your fairer friends
Make chaste and elegant amends.

The dreadful sameness of the year
The turning lathe perhaps may cheer,
And you perhaps will find it handy
To make a vice of sugar candy.
These, Israel, be thy Gods! with these
Frugal repasts, financial ease,
And *sanctae matris sancta mater*,
The columns of the chaste *Spectator*.'

SELECTED POEMS

Songs and Little Odes

Songs

I

Lo! in thine honest eyes I read
The auspicious beacon that shall lead,
After long sailing in deep seas,
To quiet havens in pure ease.

Thy voice sings like an inland bird
First by the seaworn sailor heard;
And like roads sheltered from life's sea
Thine honest heart is unto me.

II

The Blackbird

My heart, when first the blackbird sings,
    My heart drinks in the song:
Cool pleasure fills my bosom through
    And spreads each nerve along.

My bosom eddies quietly,
    My heart is stirred and cool
As when a wind-moved briar sweeps
    A stone into a pool.

III

1

I dreamed of forest alleys fair
    And fields of gray-flowered grass,
Where by the yellow summer moon
    My Jenny seemed to pass.

I dreamed the yellow summer moon,
    Behind a cedar wood,
Shone white on rippling waves of grass
    Where I and Jenny stood.

I dreamed, but fallen through my dream
    In a rainy land I lie,
Where wan, wet morning crowns the hills
    Of grim reality.

2

I am as one that keeps awake
    All night in the month of June,
That lies awake in bed to watch
    The trees and great white moon.

For memories of love are more
    Than the white moon there above,
And dearer than quiet moonshine
    Are the thoughts of her I love.

3

Last night, I lingered long without
    My last of loves to see.
Alas! the moon-white window-panes
    Stared blindly back on me.

Today I hold her very hand,
    Her very waist embrace –
Like clouds across a pool, I read
    Her thoughts upon her face.

And yet, as now, through her clear eyes
    I seek the inner shrine –
I stoop to read her virgin heart,
    In doubt if it be mine –

O looking long and fondly thus,
    What vision should I see?
No vision, but my own white face
    That grins and mimics me.

4

Once more upon the same old seat
    In the same sunshiny weather,
The elm-trees' shadows at their feet
    And foliage move together.

The shadows shift upon the grass,
    The dial point creeps on;
The clear sun shines, the loiterers pass,
    As then they passed and shone.

But now deep sleep is on my heart,
    Deep sleep and perfect rest.
Hope's flutterings now disturb no more
    The quiet of my breast.

5

St Martin's Summer

As swallows turning backward
  When halfway o'er the sea,
At one word's trumpet summons
  They came again to me –
The hopes I had forgotten
  Came back again to me.

I know not which to credit,
  O lady of my heart!
Your eyes that bade me linger,
  Your words that bade us part –
I know not which to credit,
  My reason or my heart.

But be my hopes rewarded,
  Or be they but in vain,
I have dreamed a golden vision,
  I have gathered in the grain –
I have dreamed a golden vision,
  I have not lived in vain.

6

Dedication

My first gift and my last, to you
I dedicate this fascicle of songs
The only wealth I have:
Just as they are, to you.

I speak the truth in soberness, and say
I had rather bring a light to your clear eyes,
Had rather hear you praise
This bosomful of trifles,

Than that the whole, hard world with one consent
In one continuous chorus of applause
Poured forth for me and mine
The homage of due praise.

I write the *finis* here against my love,
This is my love's last epitaph and tomb.
Here the road forks, and I
Go my way, far from yours.

IV

Dawn

About the sheltered garden ground
　　　　The trees stand strangely still.
The vale ne'er seemed so deep before,
　　　　Nor yet so high the hill.

An awful sense of quietness,
　　　　A fullness of repose,
Breathes from the dewy garden-lawns,
　　　　The silent garden rows.

As the hoof-beats of a troop of horse
　　　　Heard far across a plain,
A nearer knowledge of great thoughts
　　　　Thrills vaguely through my brain.

I lean my head upon my arm,
　　　　My heart's too full to think:
Like the roar of seas, upon my heart
　　　　Doth the morning stillness sink.

V

After Reading 'Antony and Cleopatra'

As when the hunt by holt and field
　　　　Drives on with horn and strife,
Hunger of hopeless things pursues
　　　　Our spirits thorough life.

The sea's roar fills us aching full
　　　　Of objectless desire –
The sea's roar, and the white moon-shine,
　　　　And the reddening of the fire.

Who talks to me of reason now?
　　　　It would be more delight
To have died in Cleopatra's arms
　　　　Than be alive tonight.

VI

I know not how, but as I count
　　　　The beads of former years,
Old laughter catches in my throat
　　　　With the very feel of tears.

VII

Spring Song

The air was full of sun and birds,
          The fresh air sparkled clearly.
Remembrance wakened in my heart
          And I knew I loved her dearly.

The fallows and the leafless trees
          And all my spirit tingled.
My earliest thought of love, and Spring's
          First puff of perfume mingled.

In my still heart the thoughts awoke,
          Came bone by bone together –
Say, birds and Sun and Spring, is Love
          A mere affair of weather?

VIII

The summer sun shone round me,
          The folded valley lay
In a steam of sun and odour,
          That sultry summer day.

The tall trees stood in the sunlight
          As still as still could be,
But the deep grass sighed and rustled
          And bowed and beckoned me.

The deep grass moved and whispered
          And bowed and brushed my face,
It whispered in the sunshine
          'The winter comes apace.'

IX

You looked so tempting in the pew,
          You looked so sly and calm –
My trembling fingers played with yours
          As both looked out the Psalm.

Your heart beat hard against my arm,
          My foot to yours was set,
Your loosened ringlet burned my cheek,
          Whenever they two met.

O little, little we hearkened, dear,
        And little, little cared,
Although the parson sermonized,
        The congregation stared.

X

Love's Vicissitudes

As Love and Hope together
        Walk by me for a while,
Link-armed the ways they travel
        For many a pleasant mile –
Link-armed and dumb they travel,
        They sing not, but they smile.

Hope leaving, Love commences
        To practise on the lute;
And as he sings and travels
        With lingering, laggard foot,
Despair plays *obligato*,
        The sentimental flute.

Until in singing garments,
        Comes royally, at call –
Comes limber-hipped Indiff'rence
        Free-stepping, straight and tall –
Comes singing and lamenting,
        The sweetest pipe of all.

XI

Duddingston

1

With caws and chirrupings, the woods
        In this thin sun rejoice,
The Psalm seems but the little kirk
        That sings with its own voice.

The cloud-rifts share their amber light
        With the surface of the mere –
I think the very stars are glad
        To feel each other near.

Once more my whole heart leaps and swells
        And gushes o'er with glee:

The fingers of the sun and shade
    Touch music stops in me.

2

Now fancy paints that bygone day
    When you were here, my fair –
The whole lake rang with rapid skates
    In the windless winter air.

You leaned to me, I leaned to you,
    Our course was smooth as flight –
We steered – a heel-touch to the left,
    A heel-touch to the right.

We swung our way through flying men,
    Your hand lay fast in mine,
We saw the shifting crowd dispart,
    The level ice-reach shine.

I swear by yon swan-travelled lake,
    By yon calm hill above,
I swear had we been drowned that day
    We had been drowned in love.

3

Apologetic Postscript of a Year Later

If you see this song, my dear,
    And last year's boast,
I'm confoundedly in fear
You'll be serious and severe
    About the boast.

Blame not that I sought such aid
    To cure regret:
I was then so lowly laid
I used all the Gasconnade
    That I could get.

Being snubbed is somewhat smart,
    Believe, my sweet;
And I needed all my art
To restore my broken heart
    To its conceit.

Come and smile, dear, and forget
    I boasted so.

I apologise – regret –
It was all a jest and – yet
I do not know.

XII

Prelude

By sunny market-place and street
Wherever I go my drum I beat,
And wherever I go in my coat of red
The ribbons flutter about my head.

I seek recruits for wars to come –
For slaughterless wars I beat the drum,
And the shilling I give to each new ally
Is hope to live and courage to die.

I know that new recruits shall come
Whenever they hear the sounding drum,
Till the roar of the march by country and town
Shall shake the tottering Dagons down.

For I was objectless as they
And loitering idly, day by day,
But whenever I heard the recruiters come,
I left my all to follow the drum.

XIII

The Vanquished Knight

I have lost all upon the shameful field,
        Honour and Hope, my God, and all but life;
Spurless, with sword reversed and dinted shield,
        Degraded and disgraced, I leave the strife.

From him that hath not, shall there not be taken
        E'en that he hath, when he deserts the strife?
Life left, by all life's benefits forsaken –
        Fulfill the promise, Lord, and take the life!

XIV

Away with funeral music – set
        The pipe to powerful lips –
The cup of life's for him that drinks
        And not for him that sips.

Little Odes

I

To Sydney

Not thine where marble-still and white
Old statues share the tempered light
And mock the uneven modern flight,
            But in the stream
Of daily sorrow and delight
            To seek a theme.

I too, O friend, have steeled my heart
Boldly to choose the better part,
To leave the beaten ways of art
            And wholly free
To dare, beyond the scanty chart,
            The deeper sea.

All vain restrictions left behind,
Frail bark! I loose my anchored mind
And large, before the prosperous wind
            Desert the strand –
A new Columbus sworn to find
            The morning land.

Nor too ambitious, friend. To thee
I own my weakness. Not for me
To sing the enfranchised nations' glee,
            Or count the cost
Of warships foundered far at sea
            And battles lost.

High on the far-seen, sunny hills,
Morning-content my bosom fills;
Well pleased, I trace the wandering rills
            And learn their birth.
Far off, the clash of sovereign wills
            May shake the earth.

The nimble circuit of the wheel,
The uncertain poise of merchant weal,
Horror of famine, fire and steel
            When nations fall;
These, heedful, from afar I feel –
            I mark them all.

But not, my friend, not these I sing,
My voice shall fill a narrower ring.
Tired souls, that flag upon the wing,
     I seek to cheer.
Brave wines to strengthen hope I bring,
     Life's cantineer!

Some song that shall be suppling oil
To weary muscles strained with toil,
Shall hearten for the daily moil,
     Or widely read
Make sweet for him that tills the soil
     His daily bread –

Such songs in my flushed hours I dream
(High thought), instead of armour gleam
Or warrior cantos ream by ream
     To load the shelves –
Songs with a lilt of words, that seem
     To sing themselves.

II

To —

Though deep indifference should drowse
The sluggish life beneath my brows,
And all the external things I see
Grow snow-showers in the street to me,
Yet inmost in my stormy sense
Thy looks shall live an influence.

Though other loves may come and go
And long years sever us below,
Shall the thin ice that grows above
Freeze the deep centre-well of love?
No, still below light amours, thou
Shalt rule me as thou rul'st me now.

Year following year shall only set
Fresh gems upon thy coronet;
And Time, grown lover, shall delight
To beautify thee in my sight;
And thou shalt ever rule in me
Crowned with the light of memory.

III

The relic taken, what avails the shrine?
The locket, pictureless? O heart of mine,
     Art thou not less than that?
Still warm, a vacant nest where love once sat.

Her image nestled closer at my heart
Than cherished memories, healed every smart,
     And warmed it more than wine
Or the full summer sun in noon-day shine.

This was the little weather-gleam that lit
The cloudy promontories. The real charm was it
     That gilded hills and woods
And walked beside me through the solitudes.

That sun is set. My heart is widowed now
Of that companion thought. Alone I plough
     The seas of life, and trace
A separate furrow far from her and grace.

IV

To Marcus

O South, South, South! O happy land!
Thou beckon'st me with phantom hand.
Sweet memories at my bedside stand
     All night in tears.
The roar upon thy nightly strand
     Yet fills mine ears.

The young grass sparkles in the breeze,
The pleasant sunshine warms my knees,
The buds are thick upon the trees.
     The clouds float high.
We sit out here in perfect ease –
     My pipe and I.

Fain would I be, where (winter done)
By dusty roads and noontide sun,
The soldiers, straggling one by one,
     Marched disarrayed
And spoiled the hedge, till every gun
     A Rose displayed.

Or, O flower-land, I would be where
(The trivial, well-beloved affair!)
The bird-watch drew with gentle care
      From up his sleeve
And gave me, fluttering from the snare,
      A *Mange-Olive*.

Aye, dear to me the slightest tie
That binds my heart to thee, O high
And sovereign land for whom I sigh
      In pain to see
The Springtime come again, and I
      So far from thee!

But hush! the clear-throat blackbird sings.
From haugh and hill the Season brings
Great armfuls of delightful things
      To stop my mouth
Though still (caged-bird) I beat my wings
      Toward the South.

V

Consolation

Though he that ever kind and true
Kept stoutly step by step with you
Your whole long gusty lifetime through,
      Be gone awhile before,
Be now a moment gone before,
Yet, doubt not, soon the seasons shall restore
      Your friend to you.

He has but turned a corner. Still
He pushes on with right good will,
Through mire and marsh, by heugh and hill,
      That self-same arduous way,
That self-same upland, hopeful way
That you and he through many a doubtful day
      Attempted still.

He is not dead, this friend – not dead,
But in the path we mortals tread
Got some few trifling steps ahead
      And nearer to the end;
So that you too, once past the bend,
Shall meet again, as face to face, this friend
      You fancy dead.

Push gaily on, strong heart! The while
You travel forward mile by mile,
He loiters with a backward smile
    Till you can overtake,
And strains his eyes to search his wake,
Or whistling, as he sees you through the brake,
    Waits on a stile.

VI

This gloomy northern day,
   Or this yet gloomier night,
      Has moved a something high
      In my cold heart; and I,
That do not often pray,
   Would pray tonight.

And first on thee I call
   For bread, O God of might! –
Enough of bread for all, –
      That through the famished town
      Cold Hunger may lie down
With none tonight.

I pray for hope no less
   Strong-sinewed hope, O Lord,
      That to the struggling young
      May preach with brazen tongue
Stout Labour, high success
   And bright reward.

And last, O Lord, I pray
   For hearts resigned and bold
To trudge the dusty way –
      Hearts stored with song and joke
      And warmer than a cloak
Against the cold.

If nothing else he had,
   He who has this, has all.
      This comforts under pain:
      This, through the stinging rain,
Keeps ragamuffin glad
   Behind the wall.

This makes the sanded inn
A palace for a Prince,
And this, when griefs begin
And cruel fate annoys,
Can bring to mind the joys
Of ages since.

Poems: 1869–70

I

The Light-keeper

1

The brilliant kernel of the night,
The flaming lightroom circles me:
I sit within a blaze of light
Held high above the dusky sea.
Far off the surf doth break and roar
Along bleak miles of moonlit shore,
Where through the tides the tumbling wave
Falls in an avalanche of foam
And drives its churnèd waters home
Up many an undercliff and cave.

The clear bell chimes: the clockworks strain:
The turning lenses flash and pass,
Frame turning within glittering frame
With frosty gleam of moving glass:
Unseen by me, each dusky hour
The sea-waves welter up the tower
Or in the ebb subside again;
And ever and anon all night,
Drawn from afar by charm of light,
A sea-bird beats against the pane.

And lastly when dawn ends the night
And belts the semi-orb of sea,
The tall, pale pharos in the light
Looks white and spectral as may be.
The early ebb is out: the green
Straight belt of sea-weed now is seen,
That round the basement of the tower
Marks out the interspace of tide;
And watching men are heavy-eyed,
And sleepless lips are dry and sour.

The night is over like a dream:
    The sea-birds cry and dip themselves;
And in the early sunlight, steam
    The newly-bared and dripping shelves,
Around whose verge the glassy wave
With lisping wash is heard to lave;
    While, on the white tower lifted high,
With yellow light in faded glass
The circling lenses flash and pass,
    And sickly shine against the sky.

2

As the steady lenses circle
With a frosty gleam of glass;
And the clear bell chimes,
And the oil brims over the lip of the burner,
Quiet and still at his desk,
The lonely light-keeper
Holds his vigil.

Lured from afar,
The bewildered sea-gull beats
Dully against the lantern;
Yet he stirs not, lifts not his head
From the desk where he reads,
Lifts not his eyes to see
The chill blind circle of night
Watching him through the panes.
This is his country's guardian,
The outmost sentry of peace.
This is the man,
Who gives up all that is lovely in living
For the means to live.

Poetry cunningly gilds
The life of the light-keeper,
Held on high in the blackness
In the burning kernel of night.
The seaman sees and blesses him.
The Poet, deep in a sonnet,
Numbers his inky fingers
Fitly to praise him.
Only we behold him,
Sitting, patient and stolid,
Martyr to a salary.

II

The Daughter of Herodias

Three yellow slaves were set to swing
      The doorway curtain to and fro,
With rustle of light folds and ring
      Of little bells that hung below:
The still hot night was tempered so.

And ever, from the carven bed,
      She watched the labour of the men;
And saw the band of moonlight spread,
      Leap up upon her feet and then
Leap down upon the floor again;

And ever, vexed with heat and doubt,
      Below the burthen of their shawls,
The still gray olives saw without
      And glimmer of white garden walls,
Between the alternate curtain falls.

What ailed the dainty lady then,
      The dainty lady, fair and sweet?
Unseen of these three silent men,
      A something lay upon her feet,
Not comely for such eyes to meet.

She saw a golden salver there.
      And, laid upon it, on the bed,
The white teeth showing keen and bare
      Between the sundered lips, a head
Sallow and horrible and dead.

She saw upon the sallow cheek
      Rust-coloured blood stains; and the eye
Her frightened glances seemed to seek
      Half-lifting its blue lid on high,
Watching her, horrible and sly.

Thus spake she: 'Once again that head!
      I ate too much pilau tonight,
My mother and the eunuchs said.
      Well, I can take a hint aright –
Tomorrow's supper shall be light.'

III

The Cruel Mistress

Here let me rest, here nurse the uneasy qualm
That yearns within me;
And to the heaped-up sea,
Sun-spangled in the quiet afternoon,
Sing my devotions.

In the sun, at the edge of the down,
The whin-pods crackle
In desultory volleys;
And the bank breathes in my face
Its hot sweet breath –
Breath that stirs and kindles,
Lights that suggest not satisfy –
Is there never in life or nature
An opiate for desire?
Has everything here a voice,
Saying: '*I am not the goal;*
Nature is not to be looked at alone:
Her breath, like the breath of a mistress,
Her breath also,
Parches the spirit with longing,
Sick and enervating longing.'

Well, let the matter rest.
I rise and brush the windle-straws
Off my clothes; and lighting another pipe
Stretch myself over the down.
Get thee behind me, nature!
I turn my back on the sun
And face from the gray new town at the foot of the bay.
I know an amber lady
Who has her abode
At the lips of the street
In prisons of coloured glass.
I had rather die of her love
Than sicken for you, O nature!
Better be drunk and merry
Than dreaming awake!
Better be Falstaff than Obermann!

IV

Storm

The narrow lanes are vacant and wet.
The rough wind bullies and blusters about the township,
And spins the vane on the tower
And chases the scurrying leaves,
And the straw in the damp innyard.
See – a girl passes,
Tripping gingerly over the pools,
And under her lifted dress
I catch the gleam of a comely, stockinged leg.
Pah! the room stifles me,
Reeking of stale tobacco,
With the four black, mealy, horrible prints
After Landseer's pictures.
I will go out.

Here the free wind comes with a fuller circle,
Sings, like an angry wasp, in the straining grass
Sings and whistles;
And the hurried flow of rain
Scourges my face and passes.
Behind me, clustered together, the rain-wet roofs of the town
Shine, and the light vane shines as it veers
In the long pale finger of sun that hurries across them to me.
The fresh salt air is keen in my nostrils,
And far down the shining sand,
Foam and thunder
And take the shape of the bay in eager mirth,
The white-head hungry billows.
The earth shakes
As the semicircle of waters
Stoops and casts itself down;
And far outside in the open,
Wandering gleams of sunshine
Show us the ordered horde that hurries to follow.

Ei! merry companions,
Your madness infects me.
My whole soul rises and falls and leaps and tumbles with you!
I shout aloud and incite you, O white-headed merry companions.
The sight of you alone is better than drinking.
The brazen band is loosened from off my forehead,
My breast and my brain are moistened and cool;
And still I yell in answer
To your hoarse inarticulate voices,

O big, strong, bullying, boisterous waves,
That are of all things in nature the nearest thing to human,
Because you are wicked and foolish,
Mad and destructive.

V

Stormy Nights

I cry out war to those who spend their utmost,
Trying to substitute a vain regret
For childhood's vanished moods,
Instead of a full manly satisfaction
In new development.
Their words are vain as the lost shouts,
The wasted breath of solitary hunters
That are far buried in primeval woods –
Clamour that dies in silence,
Cries that bring back no answer
But the great voice of the wind-shaken forest,
Mocking despair.

No – they will get no answer;
For I too recollect,
I recollect and love my perished childhood,
Perfectly love and keenly recollect;
I too remember; and, if it could be,
Would not recall it.

Do I not know, how, nightly, on my bed,
The palpable close darkness shutting round me,
How my small heart went forth to evil things,
How all the possibilities of sin
That were yet present to my innocence
Bound me too narrowly,
And how my spirit beat
The cage of its compulsive purity:
How – my eyes fixed,
My shot lip tremulous between my fingers
I fashioned for myself new modes of crime,
Created for myself with pain and labour
The evil that the cobwebs of society,
The comely secrecies of education,
Had made an itching mystery to meward.

Do I not know again,
When the great winds broke loose and went abroad

At night in the lighted town –
Ah! then it was different –
Then, when I seemed to hear
The storm go by me like a cloak-wrapt horseman
Stooping over the saddle –
Go by, and come again and yet again,
Like someone riding with a pardon,
And ever baffled, ever shut from passage: –
Then when the house shook and a horde of noises
Came out and clattered over me all night, –
Then, would my heart stand still,
My hair creep fearfully upon my head
And, with my tear-wet face
Buried among the bed-clothes,
Long and bitterly would I pray and wrestle
Till gentle sleep
Threw her great mantle over me,
And my hard breathing gradually ceased.

I was then the Indian,
Well and happy and full of glee and pleasure,
Both hands full of life.
And not without divine impulses
Shot into me by the untried non-ego;
But, like the Indian, too,
Not yet exempt from feverish questionings
And on my bed of leaves,
Writhing terribly in grasp of terror,
As when the still stars and the great white moon
Watch me athwart black foliage,
Trembling before the interminable vista,
The widening wells of space
In which my thought flags like a wearied bird
In the mid-ocean of his autumn flight –
Prostrate before the indefinite great spirit
That the external warder
Plunged like a dagger
Into my bosom.

Now, I am a Greek
White-robed among the sunshine and the statues
And the fair porticos of carven marble –
Fond of olives and dry sherry,
Good tobacco and clever talk with my fellows,
Free from inordinate cravings.

Why would you hurry me, O evangelist,
You with the bands and the shilling packet of tracts
Greatly reduced when taken for distribution?
Why do you taunt my progress,
O green-spectacled Wordsworth! in beautiful verses,
You, the elderly poet?
So I shall travel forward
Step by step with the rest of my race.
In time, if death should spare me,
I shall come to a farther stage,
And show you St. Francis of Assisi.

VI

Song at Dawn

I see the silent dawn creep round the world,
Here damm'd a moment backward by great hills,
There racing o'er the sea.
Down at the round equator,
It leaps forth straight and rapid
Driving with firm sharp edge the night before it.
Here gradually it floods
The wooded valleys and the meads
And the still smokeless cities.
The cocks crow up at the farms:
The sick man's spirit is glad:
The watch treads brisker about the dew-wet deck:
The light-keeper locks his desk,
As the lenses turn,
Faded and yellow.

The girl with the embroidered shift
Rises and leans on the sill,
And her full bosom heaves
Drinking deep of the silentness.
I too linger and watch
The healing fingers of dawn –
I too drink from its eyes
The unaccountable peace –
I too drink and am satisfied as with food.
Fain would I go
Down by the winding crossroad by the trees,
Where at the corner of wet wood,
The blackbird in the early gray and stillness
Wakes his first song.

Peace, who can make verses clink,
Find ictus following surely after ictus,
At such an hour as this, the heart
Lies steeped and silent.
Get back to bed,
Girl with the lace-bosomed shift,
O leaning, dreaming girl, I too grow cold,
I do the same.
Already are the sovereign hill-tops ruddy,
Already the gray passes, the white-streak
Brightens above dark woodlands. Day begins.

VII

My brain swims empty and light
Like a nut on a sea of oil;
And an atmosphere of quiet
Wraps me about from the turmoil and clamour of life.

I stand apart from living,
Apart and holy I stand,
In my new-gained growth of idleness, I stand,
As stood the Shekinah of yore in the holy of holies.

I walk the streets smoking my pipe
And I love the dallying shop-girl
That leans with rounded stern to look at the fashions;
And I hate the bustling citizen,
The eager and hurrying man of affairs I hate,
Because he bears his intolerance writ on his face
And every movement and word of him tells me how much he hates me.

I love night in the city,
The lighted streets and the swinging gait of harlots.
I love cool pale morning,
In the empty bye-streets,
With only here and there a female figure,
A slavey with lifted dress and the key in her hand,
A girl or two at play in a corner of a waste-land
Tumbling and showing their legs and crying out to me loosely.

Sonnets and Rondeaux

Sonnets

1

The roadside lined with ragweed, the sharp hills
 Standing against the glow of eve, the patch
  Of rough white oats 'mongst darkling granite knolls,
 The ferny coverts where the adders hatch,
The hollow that the northern sea upfills,
 The sea-gull wheeling by with strange, sad calls,
All these, this evening, weary me. Full fain
 Would I turn up the little elm tree way
And under the last elm tree, once again
 Stretch myself with my head among the grass;
 So lying, tyne the memories of day
 And let my loosed, insatiate being pass
Into the blackbird's song of summer ease,
Or, with the white moon, rise in spirit from the trees.

2

Lines to be Sent with the Present of a Sketch Book

So shall this book wax like unto a well,
 Fairy with mirrored flowers about the brim,
 Or like some tarn that eager curlews skim,
Glassing the sallow upland or brown fell;
And so, as men go down into a dell
 (Weary of noon) to find relief and shade,
 When on the uneasy sick-bed we are laid,
We shall go down into thy book, and tell
The leaves, once blank, to build again for us
 Old summer dead and ruined, and the time
  Of later autumn with the corn in stook.
So shalt thou stint the meagre winter thus
 Of his projected triumph, and the rime
  Shall melt before the sunshine in thy book.

3

I have a hoard of treasure in my breast:
 The grange of memory strains against the door,
 Full of my byegone lifetime's garnered store,
Old pleasures crowned with sadness for a zest,
Old sorrow grown a joy, old penance blest,

Chastened remembrance of the sins of yore
That like a new evangel, more and more
Supports our halting will towards the best.
Ah, what to us the barren after years
May bring of joy or sorrow, who can tell?
Or, knowing not, who cares? It may be well
That we shall find old pleasures and old fears
And our remembered childhood seen through tears
The best of Heaven and the worst of Hell.

4

Not undelightful, friend, our rustic ease
To grateful hearts; for by especial hap
Deep nested in the hill's enormous lap
With its own ring of walls and grove of trees
Sits, in deep shelter, our small cottage – nor
Far off is seen, rose-carpeted and hung
With clematis, the quarry whence she sprung,
O matre pulchra filia pulchrior.
Thither in early Spring, unharnessed folk,
We join the pairing swallows, glad to stay
Where, bosomed in the hills, remote, unseen,
From its tall trees it breathes a slender smoke
To Heav'n, and in the noon of sultry day
Stands coolly buried to the neck in green.

5

As in the hostel by the bridge, I sate
Mailed with indifference fondly deemed complete
And (O strange chance, more sorrowful than sweet)
The counterfeit of her that was my fate,
Dressed in like vesture, graceful and sedate,
Went quietly up the vacant village street.
The still small sound of her most dainty feet
Shook, like a trumpet blast, my soul's estate.
Instant revolt ran riot through my brain;
And all night long thereafter, hour by hour,
The pageant of dead love before my eyes
Went proudly; and old hopes, broke loose again
From the restraint of wisely temperate power,
With ineffectual ardour sought to rise.

6

As Daniel, bird-alone in that far land,
Kneeling in fervent prayer, with heart-sick eyes
Turned through the casement toward the westering skies;
Or as untamed Elijah, that red brand
Among the starry prophets; or that band
And company of faithful sanctities
Who, in all times, when persecutions rise
Cherish forgotten creeds with fostering hand;
Such do ye seem to me, light-hearted crew,
O turned to friendly arts with all your will,
That keep a little chapel sacred still,
One rood of Holy-land in this bleak earth
Sequestered still (an homage surely due!)
To the twin Gods of mirthful wine and mirth.

7

I am like one that for long days had sate,
 With seaward eyes set keen against the gale,
 On some long foreland, watching, sail by sail,
The portbound ships for one ship that was late;
And sail by sail, his heart burned up with joy,
 And cruelly was quenched, until at last
 One ship, the looked-for pennant at its mast,
Bore gaily, and dropt safely past the buoy;
And lo! the loved one was not there, was dead.
Then would he watch no more; no more the sea
 With myriad vessels, sail by sail, perplex
His eyes and mock his longing. Weary head,
Take now thy rest; eyes, close; for no more me
 Shall hope untried elate, or ruined vex.

For thus on love I waited; thus for love
 Strained all my senses eagerly and long;
 Thus for her coming ever trimmed my song;
Till in the far skies coloured as a dove,
A bird gold-coloured flickered far and fled
 Over the pathless water waste for me;
 And with spread hands I watched the bright bird flee
And waited, till before me she dropped dead.
O golden bird in these dove-coloured skies
How long I sought, how long with wearied eyes
 I sought, O bird, the promise of thy flight!
And now the morn has dawned, the morn has died,
 The day has come and gone; and once more night
About my lone life settles, wild and wide.

8

Music at the Villa Marina

From some abiding central source of power,
   Strong-smitten steady chords, ye seem to flow
   And, flowing, carry virtue. Far below,
The vain tumultuous passions of the hour
Fleet fast and disappear; and as the sun
   Shines on the wake of tempests, there is cast
   O'er all the shattered ruins of my past
A strong contentment as of battles won.

And yet I cry in anguish, as I hear
   The long-drawn pageant of your passage roll
   Magnificently forth into the night.
To yon fair land ye come from, to yon sphere
   Of strength and love where now ye shape your flight,
   O even wings of music, bear my soul!

Ye have the power, if but ye had the will,
   Strong-smitten steady chords in sequence grand,
   To bear me forth into that tranquil land
Where good is no more raveled up with ill;
Where she and I, remote upon some hill
   Or by some quiet river's windless strand,
   May live, and love, and wander hand in hand,
And follow nature simply, and be still.

From this grim world, where, sadly prisoned, we
   Sit bound with others' heart-strings as with chains,
   And, if one moves, all suffer, – to that goal,
If such a land, if such a sphere, there be,
   Thither, from life and all life's joys and pains,
   O even wings of music, bear my soul!

9

Fear not, dear friend, but freely live your days
   Though lesser lives should suffer. Such am I,
   A lesser life, that what is his of sky
Gladly would give for you, and what of praise.
Step, without trouble, down the sunlit ways.
   We that have touched your raiment, are made whole
   From all the selfish cankers of man's soul,
And we would see you happy, dear, or die.

Therefore be brave, and therefore, dear, be free;
Try all things resolutely, till the best,
Out of all lesser betters, you shall find;
And we, who have learned greatness from you, we,
Your lovers, with a still, contented mind,
See you well anchored in some port of rest.

10

The Touch of Life

I saw a circle in a garden sit
Of dainty dames and solemn cavaliers,
Whereof some shuddered at the burrowing nit,
And at the carrion worm some burst in tears:
And all, as envying the abhorred estate
Of empty shades and disembodied elves,
Under the laughing stars, early and late,
Sat shamefast at their birth and at themselves.
The keeper of the house of life is fear:
In the rent lion is the honey found
By him that rent it; out of stony ground
The toiler, in the morning of the year,
Beholds the harvest of his grief abound
And the green corn put forth the tender ear.

11

The Arabesque
(Complaint of an Artist)

I made a fresco on the coronal,
Amid the sounding silence and the void
Of life's wind-swept and unfrequented hall.
I drew the nothings that my soul enjoyed;
The petty image of the enormous fact
I fled; and when the sun soared over all
And threw a brightness on the painted tract,
Lo, the vain lines were reading on the wall!
    In vain we think; our life about us lies
O'erscrawled with crooked writ; we toil in vain
To hear the hymn of ancient harmonies
That quire upon the mountain or the plain;
And from the august silence of the skies
Babble of speech returns to us again.

Rondeaux

1

Nous n'irons plus au bois

We'll walk the woods no more
But stay beside the fire,
To weep for old desire
And things that are no more.
  The woods are spoiled and hoar,
The ways are full of mire;
We'll walk the woods no more
But stay beside the fire.
  We loved in days of yore
Love, laughter and the lyre.
Ah God but death is dire
And death is at the door –
We'll walk the woods no more.

2

Far have you come my lady from the town,
And far from all your sorrows, if you please,
To smell the good sea-winds and hear the seas
And in green meadows lay your body down.
To find your pale face grow from pale to brown,
Your sad eyes growing brighter by degrees;
Far have you come my lady from the town
And far from all your sorrows if you please.

Here in this seaboard land of old renown,
In meadow grass go wading to the knees;
Bathe your whole soul awhile in simple ease;
There is no sorrow but the sea can drown;
Far have you come my lady from the town.

3

'Since I am sworn to live my life
And not to keep an easy heart,
Some men may sit and drink apart,
I bear a banner in the strife.

'Some can take quiet thought to wife,
I am all day at *tierce* and *carte*,

Since I am sworn to live my life
And not to keep an easy heart.

'I follow gaily to the fife,
Leave Wisdom bowed above a chart,
And Prudence brawling in the mart,
And dare Misfortune to the knife,
Since I am sworn to live my life.'

4

In Autumn when the woods are red
And skies are gray and clear,
The sportsmen seek the wild fowls' bed
Or follow down the deer;
And Cupid hunts by haugh and head,
By riverside and mere.
I walk, not seeing where I tread
And keep my heart with fear.
Sir, have an eye on where you tread,
And keep your heart with fear,
For something lingers here;
A touch of April not yet dead,
In Autumn when the woods are red.

5

Of his Pitiable Transformation

I who was young so long,
    Young and alert and gay,
    Now that my hair is gray,
Begin to change my song.

Now I know right from wrong,
    Now I know *pay* and *pray*,
    I who was young so long,
Young and alert and gay.

Now I follow the throng,
    Walk in the beaten way,
    Hear what the elders say,
And I own that I was wrong –
I who was young so long.

Poems: 1879–80

I

Know you the river near to Grez,
   A river deep and clear?
Among the lilies all the way,
That ancient river runs today
   From snowy weir to weir.

Old as the Rhine of great renown,
   She hurries clear and fast,
She runs amain by field and town,
From south to north, from up to down.
   To present on from past.

The love I hold was borne by her;
   And now, though far away,
My lonely spirit hears the stir
Of water round the starling spur
   Beside the bridge at Grez.

So may that love for ever hold
   In life an equal pace;
So may that love grow never old,
But, clear and pure and fountain-cold,
   Go on from grace to grace.

II

The wind blew shrill and smart,
   And the wind awoke my heart
Again to go a-sailing o'er the sea,
   To hear the cordage moan
   And the straining timbers groan,
And to see the flying pennon lie a-lee.

O sailor of the fleet,
   It is time to stir the feet;
It's time to man the dinghy and to row!
   It's lay your hand in mine
   And it's empty down the wine,
And it's drain a health to death before we go!

To death, my lads, we sail;
   And it's death that blows the gale
And death that holds the tiller as we ride.

For he's the king of all
In the tempest and the squall,
And the ruler of the Ocean wild and wide!

III

The cock's clear voice into the clearer air
    Where westward far I roam,
Mounts with a thrill of hope,
    Falls with a sigh for home.

A rural sentry, he from farm and field
    The coming morn descries,
And, mankind's bugler, wakes
    The camp of enterprise.

He sings the morn upon the westward hills
    Strange and remote and wild;
He sings it in the land
    Where once I was a child.

He brings to me dear voices of the past,
    The old land and the years:
My father calls for me,
    My weeping spirit hears.

Fife, fife, into the golden air, O bird,
    And sing the morning in;
For the old days are past
    And newer days begin.

IV

Of where or how, I nothing know,
    And why I do not care.
    Enough if even so,
My travelling eyes, my travelling mind can go
By flood and field and hill, by wood and meadow fair,
Beside the Susquehanna and along the Delaware.

I think, I hope, I dream no more
    The dreams of otherwhere,
    The cherished thoughts of yore;
I have been changed from what I was before,
Or breathed perchance too deep the lotus of the air
Beside the Susquehanna and along the Delaware.

Though westward steers the train, my soul
   Shall for the East declare;
   Shall take the East for goal,
Outward and upward bound; and still shall roll,
And still unconquered live, as now she spurns despair
Beside the Susquehanna and along the Delaware.

Unweary, God me yet shall bring
   To lands of brighter air,
   Where I, now half a king,
Shall with superber spirit boldlier sing,
And wear a bolder front than that which now I wear,
Beside the Susquehanna and along the Delaware.

V

It's forth across the roaring foam and on towards the west,
It's many a lonely league from home, o'er many a mountain crest,
From where the dogs of Scotland call the sheep around the fold
To where the flags are flying beside the Gates of Gold.

Where all the deep-sea galleons ride that come to bring the corn,
Where falls the fog at eventide and blows the breeze at morn,
It's there that I was sick and sad, alone and poor and cold,
In yon distressful city beside the Gates of Gold.

I slept as one that nothing knows; but far along my way
Before the morning God arose and planned the coming day;
Afar before me forth he went, as through the sands of old,
And chose the friends to help me beside the Gates of Gold.

I have been near, I have been far, my back's been at the wall
Yet aye and ever shone the star to guide me through it all;
The love of God, the help of man, they both shall make me bold
Against the gates of darkness as beside the Gates of Gold.

VI

What man may learn, what man may do,
Of right or wrong, of false or true,
While, skipper-like, his course he steers
Through nine and twenty mingled years:
Half misconceived and half forgot
So much I know and practise not.

Old are the words of wisdom, old
The counsels of the wise and bold:
To close the ears, to check the tongue,
To keep the pining spirit young;
To act the right, to say the true,
And to be kind whate'er you do.

Thus we across the modern stage
Follow the wise of every age;
And, as oaks grow and rivers run
Unchanged in the unchanging sun,
So the eternal march of man
Goes forth on an eternal plan.

VII

The Piper: 'Inveni Portum'

Again I hear you piping, for I know the tune so well –
    You that rouse the heart to wander and be free,
Tho' where you learned your music, not the God of song can tell
    For you pipe the open highway and the sea.
O piper, lightly footing, lightly piping on your way,
    Tho' your music thrills, and pierces far and near,
I tell you you had better pipe to some one else today,
    For you cannot pipe my fancy from my dear.

You sound the note of travel through the hamlet and the town;
    You would lure the holy angels from on high;
And not a man can hear you, but he throws the hammer down
    And is off to see the countries ere he die.
But now no more I wander, now unchanging here I stay;
    By my love, you find me safely sitting here;
And pipe you ne'er so sweetly, till you pipe the hills away,
    You can never pipe my fancy from my dear.

VIII

Small is the trust when love is green
    In the sap of early years;
A little thing steps in between
    And kisses turn to tears.

Awhile – and see how love be grown
    In loveliness and power!
Awhile, it loves the sweets alone,
    But next it loves the sour.

A little love is none at all
    That wanders or that fears;
A hearty love dwells still at call
    To kisses or to tears.

Such then be mine, my love, to give
    And such be yours to take: –
A faith to hold, a life to live,
    For loving kindness' sake: –

Should you be sad, should you be gay,
    Or should you prove unkind,
A love to hold the growing way
    And keep the helping mind: –

A love to turn the laugh on care
    When wrinkled care appears,
And, with an equal will, to share
    Your kisses and your tears.

More Pieces in Scots

I

To the Commissioners of Northern Lights, with a Paper

I send to you, commissioners,
A paper that may please ye, sirs,
(For troth they say it micht be worse
    An' I believ't)
And on your business lay my curse
    Before I leav't.

I thocht I'd serve wi' you, sirs, yince,
But I've thocht better of it since;
The maitter I will nowise mince,
    But tell ye true:
I'll service wi' some ither prince,
    An' no wi' you.

I've no been very deep, ye'll think,
Cam' delicately to the brink
An' when the water gart me shrink
    Straucht took the rue,
An' didna stoop my fill to drink –
    I own it true.

I kent on cape and isle, a light
Burnt fair an' clearly ilka night;
But at the service I took fright,
      As sune's I saw,
An' being still a neophite
            Gaed straucht awa.

Anither course I now begin,
The weeg I'll cairry for my sin,
The court my voice sall echo in,
      An' – wha can tell? –
Some ither day I may be yin
            O' you mysel'.

II

To Mesdames Zassetsky and Garschine

The wind may blaw the lee-lang way
And aye the lift be mirk an' gray,
An' deep the moss and steigh the brae
      Where a' maun gang –
There's still an hoor in ilka day
            For luve and sang.

And canty hearts are strangly steeled.
By some dikeside they'll find a bield,
Some couthy neuk by muir or field
      They're sure to hit,
Where, frae the blatherin' wind concealed,
            They'll rest a bit.

An' weel' for them if kindly fate
Send ower the hills to them a mate;
They'll crack a while o' Kirk an' State,
      O' yowes an' rain:
And when it's time to tak' the gate,
            Tak' ilk his ain.

– Sic neuk beside the southern sea
I soucht – sic place o' quiet lee
Frae a' the winds o' life. To me,
      Fate, rarely fair,
Had set a freendly company
            To meet me there.

Kindly by them they gart me sit,
An' blythe was I to bide a bit.
Licht as o' some hame fireside lit
    My life for me.
– Ower early maun I rise an' quit
    This happy lee.

III

To Charles Baxter

Noo lyart leaves blaw ower the green,
Reid are the bonny woods o' Dean,
An' here we're back in Embro, frien':
    To pass the winter,
Whilk noo, wi' frosts afore, draws in,
    An' snaws ahint her.

I've seen 's hae days to fricht us a',
The Pentlands poothered weel wi' snaw,
The ways half smoored wi' liquid thaw
    An' half congealin', –
The snell an' scowtherin' norther blaw
    Frae blae Brunteelan'.

I've seen 's been unco sweir to sally
And at the door-cheeks daff an' dally –
Seen 's daidle thus an' shilly shally
    For near a minute,
Sae cauld the wind blew up the valley,
    The deil was in it!

Syne spread the silk an' tak the gate,
In blast an' blaudin' rain, deil hae 't!
The hale toon glintin', stane an' slate,
    Wi' cauld an' weet,
An' to the Court, gin we 'se be late,
    Bicker oor feet.

And at the Court, tae, aft I saw
Whaur Advocates by twa an' twa
Gang gesterin' end to end the ha'
    In weeg an' goon,
To crack o' what ye wull but Law
    The hale forenoon –

That muckle ha', maist like a kirk,
I've kent at braid mid-day sae mirk
Ye'd seen white weegs an' faces lurk
      Like ghaists frae Hell,
But whether Christian ghaists or Turk
      Deil ane could tell.

The three fires lunted in the gloom,
The wind blew like the blast o' doom,
The rain upo' the roof abune
      Played Peter Dick –
Ye wadnae'd licht enough i' the room
      Your teeth to pick.

But, freend, ye ken how me an' you,
The ling-lang lanely winter through,
Keep'd a guid speerit up, an' true
      To lore Horatian,
We aye the ither bottle drew –
      To inclination.

Sae let us in the comin' days
Stand sicker on oor auncient ways, –
The strauchtest road in a' the maze
      Since Eve ate apples;
An' let the winter weet oor cla'es –
      We'll weet oor thrapples.

IV

*To the same, on the death of their common
friend, Mr John Adam, Clerk of Court*

An' Johnie's deid. The mair's the pity!
He's deid, an' deid o' Aqua-vitae.
O Embro', you're a shrunken city,
      Noo Johnie's deid!
Tak hands, an' sing a burial ditty
      Ower Johnie's heid.

To see him was baith drink an' meat,
Gaun linkin' glegly up the street.
He but to rin or tak a seat,
      The wee bit body!
Bein' aye unsicker on his feet
      Wi' whusky toddy.

To be aye tosh was Johnie's whim.
There's nane was better tent than him,
Though whiles his gravit-knot wad clim'
          Ahint his ear,
An' whiles he'd buttons oot or in
          The less or mair.

His hair a'lank about his bree,
His tap-lip lang by inches three –
A slockened sort o' mou', to pree
          A'sensuality –
A drouthy glint was in his e'e,
          An' personality.

An' day an' nicht, frae daw to daw,
Dink an' perjink an' doucely braw,
Wi' a kind o' Gospel look ower a',
          May or October,
Like Peden, followin' the Law
          An' no that sober.

An' wow! but John was unco sport.
Whiles he wad smile aboot the Court
Malvolio-like – whiles snore an' snort,
          Was heard afar.
The idle writer lads' resort
          Was aye John's bar.

Whusky an' he were pack thegether.
Whate'er the hour, whate'er the weather,
John kept himsel' wi' mistened leather
          An' kindled spunk.
Wi' him, there was nae askin' whether –
          John was aye drunk.

The auncient heroes gash an' bauld
In the uncanny days of Auld,
The task ance found to which th'were called,
          Stack stenchly to it.
His life sic noble lives recalled,
          Little's he knew it.

Single an' straucht, he went his way.
He kept the faith an' played the play.
Whusky an' he were man an' may
          Whate'er betided.
Bonny in life – in death, thir twae
          Were no' divided.

What's merely humorous or bonny
The warl' regairds wi' cauld astony.
Drunk men tak' aye mair place than ony;
    An' sae, ye see,
The gate was aye ower thrang for Johnie –
    Or you an' me.

John micht hae jingled cap an' bells,
Been a braw fule in silks an' tells,
In ane o' the auld warl's canty hells,
    Paris or Sodom.
O – I wadnae had him naething else
    But Johnie Adam.

He suffered – as have a' that wan
Eternal memory frae man,
Sin' e'er the weary warl' began –
    Mister or Madam,
Keats or Scots Burns, the Spanish Dan
    Or Johnie Adam.

We leuch, an' Johnie deid. An', fegs!
Hoo he had keept his stoiterin' legs
Sae lang's he did, 's a fact that begs
    An explanation.
He stachers fifty years – syne flegs
    To's destination.

V

Song

Sit doon by me, my canty freend,
    Sit doon, an' snuff the licht!
A boll o' bear's in ilka glass
    Ye'se drink wi' me the nicht!

CHORUS
Let preachers prate o' soberness
    An' brand us ripe for doom,
Yet still we'll lo'e the brimmin' glass,
    And still we'll hate the toom.

There's fire an' life in ilka glass,
    There's blythesomeness an' cheer,
There's thirst an' what'll slocken it,
    There's love and laughter here.

O mirk an' black the lee-lang gate
　　That we maun gang the nicht,
But aye we'll pass the brimmin' glass
　　An' aye we'll snuff the licht.

We'll draw the closer roond the fire
　　And aye the closer get.
Without the ways may thaw or freeze,
　　Within we're ravin' wet!

VI

Auld Reekie

When chitterin' cauld the day sall daw,
Loud may your bonny bugles blaw
　　And loud your drums may beat.
Hie owre the land at evenfa'
Your lamps may glitter raw by raw,
　　Along the gowsty street.

I gang nae mair whaur ance I gaed,
By Brunston, Fairmileheid, or Braid;
　　But far frae Kirk and Tron.
O still, ayont the muckle sea,
Still are ye dear, and dear to me,
　　Auld Reekie, still and on!

VII

To C. W. Stoddard

Ne sutor ultra crepidam;
An', since that I a Scotsman am,
The Lallan ait I weel may toot
As ye can blaw the English flute;
An' sae, without a wordie mair
The braidest Scots ma turn sail sair'.

Of a' the lingo's ever prentit
The braidest Scot's the best inventit,
Since, Stoddard, by a straik o' God's,
The mason-billies cuist their hods,
And a' at ance began to gabble
Aboot the unfeenished wa's o' Babel.

Shakespeare himsel' (in Henry Fift)
To clerk the Lallan made a shift;

An' Homer's aft been heard to mane:
'Waesucks, could I but live again!
Had I the Scottish Language kennt,
I wad hae clerk't the *Iliad* in't!'

(*Follows the Aria*)

Far had I rode an' muckle seen
    An' witnessed mony a ferlie,
Afore that I had clappit e'en
    Upo' my billy, Chärlie.

Far had I rode an' muckle seen
    In lands accountit foreign,
An' had foregather'd wi' a wheen
    Or I fell in wi' Warren.

Far had I rode an'muckle seen,
    But ne'er was fairly doddered
Till I was trystit as a frien'
    Wi' Chärlie Warren Stoddard!

VIII

When I was young and drouthy
    I kent a public hoose
Whaur a' was cosh an' couthy;
    It's there that I was crouse!
It's there that me an' Thamson
    In days I weep to mind,
Drank Wullywauchts like Samson
    An' sang like Jenny Lind.
We cracked o' serious maitters
    We quarrelt and we grat;
Like kindly disputators
    Our whustles weel we wat.

A grieve frae by Langniddry,
    Wha drank hissel to death,
Was great upon sculdiddry
    And curious pints o' faith.

The grieve was in the centre,
    Wi' Thamson close anigh,
An' Doctor Brown's prezentor
    Was often there forby.

Wi' mair I neednae mention
Tho' a' were decent folk –
That public hoose convention
Is now forever broke!

(Air: *Jerusalem the Golden*)

For some are deid an' buried
An' dootless gane to grace;
And ither some are merried,
Or had to leave the place.

And some hae been convertit
An' weirs the ribbon blue
And few, as it's assertit,
Are gude for muckle noo!

IX

O dinnae mind the drams ye drink
Nor whatten things betide.
There's naething maitters noo or syne:
The Lord'll can provide!

Tho' weans, frae different mithers, thrang,
O dinnae cease to ride!
It's only haulf-a-croon a week:
The Lord'll can provide!

Tho' muckle-bellied creditors
Spring gleg on ilka side,
O borrow, borrow, borrow the mair:
The Lord'll can provide!

Tho' jolterin hands the toddy spill
An' Tremens claim his bride,
O never ye fash, for health or cash:
The Lord'll can provide!

Of a' the wauf and shiftless lairds
Frae Coppersmith to Clyde,
What maitters if the warst's yersell:
The Lord'll can provide.

What though your wee bit shoppie's steeked?
An' what though alms' denied?

An elder still you'll hae your will:
The Lord'll can provide.
                        Thomson
                      Toddy hill
                    By Sculduddery
                    Glen Tosh

X

Athole Brose

Willie an' I cam doun by Blair
    And in by Tullibardine,
The kye were at the waterside,
    An' bee-skeps in the garden.
I saw the reek of a private still –
    Says I, 'Gud Lord, I thank ye!'
As Willie and I cam in by Blair
    And out by Killiecrankie.

Ye hinny bees, ye smuggler lads,
    Thou, Muse, the bard's protector,
I never kent what kye were for
    Till I had drunk the nectar!
And shall I never drink it mair?
    Gud troth, I beg your pardon!
The neist time I come doun by Blair
    And in by Tullibardine.

XI

Impromptu Verses Presented to Girolamo, Count Nerli

Did ever mortal man hear tell of sae singular a ferlie,
As the coming to Apia here of the painter, Mr Nerli?
He cam; and O, for a hunner pound, of a' he was the pearlie
The pearl of a' the painter folk was surely Mr Nerli.
He took a thraw to paint mysel, he painted late and early:
O wow! the mony a yawn I've yawned in the beard of Mr Nerli!
Whiles I would sleep an' whiles would wake, an' whiles was mair than surly.
I wondered sair as I sat there fornenst the eyes of Nerli:
'O, will he paint me the way I want, as bonny as a girlie,
Or will he paint me an ugly tyke, and be damned to Mr Nerli!'
But still and on and whichever it is, he is a canty Kerlie.
The Lord proteck the back and neck of honest Mr Nerli.

Vailima, Samoa. Sept. 1892.

The Vailima Family

I

Mother and Daughter

High as my heart! – the quip be mine
That draws their stature to a line,
My pair of fairies plump and dark,
The dryads of my cattle park.
Here by my window close I sit
And watch (and my heart laughs at it)
How these my dragon-lilies are
Alike and yet dissimilar.
From European womankind
They are divided and defined
By the free limb and the plain mind,
The nobler gait, the naked foot,
The indiscreeter petticoat;
And show, by each endearing cause,
More like what Eve in Eden was: –
Buxom and free, flowing and fine,
In every limb, in every line,
Inimitably feminine.
Like ripe fruit on the espaliers
Their sun-bepainted hue appears,
And the white lace (when lace they wear)
Shows on their golden breast more fair.
So far the same they seem. And yet
One apes the shrew, one the coquette: –
A sybil or a truant child,
One runs – with a crop halo – wild;
And one, more sedulous to please,
Her long dark hair, deep as her knees
And thrid with living silver, sees.

What need have I of wealth or fame,
A club, an often-printed name?
It more contents my heart to know
Them going simply to and fro;
To see the dear pair pause and pass
Girded, among the drenching grass,
In the resplendent sun; or hear,
When the huge moon delays to appear,
Their kindred voices sounding near
In the verandah twilight. So
Sound ever; so for ever go
And come upon your strong brown feet:

Twin honours, to my country seat
And its too happy master lent:
My solace and its ornament!

II

The Daughter

TEUILA – HER NATIVE NAME – THE ADORNER

Man, child or woman, none from her,
The insatiable embellisher,
Escapes! She leaves, where'er she goes,
A wreath, a ribbon, or a rose:
A bow or else a button changed,
Two hairs coquettishly deranged,
Some vital trifle, takes the eye
And shows the Adorner has been by.
Is fortune more obdurate grown?
And does she leave my dear alone
With none to adorn, none to caress?
Straight on her proper loveliness
She broods and lingers, cuts and carves,
With combs and brushes, rings and scarves.
The treasure of her hair she takes;
Therewith a new presentment makes.
Babe, goddess, naïad of the grot; –
And weeps if any like it not!

Her absent, she shall still be found,
A posse of native maids around
Her and her whirring instrument
Collected, and on learning bent.
Oft clustered by her tender knees
(Smiling himself) the gazer sees,
Compact as flowers in garden beds,
The smiling faces and shaved heads
Of the brown island babes: with whom
She exults to decorate her room,
To draw them, cheer them when they cry,
And still to pet and prettify.

Or see, as in a looking-glass,
Her pigmy, dimpled person pass,
Nought great therein but eyes and hair,
On her true business here and there:
Her huge, half-naked staff, intent,

See her review and regiment,
An ant with elephants! and how
A smiling mouth, a clouded brow,
Satire and turmoil, quips and tears,
She deals among her grenadiers!
Her pantry and her kitchen squad,
Six-footers all, hang on her nod,
Incline to her their martial chests,
With schoolboy laughter hail her jests,
And pay her in her girded dress
Obsequious obeisances.

But rather to behold her when
She plies for me the unresting pen
And while her crimson blood peeps out,
Hints a suggestion, halts a doubt,
Laughs at a jest; or with a shy
Glance of a particoloured eye
Half brown, half gold, approves, delights
And warms the slave for whom she writes!

So, dear, may you be never done
Your pretty, busy round to run,
And show, with changing frocks and scents,
Your ever-varying lineaments:
Your saucy step, your languid grace,
Your sullen and your smiling face,
Sound sense, true valour, baby fears,
And bright unreasonable tears:
The Hebe of our aging tribe:
Matron and child, my friend and scribe!

III

About my fields, in the broad sun
And blaze of noon, there goeth one
Barefoot and robed in blue, to scan
With the hard eye of the husbandman
My harvests and my cattle. Her,
When even puts the birds astir
And day has set in the great woods,
We seek, among her garden roods,
With bells and cries in vain: the while
Lamps, plate and the decanter smile
On the forgotten board. But she,
Deaf, blind, and prone on face and knee,

Forgets time, family and feast
And digs like a demented beast.

IV

Tall as a guardsman, pale as the east at dawn,
Who strides in strange apparel on the lawn?
Rails for his breakfast? routs his vassals out
(Like boys escaped from school) with song and shout?
Kind and unkind, his Maker's final freak,
Part we deride the child, part dread the antique!
See where his gang, like frogs, among the dew
Crouch at their duty, an unquiet crew;
Adjust their staring kilts; and their swift eyes
Turn still to him who sits to supervise.
He in the midst, perched on a fallen tree,
Eyes them at labour; and, guitar on knee,
Now ministers alarm, now scatters joy,
Now twangs a halting chord – now tweaks a boy.
Thorough in all, my resolute vizier,
Plays both the despot and the volunteer,
Exacts with fines obedience to my laws,
– And for his music, too, exacts applause.

V

What glory for a boy of ten,
Who now must three gigantic men,
And two enormous, dapple gray
New Zealand pack-horses, array
And lead, and, wisely resolute
Our day-long business execute
In the far shore-side town. His soul
Glows in his bosom like a coal;
His innocent eyes glitter again,
And his hand trembles on the rein.
Once he reviews his whole command
And chivalrously planting hand
On hip – a borrowed attitude –
Rides off downhill into the wood.

VI

The old lady (so they say) but I
Admire your young vitality.
Still brisk of foot, still busy and keen,

In and about and up and down.
To hear you pass with bustling feet
The long verandah round and beat
Your bell, and 'Lotu, lotu' cry:
Thus calling our queer company
At morning or at evening dim,
To prayers and the oft mangled hymn.

VII

Tusitala

I meanwhile, in the populous house apart,
Sit snugly, chambered, and my silent art
Uninterrupted, unremitting ply,
Before the dawn by morning lamplight, by
The glow of sweltering noon, and when the sun
Dips past my westward peak and day is done:
So, bending still over my trade of words,
I hear the morning and the evening birds,
The morning and the evening stars behold.
So there apart I sit, as once of old,
Napier in wizard Merchiston; and my
Brown innocent aides in house and husbandry
Wonder askance. *What ails the Boss?* they ask.
Him, richest of the rich, an endless task
Before the earliest birds or servants stir
Calls, and detains him daylong prisoner.
He, whose innumerable dollars hewed
This cleft in the boar- and devil-haunted wood,
And bade therein, far seen to seas and skies,
His many-windowed, painted palace rise,
Red-roofed, blue-walled, a rainbow on the hill,
A wonder in the wild-wood glade: he still,
Unthinkable Aladdin, dawn and dark,
Scribbles and scribbles like a German clerk.
We see the fact, but tell, O tell us why?
My reverend washman and wise butler cry,
And from their lips the unanswered questions drop:
How can he live that does not keep a shop?
And why does he, being acclaimed so rich,
Not dwell with other gentry on the beach?
But harbour, impiously brave,
In the cold uncanny wood, haunt of the fleeing slave?
The sun and the loud rain here alternate:
Here, in the unfathomable bush, the great
Voice of the wind makes a magnanimous sound;

Here too, no doubt, the shouting doves abound
To be a dainty; here, in the twilit stream
That brawls adown the forest, frequent gleam
The jewel-eyes of crawfish. These be good:
Grant them! and can the thing be understood?
That this white chief, whom no distress compels,
Far from all compeers, in the mountain dwells?
And finds a manner of living to his wish
Apart from high society – and sea fish!

VIII

These rings, O my beloved pair,
For me on your brown fingers wear:
Each, a perpetual caress,
To tell you of my tenderness.

Let – when at morning as ye rise
The golden topaz takes your eyes –
To each her emblem whisper sure
Love was awake an hour before.

Ah yes! an hour before ye woke
Low to my heart *my* emblem spoke,
And grave, as to renew an oath,
It I have kissed, and blessed you both.

Occasional Verse

Epistles and Verses Addressed to Friends and Family

I

To Charles Baxter

(a)

Reaped grain should fill the reaper's grange.
My fate for thine I would not change.
Thy pathway would to me be strange,
　　And strange to thee
The limits of the daily range
　　That pleases me.

For me, I do but ask such grace
As Icarus. Bright breathing space –

One glorious moment – face to face,
        The sun and he!
The next, fit grave for all his race,
        The splendid sea.

The father, rich in forty years
Of poor experience culled in tears,
Meanly restrained by sordid fears
        Went limping home
And hung his pinions by the spears,
        No more to roam.

O more to me a thousand fold
The son's brief triumph, wisely bold
To separate from the common fold,
        The general curse,
The accustomed way of growing old
        And growing worse.

O happy lot! A heart of fire,
In the full flush of young desire,
Not custom-taught to shun the mire
        And hold the wall,
His sole experience to aspire,
        To soar and fall.

His golden hap it was to go
Straight from the best of life below
To life above. Not his to know
        O greatly blest,
How deadly weary life can grow
        To e'en the best.

Sad life, whose highest lore, in vain
The nobler summits to attain,
Still bids me draw the kindly strain
        Of love more tight,
And ease my individual pain
        In your delight.

For I, that would be blithe and merry,
Prefer to call Marsala sherry,
When duty-bound to cross the ferry
        Believe it smooth,
And under pleasant fictions bury
        Distasteful truth.

And hence I banish wisdom, set
The sole imperial coronet
On cheerful Folly, at regret
    Pull many a mouth,
Drown care in jovial bouts – and yet
    Sigh for the South!

(b)

Blame me not that this epistle
  Is the first you have from me.
    Idleness has held me fettered;
    But at last the times are bettered
And once more I wet my whistle
  Here, in France beside the sea.

All the green and idle weather
  I have had in sun and shower
    Such an easy, warm subsistence,
    Such an indolent existence
I should find it hard to sever
  Day from day and hour from hour.

Many a tract-provided ranter
  May up-braid me, dark and sour,
    Many a bland Utilitarian
    Or excited Millenarian,
  – 'Pereunt et imputantur
  You must speak to every hour.'

But (the very term's deceptive)
  You at least, my friend, will see
    That in sunny grassy meadows
    Trailed across by moving shadows
To be actively receptive
  Is as much as man can be.

He that all winter grapples
  Difficulties – thrust and ward –
    Needs to cheer him thro' his duty
    Memories of sun and beauty,
Orchards with the russet apples
  Lying scattered on the sward.

Many such I keep in prison,
  Keep them here at heart unseen,
    Till my muse again rehearses

Long years hence, and in my verses
You shall meet them re-arisen
    Ever comely, ever green.

You know how they never perish,
    How, in time of later art,
        Memories consecrate and sweeten
        These defaced and tempest-beaten
Flowers of former years we cherish,
    Half a life, against our heart.

Most, those love-fruits withered greenly,
    Those frail, sickly amourettes,
        How they brighten with the distance
        Take new strength and new existence
Till we see them sitting queenly
    Crowned and courted by regrets!

All the loveliest and best is,
    Aureole-fashion round their head,
        They that looked in life but plainly,
        How they stir our spirits vainly
When they come to us Alcestis-
    Like, returning from the dead!

Not the old love but another,
    Bright she comes at Memory's call,
        Our forgotten vows reviving
        To a newer, livelier living,
As the dead child to the mother
    Seems the fairest child of all.

Thus, our Goethe, sacred master,
    Travelling backward thro' his youth,
        Surely wandered wrong in trying
        To renew the old, undying
Loves that cling in memory faster
    Than they ever lived in truth.

(c)

The wind is without there and howls in the trees,
    And the rain-flurries drum on the glass:
Alone, by the fireside, with elbows on knees
    I can number the hours as they pass.
Yet now, when to cheer me the crickets begin
    And my pipe is just happily lit,

Believe me, my friend, tho' the evening draws in,
    That not all uncontented I sit.

Alone, did I say? O no, nowise alone
    With the Past sitting warm on my knee,
To gossip of days that are over and gone
    But still charming to her and to me.
With much to be glad of and much to deplore,
    Yet, as these days with those we compare,
Believe me, my friend, tho' the sorrows seem more
    They are somehow more easy to bear.

And thou, faded Future, uncertain and frail,
    As I cherish thy light in each draught,
His lamp is not more to the miner – their sail
    Is not more to the crew on the raft.
For Hope can make feeble ones earnest and brave,
    And, as forth thro' the years I look on,
Believe me my friend, between this and the grave
    I see wonderful things to be done.

To do or to try; and, believe me my friend,
    If the call should come early for me,
I can leave these foundations uprooted, and tend
    For some new city over the sea.
To do or to try; and, if failure be mine,
    And if fortune go cross to my plan,
Believe me my friend, tho' I mourn the design,
    I shall never lament for the man.

II

To W. E. Henley

The Gods are dead. Perhaps they are. God knows.
They dwell, at least, in Lemprière undeleted;
And I, lone wandering in a world of prose,
Prefer to think them gracefully retreated
In some still land of lilacs and the rose.

There let them rule some province of repose!
And yet I think I hear the words repeated,
Plangent and sad, on every wind that blows:
    The Gods are dead.

Once high they sat; and high o'er earthly shows,
At their good pleasure all mankind entreated:

Once ... long ago; but now the story goes
That one and all, the awful, the jocose
    Gods are dead.

III

To Horatio F. Brown

Brave lads in olden musical centuries
Sang, night by night, adorable choruses,
    Sat late by ale-house doors in April
Chaunting in joy as the moon was rising.

Moon-seen and merry, under the trellises,
Flush-faced they played with old polysyllables
    Spring scents inspired, old wine diluted,
Love and Apollo were there to chorus.

Now these, the songs, remain to eternity,
Those only, those, the bountiful choristers
    Gone – those are gone, those unremembered
Sleep and are silent in earth forever.

So man himself appears and evanishes,
So smiles and goes; as wanderers halting at
    Some green-embowered house, play their music,
Play and are gone on the windy highway;

Yet dwells the strain enshrined in the memory
Long after they departed eternally,
    Forth-faring toward far mountain summits
Cities of men or the sounding ocean.

Youth sang the song in years immemorial
Brave chanticleer he sang and was beautiful;
    Bird-haunted, green tree-tops in April
Heard and were pleased by the voice of singing.

Youth goes and leaves behind him a prodigy –
Songs sent by thee afar from Venetian
    Sea-gray lagunes, sea-paven highways,
Dear to me here in my Alpine exile.

IV

To Mrs MacMorland

Im Schnee der Alpen – so it runs
    To those divine accords – : and here
We dwell in Alpine snows and suns,
    A motley crew, for half the year:
A motley crew we dwell, to taste –
    A shivering band in hope and fear –
That sun upon the snowy waste,
    That Alpine ether cold and clear.

Up from the laboured plain, and up
    From low sea-levels, we arise
To drink of that diviner cup,
    The rarer air, the clearer skies;
For, as the great, old, godly King
    From mankind's turbid valley cries,
So all we mountain-lovers sing:
    I to the hills will lift mine eyes!

The bells that ring, the peaks that climb,
    The frozen snow's unbroken curd
Might well revindicate in rhyme
    The pauseless stream, the absent bird:
In vain – for to the deeps of life
    You, lady, you, my heart have stirred;
And since you say you love my wife,
    Be sure I love you for the word.

Of kindness, here, I nothing say –
    Such loveless kindnesses there are
In that grimacing, common way,
    That old, unhonoured social war:
Love but my dog and love my love,
    Adore with me a common star –
I value not the rest above
    The ashes of a bad cigar.

V

To A. G. Dew-Smith
In return for a box of cigarettes

Figure me to yourself, I pray –
    A man of my peculiar cut –
Apart from dancing and deray,
    Into an Alpine valley shut:

Shut in a kind of damned Hotel
    Discountenanced by God and man:
The food? – Sir, you would do as well
    To cram your belly full of bran!

The company? Alas the day,
    That I should dwell with such a crew
With devil anything to say
    Nor anyone to say it to!

The place? – Although they call it Platz,
    I will be bold and state my view:
Its not a place at all – and that's
    The bottom verity, my Dew.

There are, as I will not deny,
    Innumerable inns; a road;
Several Alps indifferent high,
    The snow's inviolable abode;

Eleven English parsons, all
    Entirely inoffensive; four
True human beings – what I call
    Human – the deuce a cipher more;

A climate of surprising worth;
    Innumerable dogs that bark;
Some air, some weather, and some earth;
    A native race – God save the mark!

A race that works yet cannot work,
    Yodels but cannot yodel right,
Such as, unhelpt, with rusty dirk,
    God help me, I could wholly smite;

A river that from morn to night
    Down all the valley plays the fool;
Nor once she pauses in her flight;
    Nor knows the comforts of a pool;

But still keeps up, by straight or bend,
    The self-same pace that she begun –
Still hurry, hurry, to the end –
    Good God, is that the way to run?

If I a river were, I hope
    That I should better realise

The opportunities and scope
 Of that romantic enterprise.

I should not ape the merely strange,
 But aim besides at the divine;
And continuity and change
 I still should labour to combine.

Here should I gallop down the race,
 Here charge the sterling like a bull;
There, as a man might wipe his face,
 Lie, pleased and panting, in a pool.

But what, my Dew, in idle mood,
 What prate I, minding not my debt?
What do I talk of bad or good? –
 The best is still a cigarette.

Me, whether evil fate assault,
 Or smiling providences crown –
Whether on high the eternal vault
 Be blue, or crash with thunder down –

I judge the best, whate'er befall,
 Is still to sit on one's behind
And, having duly moistened all,
 Smoke with an unperturbèd mind.

So sitting, so engaged, I write;
 So puffing, so puffed up, I sing,
In modest climates of delight
 And from the islands of the Spring:

My manner, even as I can:
 My matter – Frenchly – to agree
As from a much delighted man,
 A *gift unspeakable to me.*

VI

To Frederick Locker-Lampson

Not roses to the rose, I trow,
 The thistle sends, nor to the bee
Do wasps bring honey. Wherefore now
 Should Locker ask a verse from me?

Martial, perchance – but he is dead;
    And Herrick now must rhyme no more:
Still burning with the Muse, they tread
    (And arm in arm!) the shadowy shore.

They, if they had lived, with dainty hand,
    To music as of mountain brooks,
Might bring you worthy words, to stand
    Unshamed, dear Locker, in your books.

But though these fathers of your race
    Be gone before: yourself a sire
Today you see before your face
    Your stalwart youngsters touch the lyre.

On these, on Lang or Dobson, call,
    Long leaders of the songful feast.
They lend a verse your laughing fall –
    A verse they owe you at the least!

VII

To Master Andrew Lang
On his re-editing of Cupid and Psyche

You, that are much a fisher in the pool
Of things forgotten, and from thence bring up
Gold of old song and diamonds of dead speech,
The scholar, and the angler, and the friend
Of the pale past, this unremembered tale
Restore and this dead author re-inspire;
And lo, oblivion the iniquitous
Remembers, and the stone is rolled away.
And he, the long asleep, sees once again
The busy bookshop; once again is read.

Brave as at first, in his new garb of print,
Shines forth the Elizabethan. But when death,
The unforgetful shepherd, shall have come
And numbered us with these, the numberless,
The inheritors of slumber and neglect –
O correspondent of the immortal dead,
Shall any pious hand re-edit us?

VIII

To Harriet Baker

I was a barren tree before,
    I blew a quenchèd coal,
I could not, on their midnight shore,
    The lonely blind console.

A moment, lend your hand – I bring
    My sheaf for you to bind –
And you can teach my words to sing
    In the darkness of the blind.

Dedications and Presentations

I

To the Hesitating Purchaser
Prefatory verses to *Treasure Island*

If sailor tales to sailor tunes,
    Storm and adventure, heat and cold,
If schooners, islands, and maroons
    And Buccaneers and buried Gold,
And all the old romance, retold
    Exactly in the ancient way,
Can please, as me they pleased of old,
    The wiser youngsters of today:

– So be it, and fall on! If not,
    If studious youth no longer crave,
His ancient appetites forgot,
    Kingston, or Ballantyne the brave,
Or Cooper of the wood and wave:
    So be it, also! And may I
And all my pirates share the grave
    Where these and their creations lie!

II

To Mr and Mrs Robert A. Robertson
Presentation inscription in a copy of *A Child's Garden of Verses*

Before this little gift was come,
The little owner had made haste for home;
And from the door of where the eternal dwell,
Looked back on human things and smiled Farewell.

O may this grief remain the only one!
O may your house keep still a garrison
Of smiling children; and forever more
The tune of little feet be heard along the floor!

III

To H. C. Bunner
Presentation verses with a copy of A Child's Garden of Verses

You know the way to Arcady
Where I was born;
You have been there, and fain
Would there return.
Some that go thither bring with them
Red rose or jewelled diadem
As secrets of the secret king:
I, only what a child would bring.
Yet I do think my song is true;
For this is how the children do:
This is the tune to which they go
In sunny pastures high and low;
The treble pipes not otherwise
Sing daily under sunny skies
In Arcady the dear;
And you who have been there before,
And love that country evermore,
May not disdain to hear.

IV

To Virgil and Dora Williams
Presentation inscription in a copy of The Silverado Squatters

Here from the forelands of the tideless sea,
Behold and take my offering, unadorned
Or – shall we say? defaced by Joseph's art.
In the Pacific air, it sprang; it grew
Among the silence of the Alpine air;
In Scottish heather blossomed; and at last
By that unshaken sapphire, in whose face
Spain, Italy, France, Algiers and Tunis view
Their introverted mountains, came to fruit.
Back now, my Booklet! on the diving ship
And posting on the rails, to home return –
Home, and the friends whose honouring name you bear!

V

To Nelly Van de Grift Sanchez
Presentation verses with a copy of *Prince Otto*

Go, little book – the ancient phrase
And still the daintiest – go your ways,
My Otto, over sea and land,
Till you shall come to Nelly's hand.

How shall I your Nelly know?
By her blue eye and her black brow,
By her fierce and slender look,
And by her goodness, little book!

What shall I say when I come there?
You shall speak her soft and fair:
See – you shall say – the love they send
To greet their unforgotten friend!

Giant Adulpho you shall sing
The next, and then the cradled king:
And the four corners of the roof
Then kindly bless; and to your perch aloof,
Where Balzac all in yellow dressed
And the dear Webster of the west
Encircle the prepotent throne
Of Shakespeare and of Calderon,
Shall climb an upstart.
     There, with these,
You shall give ear to breaking seas
And windmills turning in the breeze,
A distant undetermined din
Without; and you shall hear within
The blazing and the bickering logs,
The crowing child, the yawning dogs,
And ever agile, high and low,
Our Nelly going to and fro.

There shall you all silent sit,
Till, when perchance the lamp is lit
And the day's labour done, she takes
Poor Otto down, and, warming for our sakes,
Perchance beholds, alive and near,
Our distant faces reappear.

VI

To Katharine de Mattos
Ave!

Bells upon the city are ringing in the night;
High above the gardens are the houses full of light;
On the heathy Pentlands is the curlew flying free;
And the broom is blowing bonnie in the north countrie.

It's ill to break the bonds that God decreed to bind,
Still we'll be the children of the heather and the wind;
Far away from home, O, it's still for you and me
That the broom is blowing bonnie in the north countrie!

VII

To Fanny Stevenson

(a)
Verse for her birthday (1887)

What can I wish, what can I promise, dear,
To make you gladder in the coming year?
I wish you – ah, if I could promise too! –
A kinder husband than you ever knew.

(b)
Verse for her birthday (1894)

To the stormy petrel:
                        Ever perilous
And precious, like an ember from the fire
Or gem from a volcano, we today
When the drums of war reverberate in the land
And every face is for the battle blacked,
Nor less the sky that, over sodden woods,
Menaces now in the disconsolate calm
The hurly-burly of the hurricane,
Do now most fitly celebrate your day.

Yet amid turmoil keep for me, my dear,
The kind domestic faggot. Let the hearth
Shine ever as (I praise my honest gods)
In peace and tempest it has ever shone.

(c)
Dedication for *Weir of Hermiston*
To My Wife

I saw rain falling and the rainbow drawn
On Lammermuir. Hearkening I heard again

In my precipitous city beaten bells
Winnow the keen sea wind. And here afar,
Intent on my own race and place, I wrote.
Take thou the writing: thine it is. For who
Burnished the sword, blew on the drowsy coal,
Held still the target higher, chary of praise
And prodigal of censure – who but thou?
So now, in the end, if this the least be good,
If any deed be done, if any fire
Burn in the imperfect page, the praise be thine!

VIII

Dedication {intended for *Songs of Travel?*}

To friends at home, the lone, the admired, the lost,
The gracious old, the lovely young, to May
    The fair, December the beloved,
These from my blue horizon and green isles,
These from this pinnacle of distance, I,
    The unforgetful, dedicate.

IX

To Thomas Hutchinson
Presentation inscription in his copy of *Memories and Portraits*

        Much of my soul lies here interred,
            My very past and mind;
        Who listens nearly to the printed word,
            Shall hear the heart behind.

Epigrams and Satire

I

Here he comes big with Statistics,
    Troubled and sharp about fac's.
He has heaps of the *Form* that is thinkable –
    The *stuff* that is feeling, he lacks.

Do you envy this whiskered absurdity,
    With *pince-nez* and clerical tie?
Poor fellow, he's blind of a sympathy!
    I'd rather be blind of an eye.

II

Browning made the verses,
Your servant the critique.
Browning couldn't sing at all –
I fancy I could speak.
Although his book was clever
(To give the deil his due)
I wasn't pleased with Browning's verse,
Nor he with my review.

III

I had companions, I had friends,
I had of whisky various blends.
The whisky was all drunk; and lo!
The friends were gone for evermo!
And when I marked the ingratitude,
I to my maker turned, and spewed.

IV

Epitaph

The angler rose, he took his rod;
He kneeled and made his prayers to God.
The living God sat overhead:
The angler tripped, the eels were fed.

V

Epigrams from Notebooks

(a)

Of a pair of married folk
Which shall bear the other's yoke?
Oft the mind of lesser stature,
Ofter still the better nature.

(b)

Once a week arrayed anew
People troop to bench and pew;
They give that poor relation, God,
A copper and a distant nod.

(c)

I wrote her name in snow last year
And thought to grave my love in stone;
She spoke three words, the sun broke forth,
And lo! both love and snow were gone.

VI

O Pilot! 'tis a fearful night,
    And I am fearful too;
The billows are a bloody height,
    The vessel far from new.
You strike me as a trifle tight,
    The Captain's worse than you,
I'm sure there's nothing really right
    In either ship or crew.

VII

Awhile you have paused amongst our semi-nude
Brown tattooed islanders, and in our stern
Intensity of forest solitude.
Now to the applauding theatre return
And be the idol of the multitude.

VIII

Let no sour looks degrade my burial day
And when my bones are in the ground
Let the sun shine and the good word go round.
Be to my faults that day a little blind,
My trivial virtues, call them all to mind.

IX

I, whom Apollo sometime visited,
Or feigned to visit, now, my day being done,
Do slumber wholly; nor shall know at all
The weariness of changes, nor perceive
Immeasurable sands of centuries
Drink up the blanching ink, or the loud sound
Of generations beat the music down.

X

Casparides

Eight scurrilous poems against a certain
pastry cook, and a painter, his brother-in-law

1

The Gull along the ocean flits,
Where on the long, sea-levelled sands
The falling breakers toss their hands:
By Babel's old foundation pits,
The lone, besotted Buzzard sits,
Deserted in deserted lands.

Buzzard and gull am I, alas!
And well had borne that shameful pass;
But to be gull to such a crew,
And buzzard to the likes of you,
O Clan Casparis! – fills the glass
And double-donkeyfies the ass.

2

[*Cor meum eructavit.*]

May you, O Sigrist Maler – you
And that uncircumcised Jew,
Your brother, although not by birth,
Full brother in the lack of worth,
Casparis: – may you live and lie,
Beg bestial viands ere you die,
Truckle and juggle, fawn and crawl,
And be rebuffed by one and all!
May, Sigrist, you, some early date
Eat of the fruit your singer ate;
Cheats out of all the winds that blew
Gather to make a gull of you;
Indignant death his sword upraise
To close the scandal of your days;
You and your race together rot
In some forlorn, unsacred spot –
You and your aunts and cousins spoil
Ten thousand fathom deep in soil
Such as, by subterranean sewers,
The million-privied city pours!

3

One day, mustachio'd Sigrist Maler
Choked upon an ill-gotten thaler.

His brother the polite Casparis
Flew to consult the Alpine fairies.
'Save, I beseech you, save my Sigrist
Lest to the devil's mill he bé grist!'
– 'Never,' they said, '*the world and God,*
The retching nations all abroad,
And Satan striving not to spew,
Are all dead sick of him and you.'

4

'*Not for a hundred francs,*' he said,
    Would I so base an action do.'
It somehow slipped into my head:
    'Perhaps you might, you know, for two.'

5

Jacob the first, in Holy Writ,
At least had antenatal wit.
Jacob the Second at Davos
With conscious idiocy glows.
In royal state, mid tarts and pies,
With smiling lips, with goggling eyes,
And smoothing his enormous hands,
The Casparidian Jacob stands.
O not for him, a thousand fold,
The glories of the rogues of old,
The skilful fraud, the loaded dice,
The intellectual parts of vice!
Him rather hath the Lord designed,
In radiant vacancy of mind,
To gape and goggle, duck and grin,
And scrape dishonest groschen in.
He triumphs by his idiot smile;
For who suspects a louse of guile?

6

Sovereign, among its frozen snows,
The jurisdiction of Davos!
Death in the old Landamman's hand –
Death and the ignominious brand
Reside: O wherefore then, my heart
So long delays the avenging dart?
And you, O judge of all your kind
Wherefore to Sigrist still be blind?
Take, then, and at your chariot wheels
Drag, shrieking, by their tethered heels,

Woman by woman, man by man,
Deathward, the whole Casparis Clan!
Clear throughly from their native place
That old predestinated race;
Nor longer in your midst permit
Yon thieving pastry-cook to sit;
His head of wood, his smile of brass,
Forever into limbo pass;
Nor longer shall Casparis dare
Soil with his breech a human chair;
Nor Sigrist of the evasive eye
Longer exist or longer lie.

7

I mark the magistracy pause,
Fear to disgrace the pomp of laws;
And the poor catchpole hanging back,
And bench and dock and clerk in black,
From that vile duty they discharge
And leave my gruesome thieves at large.
Such are the men, I joy to own,
Who from disgust leave vice alone,
And all their righteous blood aboil,
From such as Sigrist back recoil.
He that unblushing crushed a toad
Spares Jacob in his vile abode;
There, let him munch his theftuous nuts
And nourish venom in his guts;
There he and Sigrist, turn by turn,
With fear and envy freeze and burn.

Yet, O Landamman of the Kreis,
You once, they tell, were not so nice.
At your high throne, when calves complained,
A dog was once – a dog – arraigned:
Rickets, the hero of the vale,
Old Rickets of the fleshy tail.

I hear you speak, I hear and bow,
I hear you and am silent now.
'Rickets at least,' I hear you say
'Was noble, dignified and gay.
The calf with all his fathers slept,
None the less nobly Rickets stept.
Him I could judge; but not that man,
Reproach of a dishonoured clan,
Who wriggling on through ill and well,

Reaps hate from Heaven and scorn from Hell.
You take me? I could bring to book
A dog, but not that pastry cook.'

8

[*Exegi monumentum.*]

Muse of my indignation, since
For the first time I felt you wince,
Since into life, O Goddess, first
Your loud octosyllabics burst
And like heroic verses trod
The echoing judgement courts of God:
Since then, O muse, I heretofore
So small a voice among the roar,
So small a figure in the crowd,
I also venture to be proud.

For say, O Goddess, have we not,
In marching measures unforgot,
Immortalised with glee and grief
The trembling and the leering thief,
And placed them by the chemist's door
Pickled and jar'd for evermore.

XI

Brasheana
A sequence of sonnets dedicated to Charles Baxter

1

We found him first as in the dells of May
   The dreaming damsel finds the earliest flower;
   Thoughtless we wandered in the evening hour;
Aimless and pleased we went our random way:
In the foot-haunted city, in the night,
   Among the alternate lamps, we went and came
   Till like a humorous thunderbolt, that name,
The hated name of Brash, assailed our sight.

We saw, we paused, we entered, seeking gin.
   His wrath, like a huge breaker on the beach,
      Broke instant forth. He on the counter beat
      In his infantile fury; and his feet
Danced impotent wrath upon the floor within.
   Still as we fled, we heard his idiot screech.

2

Sir, in one thing, I will commend myself,
   And, doing thus, you also I commend,
My fellow Brashite and most honoured friend,
Of common worth in this: that love of pelf,
Nor love of fame, nor the luxurious feast,
   Nor any piety or fear withheld,
   When once his putty face we had beheld,
Our most invidious visits from the Beast.

Contrariwise, the moon's most holy face
   Beheld us, and the morn beheld, and noon,
Still, as the enamoured hunter drives the chase,
   Brashward our steps directing; and eftsoon
Earth shuddered as it heard, through treble and bass,
   The tortured idiot bawl like a baboon.

3

We found him and we lost. The glorious Brash
   Fell, as the cedar on the mountain side
   When the resounding thunders far and wide
Redoubling grumble, and the instant flash
Divides the night a moment and is gone;
   He fell not unremembered nor unwept;
   And the dim shop where that great hero stept
Is sacred still. We, steering past the Tron,
And past the college southward, and thy square
   Fitz-Symon! reach at last that holier clime,
And do with tears behold that pot-house, where
   Brash the divine once ministered in drink,
Where Brash, the Beershop Hornet, bowed by time,
   In futile anger grinned across the zinc.

4

There let us often wend our pensive way,
   There often pausing celebrate the past;
   For though indeed our Brash be dead at last,
Perchance his spirit, in some minor way,
Nor pure immortal nor entirely dead,
   Contrives upon the farther shore of death
   To pick a rank subsistence, and for breath
Breathes ague, and drinks Acetate of Lead.

There, on the way to that infernal den,
   Where burst the flames forth thickly, and the sky
     Flares horrid through the murk, methinks he doles
     Damned liquors out to Hellward-faring souls,

And as his impotent anger rages high
Gibbers and gurgles at the shades of men.

5

Brash, while he lived, we not deserted; nor,
   When his long rage was over, and his head
Had bowed before the uncomely conqueror,
   Were his achievements disrememberèd.
O not, my friend, by us: we day by day
   Revisit still with ceremonious tread
   The confines of the country of the dead,
And, having briefly jeered him, turn away.

For that which is ideal, shines above
   The powers of observation; – She of Troy,
Still spherèd in the rosy light of love,
   Numbers her lovers: – He, our vanished joy,
     Brash the immortally absurd, receives
     Post-mortem insults still as thick as Autumn leaves!

6

Alas! that while the beautiful and strong,
   The pious and the wise, the grave and gay,
   All journey downward by one common way,
Bewailed and honoured yet with flowers and song,
There must come crowding with that serious throng,
   Jostling the ranks of that discreet array,
   Infirm and scullion spirits of decay,
The dull, the droll, the random and the wrong.

An ape in church, an artificial limb
   Tacked to a marble god serene and blind –
   For such as Brash, high death was not designed,
That canonising rite was not for him;
   Nor where the Martyr and the Hero trod
   Should idiot Brash go hobbling up to God.

7

As the great artists, at the writing desk,
   Or by the enchanted easel, brush in hand,
   Not always lingered in the ideal land,
But stooped with smiling eyes to the Grotesque:
Ev'n thus the Master-Artist, laughing low,
   His Parian clay, his golden moulds, laid by,
   And taking mud and urine, winked his eye
And stirred the abhorrent mixture in a poe.

Long time the broth he simmered, and the excess
 Poured, shuddering, down the sewers that lead to Hell;
 The gross deposit, next, he kneaded well
And formed a goblin from the plastic mess:
 Last, sniggering loud, he dealt the gnome a prod,
 And there was Brash – the Caliban of God!

8

Who that hath walked with nature in her mirth
 But loves the untutored hedgehog in the brush?
 The spotted, wayside toad, who turns to crush,
Or tread the nippered ear-wig in the earth?
All things are lovely as a summer cloud;
 And the bald-headed bard, beside the newt,
 Hath often stayed his meditative foot,
Or o'er the bare-arsed buzzard, wept aloud!

Such is the gospel, such the higher law;
Thus was it both with that immortal goose,
Wordsworth, the poet, and with us, who saw
Nature from forth her caravan produce
 Her Ugliest Bugbear, and with glad surprise
 Fed upon Brash our nature-loving eyes.

9

His gory helm the soldier must unbrace
 Nor always deal destruction on his foes;
The wakefullest watcher seize a breathing space;
 The weary King his coronet depose.
Some count the pustules on the planet's face;
 Some mark the poet while he picks his nose,
And some the monarch as, with stealthy pace
 And shielded taper, toward the Forth he goes.

Among his whelps, around the household fire,
 Brash too may have been human – may perchance,
 As when the graceful dancer leaves the dance,
Have laid aside his ineffectual ire.
 He may. But for the love of all romance,
Breathe not the irreverent fancy, O my lyre!

10

Goodness or Greatness: to be good and die,
 Or to be great and live forever great:
 To be the unknown Smith that saves the state
And blooms unhonoured by the public eye:

To be the unknown Robinson or Brown
  Whose piping virtues perish in the mud;
  Or triumphing in blasphemy and blood,
The imperial pirate, pickled in renown.

Unfaltering Brash the latter member chose
  Of this eterne antithesis; and still
The flower of his immortal memory blows
Where'er the spirits of the loathed repose
  Where'er the trophy of the gibbet hill
Dejects the traveller and collects the crows.

11

Rain, that effaces epitaphs; the gale
  That can the mortared pyramid uproot;
  Irreverent hands; the unregarding foot.
These – while the years, falling, like veil on veil,
Enshroud men's reputations – these assail
  Their unenduring trophies, city or tomb,
Confound the engraven legend of the tale,
  And, man and memory both, involve in gloom.

Type, type, alone survives; and these my lays,
  And him they celebrate, shall yet o'erleap
Our narrow margin of deciduous days,
  And thanks to *Baxter*, shall forever keep
When all their painted fanes have gone to smash,
  Fragrant and green the memory of *Brash*.

XII

Ode by Ben Jonson, Edgar Allan Poe, and a bungler

Long, long ago,
  (It was in the Lothian Road)
I saw two fellows wander long ago.
  So merrily they strode
  So high their spirits glowed,
With twopence in their pockets long ago.

Brash, Brash is dead,
  That immortal Brash is gone
  And the crowds go streaming on,
They go streaming, streaming forward, seeking Brash!
But he
I can see,
On the great Olympus dwells, dispensing trash.

Gin, gin he sells,
    Then as now;
And with infuriate brow
Light-minded drinkers forth he drives, who bow
Not duly unto Brash.

Brash, Brash, Brash,
    How musical they clash
Words of pleasant savour, words endeared of yore!
    But Brash has gone before,
    Godlike Brash is gone.
    From earth's phantasmal shore
      In a flash
      Immortal Brash
    Burst, like Elijah, upward and was gone!

Yet fear not – we shall follow; for wherever
    Great Brash his way made plain, the common herd
    May follow that extraordinary turd
And with no unusual endeavour:
Brash was not wise, nor amiable nor clever;
    Brash was a beast as I have always heard;
    Fate could not act more palpably absurd
Than the dead Brash from other fools to sever.

Let us be fools, my friend, let us be drunken,
    Let us be angry and extremely silly;
        Then though divines and commentators clash,
We, when once dead and dry, dusty and shrunken,
        Buried and bundled hence, shall, willy-nilly,
        Share the eternal destiny of Brash.

Miscellaneous Verse

I

The old Chimaeras, old receipts
    For making 'happy land',
The old political beliefs
    Swam close before my hand.

The grand old communistic myths
    In a middle state of grace,
Quite dead, but not yet gone to Hell,
    And walking for a space,

Quite dead, and looking it, and yet
    All eagerness to show
The Social-Contract forgeries
    By Chatterton – Rousseau –

A hundred such as these I tried,
    And hundreds after that,
I fitted Social Theories
    As one would fit a hat!

Full many a marsh-fire lured me on,
    I reached at many a star,
I reached and grasped them and behold –
    The stump of a cigar!

All through the sultry, sweltering day
    The sweat ran down my brow,
The still plains heard my distant strokes
    That have been silenced now.

This way and that, now up, now down,
    I hailed full many a blow.
Alas! beneath my weary arm
    The thicket seemed to grow.

I take the lesson, wipe my brow
    And throw my axe aside,
And, sorely wearied, I go home
    In the tranquil eventide.

And soon the rising moon, that lights
    The eve of my defeat,
Shall see me sitting as of yore
    By my old master's feet.

II

I look across the ocean,
    And kneel upon the shore,
I look out seaward – westward
    My heart swells more and more.

I see the great new nation,
    New spirit and new scope
Rise there from the sea's round shoulder –
    A splendid sun of hope!

I see it and I tremble –
    My voice is full of tears –
America tread softly,
    You bear the fruit of years.

Tread softly – you are pregnant
    And growing near your time.

III

My summer health is gone away,
    That good companion that went hand in hand
With me through many a pleasant day.
    Perhaps on winter's farther side,
Perhaps as playful children hide
He hides a moment.
    And in the time of early flowers
    He may leap out with joy – that truant one –
Leap out all wet with April showers
      And flushed with April sun!
    Or if the hope be vain, and if, O friend,
I shall not hear the blackbird sing
Nor taste the pleasant sun, next spring,
And all our doubled hopes are at an end,
Still, with such heart as I have trod
The difficult ways of life, may I not tread
    The strait of death and go to God
      As children go to bed.

IV

Ne Sit Ancillae Tibi Amor Pudori

There's just a twinkle in your eye
That seems to say I *might*, if I
Were only bold enough to try
    An arm about your waist.
I hear too as you come and go,
That pretty nervous laugh, you know;
And then your cap is always so
    Coquettishly displaced.

Your cap! the word's profanely said,
That little topknot, white and red,
That quaintly crowns your graceful head,
    No bigger than a flower,

Is set with such a witching art,
Is so provocatively smart,
I'd like to wear it on my heart,
   An order for an hour!

O graceful housemaid, tall and fair,
I love your shy imperial air,
And always loiter on the stair,
   When you are going by.
A strict reserve the fates demand;
But, when to let you pass I stand,
Sometimes by chance I touch your hand
   And sometimes catch your eye.

V

Schumann's 'Frölicher Landmann'

Come, here is adieu to the city
   And hurrah for the country again!
The broad road lies before me
   Watered with last night's rain.

O I that have slept all winter
   Am wakened again today
And the breeze blows into my spirit
   And brushes the cobwebs away.

The tumbled country woos me
   With many a hill and hough,
And away in the shining furrow
   The ploughman follows his plow.

The whole year's sweat and study
   And the whole year's sowing time
Comes now to the perfect harvest
   And ripens now into rhyme.

For we that sow in the autumn,
   We reap our grain in the spring,
And we that go sowing and weeping
   Return to reap and sing.

VI

Inscription for the Tankard of a Society Now Dissolved

1

Take this Tankard. You and I,
  Loyal comrades, met and duly
Drank it three or four times dry,
  Three or four times filled it newly.
Once a week, each Monday night
  Thorough all the winter weather
Saw this Tankard filled and bright,
  Saw us gladly met together.

2

What a fund of wit and mirth,
  What a lusty inspiration,
What broad laughter once had birth
  From this tankard's exhalation.
In this well of amber ale
  Deeply drowned lay all our troubles;
And at each new jest or tale
  Slyly winked its beaded bubbles.

3

All those days are gone; and now
  Never more in winter weather
Shall we sit with smoothened brow
  Round this drinking-cup together.
Yet may he that drains it well,
  Drains this tankard long hereafter,
In the lisp of breaking bell
  Echoed, hear our former laughter.

4

Poor its stuff may once have been:
  Now may no one dare to flout it,
Our old memories bound, a green
  Sweetly scented wreath, about it.
Drink one silent toast to me
  And my friends, O future races –
Stoop, and in the metal see,
  Flushed and glad –, our mirrored faces!

VII

A Valentine's Song

Motley I count the only wear
    That suits, in this mixed world, the truly wise,
Who boldly smile upon despair
    And shake their bells in Grandam Grundy's eyes.
Singers should sing with such a goodly cheer
    That the bare listening should make strong like wine,
At this unruly time of year,
    The Feast of Valentine.

We do not now parade our 'oughts'
    And 'shoulds' and motives and beliefs in God.
Their life lies all indoors: sad thoughts
    Must keep the house, while gay thoughts go abroad.
Within we hold the wake for hopes deceased;
    But in the public streets, in wind or sun,
Keep open, at the annual feast,
    The puppet-booth of fun.

Our powers, perhaps, are small to please
    But even negro-songs and castanettes,
Old jokes and hackneyed repartees
    Are more than the parade of vain regrets.
Let Jaques stand Werthering by the wounded deer –
    We shall make merry, honest friends of mine,
At this unruly time of year,
    The Feast of Valentine.

I know how, day by weary day,
    Hope fades, love fades, a thousand pleasures fade.
I have not trudged in vain that way
    On which life's daylight darkens, shade by shade.
And still, with hopes decreasing, griefs increased,
    Still, with what wit I have shall I, for one,
Keep open, at the annual feast,
    The puppet-booth of fun.

I care not if the wit be poor,
    The old worn motley stained with rain and tears,
If but the courage still endure
    That filled and strengthened hope in earlier years,
If still, with friends averted, fate severe,
    A glad untainted cheerfulness be mine
To greet the unruly time of year,
    The Feast of Valentine.

Priest, I am none of thine and see
    In the perspective of still hopeful youth
That Truth shall triumph over thee –
    Truth to one's self – I know no other truth.
I see strange days for thee and thine, O priest,
    And how your doctrines, fallen one by one,
Shall furnish, at the annual feast,
    The puppet-booth of fun.

Stand on your putrid ruins – stand,
    White-neckcloth'd bigot, fixedly the same,
Cruel with all things but the hand,
    Inquisitor in all things but the name.
Back, minister of Christ and source of fear –
    We cherish freedom – back with thee and thine
From this unruly time of year,
    The Feast of Valentine.

Blood thou mayest spare; but what of tears?
    But what of riven households, broken faith –
Bywords that cling through all men's years
    And drag them surely down to shame and death?
Stand back, O cruel man, O foe of youth,
    And let such men as hearken not thy voice
Press freely up the road to truth,
    The King's highway of Choice.

VIII

Hail! childish slaves of social rules
    You had yourselves a hand in making!
How I could shake your faith, ye fools,
    If but I thought it worth the shaking.
I see, and pity you; and then
    Go, casting off the idle pity,
In search of braver, better men,
    My own way freely through the city.

My own way freely, and not yours;
    And careless of a town's abusing,
Seek real friendship that endures
    Among the friends of my own choosing.
I'll choose my friends myself, you hear?
    And won't let Mrs Grundy do it,
Tho' all I honour and hold dear
    And all I hope should move me to it.

I take my old coat from the shelf –
    I am a man of little breeding,
And only dress to please myself
    I own, a very strange proceeding.
I smoke a pipe abroad, because
    To all cigars I much prefer it
And as I scorn your social laws
    My choice has nothing to deter it.

Gladly I trudge the footpath way,
    While you and yours roll by in coaches
In all the pride of fine array,
    Through all the city's thronged approaches.
O fine, religious, decent folk,
    In Virtue's flaunting gold and scarlet,
I sneer between two puffs of smoke,
    Give me the publican and harlot.

Ye dainty-spoken, stiff, severe
    Seed of the migrated Philistian,
One whispered question in your ear –
    Pray, what was Christ, if you be Christian?
If Christ were only here just now,
    Among the city's wynds and gables
Leading the life he taught us, how
    Would he be welcome to your tables?

I go and leave your logic-straws,
    Your former-friends with face averted,
Your petty ways and narrow laws,
    Your Grundy and your God deserted.
From your frail ark of lies, I flee
    I know not where, like Noah's raven.
Full to the broad, unsounded sea
    I swim, from your dishonest haven.

Alone on that unsounded deep,
    Poor waif, it may be I shall perish,
Far from the course I thought to keep,
    Far from the friends I hoped to cherish –
It may be I shall sink, and yet
    Hear, thro' all taunt and scornful laughter,
Through all defeat and all regret,
    The stronger swimmers coming after.

IX

If I had wings, my lady, like a dove
    I should not linger here,
But through the winter air toward my love,
    Fly swift toward my love, my fair,
If I had wings, my lady, like a dove.

If I had wings, my lady, like a dove,
    And knew the secrets of the air,
I should be gone, my lady, to my love,
    To kiss the sweet disparting of her hair,
If I had wings, my lady, like a dove.

If I had wings, my lady, like a dove,
    This hour should see my soul at rest,
Should see me safe, my lady, with my love,
    To kiss the sweet division of her breast,
If I had wings, my lady, like a dove.

For all is sweet, my lady, in my love;
    Sweet hair, sweet breast and sweeter eyes
That draw my soul, my lady, like a dove
    Drawn southward by the shining of the skies;
For all is sweet, my lady, in my love.

If I could die, my lady, with my love,
    Die, mouth to mouth, a splendid death,
I should take wing, my lady, like a dove,
    To spend upon her lips my all of breath,
If I could die, my lady, with my love.

X

Death, to the dead for evermore
A King, a God, the last, the best of friends –
Whene'er this mortal journey ends
Death, like a host, comes smiling to the door;
Smiling, he greets us, on that tranquil shore
Where neither piping bird nor peeping dawn
Disturbs the eternal sleep,
But in the stillness far withdrawn
Our dreamless rest for evermore we keep.

For as from open windows forth we peep
Upon the night-time star beset
And with dews forever wet;

So from this garish life the spirit peers;
And lo! as a sleeping city doth outspread,
Where breathe the sleepers evenly; and lo!
After the loud wars, triumphs, trumpets, tears
And clamour of man's passion, Death appears
And we must rise and go.

Soon are eyes tired with sunshine; soon the ears
Weary of utterance, seeing all is said;
Soon, racked by hopes and fears,
The all-pondering, all-contriving head,
Weary with all things, wearies of the years;
And our sad spirits turn toward the dead;
And the tired child, the body, longs for bed.

XI

I have a friend; I have a story;
    I have a life that's hard to live;
I love; my love is all my glory;
    I have been hurt and I forgive.

I have a friend; none could be better;
    I stake my heart upon my friend!
I love; I trust her to the letter;
    Will she deceive me in the end?

She is my love, my life, my jewel;
    My hope, my star, my dear delight.
God! but the ways of God are cruel, –
    That love should bow the knee to spite.

She loves, she hates: – a foul alliance!
    One king shall rule in one estate.
I only love; 'tis all my science;
    A while, and she will only hate.

XII

Poem for a Class Reunion

Whether we like it, or don't,
    There's a sort of a bond in the fact
That we all by one master were taught,
    By one master were bullied and whackt.
And now all the more, when we see

Our class in so shrunken a state
And we, who were seventy-two,
  Diminished to seven or eight.

One has been married; and one
  Has taken to letters for bread,
Several are over the seas;
  And some I imagine are dead.
And that is the reason you see
  Why, as I have the honour to state,
We, who were seventy-two,
  Are now only seven or eight.

One took to heretical views,
  And one, they inform me, to drink;
Some construct fortunes in trade,
  Some starve in professions, I think.
But one way or other alas!
  Through the culpable action of Fate
We, who were seventy-two,
  Are now shrunken to seven or eight.

So, whether we like it or not,
  Let us own there's a bond in the past,
And, since we were playmates at school,
  Continue good friends to the last.
The roll-book is closed in the room,
  The clackan is gone with the slate,
We, who were seventy-two,
  Are now only seven or eight.

We shall never, our books on our back,
  Trudge off in the morning again,
To the slide at the Janitor's door,
  By the ambush of cads in the lane!
We shall never be sent for the tawse,
  Nor lose places for coming too late;
We shall never be seventy-two,
  Who are now but seven or eight!

We shall never have peeries for luck,
  We shall never be strapped by Maclean,
We shall never take Lothian down,
  Nor ever be schoolboys again.
But still for the sake of the past,
  For the love of the days of lang syne
The remnant of seventy-two
  Shall rally together to dine.

XIII

*To the Thompson Class Dinner Club
from their Stammering Laureate*

1

Friends, that here together met
 Toast the flying year,
Do not at the board forget
 Friends afar from here.

2

All together once we went
 In by Jenny's gate,
Every Monday, schoolward sent,
 Somewhat after eight.

3

Now from other lands, we look
 Backward on the past,
When with clackan, board and book
 Hurried in the last.

4

Nevermore the bell shall beat,
 Catching us afar
Somewhere down in Brandon Street
 Or the lane of war.

5

All the panic, all the plays,
 Gone for evermore,
We have now outgrown the ways –
 And the clothes of yore.

6

Still, as feasted, rosy, warm,
 Round the board you sit,
Vanished schoolday faces swarm,
 Vanished figures flit.

7

Still at mirth's returning tide,
 Kind at heart and true,
Absent schoolmates side by side
 Here sit down with you.

8

Dux and booby, fill your glasses
    And with beaming eye
To your friends of Thompson's classes
    Drain the goblet dry.

9

Dux and booby, dull and clever,
    Humble soul and vain,
We are not yet old, but never
    Shall be young again.

10

Here for years we still may tarry
    Tending still the fire;
Like MacEwen we may marry
    And for babes aspire;

11

Loves and friendships still increasing
    Round us grow and spread,
As the wings of time unceasing
    Beat above our head;

12

But for all – the best befriended,
    Best beloved or praised –
Still the past, the past is ended
    And the school erased.

13

We are now not very many –
    We shall ne'er be more –
Nor till time is done, shall any
    Join the dwindling score.

14

Then, companions, fill your glasses
    Fill and drain the wine,
For the friends of Thompson's classes,
    And for Auld Lang Syne.

XIV

Praise and Prayer

I have been well, I have been ill,
  I have been rich and poor;
I have set my back against the wall
  And fought it by the hour;

I have been false, I have been true;
  And thoro' grief and mirth,
I have done all that man can do
  To be a man of worth;

And now, when from an unknown shore,
  I dare an unknown wave,
God, who has helped me heretofore,
  O help me wi' the lave!

XV

John Cavalier

These are your hills, John Cavalier.
Your father's kids you tended here,
And grew, among these mountains wild,
A humble and religious child. –
Fate turned the wheel; you grew and grew;
Bold Marshals doffed the hat to you;
God whispered counsels in your ear
To guide your sallies, Cavalier.

You shook the earth with martial tread;
The ensigns fluttered by your head;
In Spain or France, Velay or Kent,
The music sounded as you went. –
Much would I give if I might spy
Your brave battalions marching by;
Or, on the wind, if I might hear
Your drums and bugles, Cavalier.

In vain. O'er all the windy hill,
The ways are void, the air is still,
Alone, below the echoing rock,
The shepherd calls upon his flock. –
The wars of Spain and of Cevennes,
The bugles and the marching men,
The horse you rode for many a year –
Where are they now, John Cavalier?

All armies march the selfsame way
Far from the cheerful eye of day;
And you and yours marched down below
About two hundred years ago.
Over the hills, into the shade,
Journeys each mortal cavalcade;
Out of the sound, out of the sun,
They go when their day's work is done;
And all shall doff the bandoleer
To sleep with dead John Cavalier.

XVI

The Iron Steed

In our black stable by the sea,
Five and twenty stalls you see –
Five and twenty strong are we:
The lanterns tossed the shadows round,
Live coals were scattered on the ground,
The swarthy ostlers echoing stept,
But silent all night long we slept.
Inactive we, steeds of the day,
The shakers of the mountains, lay.
Earth's oldest veins our dam and sire,
Iron chimeras fed with fire.
All we, the unweary, lay at rest;
The sleepless lamp burned on our crest;
And in the darkness far and nigh,
We heard our iron compeers cry.

XVII

Here you rest among the valleys, maiden known to but a few;
    Here you sleep unsighing, but how oft of yore you sighed!
And how oft your feet elastic trod a measure in the dew
    On a green beside the river ere you died!

Where are now the country lovers whom you trembled to be near –
    Who with shy advances, in the falling eventide,
Grasped the tightlier at your fingers, whispered lowlier in your ear,
    On a green beside the river ere you died?

All the sweet old country dancers who went round with you in tune,
    Dancing, flushed and silent, in the silent eventide,
All departed by enchantment at the rising of the moon
    From the green beside the river when you died.

XVIII

On Some Ghastly Companions at a Spa

That was an evil day when I
To Strathpeffer drew anigh,
For there I found no human soul
But ogres occupied the whole.

They had at first a human air
In coats and flannel underwear.
They rose and walked upon their feet
And filled their bellies full of meat.
They wiped their lips when they had done,
But they were ogres every one.

Each issuing from his secret bower,
I marked them in the morning hour.
By limp and totter, list and droop,
I singled each one from the group.
I knew them all as they went by –
I knew them by their Blasted Eye!

Detested ogres, from my sight
Depart to your congenial night!
From these fair vales, from this fair day,
Fleet, spectres, on your downward way,
Like changing figures in a dream,
To Muttonhole or Pittenweem!
As, by some harmony divine
The devils quartered in the swine,
If any baser place exist
In God's great registration list –
Some den with wallow and a trough –
Find it, ye ogres, and be off!

XIX

Since years ago for evermore
My cedar ship I drew to shore;
And to the road and river-bed
And the green, nodding reeds, I said
Mine ignorant and last farewell:
Now with content at home I dwell,
And now divide my sluggish life
Betwixt my verses and my wife:
In vain: for when the lamp is lit
And by the laughing fire I sit,

Still with the tattered atlas spread
Interminable roads I tread.

XX

My wife and I, in our romantic cot,
The world forgetting, by the world forgot,
High as the gods upon Olympus dwell,
Pleased with the things we have, and pleased as well
To wait in hope for those which we have not.

She burns in ardour for a horse to trot;
I pledge my votive prayers upon a yacht:
Which shall be first remembered, who can tell –
         My wife or I?

Harvests of flowers o'er all our garden plot
She dreams; and I to enrich a darker spot,
My unprovided cellar; both to swell
Our narrow cottage huge as a hotel
That portly friends may come and share the lot
         Of wife and I.

XXI

At morning on the garden seat
I dearly love to drink and eat.
To drink and eat, to drink and sing,
At morning, in the time of Spring.
In winter honest men retire
And sup their possets by the fire,
But when the Spring comes round, you see,
The garden breakfast pleases me.
The morning star that melts on high
The fires that cleanse the changing sky,
The air that smells so new and sweet,
All put me in the cue to eat
   A pot at five, a crust at four,
   At half past six a pottle more.

XXII

To Time

God of the business man, to thee,
O Time, I bow the suppliant knee,

And to thy dwarfish temple bring
My books as a peace-offering.
Thou cleaver of the crowded woods,
That drivest from green solitudes
The sylvan deer; and dost conspire,
Or for the shipyard or the fire,
The fall of woodland colonnades;
O Time, that lovest in the glades
To cheer the ringing axe's din
And let the untrammelled sunshine in:
Think but once more, nor let this be,
Thy servant should survive to see
His native country and his head
Lie both alike disforested.

XXIII

God gave to me a child in part
Yet wholly gave the father's heart: –
Child of my soul, O whither now,
Unborn, unmothered, goest thou?

You came, you went, and no man wist;
Hapless, my child, no breast you kisst;
On no dear knees, a privileged babbler, clomb,
Nor knew the kindly feel of home.

My voice may reach you, O my dear –
A father's voice perhaps the child may hear;
And pitying, you may turn your view
On that poor father whom you never knew.

Alas! alone he sits, who then,
Immortal among mortal men
Sat hand in hand with love, and all day through
With your dear mother wondered over you.

XXIV

Now bare to the beholder's eye,
Your late denuded lendings lie,
Subsiding slowly where they fell,
A disinvested citadel:
The obdurate corset, cupid's foe,
The Dutchman's breeches frilled below,
Hose that the looker loves to note,
And white and crackling petticoat.

From these, that on the ground repose,
Their lady lately re-arose;
And laying by the lady's name
A living woman re-became.
Of her, that from the public eye
They do inclose and fortify,
Now, lying scattered as they fell
An indiscreeter tale they tell:
Of that more soft and secret her
Whose daylong fortresses they were,
By fading warmth, by lingering print,
These now discarded scabbards hint.

A twofold change the ladies know.
First, in the morn the bugles blow,
And they, with floral hues and scents,
Man their be-ribboned battlements.
But let the stars appear, and they
Shed inhumanities away;
And from the changeling fashion sees,
Through comic and through sweet degrees,
In nature's toilet unsurpassed,
Forth leaps the laughing girl at last.

XXV

Verses on Bogue [RLS's dog]

1

He can't live as long as I
But must grow early old and die.
His little heart shall cease to beat
And rest receive his faltering feet.
In his dear eyes the light shall fade
And for my dog the grave be made.

2

Dear Bogue when your pads are as white as the snow
From trotting in summer's sweet dust as you go;
When your tail is expanded in conquering fold
As black as the flag of the pirates of old;
When trotting in front in remarkable grime,
You turn and look round with your bramble-dew eyes;
When I see from the rice grains that serve you as teeth
That rose leaf, your tongue, hanging flaunted beneath;
When at each of the corners with one foot in air

You pause with a smile, asking whither we fare;
The first thing at morning, the last thing at night,
I praise my dear Boguey, my child and delight!

The wisest of mankind, no wiser than you
Find, once out of twenty, the right thing to do.
And the once that they find it and do it, I swear,
They contrive to spoil all with their sanctified air;
But you my dear Bogue, whether erring or right
You are still the bright image of love and delight.

At the end of the road that we travel today
What future awaits, no prophet can say.
To wealth or to woe, to the goal or to jail,
You follow your master with fluttering tail.

3

To A Warrior Dead

*In memory of 'Bogie', whose picture by RANDOLPH CALDECOTT
is now in the Print Room of the British Museum.*

We knew you better, dear, than you believed,
Pierced all the baseless notions you conceived,
And plumbed with too much gusto to despise
The human humour of your acted lies.
Your valour that (with someone to admire)
Swole vast as Atlas and inflamed your ire
And (you that could not fight and would not yield)
Still made you challenge and engage the field:
Your pride that in your private hours of life
Not well became, – but when you sprang in strife
And in unequal battle bit the ground,
From all approach of weakness mailed you round:
Aye, all we knew, and now no more than pray,
When like a hillside lion in the way,
Sudden and sharp, your soldier's end you met,
No venomed penitence or vain regret,
No yearning for the friends that loved you best,
Disturbed your moments as you swooned to rest:
But just the weakening heart – the stiffening limb –
Your wild, bright eye that grew forever dim!

Poor soul, had you but known the strumpet's name,
How you had longed and laboured after Fame!
How it had thrilled through all your fiery clay,
To know her yours, as yours she is today!

To you she came uncalled. To you belong
Some passing mention in a martial song
And an immortal icon. For to you
Art brought the gift she brings to but a few:
And in the pillared house of jealous doors,
Where all the nation treasures and adores,
And all the Caesars and the Pharaohs are –
With others dear to art and dead in war,
You dwell enshrined, nor shall be quite forgot
While London stands and men love Caldecott.

XXVI

Ye chimney pots of London
    The winds shall blow ye down
The foot shall tread ye under,
    Ye pots of London town.

O dreary pots of London
    That poison many a mile,
O dreary streets of stucco
    And dreary fields of tile!

They sang to me in childhood
    Your streets were paved with gold,
A most unsightly city
    Is all that I behold.

O cats and iron chimneys
    A screeching in the night!
O clouds of ugly vapour
    That quench the brightest light!

Ye chimney pots of London,
    Your day is near to hand
When ye, with your defilement
    Shall poison all the land.

When London and the country
    In London fog is drowned,
When all the little cockneys
    Lie choked upon the ground.

XXVII

The Far Farers

The broad sun,
  The bright day:
White sails
  In the blue bay: –
The far farers
  Draw away.

Light the fires
  And close the door.
To the old homes
  To the loud shore,
The far farers
  Come no more.

XXVIII

The Fine Pacific Islands
Heard in a Public-house at Rotherhithe

The jolly English Yellowboy
  Is a 'ansome coin when new,
The Yankee Double-eagle
  Is large enough for two.
O, these may do for seaport towns,
  For cities these may do;
But the dibbs that takes the Hislands
  Are the dollars of Peru:
    O, the fine Pacific Hislands,
    O, the dollars of Peru!

It's there we buy the cocoanuts
  Mast 'headed in the blue;
It's there we trap the lasses
  All waiting for the crew;
It's there we buy the trader's rum
  What bores a seaman through …
In the fine Pacific Hislands
  With the dollars of Peru:
    In the fine Pacific Hislands
    With the dollars of Peru!

Now, messmates, when my watch is up,
  And I am quite broached to,
I'll give a tip to 'Evving

Of the 'ansome thing to do:
Let 'em just refit this sailor-man
And launch him off anew
To cruise among the Hislands
With the dollars of Peru:
In the fine Pacific Hislands
With the dollars of Peru!

XXIX

As with heaped bees at hiving time
The boughs are clotted, as (ere prime)
Heaven swarms with stars, or the city street
Pullulates with passing feet;
So swarmed my senses once; that now
Repose behind my tranquil brow,
Unsealed, asleep, quiescent, clear;
Now only the vast shapes I hear
Hear – and my hearing slowly fills –
Rivers and winds among the twisting hills,
And hearken – and my face is lit –
Life pacing; death pursuing it.

XXX

Early in the Evening

Light foot and tight foot
    And green grass spread,
Early in the morning –
    But hope is on ahead.

Stout foot and proud foot
    And gray dust spread,
Early in the evening –
    And hope lies dead.

Long life and short life,
    The last word said,
Early in the evening
    There lies the bed.

Brief day and bright day
    And sunset red,
Early in the evening,
    The stars are overhead.

XXXI

Student Song

They say that at the core of it
    This life is all regret;
But we've scarce yet learned the lore of it,
    We're only youngsters yet.
We only ask some more of it, some more of it,
        We only ask some more of it
        – The less we're like to get!

Though ill may be the close of it,
    It's fair enough at morn;
And the manner to dispose of it
Is just to pluck the rose of it
    When first the rose is born.
Is first to pluck the rose of it, the rose of it, the rose of it,
    Is just to pluck the rose of it,
    The de'il may take the thorn!

The opinions of the old of it
    Depict a doleful land;
For the guide-books that are sold of it,
    The ill that we are told of it,
    Would make Columbus stand.
But come let's take a hold of it, a hold of it, a hold of it,
    But come let's take a hold of it
    With Alexander's hand.

When sages call the roll of it
    How sad their looks appear!
    But there's fire in every coal of it
    And hope is in the soul of it
    And never a word of fear.
So love we then the whole of it, the whole of it, the whole of it,
    So love we then the whole of it
    For as long as we are here.

TEXTUAL NOTES

Preface

'Shall any pious hand re-edit us?', a question posed in *To Master Andrew Lang* by Stevenson, must give pause to any editor assembling a volume such as this one. The poet was fastidious in selecting, from among masses of his MS verse, only a few pieces for publication. He also scoffed at learned pedantry, which he embodied in his imaginary German scholar Bummkopf, who (in Colvin's words) 'cannot clear his edifice of its scaffolding, nor set forth the results of research without intruding on the reader all its processes, evidences and supports' (*LETBM*, Vol. II, No. 637).

It is not the present editor's intention to emulate Herr Bummkopf by overwhelming the reader with an avalanche of erudition. The following Notes try to put the poems in contexts which will enhance enjoyment and understanding of them. Assuming that the reader will want to see exactly what the poet intended as a final version, the editor has specified a copy-text, that is, a MS or printed version having the greatest authority, for every poem. Detailed accounts are given of all authoritative editions, both English and American, of each of the four collections of poetry that Stevenson readied for press. Since first editions of his poems have fetched as much as US$8,500 on the antiquarian book market, what bibliographers and collectors call 'points' about them are worth noting.

Though somewhat daunted by the fear of falling into Bummkopfery, the editor has nevertheless included full scholarly apparatus and followed standard academic practices. Original or early editions of all sources cited or quoted are fully identified. Where an accessible reprint of a rare original exists, I have noted the fact, but most references to Stevenson's texts in verse or prose point the reader to first editions, the Edinburgh Edition of his *Works*, Janet Adam Smith's *Collected Poems*, the Yale *Letters*, Colvin's *Letters* and Balfour's *Life*. The eight-volume Yale *Letters* (*LETBM*) is the source of many dates and other specific references to poems: co-editor Ernest Mehew has declared that all dating and annotation in that work was done by him. When a letter is cited but not quoted (e.g. as the source for a date), I give volume and letter number; when a letter is quoted, I give volume and page number(s).

I refer often to Smith's *Collected Poems* (CP) because it has been the standard for fifty years: it brought order to the chaos she found in editions of Stevenson's poetry. Prominence is given also to the work of those with special authority on matters Stevensonian, for example Colvin, Balfour and various family members such as Fanny Stevenson, Lloyd Osbourne and Isobel Strong. However venal we may think some of them to be for trying to transmute Stevenson's literary remains into hard cash, they were eyewitnesses to his life.

Where possible, dates of composition are those supplied by the poet himself. For each poem I try to give place of composition and, if not an exact date, one with a *terminus ad quem* or *a quo* or a time period in which it was probably composed, for example 'Edinburgh student days' or 'Samoan period'. Place/date references are followed by a source identified briefly in parentheses, for example a dated MS or fair copy, Balfour's list of dates, LETBM, internal evidence from a notebook. The first appearance in print is given for uncollected poems and for those which came out in periodicals or books before they were published in one of the four collections or the Edinburgh Edition. As a rule, magazine publication has been noted in this edition only if it had Stevenson's authority; a full listing of periodical printings of verse may be found in Volume II of McKay's Catalogue. 'Printed text' for uncollected poems identifies the first appearance of the text in print after the poet's death: such sources are Colvin's *Letters*, Balfour's *Life*, and family compilations presenting hitherto unpublished poems; other poems appeared for the first time in periodicals, private printings and collected editions such as Pentland, Swanston and Vailima. For the multitude of verse that came out posthumously and variously under such headings as *New Poems*, the standard reference is *Poems* Vol. II in the Tusitala Edition (*NP*).

Cross-referencing in the Textual Notes guides the reader to fuller discussion in the Explanatory Notes of such matters as the poet's family background, relevant historical events or literary questions. These Notes also identify people and places mentioned in the poems.

Editorial procedure follows William Proctor Williams and Craig S. Abbot, *An Introduction to Bibliographical and Textual Studies*, 2nd edn, New York, Modern Language Association, 1989. A full list of variants is provided, except where it is explicitly stated that variants have been selectively recorded. Copy-texts and rationales for selecting them, either in the case of a single poem or a collection of them, are described and explained below.

RLS misspelled so many words that successive copy-editors have not yet managed to correct them all: one still sees 'wier', 'guager', 'blythe' and the like in contemporary re-issues. All spelling mistakes, Americanisations and errors in grammar, syntax and punctuation have been silently corrected, although RLS's idiomatic punctuation has been retained: on this point the reader is referred to Barry Menikoff's important disquisition on 'The Accidentals' (1984: 32–57). He was inconsistent in his use of hyphens: where it has been possible to take out a hyphen, I have taken it out – in this edition his 'to-day' appears as 'today'.

In recording variants I have placed all MS citations in parentheses, abbreviating the lengthy ones. Stevenson's own annotations and numbered footnotes are included with the text; in *Ballads* the lines are numbered. Some features of the first editions have not been followed, for example the small font in *Ballads*, the breaking-up of long lines, placing each poem on its own page and capitalising the first word of each poem.

A Child's Garden of Verses

History of Composition and Publication

RLS's first volume of poetry was published in London by Longmans Green on 6 March 1885 and in the USA by Scribner's on 16 April. According to his mother's Diary Notes, he began to write his verses for children in the summer of 1881 at Braemar, in the Scottish Highlands; she records that he picked up her copy of Kate Greenaway's newly published and best-selling *Birthday Book for Children*, with verses by Mrs Sale Barker, and commented, 'These are rather nice rhymes and I don't think they would be difficult to do' (*VAIL*, Vol. 26, p. 338). In fact he did them so easily at first that he wrote nos 1–14 of CGV before leaving Braemar, then the next three before returning to the more urgent matter of *Treasure Island*, which was appearing serially (Balfour I, pp. 228–9). Financially pressed at this time, RLS seems to have taken up what has more recently become known as children's literature because he thought it was likely to yield 'more coin' than the travel books, essays and other *belles-lettres* with which he had begun to establish his literary reputation (*LETBM*, Vol. III, p. 224). What began as fun and games with his young stepson, Lloyd Osbourne, the Davos-Platz pamphlets they made on a hand-press and the map they devised showing buried treasure on an island, became for RLS an opportunity to pursue commercial success as a writer of children's books.

Usually RLS composed verse as a relief from the serious labour of writing for money, often when he was bedridden or otherwise unable to get on with his prose: as he once put it to his mother, 'when I spit blood I write verses' (*LETBM*, Vol. IV, p. 228). After the first seventeen numbers, the CGV poems were written piecemeal over the next three and a half years and are therefore difficult to date. In the autumn of 1881 he began sending them to Fanny Sitwell. Encouraging Louis' poetic efforts as she had been doing for several years, she made fair copies of them, building up a portfolio which, when it included forty-eight poems in the autumn of 1883, was sent off to be privately printed at Cambridge University Press: the result was the rarest of all Stevensoniana, the trial pamphlet *Penny Whistles*, of which only three copies survive.

The project begun in Braemar was taken up again in Marseilles in late January 1883 at the urging of Henley, to whom he wrote: 'I ought to have the scrolls of the Nursery Muse somewhere in a blank paper book; but I can't find them. I pray God the originals are not lost. I inclose four new ones, and am capable of producing them steadily if more are wanted – at least I think so' (*LETBM*, Vol. IV, p. 61). By mid-February he had completed thirty-five poems of the collection he was now calling *Songs of Innocence* (*LETBM*, Vol. IV, No. 1058). He decided to dedicate the volume to 'Cummy', his nurse Alison Cunningham, telling her with affecting simplicity, 'this little book which is all about my childhood should indeed go to no other person but you, who did so much to make that childhood happy' (*LETBM*, Vol. IV, p. 76). The first version was completed at Chalet La Solitude, Hyères, on the south coast of France, the only place (he later told Colvin) where he had ever been happy (*LETBM*,

Vol. VII, p. 93). Fanny Sitwell sent him her fair copies in April; he told her, 'I have struck out two, and added five or six; so they now number forty-five; when they are fifty, they shall out on the world' (*LETBM*, Vol. IV, p. 102). By early May he was ready to start negotiations with an illustrator, printer and book designer, as he told Henley: 'This is to announce to you the MS of *Nursery Verses*, now numbering XLVIII pieces or 599 verses, which of course one might augment *ad infinitum*.' He goes into detail about his wishes concerning format, type, size, paper, number of pages, binding and the all-important illustrations: he wanted to collaborate with one of the leading children's book illustrators of the day – Kate Greenaway, Walter Crane or Randolph Caldecott. Finally he considered the title:

> O I forgot. As for the title, I think *Nursery Verses*, the best. Poetry is not the strong point of the text, and I shirk any title that might seem to claim that quality; otherwise we might have *Nursery Muses* or *New Songs of Innocence* (but that were a blasphemy), or *Rimes of Innocence*: the last not bad, or – an idea – *The Jews' Harp*, or Now I Have It: – *The Penny Whistle*.
>
> THE PENNY WHISTLE:
NURSERY VERSES
BY
ROBERT LOUIS STEVENSON
ILLUSTRATED BY
>
> And here we have an excellent frontispiece, of a party playing on a P.W. to a little ring of dancing children.
>
> THE PENNY WHISTLE
is the name for me.
>
> Fool! this is all wrong, here is the true name: –
>
> ~~PENNY WHISTLES~~
For Small Whistlers
>
> The second title is queried, it is perhaps better, as simply PENNY WHISTLES … Crossed penny whistles on the cover, or else a sheaf of 'em.'
>
> (LETBM, Vol. IV, pp. 112–14)

In the autumn Henley and Colvin arranged for the printing of a twelvemo of twenty-two pages containing forty-eight poems without title-page or wrappers, having only the dropped-head title *Penny Whistles* at the top of page one and the printer's imprint at the bottom of page twenty-two. Proofs were taken and distributed, not only to potential illustrators but also to family, former playmates and friendly critics. The most interesting of the three surviving copies of these proofs is the one in BRBML because it has corrections and marginal annotations by both Colvin and Henley suggesting revisions and deletions. After reviewing these and other improving suggestions from friends, the poet responded to Colvin with evident frustration and with yet another change of title:

> 'In the multitude of councillors the Bible declares there is wisdom,' said my great-uncle, 'but I have always found in them distraction.' It is extraordinary how tastes vary; these proofs have been handed about it appears, and I have had several letters; and – distraction … I will delete some of those condemned, but not all. I don't care for the name *Penny Whistles*; I sent a sheaf {of names} to Henley when I sent 'em. But I've forgot the others. I would just as soon call 'em *Rimes for Children*, as anything else.'
> (*LETBM*, Vol. IV, pp. 198–9)

RLS deleted nine of the forty-eight poems; for details see the comparison of *PW* with *CGV* on pp. 344–6. These omitted pieces were privately printed in 1912 by the poet's bibliographer Luther S. Livingston in an issue of 100 copies called *Verses by R. L. S.* They are printed here in the Textual Notes on Individual Poems in the order in which they appeared in *PW*.

For many reasons, this project lapsed again during the winter of 1883/4. RLS was diffident about his debut as a poet and his protective literary circle feared a harsh critical reception. His *PW* MSS are tattooed with revisions, alternate readings and variations in order, reflecting his anxiety about what he called the cold light of print. 'His friends,' wrote Edmund Gosse, 'were as timid as hens about this new experiment of their duckling's; they hesitated and doubted to the last' (Hammerton 1903: 155). All agreed that the penurious writer should publish nothing that might damage his modestly advancing reputation and hence his earning power. Against the argument that Thomas and Margaret Stevenson could afford to advance their son all the money he needed, it must be said that RLS viewed such bail-outs as a defeat: he strove to demonstrate, to his father in particular, that he could earn a living as a professional writer. Then, at the close of 1883, two incidents broke the momentum driving *PW* towards the public's judgement. *Treasure Island* was published in book form for the Christmas season, bringing the writer his first taste of large-scale popular success and big cheques; with the prospect of earning £500 in 1884, he could afford to slow down his literary production. Then, in January, he was unexpectedly prostrated by lung problems that almost killed him. Although he continued to write new children's verses at Hyères, the ensuing convalescence sharply limited his capacity to see work through the press. A further impediment was that none of the illustrators Louis wanted was available.

Early in March 1884, RLS asked Henley to prepare another proof issue, to be sent to Cassell & Co., of the collection he was now calling *A Child's Garden of Verses*. Cassell's had earlier declined to publish *PW*, so the poet revised and enlarged it, bringing the total number of poems to the desired fifty. Henley arranged for six of them to be published in the March and July issues of Cassell's *Magazine of Art*, which he was editing: they were nos VIII, XVI, XXIII, XXV, XXVII and XLI. By June the volume had been extensively rearranged and completed by the addition of new poems, the 'Garden Days' section and the six concluding 'Envoys', for a total of sixty-four poems, the number it contained when finally published. With the help of Andrew Lang, Henley secured a contract with Longmans Green to publish the volume, though without illustrations. This formal agreement, dated 24 December 1884, offered '£30 (in advance) for the first thousand, and £20 per five hundred up to a total of 2500' (*LETBM*, Vol. V, p. 51, n. 1). The retail price asked was five shillings.

RLS continued his quest for an illustrated edition through the good offices of his American friend Will. H. Low, an artist. After proofing it, the poet sent Low the Longmans edition in sheets. Although unable himself to illustrate it or to find another artist to do so, Low did manage to generate an offer from Scribner's to publish an American edition, which RLS accepted on 12 March 1885 (*LETBM*, Vol. V, p. 86). The first illustrated edition, published by Scribner's in New York and The Bodley Head in London, did not appear until 1895–6. RLS had been consulted about it but, far away in Samoa, he seems to have taken no interest and died in 1894 before seeing any sketches or proofs.

To Edmund Gosse on 12 March 1885, RLS sent this account of his reaction to publication:

They look ghastly in the cold light of print; but there is something nice in the little ragged regiment for all; the blackguards seem to me to smile; to have a kind of childish treble note that sounds in my ears freshly: not song, if you will, but a child's voice. (*LETBM*, Vol. V, p. 85)

Location and Description of Manuscripts

The MSS for the earliest poems are in BRBML. They are to be found for the most part in one of the more than fifty notebooks that RLS made entries in, the one identifed as 'C'. Specific reference to these documents is difficult because of RLS' habit of turning his notebooks upside down and writing from the back towards the middle: page numbering often proceeds front to middle and back to middle as well, so that many page numbers are duplicated. In McKay vols five and six, where the MSS are catalogued, each discrete unit in a notebook, even if only one line of verse, is given a McKay number beginning with 'B', for example *Bed in Summer* MSS are B6007 and B7140; even though they are on the same page of Notebook 'C', McKay did not recognise them as parts of the same poem. These numbers may refer to verse on notebook pages or in remnants of disbound notebooks (see Introduction) or to an individual MS. The notebooks themselves have no McKay numbers but are catalogued by BRBML according to their individual numbers, letters and/or subtitles.

Notebook 'C', dating from 1880 to 1882, has eighty-eight pages; CGV material occurs on pp. 54–65. There is also CGV material on pages 13, 23 and 31 of Notebook 'A.269 *Verses used and incomplete*' dating from 1880 to 1881 and having sixty-three pages. Other CGV drafts will be found in Notebooks 51, 53 and 59. There are individual MSS of poems (for example, *Lesson on the Sea* is B6507) and of course the unique copy of *PW* with annotations by Colvin and Henley.

HL has three collections of material important to CGV. H2460 is sixteen pages of unbound folio containing MSS of 21 poems: 16 occur in CGV, 14 in *PW* and 10 in both; one originally intended for CGV, *A Visit from the Sea*, became UW VI. H2404, Notebook 'A270 *Places I have slept in, Child's Garden etc.*', seventy-two pages, has drafts on pp. 1–4. H2407 is Notebook 'D. *Book Poems, Child's Garden No.A.156*', containing eighty-nine pages. There are CGV drafts on pp. 1, 8–27, 42–3, 50–2, 60–1, 74–6 and 80–1. The HL material is later than the BRBML MSS, belonging mostly to 1883–4; it includes early pencil drafts of most of the 'Garden Days' poems.

NYPL has a bound morocco volume called 'Stevenson/Child's Garden of Verses/ Unpublished Manuscript'. It contains MSS of XXIV, XXXV, 2-V and 2-VIII. NLS has an early MS of XL.

From *Penny Whistles* to *A Child's Garden of Verses*

Below are listed the contents of the 1883 trial pamphlet *PW*, which was not divided into parts with subtitles; deletions, rearranging and additions are noted:

I.	*Bed In Summer.*
II.	*A Thought.*
III.	*At The Sea-Side.*
IV.	*Young Night Thoughts.*
V.	*Whole Duty Of Children.*
VI.	*Bull Hunt.* {deleted 1883}

VII.	*Rain.*
VIII.	*Pirate Story.*
IX.	*Foreign Lands.*
X.	*Windy Nights.*
XI.	*Travel.*
XII.	*Singing.*
XIII.	*My Ship And I.* {became II. in 'The Child Alone'}
XIV.	*Looking Forward*
XV.	*A Good Play.*
XVI.	*Where Go The Boats?*
XVII.	*Auntie's Skirts.*
XVIII.	*The Land Of Counterpane.*
XIX.	*The Land Of Nod.*
XX.	*My Shadow.*
XXI.	*The Hunt Interrupted.* {deleted 1883}
XXII.	*The Garden Door.* {deleted 1883}
XXIII.	*A Song Of Days.* {deleted 1883}
XXIV.	*System.* {became XIX. in CGV}
XXV.	*A Good Boy.*
XXVI.	*Escape At Bedtime.*
XXVII.	*Marching Song.*
XXVIII.	*The Cow.*
XXIX.	*My Treasures.* {became V. in 'The Child Alone'}
XXX.	*Happy Thought.*
XXXI.	*The Wind.*
XXXII.	*Lesson On The Sea.* {deleted in 1883}
XXXIII.	*Keepsake Mill.*
XXXIV.	*Time To Rise.*
XXXV.	*Good And Bad Children.*
XXXVI.	*A Proper Pride.* {deleted 1883}
XXXVII.	*Foreign Children.*
XXXVIII.	*Birthday Party.* {deleted 1883}
XXXIX.	*The Sun's Travels.*
XL.	*The Lamplighter.*
XLI.	*Little Boy Blue.* {deleted 1883}
XLII.	*My Bed Is A Boat.*
XLIII.	*The Moon.*
XLIV.	*My Kingdom.* {became III. in 'The Child Alone'}
XLV.	*The Unseen Playmate.* {became I. in 'The Child Alone'}
XLVI.	*Good News.* {deleted 1883}
XLVII.	*The Land Of Story-Books.* {became VII. in 'The Child Alone'}
XLVIII.	*The Swing.*

Additions were made as follows:

By November 1883: *North-West Passage* (XLI.), *Picture-Books in Winter* (2-IV.), *Block City* (2-VI.)

By March 1884: Dedication

By June 1884: *Armies in the Fire* (2-VIII.), *The Little Land* (2-IX.), all of 'Garden Days' and all of 'Envoys'

MS Fragments

These unused passages from notebooks were not clearly intended to be part of any *PW* or *CGV* poem but seemed nevertheless related to them through theme, tone or image. They are identified by MS number and, where possible, by notebook page:
{From Notebook 'C':}

> 'My dear Papa must buy the cake,
>> The currants are from Greece,
> My dear Mama, for my dear sake,
>> Shall cut it piece by piece.'

(B6603, p. 54)

> 'You must not suppose that a child is a fool
> For I have been thinking for long
> That a man is no better for going to school
> And the old people all in the wrong
> <That playthings are better than battles I know,>'

(B7200, p. 55)

> 'Bring out the dolls, bring out the blocks
>> <The soldiers tin array>
>> ^Bring out the horse and dray^
> And let us in our oldest frocks
>> At once proceed to play.
> <Let us get all the playthings out
>> And have a splendid play
> Get out the dolls, get out the ships,
>> The leaden soldiers bring>
>> <So fine a chance we see
> Mama in such a dreadful rain
>> Will surely let us be
> Lest such a day should pass in vain
>> Let us at once agree>'

(B6054, p. 57)

{List of proposed poem topics and titles?}

'ships in bath tub	Apothecary's bottles
Sick child	Prayer
The doctor	Lamplighter
Wind at night	[?The Divination]' (B6840, p. 57)

> '<All the fish were eating flies,>
> And all the squirrels up the trees

Were eating beechnuts, if you please.
This was a very pleasant day
When nurse and I went out to play,
All the trees that stood around
Dropped crumpled leaves upon the ground
All the winds, so soft and sweet
Kept chasing leaves away to eat.'

(B6975, p. 58)

'In all the tidy chemist's shops
<When nurse and I go there>
They have things full of lollipops.
How can they leave the sweets about
And then give nasty medicines out?'

(B6404, p. 59)

'I wish I had the lolly pops
From all the apothecary's shops,
They only give me one a day
To take the nasty taste away.'

(B6381, p. 62)

'The pleasant waters run, a shining in the sun,
        And the [? water hens] are standing in a row
And all the little trout are running in and out
        For they can't imagine where they ought to go.
Sometimes they live a day, to lie about and play
        A turning round the bubbles in a pool.'

(B6723, p. 60)

'Jim would be a sailor and Tom would be a sweep,
Rose would be a baker to eat the sugar-bread
But Will would be a soldier, with the [?]
And he himself a marching so finely at the head.'

(B6476, p. 60)

'Across the road and past the dene
I know a meadow white and green.
So high the grass and daisies grow
It must be where the fairies go.'

(B5938, p. 63)

'This is the mill that makes the bread
        The river makes it go'

(Ibid., p. 63)

'<The dog is barking loud and long
        The cock is crowing clear;
O John and Peter, shout with me
        And boys and girls come here
O John and Peter shout aloud,>
And we shouted out together all the day
And a jolly, jolly time we had of play.'

(B6162, p. 64)

{H2407, Notebook 'D', contains drafts of most of the 'Garden Days' poems written in the spring of 1884; it also has the following unused fragments that echo this section:}

'It is time to be sure, to be out of the town
        And off to the shores of the sea
To run in the wind on the top of the down
        And dig in the sand in the lee.'

(p. 1)

'In the cold and early spring
Snowdrops blossom, robins sing
Ploughman driving up and down
Then it is I leave the town.
In the corners all about
Tiny blades begin to sprout.
If I could go to sleep and know
How the pinks and pansies feel,
In the borders as they grow
Hoed and raked and watered well.'

(pp. 22–3)

{The following long fragment begins on the same page as *The Little Land*:}

'All in a garden green I play
Every shining summer day
All with rare carnations set
Marigold and mignonette.
Where the bees and shadows dance,
Here is England, there is France.
Here the gravel drive withal,
That I the bridgeless river call.
Bridgeless river, clear I see
Little waves and fish in thee;
Down along thy sheer brink
Bears and Indians come to drink
You are deeper I pretend,
River, at the laurel end
When I pass from shore to shore

I do not walk but wade thee o'er.
Here the prairie, there the woods,
Sunny, solemn solitudes,
Here the hopping fairies dwell
In the dim and daisied dell;
Here is piping shepherd's land
Where for sheep the daisies stand;
There along the ivied wall
Witches walk and goblins crawl.
To and fro my shadow goes
Now on ivy, now on rose.
Here I [?quake] and there I sing,
Everywhere the garden king!
Now to the witches walk I go,
Bold of heart but rather slow,
Now in the grass my head I bend
And see the fairy armies wend
Is the world from side to side
Wider than my garden wide?
Far along the kitchen plots
Giant cook collects shallots;
In the borders brown and big,
See the giant gardener dig,
They like shadows go and come;
Faint I hear their voices hum;
Shadows, echoes, sound and smoke:
They are only real folk,
But my fairies bright and good,
And my lions in the wood
Butterflies with flimsy wings
And the fairy garden things
They and I are child and child;
Happy, honest, laughing, wild
They and I shall all the day
Come and go and run and play.
Everywhere I turn my eye,
Something has but flitted by
And if I could quicker be,
Something surely I should see
<In the garden, in and out
Something lives and moves about,>
For there wanders, well I know,
Something living to and fro,'

(pp. 8–9)

'Children high above it like the blowing trees
Now their shadows over it like shadows of the clouds:

But it's all down below us in the green grass seas
That the insects and the fairies go in crowds.
Stoop your face adown and where the army goes
You shall see the fairy flags and towers wind along,
And away down below you where the green grass grows;
You shall hear the tiny trumpet and the song.
O to be so small and to wander in the wood
Find the fairy palaces and meet the fairy kings,
For they're all down below us in the green grass sea
All the land of stories and the princes of the rings.'

(p. 13)

'Now the day draws near an end,
O green garden, flowery friend,
In the night, when all your flowers
Grow in the dim and dewy hours
Silly snow white mushrooms sprout
And the cattle field about
I shall drive by dark ways'

(p. 25)

'All in the dark to town we go;
Wonderful shapes the coach lamps throw;
Wonderful shadows flee in front'

(p. 25)

'Down by the side of the wall and under the lilac tree
This is a part of the garden where nobody comes but me;
Nobody comes but the King, and who is the King but me?
Daisies are on the grass and birds in the lilac tree.'

(p. 25)

'White is the moon that rides the night
And the sheep are daisy white;
Below a mushroom I will camp
A glowworm I will take to lamp,' p.28

Printed Text

The copy-text chosen is the first issue of the first English edition, fully described below; it
was seen through the press by RLS and represents his final intentions. In some cases readings
have been adopted from MSS: these emendations are fully explained in the Textual Notes
on Individual Poems.

First Edition, First Issue

A CHILD'S GARDEN / OF VERSES / BY / ROBERT LOUIS STEVENSON / [Publisher's
Device] / LONDON / LONGMANS, GREEN, AND CO. / 1885

Pott. 8vo. [A]⁴ a² B–G⁸ H⁴ pp. xii + 104: [–] [iii–vii] viii–x [1–3] 4–101 [102–104]. Bound in peacock-blue cloth boards with cream end-papers, publisher's device 'The Sign of the Ship' stamped in gold on the upper left-hand corner of the front cover. Lettered in gold across the back, A / Child's / Garden / of / Verses. / Stevenson / Longmans & Co. Copies were issued with gilt edges, some with gilt top, other edges uncut, and some entirely uncut.

Variants

Binding variants are fully described in Wainwright 1971: 12–13. The Second Edition (1885) is not a resetting but a re-issue with the same collation as the first issue. The lists of books By the same Author (verso on A¹) differ slightly and the number for page 8, missing in the first issue, is present in the second one.

The American Edition of 1885, also called the Author's Edition to distinguish it from piracies, was set up by Scribner's from the sheets of the Longmans edition but has several variants. It was not corrected by RLS. The binding is paper-covered boards with cloth spine, copies issued in blue but also in green.

In addition to the annotated copy of PW at BRBML, there are copies at the Houghton Library, Harvard University and at the Firestone Library, Princeton University.

Textual Notes on Individual Poems

Dedication: To Alison Cunningham
Date of composition: [early May 1883] (see letters 3 and 4 below)
Letters 1. RLS to Alison Cunningham, 16 February 1883 (LETBM, Vol. IV, p. 76): 'the real reason why you have been more in my mind than usual, is because of some little verses that I have been writing and that I mean to make a book of; and the real reason of this letter … is that I have just seen that the book in question must be dedicated to
Alison Cunningham,
the only person who will really understand it. I don't know when it may be ready, for it has to be illustrated; but I hope in the meantime you may like the idea of what is to be; and when the time comes, I shall try to make the dedication as pretty as I can make it. Of course, this is only a flourish, like taking off one's hat; but still a person who has taken the trouble to write things, does not dedicate them to anyone without meaning it; and you must just try to take this dedication in place of a great many things I might have said and that I ought to have done to prove that I am not altogether unconscious of the great debt of gratitude I owe you.'

2. RLS to his mother, 3 March 1883 (LETBM, Vol. IV, pp. 84–5): 'I stick to what I said about Cummy: which was that she was the person entitled to the dedication; if I said she was the only person who would understand, it was a fashion of speaking; but to Cummy the dedication is due because she has had the most trouble and the least thanks. Ecco! As for Auntie, she is my aunt, and she is a lady, and I am often decently civil to her, and I don't think I ever insulted her: four advantages that could not be alleged for Cummy. That was why, out of the three of you, I chose Cummy; and that is why I think I chose right.'
{Evidently Margaret Stevenson had objected, both on her own behalf and on that of RLS's aunt, Jane Balfour, to her son's decision to dedicate CGV to his nurse; perhaps the late-

added *Envoys* 'To My Mother' and 'To Auntie' (see *LETBM*, No. 1274) were meant to appease these feelings of resentment.}

3. RLS to Henley [early May 1883] (*LETBM*, Vol. IV, p. 113): 'I forgot to mention that I shall have a dedication; I am going to dedicate 'em to Cummy; it will please her, and lighten a little my burthen of ingratitude. A low affair is the Nurse business.'

4. RLS to Henley [early May 1883] (*LETBM*, Vol. V, p. 117): 'I also write to inclose the dedication to *Penny Whistles* ...'
{*Penny Whistles* was at this time the working title for CGV; this dedication did not, however, appear in the trial version of the children's poems printed under that title in the autumn of 1883. It does not seem to have been set up in print until March 1884, when RLS ordered a new (second) proof of the expanded and retitled book (*LETBM*, Nos 1232, 1254).}

5. RLS to Alison Cunningham [late November 1883] (*LETBM*, Vol. IV, p. 208): 'I have been adding some more poems to your book. I wish they would look sharp about it; but you see they are trying to find a good artist to make the illustrations, without which no child would give a kick for it. It will be quite a fine work, I hope. The dedication is a poem too; and has been quite a long while written. But I do not mean you to see it, till you get the book: keep the jelly for the last, you know, as you would often recommend in former days; so now you can take your own medicine.'
MSS: None

I *Bed in Summer*
Date of composition: summer 1881 (Balfour)
MSS: B6007, B7140, *PW*, p. 1
Line
  2 candle-light.] candle light; (B6007)
  7 grown-up] older (B6007)
{B7140 seems to continue this poem for nine lines beyond the three published stanzas:

> 'When big and strong and wise I grow,
> I forth to foreign lands will go
> And pleasant places I shall see
> With berries growing in the tree.
>
> Lions and tigers, dogs and trees
> And [?bullpups] march along with these
> I shut my eyes for all are shy,
> Still in my bed I seem to <lay>^lie^:
>
> Yet as the crowd' {MS breaks off}

II A *Thought*
Date of composition: summer 1881 (Balfour)
MSS: B6981, *PW*, p. 1

Line
1   very] so very (B6981, *PW*)
2   drink,] drink (B6981)
3   grace] grace, (B6981)

III *At the Sea-side*
Date of composition: summer 1881 (Balfour)
MSS: B5990, *PW*, pp. 1–2

IV *Young Night Thought*
Date of composition: summer 1881 (Balfour)
Letter: RLS to Henley [early May 1883] (*LETBM*, Vol. IV, p. 114):
{RLS suggested an illustration as follows:}
'The procession – the child running behind it. The procession tailing off through the gates of a cloudy city.'
MSS: B7203, *PW*, p. 2
Title: *Thought*] *Thoughts* (*PW*)
Line
1   night,] night (B7203)
2   When my mamma] As soon as Mama (B7203)
                              When my mama (*PW*)
3   by,] by (B7203)
4   day, ~ eye.] day ~ eye (B7203)
5   kings,] kings (B7203)
7   grand a way,] strange a way (B7203)
8   You] I (B7203)
9   seen,] seen (B7203)
10   green;] green (B7203)
11–12   For every kind of beast and man
        Is marching in that caravan.] {omitted in (B7203)}
        Though I'm so sleepy, yet I find
        That I can never stay behind (*PW*)
13   slow,] slow. (B7203)
14   go,] go (B7203)
16   we reach the town of Sleep.]
        <they pass the gates of sleep. >^we reach the town of sleep. ^ (B7203)

V *Whole Duty of Children*
Date of composition: summer 1881 (Balfour)
MSS: B7158, *PW*, p. 2
Line
1   always say what's true] <do his best to grow>^ ~ ^ (B7158)
2   to,] to (B7158)
3   table:] table, (B7158) table; (*PW*)

{On p. 2 of *PW Bull Hunt* follows as No. VI but on the annotated copy of *PW* at BRBML is marked for deletion by Henley, Colvin and RLS; this printed text, a later version of B6058, follows:}

> 'Papa is away to the office I see,
>   And Johnnie has gone to the school.
> Come, Peter, and sit in the corner with me,
>   And pretend to be hunting a bull.'

VI *Rain*
Date of composition: summer 1881 (Balfour)
MSS: B6747, B6644, *PW*, p. 3
Line
 2   field and tree,] <tower>^field^ and tree. (B6747)
 3   on the umbrellas here,] <upon the grassy ground,>^on the umbrellas here,^ (B6747)
 4   And on the ships] And out on ships B6747, *PW*
{In B6644 there is an unpublished second quatrain as follows:}

> 'Now all the roads are full of mire,
>   Both in and out of town;
> And children sit beside the fire
>   And hear it patter down.'

VII *Pirate Story*
Date of composition: summer 1881 (Balfour)
Letter: RLS to Henrietta Milne, [?23 October 1883] (*LETBM*, Vol. IV, p. 189:
{While reading this poem in the just-printed *PW*, RLS's cousin Henrietta had recognised herself and her brother Willie Traquair.}
'Certainly; who else would they be? More by token, on that particular occasion, you were sailing under the title of Princess Royal; I, after a furious contest, under that of Prince Alfred, and Willie, still a little sulky, as the Prince of Wales. We were all in a buck basket about halfway between the swing and the gate; and I can still see the Pirate Squadron heave in sight upon the weather bow.'
MSS: B6718, *PW*, p. 3
Line
 1   afloat] <were out><at sea>^afloat^ (B6718)
 2   on the lea.] <for the clothes><for the wash>^on the lea.^ (B6718)
 3   Winds are in the air, they are blowing in the spring,]
         <Winds were in the air, blowing in the Spring.>
         ^Winds were in the air, they were blowing in the Spring.^ (B6718)
                                                          ~ Spring, (*PW*)
 4   And waves are on the meadow] <Waves were in the grass,>
                                   ^And waves were on the meadow^ (B6718)
 5   Where shall we adventure, today that we're afloat,]
         ~ adventure <now>^today^ ~ afloat? (B6718)
 6   Wary of the weather and steering by a star]
         <This shall be the compass for a bearing by a star;>
         ^Watchful of the weather and steering by a star;^ (B6718)

7   Shall it be to Africa,] <Shall we go to India>^Shall it be to India^ (B6718)
8   To Providence, or Babylon,] To Providence or <Egypt>^Malaga,^ (B6718)

                                        Malaga, (PW)

         {RLS may have changed 'Malaga' to 'Babylon' because Colvin, annotating the Yale
         copy of PW, criticised the terminal 'a' followed by 'or' as awkward.}
9–12   <Here we <<saw>>^see^ a pirate a rowing in the field,
         Quick and to the oars, for the pirate is anear;
         The wicket is the harbour and the garden is the <<shore>>^land.^ > (B6718)
9   Hi! but here's a squadron a-rowing on the sea –]
         <I am the><Hey>^Hi!^ but here's a <rower>^squadron^ a rowing in the
         <field>^sea^ (B6718)
10   Cattle on the meadow a-charging with a roar!]
         Cattle in the meadow <are> a-charging with a roar; (B6718)
11   Quick, and we'll escape them, they're as mad as they can be,]
         ~ escape – they're as <bad>^wild^ ~ (B6718)
         ~ escape, they're ~ (PW)

VIII *Foreign Lands*
Date of composition: summer 1881 (Balfour)
Letters and sources: 1. {In 1880 RLS recorded this reminiscence of Colinton Manse:}
'I remember … another outlook, when I climbed a hawthorn near the gate, and saw over the
wall upon the snuff-mill garden, thick with flowers and bright with sunshine, a paradise not
hitherto suspected' ('Memoirs of Himself', *VAIL*, Vol. XXVI, p. 212).

2. RLS to Henley [early May 1883] (*LETBM*, Vol. IV, p. 114):
{RLS suggested illustrations as follows:} 'This will I think want two plates: the child
climbing, his first glimpse over the garden wall with what he sees – the tree shooting higher
and higher like the beanstalk, and the view widening. The river slipping in. The road
arriving in Fairyland.'
MSS: B6236, *PW*, pp. 3–4
First publication: included with *A Child's Fancies* in Cassell's *Magazine of Art*, London: July
1884
Line
1   Up into the cherry tree] <Into the old red hawthorn tree>^Up into the cedar tree^
         (B6236)
2   me?] me (B6236)
3   with both my hands] in both my hands (B6236) ~hands, (MA)
5   next door garden lie,] <old mill>^next door^ garden lie (B6236)
6   Adorned with flowers, before my eye,]
         <Wholly<<disclosed before>>uncovered to> ^ ~ ^ (B6236)
                                        ~ eye; (PW, MA)
7   pleasant] other (B6236)
9   dimpling river pass] river <stealing>^dimple^ by, (B6236)
                                        river dimple by (PW)
10   And be the sky's blue looking-glass;]
         Holding its face up to the sky; (B6236, PW)
11   down] down, (B6236, MA)

12		in to town.] into town. (*PW*)
		{trial fragments for lines 11–12 in (B6236):}
		I saw the road go up and down
		I saw the mill wheel turning round
		And from
		Making a most melodious sound.
		The garden set with scarlet flowers,
15–16	To where the grown-up river slips
		Into the sea among the ships,]
		Till I at last should catch a glance
		 Of vessels sailing off to France. (B6236)
		{trial fragments for lines 15–16 in (B6236):}
		<To>Where the roads and river
		From town to city journey on
		<That river, between harbour walls
		Into the bright Atlantic falls.>
		To where the <full>grown-up river slips
		<Along>Seaward, between the anchored ships.
		And lastly between harbour walls
		Into the bright Atlantic falls.
17		To where the roads on] <To>^Or^ ~ from (B6236)
							Or ~ *PW*, MA
18		Lead onward into fairy land,]
		Lead forth into the fairy land (B6236)
19		all the children dine at five,] little children dine at five (B6236)

IX *Windy Nights*
Date of composition: summer 1881 (Balfour)
Letters and sources: 1. 'Notes of Childhood', 18 May 1873, quoted by Balfour (Vol. I, p. 38):
'I had an extreme terror of Hell, implanted in me, I suppose, by my good nurse, which used
to haunt me terribly on stormy nights, when the wind had broken loose and was going about
the town like a bedlamite. I remember that the noises on such occasions always grouped
themselves for me into the sound of a horseman, or rather a succession of horsemen, riding
furiously past the bottom of the street and away up the hill into town; I think even now that
I hear the terrible *howl* of his passage, and the clinking that I used to attribute to his bit and
stirrups. On such nights I would lie awake and pray and cry, until I prayed and cried myself
asleep.'

2. RLS to Frances Sitwell [21 October 1874] (*LETBM*, Vol. II, pp. 65–6): 'Last night, it blew
a fearful gale; I was kept awake about a couple of hours, and could not get to sleep for the
horror of the wind's noise; the whole house shook; and mind you our house *is* a house, a great
castle of jointed stone that would weigh up a street of English houses; so that when it quakes,
as it did last night, it means something. But the quaking was not what put me about; it was
the horrible howl of the wind round the corner; the audible haunting of an incarnate anger
about the house; the evil spirit that was abroad; and above all the shuddering silent pauses
when the storm's heart stands dreadfully still for a moment. O how I hate a storm at night!
They have been a great influence in my life I am sure; for I can remember them so far back

– long before I was six at least … the storm had for me a perfect impersonation; as durable and unvarying as any heathen deity. I always heard it, as a horseman riding past with his cloak about his head, and somehow always carried away, and riding past again, and being baffled yet once more, *ad infinitum*, all night long. I think I wanted him to get past; but I am not sure; I know only that I had some interest either for or against, in the matter and I used to lie and hold my breath, not quite frightened but in a state of miserable exaltation.'

3. RLS to Henley [early May 1883] (*LETBM*, Vol. IV, p. 114):
{RLS suggested an illustration as follows.}
'The child in bed listening – the horseman galloping.'
{Cf. his Whitmanesque treatment of these *motifs* in *Stormy Nights*.}
MSS: B7171, *PW*, p. 4
{This poem seems to originate from the following metrical scheme on B7171:

/∧∧ /∧∧ /∧ /
/∧∧ /∧∧ /∧∧ /

The first line of this dactylic scheme fits lines 5 and 11, the second fits lines 6 and 12; beneath it are these trials for lines 5–6; the onomatopoetic intention is evident:
    'Late in the night when the <lights><candles>^fires^ are out
        Why does he gallop and gallop about?'}
Line
  1   moon and stars are set,] <night is><weather is><dark and wet>
                                ^moon and stars are set^ (B7171)
  2   Whenever ~ high,] <And>whenever ~ high (B7171)
  3   the dark] dark (B7171)
  4   by.] by – (PW)
  7   the trees are crying aloud,] <the trees are fallen>
       ^the <chimneys>^^trees^^are crying aloud^ (B7171) ~aloud (PW)
  8   tossed] sinking (B7171)
  9   By, on the highway, low and loud,] By on the highway low and loud (B7171)
  10   he.] he – (PW)
{There are trial stanzas in (B7171) as follows:}

            Where is he riding at night so late?
                With nobody riding <along>^besides^
            Hark, as the cinders fall in the grate
                To the ring of his spurs as he rides.
            <Where is he riding, <<early and late>>^all night long^
                And why does he never get there?>

            Where is he riding at night so late
                Why does he ride so <hard>^fast^
            Why does he come when the wind is great
                And gallop before the blast?
            Galloping ever and all night long,
            Galloping still, when the wind is strong.

> Where and where and where can he <ride>^go?^
>   Who and who can he be?
> Maybe St. Nicholas to and fro
>   To <bring>^buy^ my presents <to>^for^ me,
> Riding and riding as hard as he can
> Bringing a drum to a good little man.

X *Travel*

Date of composition: summer 1881 (Balfour)

MSS: B7057, *PW*, p. 5; the Yale MS is a draft of this eight-line version printed in *PW*:

> O I should like to rise and go
>   And wander on my feet,
> Where all the garden apples grow
>   And things are nice to eat;
>
> All down beside the water-brooks,
>   And past the harbour bar,
> And o'er the hills, in story-books,
>   Where bears and lions are.

{B7057 has the following variants from *PW*:}

Line

2   feet,] feet

3   garden] golden

4   eat,] eat,

5   water-brooks,] water brooks

6   And past the harbour bar,] <And onward near and far,>^ ~ ^

7   o'er] over

5–8 {trial}<And over the hills in story books,
         Where bears and lions are.
         All down beside the water brooks,>

XI *Singing*

Date of composition: summer 1881 (Balfour)

MSS: B8354, *PW*, p. 5

Line

1   Of speckled eggs the birdie sings] <The birdies sing><The birds sing>
                                      ^ ~ sings,^ (B8354) ~ sings, (*PW*)

2   trees;] trees (B8354)

3   sailor sings of ropes and things] sailors sing of ropes'n things (B8354)

4   In] And (B8354)

6   Spain;] Spain, (B8354)

7   with the organ man] <and>^with^ the organ man, (B8354)

XII *Looking Forward*

Date of composition: summer 1881 (Balfour)

Letter: RLS to Colvin [early November 1883] (*LETBM*, Vol. IV, p. 198):
{Colvin, writing on the Yale copy of *PW*, which he has just returned to the poet, had
objected to the final line as follows: 'Jerky metre, I don't think the dropping of a first syllable
suddenly at the beginning of a line is permissible in a set of poems like this.' Henley con-
tradicted him, crossing out Colvin's comment and writing above it, 'Don't matter a bit.' In
this letter RLS remarked, 'I love the occasional trochaic line; and so did many excellent
writers before me.' Colvin also queried 'tell' in line 3, suggesting 'teach' instead.}
MSS: *PW*, p. 5; cf. first 4 lines of B7140 quoted above on p. 352

XIII *A Good Play*
Date of composition: summer 1881 (Balfour)
Letter: RLS to Henley [early May 1883] (*LETBM*, Vol. IV, p. 114):
{RLS suggested an illustration as follows:}
'Building of the ship – Storing her – Navigation – Tom's accident, the other child paying no
attention.'
MSS: B6263, *PW*, p. 6
Line
  1   stairs] stairs, (B6263)
  3   And filled it full of sofa pillows] <We loaded it with>^And filled it full of
                                                          sofa pillows,^ (B6263)
  5   We took a saw and several nails,] <We took a hat of my papa's>^ ~ nails^ (B6263)
       ~nails (*PW*)
  7   said, 'Let us] said let us (B6263)
  8   An … cake'; –] <This>^An^ … cake (B6263) ~ cake;' (*PW*)
       {Two trial lines follow at this point in B6263:}
       <We had a plate of breakfast crumbs,
       And half an ounce of sugar plums,>
  9   me] me, (B6263)
  10 go a-sailing] {'go' omitted} a sailing (B6263)
  11 days,] days (*PW*)
  12 plays;] plays, (B6263)

XIV *Where Go the Boats?*
Date of composition: summer 1881 (Balfour)
MSS: H2460, *PW*, p. 6
Line
  2   sand.] sand, (*PW*)
  3   for ever,] for ever (H2460)
  4   hand.] hand, (*PW*)
  16 bring] {unadopted marginal alternative} 'fetch' (H2460)

XV *Auntie's Skirts*
Date of composition: summer 1881 (Balfour)
MSS: H2460, *PW*, p. 7
Line
  2   sound;] sound. (H2460)
  3   floor,] floor (H2460)

XVI *The Land of Counterpane*

Date of composition: summer 1881 (Balfour)

Letter: RLS to William Archer, 29 March 1885 (*LETBM*, Vol. V, pp. 97–8): {Archer had reviewed *CGV* in the *Pall Mall Gazette* for 24 March 1885: in this letter the poet thanks him for 'the best criticism I ever had.'} 'You are very right about my voluntary aversion from the painful sides of life. My childhood was in reality a very mixed experience, full of fever, nightmare, insomnia, painful days and interminable nights; and I can speak with less authority of Gardens than of that other "land of counterpane". But to what end should we renew these sorrows? The sufferings of life may be handled by the very greatest in their hours of insight; it is of its pleasures that our common poems should be formed; these are the experiences that we should seek to recall or to provoke; and I say with Thoreau, "What right have I to complain, who have not ceased to wonder?" and, to add a rider of my own, who have no remedy to offer.'

MSS: B6486, H2460, *PW*, p. 7

First publication: included with *A Child's Fancies* in *Magazine of Art* July 1884

{B6486 is an early rough draft, with false starts and erased and alternate lines as follows:}

'<Once a week at candle light

   The organ man> ^Once a week at candlelight

When all the lamps are lit^

When I was ill & lay in bed

I had 2 pillows at my head;

<I <<wanted>>called my soldiers out><My playthings all>^And all my toys beside me lay^

<Upon my knees and in a tray.>

^To keep me happy all the day.^

Sometimes for an hour or so

I watched my leaden soldiers go

{alternate} I placed my soldiers row by row

{alternate} And then I sat and watched {them go?}

With different uniforms and drills

Among the bedclothes, through the hills,

And sometimes sent my ships in fleets

All up and down across the sheets;

Or brought my trees and houses out

And set them here and there about

<Hill, valley, road and>^To make a country all complete.^'

I was the giant, great and still' {rest of draft identical with copy-text}

Line

  1   a-bed] abed (H2460)

  5   sometimes for an hour or so] sometimes, for an hour or so, (H2460)

 11 out,] out (H2460)

 13 giant great and still] giant, great and still, (H2460)

 15 dale and plain,] field and plain, (H2460, *PW*)

 16 counterpane.] Counterpane. (H2460)

XVII *The Land of Nod*

Date of composition: summer 1881 (Balfour)

MSS: B6487, H2460, *PW*, pp. 7–8

{In B6487, a version of lines 5–8 of the copy-text appears as lines 13–16; at the top of this MS there are twelve words which rhyme with 'nod'.}

Line

2   stay;] stay (B6487)

4   Nod.] nod. (B6487)

5   All by myself I have to go,] <Every night I find the way>
                   ^And all alone, I have to go – ^ (B6487)

6   With none to tell me what to do –] Its very dangerous, don't you know – (B6487)

8   mountain-sides] mountain sides (B6487, PW) mountainsides (H2460)

9   The strangest] Curious (B6487, H2460 {H2460 has 'The strangest' in the margin})

10 see,] see; (B6487)

11 And many frightening sights abroad] <And curious people go abroad>
             ^And many frightening <things>^^sights^^ abroad^ (B6487)

12 Nod.] nod. (B6487)

13 Try as I like to find the way,]<Every night I find the way>^Try ~ way^ (B6487)

14 get back] get there (B6487)

XVIII *My Shadow*

Date of composition: c. summer 1881 (pp. 63–5, Notebook 'C')

MSS: B5989, B6324, B6359, B6613, B6614, H2460, *PW*, p. 8

{From Notebook 53 (BRBML) – variations on *My Shadow*?}

    'At night I leave my little bed
        Upon the upper floor;
    I cross the room with naked tread
        And slip from out the door
    I peer between the railings tall
        And see all and about
    The great big hollow of the hall,'

                         (B5989)

    'How tall the grass and daisies grow
        Here in the valley where I go.
    <I rose before the sun was up>
        Before the sun began to peep
    When all the children were asleep,
        I rose and went abroad.
    What do you think?
        All the shadows were still abroad.'

                         (B6324)

{On p. 63 of Notebook 'C', B6613 consists of the following lines:}

    'I have a little shadow that goes always round with me,
    He gets into bed before me every night
    <And when>'

{Just below, on the same page, B6359 consists of these lines:}

'I rose before they told me to
When all the \<grass>^lawn^ was thick with dew,
It was the very peep of day,
And night had hardly gone away
The dew stood in the buttercup,
Only the birds and me were up.
All the trees stood very still
Both \<in the garden>^round the house^ and on the hill;
And all the shadows lay so long'

{After several tentative, fragmentary lines unconnected with CGV or with one another, on the next pages of Notebook 'C' (64–5) there is a full draft of My *Shadow* (B6614) which, however, varies from the copy-text in the order in which the couplets are arranged; this MS gives the printed lines as follows: 1–4, 11–12, 9–10, 13–16, 5–8; H2460 follows the same line order as the copy-text.}

Line
  1 me,] me; (H2460)
  2 of him] of it (B6614) of him, (H2460)
  3 He is very, very … head;] \<It>^He^ is shaped exactly … head (B6614)
  4 see him] see it (B6614)
  5 grow –] grow, (B6614)
  7 shoots up … india-rubber] jumps up … india rubber (B6614)
 10 sort] kind (B6614)
 11 He stays so close beside me, he's a coward you can see;]
     He \<sticks>^stays^ so close beside \<me you can see that he's afraid.>
     ^me, he's a coward you can see^ (B6614) he's a coward, you can see; – (H2460)
 12 I'd think shame to stick to nursie as that shadow sticks to me!]
        \<Go, out, and take a run you \<\<little fool>>^timid fool,^ I said.>
        \<But no; the> ^ ~ me.^ (B6614)
 13 early, before] early and before (B6614)
 14 on every buttercup;] in every buttercup. (B6614)
     I rose] {marginal query} I went out (H2460)
 15 But my lazy little shadow, like an arrant sleepy-head,]
     And do you know? my shadow, \<that>^like^ an arrant sleepyhead (B6614)

{On p. 8 of *PW*, *The Hunt Interrupted* follows as No. XXI but on the Yale copy of *PW* it is marked for deletion; this printed text, a later version of both B6325 and four lines on p. 3 of H2460, follows close on My *Shadow* in both MSS so was probably written about the same time (summer of 1881): the *PW* text follows:}

'Hi! nursie, you come back again,
Behind the deodar,
For that's the place I'm going to hunt
Where all the tigers are.'

{RLS recorded this memory from a summer afternoon at Colinton Manse:} 'Once as I lay, playing hunter, hid in a thick laurel, and with a toy-gun upon my arm, I worked myself so hotly into the spirit of my play, that I think I can still see the herd of antelope come sweeping down the lawn and round the deodar; it was almost a vision' ('Memoirs of Himself', *VAIL*, Vol. XXVI, pp. 211–12).

{On p. 9 of *PW*, No. XXIII, *A Song of Days*, is marked for deletion on the Yale copy; it is identical with the MS version in H2460 and follows here:}

> 'Wheat bread and honey,
> Ice-cake and fool,
> Saturday for money,
> Monday for school!
>
> Play and work and eating
> All the week along –
> Sunday go to meeting
> With the new clothes on!'

XIX *System*
MS: *PW*, p. 9. {Colvin advised deletion; Henley wrote 'stet'.}

XX *A Good Boy*
Letters: 1. RLS to Henrietta Milne [?23 October 1883] (*LETBM*, Vol. IV, p. 190):
{See notes to *Pirate Story* above, pp. 354–5} 'You were a capital fellow to play: how few there were who could! None better than yourself. I shall never forget some of the days at Bridge of Allan; they were one golden dream: see *A Good Boy* in the *Penny Whistles*, much of the sentiment of which is taken direct from one evening at B. of A. when we had a great play with the little Glasgow girl … Generally speaking, whenever I think of play, it is pretty certain that you will come into my head. I wrote a paper called *Child's Play* once, where, I believe, you or Willie would recognise things.' {This paper, written in 1878, appears in *EDIN*, Vol. III, pp. 157–71.}

2. RLS to Colvin [early November 1883] (*LETBM*, Vol. IV, p. 198):
{Colvin wrote 'priggish' opposite this poem's title on the Yale *PW*, suggesting deletion. Henley agreed, but RLS stood his ground, telling Colvin, 'If you don't like *A Good Boy*, I do.' MSS: B6261, H2460, *PW*, pp. 9–10; H2460 and *PW* have three couplets not included in B6261 or the copy-text; the earliest version appears to be B6261, transcribed below:}

> '<The children all go homeward – you can hear the mothers <<call>>^cry^
> The little birds are silent now upon the treetops high.>
> At last the golden sun begins to go behind the wood.
> Another day is over and I know that I've been good.
> <For I was happy in the {word omitted} when I woke and happy at my play>
> I love the even shadow as I loved the noonday sun
> And <my>cousin Tom has painted me the picture of a gun.
> I pounded little pebbles on the beach below the <firs>^trees^
> <And read the tale of <<Twoshoes and the fractious [?]>>Goody and the evil [?]>
> And climbed the sandy mountain <with>^in^ the <prickles>^nettles^ to my knees.
> <And>^So^ now along the shadow I'm returning home to bed,

<With the><And soon>^And then^, when all is over, <when I'm>and my evening
   prayer is said
<I shall>I'll lie among the pleasant sheets and close my happy eyes,
And wait until time comes to call me by surprise.'

{In H2460 and *PW*, there are three couplets between lines 4–5, as follows:}

'You know, with naughty children, one is always naughty too;
But I was playing all the day alone or with a few.
We scared the sandy martens and we almost caught the hares;] <hare>^hares;^ (H2460)
We played at being princes and we played at being bears;] Princes ~ Bears; (H2460)
We told each other fairy tales till all of us were sad;
Among the golden furzes, we clambered and were glad.'

Line
 4   happy, for] happy for (H2460, *PW*)
 5   fair,] fair. (H2460)
 6   sleepsin-by,] Sleepsin-by, (H2460) prayer.] prayer! (H2460, *PW*)
 7   that, till … arise,] that till … arise (H2460, *PW*)
 9   dawn,] dawn<,> (H2460) dawn (*PW*)
10   lawn.] lawn<!>^.^ (H2460)

{On p. 9 of *PW* this text of *The Garden Door*, omitted from CGV, is No. XXII:}

'The world is quite a foreign place for little children's feet,
     There are so many borders where we're not allowed to go;
The flowers that are so beautiful, we are not meant to eat;
     And many things we ask about, we're told we're not to know.

But patience, little children, let us wait a year or more;
     We're growing very rapidly and soon we shall be men.
When we're a little older, we'll unbar the garden door,
     And off to follow fortune over mountain, over glen!'

MSS: H2460, *PW*, p. 9; the following variants occur in H2460:
Line
 1   feet,] feet –
 5   children,] children –
 6   men,] men<;>^.^ {Here the MS reading is better than the printed one as the syntax
      requires a full stop: it has been adopted.}
 8   over mountain, over glen!] in the mountain and the glen!

XXI *Escape at Bedtime*
Letter: RLS to Colvin [early November 1883] (*LETBM*, Vol. IV, pp. 198–9):
{For line 12 Colvin suggested, on the Yale *PW*, 'Twinkled half full' instead of 'Would be half
full'. RLS sharply rejected this: '"Twinkled" is just the error; to the child the stars appear to
be there; any word that suggests illusion is a horror.'}
MS: *PW*, p. 10; the following variants from the copy-text occur:

Line

 3   high overhead] just overhead

 6   Nor] Or

 7   me,] me

11   These shone] These above

15   eyes,] eyes

XXII *Marching Song*

Date of composition: before mid-February 1883 (*LETBM*, No. 1058)

MSS: H2460, *PW*, p. 11

Line

 5   party,] party (H2460, *PW*)

 8   Grenadier!] grenadier! (H2460)

10   Marching] Marching, (H2460)

11   Waves] <Blows>^Waves^ (H2460)

14   {Colvin suggested on the Yale *PW* that 'Great Commander Jane' be altered to 'Captain
     Mary Jane' but RLS made no change.}

16   again.] again! (H2460)

XXIII *The Cow*

MSS: H2460, *PW*, p. 11

First publication: included with *A Child's Fancies* in *Magazine of Art*, July 1884

Line

 1   cow] cow, (MA)

 2   heart:] heart. (H2460) heart; (MA)

 7   open air,] open-air, (MA)

 9   pass] pass, (MA)

11   meadow grass] meadow-grass (MA)

12   meadow flowers] meadow-flowers (MA)

XXIV *Happy Thought*

MSS: B7182, Berg: CGV, *PW*, p. 12

{B7182 may be the first effort at any CGV poem; it appears on p. 54 of Notebook 'C' as
follows:

> 'The world is so great and I am so small
> I do not like it at all at all'

These lines are opposite in meaning to *Happy Thought*. Balfour (Vol. I, p. 40) speculates that
the following nightmare may have inspired this first draft, later modified into RLS's
characteristic idiom of brave optimism: 'I dreamed I was to swallow the world, and the terror
of the fancy arose from the complete conception I had of the hugeness and populousness of
our sphere. Disproportion and a peculiar shade of brown, something like that of sealskin,
haunted me particularly during these visitations' ('Memoirs of Himself', *VAIL*, Vol. XXVI,
pp. 210–11).

The Berg MS is a photostat of a Notebook page (unidentified) containing drafts of *Happy
Thought* and *My Treasures*, the poem preceding it in *PW*. The two lines from B7182 are here
transposed and given a title, as follows:

'<A Thought>^Happy Thought^
I'm sure we should all be as happy as kings!
The world is so full of a number of things, –'

But the dash in line 2 is cancelled and the lines are marked for transposition. *PW* and the
copy-text are identical.}

XXV *The Wind*
Date of composition: before mid-February 1883 (*LETBM*, No. 1058)
Letters: 1. RLS to Henley [mid-February 1883] (*LETBM*, Vol. IV, p. 73):
{Henley had written to RLS, asking him, 'Try and draw me your idea of "The Wind" ' so he
could send it to potential illustrators such as Walter Crane, Kate Greenaway and Randolph
Caldecott.} 'If Crane can catch it, the Wind is the fellow to illustrate. Ah, if I could only
draw! I see the blame thing so clearly in outline; and if I try to put it down – but you have,
ahem! seen my work.'

2. RLS to Colvin [early November 1883] (*LETBM*, Vol. IV, pp. 198–9):
{In his annotations, Colvin had marked 'sings' in the final line of the refrain, complaining,
'It won't do: the vocative demands a second person in the verb: "singest"; or else the line
must be differently turned.' Henley drew a line through Colvin's notes and RLS said, 'I don't
care: I take a different view of the vocative.'}
MSS: *PW*, pp. 12–13
First publication: included with *A Child's Fancies* in *Magazine of Art*, July 1884; this printing
varies from the copy-text as follows:
Line
5, 11, 17   long,] long'
8   hid.] hid;

{Following *The Wind* as No. XXXII in *PW* is *Lesson on the Sea*, omitted from CGV: the
printed text follows:

'The sea is the largest of waters I hear,
        And behold! it is full to the brim,
For the sun to go down in when evening draws near
        And the birds and the boaties to skim.

The ships may go sailing before them for days,
        And the birds may go flying at will,
But they never arrive at the end of their ways,
        For the sea is in front of them still.

It tosses the seaweed and shells on the sand
        For the children to play with on shore;
And it tumbles and roars at the edge of the land
        As the beasts in menageries roar.

The rain of the sky and the rivers that haste,
        All run to the sea without halt;

But the rain and the rivers are sweet to the taste,
And the sea is unpleasantly salt.

Most wonderful things are observed on the land,
    Like the wind and the Chinaman's wall,
There are thousands of things that we can't understand,
    But the sea is the greatest of all!'

MSS: B6507, PW, p. 13; these MSS are identical except that B6507 omits the comma following line 5. B6507 is not in a notebook but is a separate page.

XXVI *Keepsake Mill*
MSS: H2460, PW, p. 14; on the annotated PW Henley drew an 'x' through the text with the marginal note, 'I don't like this one at all.' Colvin disagreed, but marked the last stanza for deletion, saying 'ends much better at stanza 5'.
Line
 7   under –] under, (H2460) under, – (PW)
 9   village] hamlet (H2460)
10   hill;] hill, (H2460), (PW)
13   river] river<,> (H2460) river, (PW)
15   for ever] forever (H2460)
18   soldiers we] soldiers, we (H2460)
20   churning] cheering (PW)
21   gave when we quarrelled,] gave you on Friday, (H2460, PW)
23   Honoured and old and all gaily apparelled,]
     Shining with epaulettes, upright and tidy, (H2460, PW)
24   and remember] to remember (PW)

XXVII *Good and Bad Children*
Letter: RLS to Colvin [early November 1883] (*LETBM*, Vol. IV, pp. 198–9):
{On the Yale PW, Colvin called the rhyming of 'bewild'ring' and 'children' in lines 7–8 a 'Cockney rhyme'. Henley crossed this out, remarking 'Cf. Keats & Mrs. Browning'. RLS responded, 'Bewildering and childering are good enough for me. These are rhymes, jingles; I don't go for eternity and the three unities.' Colvin was engaging in the same kind of neo-classical pedantry that Ruskin displayed when he chastised Rossetti for his 'Cockney rhyme' of 'Jenny' with 'guinea' in the first couplet of the monologue *Jenny*.}
MSS: H2460, PW, pp. 14–15
First publication: included with *A Child's Fancies* in *Magazine of Art*, July 1884.
Line
 2   brittle;] brittle: (H2460)
13   unruly,] unruly (MA, PW)
16   story!] story. (MA)
18   gabies,] gabies (MA)

{Following *Good and Bad Children* as No. XXXVI in PW, *A Proper Pride* was omitted from CGV; the printed text follows here:}

'Now, Jenny, don't be silly, there are girls and there are boys,
And different kinds of children must have different kinds of toys.
For some are all for driving whips and things with which to strike,
And others take to tea-cups and to rattles and the like;
And some can play with soldiers, and the rest with women dolls –
So I'll play with you at keeping shop but not at making calls!'

MSS: H2460, PW, p. 15; H2460 has the following variants:
Line
  1   silly,] silly –
  4   take to tea-cups] <are for tea>^take to tea-cups^
  5   can play] <must play>^can play^
  6   shop] shop,

XXVIII *Foreign Children*
Letter: RLS to Henley [early May 1883] (*LETBM*, Vol. IV, pp. 114–15):
{RLS suggested an illustration as follows:} 'The foreign types dancing in a jing-a-ring, with the English child pushing in the middle. The foreign children looking and showing each other marvels. The English child at the leeside of a roast of beef. The English child sitting thinking with his picture-books all round him, and the jing-a-ring of the foreign children, in miniature dancing over the picture-books.'
MS: PW, pp. 15–16; in *PW*, the first stanza is repeated as a refrain after each of the following three stanzas whereas in the copy-text it is repeated only once as the final stanza. Other variants are as follows:
Line
  4, 20   O! don't] Don't
  16   safe and live] safe alive
  19   Turk or] Turk, or

{On the Yale *PW*, No. XXXVIII, *Birthday Party*, which follows *Foreign Children*, is marked for deletion by both Colvin and Henley; the former wrote 'I've read almost the same lines on Christmas crackers.' It did not appear in CGV. The *PW* text is as follows:}

'Laughing and leaping and blind-man's-buff,
All of us merry and none of us rough!

Now for the supper, and what do you think?
Trifle and ices, and negus to drink!

Cracker and caramel, apple and quince,
Here is a birthday to honour a Prince!'

XXIX *The Sun's Travels*
MS: PW, pp. 16–17; the only variant occurs in line 6, as follows:
We round the sunny garden play,] We drive or round the garden play,

XXX *The Lamplighter*
MS: PW, p. 17; in the margin of the Yale *PW*, Colvin advised deletion, 'the lamplighter being an extinct animal to the modern child'.

{The poem following *The Lamplighter* as No. XLI in *PW*, *Little Boy Blue*, was marked for deletion by both Colvin and Henley, the former having written 'not very good'. It did not appear in *CGV*. The *PW* text follows}

'Little Boy Blue
   Come blow me your horn!
We are all going through
   The clover and corn.

Before I was up,
   You blew from the hill,
The swallows had heard you
   And sang on the sill.

Come out to play –
   It was that, that you said –
All the long day,
   And go weary to bed!

Little Boy Blue,
   Go trotting before!
Give us a lead
   And a tune or two more.

Little Boy Blue,
   Come blow us your horn!
We are all going through
   The clover and corn.'

XXXI *My Bed is a Boat*
Letter: RLS to Henley [early May 1883] (*LETBM*, Vol. IV, p. 115):
[RLS suggested an illustration as follows:} 'The child being started off. The bed sailing, curtains and all, upon the sea. The child waking and finding himself at home, the corner of toilette might be worked in to look like the pier.'
MS: *PW*, p. 18; the only variant is in line 6, as follows: good-night] good night.

XXXII *The Moon*
MS: *PW*, p. 19
Line
  9 But all of the things] But all the things
 12 Till up in the morning the sun shall arise.]
      Till morning returns and rekindle the skies.

{On the annotated *PW*, No. XLVI, *Good News*, which follows *The Moon*, is marked for deletion by both Colvin and Henley, the former noting that it is 'out of the key'. It did not appear in *CGV*. The *PW* text follows:}

'God's in the blue, and cares for you;
    Angel and fairy fly.
Sunshine and sleep, and swallows and sheep,
    And flowers to please the eye!

Merry to bed, O flaxen head!
    Merrily rise to play!
There is no fear – your mother is near,
    And bright is the face of day!'

XXXIII *The Swing*
MS: *PW*, p. 22; Colvin wrote 'commonplace' next to this poem, as No. XLVIII the final item
in the trial printing; he advised deletion but Henley wrote 'stet'.
Line
  1   swing,] swing
  3   Oh, I do] – O I do

XXXIV *Time to Rise*
MS: *PW*, p. 14

XXXV *Looking-glass River*
MS: Berg: CGV; this MS has two unpublished stanzas following line 12:

'See upon it, fairy-painted,
    Leafy green and airy-blue
        Larks half fainted
        Beyond man's view.

Crested clouds aloft and steady
    Humming flies that cross and pass –
        Till a silver eddy
        Break the looking-glass;'

Line
24   by-and-by.] by and by.

XXXVI *Fairy Bread*
MSS: None found.

XXXVII *From a Railway Carriage*
MSS: None found.

XXXVIII *Winter-time*
Date of composition: [November 1884] (*LETBM*, No. 1335)
Letter: RLS to Henley [November 1884] (*LETBM*, Vol. V, p. 35): 'By return, send me the
three poems (1) *Hayloft*; (2) *Good-bye to Farm*; (3) *Winter*, I sent you to add to the *corpus*.'
MSS: H2407, H2404; RLS Notebook 'D', H2407, has on its first page these four cancelled
lines which might be a draft of the first stanza:

> 'In winter when the frost is white
> The days are short and cold;
> The moon is up by three o'clock
> The sun is down by four.'

H2404 is RLS Notebook No. A270; scattered on the first two leaves are draft stanzas and lines for *Winter-time* which vary from the copy-text as follows:
Line

1   a-bed,] abed,

6   in the dark] \<before the day>\<by>^in the dark^

8   bathe and dress.] \<I must>bathe and dress.

       {Trial fragments follow:}

> '\<Forth from>When through the frosted panes I peer,
> \<I see the street lamps>far and near,
> \<I see the street lamps shine>\<In the blue dark>
> And lamplight glittering on the rime
> At morning in the winter time.
> In the blue dark abroad I see
> The lamps not yet put out,'

9   sit] sit,

11   Or with a reindeer-sled, explore]
       Or \<go on arctic trip>\<like a>\<polar>^with a reindeer sled, explore^

12   The colder countries round the door.]
       \<To the>^The^ \<cold>^colder^ countries \<near>^round^ the door.

13–16 When to go out, my nurse doth wrap
       Me in my comforter and cap:
       The cold wind burns my face, and blows
       Its frosty pepper up my nose.]
       And when at last myself I wrap
       In winter comforter and cap,
       How the wind burns my face and blows
       Its frosty pepper up my nose!

17   silver sod;] silver sod

19   lake,] lake

20   wedding-cake.] wedding cake.

XXXIX *The Hayloft*
Date of composition: [November 1884] (*LETBM*, No. 1335)
MSS: None found.

XL *Farewell to the Farm*
Date of composition: [November 1884] (*LETBM*, No. 1335)
From Margaret Stevenson's Diary Notes for 1856: 'We spent June and July at Colinton this year; we lived in Mr Macfarlane's house … Two families of cousins were home from India and then he [RLS] had his cousins Henrietta and Willie Traquair at the Farm so he had a very happy time' (*VAIL*, Vol. XXVI, p. 290).

MSS: NLS3793, H2404; NLS3793 is a much-revised early version, as follows:

'The coach is at the door at last;
The eager children, mounting fast
And kissing hands, in chorus sing
Good-bye, good-bye, to everything.
Good-bye, O farm of
O leafy trees we loved to climb,
<Here are the>O playing fields of summertime!
<O hollyhock, O stable stalls,
O lilac and O laurel woods, {then the 'O's become 'To's}
To garden seat and garden wall,
To rick and roller, sty and stall,>
To the kind house and garden ground,
And all the kindly fields around

<Farewell>And fare you well for evermore,
O ladder at the hayloft door,
<O>^To^ pump and barrow, lawn and swing,
Good bye! – Good bye to everything!

Now all your summer playmates go;
And your June garden
Be nothing that we loved forgot; –

To each and all, O kiss the hand;
Let nothing here neglected stand.
Be nothing that we loved forgot,
Round all the dear & happy spot.

We pass the gate; <we climb the hill;>^and as we go^
The trees and houses smaller grow;
<And><Then>^Now^ round the woody turn we swing:
Good bye, Good bye, to everything!'

{H2404 varies from the copy-text as follows:}
Line
title *Farewell to the Farm*] {untitled}
  2   children,] children
  4   good-bye,] good bye, {and so throughout}
  6   The meadow-gates ... upon,] <To>^The^ meadow gates ... upon
  7   tree and swing,] <lawn>^tree^ and swing
  8   Good-bye, good-bye,] Good bye! good bye
  9   for evermore,] forevermore,
 10   door,] door!
 12   Good-bye, good-bye,] Good bye! – good bye
 14   trees] <field>trees

XLI *North-West Passage*
Date of composition: [November 1883] (*LETBM*, No. 1183)
Letters: 1. RLS to Henley, [?23 November 1883] (*LETBM*, Vol. IV, pp. 206–7).
{Around this time RLS added in MS the titles of three new poems at the bottom of p. 22 of
the Yale *PW*: they were, 'XLIII. *Northwest Passage*,' 'XLIV. *Block City*' and 'XLV. *Picture Story
Books*' (*Picture-Books in Winter* in CGV). The numbering had been adapted on these proofs
to accommodate the poet's deletions.} 'Near upon 90 more lines of *Penny Whistles*: *inter quos*,
you will remark the 'Picture Books', of which I refuse to sanction the separate publication
{in the *Magazine of Art*}. I have not been happily inspired. But on the other hand: I will
gladly let you take the *Nor'West Passage*, by which I am content that men should judge me:
come a good movement: two pages of pictures and poethry. For the N.W.P. is very nearly
poethry, penpoetry we'll call it; and it would make fine pic's. If however you insist on having
a single page, take *The Land of Story Books* out of the proof {No. XLVII in *PW*} ... *The Land*
is very suitable for ulceration {he means illustration} by the Lord! Or if you are too proud you
must just wait till I have a happy moment; this picture book affair took me merely metrically,
and as metre is my weak point, lo! the poor Indian!'

2. RLS to Henley [mid-December 1883] (*LETBM*, Vol. IV, p. 218): {Having decided to print
North-West Passage in the March 1884 issue of the *Magazine of Art*, RLS was now trying to
decide on a collective title for these three poems; here he offers Henley a choice between
'Nor'West Passage: a Memory of Childhood' and 'Nor'West Passage: A Childish Memory'. The
poems appeared under the title: 'North-West Passage: a Childish Memory'.}
MSS: H2407
First publication: *Magazine of Art*, March 1884.
{H2407, RLS Note Book 'D', has two versions, on p. 1 and p. 74; the first one is a fragmentary
sketch for '*1. GOOD NIGHT*' only, as follows:}

> 'The big red orange of the sun
> <Drops>Now downward when the day is done.
> <When>Now are the parlour candles lit,
> And close about the fire we sit
> <When the>Now when the darker hues begin
> The parlour lamp is carried in;
> <Day dwindles>And now <do> the windows, fallen black,
> Reflect our frightened faces back,
> {alt.}Our faces painted as we pass
> Like pictures on the window glass.
> Must we <to bed>begone, indeed? Well then,
> Let us arise and go like men,
> And face with an undaunted tread
> The long black passage up to bed.
> <In such a passage long ago>'

{The following variants occur on H2407, p. 74:}

1. GOOD NIGHT
Line
subtitle   *1. GOOD NIGHT*] 1

2   begin;] begin,
3   without, … lane,] without … lane
6   hearth;] hearth,
7   pass,] pass
8   pictures, … window-glass.] pictures … window glass.
10 men,] men
13 Farewell, O brother,] Farewell O brother,
15 tell,] tell –
16 tomorrow, fare] tomorrow – fare

2. SHADOW MARCH
subtitle   *2. SHADOW MARCH*] 2
2   window-pane;] window pane;
3   corners, … light,] corners … light
5   Now my … drum,] My … drum

3. IN PORT
subtitle   *3. IN PORT*] 3
1   Last,] Last
2   nigh,] nigh.
    {trial for stanza two}
    <There shall kind dreams and angels keep
    Their watch about my <silent>^quiet^ sleep;
    And doors and curtains shall keep out
    Bogies and shadows, tears and doubt.>
    There, <quick as thought>safe arrived,<the door we shut>we turn about
8   past.] passed. {Here the copy-text has been emended from this MS.}
9   Then,] There,
10 tread,] tread
    {Trial fragments at bottom of page}
    <There when the door we close,
    Safe in my castle I repose,
    There, kneeling down, my prayers I say
    And feel as easy as by day
    There is my castle, there my den
    Safe from all shades and wicked men.>

The Child Alone

I *The Unseen Playmate*
MS: *PW*, pp. 20–1
Line
18 go to your sleep] go to sleep
19 in cupboard or shelf,] in cupboard, on shelf,

II *My Ship and I*
Letter: RLS to Henley [early May 1883] (*LETBM*, Vol. IV, p. 114): {RLS suggested an illustration as follows:} 'The child helplessly watching his ship – then he gets smaller and

the doll joyfully comes alive – the pair landing on the island – the ship's deck with the doll steering and the child firing the penny cannon. Query two Plates? The doll should never come properly alive.'
MSS: B6615, *PW*, p. 5
Line
  1   O it's I that am the captain] I'm the happy little owner (B6615)
                        It's I that am the captain (*PW*)
  2   Of a ship that goes a-sailing on the pond;] All fit to go a sailing on the pond (B6615)
  3   a-turning … about;] <a sailing>^a turning^ … about (B6615)
  7   alive;] alive. (B6615)
  8   And with him beside to help me, it's a-sailing] <And I shall go a sailing,>
                        ^ ~ ^ (B6615)
  9   It's a-sailing on the water, when the jolly breezes blow,]
       <When the rushes keep a shaking {alt.'a heaving'} and the jolly breezes blow,>
       <And <<descend>>get down when I've a fancy to the cabin down below,>
       <I shall walk>I'll descend, when I've a fancy to the cabin down below,
                        (B6615) ~ blow (*PW*)
 10   divie] a divy (B6615)
 12   prow;] prow (B6615)
 13   For beside the dolly sailor, I'm to voyage and explore,]
       <As I sail the <<pond>> to survey and explore>
       <As I sail the [?] waters with the dolly to explore> ^ ~ ^
 14   To land upon the island where no dolly was before,]
       <And I'll>To land upon the island, where <no one>^no dolly^ was before, (B6615)
 15   And to fire] And I'll fire (B6615)

III *My Kingdom*
MS: *PW*, pp. 19–20
Line
  8   were big] were hills
 22   At last] – At last

IV *Picture-books in Winter*
Date of composition [November 1883] (*LETBM*, No. 1183)
Letters: 1. RLS to Henley [?23 November 1883] (*LETBM*, Vol. IV, p. 206). {See notes to *North-West Passage*, p. 373.}

2. RLS to Fred Holland Day [?July or August 1887] (*LETBM*, Vol. V, p. 435):
{The poet had been asked to comment on sources for this poem:} 'There was a great blue Bible Picture Book, from which the cities and the 'flowing brooks' came certainly. The sheep and shepherds and the flying fairies I can no longer place.'
MS: H2407
Line
  1   Summer fading, winter comes –] Summer fading winter comes
  3   robins, … rooks,] <red breasts>^robins^, … <books>rooks,
  4   story-books.] story books! {this phrase is unhyphenated in the MS.}
         {this trial stanza occurs between lines 4–5:}

> 'In December roses bloom
> In a corner of the room;
> Lilies keep their silver looks
> In the picture story books.'

9   by,] by
10   cyc,] cyc
11   Sheep and shepherds, trees and crooks,] <All the sheep are surely killed>
                                      <They are vanished from the field,>
                                      <Sheep and Shepherd>
13–15   We may see how all things are,
        Seas and cities, near and far,
        And the flying fairies' looks,]
        <All the stories too are here
        Tales of travel, tales of fear,
        <<And the>>Flying fair<y>^ies^ books>
        You may see how all things are
        <Towns and><Forests, cities> Seas and cities, near and far,
        And the flying fairies' looks …
17   How am I to sing your praise,] <Summer pleasures here past by>
                                      ^How am I to sing your praise^
18   chimney-corner] chimney corner
19   nooks,] nooks

V *My Treasures*
Letter: RLS to Alison Cunningham [late November 1883] (*LETBM*, Vol. IV, p. 209): 'Do
you remember making the whistle at Mount Chessie? I do not think it *was* my knife; I believe
it was yours; but rhyme is a very great monarch and goes before honesty: in these affairs,
at least. Do you remember, at Warriston, one autumn Sunday, when the beech nuts were
on the ground, seeing Heaven open? I would like to make a rhyme of that, but cannot.'
{*LETBM*, n. 1 on Mount Chessie tells us that it was 'a beautiful place near Lasswade where
the Stevensons stayed in June 1861'.}
MSS: B6371, Berg: CGV, *PW*, p. 12; B6371 is the following four lines on p. 54 of Notebook
'C' that resemble the first stanza of this poem:

> 'I went a-nutting all <alone>by myself –
> All <alone>by myself <in the trees><wood>^to the trees^
> Some of the nuts are there on the shelf,
> And the rest have been eaten by me.'

{Berg: CGV is a photostat of an unnumbered MS page from an unidentified Notebook
containing an untitled draft of *My Treasures* missing the first two lines but containing an
additional, unpublished stanza following line 16, as follows:

> 'They will not allow me to touch it at all
> In case I should injure myself when I fall,
> But at least its my own, there is none to say no,
> And its always a pleasure to have it to show.'

{*PW* runs the sixteen lines together without breaking them into quatrains.}
Line
3   autumn] Autumn (*PW*)
4   sea.] sea<!>^.^ (Berg: CGV)
5   made (and how clearly it sounds!)]
      made – and how clearly it sounds! – (Berg: CGV)
      made, and how clearly it sounds! (*PW*)

VI *Block City*
Date of composition: [November 1883] (*LETBM*, Vol. IV, No. 1183)
Letter: RLS to Henley [?23 November 1883] (*LETBM*, Vol. IV, p. 206):
{See notes to *North-West Passage*, p. 373.}
MS: H2407; {there are several fragmentary and full drafts scattered in Notebook 'D' on
pp. 1, 80 and 81. This quatrain on p. 1 seems the starting point:}

> 'When I am a king, on the top of a hill
> Shall my little block city be set;
> The flag shall be flying atop of it still
> And the weather shall never be wet.'

{This sketch is on p. 80:}

> 'I built a city with my blocks,
> Temple and tower and streets and docks
> And down the beach beside the sea
> A towered palace
>
> <I built a city>A city once I built of blocks,
> Temple<s><churches><towers & streets>^towers and docks,^
> Along the carpet-sea;
> And climbing down the footstool-hill,
> <A mighty palace>First a fort, and then a mill,
> And last a house for me.
> It was a mighty palace hall –
> I used my blocks up one and all
> To build it broad and high;
> A pillared terrace <ran>faced the sun,
> And steps descended one by one
> To where the sea was high.
> Close in front my vessels lay,
> Safe in the peaceful carpet bay,
> And far away behind
> In dismal ridges, grim and black
> The mountains of the sofa back
> <Towered high above it, great and black>
> And through the windows
> The real sun fell.

All round the town the churches rang,
From the ships the sailors sang.
And down the palace stairs,
<Fairy figures came and went,><And from within>
I played that little people went.'

{This version is on p. 81:}

'O the little city, the city on the bay,
<The city><of my>which I <builded>^built^ on a rainy, rainy day>
All without the rain came down,
When I built my fairy town
Along the carpet sea;
Built my little city
My city, on the sea
First a fort and then a mill
And houses further down the hill
And last a house for me
O the little city, the city by the sea.'

{Also on p. 81 is a full draft which varies as follows from the copy-text:}
Line
  2   Castles and palaces, temples and docks.]
          Temples and palaces, mountains and docks;
  3   Rain may keep] <And once when>
  4   be happy and] <keep>^be^ happy, and
  5   Let the sofa be mountains, the carpet be sea,]
          <Now for the carpet, imagine a sea,>^ ~ sea;^
  6   There I'll establish a city for me:] There I will {blank} a city for me,
  7   A kirk and a mill] A fort <at the top>and a <kirk>mill
  8   as well] with piers
  9   pillar] pillar<s>
 10   all,] all
 11   coming down] leading down
13–14   This one is sailing and that one is moored:
          Hark to the song of the sailors on board!]
          <And><Soon as I look, it appears to be true>
          Hark, how the bells in the city resound!
          See, although still, how the millwheels go round!
 15   And see … the kings] <And>See on … the <folk>^kings^
 16   things!] things.
 17   ~ go!] <Little and lovely> ~ go;
 18   moment … low.] moment, … low;
 19   Block upon block … free,] <The carpet has ceased to>^ ~ free^
 22   The kirk … men,] The church … men;
 23   where'er I may be,] wherever I be,

VII *The Land of Story-books*
Letter: RLS to Henley [early May 1883] (*LETBM*, Vol. IV, p. 115):
{RLS suggested an illustration as follows:} 'The lighted part of the room, to be carefully distinguished from my child's dark hunting grounds. A shaded lamp.'
{See also *LETBM*, No. 1183 and notes to *North-West Passage*, p. 373.}
MSS: B6488, *PW*, pp. 21–2. In the poet's MS recollections of his childhood written during 1872–3, he gives this account of the dining-room at Colinton Manse: 'Now I come to the crown of my dining-room reminiscences, for after dinner, when the lamp was brought in and shaded, and my aunt sat down to read in the rocking chair, there was a great open space behind the sofa left entirely in the shadow. This was my especial domain: once round the corner of the sofa, I had left the lightsome, merry indoors, and was out in the cool, dark night. I could almost see the stars. I looked out of the back window at the bushes outside. I lay in the darkest corners, rifle in hand, like a hunter in a lonely bivouac. I crawled about stealthily, watching the people in the circle of lamplight' (Balfour 1901: Vol. I, 55).
{B6488 is a sprawling draft on p. 31 of Notebook 'A.269' which has erased passages, variations in line and stanza order and lacks the final stanza.}
Line
1   evening, when the lamp is lit,] evening when the lamp is lit (B6488, *PW*)
2   Around the fire my parents sit;] <Away behind the chairs I sit,>
        ^Around the fire <they like to>^^my parents^^ sit;^ (B6488)
3   home and] home, and (B6488)
4   And do not play at anything.] And don't pretend to anything. (B6488)
5–6 Now, with my little gun, I crawl
    All in the dark along the wall,] But I keep <far off><But far away where all is dark>
    (B6488)
7–8 And follow round the forest track
    Away behind the sofa back.]
    <And wander <<in the space of>> ^off where all is^ black>
    Away behind the sofa back
    I keep my silent bivouac. (B6488)
9   spy,] spy (B6488)
13   woods,] woods (B6488)
14   solitudes;] solitudes (B6488)
15   And there the river by whose brink] <There as I lay me down to think>
        There, ~ (B6488)
16   The roaring lions come to drink.]<And the wild beasts come down to
        drink.>^And hear the lions come to drink.^ (B6488)
17   away] away, (B6488)
19   Indian scout,] indian scout (B6488)
20   their party] <this>^their^ party {a Colvin correction on the Yale *PW* adopted by the poet}
21   me,] me (*PW*)

VIII *Armies in the Fire*
MS: Berg: CGV; this draft is No. LXI following No. LX, *Looking-glass River*, on pages numbered 4 and 5 but is incomplete, ending at line 16; doubtless it continued on the missing page 6. It has an unpublished stanza following line 8. These two poems were not in *PW* and

seem to have been added late to CGV: they may have been among those sent to Colvin in early June 1884 (see *LETBM*, No. 1279). This MS varies from the copy-text as follows:
Line
3   slowly falls] <slow descends>^slowly falls^
6   empty room:] ghostly room,
     {additional stanza following line 8:}

> 'The breathing shadows swell and sink;
> The lovely, dozing embers blink;
> And gazing through the coal-black arch,
> I see the phantom armies march.'

12   dies.] dies; –

IX   *The Little Land*
Date of composition: [early June 1884] (*LETBM*, Vol. IV, No.1279)
Letter: RLS to Colvin [early June 1884] (*LETBM*, Vol. IV, p. 301):
{The poet added this poem and three others to CGV at the last moment.}
'Are these four in time? No odds about order … You see how this d__d poeshie flows from me in sickness: are they good or bad? wha kens? But I like *The Little Land* I think, as well as any. As time goes on, I get more fancy in …
P.S. It does not matter of course about order. As soon as I have all the slips, [proofsheets] I shall organise the book for the publisher. A set of eight will be put together under the title *An Only Child*; another cycle of ten will be called *In the Garden*; and other six called *Bedtime* to end all up. It will now make quite a little volume of a good way upwards of 100 pp. {CGV had 104 pages.} The Envoys will conclude the volume of course.' {RLS had just sent Colvin MSS of the six *Envoys*: see *LETBM*, No. 1274.}
MSS: H2404, H2407; sketches of other 'little lands' are scattered across pp. 9, 13 and 25 of Notebook 'D' (H2407) – these are assembled in *MS Fragments*, pp. 348–50. On p. 1 of Notebook 'A.270' (H2404), there is a sketch of lines 24–30, as follows:

> 'Where the ladybird alit;
> I can climb the jointed grass,
>   And from on high
> See the <great cloud-mountains>^greater swallows^ pass
>   In the sky,
> And the round sun rolling by
> Marking no such things as I.'

Lines 10, 36, 40, 61: RLS was inconsistent in his spelling of 'rainpool', usually but not always omitting the hyphen. In *EDIN*, Colvin followed the hyphenated spelling throughout, a practice repeated in *TUS* and other subsequent editions. I have eliminated the hyphen.

Garden Days

I   *Night and Day*
Date of composition: winter 1883–4 (see note on H2460 below)
MS: H2460, H2407 ; the first six poems of *Garden Days* plus *A Visit from the Sea*, numbered

XLVI–LII, are found consecutively on eight pages of H2460. *Verso* on the last of these pages is written 'F.S. Jan. 84'. We know that Fanny Sitwell made fair copies of the *Penny Whistles* poems; perhaps she did so again for the new ones he had written since the trial book was printed in the autumn of 1883. While he was ill during that winter at Hyères, he wrote more children's poems, asking Henley in March to prepare a second, expanded proof of *CGV* for resubmission to Cassell's (see *LETBM*, No. 1228). There are three additional stanzas to this poem in H2460. Each stanza of *Garden Days* poems I through V in this MS is preceded by an arabic number and a period. Variants from the copy-text are as follows:

Line

5–6   As the blinding shadows fall,
        As the rays diminish,]
      <First the faraway and small
         Then the near diminish,>^ ~ ^

11   Glow-worm] glowworm
15   Till on all,] Till, on all,
       {two unpublished stanzas follow line 16:}

            'Then for every starry eye
                Lampless watches follow;
            In the deep dark, dreamers lie
                Quiet on the pillow.

            Only on the silent sod
                Or the chinking gravel,
            In the blotted night abroad
                Hooded angels travel.'

18   east] East
21   darkness shapes of things,] darkness, shapes of things –
22   hedges,] hedges –
       {an unpublished stanza follows line 28: a version of these lines follows a draft of *Nest Eggs* on p. 14 of Notebook 'D' (MS H2407)}
       ['<Clearly peeps the day;>]
            There the sun shall meet the sky
            Then the east shall golden grow
                And the clouds shall glisten;
            Till with farm-yard view-hallo,
                Lo! the sun arisen!'

                                        (H2460, H2407)

38   roses,] roses
40   reposes,] reposes –

II *Nest Eggs*

Date of composition: winter 1883–4

MSS: H2460, H2407; these are not separate drafts but contain much common matter, including several unadopted lines and stanzas; variants from the copy-text follow:

Line
1   sunny day] day long (H2407)
2   Flutter] Make friends (H2407)
3   arbour-like] arbourlike (H2460, H2407)
4   laurel.] Laurel. (H2460)
6   seated;] seated (H2407)
8   keeps heated.] <had><has>^keeps^ heated; (H2407)
        {unpublished stanza follows:}

> 'Soft, and disturb her not –
> Softly regard her,
> Bright-eyed and brown-bodied
> Mother and warder.'

                                        (H2460, H2407)

9–12   {This stanza is not in H2460 or H2407}
13   frail eggs] <thin>^frail^ shells (H2407)
14   Chip,] <Chirp,>^ ~ ^ (H2407)
15   Make] <Let> ^ ~ ^ (H2407)
16   Merry with] <Loud with their>^ ~ ^ (H2407)
17   Younger than we are,] Younger <and smaller>^than we are^ (H2407)
18   and frailer,] <thin>and frailer, (H2407)
19   in blue air they'll be,] in <blue>air <shall each>^they'll be^ (H2407)
21–4   We, so much older,
            Taller and stronger,
        We shall look down on the
            Birdies no longer.]
21   We,<then, the older>^growing older^ so much older
22   <<The>><Stronger and taller,> Taller and stronger,
23   <We still on earth must stay>We shall behold them fly
                                We shall look down on the
24   <On the><Smaller and smaller.>Birdies no longer. (H2460, H2407)
21–4   {alternate version}
21   We, then, the <wise>^human^ ones
        But we/the poor sons of men
22   <Ne'er can>^Only^ rise higher
23   By climbing the green trees
24   Or up <on>^to^ the spire. (H2460, H2407)
25–8   They shall go flying
            With musical speeches
        High overhead in the
            Tops of the beeches.]
        <Soon each young bird shall<<go>>^fly^
            Brimming with speeches
                    ~   > (H2407)

        <Higher and higher still,
            Louder and sweeter

And hear with <<delight>>^surprise^ all their
<<Their>>Musical speeches.>
{alternate for lines 25–8}

High overhead in the
    Tops of the beeches
They shall go flying
    With musical speeches.

                                                  (H2407)

29–32 In spite of our wisdom
          And sensible talking,
     We on our feet must go
          Plodding and walking.]
     {There are three alternate versions in H2407, as follows:}
     <For the <<poor>>human child
          <<Both>>Stronger and weaker>
     Is fastened to earth
          A walker and speaker.

     <We growing older,
          Stronger and weaker
     Still on the earth must stay
          Walker and speaker.>

     In spite of their wisdom
          And sensible talking
     They on their feet must go
          Plodding and walking.

     {This final stanza was not adopted.}
     And never go <sailing><winging> ^raking^
          In moments of <pleasure>^leisure^
     Round the cloud mountain tops
          Up in the azure.

                                  (H2460, H2407)

III *The Flowers*
Date of composition: winter 1883–4
MSS: H2460, H2407
Line
  2 purse,] purse (H2460)
  3 buttons, … smock,] Buttons, … Smock, (H2460)
     {in H2460 stanzas 3 and 4 are reversed but marked by RLS for transposition to the
     printed order.}
  9 Tiny woods below whose boughs] <In the shadows of their>
                       ^Tiny woods, below whose boughs^ (H2407)

11   tree-tops, rose or thyme,] <tree-tops – >^tree-tops,^ ~ (H2460)
      treetops … thyme (H2407)
12   climb!] climb. (H2407)
13   trees,] trees (H2460)
15   Where if] Where, if (H2460)

IV *Summer Sun*
Date of composition: winter 1883–4
MSS: H2460, H2407
Line
   1–2   Great is the sun, and wide he goes
          Through empty heaven without repose;]
          In the broad noon the splendid sun
          <That through the blue>Lights up the world from end to end; (H2407)
   1   sun,] sun (H2460, H2407)
   3   glowing] sunny (H2407)
   4   More thick] <Thicker>^More thick^ (H2407)
          {Unpublished stanza follows here in both MSS:}
          'Straight {alt. "swift") as the {alt. "a"} train along the rails,
          Sometimes alone the blue {alt. "sky"} he sails;
          <High over all>
          And sometimes eagles <wing>^winging^ strong
          Or the white clouds around him throng.' (H2407, H2460)
   5–8   Though closer still the blinds we pull
          To keep the shady parlour cool,
          Yet he will find a chink or two
          To slip his golden fingers through.]
   5   <Close up the shutter, bar the door> (H2407)
          <As with shutters and blinds we try> (H2460)
          Up with the blind and shutter if we try
   6   Our home from heat to frosts fly. (H2407)
   5–6   Though blinds and shutters all complete
          Do fortify the house from heat. (H2460, H2407)
   9   attic spider-clad] attic, spider clad, (H2407)
   10   He, through the keyhole,] He through the keyhole (H2407)
   11   tiles,] tiles (H2407)
   12   hay-loft] hayloft (H2460)
          {These lines seem to be a largely unused sketch for lines 13–16:}

              '<Chil>The flowers are stronger-eyed <than we>^and stare^
              <And look straight up>
              Children and flowers and birds and bees

              As if the sun were but the moon
              They give him stare for stare all noon.
              The flowers are blind, and have no eyes
              To fear the glory of the skies

> But if like them <our lids>^the eye^ we close
> And blindly in the sunlight <sit>^lie;^'

13	Meantime] Meantime, (H2460)
14	the garden] on garden (H2407)
16	Among] <Into>^Among^ (H2407)
17	Above the hills,] Across the hill, (H2407)
18	true,] true <the sun's swing> (H2407)
19–20	To please the child, to paint the rose,

> The gardener of the World, he goes.]
> The gardener of the World, he strays
> And every plant and child surveys; (H2407)
> <The Gardener of the World> (H2460)

V *The Dumb Soldier*

Date of composition: winter 1883–4
MSS: H2460, H2407
Line

1	mown,] mown (H2407)
5	apace;] apace (H2407)
6	hide] hid {both MSS have 'hid', a reading which has been adopted.}
	place;] place (H2407)
9	alone he lies,] secure he lies (H2460, H2407)
10	eyes,] eyes (H2407)
11	gun,] gun (H2407)
15	clear,] clear (H2407)
16	my hole] the hole (H2407)
17	fear,] fear (H2407)
18	grenadier;] grenadier: (H2407)
19	{These lines, mostly cancelled, are a sketch for 19ff.:}

> <But of all <<that>>his nights and days>Gun at shoulder, coat of red
> Military cap at head
> <Not a word of blame or
> Of his terrors and delights
> Frosty mornings, rainy nights
> All he saw with sleepless lid
> In the gravel pothole lived.> (H2407)

19	gone and come,] <come and gone>^gone and come^ (H2407)
20	I shall find] <Find> (H2407)
21	He has lived,] <What a life> ^ ~ ^ (H2407)
22	spring;] Spring; (H2460)
23	Done, if he could tell me true,] <In rain and wind and dew> ^ ~ ^ (H2407)

> {There are several sketches in H2407 for lines 25ff.:}
> <Beetles creeping, buzzing flies
> Visitors with insect eyes.
> And the fairy things that pass
> <<The humming>>In the forests of the grass:>

lain and wondered, close at hand,
At the games of fairyland;
<At the dropping of the>

<At high noon><The forest of the grass is>
There is a forest green and deep
Where the fairy ...
And the fairy armies pass
Through the forest of the grass. (H2407)

26   And the springing of the flowers;] <And the morn> ^ ~ flowers,^ (H2407)
30   ladybird,] ladybird; (H2407)
31   butterfly] Butterfly (H2407)
33   disclose,] disclose – (H2407) disclose (H2460)
34   knows.] knows; (H2407) knows<;>^.^ (H2460)
35   shelf,] shelf (H2407, H2460)

VI *Autumn Fires*
Date of composition: winter 1883–4
MSS: H2460, H2407; consisting of twenty-four lines, the draft in H2407 seems the starting
point for this poem and is transcribed below from p. 19 of Notebook 'D':

'In the other gardens and
All up the <valley>^vale^
<Round about the>From the autumn bonfires
<O the children rally.> See the smoke trail.
Autumn robins singing
In the Autumn <weather>time,
Short days, gray days,
And morning rime.

{In H2460 the above four lines appear after line 4 but are bracketed in ink,
marked with a marginal query 'Dele?' and cancelled in pencil.}

Pleasant summer over
<All the summer flowers>^And all the summer hours^
<There are the weeds
That once were the flowers>
The red fire blazes
The gray smoke towers
<Feed, feed the bonfire
Warm, warm the hands
<<Ready>>Stiff and straight
The gardener stands.
The red fire crackles
The flame expands>
<Happy, happy>Sing a song of seasons:
Something bright in all:

> Flowers in the summer,
> Fire in the fall!'

(II2407)

{The following variants from the copy-text occur in H2460:}
Line
3   autumn] Autumn
5, 11   summer] <summer>^Summer^
6   summer flowers,] <summer roses>^Summer flowers,^
12   Fires in the fall!] Fire in the Fall!

VII *The Gardener*
Date of composition: winter 1883–4: there is no version of this poem in H2460 but on pp.
26–7 of Notebook 'D' (H2407), there is a rough draft among similarly early versions of the
first six *Garden Days* poems written during this time.
MS: H2407
Line
1–2   The gardener does not love to talk,
         He makes me keep the gravel walk;]
         The gardener will not let me go,
         Across the borders to and fro,
         [He] does not like to talk,
         He bids <me>^thee^ keep the gravel walk
5–6   Away behind the currant row
         Where no one else but cook may go,]
         Far in the borders, <stooping low,>
         Far in the <plots where greens run>
         <Where>^And^ no one else but cook may go.
7   plots, … dig] plots … dig,
8   big.] big;
9–10   He digs the flowers, green, red and blue,
         Nor wishes to be spoken to.]
         The gardener's name, you know, is John.
         He digs the flowers; green, red and blue,
         Nor wishes to be spoken to
11–12   He digs the flowers and cuts the hay,
         And never seems to want to play.]
         <He sets his foot upon his spade>
         He digs the plot and cuts the hay
         <All through the summer, day by day>
         <He>^And^ never seems to want to play.
13–16   Silly gardener! summer goes,
         And winter comes with pinching toes,
         When in the garden bare and brown
         You must lay your barrow down.]
         <Swiftly gardener, old and brown,
         Lay your spade and barrow down>

            <Come and lay your spade aside>
13   <O>Silly gardener, ~
15   brown] brown,
16   down.] down!
17–20   Well now, and while the summer stays
            To profit by these garden days
            O how much wiser you would be
            To play at Indian wars with me!]
            <But> ^Now,^ while all is warm and blue,
            And all the flowers are bright and gay,
            Silly gardener, come and play,

            Up, while the flowers are …
            Up and bring your rake for gun.
17   now,] now
18   garden days] shining days,
19   O] O!
20   me!] me,
            <To rise and with a rake for gun
            To see the>

VIII *Historical Associations*
MSS: None found. In the US edition of CGV and in Thistle and many other subsequent
editions, the last five stanzas of this poem are omitted.

Envoys

Date of composition: spring 1884 (*LETBM*, Vol. IV, No. 1274)
Letter: RLS to Colvin [?25 May 1884] (*LETBM*, Vol. IV, p. 297):
{The six *Envoys* were enclosed with this letter; MSS of the first five seem not to have
survived.} 'I send herewith a kind of postscript to the *Child's Garden*. It will add ten pages
to the bulk of the volume which is a consideration and they are all sure to give pleasure
to someone. They have begun by giving pleasure to me. If they are not in time they can be
printed separate. They certainly finish and, so to speak, hedge in the Garden.'

VI *To Any Reader*
MSS: B5981; Yale *New Arabian Nights*; BBS I, 1916, pp. 225–7. {The starting point for this
poem may be the following lines transcribed (without corrections or variants) from a rough
sketch on p. 2 of Notebook 51 (B5981):

            'As long then as the day endures
            These happy woods are wholly yours,
            Wherein to wander, hear and see
            Until the hour returns for tea;
            There you shall hear the sunset gun …

            But you like Gerda following Kay
            Shall, wandering in a charming way,

As Alice through the looking glass
From pleasure to pleasure pass.
For there before your shining eyes,
The bright land of adventure lies
And when you come and when you go
No-one but yourself shall know.'

{The earliest full draft of thirty-nine lines is written in pencil on the dedication and title pages of a Yale copy of *New Arabian Nights*, identified by Belle Strong as 'From the library of RLS' (Ip St.48 Beinecke 882 ndc). McKay described this one-volume 1884 edition as B144 in Vol. I, p. 66, noting that 'Verses in Stevenson's hand are written on pp. [iv] and [vi].' This unpublished version reads as follows:}

'Whether upon the garden seat
You lounge with your uplifted feet
Under the May's whole heaven of blue;
Or whether on the sofa you,
<Your>No meddling elders being by
A cosy corner occupy. <some [?] position try>
Take you this volume in your hands
To lead you {alt. 'And enter'} into other lands.
For lo! (as children tell) suppose
You <hunted><found>behind all the garden rows
Or in the lumbered attic or
The cellar, a nail-studded door
And dark-descending stairway found
That led to kingdoms underground,
A door <thro>^by^ which in easy style
From your nice nurseries you <could>^may^ pass
Like Alice through the Looking Glass
To places where Aladdin played,
The coasts where Sinbad {alt. 'Crusoe'} once strode,
Just so this little volume can
Transport each little maid or man
Presto, from where they live away
<To where the other children play>
^Where other children used to play.^
As from the house your friends can see
You playing round the cherry tree
For you shall see, if you but look
<Within the binding> of this book
<As through the window, clearly seen>
Another child <another day>^some other day^
And in another garden play.
But do not think you can at all
By knocking at the window call
That child to hear you. He, intent
Is still on his play-business bent:

He cannot hear, he will not look
Nor yet be lured out of this book:
For long ago, the truth to say,
He has grown up and gone away
And it is <just>^but^ a child of air
That lingers in the garden there.'

{The MS followed in the BBS printing of a 44-line version of this poem was in the Sotheby's sale of Nov. 1949 as lot 405. As its present location remains unknown, and I have been unable to check it against the unreliable transcription of George Hellman. The collation below compares BBS, copy-text for the long variant version as it is set up from a later draft, against Yale, the poet's obviously earlier pencil sketch. There is a cancelled variant for lines 15–20 in the later MS that BBS prints in a footnote.}

Line
3   Heaven] heaven
5   No grown up person] No meddling elders
6   Do some soft corner occupy:] A cosy corner occupy.
7   lands,] lands.
9   feign] tell
10   You, hunting in ... rows,] You behind all ... rows
12   cellar –] cellar,
13   dark, descending] dark-descending
14   underground:] underground,
15–20   There standing, you should hear with ease
         Strange birds a-singing, or the trees
         Swing in big robber woods, or bells
         On many fairy citadels:
         There passing through (a step or so
         Neither mamma nor nurse need know!)]
         Wherethrough, if you but turn the key,
         Shall come a sobbing of the sea
         Tossing of robber woods, and bells
         Of many fairy citadels;
         Wherethrough for half an hour or so
         You may on foreign travels go. (BBS) {footnote variant: no version of these six lines
         is present in Yale}
21   would pass] may pass
23–4   Or Gerda following little Kay
         To wondrous countries far away.]
         To places where Aladdin played,
         The coasts where Sinbad once strode,
25   Well, and just so this volume can]
         Just so this little volume can
26   man,] man
27   Presto from] Presto, from
29   Your mother sees] Your friends can see
30   garden trees] cherry tree

31	So you may] For you shall
32	Through the windows] Within the binding
34	garden, play] garden play
36	on the window, call] at the window call
37	He intent] He, intent
38	bent.] bent:
39	He does not hear, he will not look,]
	He cannot hear, he will not look
40	book.] book:
42	away;] away
	{CGV varies from *BBS* lines 29–44 as follows; I give the line numbering of the first edition:}
2	trees.] trees
3	if you will look] if but you look
4	book,] book
5	away,] away
7	all,] all
10	all] still
11	hear;] hear,
13	For,] For
14	away,] away;

Underwoods

History of Composition and Publication

Underwoods was published on 26 August 1887 by Chatto and Windus in London and by Scribner's in the USA. Like *A Child's Garden of Verses*, this collection had its early development at Chalet La Solitude, Hyères, but was completed at Skerryvore, Bournemouth. The fifty-four poems in the volume were written between 1869 and 1887; of this number eighteen appeared in print, usually in periodicals, before being collected: these were, from Book I, Nos II, IV–VII, XI, XV, XXIV–XXVIII, XXXII–XXXIII; and, from Book II, Nos II, IV–V, X and XII. For forty-nine of these poems, the place of composition for each was written by the poet in his mother's copy, now at NLS (see Scally 1998: 27); locations for the other five had been printed below the text.

RLS soon learned, after his return from America with a wife and family to support, that editors of magazines paid handsomely to fill up odd spaces with bits of poetry. In the autumn of 1880, he boasted to his cousin Bob Stevenson, 'I am now quite the poet,' pointing to four of his verse compositions scheduled to appear shortly in *The Atlantic Monthly*, *Cornhill* and *Fraser's*: they were all eventually included in *UW* (*LETBM*, Vol. III, p. 101). The first indication that he was thinking of collecting his poems may have been this advice to Henley in a letter of December 1882:

> Why not publish your verses? It's always pleasant to be in print – and everybody does it – and some of yours are good, and others bad, which is better than can be said for all. I'd go into print if I felt like it, like a shot. (*LETBM*, Vol. IV, p. 39).

From Hyères he wrote to Henley in April 1884:

> You may be surprised to hear that I am now a great writer of verses: that is, however, so. I have the mania now like my betters ... Really I have begun to learn some of the rudiments of that trade, and have written three or four pretty enough pieces of octosyllabic nonsense, semi-serious, semi-smiling. A kind of prose Herrick, divested of the gift of verse, and you behold the Bard. But I like it. (*LETBM*, Vol. IV, p. 267)

Even as the vein of children's poems dried up in the spring of 1884, a new one opened. RLS was delighted when a New York magazine offered him $75 for *The Canoe Speaks* (Book I, No. III). At the end of 1886, he began to collect the various verses he had sent to periodicals or presented to friends; for instance, he asked Will Low for the original MS of lines addressed to Mrs Low earlier in 1886 (Book I, No. XII), explaining, 'I am thinking of a volume of verses' (*LETBM*, Vol. V, p. 335). What poetry he had gathered by the end of 1886 he sent to his Edinburgh printer R. and R. Clark with these instructions:

A mass of MS … will speed north to you tomorrow: verses, I regret to say: both Scots and English. I wish them set up and sent me on galleys … I don't want it to cost too much, as I shall have to pay for it, and there is a high improbability of its ever paying for itself … As to cheapness, I may add that the sight of verses in cold type is often singularly disenchanting; so it is possible the enterprise may go no farther. (*LETBM*, Vol. V, pp. 337–8).

An inscribed and signed copy of the resulting set of proofs from Clark, dated July 1887, was given to Adelaide Boodle, his neighbour at Skerryvore, and is now part of the Widener Collection at Harvard. The total number of pages is the same as in the first edition but the text and make-up differ significantly and there are corrections in the poet's hand: these variants are recorded in the textual notes to individual poems. Early in March he sent *UW* in sheets to fellow Scot William Sharp, who was then writing an article on RLS and later pleased him with his review of *UW* (*LETBM*, Vol. VI, No. 1909). By 30 May he had the book almost done, and was engaging in his customary last-minute dithering, as he told Clark's:

I return you the whole manuscript ready for press except as to the numeration; for as I have struck out a considerable number of the last additions, this numbering will have to be closely noticed. There will probably be another Scots one, but this will come last or second last, and as I shall send it you on my arrival in Bournemouth … do not fancy this should cause delay. There will also be a little prose note or a quatrain to go on the title or on the back of the title, which I shall see to as soon as possible. Messrs Chatto are to publish. I fancy the simplest (cheapest I mean) way would be to throw off a thousand copies. (*LETBM*, Vol. V, pp. 417–18)

On 15 July *UW* was sent in sheets to Scribner's: 1,040 copies had been printed by Chatto and Windus before the end of the month. The second edition of 1,000 books was ready by 9 September. The large paper edition of fifty copies appeared in early October. In November, RLS sought the opinion of critic J. A. Symonds, while reflecting on how his first volume of 'grown-up' poetry had been received:

I wonder if you saw my book of verses? It went into a second edition, because of my name, I suppose, and its *prose* merits. I do not set up to be a poet. Only an all-round literary man: a man who talks, not one who sings. But I believe the very fact that it was only speech served the book with the public. Horace is much a speaker, and see how popular! Most of Martial is only speech, and I cannot conceive a person who does not love his Martial; most of Burns also, such as the 'Louse', the 'Toothache', the 'Haggis' and lots more of his best. Excuse this little apology for my muse; but I don't like to come before people who have a note of song, and let it be supposed I do not know the difference. (*LETBM*, Vol. VI, p. 65).

Location and Description of Manuscripts

Most of the MSS are at Yale; BRBML has MS versions of thirty-two out of the fifty-four poems, many of them in notebooks and notebook fragments (see Appendix One). The most important of these are Notebook 'C', Notebook '*No. A–154 Book poems/and essay*' and the disbound '*Book full of poems No. A.155*'. HL has drafts of most of the longer Scots poems in

H2404, Notebook 'A270'. Other MSS are found in H2408, Notebook 'G', the Cevennes Journal, and in H2407, Notebook 'D'. Many separate MSS of individual poems are also to be found at Yale and Huntington. *LETBM* transcribes MSS originally copied out and sent to correspondents. Harvard has corrected proofs. Other repositories holding MSS are the Parrish Collection at Princeton; the Berg Collection at NYPL; Silverado; NLS and The Writers' Museum, Edinburgh.

Printed Text

The copy-text chosen is the first issue of the first English edition, seen through the press by RLS. In some cases readings have been adopted from MSS: these emendations are fully explained in the Textual Notes on Individual Poems below.

First Edition, First Issue

UNDERWOODS / BY / ROBERT LOUIS STEVENSON / [Publisher's Device] / LONDON / CHATTO AND WINDUS, PICCADILLY / 1887
Crown 8vo. [A] ^{10} B – I ^{8} K ^{6} pp. xviii + 140: [–] [i–v] vi–vii [viii–ix] x–xii [xiii] xiv–xv [xvi–xviii] [1–2] 3–137 [138–140]. Tipped in at the end is 'A List of Books published by Chatto and Windus' dated July 1887, pp. [1]–32. Bound in dark blue-green cloth over boards with black or brown end-papers (reverse white). Lettered in gold across the back, [rule] *Underwoods* / [rule] *Robert Louis* / *Stevenson* / [Publisher's device] / *Chatto & Windus* / [rule]. Wove paper. Edges uncut.

Variants

The Second Edition (1887) is not a resetting but a re-issue with the same collation as the first issue. On the title page, 'Second Edition' appears under the publisher's device. There are differences from the First Edition, in alignment of title with text, on pp. 16, 17, 29, 31 and 45. The large paper issue of fifty copies, ordered to be printed on 9 September, has the text and pagination of the Second Edition but the signatures differ, as follows: [–] ^{2} [a] – b ^{4} A – R ^{4} S ^{2}. Bound in white buckram with cream end-papers, it was printed on handmade laid paper. On p. [ii] a Certificate of Issue replaces the 'By the same author' list of titles in the First Edition.

The Third Edition (1888) is a re-issue of the second, with the appropriate changes to the title-page. It lacks the 32-page Chatto and Windus advertisement.

The American edition of 1887, called the Author's Edition to distinguish it from piracies, was set up by Scribner's from the sheets of the first Chatto and Windus printing; it has the same collation but no advertisements. Not corrected by RLS, it has several variants: for example on p. 101, line 14; p. 131, line 6 and p. 134, line 17. The binding of this edition and its re-issues is tan paper over boards, tan cloth spine, top edge gilt and plain end-papers. The title and author's name are stamped in black on the front cover and in gold on the spine. A full bibliographical description may be found in McKay, Vol. I, Nos 445–7.

Preliminary Material

It is necessary at the outset to clarify what and where the preliminary material is in the copy-text. Following the half-title and title-pages, there is an epigraph in verse, a Dedication in prose and a Note which is really a preface to 'Book II. – In Scots'. CP begins with the epigraph but consigns the Dedication and Note to the apparatus, prefixing the former to notes on 'Book I. – In English' and the latter to notes on Book II. In VAIL, TUS and some other subsequent collected editions, a poem titled *Dedication* with the first line 'To her, for I must still regard her' is added to Book I as No. XXXIX, the final poem: this absurdity of a dedication appearing at the end of a collection is compounded by the fact that the poem is entirely unconnected with *UW*. CP prints this poem where it belongs, in the 'Light Verse' section (p. 336): it is a private joke, shared in a letter to Colvin, at the expense of *The Spectator* (*LETBM*, Vol. III [?27 August 1880], pp. 96–7). Like so many textual blunders that got into editions of RLS's poetry, this one can be traced back to George S. Hellman (see Introduction pp. 16ff.). Tearing the MS from a notebook he had disbound, he misdated it 1886 and styled it a projected Dedication to *UW*.

The four-line epigraph *verso* on the title-page, alluding to RLS's appropriation of Ben Jonson's title *Underwoods*, was added at the last minute; returning to his printer 'the whole manuscript ready for press', he warned him that 'There will also be a little prose note or quatrain to go on the title or on the back of the title, which I shall see to as soon as possible' (*LETBM*, Vol. V [30 May 1887], pp. 417–18).

The Dedication was gently mocked by Edmund Gosse in his review of *UW* ('Mr R. L. Stevenson as a Poet', *Longman's Magazine*, October 1887, repr. Maixner 1981: 273–9): 'This volume is dedicated, if you please, to eleven physicians, and it is strange that one so all compact of humour as Mr Stevenson should not have noticed how funny it is to think of an author seated affably in an armchair, simultaneously summoning by name eleven physicians to take a few words of praise each, and a copy of this little book.' RLS responded to 'the touch about the doctors' on 8 October as follows: 'you were right; that dedication has been the subject of some pleasantries that made me grind, and of your happily touched reproof which made me blush. And to miscarry in such a dedication is an abominable form of book-wreck; I am a good captain, I would rather lose the text and save my dedication' (*LETBM*, Vol. VI, p. 24).

There is evidence that at some point RLS intended to include a Preface. At BRBML there are the ruins of five RLS notebooks mutilated by Hellman: they are stored in the vault as 'Copy Books and Copy Book Covers'. One of them, labelled on the front cover '*Book full of poems No A.155*', contains typescripts and three pages of notes by Hellman detailing what seem to be the former contents of the notebook: these include lists of poems organised (as they presumably were) into projected collections, one to be called *Little Odes and Songs* and another which seems to be a prototype of *UW*, being divided into two sections, one in Scots and one in English. Another note, probably by Edwin J. Beinecke, who acquired this sad wreck, says, 'These 3 pp. in Hellman's hand list 83 poems as he notes inside cover before dismembering them.' Hellman's note on the inside back cover of the now-empty notebook reads as follows: 'ROBERT LOUIS STEVENSON / ORIGINAL MSS OF 83 POEMS / of which 9 are published including / the famous "Requiem" / and 74 unpublished / This is the most notable volume in / existence of unpublished poems of a / famous author.'

One of the typescripts (transcribing MS B6729) is this fragmentary trial preface which Hellman presumes, not without reason, was intended for what eventually became *UW*, although RLS may have projected a preface for all the poems originally included in Notebook A.155:

It may be asked why a gentleman not in any way favoured of the muses should write and print his verses; and whether or not by the promptings of self-deception, I conceive I have found an answer. There are many pleasant thoughts of too little consistence for prose; they would not bear to be laid and beaten on that rude anvil; they do not enter organically into the process of any argument, nay even some of their charm may spring from isolation. On these the poet who has the gift of perfect utterance confers a delightful immortality and we have what is not the least precious of man's possessions, Catullus, Martial, Herrick, Heine; and here and there, a poppy in a field of tares, snatches like the song of 'Rose Aylmer'. So far I carry my audience along with me; but when we approach the case of the man who has no such gifts, who stammers verses.

The typed list headed 'Pieces in Lallan' accurately represents what this notebook (or perhaps some other disbound exercise book) once contained: of the fifteen titles, eleven were included in the Scots part of UW (though in a very different order); the four not selected by RLS for publication appear in this book on pp. 272ff. and were printed as *Pieces in Lallan* on pp. 101–8 of CP. The list, headed 'Page A', contains the following:

I.   *To the Commissioners of Northern Lights*
II.   *To Mesdames Zassetsky and Garschine*
III.   *To W.E. Henley: 'It's rainin'* {UW VII. *The Blast* – 1875}
IV.   *To Charles Baxter: 'Noo lyart leaves'*
V.   *To The Same*
VI.   *Ille Terrarum* {UW II}
VII.   *'When aince Aprile'* {UW III}
VIII.   *Embro Hie Kirk* {UW XI}
IX.   *A Mile an' a Bittock* {UW IV}
X.   *The Spaewife* {UW VI}
XII.   [no No. XI included] *Their Laureate to an Academy Class Dinner Club* {UW X}
XIII.   *'It's an owercome sooth for age an' youth'* {UW XVI}
XIV.   *The Counterblast* – 1886 {UW VIII}
XV.   *The Counterblast Ironical* {UW IX}
XVI.   *A Lowden Sabbath Morn* {UW V}

The twenty poems in the list headed 'Pieces in English' on 'Page B' include only two from UW, *The Canoe Speaks* (III) – mentioned twice, appearing a second time under a working title, *Phasellulus Loquitur* – and *A Portrait* (XXX), here given its working title *Mallock Loquitur*. The list begins with the bogus dedication poem mentioned above. The other seventeen titles are drawn from those *not* selected for UW or ST.

Notebook 'A.270' at HL (H2404) has many sketches of the Scots poems in UW and, on leaf 15, a fragment of the 'Note' on the use of the Scots language that precedes the Contents pages in the copy-text; I do not include it as it does not vary significantly from the printed text. In the Harvard proofs, the 'Table of Common Scottish Vowel Sounds' follows the 'Note' but RLS has there moved it to the *verso* of the half-title for Book II (p. 76) where it appears in the copy-text. In the 'Note' he also changed 'native maker' on p. xii to 'native Maker' during proofing.

Textual Notes on Individual Poems
Book I – *In English*

I *Envoy*
Place/date of composition: Hyères, 1883–4. Will. H. Low's *A Chronicle of Friendships* (1908)
notes that this poem was suggested to RLS in the summer of 1875 during his visit to the
Lows' house on the riverbank at Montigny-sur-Loing; Balfour agrees (Vol. I, 157).
MSS: H2407; W. H. Arnold 1923: 289. There is a rough pencil draft on pp. 75–7 of H2407,
Notebook 'D', as follows:

> '<With hope before me, and joy behind,>
> <Peace of mind may you enjoy, serious and kind>
> <And married mirth and peace of mind>
> Flowers in the garden, meat in the hall;
> Go, little book, and {alt. "wish"}say to all,
> <Smiles in the morning, mirth at night>
> <And><A humble and sufficient store,>
> <A living river by the door>
> <A blackbird <<by>>^on^ the garden wall>
> <Go little book and wish to all.>
> An active conscience <all through>; honoured life;
> A tender and a laughing wife;
> Still to enjoy
> The genial and awful earth;
> And calmly wait the
> <Still on the garden>
> Smiles in the morning, mirth at night
> <Music and books and friendly wit;>
> A bin of wine, a spice of wit
> A house with lawns enclosing it;
> A living river by the door,
> <A blackbird on the garden wall.>
> A nightingale in the sycamore
> <Go, little book, and wish to all.>'

The untraced MS transcribed in *BBS* II, p. 139, is printed in facsimile on p. 289 of W. H.
Arnold's 'My Stevensons' article in his book *Ventures in Book Collecting*, where he mistakenly
claims it was written at Bournemouth to describe Skerryvore, RLS's home there between
1884 and 1887. At the top of this MS is written 'Book I In English'; variants are as follows:
Line
1   book, and] book and
2   hall,] hall
{between lines 2 and 3 the following lines, not in *UW*, are inserted:}
> <A tender>An active conscience, honoured life
> A tender and a laughing wife,

II *A Song of the Road*
Place/date of composition: Hyères, summer 1878 (MS B6891 dated at end)

Letter: RLS to Charles Baxter, [7 or 14 December 1872] (*LETBM*, Vol. I, p. 260): 'The general chorus of all my thoughts just now is "Over the hills and far away," as it must be of any well-regulated person in this double-damned place {Edinburgh} at the beginning of winter.' {The quote, used in the first and last stanzas of the poem, is the refrain of a popular song.}

Source: there is a prose version of the anecdote of the gauger's flute in Chapter X of RLS's 1878 *Edinburgh: Picturesque Notes* (*EDIN*, Vol. I, pp. 73–4) but RLS sketched a draft of it in his Cevennes Journal (Notebook 'G', H2408) in the summer of 1878: W. H. Arnold, who owned the notebook before it was mutilated by Hellman (and possibly others), prints that version following a facsimile of the first stanza of the poem (also written out in Notebook 'G'), titled in MS *The Gauger's Flute*. To understand this anecdote, one must know that a gauger is an exciseman, a tax collector, and perhaps also one should remember that Burns was a gauger:

> Down below upon a stream the road passes Bow Bridge, now a dairy farm, but once a distillery of whiskey. It chanced in the last century, that the distiller was on terms of good fellowship with the visiting officer of excise. This latter was a man of an easy, friendly disposition, and a master of convivial accomplishments. Every now and again, he walked out of Edinburgh to measure his friend's stock; it was a double-faced predicament, agreeable enough when one's business led one in a friend's direction, but painful to be the cause of loss to a host. Accordingly when he got to the level of Fairmilehead the gauger would take his flute, without which he never travelled, from his pocket, fit it together, and as if inspired by the beauty of the neighbourhood, proceed to play a certain air as hard as ever he could. At the first note, the distiller pricked his ears. A flute at Fairmilehead? and playing 'Over the hills and far away?' It was his friend the Gauger. Instantly, a horse was put to: and sundry barrels were got upon a cart and driven furiously round by Hill-End, and concealed in the mossy glen behind Kirk Yetton. At the same time, you may be sure, a fat fowl was put to the fire, and the best napery brought out. A little after, the Gauger having had his fill of music for the moment walked down with the most innocent air, and found the good people at Bow Bridge taken entirely unaware by his arrival, but nonetheless glad to see him. In the evening, the gauger's flute and the distiller's liquors would combine to pass the rosy hours; and I daresay, when both were a little mellow, the proceedings would terminate with 'Over the hills and far away', to an accompaniment of knowing glances. (Arnold 1923: 283–4)

MSS: B6889, B6890, B6891, B6892, H2408, Silverado (Foot), Arnold 1923: 282–3
{The label on the front cover of H2408, Notebook 'G', states that it contains three poems: *The Gauger's Flute, John Cavalier* and *Praise and Prayer*. It no longer does. HL catalogued it as having eighty-one leaves but it has only seventy-seven. Four leaves have been torn from the back, evidently the ones bearing the MSS of these three poems. The notebook was intact when Arnold first published 'My Stevensons' in January of 1922 in *Scribner's Magazine*, because he describes these three poems as 'written on several back pages' (p. 282) and he printed facsimiles of some of *UW* II and all of *Praise and Prayer* while transcribing all thirty-four lines of *John Cavalier* – these last two were printed in *CP*, p. 98. But by the Arnold Sale of 1924 Notebook 'G' had been mutilated, because what became H2408 sold as item 837 whereas the three poems on four leaves torn from the notebook sold separately as items 823, 824 and 829. *The Gauger's Flute* is now at Silverado among their MSS acquired from

Isaac Foot; comparison of the first stanza as printed by Arnold out of Notebook 'G' shows it to be identical with this MS, the paper being the same colour (blue) and size as that in the notebook. B6889 is a photostat of the first stanza as printed by Arnold. Thus, there seem to be four MSS extant:

1. B6890: A pencil version in Notebook 'F'
2. Foot: A version torn out of Notebook 'G'
3. B6891: An untitled fair copy, dated 'Summer 78', No. 42 on pp. 52–3 of the notebook containing eighty-three poems dismembered by Hellman
4. B6892: A copy titled 'II A Song of the Road' on a page numbered 2, presumably from another notebook}

First publication: *Magazine of Art*, January 1886
Title: *A Song of the Road*] The Gauger's Flute (B6890, Foot) {no title – B6891}
Line

1   gauger] Guager all MSS {RLS misspelled it thus throughout; it has been silently corrected; the word is capitalised throughout MA}
1   foot,] foot; (B6892)
4   *hills and far away?*] Hills and Far Away? MA {also in line 28}) *away.* (B6890)
5   pack] pack, (MA)
6   foot it gaily] gaily foot it (B6890)
7   gauger, long since dead,] gauger long ~ (B6890, MA) ~ dead! (B6891, B6892, Foot)
9   self-same way –] selfsame way, – (B6890) self same way – (B6891, Foot)
10   self-same] selfsame (B6890), self same (B6891, Foot)
11   think … you] think, … you, (B6890, B6891, Foot, MA)
13   would] could (B6890, Foot)
14   or] and (MA)
15   Heav'n] heaven (B6890, B6891, Foot, MA)
16   travelling] trav'ling (B6890) trav'lling (B6891, Foot)
17   begin,] begin (B6891, Foot)
18   therein;] therein, (B6891) therein (Foot)
19   tend,] tend (B6891)
20   Be sure … end.] Be sure, ~ (B6890, Foot) ~ end! (MA)
21   follow you,] follow, you, (MA)
22   sky.] sky; (B6890, Foot) sky, (B6891, B6892, MA)
23   streams in civil mode] streams, in civil mode, (B6891, Foot)
24   road;] road. (B6890, Foot, MA)
25   For one and all,] For one <or>^and^ all, (Foot)
26   lead] bring (MA)
28   *away!*] Away. (MA)
{place/date at bottom left}
Forest of Montargis, 1878.] Forest of Montargis (B6890) Summer. 78. (B6891)
                {MA, B6892 have no place/date   Foot has place only at bottom right.}

III   *The Canoe Speaks*
Place/date of composition: Hyères, 17 March 1884 (MS H8914 so dated)
Letters: 1. RLS to Will. Low [?late March 1884] (*LETBM*, Vol. IV, pp. 264–5): 'Herewith are a set of verses {H8914, a fair copy by RLS of this poem} which I thought pretty enough

to send to press. Then I thought of the *Manhattan*, towards which I have guilty and compunctious feelings. Last, I had the best thought of all: to send them to you in case you might think them suitable for illustration. It seemed to me quite in your vein. If so, good; if not, hand them on to *Manhattan*, *Century* or *Lippincott*, at your pleasure, as all these desire my work or pretend to. But I trust the lines will not go unattended. Some riverside will haunt you; and O! be tender to my bathing girls.'

2. RLS to Bob Stevenson [mid-April 1884] (*LETBM*, Vol. IV, p. 269): 'I am now, having been ill with fever, and my new Arabians interrupted, writing a lot of sort of dickering verse; of no interest to you … being flat and tame and pretty soulless; but a great diversion to myself. I sent one shitty thing to Low to illustrate for an American paper: I don't know if he will care: it is about canoeing. I have another on female underclothes which is my own favourite, as that is about the deepest poetry I have.' {RLS here refers to *Now Bare To The Beholder's Eye*, a poem that may be contemporary with *The Canoe Speaks* since they both appear in the disbound Notebook A.155. Henley wrote to Charles Baxter 19 April 1884: 'Louis has confessed that female underclothing – smocks, hose, garters, drawers – are his fate, and that the noblest sight in the world is a washing. That we shall all develop into Bawdy Noblemen is evident' (*LETBM*, Vol. IV, p. 269).}

3. RLS to Henley [June 1884] (*LETBM*, Vol. IV, pp. 309–10): {Low wrote on 5 June to tell the poet that *Manhattan* would pay $75 for *The Canoe Speaks*; the editor of *The Century* declined it, fearing to corrupt the young persons for whom he is obliged to cater, as illustrations for the poem would likely be 'a little nude'. Amused by the size of his promised payment, RLS ended his letter to Henley with this:}

> When I wrote prose, which I write well,
> I was as pauperised as hell;
> When I wrote verse, which I write ill,
> The eager asses brimmed my till.

{RLS never got his money as *Manhattan* went defunct that autumn. These verses were not published before they appeared in *UW*.}
MSS: B6065, B6066, B6067, B6068, B6069; BBS II, p. 140; H8914; BRBML 370
{B6065, an untitled fragment, seems to be the earliest sketch; the poem may have been suggested by RLS's canoe trip with Sir Walter Simpson which resulted in his first book, *An Inland Voyage* (1878); the sketch is as follows:}

> On the great streams <to and fro>the ships may go
> About man's business to and fro.
> I rather with the leaping trout
> Wind, [?moving] the sedges in and out.
> I, the unnamed, inviolate,
> Green, rustic rivers navigate.
> <Rathe rivers, stripling rivers, sail.>
> My deviating craft I steer
> By humming mill and splashing weir
> <By singing rapid, reedy bend,
> By the house back and garden end.>

The dusty miller comes and stands,
Sings to the trees and dusts his hands;
He watches with contented eye,
The mystic water twirling by.
<And [?hears] with>And broken eddies gray and blue
Dance round the prow of the canoe.
Miller, you stay forever still,
<By the>There in the long green valley's end
Miller and mill go by; the stream
Ever along with bubble and gleam
Runs singing to the woods and meads
Runs among the nodding reeds,
<Its private, pathless country ways>
<Ever along, by night and day>
<Runs its private country way>
<The shining fish, the nested>
Far from the beaten ways of men,
We coast {word omitted} the nested water hen;
The fishing bird of heavenly blue,
Sails neck and neck with the canoe;
The silver fish, the lurking rat,
Flit from my
And from the hazel shore anigh,
The wandering children cheer me by.
Farewell, my tiny craft; of yore
The stripling rivers to explore.'

{Below is a collation of MSS B6066, B6067, B6069 and BBS with the copy-text:
Title: *The Canoe Speaks*] *Phasellulus loquitur* (B6067, BBS) {no title – B6069}
Line
2   fro.] fro: (B6066) fro; (B6067)
3–4   But I, the egg-shell pinnace, sleep
       On crystal waters ankle-deep:]
3   <   ~ haunt
4   Far from the <<seas>>^forths^ where ensigns flaunt>
3   <   ~ frail
4   In ankle-wetting waters sail>
3   ~
4   Upon bright waters, ankle-deep (B6066)
4   <Upon bright><In living>^On lilied^ ~ (B6067)
       <Upon bright><On lilied>^On crystal^ (BBS)
5   diminutive] destructible (B6066, B6067, BBS)
6–8   Of sweeter cedar, pithier pine,
       Is fashioned on so frail a mould,
       A hand may launch, a hand withhold:]
       Of the sweet cedar and strong pine
       Fairily <finished>^fashioned^, fairy <small>^slight,^

Seems moulded for a maid's delight; (B6066)
{B6067 has this reading without revisions; BBS is corrected from this reading to
that of the copy-text.}

9   I, rather,] I rather (B6066) I, rather (B6067)
17   nested angler fare,] nested <fisher>^angler^ fare (B6067)
19–20   By willow wood and water-wheel
          Speedily fleets my touching keel;]
          In by the marsh, out by the weir
          By dim recess and dripping weir
          Unsurveyed by the engineer
          And down the shallows I career. (B6069 {these are fragments})
22   Where prosper dim] Where <blow the dim>^prosper dim^ (B6069)
21–36   {RLS had trouble ending this poem; evidently it remains incomplete; B6066 ends
          as follows:}

'By where the map ignores, by where
The peering poacher spreads his snare
And where in the gross heats of noon
Unfearing maidens cast their shoon
And <shed>^loose^ their girdle, <and step>^stepping^ free
Each from her ring of clothes, each she
Bare as a flower {then these last three lines altered to read as follows:}
And loose their girdle on the grass,
And stepping here, each breathing lass,
From her discarded ring of clothes,
Into the crystal coolness goes.'

{B6067 and BBS have slight variations on the above; the fragmentary B6069
follows the copy-text from lines 21 to 30, then ends as follows:}

'One moment, in the naked air,
She stands, as stands the nymph in prayer;
<Next>Then, bounding from her ring of clothes,'

{B6068 and H8914, the MS included with RLS's letter to Henley (No. 1 above), are fair
copies with minor variants; the same is true of BRBML 370, an uncatalogued MS. Collation
of these three with the copy-text follows:}
Title: *The Canoe Speaks*] *Phasellulus loquitur: the Canoe speaks* (B6068, H8914)
                      <Phasellulus Loquitur:> The Canoe Speaks (370)

Line
3   egg-shell] eggshell (H8914)
5   design,] design (B6068)
8   launch,] launch – (H8914)
9   trout] trout, (H8914)
11   inviolate,] inviolate (B6068)
12   Green, rustic … navigate;] Green rustic ~ (B6068) ~ navigate. (H8914)
16   garden-end;] garden-end, (H8914)
17   fare,] fare (B6068)
19   willow wood] willow-wood (B6068)

25 grass.] grass: (H8914)
26 Ah! ... glass] Ah, ... glass, (B6068, H8914)
30 divinity.] divinity! (B6068, H8914)
31 When,] If, (B6068, H8914)
32 this scene I look,] that scene I look (B6068, H8914)
34 bathing-place,] bathing place, (B6068, H8914, 370)
35 about] about, (B6068)
36 abandoned ...] abandoned. – (H8914, 370)
           abandoned. {with solid line drawn under whole line} (B6068)

IV 'It is the season now to go'
Place/date of composition: Hyères, 1883–4
MSS: B6467, H2404
First publication: *Magazine of Art*, December 1885
{H2404, labelled '*Notebook kept during a severe illness, while not allowed to speak*' dates from
the Hyères period and contains on leaves 2v.–3r. this very early sketch, transcribed selec-
tively as follows:}

> 'Her whom with rude uplifted hand
> Shouting, he chased with his command
> He blushes not to worship, nor
> To linger at the window for.'
>
> 'Now angered by her loveliness
> He trembles at the touch [ ] her dress'
>
> 'Her whom he chased by bank and green
> <Her whom he divined on the green>
> Love, love has consecrated queen.'
>
> 'He like a comrade
> He that with her the brook would wade
> Now to touch her hand afraid
> Now quails before her womanhood'

Title: untitled] *It is the Season* MA {MA also numbers the stanzas}
Line
   4 fairy land.] fairy-land. (MA)
   7 Now meet ... brook] Do meet ~ (B6467) ~ brook, (MA)
   9 ago, and] ago and, (B6467)
  10 rough-and-tumble ... shared;] rough and tumble ~ (B6467) ~ shared, (MA)
  11 quarrelled, ... cried,] quarrel'd ... cried (MA)
13–16 {MA omits stanza 4, including in its place the following stanza:}

> 'Her, whom with rude, uplifted hand
> He did bethreaten or command –
> Her, in a somewhat longer dress,
> He now would tremble to caress.'

19   sighs] sighs, (MA)
21   is] is, MA
25   Now when] Now, when MA

V *The House Beautiful*
Place/date of composition: Hyères, 1883–4
MS: B6321
First publication: *Speculum Universitatis: Alma Mater's Mirror*, ed. Baynes and Campbell,
Saint Andrews, 1887
{B6321 is identical with the copy-text but the book printing has these variants:}
Line
 3   *fruit*] *fruit,*
11   And when] And – when
12   chase,] chase, –
13   again,] again
27   rime;] rime,
28   pool] pool,

VI *A Visit from the Sea*
Place/date of composition: Hyères, 1883–4
MSS: H2407, H2460, BRBML 734
First publication: *Magazine of Art*, December 1885
{This poem was originally intended for CGV, like many other sketches in Notebook 'D'
(H2407), where it appears on p. 20, with line 13 reading, 'Pity the child that has wandered.'
It is actually included in the CGV section in H2460: it is on p. 6 of eight pages containing
twenty-one poems, all of them except this one eventually part of either *PW* or *CGV*. It is
numbered L, between *Summer Sun* and *The Dumb Soldier*. The uncatalogued Yale MS was
once a single sheet of foolscap but has been chopped into several bits, mounted on six pages
and dolled up with a printed version and etched portrait of RLS. H2407 has an order of lines
different from the other MSS, as follows: 3, 4, 1, 2; 5, 8, 7, 6; third stanza as in copy-text;
17–20; 13–16; a final quatrain not in other MSS, cancelled. Collation follows:
Line   {MA numbers the stanzas}
 1   loud sea beaches] <salt>^loud^ sea-beaches, (H2407)
 2   he goes fishing and crying,] <they go flying> ^ ~ ^ (734)
 3   inland garden] {'inland' omitted} (734)
 4, 20 sea-gull] sea gull (H2460)
 7   rustling.] rustling (H2407, MA) rustling – (H2460)
 8   to sea!] to sea. (H2407 to the sea! (MA)
 9   water] water, (H2407)
10   rushes;] rushes. (H2407)
11   the sea-gull] a sea gull (H2460) a sea-gull (H2407) the sea-gull, (MA)
12   thrushes.] thrushes! (H2460) thrushes; (734)
13   bird … wandered!] child … wandered (H2407) <child>^bird^ ~ (H2460)
14   ashore!] ashore. (H2407)
15   Hurry him home to the ocean,] <Home to his deep bays send him,>^ ~ ^ (H2407)
16   more!] more (H2407)

17   on the sea-cliff ledges] on <its>^the^ cliff's steep ledges (H2407)
                                on the <cliff's steep>sea cliff's ledges (H2460)
        on the sea cliff's ledges, (MA) on the sea cliff edges (734)
18   The white gulls are trooping and crying,] <Its hungry young are crying,>
                                ^Its friends are trooping and crying;^ (H2407)
                                <His brothers>^The white gulls^ ~ crying; (H2460)
        ~ crying; (MA) ~ <crying>trooping and crying. (734)
19   roses,] roses (H2407, MA)
        {additional stanza in H2407:}

> 'Once of the swinging surges
> <And crystal <<deeps>>^wells^ below,
> Once of your deep sea fishing
> Sing us a song, and go!'

VII *To a Gardener*
Place/date of composition: Hyères, 1883
Letters: Written at, and about, Chalet La Solitude and its garden at Hyères (this location appears below the copy-text, bottom left), these verses and their forerunner *The Salad*, convey the happiness RLS experienced in this idyllic location, a happiness often expressed in his letters from La Solitude in the spring of 1883 (see *LETBM*, Vol. IV, Nos 1086 and 1105, and p. 79, where Fanny's description of the chalet and its setting is quoted).
MSS: H2407, Princeton (Parrish) CO171
First publication: *Magazine of Art*, June 1886
{There are fragmentary sketches of parts of this poem under the title, *The Salad*, on pp. 51–2 of Notebook 'D' (H2407), as follows:

> 'At first the onion, <rose of roots>^queen of all,^
> <Wine-flavoured onion>
> Tender and crisp and virginal,
> The darling of the sun-burnt south
> {alt. Queen mother of the <enraptured>^unshrinking^ south}
> The touchstone of a comrade's mouth.'

> 'Let first the onion flourish there –
> Rose among roots, the maiden-fair,
> Wine-flavoured
> Earth saving spirit of the dish
> Dutch painter's darling, seaman's wish, {alt. cook's delight}
> Earth saving and poetic soul
> Of the capacious salad bowl.'

> 'Spare, spare the weeds awhile'

> 'And saffron soul of bouillabaisse
> The mediaeval condiment'

{The following collation includes the fullest of the Notebook 'D' fragments, the Princeton

fair copy and the MA printing, which was so carelessly punctuated that I have not recorded its punctuation variants:}
Line
   1   mountain-side] mountainside (H2407, CO171)
   2   My plain-beholding, rosy, green] Untendable, my rosy, green
                    <My rosy, plain-beholding, serene green>^ ~ green,^ (H2407)
   3   garden-ground,] garden ground (H2407)
   7   Wine-scented] Wine-flavoured (MA)
  11   The lover of the shallow brook,] <That wants><That loves the
                    <<margins>>^shallows^ of the brook > ^ ~ brook^ (H2407)
  12   my plots] our plots (H2407)
  14   Pease-cods] Peasecods (MA, CO171)
  20   Outsavours] Out savours (MA)
  26   garden door.] kitchen door. (MA)
          {There is a one-line space after line 26 in MA and CO171}
  27   thus,] thus. 2nd edn

VIII *To Minnie*
Place/date of composition: Edinburgh, 19 November 1869 (dated in B8358 by Margaret Stevenson)
Source: {From Margaret Stevenson's Diary Notes for 1869:} 'On the 19th of Nov. Lou has a cold and cannot go to his cousin Cecilia Balfour's birthday party. I suggest that he might send her a hand mirror and write some lines; he sat down at once and dashed off "A picture frame for you to fill"' (VAIL, Vol. XXVI, p. 314). {See Explanatory Note on 'Minnie' (below p. 623) and CGV Envoy IV, above pp. 62–3.]
MSS: B7015, B8358 {the first of these was part of the *Little Odes* collection (folder B7032). The second is on two pages of Margaret Stevenson's diary for 1869, written out in her hand. Collation is as follows:}
Title: *To Minnie / (With a hand-glass)*] *To Minnie with a hand mirror on her / 17th*
                    birthday Nov 19th 1869. (B8358)
                    To Minnie, with a Hand-glass. (B7015)
Line
   5   I send (unhappy I that sing] I send it – I, poor I, that sing (B7015)
   6   shelf)] shelf – (B7015)
   7   would] dared (B8358)
   8   Less charming than you are yourself.] That was less charming than yourself. (B7015)
{Lines 9 and 11 of the copy-text are lacking in B7015, which ends with,

           'Dumb thing! I envy its delight
           And look upon your face tonight.'

The date of '1869.' at bottom left is lacking in B7015.}

IX *To K. de M.*
Place/date of composition: Hyères, 1883–4
MSS: Harvard proofs; BBS II, p. 142; BBS describes a MS of the poem with two additional stanzas. The following eight lines appear after line 14:

'More human grown, yet more divine
You now outsavour, now outshine,
The golden lamps that rare and far
Along the blue embankments are,
The salty smell of running tides,
The rowan wild on mountain sides,
The silver and the saffron dawn
Across the arched orient drawn.'

In the margin eight more lines are written, identified in BBS as unpublished; in fact, they appear later in UW as No. XIX, *Katharine*. See Explanatory Note on her, p. 623.
Harvard has two variants, as follows:
Line
  4 brook,] brook
18 rain,] rain –

X *To N.V. de G.S.*
Place/date of publication: Oakland, April/May 1880
Letter: RLS to Colvin [mid-April 1880] (*LETBM*, Vol. III, pp. 76–7): {RLS wrote a group of poems addressed to friends and family while recovering from grave illness in Fanny's home in East Oakland. Fanny's sister Nellie was a member of the household who helped nurse RLS through this crisis in April/May 1880:} 'I am now out of danger; in but a short while … F. and I marry and go up to the hills to look for a place … Thence, as my strength returns, you may expect works of genius. I always feel as if I must write a work of genius some time or other; and when is it more likely to come off, than just after I have paid a visit to Styx and go thence to the eternal mountains … When we get installed, Sam {Lloyd Osbourne} and I are going to print my poetical works; so all those who have been poetically addressed shall receive copies of their addresses. They are, I believe, pretty correct literary exercises, or will be, with a few filings;'
MS: Harvard proofs: p. 20 has these ten lines at the end of the poem that were omitted from the copy-text – they cause a pagination change in the proofsheets:

'As from a bark, I have perceived thee dwell
Lone like an island, for it pleased thee so;
And as upon a bark, I came not near
But from the sea saluted. Happy they
Who land and dwell with thee! For I have seen
Promise in thy refusals, love behind
Thy hatred, virtue woven with thy faults;
And when thy land thou praisest, like a maid
In old republics nurtured and brave days,
I feel my alien heart swell and grow warm.'

XI *To Will. H. Low*
Place/date of composition: Bournemouth, 2 January 1886 (MS sent with letter of that date)
Letters: 1. RLS to Will. H. Low, 2 January 1886 (*LETBM*, Vol. V, pp. 163–5): {See Explanatory Note on Low and his wife Berthe, p. 623. Low had dedicated his illustrated edition of Keats' *Lamia* to RLS, who responded with this letter and poem:} 'I have copied out

on the other sheet some bad verses, which somehow your pictures suggested: as a kind of image of things that I pursue and cannot reach, and that you seem – no, not to have reached – but to have come a thought nearer to than I. This is the life we have chosen: well, the choice was mad, but I should make it again.'

2. RLS to Edmund Gosse [17 February 1886] (*LETBM*, Vol. V, p. 208): {RLS protests his mock outrage at being paid five pounds by *The Century* 'for a set of shambling lines {i.e. the verses to Low} that don't know whether they're trochees or what they are, that you or any of the crafty ones would blush all over if you had so much as thought upon, all by yourselves, in the water-closet'.

MSS: *LETBM*, Vol. V, No. 1503

First publication: *The Century*, New York, May 1886. Collation follows:

Title: *To Will. H. Low*] *To Will H. Low: / Damned bad lines in return for a beautiful book.* (1503)

        To Will H. Low: In Acknowledgement of the Dedication of his Drawings for Keat's 'Lamia.' (*The Century*)

Line

1   foot,] foot. (both MSS)

2   flute,] flute; (1503)

3   Rarer songs of gods; and still] Rarer songs of Gods. / And still, (1503)

        Rarer songs of gods, – / And still (*The Century*)

   {In both MSS there is a space where line 3 ends with 'gods;', 'and still' becoming line 4.}

7   flits but] flits, but (*The Century*)

8   flees but] flees, but (*The Century*)

9   home,] home (1503) home, – (*The Century*)

10 follow, all] follow – all (both MSS)

13 sun and] sun, and (both MSS)

14 Late with] Late, with (both MSS)

15 trees, and] trees and (*The Century*)

17 roof:] roof. (both MSS)

19 clouds and kiss't] clouds, and kissed (both MSS)

   {the copy-text has a triple line space between lines 20 and 21}

21 lane,] lane (both MSS)

22 pant and pound] pound and pant (both MSS)

23 leaden] earthy (both MSS)

25 Still with gray hair we … on,] Still, with gray hair, we … on (1503)

        Still, with gray hair, ~ (*The Century*)

26 Till, behold, the vision gone!] Till – behold! – the vision gone! (1503)

        Till – behold! – the vision gone. (*The Century*)

27 hath] has (both MSS)

28 dead.] dead! (1503) dead: (*The Century*)

   {*The Century* has a line space between lines 28 and 29.}

29 Life is over, life was gay:] Life is gone, but life was gay: (both MSS)

30 way.] way! (both MSS)

{On p. 165 of Letter 1, RLS queries whether the last two lines should be omitted.}

XII *To Mrs Will. H. Low*
Place/date of composition: Paris, August 1886 (*LETBM*, Vol. V, No. 1711)
Letter: RLS to Will. H. Low [late September/early October 1886] (*LETBM*, Vol. V, p. 326):
'Send me a copy of my verses, will you? I have them not.' {This poem addressed to Berthe
Low was written during RLS's visit to the Lows at the Paris address which appears below the
text; he was now gathering material for publication.}
MSS: None found.

XIII *To H. F. Brown*
Place/date of publication: Hyères, 1884 (the 'dangerous sickness' mentioned in the subtitle
occurred in May 1884)
MSS: None found.
{See the other poem addressed to Brown and the Explanatory Note on him above p. 292 and
below p. 623.}

XIV *To Andrew Lang*
Place/date of composition: Bournemouth, March 1886 (B6992 dated)
Letter: RLS to Lang [c. 10 March 1886] (*LETBM*, Vol. V, pp. 226–7): {Having just read
Lang's miscellany, *Letters to Dead Authors*, RLS included these lines with his letter:}'I treated
myself to your *Dead Authors* … and I can fancy none better … If I send you the following
insulting lines, blame yourself and not me.'
MSS: B3180, B6992, B7260, BRBML 370 {B3180 includes an untitled fair copy of the poem
with the letter, while B6992 is a sketch with revisions. 370 is an uncatalogued MS with one
variant, in line 6.}
Line
  1   Andrew, with … hair,] Andrew, of ~ (B3180) ~ hair (B6992)
  2   glory] glories (B6992) {B3180 has 'glory' with a marginal query, 'or glories? I don't know
       grammar, no not I!'}
  3   arm, … reed,] <hand>^arm^ ~ (B6992) ~ reed (B6992, B3180)
  4   and … and Tweed:] <and>^or^ … or Tweed: (B6992) or … or Tweed; (B3180)
  6   throw:] throw. (B6992, B3180, 370)
  8   He] he (B6992, B3180)
 11   by] in (B6992)
 13   streets, or] streets or (B6992)
 14   sanhedrin,] sanhedrim (B6992) {See Explanatory Note, p. 624.}
 17   and] or (B3180)
 19   follow] flutter (B3180)
 20   the … pane;] your … pane: (B6992) your … pane –: (B3180)
 21   peel,] peel (B6992)
 23   forth,] forth; (B6992)
 27   moment, or] moment or (B6992, B3180)
 28   May;] May, (B3180)
 30   gods:] gods. (B6992, B3180)
 31   page] pen (B6992, B3180)
{Lang's response was to publish the following verses in his causerie 'At the Sign of the Ship'
in *Longman's Magazine*, Vol. X, p. 686, October 1887:}

'To R.L.S.
(See *Underwoods*.)
Dear Louis of the awful cheek,
Who told you it was right to speak,
Where all the world might hear and stare,
Of other fellows' 'brindled hair'?

'Shadows we are,' the sophist knew –
Shadows – 'and shadows we pursue.'
For this my ghost shall chase your shadow
From Skerryvore to Colorado.'

{In October 1881 RLS had sent a less complimentary set of verses on Lang to Henley:}

'My name is Andrew Lang,
Andrew Lang,
That's my name,
And criticism and cricket is my game.
With my eyeglass in my eye
Am not I,
Am I not,
A lady-dady Oxford kind of Scot.'

(*LETBM*, Vol. III, p. 241)

XV *Et Tu in Arcadia Vixisti*
      (To R.A.M.S.)
Place/date of composition: Oakland, 1880 (*LETBM*, Vol. III, No. 717, [Postmark 1 September 1880])
Letter: No. 717 (above) asked the printer Smith, Elder to alter the printed signature on this poem to 'R.L.S.' from 'W.P. Bannatyne' since it was to be published in *Cornhill Magazine* and Leslie Stephen urged the poet to use his real name; Bannatyne, a pseudonym also used on MSS of *UW* XXIII and XXXIII, and in *Travels With A Donkey*, was a private joke between RLS and Bob Stevenson (R.A.M.S.) dating back to their childhood games (see *LETBM*, Vol. II, No. 604, n.3 and Explanatory Note on Bob, below p. 624).
MS: Harvard proofs
First publication: *Cornhill Magazine*, London, February 1881
Line
10   rod'st] rode (*Cornhill*)
18   took'st] took (*Cornhill*) tookst (Harvard)
21   the Pelethronian antre,] a vast mountain antre, (*Cornhill*)
51   Dakota] Dakotah (Harvard)
74   And O,] And oh, (*Cornhill*)
      {Scribner's Author's Edn (1887) (see above, p. 394) omits the colon at the end of line 21 and is followed in this error by Thistle and other editions.}

XVI *To W. E. Henley*
Place/date of composition: Oakland, Spring 1880
MSS: None found.

XVII *To Henry James*

Place/date of composition: Bournemouth, 19 May 1885 (*LETBM*, Vol. V, No. 1433, n. 2)

On 19 May 1885 Fanny and RLS celebrated their wedding anniversary with a dinner party at Skerryvore. Fanny told the poet's mother that under each napkin were verses written by RLS for each guest; this poem awaited Henry James (Sanchez 1920: 123).

MS: H2389

No. XVII] <XII>^XVI^

Title: *Henry James*] <*To Henry James.*>

Line

  1   ope] close
  2   walls, can] walls can
  3   now] do
  8   *De Mauves,*] *de Mauves,*
 11 and] and –

XVIII *The Mirror Speaks*

Place/date of composition: Bournemouth, March 1886 (B6583 dated at end)

Letters: 1. Fanny Stevenson to Henry James [25 February 1886] (*LETBM*, Vol. V, p. 210): {James had sent the Stevensons a mirror, which they hung in their drawing room at Skerryvore.} 'A magic mirror has come to us which seems to reflect not only our own plain faces, but the kindly one of a friend entwined in the midst of all sorts of pleasant memories. Louis felt that verse alone would fitly convey his sentiments concerning this beautiful present, but his muse, I believe, has not as yet responded to his call. As for me, to whom the gift of song has been denied in common with the modest hen canary, I can only attempt to express my thanks in plain prose.'

2. RLS to Henry James [7 March 1886] (*LETBM*, Vol. V, pp. 222–3): 'This is what the glass says:' {MS of poem follows:}

MSS: B6583, B6584, Letter 2 (1573)

Title: *The Mirror Speaks*] *To Henry James.* / *(The mirror speaks)* (B6583)

                    The Mirror Speaks / <*To Henry James*> B6584 {untitled} (1573)

Line

  1   sea] sea, (1573)
  4   sung;] sung, (B6583)
  5   heard, … well,] heard … well (B6583)
  8   looked,] looked; (1573)
 12 said;] said. (1573)
 15 glowed,] glowed; (1573) glowed (B6583)
 16 men;] men. (all MSS)
 17 straw,] straw (B6583)
 18 Long I none but] And no one but the (B6583, 1573)
 19 eye] eye, (B6583)
 20 One that sees] One who Sees (1573)
 21 grace,] grace (B6583)
 24 Where] And (1573)
 25 Prince of Men,] Prince of men, (1573)

{Like Lang, James had been the target of a private lampoon sent from Davos to Henley in November 1881:}

> 'H. James:
> Not clad in transatlantic furs,
>   But clinking English pence,
> The young republic claims me hers
>   In no parochial sense.
>
> A bland colossus, mark me stride,
>   From land to land, the sea,
> And patronise on every side
>   Far better men than me.
>
> My books, that models are of wit
>   And masterworks of art,
> From occident to orient flit
>   And please in every part.
>
> Yet I'm a sentimental lot;
>   And freely weep to see
> Poor Hawthorne and the rest, who've not
>   To Europe been, like me.'

(*LETBM*, Vol. III, p. 245)

XIX *Katharine*
Place/date of composition: Hyères, 1883–4
MSS: B6477; BBS II,142 {B6477 is identical with the copy-text. *BBS*, a transcription of lines written on the margin of a MS of *UW* IX (see above, p. 407), varies from the copy-text as follows:}
Line
  4   quiet, clear and cool;] clear and beautiful;
  5   glass,] glass

XX *To F.J.S.*
Place/date of composition: Mentone, France, 15 November 1873 (B6998 dated at bottom)
Letter: RLS to Frances Sitwell [c. 15 November 1873] (*LETBM*, Vol. I, pp. 370–1): 'Here is what I have often said in good prose, put into bad verse. {Enclosed is an untitled 33-line draft of this poem with four more stanzas than appear in *UW*.}
    I send you this rubbish just to show you, my dear Amalia (which is the name of your *face*, I have found no name yet for your spirit) that I thought of you. Don't criticise it, for the love of Charity, but remember that it was written by a – an imbecile I was going to say and I'm not much better.'
MSS: B6998, B3274, BRBML 734 {B6998, reproduced in facsimile in McKay Vol. V opp. p. 2013, also contains thirty-three lines and seven stanzas; B3274 is the MS of *LETBM*, No. 173 and 734 is an uncatalogued MS which is identical to the copy-text. Collation follows:

Title: *To F.J.S.*] <XIX *To Claire*> {Beside this cancelled title on B6998 RLS pencilled 'XX
To F.J.S. First 3 stanzas publish'. He may have been following his usual
practice of marking sections of his MSS and notebooks for publication. His
MS is one of those torn from Notebook A.155. See Explanatory Note on
this poem, p. 624.}

Line

3 life,] life (both MSS)
4 sun-chequered,] sun-chequered (both MSS)
5 the far-distant fountain-head.] <the><its>far distant fountainhead. (B6998)
                                    its far distant fountainhead. (B3274)
6 your] <thy>^your^ (B6998)
7 you] thee (B6998)
10 But as some lone, wood-wandering] But, as some lone wood-wandering (both MSS)
11 home] back (B6998)
13 true] true, (both MSS)
14 you!] you. (both MSS)

{The omitted stanzas follow, based on B3274, with variants given from B6998:}

> 'And thorns. But did the sculptor spare] thorns!
> Sharp steel upon the marble, ere,] marble<,>
> After long vigils and much care] {whole line obliterated}
> And cruel discipline of blows,] <And>^Thro'^
> From the dead stone the statue rose?] stone,
>
> Think you I grudge the seed, who see] see,
> Broad armed the consummated tree?] Wide armed, the
> Or would go back if it might be] back, if it might be,
> To some old geologic time
> With Saurians wallowing in fat slime,] <When>^With^... <fat>^the^
>
> Before the rivers and the rains
> Had fashioned, and made fair with plains
> And shadowy places fresh with flowers,
> This green and quiet world of ours,] ours <,>^.^

{In B6998 this final stanza was cancelled in pencil at some point after the seven-stanza
version had been sent to Mrs Sitwell:}

> Where, as the grass in springtime heals
> The furrow of the winter's wheels,
> Serene maturity conceals
> All memory on the perfect earth] memory, on the perfect earth,
> Of the byegone tempestuous birth.'

XXI *Requiem*

Place/date of composition: San Francisco, 1879–80. Balfour dates it 1884 and CP, following
TUS, gives 'Hyères, May, 1884'. However, the earliest versions, B6790 and B6791, are dated
1879 and 1880 respectively; the letters quoted below confirm this dating.

Letters: 1. RLS to Colvin [late February 1880] (*LETBM*, Vol. III, pp. 66–7): 'Sketch of my tomb follows:

Robert Louis Stevenson
Born 1850, of a family of Engineers
Died – – – – – – – – – – – – – – – – –

Nitor Aquis

———

Home is the sailor, home from sea,
And the hunter home from the hill.

———

You, who pass this grave, put aside hatred; love kindness; be all services remembered in your heart and all offences pardoned; and as you go down again among the living, let this be your question: Can I make some one happier this day before I lie down to sleep? Thus the dead man speaks to you from the dust: you will hear no more from him.

Who knows, Colvin, but I may thus be of more use when I am buried than ever while I was alive? The more I think of it, the more earnestly do I desire this. I may perhaps try to write it better some day; but that is what I want in sense. The verses are from a beayootiful poem by me.' {A facsimile of this letter faces p. 948 in Vol. III of McKay. RLS explained *Nitor Aquis* in a letter of 8 December 1879 to Gosse: describing his poor health and severely depressed state at this point in his transcontinental pursuit of Fanny in order to make her his wife, RLS recognises that his quixotic questing may be the death of him, and soon. His present convalescence in Monterey will not be for long, because he is driven to continue his quest: 'I hear the breakers roar; I shall be steering head first for another rapid before many days; *nitor aquis*, said a certain Eton boy, translating for his sins a part of the *Inland Voyage* {RLS's first book} into Latin elegiacs; and from the hour I saw it ... and recognized its absurd appropriateness, I took it for my device in life. I have *knighted with the waters* steadily since I was nineteen, and the great billows have gone over my soul in succession till ... I have come to have moments of weariness. I am going for thirty now, and unless I can snatch a little rest before long, I have, I may tell you in confidence, no hope of seeing thirty-one ... If the knighting is to continue, I believe I must go. It is a pity in one sense, for I believe the class of work I *might* yet give out, is better and more real and solid than people fancy. But death is no bad friend; a few aches and gasps, and we are done' (*LETBM*, Vol. III, pp. 32–3).}

2. RLS to William Sharp [?mid-October 1887] (*LETBM*, Vol. VI, p. 34): 'Your article is very true and kindly put: I have never called my verses poetry: they are verse, the verse of a speaker not a singer; but that is a fair business like another. I am of your mind too in preferring much the Scotch verses, and in thinking *Requiem* the nearest thing to poetry that I have ever "clerkit".' {Sharp, the poet 'Fiona MacLeod' and biographer of D. G. Rossetti, had reviewed *Underwoods* in the *Academy* for 1 October 1887, praising the 'true and delightful Scottish poetry' but calling the English poems 'verses by a prose writer'. For *Requiem*, however, he had high praise: 'I believe it will outlive ... the whole of *Underwoods*, and perhaps, so greedy is oblivion, the greater portion of the author's prose' (see Maixner 1981: 264–71).

3. RLS to Leslie Brooke, 24 January 1893 (*LETBM*, Vol. VIII, pp. 12–13): 'I address Miss

Rhoda who has done me the compliment to take a fancy to my own favourite verses, and to set them as it seems to me with a great deal of feeling. I thank you very much for having sent it to me and Graham for having suggested it ' {Brooke's sister Rhoda, future wife of RLS biographer Graham Balfour, had set *Requiem* to music.}

MSS: B6790, B6791, H1998. {B6790 is the earliest version, dated at the end in pencil 'Train August 79'. It appears as a facsimile in McKay Vol. V opposite p. 1954. No. 54 in the disbound notebook A.155 (see above, p. 434), written while RLS travelled across the USA by rail at the cheapest fares from New York to San Francisco, this draft shows the same low spirits expressed in the above-quoted letter to Gosse:

> 'Now when the number of my years
> Is all fulfilled, and I
> From sedentary life
> Shall rouse me up to die,
> > Bury me low and let me lie
> > Under the wide and starry sky,
> > Joying to live, I joyed to die,
> > Bury me low and let me lie.
>
> Clear was my soul, my deeds were free,
> > Honour was called my name,
> I fell not back from fear
> Nor followed after fame.
> > Bury me low and let me lie
> > Under the wide and starry sky, etc.
>
> Bury me low <and let me lie>^in valleys green^
> And where the milder breeze
> Blows fresh along the stream,
> Sings roundly in the trees –
> > Bury me low etc.'

B6791, also removed from a disbound notebook, is a three-stanza version dated at the end in pencil, '1880 Jan. S.[an] F.[rancisco]'; it appears in facsimile in McKay Vol. V opp. p. 1955. H1998 (see illustration p. 87) is identified by HL as being in the hand of Isobel Strong, but there seems to be no evidence supporting this statement. This MS was formerly owned by W. H. Arnold, who reproduced it in his book (Arnold 1923: 290). It has the suppressed second stanza but is closer to the copy-text than B6791:

Title: XX. *Requiem*] {untitled} (B6791)
Line
1   sky,] sky (B6791)
3   die,] die (H1998)
{5–8 suppressed in copy-text}
> 'Here may the winds about me blow;
> Here the clouds may come and go;
> Here shall be rest for evermo,
> > And the heart for aye shall be still.' (both MSS)

9   This be] <That be>^This be^ (B6791)

10–12   {underlined for italicization} (H1998)

{*Requiem* is part of a panel cast in bronze on RLS's tomb on Mount Vaea near his Samoan home at Vailima: see 'Epilogue: The Death of Stevenson' in *LETBM*, Vol. VIII, pp. 401–10. Following the poet's sudden death on 3 December 1894, these elegiac verses by A. E. Housman appeared in the *Academy*:}

'R.L.S.

Home is the sailor, home from sea:
    Her far-borne canvas furled
The ship pours shining on the quay
    The plunder of the world.

Home is the hunter from the hill:
    Fast in the boundless snare
All flesh lies taken at his will
    And every fowl of air.

'Tis evening on the moorland free,
    The starlit wave is still:
Home is the sailor from the sea,
    The hunter from the hill.'

XXII *The Celestial Surgeon*

Place/date of composition: Davos, 1882 (Balfour)

~~MS: Notebook 'T' (1882–3), NLS MS19637 {The NLS sketch is 10 lines, as follows:}~~

'If I have faltered more or less
In my great task of happiness;
If I, a midnight figure, stand
In this great April orchard-land;
Lord thy most pointed pleasure take
And stab my spirit broad awake;
Or choose a piercing sorrow out,
A timely sin, an eating doubt,
And with the red fires of distress
Wake me again to happiness.'

{A working title for this poem was *Indifference*.}

XXIII *Our Lady of the Snows*

Place/date of composition: Edinburgh, 1879. {A draft of this poem dating from September 1878, when RLS stayed at Our Lady of the Snows Monastery in France, appears in the Cevennes Journal, which was the basis for *Travels with a Donkey* (Golding 1978: 142). B6705, a later MS version, is dated 'Edin. Feb.79.'}

Letters: RLS to Henley [early April 1879] (*LETBM*, Vol. II, Nos 606–7), pp. 308–10: {Asked to comment on a version of this much-revised Arnoldian effusion, Henley had done so freely in an effort to get RLS to improve it, saying, 'the verses are not in the least like doggerel.

They seem to me, on the contrary, to be very genuine and pleasant stuff indeed … The matter with it is, that it wants weight and dignity. Your verse is too lax and light. If you cannot brace and straighten it up to the kind of Andrew Marvell standing this octosyllabic rhyme must not be used to moralise in.' Henley had attacked the opening couplet as weak, which in the version he had annotated read,

> 'Out of the world, out of the sun
> My steps went slowly one by one,'

RLS responded as follows:}
'You have the brass to ask me *why* 'my steps went one by one'? Why? Powers of man! To rhyme with *sun*, to be sure … I am a weak brother in verse. You ask me to rewrite things that I have already managed just to write with the skin of my teeth. If I don't rewrite them, it's because I don't see how to write them better, not because I don't think they should be.' {Henley also condemned lines 27–8,

> 'My undissuaded heart I hear
> Whisper courage in my ear.'

drawing this response from the poet:}
'I did not try to make good verse, but to say what I wanted as well as verse would let me. I don't like the rhyme "ear" and "hear". But the couplet is exactly what I want for the thought, and to me seems very energetic, as speech, if not as verse. Would "daring" be better than "courage"? … No, it would be ambigous, as though I had used it licentiously for "daringly", and that would cloak the sense.'
MSS: H2408, B6704, B6705, B6706
{H2408 is Notebook 'G' containing the Cevennes Journal of 1878. Opposite p. 31 is written this sixteen-line draft, the seminal version of *UW* XXIII, signed 'W.P. Bannatyne', an imaginary character from childish games with Bob Stevenson: RLS also signed this pseudonym to MSS of *UW* XV and XXXIII. Evidently the poet had at one time intended to use these lines by 'Bannatyne' as a 'motto' or epigraph preceding the chapter 'Our Lady of the Snows' in *Travels with a Donkey*; he did preface another chapter in that book, 'The Country of the Camisards', with the *UW* poem of the same title, there also ascribed to 'Bannatyne'. The 'motto' ultimately chosen for the chapter half-title page introducing 'Our Lady of the Snows' comes from a real poet, Matthew Arnold, and precedes these sixteen lines in Notebook 'G': it is lines 64–6 of *Stanzas from the Grande Chartreuse*, an elegiac poem of 1855 recording Arnold's visit to a remote Carthusian monastery in the mountains near Grenoble, France:

> 'I behold
> The House, the Brotherhood austere –
> And what am I, that I am here?'

RLS's very rough draft follows:}
> 'O better in the great {alt. "wild"} world tempest-tossed
> To serve and sin,
> Than here, grave-clad, an empty peace to win,
> Than here, unkindly quiet in a cell,
> With loving joy and laughing service lost
> <In that last cell>To breathe your breath

Where, neighbouring \<on the\>with the royalty of death,
Mankind's deserters, mankind's wounded dwell.

Here the tongue ceases, here the heart is dead;
Here in a cell
Mankind's deserters, mankind's wounded dwell,
And life continues with life's purpose fled,
O better, in the wild world tempest-tossed,
To serve and sin,
Than, O \<unkindly\>ironically perfect \<dwell herein\> lost
To man and mankind, \<cold\> deadly \<live\>dwell herein!

W. P. Bannatyne'

B6704, 6pp. and 112 lines, a very early and much-revised pencil draft, follows:

'Poor passionate man, still clothed afresh
In that Nessus robe of flesh,
Whom the clear eyes solicit still
To some bold output of the will;
\<And\>Whom the \<red\>bold heart beating high,
Yet prompts to suffer and enjoy,
\<And\>like the soldier's drum, its sound
Recruits and calls the passions round.
O little boots it thus to dwell
On the remote, unneighboured hill;
To hold the peace, to fold the hands,
And in unnoticeable sands
Drain out the useless lees of time,
Far from virtue, far from crime.
O to be up and doing, O
Unfearing and unshamed, to go
In all the uproar and the press
\<Upon\>About my \<father's\>human business!

Out of the \<life\>world, out of the sun,
My \<two\>feet went slowly, one by one,
Across the moor and through the wood
To where the monastery stood.
\<Where the tongue ceases\>
\<Death's \<\<little\>\>silent outpost, it looks \<\<forth\>\>\<\<out on\>\>far apart\>
\<Patient upon life's seething rout\>
\<Uncaring, and it looks about\>
\<On life's\>\<A blot on life's\>
\<\<\<Here\>\>Uncaring, patient, dead, they see in life\>
\<They watch far off the undying\>\<evil and strife\>
Its silent, untouched denizen
Watches from far the evil of men
\<The sunlit, swift, uproarious \<\<dream\>\>stream,\>

<The call, the glamour, and the dream,>
Where love and honour <up and down>travel by
<Wrestle to win> To dare, to suffer and to die.
Hearts have no heart [? illegible] to tell
And nothing speaks except the bell.

My undissuaded heart I hear
Whisper courage in my ear;
With voiceless calls, the world of earth
Calls me from my private hearth
<Ye>Thou, O my love, ye, O my friends
The gist of life, the end of ends
<The suffering God in each>
<In all your ways the sinner trod;>
In each, I knew a suffering God;

And moves <the heart>like <song>music the undefended soul,
Speak, and mankind from pole to pole

<Upon>Alike on foe, alike on friend
Our educating eyes attend;
<We look, we listen, we are prompt to reap>
In all the mingled brotherhood,
<We see the>O prompt and proud to <find them>mark the good?
<By>Each pure design, <by>each honest word
Flies heavenward <like a singing bird>singing like a bird
And by the song are all the nations stirred.
<In pure>Just is my foe? – Then juster I!
<So, the brief hour before they die,>
<The noble souls of men, their splendid>
The pathos of your human looks
Speaks clearer than the best of books
To laugh, to love, to give, to die,
Ye call me by the ear and eye.
The thrill, the tremor of your speech <voice>
Can to the inmost feeling reach
<Ye speak beside the>Speak, and the word's a trumpet call,
And the brave heart and rampired city fall.

And ye, O silent brothers, what if God
When from <the>heaven's top, he spies abroad
And sees on this tormented stage
<And sees red battle of mankind>
The red war of mankind rage
<Undaunted to fulfill the age>
On all his ranked battalions, <here below,><and appears;>
And sees the pennons flying. <and blood and tears>

What if his vivifying eye,
Intent on those who do and die,
O silent monks, should pass your corner by?
For God is God of might;
In deeds he takes delight;
He sniffs the wind of battle; <he drinks in>war in his sight
<From that great whirlwind where we sin and sin,>
<Love><Life, the great drama,>
<All>Not virtue only, but the good that lives in sin,
Do <I>we a nicer honour spy? –
That shall be <mine>ours as <on the>in the quest <I>we die!
Forth from <your trench>the casemate, on the plain,
Where honour has the world to gain,
<Forth the unshielded human heart>
<Goes bravely {blank space} at its part>
Pour forth and bravely do your part,
O knights of the unshielded heart!
War oft its noblest task secretes
In well supporting ill defeats.
Not all who run shall reach the goal,
<Or do the ranks of evil flee,>
<Well struck>Or back returning, like a sea
<What boots it? To vanquish or be vanquished>
Victor or vanquished, O my soul
Look clearly heavenward and be glad –
<Look>Rise up and sing <my soul>; such honour as we had
<To fight though not to conquer, to be true>
<No other honours are>
<That, striving near and far,><Is true worth>
Shines like an inward star:
A cheerful planet, still shall cheer the way!
And <that>through disgrace and <through>past defeat,
A comfortable planet, guides our feet.
<Fate can deny not virtue to the brave>
<May fate and fortune stain the life,>
Fate much can do, yet courage more;
I beat through evil, seeing good before,
[?]<the worst>bad befall, though we move in fear
O little boots it, if to good we steer,
<A sin, a crime, is but a wound received>
<In these hot ranks of war>
Success is ever by the fates denied:
The true success is to have bravely tried.'

B6705, an untitled draft of 4pp. and 86 lines, is collated below against the copy-text:
Line
1–2   Out of the sun, out of the blast,

	Out of the world, alone I passed]
	Out of the world, out of the sun
	My \<feet\>steps went slowly one by one,
3	wood] wood,
9	unhelpful, and] unhelpful and
10	The prisoners of the iron mind,] Each prisoner in his lonely mind,
13	Poor passionate men, still] Poor, passionate men still
14	With agonising folds] In the Nessus robe
16	will,] will;
17–20	{these MS lines have no equivalent in the copy-text:}
	Whom the red heart beating high
	Yet prompts to suffer and enjoy,
	And like the soldier's drum, its sound
	Recruits and calls the passions round –
21	O, little] O little
23	doing, O] doing – O,
24	unshamed to go] unshamed, to go
34ff.	{MS lines 35–47, which follow, have no equivalent in the copy-text:}
	The pathos of your human looks
	Speaks clearer than the best of books.
	The thrill, the tremor, of your speech
	Can to the inmost feeling reach;
	Speak, and the word's a trumpet call,
	And the brave heart and rampired city fall.
	Alike on foe, alike on friend,
	Our educating eyes attend,
	In all the mingled brotherhood
	O prompt and proud to mark the good!
	Just is my foe – then juster I!
	Do we a nicer honour spy? –
	That shall be ours as in the quest we die?
39ff.	{MS lines 52–5, which follow, were inserted after line 38 and have no equivalent in the copy-text:}
	O brave defeats where hope remained!
	O honour fall'n and yet unstained!
	O gentle valour, tender-souled!
	O arms of iron, hearts of gold!
47	brethren] \<silent brothers\>^brethren^
48	Heav'n's] heav'n's
50	rage:] rage,
51	What if] What, if
52	{MS line 70 follows line 51 here:} Intent on those who dare and die,
	O monks,] O silent monks
53–4	For still the Lord is Lord of might;
	In deeds, in deeds, he takes delight;]
	For God is God of might;

                In deeds he takes delight;
                {MS line 74 inserted here:} He marks the battle and the armour bright;
56ff.   {MS lines 77–8 inserted here:} His looks all-fatherly approve
                                         Kind lovers and their simple love;
59   in the rocks;] on the rocks;
60   To him,] And as to him,
61   {Lines 57–8 and 61–70 of the copy-text are not present in B6705}
75   General] <general>^General^
{B6706 varies only slightly from the copy-text, as follows:}
  9   unhelpful, and] unhelpful and
 18   Memory-Hold-the-door] Memory-hold-the-door
 50   rage:] rage –
 60   To him,] And as to him,
 64   caryatides.] cariatides. {changed during proofing}
 66   maid,] maid;
 75   General] general
{In the first and subsequent editions line 11 ends with 'hell' but B6704 and B6705 have 'bell'.
Obviously the MSS are correct and 'hell' is a printer's error.}

XXIV 'Not yet, my soul, these friendly fields desert'
Place/date of composition: Oakland, April 1880 (LETBM, Vol. III, Nos 699, 704)
Letters: {RLS was both dangerously ill and severely depressed in California during
March–April 1880. Some letters of this period, and this poem, record his sense of a bitter
struggle against death. See notes on UW X.}

1. RLS to Edmund Gosse, 16 April [1880] (LETBM, Vol. III, pp. 77–8): 'For about six weeks
I have been in utter doubt; it was a toss up for life or death all that time; but I won the toss,
sir, and Hades went off once more discomfited … I have cause to bless God, my wife that is
to be, and one Dr Bamford … that I have come out of all this, and got my feet once more
upon a little hill-top, with a fair prospect of life and some new desire of living. Yet I did not
wish to die, neither; only I felt unable to go on farther with that rough horseplay of human
life; a man must be pretty well to take the business in good part. Yet I felt all the time that
I had done nothing to entitle me to an honourable discharge, that I had taken up many
obligations and begun many friendships which I had no right to put away from me; and that
for me to die was to play the cur and slinking sybarite, and desert the colours on the eve of
the decisive fight … Of course I have done no work for I do not know how long … I have
been reduced to writing verses for amusement … But I'll have them buried with me, I think;
for I have not the heart to burn them while I live.'

2. RLS to William Dean Howells [early June 1880] (LETBM, Vol. III, p. 85): 'I have been
for some four months inhabiting the immediate borderland of death. I was unable to write
any prose, I amused myself with verse, my heart softened to these children of the sickroom,
my wife … fancied they had merit.' {RLS was sending three poems, this one and possibly
others written in 1880, to Howells, the American novelist who was then editor of the
Atlantic Monthly, in which this poem appeared.}
MS: Harvard proofs
First publication: Atlantic Monthly, October 1880

Collation of printed sources with copy-text:

Line

3   hadₛtᵢ] hadᵢ (AM)

11 love for love,] love for love; (Harvard)

15 grows –] grows, – (AM)

16 growth;] growth: (AM)

21 desert] desert, (AM)

34 fortune] Fortune (AM)

XXV 'It is not yours, O mother, to complain'

Place/date of composition: Oakland, 1880 (Balfour)

MS: Harvard proofs

First publication: *Voluntaries for an East London Hospital*, London, Stott, 1887

Title: untitled}] *Ad Matrem* (Voluntaries)

Line 21 flee,] flee (both printed sources)

XXVI *The Sick Child*

Place/date of publication: Bournemouth, 1884–6

Sources: 1. 'Notes of Childhood', 18 May 1873, quoted by Balfour (Vol. I, 39): 'My ill-health principally chronicles itself by the terrible long nights that I lay awake, troubled continually with a hacking, exhausting cough, and praying for sleep or morning from the bottom of my shaken little body. I principally connect these nights, however, with our third house, in Heriot Row; and cannot mention them without a grateful testimony to the unwearied sympathy and long-suffering displayed to me on a hundred such occasions by my good nurse. It seems to me that I should have died if I had been left there alone to cough and weary in the darkness. How well I remember her lifting me out of bed, carrying me to the window, and showing me one or two lit windows up in Queen Street across the dark belt of gardens; where also, we told each other, there might be sick little boys and their nurses waiting, like us, for the morning.'

2. 'Memoirs of Himself', 1880: 'These were feverish, melancholy times; I cannot remember to have raised my head or seen the moon or any of the heavenly bodies; my eyes were turned downward to the broad lamplit streets, and to where the trees of the garden rustled together all night in undecipherable blackness; yet the sight of the outer world refreshed and cheered me; and the whole sorrow and burden of the night was at an end with the arrival of the first of that long string of country carts that, in the dark hours of the morning, with the neighing of horses, the cracking of whips, the shouts of drivers and a hundred other wholesome noises, creaked, rolled, and pounded past my my window.' (*VAIL*, Vol. XXVI, p. 210)

{Cf. similar accounts in a letter to Fanny Sitwell (*LETBM*, Vol. I, p. 317) and 'Nuits Blanches', *EDIN*, Vol. XXI, pp. 34–7.}

MSS: B6842, Silverado MR-VII #3: A-18

First publication: *The State*, London, 10 April 1886

Both MSS and the magazine printing have two five-line stanzas at the end omitted in the copy-text; these have been printed in BBS II, 146–7 and CP 482. Collation of all three sources follows; the additional ten lines are taken from MR-VII with variants shown to the right of each line:

Line
15 begin] begin. (MR-VII)
17 kind,] <good>^kind^ (B6842)
18 window-blind,] window blind. (MR-VII)
19 asleep,] to sleep (MR-VII)
20 And dream of the birds and the hills of sheep.]
     To dream of the <hills>^birds^ and the <fields>^hills^ of sheep. (MR-VII)

{In MR-VII the final ten lines are separated from the published lines by a solid line, thus ———.}

'So in the dream-beleaguered night,] So, in (B6842)
     While the other children lie
     Quiet, and the stars are high,
The poor, unused and playful mite
Lies strangling in the grasp of fright.

<So>^O^, when all golden comes the day,
     And the other children leap
     Singing from the doors of sleep,
Lord, take thy heavy hand away!] Lord take (B6842) Thy (The State)
Lord, in thy mercy, heal or slay.] in Thy mercy heal (The State)

XXVII *In Memoriam F.A.S.*
Place/date of composition: April 1881 (Private issue dated 'Davos, April 3, 1881')
Letters: 1. RLS to Colvin [c. 12 March 1881] (*LETBM*, Vol. III, pp. 161–2): {F.A.S. was Francis Albert Sitwell, Fanny Sitwell's son Bertie, who died of tuberculosis in his mother's arms at age eighteen.} 'As to Bertie, … I know the thing to be terribly perilous; I fear it to be now altogether hopeless … In her true heart, the mother hopes no more. But – well, I feel a great deal, that I either cannot or will not say, as you well know. It has helped to make me more conscious of the wolverine on my own shoulders; and that also makes me a poor judge and poor adviser.'

2. RLS to his mother [4 April 1881] (*LETBM*, Vol. III, p. 168): 'Poor Bertie died yesterday morning … The boy is beyond all evil, and has had a most bright and harmless life.'
First publication: a single 8vo leaf printed privately, headed 'To F.J.S. / Davos, April 3, 1881' and signed 'R.L.S.'. There is a facsimile in the Widener Catalogue, p. 44.
MSS: B5979, B5980, B5985, B6394, B6999, B7000.
{As RLS remarked in the above letter to Colvin, he found it very difficult to express his feelings about this horrific death: the first six MSS listed above, containing more than 160 lines in total, are attempts at it, and record the tortuous process by which he finally arrived at the sixteen-line elegy. McKay, *BBS* and *CP* all treat this material as several separate poems, but a close examination of the MSS provides evidence to support the argument that RLS was working towards a single expression of elegiac consolation that he could offer to Bertie's mother, and that would also mean something to him. The seminal draft occurs over pp. 36–40 of Notebook 'C' (BRBML); an equally extensive experiment with similar themes and images can be seen in B6999, three pages numbered 70–2 and headed No. 58, torn from

disbound notebook A.155. B6394 (Notebook 'C' pp. 36–7) starts off in blank verse, then modulates uncertainly into quatrains with an abab rhyme scheme, as follows:}

> '<Small is that>
> If that which should be is not; that which is
> O God, so greatly should not be; and all
> From dawn to sunset and from birth to <death>^grave^
> Be, or appear, <alas> oh God, evil alone;
> <Alas> If that be so, <all>then silence were the best,
> Yet, O broken heart remember, O remember,
> All has not been evil from the start,
> April came to bloom at least, and no December
> Laid its chilling frosts upon the head or heart,
> Life indeed of months, and not of years; a being
> Trod the flowery April <and went>blithely for a while,
> Took his fill of music, joy of thought and seeing,
> Came and stayed and went nor ever ceased to smile.
> Yours the pang; but his, O his the undiminished
> Undecaying glory, [line left unfinished]
> <Came and went <<and now>> a dream, and now when all is finished,>
> ^Came and went, a dream; and now when all is finished,^
> You alone have trod the melancholy stream,
> Yours the pang but his, O his the undiminished
> Undecaying glory, undisturbed dream.
> All that life contains of <rough and foul and evil,>^torture, toil and treason^
> Shame, dishonour, death to him were but a name,
> Here for all his youth he dwelt
> <And>Ere the day of sorrow departed as he came.
> Here a youth he stayed through all the singing season.'

{B5985 continues B6394 on p. 37 with the first draft of an extended simile about migrating songbirds, much worked on but ultimately abandoned:}

> '<he lived a whi[lle]>
> <Hear me again>
> As to these vales the blackbirds came awhile
> As <to these>in the mountain valleys for awhile
> In March, the blackbird sings
> And ere the summer, many a mile
> Forth voyaging, sings,
>
> He knew not; who should know?'

{B5979, on pp. 38–40, expands the above simile to a sprawling fifty-four lines. B5980, three pages from another notebook, immediately follows a late draft containing few variants (B6999) and reduces the fifty-four lines to thirty-one. This MS has been printed as a separate poem by *BBS*, I, pp. 189–90 (there misdated 1880); it was reprinted in *NP*, p. 164 and *CP*, pp. 300–1 and reads as follows:

'As in their flight the birds of song
Halt here and there in sweet and sunny dales
But halt not overlong;
The time one rural song to sing
They pause; then following bounteous gales
Steer forward on the wing:
Sun-servers they, from first to last,
Upon the sun they await
To ride the sailing blast.

So he a while in our contested state,
A while abode, not longer – for his Sun –
Mother we say, no tenderer name we know –
With whose diviner glow
His early days had shone,
Now to withdraw her radiance had begun.
Or lest a wrong I say, not she withdrew,
But the loud stream of men day after day
And great dust columns of the common way
 Between them grew and grew:
And he and she for evermore might yearn,
But to the spring the rivulets not return
Nor to the bosom comes the child again.

And he (O may we fancy so!)
He, feeling time for ever flow
And flowing bear him forth and far away
From that dear ingle where his life began
And all his treasure lay –
He, waxing into man,
And ever farther, ever closer wound
In this obstreperous world's ignoble round
From that poor prospect turned his face away.'

{Variants between B5979 and B5980 are too numerous to give in full, but the following example, pertaining only to the final line, should suffice:}
Line
31   From that poor prospect turned his face away.] (B5980)
     <Saw what a fall before him><And in the><Saw><Judged this>
     Saw that from good to ill he trod,
     And <fled>fearing more, he fled to God.
     <Or if not he, at least some kindly power>
     <Or not himself, but kindlier God,>Or rather
     <Saw from good to worse>
     Saw how from good to ill
     <That forth conducted still,>
     And rather chose to die.' (B5979, Notebook 'C', pp. 39–40)

Collation of B6999, B7000 and To F.J.S. with copy-text:
Title: *In Memoriam F.A.S.*] *To F.J.S.* / *Davos, April 3, 1881* (To F.J.S.)
[untitled] (B6999, D7000)

Line
1   Yet, O ... remember] Yet O ... remember, (B6999)
2   human days ... part.] mortal days ~ (B7000) mortal days ... part; (To F.J.S.)
3   bloom and never] bloom, nor ever (B7000, To F.J.S.)
4   the head or heart.] his ~ (B7000) his head and heart. (To F.J.S.)
5   Winter, only Spring,] winter ~ (B6999) winter, only spring, (B7000, To F.J.S.)
6   for a while,] for awhile, (B7000) for awhile; (To F.J.S.)
9   went, ... finished,] ~ finished (B6999) went; ~ (B7000, To F.J.S.)
10   stream,] stream. (B7000) stream; (To F.J.S.)
11   pang, but his, O his, the undiminished] pang but his, O his the ~ (B6999)
~ O his the undiminished, (To F.J.S.)
13   toil, and] toil and (B6999) toil, or (To F.J.S.)
14   death, to ... name.] death to ~ (B6999) ~ name; (To F.J.S.)
15   season] season, (all MSS)
Signature at bottom: Davos, 1881] {no date/place} (B6999)
Davos, Apr.3, 1881 (B7000) R.L.S. (To F.J.S.)

XXVIII   *To My Father*
Place/date of composition: Oakland, spring 1880
MS: Harvard proofs
Line
22   beach.] beach;
23   speaks.] speaks;

XXIX   *In the States*
Place/date of composition: San Francisco, January 1880 (McKay, Vol. V, p. 1855)
MS: B6447 {This is No. 53 in Notebook A.155 disbound by Hellman.}
Title: *In the States*] *In America*
Line
2   by] by,
3   yet though] yet, though
6   born.] born;
10   decay:] decay.
11   States – for me,] <s>^S^tates – for me

XXX   *A Portrait*
Place/date of composition: Davos, 1881 (*LETBM*, Vol. III, Nos 792 n.4, p. 173, and 859 n.3, p. 240) {This lampoon on W. H. Mallock, a writer with whom RLS had clashed at the Savile Club, was intended to be part of the projected satire *Diogenes*, on which Henley and RLS were working in the autumn of 1881, and for which RLS had written his lampoons on Andrew Lang and Henry James (see above, pp. 410, 412 and Explanatory Note on Mallock p. 625).}
MSS: B6733, B6734, NLS, H2459
{At the top of B6733 there is a note in pencil signed and dated, 'Isobel Strong, May 20 1911,

Santa Barbara' which identifies this poem as 'written in the character of Mallock after reading some of his work'.}
Title: *A Portrait*] *Mallock Loquitur*
Line
  2   eyes;] eyes.
  3   blue-behinded] blue-behind-ed
  4   Upon] <About>^Upon^
  9   {MS omits quotation marks}
13   still, ... pale,] still ... pale
16   place;] place.
{There are three additional stanzas following line 4 and one following line 12, as follows:}

> 'Now naked – now intent on ill,
>   Ensconced in a monastic cowl –
> The angel lawns of life I still
>   With great activity befoul.
>
> None can compare with me, I think,
>   In all that makes a man adored,
> In raising an outrageous stink
>   Or heaping filth upon the board.
>
> And all the time – the wondrous sly,
>   The king of impudence and rape
> The primal man of mankind – I
>   Dissemble like a theftuous ape.
>
> Is life worth living? Ah, you prod
>   My fibre in a queasy place! –
> To me, if not worthwhile – my God,
>   It cannot be so to the race!'

{B6734 is a fair copy, identical with the copy-text, watermarked 1883. The *Diogenes* fragment at NLS is in the hand of Henley, consisting of pp. 11–13 filed as folios 241–2 and 298 in the bound volume of letters RLS wrote to Henley. In these pages Mallock (described as 'a young man of swarthy exterior') sings his song to the cynic Diogenes. It is headed, 'Song of the Young Man of Swarthy Exterior' and gives the text of *A Portrait* plus the first of the additional stanzas quoted above. Diogenes smiled and extemporised the following in reply:}

> 'I saw him reach with several other birds
> The Isle of the Eternal Sages who
> On being pertly questioned in these words,
> "Is Life worth Living?" answered, "Not for You!"'

{H2459 is a copy of the verses in the NLS MS, including the above epigram, written out by Henley and given by him to Gosse in 1882. Gosse claimed to have been an eye-witness to the altercation between RLS and Mallock, which he described as 'a certain clash of temperaments, very unfortunate and rather inexplicable, in the course of which the fault lay not on Stevenson's side. *A Portrait* ... was written that afternoon, in what was certainly a ruffled mood of high spirits; and I possess the MS of another epigram, directed, at the same time, against the same author' (Gosse 1908: 71). H2459 was given to HL by Philip Gosse. JAS (CP, 1950) was the first to identify Mallock as the subject of the poem after she had examined what became Yale MS B6733 at Sotheby's in 1949.}

XXXI 'Sing clearlier, Muse, or evermore be still'
Place/date of composition: Oakland, spring 1880
MSS: None found.

XXXII A Camp
Place/date of composition: Mont Lozère, Cevennes, 1878 (drafted in H2408, Notebook 'G', Cevennes Journal, which dates from that year)
Letter: RLS to Henley, [c. 23 March 1879] (LETBM, Vol. II, No. 604, p. 306): {RLS was working on 'mottoes' for Travels with a Donkey (1879), verse epigraphs to precede sections of the book based on his Cevennes Journal; enclosed with this letter were verse sketches which eventually got reprinted as UW XXXII and XXXIII following their publication in Travels.}
'Look here: here's a hitch. I can't get mottoes for some of my sections and took to making them; for I wished rather to have the precise sense than very elegant verses. Still I don't wish to be a public fool. Ferrier thought they would do – for mottoes; but then he's indulgent – and then he helped me with them. So I apply to you.' {Henley, who had been told not to judge these efforts as though they were works of Shakespeare, replied as follows: 'Your verses are pretty and almost companionable ... They are like your prose diluted and weakened. I like them.'}
MSS: H2408; LETBM, No. 604
{H2408 is Notebook 'G', Cevennes Journal; this poem and UW XXXIII are written verso of p. 29 in that MS. As an epigraph for the chapter 'Upper Gévaudan (continued)', it is attributed to another source, in this case a fictitious one, 'Old Play'. RLS may have adopted this practice from Sir Walter Scott, who follows it in the Waverley Novels.}
Title: A Camp] {untitled} (H2408) Motto First (604)
Line
  2 lit;] lit, (both MSS)
  3 still, the water ran,] sweet, the water ran; (H2408) sweet, ~ (604)
  4 was there] there was (H2408)
  5 up, my ass and I,] up my ass and I, (H2408) ~ and I (604)

XXXIII The Country of the Camisards
Place/date of composition: Edinburgh, 1879 (but drafted in H2408, Notebook 'G', Cevennes Journal, which dates from 1878)
Letter: RLS to Henley, LETBM, Vol. II, No. 604 (see note on XXXII above)
MSS: H2408; LETBM, No. 604 (see note on XXXII above)
This 'motto', used to open the chapter 'The Country of the Camisards', in Travels with a Donkey, is attributed in H2408 to W. P. Bannatyne, an imaginary character invented by RLS and his cousin Bob as children, who is also used to sign MSS of UW XV and XXIII.
Title: The Country of the Camisards] {untitled} (H2408) Motto Second (604)
Line
  1 print of olden wars,] prints of olden war <alt. 'wake of wars'> (H2408) ~ wars; (604)
  2 green,] green; (both MSS)

4–5   {604 is not divided into two stanzas}
5   the children] these children (both MSS)
7   O,] O! (both MSS)

XXXIV *Skerryvore*
Place/date of composition. Bournemouth, 1885–7
Letter: RLS to Harriet Monroe [30 June 1886] (*LETBM*, Vol. V, p. 273): 'We are all very
proud of the family achievements, and the name of my house here in Bournemouth is stolen
from one of the sea-towers of the Hebrides which are our pyramids and monuments' (see
Explanatory Note on Skerryvore, p. 625).
MSS: B6862, B6863, B6864
Line
  6   I, … cot,] I … cot (B6863)
  7   a strong tower] that strong tower (B6862)

XXXV *Skerryvore: The Parallel*
Place/date of composition: Bournemouth, 1885–7
MSS: B6865, B6866
Line
  4   kneaded] clotted (both MSS)
10   glittering glass, stands, in … winds,] dazzling glass, stands … winds (B6865)
                                              ~ stands … winds (B6866)

XXXVI '*My house*, I say. But hark to the sunny doves'
Place/date of composition: Bournemouth, 1885–7
MSS: B6606, B6607
Line
   3   gable] gables (B6606)
   4   song:] song – (both MSS)
   7   *mine* the dog, and] *mine*, the dog – and (B6606)
   8   foot] tread (B6606)
   9   So too] So, too, (Author's Edn {see above, p. 394})
{[9–12]   These lines in B6606 are not in *UW*; the eight additional lines in this MS were
           printed in *BBS* II, 149:}

                     'And she, the changeful stranger in our gates,
                     That left for us the land beyond the straits,
                     That now the servant seems and now the guest –
                     Has but to say *our house* to please us best.'

10   Our] <A>^Our^ (B6606)
12   kingdom, only] kingdom only (B6606)
{[17–20] These lines are not included in *UW* but form the conclusion to both MSS:}
                     'Man, mind and beast, but for an hour we stay] stay, (B6607)
                     While the veiled owner dallies on the way;
                     Who shall erelong return, his journeys o'er,
                     And (like the gardener) show us all the door.' (B6606)

XXXVII 'My body which my dungeon is'
Place/date of composition: Bournemouth, 1885–7
MS: B6600
Line
 9   way,] way
10   (She having roamed a summer's day]
      <When night comes (having roamed all day,>
      She (having roamed <all>a summer's day
11   Along the mountain-sides] Along the mountain<s> sides
21   fishers'] fishers
29   bones] bones,

XXXVIII 'Say not of me that weakly I declined'
Place/date of composition: Bournemouth, 1885–7
Letter: RLS to Will. Low, 15 January 1894 (*LETBM*, Vol. VIII, p. 235):
{RLS here taxes himself, in the last year of his life, with the problem of the 'ineffable smallness' of modern art, why the artist today can achieve nothing beyond his art, lacking the 'all-round human sufficiency' of Julius Caesar, Montaigne, Michelangelo or Fielding:}
'I think *David Balfour* a nice little book, and very artistic, and just the thing to occupy the leisure of a busy man; but for the top flower of a man's life it seems to me inadequate. Small is the word; it is a small age, and I am of it. I could have wished to be otherwise busy in this world. I ought to have been able to build lighthouses and write *David Balfours* too.'
MSS: None found.

Book II – *In Scots*

{In the collations of the longer Scots poems, stanzas as well as lines are numbered, and recurrent minor punctuation variants are omitted, e.g. and, an', an, or, o', o.}

I *The Maker to Posterity*
Place/date of composition: Bournemouth, 1885–7
MS: H2463
Heading: BOOK II. – *In Scots*] Book II <Scotch>^In Scots^
Line
 2   see,] see
 4   rouch shouther,] rough shou'ther,
27   skeel,] skeel
31   eggs,] eggs
37   book, ... tongue,] book ... tongue
      {MS marginal note on 'clegs' in line 32: Jamieson states it ought to be pronounced 'gles' but RLS says he's never heard it pronounced that way and never wants to.}

II *Ille Terrarum*
Place/date of composition: Edinburgh, winter 1875 (B6398 so dated at end)
Letters: 1. RLS to William Sharp [?mid-October 1887] (*LETBM*, Vol. VI, p. 34): {In his *Academy* review of *UW*, Sharp had censured 'the townsman's slip' in line 32, 'the sweet-throat mavis tunes her lay;'}: 'What is the townsman's blunder? – though I deny I am a

townsman, for I have lived, on the whole, as much or more in the country: well, perhaps not so much. Is it that the thrush does not sing at night? That is possible. I only know most potently the blackbird (his cousin) does: many and many a late evening in the garden of that poem have I listened to one that was our faithful visitor; and the sweetest song I ever heard was past nine at night in the early spring, from a tree near the N.E. gate of Warriston cemetery. That I called what I believe to have been a merle by the softer name of mavis (and they are all *turdi*, I believe) is the head and front of my offence against literal severity, and I am curious to hear if it has really brought me into some serious error.' {*LETBM*, n.1 to this letter suggests that 'presumably the "slip" is that it is the male bird that does the singing'.}

2. RLS to Alison Cunningham, 16 April 1887 (*LETBM*, Vol. V, pp. 392–3): 'As I write, {from Bournemouth, in south-west England} there is a blackbird singing in our garden trees, as it were at Swanston. I would like fine to go up the burnside a bit, and sit by the pool, and be young again – ' {*Swanston Cottage* was a working title for this poem: RLS was often nostalgic for this leased country home on the slopes of the Pentland Hills, south of Edinburgh, 'the hills of home' (*ST* XLV). Balfour tells us: 'Hither at all seasons Louis would often retire alone or in the company of a friend; here he gained a knowledge of the Pentlands only to be acquired by living among them; here he saw something of the country folk, and enriched his vocabulary of Lallan; here made the acquaintance of John Todd the shepherd, and Robert Young the gardener, and the military beggarman who had a taste for Keats. This was to him *ille terrarum angulus* of *Underwoods*; on the hill above Swanston there lies the tiny pool, overhung by a rock, where he "loved to sit and make bad verses"' (Vol. I, pp. 88–9). See also the essay 'Pastoral' (*EDIN*, Vol. I, pp. 144–54), from which Balfour's quote is taken, and Explanatory Note on this poem, p. 625.}

MSS: B6398. Princeton: Parrish (CO171)
First publication: *The Scottish Church*, Vol. IV, April 1887
Title: *Ille Terrarum*] <*Swanston cottage*>^*Ille Terrarum*^ (CO171)
                    Ille terrarum mihi praeter omnes angulus ridet (B6398)
Stanza.line
  1.1   nirly, nippin', Eas'lan'] nirly nippin Eastlan' (B6398) ~ rippin' Eas'lan' (SC)
  1.2   Norlan' snaw, an'] Norlan snaw an' (B6398)
  1.6   Secure] Secŭre (CO171, SC)
  2.1   theek,] theek (B6398)
  2.3   reek,] reek. (B6398)
  2.5   windies] windows (B6398)
  2.6   green.] green. – (B6398)
  3.2   gillyflowers an' roses:] ~ an roses – (B6398) gilly-flowers ~ (SC)
  3.4   men;] men, – (B6398)
  3.5   dozes,] dozes (B6398)
  4.2   pitaty-track,] pitata track, (B6398) pitaty track, (SC)
  4.4   Jane] Jean (SC)
  5.1   ca's;] ca's, (B6398)
  5.2   gang … wa's;] <gae>^gang^ … wa's, (B6398)
  5.3   Or whiles a clan] <An' [?] whiles>^Or whiles^ a <wheen>^clan^ (B6398)
  5.4   thegether;] thegether. (B6398)
  5.5   gairden raws,] garden ~ (B6398) ~ raws (CO171)
  6.3   linkin'] <toddlin'>^linkin'^ (B6398)

6.5 mŭne maks] mune mak's (B6398) ~ <mak's>^maks^ (CO171)
6.6 trees.] trees. – (B6398)
7.1 hae] <have>^hae^ (B6398)
7.2 sat apairt,] sat apart, (B6398, CO171) set apairt, (SC)
7.3 loves] <lŭves>^luves^ (CO171) luves (B6398, SC)
7.4 mind;] mind: (B6398)
7.5 socht] soucht (B6398)
8.2 Wi' Horace, or] Wi Horace or (both MSS)
8.4 Abŭne] Abune (B6398)
8.5 gi'en a chucky-stane] gie'n a chucky stane (B6398) gi <'> en ~ (CO171)
9.1 noo … city, street] now ~ (B6398) ~ city street (CO171)
9.2 fu'o'] <fu'o'>^full o'^ (B6398)
9.4 goavin' mettle;] <wandering>^goavin'^ mettle. (B6398)
9.5 Noo … soopit] Now … sweepit (B6398)
10.1 noo … winds complain;] now … <wind complains,>^winds complain^ (B6398)
10.2 ilka lane;] <?>ilka <lanes>^lane.^ (B6398)
10.3 hizzie, … wean] <hizzies, … weans>^ ~ ^ (B6398)
10.5 In the mirk nicht, … rain] By <the>^lown^ lamplicht, … rain<s> (B6398)
        By lown lamplicht, ~ (CO171) Late in the nicht, ~ (SC)
10.6 blads.] bla'ds. (CO171)
11.1 rock,] rock (B6398)
11.2 shock,] shock (CO171)
11.5 cock,] cock – (B6398)
11.6 The kintry hame.] <Wi' scarlet kame.><A>^The kintry hame.^ (B6398)
12.1 bield;] bield B6398
12.2 Fancy traivels] fancy <travels>^traivels^ (B6398)
        ~ <traivels>^travels^ (CO171) fancy travels (SC)
12.4 sun an' Simmer:] <[?]>sun an' simmer. (B6398)
12.5 To] – To (B6398)

III 'When aince Aprile has fairly come'
Place of composition: Edinburgh
MSS: B7138, B7139
Line
1 come,] come (both MSS)
2–3 An' birds may bigg in winter's lum,
    An' pleisure's spreid for a' and some]
    An' winter turned his icy bum,
    Wi pleisand days to a' and some
                        (B7138)
    {In B7139 the earlier MS reading is cancelled in favour of the copy-text}
5 Love,] <Lŭve,>^Luve,^ (B7139) Luve, (B7138)
6 taks … gate.] tak's ~ (both MSS) ~ gate (Author's Edn {see above, p. 394})
7 micht;] micht, (B7138)
8 een] e'en (both MSS)
12 hurdies.] hurdies! (B7138)

13   An' aye as love] And aye as Luve (B7138) ~ luve (B7139)
19   snaw,] snaw (both MSS)
21   braw,] braw (B7139)
23   raw,] raw (B7139)

IV *A Mile an' a Bittock*
Place/date of composition: Hyères, 1884 (Balfour)
MSS: B6579, B6580
First publication: *Leisure Hour*, January 1887, p. 26 (see *LETBM*, Vol. V, No. 1715)
{See Explanatory Note on 'the law' p. 625.}
Line {*Leisure Hour* is not divided into stanzas.}
  4   müne] mune (B6579) {and so throughout: no umlauts are used in this MS or in *LH*;
        umlauts occur in B6580, agreeing with the copy-text}
10   twal an'] twal' and (B6579) twal, and (*LH*)
11   guidman's] gudeman's (B6579, *LH*)
13   wind ... affa] ~ affa' (B6579) wund ~ (*LH*)
15   een of a' o'] e'en of a of (B6579) ~ a' <of>^o'^ (B6580)
17   Noo, Davie ... head,] Now Davie ... head. (*LH*)
18   o' frien's ... said;] o'freen's ... said, (B6579), (*LH*) ~ said, (B6580)
19   awa'] awa (all MSS) {also in line 25}
20   shinin'] shinin (B6579)
21   crackin'] crackin (B6579)
22   cam] cam' (*LH*)
23   birds they yammert] birdies yammert (*LH*)
26   hefa' –] hefa', – (B6579)
27   law,] law (B6579)
28   clearly.] clearly! (*LH*)
        {B6579 has at the end 'Hyères'}

V *A Lowden Sabbath Morn*
Place/date of composition: Bournemouth, 1887 (Balfour)
MSS: B6551, B6552, H2387
First publication: *The Scottish Church*, Vol. IV, April 1887
{H2387 is a fair copy identical with the copy-text; B6551 is a sprawling 506 lines in
Notebook 'No. A – 154 *Book poems/and essay*' scattered across pp. 3–5, 15–17 and 19–31.
B6552 is a later version of 158 lines on six notebook pages numbered 31–6. See Explanatory
Note on this poem, p. 625.}
Title: *A Lowden Sabbath Morn*] untitled (B6551, B6552)
Stanza.line
  1.{draft} 'The clinkum-clank o Sabbath bells
              <Thro a>An through the simmer kintry tells:
                    Sings far & near
                    Its tale o' cheer
                    A peacefu' story
              <From far and near>'

                                            (B6551)

{cancelled fragments} 'Noo to the hilltop rookery wells

Noo is the gudeman's [?razor] set
The halflin collents noo are met
To [?craik] ‹acroaa›frae gairden yett to yett
    And play they're men
    Are but and ben.'

(B6551)

1.4   near,] near; (B6552)
[2.] {omitted; mistranscribed in BBS, II, p. 152, and CP, p. 489}

'<Long-leggit men hing round the dures
They that a'week are doughty do'ers>
A'legs an'airms, the dand'rin men
Hing round the <cottage gardens then>doors or down the glen –
They're naethin', wantin' work, ye ken,
        Tho' blythe to want it;
<The steerin weemin but and ben>
While weemin folk are but and ben
        An' gey fu' handit.'

(B6551, B6552)

2.1   noo, to that] noo to their (B6552)
2.6   plou'man.] plouman (B6552) plooman (SC)
3.6   painfü'] painfu (B6552)
4.1   steerin' mither strang afit] <gudewife>steerin' mither <raxes>strang afit (B6551)
4.2   Noo shoos the bairnies but a bit;] <Noo to the weans [?]>^ ~ bit^ (B6551)
                    Noo shoo's ~ bit. (B6552)
4.3   Noo cries them ben, their Sinday shüit]<An'shoos them frae the kitchen oot>
                    Noo <ca's them back>^cries them ben,^ ~ (B6551)
4.5–6 Or sweeties in their pouch to pit,
            Wi' blessin's on them.]
        <Noo deal the Sinday sweeties oot
            To keep them [?]> ^ ~ ^ (B6551)
5.1   The lasses, clean frae tap to taes,] lasses clean … taes (B6552)
        <A'>The lasses clean frae <heid>^tap^ to <feit>^taes^ (B6551)
5.2   Are … underclaes;] Sit … underclaes (B6551) ~ underclas'es (B6552)
5.3   The gartened hose, the weel-filled stays,]
        <Stockin an shift an coats an stays>^ ~ stays^ (B6551)
5.4   The nakit shift,] <A white><linen>naked shift (B6551)
5.5   days,] days (B6551)
[6.][7.][8.] {omitted: [7], [8] mistranscribed in BBS, II, p. 152 and CP, p. 489}

'<On bonny daisied greens>
They bleached upo' the daisied green,
They dipped in [?] sheen
Noo, ilka sonsie strappin' quean
        Sits doucely proud;
Clean ilka shinin' face
        An southernwood.

Again the bells begin to jowe,
And as their airn summons rowe,
Gudeman, just clapping hat on pow
        <Lest a' be late>Tak's first the gate;
An' the hale clan <follies>^comes on^ in tow,
        Wi' face sedate.

Noo under rowth o'hawthorn bloom
Whaur <thick the summer insects soom,>
        <the>simmer flees may swarf and soom,
The thrangin' gate shüne lacks for room
        As frien's foregaither
–<Gudesake,>^The day,^ the kirk'll no be toom,
        Says ane to ither.'
                               (B6551, B6552)

6.3   fyle] file (B6552)
6.5   spile] sp'ile (B6552)
7.4   coats,] coats. (B6552)
7.6   Dauvit] Johnie (B6551)
8.1   breeks,] breeks (B6552)
8.2   A'spiled … weeks,] A'sp'iled … weeks (B6552)
8.3   guidman follows closs,] gudeman follies ~ (B6552) ~ near (B6551)
8.5   sarious … at aince] solemn ~ (B6551) ~ at ince (SC)
9.2   kirkton] Kirkton (SC)
9.3   neebours, comin'] nieghbours, comin (B6552)
10.1–4 But hark! the bells frae nearer clang;
       To rowst the slaw, their sides they bang;
       An' see! black coats a'ready thrang
              The green kirkyaird;]
       '<But here we're on the hill
       And there's the kirk and here's the mill
       <<And clinking bell>>
       And see! black coats already fill
              The table stanes.>'
                  (B6551)

       '<An laigh the niebours crack; and still
       The simmer air sleeps on the hill
       An' dozes round the silent mill
       <<An sure we're at the trystin' hill>>'
          (B6551) {another draft}

       '<But here we are – we've no been lang
       The mill-dam sings its <Sunday>^Sabbath^ sang;> ~ ' (B6552)
10.5–6 And at the yett, the chestnuts spang
             That brocht the laird.]
       <And the bauld sparries
             Hop on the baird.>^ ~ ^ (B6551) ~ spang, (B6552)

11.1   at] near (B6551, B6552)
11.2   Stand drinkin' ... state:] Stand, drinking ... state, (B6551)
11.3   The practised hands as gash an' great] The <[?] that see them> ^   great,^ (B6551)
11.4   Lords o' Session;] lords o'session. (B6551)
11.5–6 The later named, a wee thing blate
                In their expression.]
        <By them the congregation files,>
        The lesser folk, a wee thing blate
        <Of a kirk session>
        An'read the grave stains as they wait
                The twentieth time. (B6551)
12.3   Syne wag a moraleesin' heid,] <they shake>^ ~ moralising heid;^ (B6551)
13.1   It's here our Merren lang has lain,] ~ there our Mer'n ~ (B6552)
        <An there's where Mer'n Blair was laid>^Its there our Mer'n for lang ~ ^ (B6551)
13.6   Lie] Sleep (B6551, B6552)
14.1   guidman ... awee] gudeman ... a wee (B6552)
14.2–3 To dwall amang the deid; to see
        Auld faces clear in fancy's e'e;]
        <To think o' things [?] a jee
        And clean past din> (B6551)
14.2   to see] and see (B6551)
14.3   clear in fancy's e'e;] <in the inward>^clear in Fancy's^ e'e, (B6551)
14.4   Belike] Perchance (B6551)
14.5   fa'in] <sunkin'>^ ~ ^ (B6551) fa'in' (B6552)
14.6   fancy's ear.] <inward ear.>^Fancy's ear.^ (B6551) Fancy's ear. (B6552)
15.1–2 {abandoned in favour of a different rhyme scheme}:
        <An'the gude man, wi' serious heid,
        <<Luves>>^Likes^ weel his <<latest>>^last^ o' ways to treid,> (B6551)
15.3   fauld ... faim'ly] <gaither>^fauld^ ... <folk><people>^family^ (B6551)
15.4   screed;] screed, (B6552)
15.5–6 An' just a wee thing nearer brings
                The quick an' deid.]
        <The parish a' thegether brings,>
        <On Sunday morning duly sings>
        <Le'en an' deid.> (B6551)
16.1–2 But noo the bell is ringin' in;
        To tak their places, folk begin;]
        <But hear, some quicker clinks the bell,>
        <But look! its time to tak your place,
        And lengthen down your Sinday face> (B6551)
16.3   himsel'] himsel (B6552)
16.5   fu' ... about] fu ~ (B6552) ~ aboot (SC)
17.1   tünes ... shüre,] tunes ... shure, (SC)
17.2   The faithfü' *French*, an'] <French without doubt>^The faithfu' French^ ~
                (B6551) ~ French an' (B6552)
17.3   prezentor, hoastin' sair,] preshentor, ~ (B6551, B6552)
                ~ <his hair>^sair^ (B6552)

17.6   queer] strange (B6551)
18.1   Follows ... readin'] Follies ~ (B6551) ~ readin (B6552)
18.2   fisslin'] fishlin' (B6551)
18.4   But] Yet (B6551, B6552)
18.6   southernwood.] Southernwood. (B6552)
19, 20   {trial fragments on various pages of B6551}
         '<For noo in casual sleep maun we>
         <For noo the kirk's a scene o' battle
         When mortal sleep, like flees in cattle,
         Aye back and back again will settle,
                    On [?] parishioners,>
         <Sleep like a cloud><Sleep in the kirk>
         <Lets a' the <<dacent>> [?] to work
                    Niddin an'nodden.'

         '<And here's a lad in
         They share the [?] betwixt them twa,
         By wile each others [?] awa,
         The guidman thunders out the law>'
         'Some, when the doctor wales the word
         And his strong rantin's a' that's heard,
         <Beside>Mark the bummlin' bee, <or>the bird
                    That sings in shaw.'
19.1   whan] <when>^ ~ ^ (B6552)
19.3   When] Whan (B6552)
19.5   An' nearly half] <An mair than haulf >^An nearly a'^ (B6551)
                                              ~ a' (B6552, SC)
20.2   sweer] swear (B6552)
20.4   windie] windy (B6552)
20.5   tak ... a-glee] tak' ... aglee (B6552)
20.6   sonsie] <bonny>^ ~ ^ (B6552)
21.1   Himsel', meanwhile,] Himsel meanwhile, (B6552) Himsel' meanwhile, (SC)
21.2   An' bobs belaw the soundin'-box,]
         <Like what they ca' a Jake i' the box,> ^ ~ ^ (B6551)
21.3   words] <words>^speech^ (B6551) <speech>^ ~ ^ (B6552)
21.5   deals] deils (B6551)
22.   {trial rhyme words on B6551: 'irks, lurks, birks, dirks, mirks, Turks, stirks,
                                       yirks, works'}
22.2   The hopes o' men that trust in works,]
         <Demolishes the trust in works> ^ ~ ^ (B6551)
22.5   Turks,] Turks (B6552)
22.6   them.] them! (B6552)
23.1–3   Bethankit! what a bonny creed!
         What mair would ony Christian need? –
         The braw words rumm'le ower his heid,]
         <A'weel, we've heard the same afore
         In their queer yairdie sleep the deid,

A blessed hearin this indeed,
But lo n' behold, [?] folk indeed
⸌⸌The gospel⸍⸍The braw words rumble over heid⸍ (B6551)
23.2   Need? –] Need? (B6552)
23.3   rumm'le] rumble (B6552)
23.5   restin'] resting (B6552)

VI *The Spaewife*
Place/date of publication: Bournemouth, 1884–7
MSS: B6903: the order of stanzas in this MS differs from the copy-text, being as follows:
2,3,1,5,4; NLS 10650 (fragment).
{See Explanatory Note on this poem, pp. 625–6.}
Line
  3   siller, … keep, … gi'e.] siller … keep … gie? (B6903)
  5   O, I] O I {so throughout both MSS} (B6903)
  6   come to be whaur we find them when we try,] ~ try (B6903)
      cam' <to be> whaur we find when we try. (NLS)
  7   claes … fishes in the sea.] cla'es … <oysters>^fishes^ in the sea? – (B6903)
                        ~ oysters … sea – (NLS)
  8   speirin',] <speiring> ^speirin',^ {B6903 has comma throughout} speering – (NLS)
  9   to ken – to … I –] to ken, to … I, (NLS)
10   a' … buy;] a … buy, (B6903, NLS)
11   An' naebody for dacency but barely twa or three.]
      An naebody for <honesty>^decency^ but <barely twa or three? – >
               <just [?] an' me>^ ~ three?^ (B6903)
      <And why the [?} the drink's sae bad for me> (NLS)
13   I –] I, {also in line 17} (B6903)
15   sae fu' o' … pree.] <wi'>sae fu' o … pree? (B6903)
19   Wi' mony anither riddle brings the tear into my e'e.]
      And <if>^gin^ ye cannae tell me I maun just lie down an' dee – (B6903)
{bottom of NLS:} 'The reason of the cause of the wherefore o' the why
               O onything in general'

VII *The Blast – 1875*
Place/date of composition: Swanston, July 1875 (B6019 dated at end)
MS: B6019
Title: *The Blast – 1875*] III. *To W. E. Henley.*/ *– a cause of Atheism –*
Line
  1   rainin' … gairden] rainin … garden
  6   wull] will
  7   Heev'n, ye] Heev'n ye
  8   puir,] puir
11   inconvenient den] stinkin' kind o' den
13   out,] oot
14   mankind are about;] bodies are aboot,
15   An' if He … doubt,] An', if he … doot,
16   plans;] plans.

19   whan … again,] when … again {this change was made on the Harvard proofs}
21   Doun … droukin'] Down … drookin'
22   Upon] Upo'
25   unco] unco'
26   an' Winter,] an Autumn, {Author's Edn (see above, p. 394) has 'Sprin,' for 'Spring,' in this line.}
27   dour-heartit] door-hearted
29   wadnae try't] wadna trie't
32   watchfü'] watchfu'
33   ither] other
34   Lassie nor God.] Lassie, nor God;
35   counsel till 'e:] coonsel till ye,
{MS dated bottom left 'Swanston. July. 1875'}

VIII *The Counterblast – 1886*
Place/date of composition: Bournemouth, 1886
MSS: B6123, B6124, B6472, B6551 {B6124 is a late version, 45 lines on three pages with one page, probably containing lines 35–61 of the published poem, missing. The other MSS are in Notebook 'No. A – 154 Book poems/and essay', 152 lines in all scattered across pp. 2, 3, 7, 9–13.}
Title: *The Counterblast – 1886*] {the only MS title appears on B6124: 'XIV. (in answer to number III).' {i.e. *The Blast – 1876*, numbered III in B6019}
Stanza.line
    1   {B6472 (p. 2 of Notebook A.154) has this rough trial:}
            '<There's folk>There's many dwaibly chields about,
            <Chields hardly worth a>That cannae thole to hirstle through't;
            <[?] they're no' worth a tinker's scoot,
            Puir whinging clerks, say, no doubt
            No guid>'
            {B6123 (p. 3 of Notebook A.254) has this rough trial:}
            'Weel, sonnie, <as ye wull please><just the way you like>
                                    hae't the way ye please;
            The world's no made for us.
            <Eh man,>My bonny man, the world, its true
            Was made for niether me nor you
            The best that any man can do
                        Is mak the best o' it.
            And mebbe when we've warstled through'
    1.2   you;] you: (B6124)
    1.3   It's just a place to warstle through,]
            Its something to be warstled through, (B6472)
    1.5   aye] still (B6472)
    1.6   mak] mak' (B6124)
            {from this point, variants are taken from B6123, unless noted otherwise}
    2.1   There's rowth o' wrang, I'm free to say:] <Sic-like in your>
            <Granted, its cauld an' hard & rank>
            <The <<world>>earth is hard and cauld & gla'ry>

<And truth I'll>there's things amiss, I'm free to say
<Bended and bowed, ill-famed & rank>
<Truth it's a ><and its hard, I'm free to say, >
<In that rough and country play,>
~ plenty wrang, ~ (B6124)

2.3   The face of earth a' fyled wi' clay]
        <Rough as a man's the face of life>
        The face of yearth<defiled n' clarty>a' filed wi' clay
                               ~ <defiled>^a' filed^ ~ (B6124)

2.4   chuckies,] chuckies;
2.5   life a rough an' land'art] Life <that>^a^ rough and landwart
3.1   An' food's anither name for clart;]<Food but anither name for dirt>
        <Luve but the [?] to strife & sturt>^An'^ Food's <jist> ~ clart
3.2   An' beasts an' brambles bite an' scart;]
        <The beasts bite; the long brambles scart>
3.3   WE be like, my heart!] we be like <dear>^my^ heart!
3.4   claethin'?] claething
3.5   – Aweel, I cannae mend your cart:]
        <We cannae mend it wi' a my heart>^ ~ <tak your part>^ ^ ~ cart^
3.6   naethin'.] naething.
4.2   this queer … passed;] ~ <damned>^queer^ … past;
                         <that>^this^ ~ (B6124)
4.3   Twa-three,] <And>twa-three
4.4   The hale transaction;] The hale [word(s) omitted]
4.5   ithers] <mair>^ithers^
4.6   Fand satisfaction.] <Make>Mak' unco licht o' it.
        {rhyme words in margin: 'cast, blast, aghast, mast'}
        {trial fragment after stanza 4:}
        <Tak it, God-sake, <<the way it comes>>as God intendet
        [?] can ne'er be mendit
        And when, some day, ye have ascendit>
5.1   Whaur braid the briery muirs expand,]
        <A weary muir, a winter's <<day>>^morn^>
        <The bite o' [?] in sic a scene,>
        ^Where ~ expand^ <Where>^Whaur^ (B6124)
5.2   waefü … land,] waefu … land (B6123, B6124)
5.3   bumblebees] bumble bees (B6123, B6124)
5.4   hingin';] hinging,
5.5   An' there the canty wanderer fand] <But there the [?] o' folk hae fand>^ ~ ^
5.6   singin'.] singing.
        {rhyme words in margin: 'band, demand, stand, sand, wand'}
6.1   Trout in the burn grow great as herr'n;]
        <Snell as the wind [?] roun' the cairn> ~ <are>^grow^ ~
7.1   Sic-like the howes o' life to some:]
        <An' barefit callants unafraid
        On that unhomely muir hae played,
        And see>

       \<No' you! O well I ken it, frien';
       In vain for you the grass is green,>^ Sic like, ~ some;^

7.2   loans … thumb,] loans, … thumb
7.3   But mark the muckle winds that come,]
       \<Where they can feel the great winds come>
       ^But mark the great winds go & come^
7.4   Soopin'] sweeping
       {in right margin, 'peonies?'}
8.1   tak;] tak',
8.2   no] not
8.3   brae, a] brae a
8.3–4 {alt.} \<An never ca' a gray thing black,
               But just plain gray.>
8.4   Addressin' daily;] \<Undaunted set>\<Bravely they set>
             \<They're settin daily>^Addressing daily^
8.5   An'up the rude, unbieldy track]\<Along the rood unshielded track> ^ ~ ^
9.1   What you would like's a palace ha',]
       \<And you, whan a' thy simple things,>\< [?] to the soul [?] wings,>
       \<But Lord!>\<But if ye cannae do with>\<Its no enough, ye say!>
       \<You wish a different place awa,>
       \<Truth, an its>Well, this is no a palace ha', ^ ~ sum palace ha'^
9.2   Or Sinday] \<A>\<Sum> Nae ^Or^ Sindy
9.3   Wi' a' things ordered in a raw] Nor the right kind o place awa'
9.4   By … leddies.] For … leddies;
9.5   Weel, … hae't:] \<Well>^Weel,^ … ha'et –
       {This omitted stanza follows stanza 9:}
       'But Lord, its no sae black's its pentit,
       Tho' whiles no very timely tentit
       Whiles just a wee thing carrion scentit
               (Under my breith.)
       An' to the devilishly discontentit
               Whiles dour as deith.'
10.1   taen] ta'en
10.2   winnae … hirsle] cannae … hirstle
10.3   fund … do –] found … do:
10.4   That's to drink speerit;] Just tak' to speerit ^ ~ speerit.^
10.5   shüne … you –] sune … you
10.6   An' blithe to hear it!] Weel pleased to hear it.
11.1   coft, … lead,] \<wear>coft, … lead
11.2   Ithers will heir when aince ye're deid;]
       \<And death, when aince ye're fairly deid>
       \<Will fa' to ithers when ye're deid.> ^ ~ deid.^
11.3   They'll … bite o' breid,] \<Some>^They'll^ … bit o' breid
11.4   sappy;] sappy,
11.5   They'll to your dulefü' house succeed,]
       \<Some>^They'll^ ~ dulefu' ~ succeed
       They'll, to your dulefu' house, succeed (B6124)

12.1   As whan] <Just as>^As when^ (B6123) ~ when (B6124)
12.3   Till, wi' a rowstin' skelp, he's taen] ~ rowsting ~ ta'en (B6124)
        Till wi' a rowsting skelp <is> ^he's^ ta'en
12.4   shoo'd to bed –] <sent>^shoo'd^ to bed
12.5   play'n',] play'n'

IX *The Counterblast Ironical*
Place/date of composition: Bournemouth, 1886–7
MSS: B6123, B6125, B6126 {B6126 is a late version, twenty-eight lines on two pages. The
other MSS are in Notebook '*No. A – 154 Book poems/and essay*', sixty lines in all scattered
across pp. 2, 4 and 6.}
Title: {none of the MSS is titled}
Stanza.line
  1.   {B6123 (p. 2 of Notebook A.154) and B6125 (p. 4) have these lines indicating that
        RLS began this poem in the Burns stanza:}
        'If things were as they ocht to be,
        God wad have kept a special e'e
        To sic-like gentlemen as me,'

            'For mere humanity.
        But for the like o' *me* to do't,
                God, what insanity!'

        '<I cannae mak' the maitter out
        That God <<should>>suld mak the worl, an' no'
        Explain the same to me.>'

        'There's many things
        I wad like to hear, to
        Why an what his plan could be
        To mak a world and can no
                Explain the same to me.'
        {From this point, variants are taken from B6125, unless noted otherwise.}
 1.1   Its strange that God should fash to frame]
        <It's a strange affair that God suld frame>^ ~ suld ~ frame,^
 1.2   The yearth ... hie,] <A>^The^ earth ~ (B6125) ~ hie <;>^ , ^ (B6126)
 1.3   clean forget] <ne'er>clean forget
        {These lines following stanza 1 were omitted:}
        '<A word is a' that I would ask>
        I ask nae mair 'n a word and nod
                And a wink but o' the e'e
        <Enough to show that God himself>
        The merest sign to show that God
                Is a gentleman like me.'
  2.   {draft} 'For kye, and hogs, and ither folk
                Nae [?] I see;

But why 'o be a word aside
For <gentlefolk>^gentlemen^ like me?'

2.1 They ... folk,] The ... folk
2.2 dree;] dree
2.3 poke] pock
2.4 gentleman like me?] <gentlemen like us>^ ~ me.^
3.1 folk their parritch eat] ~ <they eat their meat>^their breid they eat^ (B6125)
        folk, their breid they eat (B6126)
3.3 mind is no to be wyled] stamack cannae be taen (B6125) ta'en (B6126)
3.4 Wi'] <For>^In^ (B6125) For (B6126)
4.1 folk, they court their joes] folk <their joes they chuse>^ ~ ^
4.2 gloamin' on the lea;] <nicht upon>^gloaming on^ the lea (B6125)
        gloaming ~ (B6126)
4.3 But they're] <It needs a different>^They're ^ (B6125) They're (B6126)
5.1 wrang,] wrang (B6126)
5.2 bleed, or] bleed and (B6125, B6126)
5.3 a' thir] a' they (B6125, B6126)
6.1 demand,] demand (B6125, B6126)
6.2 Tho' ... be –] Tho' ... be, (B6125) Though ... be: (B6126)
6.3 A statement fair in my Maker's hand] ~ maker's ~ (B6126)
        A full confession in God's own hand (B6125)
7.2 apologie;] apologie,
7.3 Or the deevil a ceevil word to God]
        Or <there's nae>the devil a civil word for God
7.4 me.] me! (B6126)

X *Their Laureate to an Academy Class Dinner Club*
Place/date of composition: Bournemouth, 1885 (Prideaux 1917: 148)
First publication: 8vo. 4pp. *The Laureat Ste'enson / to the / Thamson Class.* [1885] Privately printed by T. and A. Constable, Edinburgh. {There is a facsimile on p. 118 of the Widener Catalogue. See the Thompson Class Reunion poems of 1875 and 1883, and Explanatory Note on these poems, p. 626.}
MSS: B6496; Princeton (Parrish): CO171
Title: B6496 is untitled; CO171 has the UW title but is grouped with *Late in the Nicht* (UW 2 XIII) under the title 'Two Poems in Scots'.
{Italicisation: reported speech is italicised only in the copy-text.}
Stanza.line
1.1 gang] gang, (1885)
1.3 hang] hang, (1885)
1.4 them!) –] them!) (1885)
2.1 Straucht, at] Straucht at (B6496)
2.2 dyke;] dyke: – (1885)
2.3 hinderlands I] hinderlands, I (1885)
2.5 although] altho (B6496)
3.2 far, sae guid] ~ weel (1885) faur ~ (B6496)
3.3 the feast,] our ~ (1885)
3.4 hopefü'] hopefu' (1885, B6496)

3.5   Yearly we … beast –] Yearly, we … beast! – (1885)
3.6   again!" '] again!" (B6496)
4.2   shurely … Muse's] surely ~ (1885, B6496) ~ muse's (CO171)
4.6   Deith to a body.] Death to a buddy! (1885, B6496) ~ boddy. (CO171)
5.1   mane,] mane – (1885)
5.2   burd-alane,] burd-alane (CO171)
5.3   findin'] findin (B6496)
5.6   No car'n] No' car'n (B6496) ~ carin' (1885)
6.1   ne'er … pingein' bairn] ~ pinge-in' bairn, (B6496) neer … pingin' ~ (CO171)
6.2   weak … pitaty-par'n' –] wake … pitaty-parin' – (1885) wake ~ (B6496)
6.3   üsed wi' guidin'] used in ~ (1885) used wi guidin (B6496)
6.4   steerin' crowdie –] steerin ~ (B6496) ~ crowdie, (1885)
6.6   howdie.] howdie? (1885, B6496)
7.1   me, for] me for (1885, B6496)
7.2   poke] pork (B6496)
7.3   lowse] <loose>^ ~ ^ (B6496)
7.4   trem'lin' handit;] trem'lin'-handit; (1885)
7.5   blaff!] bowff! (1885, B6496)
7.6   landit.] landit! (1885, B6496)
8.2   Whan … muse … tak,] When … Muse … tak', (1885) {This change was made on the Harvard proofs}
8.3   gleed e'e] glee'd ~ (B6496) ~ ee (CO171)
8.4   her; –] her; (1885) her – (B6496, CO171)
9.2   scaur,] scaur (B6496)
9.3   glaur,] glaur (1885)
9.6   she no hurt] <the brüte>^she no'^ hurt (B6496)
10.3   she, wi' … reist,] she in … reist (B6496)
10.5   your feast,] yer feast: – (1885)
10.6   Hae!] Ha'e! (1885, B6496)

XI *Embro Hie Kirk*
Place/date of publication: Edinburgh, [?1883] (See Explanatory Note on this poem, p. 626.)
MSS: B6188, H2392. {The HL MS is a fair copy identical to the copy-text.}
Title: *Embro Hie Kirk*] {untitled}
Stanza.line
1.1   Himsel'] himsel'
1.2   tünes] tunes
1.3   claes] cla'es
1.5   Preceese and … ways] Preceese, and, … ways,
2.2   prayer.] prayer –
2.3   cannae] canna
2.4   warnin'.)] warnin') –
3.1   His] his {also in 4.6}
3.4   forgotten;] forgotten,
5.2   kintry-leevin'] kintry-livin
6.1   unfaithfü'] unfaithfu',
6.2   horde;] hoard; {this change was made on the Harvard proofs}

6.3   hymn-books] hymnbooks
6.5   Hie Kirk's] Hie-Kirk's
6.6   popish] Popish
7.2   o' the reformin'] of the reformin
7.4   word, or] word or
8.2   Hoo easy 't's düne! … weans,] How easy 't's done! … weans
8.3   Wha in the Hie Street] Wha, in the High Street,
9.2   hash;] hash!
9.3   pews … stramash] pews, … stramash,
9.4   fa';] fa'!
9.5   rumlin'] rum'lin
9.6   sma'.] sma'!
10.1   Noo] Now
10.3   stammer,] stammer –
10.6   dancie.] dancey.
11.1   destroy, an'] destroy an'
11.2   square] Square
11.3   Fruin,] Fruin
11.4   Hell] hell
11.5   Tell] <Till>^ ~ ^ {this change was made on the Harvard proofs.}
11.6   Niven.] Niven!

XII   *The Scotsman's Return from Abroad*
In a letter from Mr Thomson to Mr Johnstone.
Place/date of composition: Strathpeffer, autumn 1880 (*LETBM*, Vol. III, No. 721)
Letter: RLS to Bob Stevenson [13 September 1880] (*LETBM*, Vol. III, p. 101): 'I am now quite the poet: one poem accepted by *Cornhill*, two by *Atlantic his Monthly*, and a fourth by *Fraser his Halls*. The latter {this poem} is also Scotch; it is a bleeding assault on beastly elders, clergymen and others.' {Margaret Stevenson's Diary Notes record that RLS read the poem to John Tulloch during his visit to the Ben Nevis Hotel, Strathpeffer, on 6 September and that he begged it for *Fraser's Magazine*, of which he was editor (*VAIL*, Vol. XXVI, p. 336). Fanny Stevenson stated that it was written after RLS's own return from abroad, i.e. from California in 1880, 'to amuse his father when we were stopping with his family in Strathpeffer, a dreary "hydropathic" in the Highlands' (*VAIL*, Vol. VIII, p. 85). See Explanatory Note on this poem, p. 626.}
MS: Harvard proofs
First publication: *Fraser's Magazine*, Vol. 102, November 1880, pp. 624–6; the following variants occur in this printing:
Line
 6   Wast,] Wast.
 9   thir] these
12   destitütion.] destitution.
15   kirk –] kirk, –
16   stirk –] stirk, –
17   warth a preen,] worth a preen, –
18   Aiberdeen!] Aberdeen!
25   house,] hoose,

27 bluid] blude
44 Whan … syndit] When … synded
66 doubtfü'] doubtfu'
67 digression;] digression, {This change was made on the Harvard proofs.}
68 shüne] soon
69 M 'Neil,] McNeil,
70 düne] done
79 Proud,] Prood,
84 hymn-books] hymnbooks
94 üsed] used
100 p'ints] points
102 faithfü'] faithfu'
103 here –] here, –
106 pleisure] pleesure

XIII 'Late in the nicht in bed I lay'
Place/date of composition: Bournemouth, 1884–7
MS: H2404: Notebook A 270 has drafts, both rough and finished, of most stanzas scattered across leaves 8–12 and 20–1; the order of stanzas in the notebook is uncertain; there are several drafts of some stanzas; some draft stanzas were omitted in *UW*. The following collation with the copy-text includes some cancelled lines which are for the most part legible:
Stanza.line
1 '<The weary winds a' day yestreen>Round my ticht house a' day lang
The wind had skirled an eldritch sang;
  Now <smiled>growled and thundered
  Like firin' guns.'

'I heard the skipper an' the mate
Wi' bellin' han' to ear, debate'

'An' now but we had warstlin' weather,
The winds o' heevin a' skirled together,
  An' din gin hail,
  Flay like a flail'
1.3 An' tirlin' wa's an' skirlin' wae] <And gurled until my heart was wae>
  ^Tirling the ~ ^
1.4 Through Heev'n they battered; –] <An' me fair scunnered>
  <Gurled an' thunnered>
  <On, on they blattered> ^ ~ ^
1.6 The tempest blattered.] <On the windies chattered.> ^ ~ ^
2.1–2 The masoned house it dinled through;
It dung the ship, it cowped the coo';]
<The wind fell on the bieldy coo,
And rived the breath out of her noo',>
<It dung the ship, it flayed the crew,
It cowped the meditative coo'.>

2.4   Had braved a' weathers;] <As aulds our faithers>^ ~ ^
4.   'And here was me, cosh in my bed
        And there was them,
        I minded straucht on a' their care
        <Now on the yaird><Sair>
        <An' no>In cauld an' wearyness an' fear'

        'Thru the pit-murk, my [?] ee
        [?] in the deep and muckle sea
        [?] could hear a bit, no see
                To catch a sicht o' it:
        For the puir sailor-lads – wae's me,
                An awfü nicht o't!'

        'To hear it, ye'd a' thought the stanes
        Ye'd a' thought to hear the granes
        Were fleein' Earth's <pillars>keystanes
        Greetin' like flayed weans
                Earth to her centre storms
        The hole warl, <in>towns an' hills an' plains
                Itsel' <would>wad cowpit –
        An' <in the main, its>for auld airn its smashed remains
                By God be rowpit.'
4.1   To hear in the pit-murk on hie] <An as ye heard>^ ~ hie,^
4.3   ~~The warl', they thocht, wi'] The warl' ye'd thocht <with>wi'~~
4.4   cowpit;] cowpit.
4.5   the smashed] its smashed
6.   'I dwall, as in a star apairt
        Wi' jaunt as in a braw spring-cairt
        <Dwall denty-handit [?]>
                Ower guid an' ill;
        Cosh in my house, I feed my heart
                Wi' denty [?]'

        'The deil was doubtless first afit
                In this black job.'

        'I, tae, by God's especial grace
        (Or else the deil's – a kittle case)
        Dwall denty in a bieldy place
                <An turn the wheel>Wi' fire and smile
        <An' wink – wi' an unassuming face>
        Cosh in my house, I shield my face
                Frae draughts of air;'
6.4   mainners:] mainners;
6.6   sinners!] sinners.

7.   <Safe>Cosh in my <covered>roofit housie, here
        Was I mysel'.
    No frozen feet to bed I tak '

7.2   The deil may start on the rampage; –]
    <The wicked o' the warl>^ ~ <gang>start ~ rampage^

7.3   The sick in bed, the thief in cage –] <Great winds may blaw, the
        troops engage><Winds blaw being blad or>^ ~ ^

7.5   Cosh in my house, a sober sage,]<Wi' the composure of the sage>^ .. ^

8.   'Its gay an' easy to be guid
    An' wi' braw looks an' rantin' [?]
        To please your neebours
    But let me see ye when ye've stude
        Life's griefs an' labours.'

8.5–6 'Whaur's God?' I cry, an' 'Whae is me
        To hae sic graces?']
    Whaur's God? I cry, and whae is *me*?
        To hae sic graces?

[9.]   {The following fragments seem to be part of an abandoned stanza:}
    'The God that made the earth an' sea
    Is nither mair refined than me
    Nor yet (sae far as I can see)'

    'A God that does not fear a jest
    That hears the worst, <but>that [?leaves] the best
    <And>Yet is not all on pity bent'

    'A God that's aye upon his stilts
    That blushes when a lassie kilts
    That maun be praised up to the hilts
        And in a' wathers'

    'A God that cannae thole a jeist
    A God that cannae read the breist
    A God that scunners at a priest
        And dauties elders
    'S a God that couldnae mak' a feast
        Or mill you melders.'

9.   '<Sair is the fear, but warm remains>
    <To think to>And aye to think o' peoples pains
    To think perhaps that tempest wanes
    Round sailors' wives an' sailors' weans
        Sae presst wi' fear,
    The flesh upon their eerie banes
        Maun gie to hear!'

9.1   I mind the fecht the sailors keep,] <To think o' hoastin sailors fecht>
        ^To ~ ^

9.2   But] Though's ne been

9.4   An' mind beside] Or <the lost herd>never have to hand, besides
9.6   Has wandered wide.] <Has turnt the gate.>^ ~ ^
10.   '<An' lord,>I think the hubub, the tempest wanes
         And sailors' wives an' sailors' weans
                 <Offered>Sacrificed in fear.
         The flesh upon their eerie banes
                 Grew cauld to hear it.'
10.1   weans –] weans,
10.2   causey stanes –] cause'ay stanes,
10.3   folk wi' the crazy banes,] <folks that in blawlin' rains,>^folks ~ ^
10.4   Baith auld an' puir,] <Hae dune their day>^ ~ ^
10.5   That aye maun thole the winds an' rains,] <And aye maun raxe their
                                                 crazy banes>^ ~ rains^
10.6   An' labour sair.] <Wi' young folks work>^ ~ ^
11.   'There's somethin' here that's hard to face
         For why have I the bieldy place?
         < [?]the stammerin' dinner grace?>
         An' why are ithers, far from grace,
                 Ne fine?
         <I own it's a contentious case>
         In law I have a kind o' case
         While ithers to the windows face.'

         'An', truth, its an uncanny case:
         For why maun some the tempest face?
         And why have I the bieldy place –
                 In Heeven's name?
         I've just this pickle grace at least –
                 I whiles think shame.'

         'And aye I pit my trust in God,
                 I'll hae to pay for't
         An thole (when aince I'm under sod)
                 The things o' Hell.'
11.1   a blink,] <to think> ^ ~ ^
11.3   For a' my] <Whan God><How God>^For a' this^
11.4   crumb,] crumb –
11.6   Kingdom Come.] ~ come.
12.   'Strong are the bonds my hands that bind;
         Hard is the better way to find;
         But if I'm laith, I amnae blind,
                 And wudnae wonder,
         Whan they wha thole that day the wind
                 Sall [?] me under
         And in the reamin' pat o' hell
                 <He'll see them><We rich be>I'll <<yet>>^still^ be scaddit.'

'Its aye my prayer
That God wi' this affirms [?] well
He'll <pluck>^rive^ the guid himsel
    Frae them that had it.
Wi' his Ain hands, his leevin' Sel',
He'll rive the guid (as prophets tell)
    Frae them that had it.'

12.1	whan … bell,] when … bell {this change was made on the Harvard proofs}
12.2	His ain Hand, His] his ain hands, his
12.5	Hell,] hell
12.6	scaddit.] scaddit!
13.	'But then, the humble an' the puir

Shall a' like kings be welcome there,
And [?] wi' the warl' o' cheer,
    The pick of fairin'
Amen, says I. I'll tak my stane
    To get them their ane
Like honored guests at [?] fair'

'O Lord, if this be sae <indeed><in sooth>
Raise up at once your heid,
An let the <puir> ^humble^ breik the breid –
    I'll thole the paiks.'

13.1	sae,] sae
13.2	that sair] <what>^that^sair
13.3	warl',] world,
13.4	aixe!] aix!
13.5	An' let the puir enjoy their play –] And let the humble <have their day><breik>^And let the puir ~ ^
13.6	my] <the>^ ~ ^

XIV *My Conscience*
Place/date of composition: Bournemouth, 1884–7
MSS: B6602, H2404: the HL MS is Notebook A 270, which has many untitled trials and drafts which are selectively collated against the copy-text as follows:
Stanza.line

1.1	ills … fear,] <things>^ills^ … fear
1.3	yowlin'] <bitin>^ ~ ^
1.4	nonsense –] nonsense,
1.5	bear,] bear –
1.6	An' that's] <An> ~
2.1	Whan day (an' a' excüse)]<When the lang day from earth has gane>
	When day (and a excuse)
2.2	An' wark is düne, and] <And sleep should>^ ~ düne and^
2.3–4	An' to my chalmer a' my lane
	I creep apairt,]

<When in ~
　　　　The gruesome deil> ^ ~ ^
2.5　My conscience!] <An' mercy!> ^ ~ ^
2.6　heart!] <heart.> ^ ~ ^
[3]　'<Wi' you>Its seldom that we twa agree
　　　<We count the clink ane twa an' three>
　　　When clocks are clappin twa or three
　　　　　　<Deep clappin in the nicht>
　　　My conscience! why no bide in me
　　　　　　Unless you're wanted.'

　　　'When I was young, an ken't nae mair
　　　I thought that wi' a <peck>hantle o' care <Perhaps by tryin' sair>
　　　　　　　　　　　　　　　<I micht wi' [?] care>
　　　It micht be possible to sair'
　　　　　　An please the bruit.
　　　But now I dinnae fash and hair
　　　　　　I cannae do't.'

　　　'An' if I could, I wudnae dae't
　　　For if in any special state
　　　The creature mair awakes my hate'

　　　'But when he's pleased or been to kirk
　　　He runes wi' a stansome smirk
　　　　　　O' kittled vanity.
　　　Ludsake, wad gar ye draw your dirk
　　　　　　<On all humanity> ^On Christianity.^'

3.　　'<A' day>I had a hantle <things> to <do> gay through
　　　<I've bungled>And some I did, some didnae do,
　　　<An some I>did some gay weel, <some>and ithers no –
　　　<And just contrived to warstle through>
　　　　　　<A sair-tired man>Like ither men.'
3.1　day ... view] day, ... view,
3.2　pu',] pu'
3.3　soo,] soo
3.4　man! –] man.
3.5　whan ... fu',] when ... fu'
4.1　An' there] <A' day><An>^For then^
4.2　There pleesure ... fife,] <Pleesure was>^An pleesure ... fife;^
4.3–4　There anger, wi' the hotchin' knife
　　　　　　Ground shairp in Hell –]
　　　<My conscience><you should be a wife><you that's like my wife>
　　　<shairpin at your><roasted your scalpin knife>
　　　<An sin that hides an unco knife>^An anger wi' ~ ^
　　　　　　<Instead o' helpin'><Has shairpt ~ > ^ ~ Hell.^

4.5   conscience! –] conscience!
5.1   fine: just waitin' here,] fine – <ye were> ^just … here^
5.2   gar … appear,] <mak>^gar^ … appear
5.3   To clart the guid, confüse the clear,] <Yuir nie philosopher, its clear>
                                              ^ ~ confuse ~ ^
5.4   Mis-ca'] Misca'
5.6   Whan a's ower late.] When <its>^a's^ ower late!
6.   'Than, tongueless, toothless, deef and blind,
        <He>Ye wait<s> until <we've>I've fairly sinned; –
        <The thieves may pack in a' they find>
        He lets the thieves through a' they find
                <He wags his tail>Now reid disaster,
        An' the morn's mornin', wuds the wind,
                Yokes <on mysel'>on his master.'

        'When thieves in quest o'peas and kale
        Break down the [?] garden pale
        He sits and wags a dozened tail
                At my disaster
        An' the morn's mornin', without fail
                Yokes on his master.'
6.1   Sic-like,] Siclike,
6.2   Whan … brok' … p'ind,] When … broke … pound
6.3   Has] <May>^ ~ ^
6.4   At the disaster;]<Whan thieves brok through at disaster>^ ~ disaster.^
6.5   wind,] wind
{B6602, titled and numbered XIII, collates with the copy-text as follows:}
Stanza.line
1.4   nonsense –] nonsense,
2.1   Whan] When
2.6   heart!] hairt!
3.5   whan my han's were fu',] when my <hands>^han's^ were fu,
3.6   {Author's Edn (see above, p. 394) has 'then' instead of 'than' here, an error repeated
        in some later editions.}
4.1   An'] <For>^ ~ ^
4.2   There] <And>^ ~ ^
4.3   There … knife] <And>^There^ … knife,

XV *To Doctor John Brown*
Place/date of composition: Davos and Bournemouth, December 1880 (Balfour; *LETBM*,
Vol. III, No. 763). {The proem stanza, obviously written after Brown's death in 1882, may
have been added in March 1887 when RLS sent this poem to Lady Taylor (*LETBM*, Vol. V,
No. 1775A) before including it in *UW*.}
Letters: 1. Fanny to Margaret Stevenson [16 July 1880] (*LETBM*, Vol. III, p. 89):
{Brown, a physician, writer and friend of the Stevenson family, had sent RLS and Fanny as
a wedding present a copy of his *Rab and his Friends* with the inscription, 'RLS and his *Sine*

Qua Non.} 'I was more delighted than words can express with the book *Rab and his Friends*.
I have been wishing to write to Dr Brown and thank him … '

2. RLS to his parents, 21 December 1880 (*LETBM*, Vol. III, p. 145):
'About John Brown, I have been breaking my heart to finish a Scotch poem to him. Some
of it is not really bad, but the rest will not come, and I mean to get it right before I do
anything else.' {See Explanatory Note on Brown, pp. 626–7.}
MSS: H2404, NYPL (Berg); like those for *UW* XIII and XIV, this HL MS is drawn from
Notebook A 270, where many untitled trials and drafts are scattered across leaves 12
through 16. Selective collation with the copy-text follows:
Stanza.line
Proem. 'While the dear doctor <still was> (dear to a')

        Was still amang us here belaw
        <I wrocht to make my verses braw>
        Enough to gie then but noo, Dear Doctor he's awa!
        <An n'er can see them>An n'er can hear it.
        For him I <made>wrocht my verse as braw
                As I could dae't;
                An I'm now late
        I set my <hand>lips his praise to blaw
                Wi' a' my speerit.'

1.1   Tees,] Tees
1.2   river-Dee's,] River<s> Dee's,
1.3   In Mars and Manors 'yont the seas] <When the muckle Scotland yont
                      the seas,> ^ ~ yont the seas – ^
1.4   Or here at hame,] <That well are here> ^Or here at hame – ^
1.5   Whaure'er there's kindly folk to please,] <An' where ye gang awhere
                      ye please> ^An' ~ please^
1.6   They ken your name.] <Sae loud your fame>^ ~ ^
2.1–2 '<As bees that in their theechit tyke
        We've made the honey that folk like>
        They ken your name, they ken your tyke,
        Its Rab, no you awa, they like;'
2.3   But mebbe after a' your fyke,] <But you yourself><ah sir!><for a'
                    your fish and fyke>^ ~ sir for ~ fyke^
2.4   (The trüth to tell)] <To tell you>^ ~ ^
2.5   like,] like –
2.6   An' no yoursel'.] No you yoursel!
3.1   As at the gowff, some canny]As, at the gowf, some <skeely>^canny^
3.2   a common ba' wi' care –] <'is ba'>^ ~ care,^
3.3   deleever] deliver
3.5   rise] <flie>^ ~ ^
3.6   lintie:] lintie!
[4]   'Aye, Rabbie was a well tee'd ba'
        He needed but a denty caw,
        An' through the air be succedit
        And lay in the blue lift over a''

4.1   Sae ... play,] <Just>^Sae^ ... play:
4.2   There comes to some a bonny day,] <We tee our ba's frae day to day> ^ ~ ^
4.3   When a dear ferlie] <An' in the lift>^When <the>^a^ ~ ^
4.4   strife,] strife.
4.5   clay,] clay
5.   'Its often lay, its often late
        <Before><As we can learn its aft an unco long wait>
        <We labour long to><Its lang or ithers learn the trade;>
        But you – Oude ken the way ye're made –
        A'e day into the schule ye strayed
        An' picked the fiddle up, an' played
                          Like Niel himsel.'
5.1   Ye] You
5.2   trade,] trade
5.4   schüle,] schule.
5.5   up an'] up, an'
5.6   himsel'.] himsel.
6.   'Beloved o' men must swait and swink
        To you then Doctor a' 'n a blink
        The happy moment cam'.'
6.1   fingers] hand
6.2   Ye didnae ... think,] You didna ... think
6.3   But wove, as fast as puss can link,]
        <[?] wall, you stopped to drink;>
        <And ye span and wove it in a blink – >
        Wove fast as <any>^a^ hare <could>^can^ link
6.4   wab: –] wab.
6.5   stapped ... ink,] dipped ... ink
7.   'Sin syne he <gays whaure'r a';>follows you ower
        His glad wouf-wouf aft an ha'
        Denty and canty hie an' law
        O' whatna' state in whatna' land
        They're blithe to shake ye by the hand,'
7.1   Sinsyne, whaure'er your fortune lay]
        Sin syne, whaue'er <ye tak your way><your journey lead>^ ~ ^
        {'Sin syne, ~ ' on the Harvard proofs}
7.2   dowie den, by canty brae,]<dowie mairs, by bieldy heid>^ ~ ^
7.3–4   Simmer an' winter, nicht an' day,
                          Rab was aye wi' ye;]
        <At meditation, work or play,
                          Rab's aye beside ye,> ^ ~ ^
7.5   An' a' the folk on a'] Sinsyne the folk around the
8.1   O sir, the gods are] O, sir, the Gods <were>^are^
8.2   heid,] heid;
8.3   screed] screed,
8.4   ye,] ye!
[9]   'For mind ye well your Rab's nae mair

A thing of ink, a thing of air,
   A tyke on paper.'

'For though while here you bide awee
Rab at your heels we seem to see
And we to hear him wolfin hie
   Wi' gladsome caper.
<For that which we but seem to see><Sae evident at>
Your Rabbie is in some degree
   A tyke awa.'

9.1 whaure'er yoursel' may be,] whaue'er yoursel may be
9.2 We've just … a wee,] We have <but>^just^ … awee
9.3 shüre] sure
9.4 caper: –] caper
9.6 A ghaist o' paper!] <A thing o' glimmer> ^ ~ ^
10.2 Hell a] Hell, a
10.3 please,] please:
10.5 gods] Gods
10.6 hell:] hell.
11.1 Sae the true Rabbie far has gane] <The true Rab has gone>
   <Upon a kindlier><On some far business of his ain,>
   <He on a further tryst has gone>^ ~ ^
11.3 frien's;] frien's:
11.4 stumpie tailie,] stumpy tailie
11.5 hearth stane] hearth-stane
{Berg is a fair copy in ink, numbered XIV, on three pages numbered 29–31; collation with the copy-text is as follows:}

Stanza.line
2.3 fyke,] fyke
2.4 like,] like
3.6 lintie:] lintie!
4.2 day,[day
4.5 clay,] clay
6.3 fast as puss] fast's <a cat>^a puss^
6.5 stapped] clapped
7.1 lay] lay,
8.1 O sir,] O, sir,
8.4 ye,] ye;
9.1 whaure'er yoursel'] whaureer yoursel
10.5 ease] ease,
11.2 kindlier] <kinder>^ ~ ^
11.3 frien's; an'] ~ – an'
{Author's Edn (see above, p. 394) had 'like you Rab' in line 4.5 instead of the copy-text's 'like your Rab'. This error was repeated in *Thistle* and several other editions.}

XVI 'It's an owercome sooth for age an' youth'
Place/date of publication: Bournemouth, 1884–7

MSS: B6469, B6470
Line
  2 wi'] wi (B6469)
  3 friends] {in both MSS this word is spelled variously as 'frie'ns', 'freinds' and 'friends' but
     the copy-text always has 'friends'}
  5 wi' young an' auld] for … auld, (B6469) ~ auld, (B6470)
  6 him] he (B6469)
  8 And the maist o' mines hae]<∧nd>^Yet^ the whole of mine ~ (B6469)
                                        ~ whole ~ ha'e (B6470)
10 them;] them, (B6469)

Ballads

History of Composition and Publication

Ballads was published on 13 December 1890 by Scribner's in New York and on 18 December by Chatto and Windus in London. Just as he had begun *UW* while finishing *CGV*, RLS completed his first ballad as he was sending *UW* to press. Four days after posting the MSS for his second collection of verse to his Edinburgh printer R. and R. Clark, he told Colvin, 'I have written a dam fine ballad.' *Ticonderoga* was composed in Edinburgh in the aftermath of his father's death on 8 May 1887; indeed, the MS of the poem in the BL is written on the back of a draft of RLS's essay on his father (see *LETBM*, Vol. V, pp. 416–19).

However, this volume belongs mainly to the early South Seas period, 1888–90. From Tahiti, RLS sent Henley a freshly-written ballad, *Christmas at Sea*, for inclusion in the Christmas issue of the *Scots Observer* (which Henley was then editing). 'If you don't care for it,' said the poet, 'you can put it in a drawer, till I get a volume of ballads ready' (*LETBM*, Vol. VI, 9 October 1888, p. 210). Over the next two weeks, he wrote *The Feast of Famine*, sending it to Colvin on 16 October. During his first six months in the South Seas, he immersed himself in the songs and stories of the primitive oral cultures he encountered, collecting and attempting to translate and imitate traditional Tahitian songs or *Himenes* (see *LETBM*, Vol. VI, No. 2128). RLS was struck by the resemblance of these islanders, especially in Tahiti and Samoa, to Scots Highlanders: besides performing their heroic and romantic songs, they wore kilts and belonged to clans. After exchanging names with Ori a Ori, a charismatic underchief of the Teva clan, RLS considered himself a clan member and was so recognised by the chief clansman, Tati Salmon (*LETBM*, Vol. VI, No. 2128, n.7). Early in the new year of 1889, twenty days out from Papeete on his chartered yacht *Casco*, he told Colvin he was more than halfway through another ballad, *The Song of Rahéro*, based on a Teva legend (*LETBM*, Vol. VI, No. 2130). On 5 February he announced to his Scribner's editor Burlingame his plan for a new book of poems:

> I have had great fortune in finding old songs and ballads and stories … You know *Ticonderoga*. I have written another: *The Feast of Famine*, a Marquesan story. A third is half done: *The Song of Rahéro*, a genuine Tahitian legend. A fourth dawns before me: a Hawaiian fellow this: *The Priest's Draught* … If (as I half suspect) I get enough subjects out of the Islands, *Ticonderoga* shall be suppressed; and we'll call the volume *South Sea Ballads*. (*LETBM*, Vol. VI, p. 246)

A month later he sent Scribner's some copy for *BAL* to be set up in type: *Rahéro* was now finished, though *The Priest's Draught*, estimated to run about 350 lines, was not, and *Heather Ale*, here mentioned for the first time, is included along with a revised *Ticonderoga*. Worried about accommodating his hexameters and fourteeners to the printed page, he went into detail on questions of format:

The type must be very small, for lines continually running over weary a reader, and this hexameter of mine is a verse of a formidable longitude. We cannot put less than 25 lines to the page, or it will be too squat. At this figure, leaving a triple space at each paragraph, I calculate we should have enough for a volume ... counting between 1500 and 2000 {BAL had 1,384 lines}. I mean each ballad to be introduced by a false title, following which a page is to carry the dedication *in italics*; making a gain of 4pp. to each ballad ... what I want just now is galleys: as soon as may be. (*LETBM*, Vol. VI [5 March 1889], pp. 257–8)

By mid-May he had the proofs, twenty-five lines to the page in small print, as requested.

Then his capacity to execute his poetic projects seems to have flagged. *The Priest's Draught* and other projected exercises such as *The Ballad of the Barque Moroa*, about a revolt on a slave ship, did not advance (they were never completed). In February 1890, RLS proposed for the first time to Scribner's the idea that some of his recent lyrics inspired by the South Seas might be combined with the ballads to make a stronger volume:

It begins to look as if I should not be able to get any more ballads done this somewhile; I know the book would sell better if it were all ballads; and yet I am getting half tempted to fill up with some other verses. A good few are connected with my voyage, such as *The House of Tembinoka* {ST XXXVIII}, sent herewith, and would have a sort of slight affinity to the *South Sea Ballads*. (*LETBM*, Vol. VI, p. 366–7)

Hoping to bring this revised book out by the autumn, RLS played with new titles, e.g. *Ballads and Scenes of Travel*, *Ballads and Legends* or *Ballads and Songs of Travel*, the latter one dropped because it was too similar to Swinburne's *Poems and Ballads* series. He sent the following projected Contents list to Scribner's:

Ballads and <Scenes>^Songs^ of Travel

		Songs of Travel?
Ticonderoga		
The Feast of Famine	I.	To an Island Princess {ST XXIX}
The Story of Rahéro	II.	To Mother Mary Anne {ST XXXII}
Christmas at Sea	III.	To S.C. {ST XXXVII}
	IV.	The Tropics Vanish {ST XXXVI}
	V.	To Tem Binoka
	VI.	The House of Tem Binoka {ST XXXVIII}
	VII.	In Memoriam E.H. {ST XXXIII}
	VIII.	To Dr Hake {ST XX}
	IX.	Winter {ST XVIII}
	X.	Home no more home {ST XVII}
	XI.	To Schubert's Ninth {ST I}
	XII.	To an Air of Diabelli's {ST XII}
	XIII.	To [?]
	XIV.	B.R.D.

Some of these I shall send you herewith, also a few copies of verse, of which I am doubtful whether to put them in; but suppose you condemn them all, we shall have upwards of 300 verses left, which will make quite a volume with the ballads which must stand us in about 1000. (*LETBM*, Vol. VI, pp. 370–1)

In mid-July he wrote to Burlingame from the S.S. *Janet Nicoll*, asking pointedly for constructive criticism to accompany the proofs of his new poems that he expected to find on his arrival in Sydney. But he was disappointed and began to lose confidence in the project, as he reported from Australia to Burlingame:

> The deuce is in this volume. It has cost me more botheration and dubiety than any other I ever took in hand. On one thing my mind is made up: the verses at the end have no business there, and throw them down; many of them are bad, many of the rest want nine years keeping, and the remainder are not relevant – throw them down: some I never want to hear of more, others will grow in time towards a second *Underwoods* – and in the meanwhile, down with them! At the same time, I have a sneaking idea the ballads are not altogether without merit – I don't know if they're poetry, but they're good narrative, or I'm deceived. (You've never said one word about them, for which I astutely gather you are dead set against …) You will have to judge; … (First) Either publish the five ballads, such as they are, in a volume called *Ballads*: in which case pray send sheets at once to Chatto & Windus. Or (second) write and tell me you think the book too small, and I'll try and get into the mood to do some more. Or (third) write and tell me you think the whole thing is a blooming illusion; in which case draw off some twenty copies for my private entertainment and charge me with the expenses of the whole obscene dream. In the matter of rhyme, no man can judge himself; I am at the world's end, have no one to consult, and my publisher holds his tongue. I call it unfair, and almost unmanly. (*LETBM*, Vol. VI [late August 1890], pp. 411–12)

On 2 September, he authorised Scribner's to proceed with the five-ballad collection, sending in Notes for them. But during that autumn, RLS managed to write a fair amount of poetry that pleased him; by 26 November, he had changed his mind again:

> If the *Ballads* are delayed … you may expect a welcome reinforcement *certainly* by next mail. I have XXVI pieces ready, 675 verses, and could send them now, if I had one day more. (I stick over only some ten or twenty verses {these twenty-six poems probably became B7065, *Verses*}. Only twelve of these were in the proof received at Sydney; so, if there is any merit in the truck, I have used my spare moments to some account. If they are published of course it can't be helped; the stuff will do for something else. I have finished and send them on the chance. I have no copy of many of them. Should the volume be out, I think you had better have them type-written and sent to me in that form. Please ask your printers not to *put in titles* where I have not done so; I designate unnamed pieces in the contents by the first few words or the first verse; but it strikes me as idiotic to stick these same words in capitals at the top of the piece, as was done in the Sydney proof. Only one piece, please, upon a page: no matter how short it is. It will make about 50 pp. which, with the ballads, constitutes a quite efficient little volume. Let it be called *Ballads and Verses simpliciter* … Of course if the *Ballads* are out already, it's a pity: For this would have sold it, appealing to a different class; but it can't be helped, and we'll go on and try to fill up another volume, as soon as the Muse enables. But the strange thing is I never know when I shall be able to write a verse. (*LETBM*, Vol. VII, pp. 46–7).

Ballads and Verses was stillborn. It *was* too late by the time this material, the nucleus of what in 1895, under Colvin's editorship, became *ST*, arrived in New York. And RLS was right to fear a negative response to *Ballads* unaccompanied by lyrics. Writing in the autumn of 1891 to a friend who had enjoyed them, he comments on the bad reviews and small sales:

Glad the ballads amused you. They failed to entertain a coy public: at which I own I wondered. Not that I set much account by my verses, which are the verses of Prosator; but I do know how to tell a yarn, and two of the yarns were great. *Rahéro* is for its length, I think, a perfect folk tale; savage and yet fine, full of a tailforemost morality, ancient as the granite rocks; if the historian not to say the politician could get that yarn into his head, he would have learned some of his A.B.C. But the average man at home cannot understand antiquity; he is sunk over the ears in Roman civilization; and a tale like that of *Rahéro* falls on his ears inarticulate. (*LETBM*, Vol. VII, p. 187)

Location and Description of Manuscripts

Thomas J. Wise acquired an MS of *Ticonderoga*, now part of BL as Ashley 5050; the Rosenbach Foundation Museum in Philadelphia also has a complete MS of this poem. The Pierpont Morgan Library's MA419 is a complete folio MS of *The Feast of Famine*, fourteen leaves signed and dated. At HL there are three MSS relevant to *BAL*: H2421 is titled 'The South Seas – a record of two years travel'; H2458 has an unpublished ballad fragment with a list of topics and titles for projected ballads; and H2401 has a fragmentary sketch for *Heather Ale*. BRBML has some abortive ballad trials in B6022, 'First Drafts of Poems Unpublished', including a 35-line sketch for *Heather Ale* (B6285) and several drafts of RLS's attempts to translate Tahitian songs. There are MS fragments of *The Feast of Famine* and *Heather Ale* at Silverado. MSS for *The Song of Rahéro* and *Christmas at Sea* were not found. The Scribner's archive at Princeton, Box 143, folders 6 and 7, has correspondence to and from Charles Scribner, E. L. Burlingame and others relating to *BAL*.

MS and Printed Fragments

The following draft translations of Tahitian *himenes* were sent in RLS's letter (*LETBM*, Vol. VI, No. 2128 (c. 10 December 1888)) to his Teva clan chief Tati Salmon, who assisted the poet in these exercises:

> … (*It is time to*) bathe in the water of Vaitapiha
> O dancing streams of Fatutira!
> For what am I now weeping?
> I weep for the shades of the land
> That I have left behind me at my sailing.
> The trade wind blows,
> The wind that brings the Seaward Tevas,
> Sails are filled at sea:
> The clan will muster *thick* as the hairs of the head.

> The wind roars in from seaward,
> The waves of the deep are lifted up,
> They bury the high sea cliffs,
> The perching places of (the bird) Maarua.
> Let me go now to Tepari (the sea cliffs)
> To see the hole of the fishes, there where Turi was noosed
> While the woman Ahupu passed overhead in safety.

{RLS wrote a note on the legendary Ahupu, who appears in line 52 of *The Song of Rahéro* –}

> Let me fathom out with my arms *the length* of golden-hued Tahiti
> And number one by one the lands of Tautira.
> I am seized with fear at Tepari
> I shall stop short at Vaita
> Clouds are over the sun and it blows a bad wind,
> And my home is *beyond* at Faaroa.
> At Vaiumete *is a ledge where a man must* go with the arms spread.
> I must measure with my arms the face of that weary cliff.
>
> (*LETBM*, Vol. VI, pp. 235–6)

H2458 lists, besides some of the poems ultimately published in *BAL*, the following topics/titles for ballads which he intended to write: 'The Mutineers (*Bounty*), The Captives, Inchcape Reef, Uncle John, The Scalpers, Taheia {heroine of *The Feast of Famine*}, The Dead'. This list is followed by a very rough sketch of a ballad taking place in Brazil and Peru. The following lines are from 'Book XIII' of RLS's fragmentary mock-epic *The Samoid*, written to amuse Lady Jersey during her visit to Vailima in 1892 (*LETBM*, Vol. VII, No. 2415); the verses are printed below a drawing by Belle Strong in the little booklet (now in NLS) that RLS presented to Lady Jersey. Poets haunted as RLS was by the epic mode often console themselves with translating genuine epic or composing mock-epic; this portrait in hexameters of the Samoan patriarch Popo is not mere doggerel to amuse his friends but a bardic effusion, an effort to live up to his Samoan title of *Tusitala*:

> Eighty the years of his body, and how much more of his mind
> Vigorous yet and erect, with an aquiline face designed
> Like Dante's, he who had worshipped feathers and shells, and wood,
> As a pillar alone in the desert that points where a city stood,
> Survived the world that was his, playmates and gods and tongue –
> For even the speech of his race had altered since Popo was young.
> And ages of time and epochs of changing manners bowed,
> And the silent hosts of the dead wondered and muttered aloud
> With him, as he bent and marvelled, a man of the time of the Ark,
> And saluted the ungloved hand of the Lady of Osterley Park.

RLS also attempted Hawaiian ballads, some excerpts from which (such as the following example) are recorded in Arthur Johnstone's *Recollections of Robert Louis Stevenson in the Pacific*:

> #### The High Winds Of Nuuanu
>
> Within the famous valley of that name,
> Now twice or thrice the high wind blows each year,
> Until you hear it pulsing through the gorge
> In spiteful gusts: sometimes it comes with bursts
> Of rain, in fiercer squalls; and, howling down the glen,
> It breaks great tropic fronds like stems of clay.
> Lo! then, the unbending palms and rugged dates,
> Loud-whistling, strain in each recurrent blast,

Like things alive! – or fall, with roots uptorn,
The feathered algarobas, as the gale
Treads out its wasteful pathway to the sea!
Thus twice or thrice Nuuanu's high winds rage,
Thrashing the vale till quakes the Island's heart!
Ten other months are filled with nerveless rest,
Mid cooling breezes and down-dropping showers;
At night the dark-blue vault arching the vale,
Studded with stars innumerable and bright!
While fleecy clouds outdrifting to the sea,
Make shadows in the moonlight on the sward.
Here dwell the Islanders in peace, until
The blasts again sweep down from Northern Seas.

(Johnstone 1905: 307)

According to Johnstone, this poem was undertaken at the request of the editor of the *Pacific Commercial Advertiser*, shortly after RLS arrived in Honolulu in 1893. It was not published at the time because he meant to add to it, but serious illness supervened and the poem was never completed.

Johnstone also tells us that a fragment called *The Pirate's Island* (excerpted below) was presented by RLS to his Honolulu doctor George Trousseau, who had suggested that he try to write a Polynesian ballad. In a note to Dr Trousseau accompanying these lines, RLS argued 'that prose is the best way by long odds for story-tellers who depend on realistic action for their interest. You may preserve this as a sample of how the plausible suggestions of our well-meaning friends may fail in practice':

Twas on a Monday evening we sailed forth,
And veered into the purple and gold
Of our warm Southern sea. We were but six –
Four stalwart natives and two whites – who sailed
Upon that unknown course. Never had they,
My brown Samoans, ventured so; nor would
Have ventured now, had I not been with them
To urge hearts on. When we had been five days
Or more upon the main, and yet no land
Or atoll come in sight, I knew that we
Had missed our port, for on my chart there lay,
Across our course, the sea-famed island where,
'Twas said by ancient chiefs, great treasure lay,
Hidden long years ago by pirates bold,
Who seized the lumb'ring carracks (from the Isle
Of Spices) coming far from o'er the sea.
And on this flitting isle Samoans say,
Within a hollow mountain near the shore,
Were hid canoes full of bright shining gold
In lumps and wedges, fit for kingly state;
With black and yellow pearls for Chieftain's ears,
From the warm seas that wash the shore of Ind.

It was this tale that since their childhood's day
Had pricked their curiosity, and made
Them bold to rove; to leave the *cava* bowl,
The bursting bread-fruit, and the luscious gold
Of rip'ning plantains, to follow o'er the waves,
That chance might bring to wealth, or death – or both.
So when I told them, 'Children, we are lost!'
The lad Upolu fell to wailing in
The native way until Chief Kimo sternly said,
"Now hush thee, silly one, or thou wilt shame
Thy parents and thy tribe' …

(Johnstone 1905: 308–9)

Printed Text

The copy-text chosen is the first issue of the first American edition. RLS saw this material through the press from galleys through late proofs under the direction of E. L. Burlingame (see History of Composition and Publication above), then gave the following instructions to Chatto and Windus on 2 December:

> I don't know whether you have yet had a book of *Ballads* from Scribner's. If you have not you will soon receive it in a more extended form as *Ballads and Verses*. Put it into R. and R. Clark's hands to print; and let it go on the same terms with *Underwoods*. (*LETBM*, Vol. VII, p. 50)

First Edition, First Issue

BALLADS / BY / ROBERT LOUIS STEVENSON / NEW-YORK / CHARLES SCRIBNER'S SONS / 1890
Crown 8vo. No signature marks. [A] ^{4} [B] – [F] ^{8} [G] ^{4} pp. vi + 88: [–] [i – iv] v – vi 1 – 85 [86 – 88] Bound in blue cloth with plain end-papers. The title, ornament and author's name are stamped in gold on the front cover and spine, where the publisher's name appears below. Laid paper. Top edge gilt, other edges uncut.

Variants

First English Edition
BALLADS / BY / ROBERT LOUIS STEVENSON / [Publisher's device.] / LONDON / CHATTO & WINDUS, PICCADILLY / 1890
Crown 8vo. A ^{4} B – I ^{8} K ^{4} [–] ^{2} pp. viii + 140: [i – v] vi [vii – viii] [1] – 137 [138 – 40] 2,000 copies printed. Bound in dark-blue cloth with plain end-papers, lettered in gold on the spine, *Ballads / R. Louis / Stevenson. / Chatto & Windus*. Wove paper. Top edge gilt with other edges uncut.
   The large paper (4to) copies printed by Chatto and Windus have the same collation as the regular English issue. Signatures: [A] – S ^{4} [–] ^{2} On the *verso* of the half-title page is the Certificate of Issue limiting the edition to 100 copies. Bound in white buckram with plain end-papers, gilt lettered on the spine as in the regular issue. Handmade laid paper. Edges uncut.

The USA edition is sometimes bound in olive-green or copper-brown cloth.

The English and American editions differ markedly, but it is the Scribner's issue which was set up to the poet's specifications (see LETBM, Vol. VI, pp. 257–8 and p. 297). The type is smaller than in the London issue; there is a maximum of twenty-five lines to the page, and two or three spaces are left between each verse paragraph. Thus, on the first page of text, the US edition has fourteen lines whereas the English one has six. The English edition was not corrected by RLS and several other textual variants occur. For instance, the Scribner half-title page for *The Song of Rahéro* carries those four words only, as the poet directed, whereas the Chatto and Windus setting puts the subtitle, *A Legend of Tahiti*, there with the title instead of placing it after the repeated title on page 5 where the Scribner's text begins. This variant is repeated with the other four ballads. Other variants are recorded in the Textual Notes on the Individual Poems, and emendations are explained there. Full bibliographical descriptions may be found in McKay, Vol. I, Nos 531–5.

Textual Notes on Individual Poems

The Song of Rahéro
Place/date of composition: Tautira and Honolulu, 1889 (LETBM, Vol. VI [5 March 1889], No. 2138)
Letters and sources: 1. RLS to Colvin (LETBM, Vol. VI, 14 January 1889, p. 239): 'I … wrote the half of another ballad, *The Song of Rahéro*, on a Taiarapu legend of my own clan, sir – not so much fire as *The Feast of Famine*, but promising to be more even and correct. But the best fortune of our stay at Tautira {in Tahiti} was my knowledge of Ori himself: one of the finest creatures extant. The day of our parting was a sad one. We deduced from it a rule for travellers: not to stay two months in one place: which is to cultivate regrets.'

2. RLS to Henley (LETBM, Vol. VI [?March 1889], p. 267): 'Do you remember suggesting I should try an epic? I have been trying narrative verse, I think with some measure of success. When I get a proof of *The Song of Rahéro*, I shall ask you to look at it, and condemn what is inadequate.'

3. RLS to H. B. Baildon (LETBM, Vol. VII [?October or November 1891], pp. 187–8): {This letter is quoted above, p. 461; he continues speaking of the poem as follows}: 'The *Spectator* … cannot so much as observe the existence of savage psychology when it is placed before it. I am at bottom a psychologist and ashamed of it; the tale seized me one third because of its picturesque features, two-thirds because of its astonishing psychology; and the *Spectator* says there's none. I am going on with a lot of island work, exulting in the knowledge of a new world – "a new created world" and new men; and I am sure my income will Decline and Fall Off.'

4. From Fanny's Prefatory Note to BAL, VAIL, Vol. VIII, p. 91: 'An itinerary of my husband's wanderings might almost be drawn from his collected poems. The Song of Rahéro was at first inspired by the conversation of the Princess Moë in Tautira, a village lying on the Tiarapu peninsula of Tahiti. Here we lived for several months, the guests of the princess and the chief Ori, with whom my husband 'made brothers' in the island fashion. Although Moe was then grandmother to several tall girls, she was still beautiful, with much of the grace and charm of youth. It happened, while we were in Tautira, there was some legal question to be settled

concerning lands, belonging to the princess, that lay in the country of Tiarapu. In discussing the matter she touched on the tradition of Rahéro, jestingly calling herself Ahupu Vehine. My husband, deeply interested, drew from her all she could tell him of the story, afterwards corroborated and enriched by the high chief Tati, whom we visited at Papora.'
MSS: None found. {I have inserted missing full stops at the ends of lines 142 and 183.}

The Feast of Famine
Place/date of composition: Tautira and on the yacht *Casco* sailing from Tahiti to Hawaii, 5–16 October 1888 (Morgan MS so dated)
Letter and source: 1. RLS to Colvin (*LETBM*, Vol. VI, 16 October 1888, p. 216)
{Including with his letter this just-finished 'ballant', which he describes as 'better … than I expected ever to do', he is not very confident that Colvin will like it:} 'I can imagine how you will wag your pow over it; and how ragged you will find it, etc. But has it not spirit all the same? And though the verse is not all your fancy painted it, has it not some life? And surely as narrative, the thing has some considerable merit! Read it, get a typewritten copy taken, and send me that and your opinion to the [Sandwiches.] I know I am courting the most excruciating mortification; but the real cause of my sending the thing is that I could bear to go down myself, but not to have so much MS go down with me.'

2. From Fanny's Prefatory Note to *BAL, VAIL*, Vol. VIII, pp. 91–2: 'My husband found the change from his usual work so restful and pleasant that he was encouraged to attempt another South Sea ballad, the scene to be laid in the Marquesas. This ballad, begun in Tautira, was finished on board the yacht Casco, between Tahiti and Hawaii, amid every possible discomfort. Our provisions (all we could get in Tahiti) were scant and bad; we carried a hurricane barometer all the way, and were constantly beset by squalls and baffling winds. For two days we lay becalmed off Oahu, the tantalising sight of land before our eyes. During the time we spent in Tautira we lived almost entirely on native food; this, followed by thirty days of decayed beef and stale biscuits, reduced us to a state of semi-starvation. I shall never forget our first dinner on shore at Honolulu, with its roasts and potatoes and celery, and that

> "Rose among roots, the maiden fair,
> Wine scented and poetic soul
> Of the capacious salad bowl." [*UW* VII, *The Gardener*]'

MSS: Morgan MA419, Silverado MR.VII #3: A–11. The Silverado MS is a fragmentary draft of lines 7–10 and 59–60 written *verso* on a version of the *Envoi* to *The House of Tembinoka* (ST XXXVIII), as follows:

> '<Oft rose the song of morning>
> And oft in the starry even the song rose
> Oft smoked the oven in the country of <the>foes;
> Far oft to loving hearts and waiting ears and sight,
> The lads that went to forage returned not with the night.'
> 'With a lamp at his gaping head, <in the perfect forest he lay>
> And the sacred leaves of the banyan <rustled>fell around his sleep.'

{Collation of MA419 with copy-text follows:}

Title/subtitle: *THE FEAST OF FAMINE: MARQUESAN MANNERS*
  I.   *The Priest's Vigil.*]
  THE FEAST OF FAMINE. A MARQUESAN LEGEND
  {no subtitles in MA419}

Line
  8   their] our
 19   high-built lodge, hard by] great lodge, beside
 22   breakers, like] breakers like
 23   them] us
 30   depths] deeps
 31   cocoa-husk,] coco-husk;
 36   'He ... victims;] He ... victims, {The quotation mark, an error, has been omitted.}
 39   speech;] speech:
 43   roofs lay] roofs, lay
 50   rounds, and] rounds and
 52   houses the] houses, the
 53   houses they] houses, they
 56   Two] <Three>^ ~ ^
 57   frenzy twice] frenzy, <thrice>^twice^
 59   head he] head, he
 62   the lofty] <that>^the^ high
 65   across] <along>^ ~ ^
 70   apart.] apart; {at this point in the text six lines are omitted; white space on the page
      suggests that this cut was made too late in proofing for the gap to be closed; the
      omitted MS lines follow:}
      'And the commons that know not that tattoo, drew near as they dared to draw,
      And the women, the small of account, listened and whispered with awe.
      All about and above them, motionless groves of palm;
      And every hour as it passed, through an ever-deepening calm,
      A louder boom of the sea around her eternal bars,
      A deeper azure of night, and clearer legions of stars.'
      {In the text there is a subtitle at this point: 'II. The Lovers.'}
 71   sharp –] sharp,
 73   start?] start,
 77   Sly and shy as a cat,] <Sly as a cat from her seat,>^ ~ ^
 80   Then sudden] Then, sudden
 82   foot, running,] foot; running,
 83   way over] way, over
 85   length, in] length in
 86   {after this line in MS there is a three-space break; the text has no break}
 87   'Rua,' – ... my soul, and my eyes,'] 'Rua! – *. .. my soul and my eyes!'
 88   sighs,] sighs.
 89   'Rua!' – 'Taheia, my love,' – 'Rua, star of my night,]
      'Rua! – Taheia, my love – Rua, star of my night
 90   me, and] me and
 92   living, and] living and
      {93–6 is italicised in the text; in MS it is in quotation marks.}

94   *land wind*] land-wind
95   *height;*] height
97   'Taheia,] '– Taheia
98   sundered unkindly] sundered, unkindly
103   body, and] body and
106   mimosa, and] mimosa and
108   crest] vest
112   clasp] clap
113   blue, and] blue and
114   Death,] death,
120   High-place] high-place {also in lines 261, 266, 349}
121   beast,] beast;
122   {MS has a three-space break here; the text has no break}
123   '– Rua, ... me.] 'Rua, ... me;
125   Flee] <Fly>^ ~ ^
127   'Whither] – 'Whither
128   hand;] hand:
129   isle] <island>^ ~ ^
130   beneath.] beneath,
131   sleuth,] sleuth:
133   'Love,] – 'Love,
134   love you] love, you
135   There, where] There where
137   There, in the deep recess,] There in the deep recess
142   that? If] that? if
143   every one] everyone
144   quick] <swift>^ ~ ^
151   'Taheia, ... things,] – 'Taheia, ... things.
152   things;] Kings; {The MS reading has been adopted: 'things' seems to be a misreading
       and it repeats the rhyme in the previous line.}
153   in the trees] in trees
155   'Rua, ... read;] – 'Rua, ... read:
159   agreed, and] agreed; and
163   long] long,
166   haven thee] haven, thee
       {Following this line the text has the subtitle, 'III. The Feast'.}
170   stirring, for] stirring for
172   cheeks were] <face was>^ ~ ^
174   But, quiet] But quiet
175   sun the] sun, the
180   {The text has a two-space break here; MS has no break}
182   arose] <came>^ ~ ^
183   drum, and] drum and
184   wind level and strong] wind, level and strong,
186   crowd] crowd,
187   the spiders of shadow, scattered the jewels]
       <its>^the^ spiders of shadow, <fluttered its>^scattered the^ jewels

188	throbbed] <trampled>^ ~ ^
194	labour treads] labour, treads
197	Now ... heart, and] <But>^Now^ ... heart and
200	singers nine] singers, nine
202	And, struck] And struck
205	Frenzy hurried the chaunt,] <Terror strangled the cries,>^ ~ ^
208	again descended] again, descended
	{MS has a break here; the text has none.}
212	nation one after one withdrew;] nation, one after one, withdrew.
215	nobles in] nobles, in
216	{The text has a break at this point; MS does not.}
217	brewed, and ... cocoa] brewed and ... coco
219	heart, and] heart and
221	consulted] counselled
222	nodded and ... smile:] nodded, and ... smile
223	'Rua the] 'Rua, the
224	tomorrow, since] tomorrow since
225	valley, where] valley where
226	valley the] valley, the
230	trembled] <roosted>^ ~ ^
231	there in a cleft clustered] there, in a cleft, clustered
233	overhead, with a cry, the] overhead with a cry the
234	thin perennial] thin, perennial
239	mid-day shadows,] midday shadow,
243	arose and] arose, and
244	woods, and the sea, and] woods and the sea and
245	good;] good – ;
247	groves as] groves, as
255	the grave] <a plague>^ ~ ^
257	more, through] more through
258	place] <roof>^ ~ ^
259	return; no more as] return – no more, as
261	came,] came;
263	came gleaning] came, gleaning
265	bay the ... rang,] bay, the ... <came,>^rang,^
270	{There is a break in MS here but none in the text.}
272	damp of the dew,] damps of the dew;
273	arms;] arms,
274	clasp, and] clasp and
	{There is a break in MS here but none in the text.}
276	thought;] thought:
277	tonight,] <at night,>^ ~ ^
278	torches must] torches, must
283	stars,] stars;
285	height;] height,
286	glen, fell a] glen, fell, a
287	in the eye of ... east,] on the hills of ... east;

288   sea the] sea, the
289   As, when] As when
294   drooped, and droned] and fell and rose
       {The text has a subtitle here, 'IV. The Raid'.}
296   from high] <on>^from^ high
297   yore, and time had broken, the] yore < – > and time had broken the
301   'The] – 'The
305   'What] – 'What
306   that are come,] that come,
307   vessel, and] vessel and
309   On the top of the face of the cape a ... fair,]
       <Sheer was>^On the top of^ ~ cape, a ... fair;
311   'Silence, heart! What is that?] – 'Silence ~ that
312   instant, and in an instant] instant and in the instant
314   the loop] <a>^the^ ~
315   saw, in] saw, on
318   more swift than a dolphin swims;] <swift as a porpoise>^ ~ swims; – ^
321   soul he] soul, he
323   and, behold, he] and behold he
325   Hoka a] Hoka, a
326   war, and] war and
327   cornice Rua] cornice, Rua
329   'Foes] – 'Foes
331   plan;] plan,
333   years,] years
       {The three-space break in the text here occurs in MS after line 334, where it makes
       sense; the text has been so emended.}
336   Rua and] Rua, and
341   flight, and] flight; and
343   thought as he ran, and] thought, as he ran and
347   And what though I die ere morn?] <What though I die ere the morn?>^ ~ ^
348   {There is a space at this point in MS but not in the text.}
353   anigh] anigh,
355   bees in] bees, in
356   scattered, and lie, and stagger, and] scattered and lie and stagger and
358   lay;] lay.
362   life, and] life and
363   lo! on ... benches a] lo, on ... benches, a
365   Women with] Women, with
367   quiet, and] quiet and
368   Taheia, the ... Taheia, heavy] Taheia the ... Taheia heavy
377   Thick, like ... faint, like] Thick like ... faint like
378   feet;] feet.
379   place;] place,
380   cried:] cried –
381   't is] tis
388   Fifty spears they cast, and one of fifty true!]

Fifty the spears they cast, and one out of fifty true.
389   can,] can:
390   Foretell the hour] Foretell me the hour
{MS signed at bottom thus: 'Taiti Oct.5ᵗʰ–16ᵗʰ 1888   R.L.S.'}

Ticonderoga: A Legend of the West Highlands
Place/date of composition: Edinburgh, May–June 1887 (*LETBM*, Vol. V, Nos 1827, 1830)
Letters: 1. RLS to Henley [28 May 1887] (*LETBM*, Vol. V, p. 416): 'I have written a ballant in a genteel muddle of Lord Macaulay and the old ones.'

2. RLS to Scribner's [c. 10 June 1887] (*LETBM*, Vol. V, pp. 422–3): {The ballad was enclosed with this letter:} 'I am glad to be able to reply with a MS. This I had destined for you, but had not meant to send it you at once; as I have commissioned an artist friend of mine who knows the country and the dress, to do some illustrations. I will see that these reach you in time; and I feel pretty certain that they will be found good enough. Meanwhile I send you the copy at once, and I daresay you can let me have a dozen copies or so to save my copyright in England; for small as the thing is, and out of my way, I fancy it has merit.'
   Pre-publication printings: although there are genuine private and copyright printings of this poem, Thomas J. Wise and H. Buxton Forman produced a forgery of it which they passed off as a rare private issue. For a full discussion of this tricky business, see Lewis 1995: 214–18 and Barker and Collins 1983: 218–22. *Ticonderoga* appeared, with illustrations, in *Scribner's Magazine*, December 1887. As requested, Scribner's sent a few copies in sheets of this printing, which were bound up with a covering title-page printed by Clark's in Edinburgh and bearing the imprint 'London, F. Warne, 1887': Warne was the English distributor of *Scribner's Magazine*. This genuine copyright edition is even rarer than *Penny Whistles*, surviving in only one copy at the Houghton Library, Harvard (see Lewis 1995: 228). Asked in 1891 about what was almost certainly a copy of the Wise forgery, RLS said, '*Ticonderoga* was printed to ensure copyright at home; I never even saw it' (*LETBM*, Vol. VII, p. 467). No doubt Baxter as his agent had taken care of this matter.
   In May 1889 RLS commissioned another printing, this time pulled from Scribner's setting of the poem in the forthcoming *BAL*. In February 1889, while visiting King Kalakaua of Hawaii in Honolulu, he had read his Scottish ballad to the monarch and now wished to present him with a copy, so he wrote to Burlingame as follows: 'Please have a proof of *Ticonderoga* drawn on fine paper *without the dedication*, make it up, stitch it, stick on the false title in italics "*Privately printed for his Hawaiian Majesty, King Kalakaua*", and "*From the Author*"; and have the result dispatched to H.M.' (*LETBM*, Vol. VI, p. 292).
   The resulting pamphlet, printed by the De Vinne Press of New York, was a square octavo of eight leaves sewn with red silk, only two copies of which were printed, although Barker and Collins declare that there may have been four (p. 218). Only the Harvard copy is extant. The text of the Kalakaua edition varies from both *Scribner's* and *BAL*. See the Explanatory Note on this poem, p. 627.
MSS: BL Ashley 5050; Rosenbach Foundation Museum, Philadelphia
Title: *Ticonderoga: A Legend of the West Highlands*.] *Ticonderoga* (Scrib., Ros.)
Subtitles: There are three subtitles in the text, one each for sections I–III; no subtitles appear in *Scrib.*, *Ash.* or *Ros.*, only section nos.
Line
2   night] night, (Ros.)

3   heathery hills,] <mountains dark> ^ ~ ^ (Ash.)
5   sea,] sea (Ash.)
7   dead,] dead (Ash.)
10   head:] head, (Ash.)
20   {there is a two-space break in *Scrib.*, Ash. and Ros. after this line and line 204 but
        none in the text}
21   O, what] O what (Ash.) {also line 22}
23   cold] <gash> ^ ~ ^ (Ash.)
25   about] <round> ^ ~ ^ (Ash.)
32   swords.'] swords!' (Ash.)
38   dead,] dead; (Ash.)
44   body,] belly, (Ash., Ros.)
50   red,] red; (Ash.)
51   there, in] there in (Ash.)
54   death.] death; (Ash.)
55   hands,] hands (Ash.)
67   By my sword and yonder mountain,] By the bread of life and the steel of war, (*Scrib.*,
        Ros. and Ash.)
74   den] den, (Ash.)
86   air;] air, (Ash.)
90   were] was (Ash.)
91   I couldnae ... hand,] Shall gar me ... hand (Ros.) ~ hand (Ash.)
92   Nor] Or (Ash.)
93   our father,] <my> our father (Ash.) ~ father (Ros.)
95   O, what] And what (Ash.)
96   Who] That (Ros., Ash.)
98   have lived] lived (Ros., Ash.)
99   you] ye (Ash.)
100   Fause-hearted brother] False-hearted, brother (Ash.)
102   dead] dead, (Ros., Ash.)
103   hand,] hand (Ros.)
110   on his bed,] in ~ (Ash.) ~ bed (Ros.)
111   world] world, (Ash.)
117   brother,] brother; (Ros.)
121   spoken, and] spoken and (Ash.)
126   head,] head: (Ash.)
127   – Ticonderoga,] – Ticonderoga – (Ash.)
130   the time of people's fears,] <all the time of fears,> ^ ~ ^ (Ash.)
131   walked] rose and walked (Ros.)
133   know,] know,' he thought (Ros.)
134   this;] this. (Ros.) this: (Ash.)
135   O, where shall I find me a skilly man] ~ skeely man, (Ash.) O where ~ (Ros.)
137–40 <Many a league he footed,
             On many a loch he sailed,
        Where the sowers sang in meadows
             Or above the eagle wailed.> (Ash.)
        {These four lines were cancelled in favour of the copy-text reading.}

141   went unweary,] went, unweary (Ash.) went unweary (Ros.)
143   written of old] written by men of old (*Scrib.*, Ros., Ash.)
148   ears.] ears. (Ros.)
151   mountains,] mountains – (*Scrib.*, Ros., Ash.)
154   craig] crag (*Scrib.*, Ros., Ash.)
155   Scotland,] Scotland (Ros.)
157   south,] south; (Ash.)
159   periwig'd lord of London,] periwigd ~ (Ros.) ~ in London (Ash.)
163   the sea and the heather,] sea and heather, (Ros., Ash.)
167   their fathers' tartan] the ancient costume (Ros., Ash.)
171   the olden,] the olden time, (*Scrib.*) the olden times (Ros., Ash.) {I have adopted the
       reading of the MSS: 'olden' is an adjective, not a noun.}
172   shrill;] shrill. (Ros.)
177   'O, why] 'O why (*Scrib.*, Ros., Ash.)
180   strife?] fight? (Ros.)
191   cry] <shriek> ^ ~ ^ (Ash.)
200   {four cancelled lines, illegible, in (Ash.)}
203   war-pipes] <long-pipes> ^ ~ ^ (Ash.)
205–12 {alt. text in *Kalakaua*:}
       'Many a name have I heard
          In all the tongues of men,
       Many both here and there,
          Many both now and then:
       At home in my father's house,
          In the land of the naked knee,
       Where the eagles fly in the lift,
          And the herrings swim in the sea.'
207   there,] there (Ash.)
208   then.] then: (Ash.)
214   hat –] hat: (Ash.)
217   place,] place (Ash.)
220   tree,] tree; (Ash.)
221   face,] face (Ash.)
222   The silent] <And strange> ^ ~ ^ (Ash.)
223   In a land of a strange, outlandish tongue] ~ strange outlandish ~ (*Scrib.*, Ros.)
       <And the strange outlandish speech> ^ ~ ^ (Ash.)
229   seen,] seen {also in lines 233, 249} (*Scrib.*, Ros., Ash.)
231   on] upon (Ros., Ash.)
234   this;] this, (Ash.)
242   land,] land (Ash.)
243   face,] face (Ash.)
245   the quiet] <the dark of the> ^ ~ ^ (Ash.)
246   ken;] ken, (Ros., Ash.)
252   {Three cancelled lines here:}
       <Now he was aware of a captain man
          Drew near to the waterside;
       And he had the self-same plaid on his back> (Ash.)

259   man] man, (*Scrib.*, Ash.)
260   lo!] lo, (Ash.)
265   O, you] O you (*Scrib.*, Ros., Ash.)
267   death;] death (Ash.)
270   They have called it Sault-Marie;] <They call it Sault Marie;> (Ash.)
273   word,'] <name> ^ ~ ^ (Ash.)
274   head:] head; (Ash.)
276   {Four lines cancelled:}
        <It had sung in his sleeping ears,
              It had hummed in his waking head,
        That name – Ticonderoga,
              The utterance of the dead.> (Ash.)
277   morning,] morning (Ros., Ash.)
280   at] <in the> ^ ~ ^ (Ash.)
281   hills of] <sea and the> ^ ~ ^ (Ash.)
282–4   <And the land from whence he came,>
        <He sleeps in the woody places>
        <In the place of the doomed>
        <From the eagles and the herrings
        And the land of the naked knee.> (Ash.)

Heather Ale: A Galloway Legend
Letter: RLS to E. L. Burlingame [5 March 1889] (*LETBM*, Vol. VI, p. 257): '*Heather Ale* is a good story harmlessly told.' {RLS included the MS with this letter, directing Scribner's to include this poem with BAL; it is the first time he mentions it. There is no evidence indicating when or where it was written.}
MSS: H2401; B6285; among the Foot MSS at Silverado are fragments, seemingly sketches for this ballad:

> 'To harry out of hill and den
> The swarthy and the dwarfish men
> The king all day
> <The king hunted>He drew his rein at set of day
> The leagues of the red heather lay,
> And <rolled before him>rolled in front, dale and height,
> To the fiery lintel of the night,
> <And the far>Far as the margin of the sea,
> Was neither house therein, nor tree;'
>
> 'Whom when death had overtook
> He found him straight of back and look,
> And after that so long pursuit
> Yet alert of limb and foot
> Who knew so well to wield the spear
> That never foeman came anear,
> Ale!' {next six lines illegible}

The HL fragment is as follows:

> 'Heard ye the tale of Gillebride
> King of the westland far and wide;
> {alt.}Hearken while I tell the tale
> Of Gillebride and the heather ale.
> A fell king was he on firth or field
> Dour to smite and [?] to yield?
> Gillebride was up with the day
> Faith he rode with [?] away
> Silent and with sullen cheer
> He roamed the country far and near.'

The BRBML fragment, the first line of which is read by McKay as 'Hear ye the tale of Gillehinde', is rougher than those above.

Christmas at Sea
Date of composition: October 1888 (*LETBM*, Vol. VI, No. 2110)
Letters: 1. RLS to Henley, 9 October [1888] (*LETBM*, Vol. VI, p. 210): 'Well here is a kind of potty screed in my customary break-tooth versification. If it came in time it struck me it might fill a corner {in the *Scots Observer*}. And if you don't care for it, you can put it in a drawer, till I get a volume of ballads ready.'

2. RLS to E .L. Burlingame [5 March 1889] (*LETBM*, Vol. VI, p. 258): 'I have another kind of a ballad, *Christmas at Sea*, ... I should like your opinion whether it should go in {to *Ballads*}: it is what the gross mass of the public would probably prefer, but is it up to the mark?'
MSS: None found.
First printing: *Scots Observer*, 22 December 1888.
Line
  7 We] They
23 blessèd] blessed {also in line 32}

Songs of Travel

History of Composition and Publication

Songs of Travel is a posthumous collection, first published December 1895, one year after the poet's death, in Vol. XIV of the Edinburgh Edition of his collected works. The following year, Chatto and Windus issued a separate edition of *ST* on 29 August.

RLS conceived this collection as an extension of *UW*: he referred to it as *Underwoods* Book III. The first mentions of either a posthumous poems volume or a collected works occur in this letter to his stepson Lloyd Osbourne, handed to him by RLS at Tautira, Tahiti, in December 1888, with instructions to open it after his death:

> Being rather out of health and a little downcast lest I should break down before I have repaid the capital used on this voyage, I write you this letter of direction ... The first thing to be done is to try and arrange among conflicting publishers about a uniform edition. On this I recommend you to consult Charles [Baxter]. I have always thought a good and (likely) a popular volume might be made of my *reliquiae*, little verses; certain of my letters etc. This should be edited (if he will) by Colvin. (*LETBM*, Vol. VI, p. 220)

This 'quite public letter', as RLS called it, became the posthumous authority for Baxter to produce and for Colvin to edit *EDIN* and for Colvin's 1899 *Letters*.

After his scheme of combining ballads and lyrics in a single volume proved impossible, RLS talked of 'a second *Underwoods*' (see above, pp. 458–60). E. L. Burlingame suggested in a letter of 23 January 1891 that some of the typewritten lyrics that had arrived too late for inclusion in *BAL* might be printed in *Scribner's Magazine*, but the disappointing reception of that work seems to have curtailed RLS's poetic ambitions for a time. Early in 1893 a bad influenza attack prompted more anxiety over his family's security. At that time he wrote to Baxter with a plan for publishing a selection of his letters but by the end of the year his old friend and agent had devised a far grander scheme: a collected edition of his works that would be modelled on the celebrated 48-volume edition of the *Waverley Novels* and sold by subscription – the *Edinburgh Edition*, expected to bring in more than £5,000. The delighted author threw himself into the project in the early part of 1894, sending Baxter this response to the suggestion that one volume would be exclusively poems: 'In the verse business I can do just what I like better than anything else and extend *Underwoods* with a lot of unpublished stuff' (*LETBM*, Vol. VIII, p. 227).

On 20 April 1894 Colvin sent out his proposals for the contents and order of *EDIN*. A month later RLS stated that the plan was 'entirely to my mind', although he was alarmed by the projected *Juvenilia* section. Rejecting the idea of reprinting *The Pentland Rising*, which he had dismissed to Baxter as schoolboy rubbish, he warned Colvin against 'hawking unripe fruit'. In her Introduction to *Collected Poems*, JAS quoted this admonition twice as having specific reference to poetry (pp. 49, 53) but in this letter it refers to early stories and essays; poetry is mentioned in the next section: 'I am sending you a lot of verses, which had best, I think, be called *Underwoods Book III*, but in what order are they to go?' (*LETBM*, Vol. VIII, No. 2733, pp. 287–9). Since he was enclosing, for editing and eventual publication, what became *ST*, he was probably not thinking of these verses as unripe fruit – he had been revising and rearranging them since February 1890.

On the same day he wrote Baxter a letter highly charged with emotion, immensely pleased to be associated with his dearest old friend in a monumental undertaking that would forever link his name with the other two Scottish 'Rabs', poets Fergusson and Burns. Wanting to dedicate *EDIN* to Fanny, he sent Baxter for this purpose the lines beginning 'I saw rain falling and the rainbow drawn' (see above, pp. 300–1) that were ultimately printed as a dedication to his wife in *Weir of Hermiston*. Finally, he reminded his agent to apply to Scribner's about American rights.

Ten days later a prospectus appeared over the signatures of Baxter and Colvin announcing that all RLS's publishers had agreed to co-operate in issuing *EDIN*, 'which will be revised by the author and issued under the supervision of Mr Sidney Colvin of the British Museum', the first volume to appear October 1894 (Prideaux and Livingston 1917: 239–41). RLS was right to worry about US rights. The day after the prospectus was issued, Scribner's London representative Lemuel Bangs sought information about it and was told by Charles Scribner that the firm had not been consulted in this matter (Scribner Archive, Princeton). Eventually RLS, fearing that the whole scheme could collapse over copyright difficulties, prodded Baxter into negotiations that resulted in Scribner's *Thistle Edition* of his collected works; Vol. XVI, dated 1895 like Vol. XIV of *EDIN*, was called *Ballads and Other Poems*. The American editor presented *ST* with a slightly different text, two poems not in *EDIN* and the very different title, *Underwoods / Book III / Being / Songs Of Travel And Other Verses / Written principally in the South Seas, 1888–1894*.

The question of RLS's involvement with published versions of *ST* is a complex one. He had begun by sending Colvin, as an enclosure with *LETBM*, No. 2733, what was presumably the typescript of verses returned by Scribner's after they came too late for inclusion with *BAL*, augmented by poems written since then. He continued to send in poems, constantly changing his mind about the sequence of the whole and about the merits of individual pieces, as in this letter to Colvin of 7 August 1894: 'Take care about the verses … I enclose another, possibly rubbish, that I had left out, and saw the other day with a relenting; judge' (*LETBM*, Vol. VIII, p. 345). In October 1895 a set of galley proofs was pulled for *ST* that went to Edmund Gosse, for they have his bookplate, some editor's blue-pencil marks and presumably the title Gosse gave them, *Posthumous Poems*: this volume, bound in green leather, is BRBML B642. Gosse's pencil note on these proofs is as follows:

> These first rough proofs … are here printed in the order in which R.L.S. sent them home. In the published edition they appear re-arranged by Sidney Colvin. Two pieces {XIII and XLIII} and a portion of a third {XXVI}, which are found here, are not in the published volume. Several minor differences will be discovered.

JAS seems to have misread 'home' in this note as 'to me' and therefore assumed that RLS had sent his projected *UW Book III* to Gosse as well as to Colvin (*CP*, p. 500). There is no evidence to support the idea that Gosse was a co-editor, although Colvin obviously consulted him. Bound up with these proofs are two letters from Colvin to Gosse concerning the merits of this lot of poems; obviously the two held critical discussions but there is no record of Gosse's opinions at this time. The variants in these proofs are recorded below.

As he had told Burlingame earlier in connection with *BAL*, RLS expected thoughtful criticism of his poems from his editors, but he proved to be hostile to some of Colvin's editorial decision-making. In the end he became so exasperated that he dissociated himself, as author, from Colvin's editorial procedures. At first he wanted to see proofs of the early volumes of *EDIN*, but as disagreements multiplied, over inclusions, omissions, revisions, prefaces, even usage and punctuation, he began to back off. In the autumn he backed out. In the first volume of *EDIN*, published November 1894, a slip was inserted acknowledging Colvin as editor but claiming that 'additions, omissions, and corrections (other than those merely of press) have the sanction and approval of the author'. On 4 November RLS wrote to Colvin trying to prevent this insertion:

> I take an extremely emphatic view against your proposed slip. Really, if you consider your letter of this month and the various corrections which you there indicate it must appear to the meanest capacity that you *are* the editor, and that I *did not* make all excisions, alterations and additions. I am afraid, my dear fellow, that you cannot thus play fast and loose. (*LETBM*, Vol. VIII, pp. 383–4)

One immediate issue here was *Moral Emblems*: RLS had argued vigorously in this letter for their inclusion but Colvin was refusing unless the poet revised them, being just as pig-headed about keeping them out as he was about keeping *The Pentland Rising* in. On the same day that he wrote to Colvin, the poet made the following unambiguous pronouncement to Baxter, in which he conceded *de facto* editorial control over *EDIN* to Colvin but at the same time stripped him of any authority to make editorial decisions in the author's name:

> As to the proposed slip, I put my foot down absolutely. It shall not appear. I have nothing to do with the Edition; no proofs have ever reached me; so far as I can hear no attempts are being made that any should reach me; Colvin writes me by this mail that he has been cutting and carving on my immortal text; I do not say that he is wrong: I do say that 'all excisions, alterations and additions' have not been made by me. They have been made by him and he must stand the responsibility. About *Moral Emblems*, what can I say? I have no power, and I am very glad of it. You and he are so kind as to undertake the Edition for me; I have agreed to accept your decisions, and there is an end of the matter as far as I am concerned. At the same time I express an opinion strongly that they ought to go in. I shall express it again direct to Colvin. *Et puis après, je m'en lave les mains.* (*LETBM*, Vol. VIII, pp. 389–90)

The bowdlerisations, pedantic 'corrections' and assorted anilities that Sidney Colvin inflicted on RLS's texts, especially on his letters, are thus explicitly repudiated in advance by their author. It is of course true that Colvin was devoted to RLS, a lifelong mentor and friend whose good faith cannot be challenged. But for him, as for Gosse, the literary world did not extend much beyond Bloomsbury and Charing Cross Road; RLS had been feeling increasingly alienated by the parochialism of his London friends and their failure to grasp the fact that he had changed, as writer and person, since leaving Europe. Baxter, trying to address RLS's complaint that he had seen nothing of the actual *EDIN* other than specimen pages, was carrying the first two published volumes with him on his way to Vailima for a reunion with his old friend when he heard at Port Said of RLS's death on 3 December.

Location and Description of Manuscripts

There is no concentrated, authoritative body of MSS. BRBML has the most important collection, possessing at least one separate (non-epistolary) MS for thirty-nine of the forty-six poems as well as several interim gatherings towards *ST*. In the section Ordonnance, below, these gatherings are described under the following titles: *Far Ballads and Songs of Travel*, *Vailima and other Verses*, *Posthumous Verse*, *Verses*, and the Gosse proofs. Many of these poems and trial contents lists were first sketched in notebooks, such as *First Drafts of Poems* (filed under B6022), and Notebook A.282, held with other uncatalogued accessions in Box 370; this latter one contains verse written at Apemama and at sea on the *Equator*. A vast amount of correspondence relating to *ST* is at BRBML, including the originals of many letters, some containing fair copies of poems, published in *LETBM*.

HL has six leaves of South Seas poetry filed as HM2401. Notebook A.270, filed as HM2404, contains several MSS. The Silverado Museum in St Helena, the Parrish Collection at Princeton and NLS in Edinburgh have significant MS material.

Ordonnance

Poem numbers from the text of this edition are arabic rather than roman in this section. Whenever an *ST* poem is mentioned, its number is appended in parentheses. Non-*ST* poems that appear in this edition are given page numbers.

In its embryonic stage, as represented by a list in the HL notebook fragment H2401, *ST* consisted of No. 37, *Heather Ale*, No. 35 (called *Sodales*), No. 29 (called *Moë*), No. 20, No. 30, No. 31 and No. 32. In the winter of 1890, it consisted of fourteen 'songs' plus four ballads, just a contents list in *LETBM*, No. 2211 (see above, p. 459); the first twelve of these 'songs' appear on a sixteen-poem contents list at Silverado, although in a somewhat different order. This list, found with the MS 'Tembinoka's conversation', is headed *Underwoods Book III* and also includes *ST* Nos 35 and 13 and ends with *The Trades* and *To F.V. de G. S* (Fanny); it comes from Notebook A.267, dismembered by Hellman. A further variation occurs in a BRBML MS (filed under B6159) containing fifteen lyrics (fourteen from *ST*) on thirteen pages with the title of *Far Ballads and Songs of Travel*, as follows:

1. *To Mother Maryanne* (32)
2. *To S.C.* (37)
3. *To The Muse* (28)
4. *A Voice from Home [The Tropics Vanish]* (36)
5. *Wandering Willie* (17)
6. *The Vagabond {portion}* (1)
7. *Ditty (To an Air from Bach)* (13)
8. *We have loved of yore* (12)
9. *To An Island Princess* (29)
10. *To Kalakaua* (30)
11. *To Princess Kaiulani* (31)
12. *To Dr Hake* (20)
13. *In Memoriam E.H.* (33)
14. *Winter* (18)
15. *To RLS (by Dr T. G. Hake)*

B6897, a one-page MS at BRBML, lists eighteen poems under the title *Songs of Travel*:

1. *To an island princess* (29)
2. *The Pearl* (30)
3. *The Little Princess* (31)
4. *Mother Maryanne* (32)
5. *To S.C.* (37)
6. *To The Muse* (28)
7. *The Tropics Vanish* (36)
8. *To Tembinoka, King and Bard* (38)
9. *Home of T[embinoka]* (38)
10. *To E.H.* (33)
11. *Dr Hake* (20)
12. *Winter* (18)
13. *Wandering Willie* (17)
14. *The Vagabond* (1)
15. *Over the sea to Skye* (44)
16. *The stormy evening* (19)
17. *Ditty* (13)
18. *To an Air of Diabelli's* (12)

At BRBML there is a bound volume containing both proofs and MSS. Filed under B7065, this collection, simply titled *Robert Louis Stevenson / Verses / Original Autograph Manuscript* (stamped on the red morocco cover), contains twenty-six poems and may be the enclosure of 'XXVI pieces ready, 675 verses' sent November 1890 (see above, p. 460): that package also contained both proofs (which he had received in Sydney that summer) and MSS. The contents are as follows:

1. *To Mother Maryanne* (32)	14. *I whom Apollo sometime* (p. 303)
2. *To S.C.* (37)	15. *The Last Sight* (43)
3. *The Tropics Vanish* (36)	16. *In dreams, unhappy* (4)
4. *The House of Tembinoka* (38)	17. *Early in the evening* (p. 334)
5. *To Dr Hake* (20)	18. *I will make you brooches* (11)
6. *Tropic Rain* (40)	19. *Ditty* (13)
7. *The Woodman* (39)	20. *She rested by the Broken Brook* (5)
8. *Let now your soul* (41)	21. *Madrigal* (7)
9. *Evensong* (46)	22. *To an air of Diabelli's* (12)
10. *In Memoriam E.H.* (33)	23. *Wandering Willie* (17)
11. *Winter* (18)	24. *Over the sea to Skye* (44)
12. *To my old familiars* (35)	25. *Farewell, fair day* (25)
13. *To the Muse* (28)	26. *He hears with gladdened heart* (24)

B6895, headed *Vailima, and other verses*, and B6896, headed *Posthumous Verse* (evidently in the hand of RLS), are the fullest contents lists for *ST* prior to the Gosse proofs; the former, totalling forty-three poems divided into four sections, reads as follows:

Vailima, and other verses

<Dedication>*To my wife* {it is unclear which poem he intended to put here}

1. *Let now your soul* (41)	(2) The Mother
2. *Evensong* (46)	(3) The Daughter
3. *The Woodman* (39)	(4) The Son
4. *Tropic Rain* (40)	(5) The Grandson
5. *The Family* (pp. 282–7)	(6) The Old Lady
(1) Mother and Daughter	(7) Tusitala

Notes of Travel

1. *To an Island Princess* (29)	4. *A Dream of London* (37)
2. *To Kalakaua* (30)	5. *The Tropics vanish* (36)
3. *To Mother Maryanne* (32)	6. *The House of Tembinoka* (38)

Verses

1. *To Dr Hake* (20)	8. *We uncommiserate pass* (42)
2. *Winter* (18)	9. *Farewell, fair day* (25)
3. *In Memoriam E.H.* (33)	10. *I have trod the upward* (23)
4. *To my old Familiars* (35)	11. *Is it a dream* {unpub.: Yale MS
5. *To The Muse* (28)	B6461; Harvard FMS Eng.269}
6. *To S.C.* (37)	12. *He hears with gladdened* (24)
7. *If this were enough* (26)	13. *I whom Apollo* (p. 303)

Songs

1. Ditty (13)
2. She rested by the Broken Brook (5)
3. Wandering Willie (17)
4. Over the sea to Skye (44)
5. Madrigal (7)
6. To an air of Diabelli's (12)
7. The Vagabond (1)
8. I will make you brooches (11)
9. In the highlands (16)
10. [illegible]
11. Songs (15)
12. Early in the evening (p. 334)
13. Blows the wind today (45)

Table 1 shows title and number for each poem in EDIN, Gosse proofs, Thistle and this edition (RCL):

Table 1   Title and number of poems in EDIN, Gosse proofs, Thistle and this edition (RCL). (Asterisk denotes poem with altrernate title)

Title	EDIN	Gosse	Thistle	RCL
The Vagabond	1	1	1	1
Youth and Love – I	2	2	2	2
Youth and Love – II	3	3	3	3
*In dreams, unhappy	4	4	4	4
[*The Unforgotten – I in Thistle]				
*She rested by	5	5	5	5
[*The Unforgotten – II in Thistle]				
The infinite shining	6	6	6	6
*Plain as the glistering	7	7	7	7
[*Madrigal in Gosse, Thistle, CP]				
To you, let snow and roses	8	8	8	8
Let Beauty awake	9	9	9	9
I know not how it is	10	10	10	10
I will make you brooches	11	11	11	11
We have loved of yore	12	13	12	12
Ditty	–	14	13	13
Mater Triumphans	13	15	14	14
Bright is the ring of words	14	16	15	15
In the highlands	15	17	16	16
Wandering Willie	16	18	17	17
Winter	17	19	26	18
The stormy evening closes	18	12	27	19
To Dr Hake	19	20	18	20
*To Sidney Colvin	20	21	19	21
[*To – in EDIN, Gosse, Thistle]				
The morning drum-call	21	22	20	22
I have trod the upward	22	23	21	23
He hears with gladdened heart	23	24	22	24
*Farewell, fair day	24	25	23	25
*[The Lost Occasion in Thistle]				
If this were Faith	25	26	24	26

Table 1 – *continued*

Title	EDIN	Gosse	Thistle	RCL
My Wife	26	27	25	27
To the Muse	27	29	34	28
To an Island Princess	28	30	28	29
To Kalakaua	29	31	29	30
To Princess Kaiulani	30	32	30	31
To Mother Maryanne	31	33	31	32
In Memoriam E.H.	32	34	32	33
*To My Wife	33	28	33	34
[*To The Same – follows 27 in Gosse]				
To My Old Familiars	34	35	35	35
The Tropics Vanish	35	36	36	36
To S.C.	36	37	37	37
The House of Tembinoka	37	38	38	38
The Woodman	38	39	39	39
Tropic Rain	39	40	40	40
An End of Travel	40	41	41	41
We uncommiserate pass	41	42	42	42
The Last Sight	–	43	43	43
Sing me a song	42	44	44	44
To S.R. Crockett	43	45	45	45
Evensong	44	46	46	46

Printed Text

The copy-text chosen is *Songs of Travel* as it appears in Vol. XIV of the *Edinburgh Edition*. Colvin's prefatory note on p. [276] states the pertinent facts:

> The following verses are here collected for the first time. The author had tried them in several different orders and under several different titles, as *Songs and Notes of Travel*, *Vailima*, *Posthumous Poems*, etc.; finally leaving their naming and arrangement to the present editor, with the suggestion that they should be added, as Book III, to future editions of *Underwoods*.

In the Prefatory Note to his separate edition of ST (1896), Colvin adds: 'This suggestion it is proposed to carry out.' He did not, however, do so, even though the poet's suggested addition of these poems to UW had already been carried out by the editor of *Thistle*. Despite Colvin's habit of ignoring the poet's stated intentions, there is no alternative to EDIN as copy-text. RLS explicitly designated Colvin as the editor of his verses, sending him finished copy and leaving the final ordering up to him. I have made alterations in Colvin's text: for instance I have followed *Thistle* and subsequent editions in choosing to include the two poems present in the Gosse proofs but eliminated from EDIN and ST (1896). When I emend the EDIN text from MSS, letters, proofsheets or other printed sources, I give reasons for doing so in the textual Notes on Individual Poems below.

First Edition

The Works of Robert Louis Stevenson. Edinburgh, 1894–[98]. First collected edition, known as the Edinburgh Edition. Twenty-seven volumes plus Appendix. 1,035 signed and numbered copies. Bound in dark-red buckram intended to resemble the original ruddy cloth used to bind the 48-volume set of Scott's *Waverley Novels*. Demy 8vo with printed paper labels. Handmade laid paper with 'RLS' watermark. End-papers deep brownish red or maroon. Top edges gilt; other edges uncut.
Volume XIV: 'THE WORKS OF / ROBERT LOUIS / STEVENSON / POETRY / [Publisher's device] / EDINBURGH / PRINTED BY T. AND A. CONSTABLE FOR / LONGMANS GREEN AND CO: CASSELL AND CO. / SEELEY AND CO: CHAS. SCRIBNER'S SONS / AND SOLD BY CHATTO AND WINDUS / PICCADILLY: LONDON / 1895. *Songs of Travel and other Verses* pp. [275]–326.'

Variants

A cancel leaf for pp. 291–2 was issued correcting an error in *ST*, No. XVI on p. 291, lines 15 and 16: line 15, 'Lo, the valley hollow', had been omitted and terminal punctuation for line 16 was corrected from '.' to '!' A note was also issued on a loose slip requesting that the cancel leaf might be substituted in Vol. XIV. Variants among *EDIN*, *Thistle*, the Gosse proofs and the separate edition of 1896 are recorded in the textual Notes on Individual Poems below. McKay, Vol. II, No. 737, p. 373, states that some copies of the regular issue were bound in full black morocco.

First American Edition

Volume XVI of the 27-volume *Thistle Edition* of RLS's works, December 1895:
'BALLADS AND OTHER / POEMS OF ROBERT / LOUIS STEVENSON / A CHILD'S GARDEN OF / VERSES [ornament] UNDER – / WOODS [ornament] BALLADS [ornament] / PUBLISHED IN / NEW YORK BY / CHARLES SCRIBNER'S / SONS [ornament] 1895.' Bound in red cloth with lettering and ornaments in gold on spine: [thistle ornament] *Ballads / And Other / Poems* / [thistle ornament] / *Robert / Louis / Stevenson* / [thistle ornament] / *Scribners.* Title, author's name and single-line border stamped in gold on front cover. Laid paper with watermark: CSS. Plain end-papers. Top edge gilt; other edges uncut. *Underwoods / Book III / Being / Songs of Travel and other Verses / Written principally in the South Seas, 1888–1984* is on pp. 197–265.

First Separate Edition

SONGS OF TRAVEL / AND OTHER VERSES / BY / ROBERT LOUIS STEVENSON / [printer's device] / LONDON / CHATTO & WINDUS, PICCADILLY / 1896 Crown 8vo. [A] ⁶ B – F ⁸ G ⁴ pp. x + 88: [–] [i – vi] vii – ix [x] 1 – 85 [86 – 88] Tipped in at end pp. [1] – 32: list of books published by Chatto and Windus dated July 1896. First printing of 500 copies issued 29 August 1896. Bound in dark-blue cloth with lettering in gold on spine within two single-line borders in gold: *Songs / of / Travel / R. Louis / Stevenson / Chatto & Windus.* Wove paper. Plain end-papers. The contents are the same as *EDIN*, although Colvin's prefatory note differs slightly and there are some textual variants, recorded below. There was a second printing in 1896, a re-issue.

Textual Notes on Individual Poems

I *The Vagabond*
MSS: B7076, B7077, B7078
B7076 is a rough draft of thirty-six lines with many illegible passages, as follows:

> 'Prison bond, or future cursed
>   Let what will be o'er me
> [Give the face of earth around
>   And the road before me.]
> Perish <all my loans><debt>all I owe to time
>   And all that any owe me,
> Give me but the heaven above,
>   <And>the open road below me.'
>
> 'White as meal the <frozen>wintry mire
>   And the frozen furrow
> I will build my hedgerow fire,
>   I will doze and burrow.
> <To and fro>the limping hare
>   Hirples to behold me
> Here I <lie>gypsy cold and bare
>   <For>A house would never hold me!'
>
> 'Now the pinching robin sees
>   And the frozen sparrow
> Turning toasty toes and knees,
>   Behind a broken barrow.
> I am fettered, I am bound
>   If a house be o'er me
> <Seek not>Vain the hope to roof or board
>   To window or to door me.'
>
> 'Give the jolly heaven above
>   The open road below me,
> <All the fallows fill with mire,
>   Empty my larder.>
> When the ploughman fills with mire
> Cleared the wayside, and the noonday darkles
> I will build a hedgerow fire
> And blow it <up with ardour>till it sparkles
> Cossetted old gentlemen
> Tell me that they told me!
> I but spit and stretch again ...'

B7077 contains a draft of stanzas 2 and 3:
Line
11 Give] Since

13   seek] ask
15   All I seek, the heaven above] All I ask the heav'n above,
20   finger.] finger,
21   field –] field,
22   Warm the fireside haven –] And the fire side heaven –
31   above] above, (Gosse proofs, *Thistle*)
B7078, a draft of the first fifteen lines, is a printer's copy from the MS *Far Ballads and Songs of Travel*; doubtless the MS of the other seventeen lines is lost.
Title. *The Vagabond (To an air of Schubert)*] *The Vagabond* (Schubert's Ninth)
Number I] <XII><XIV>^XV^
Line
 3   Give the ... heaven] Give me the ... heav'n
12   me.] me!
15   heaven] heav'n
{After 'me' at the end of line 30, *EDIN* and *Thistle* have a full stop, *ST* (1896) has a semicolon; as this line repeats line 14, which terminates with a semicolon, I have adopted that reading.}

II *Youth and Love – I*
MS: B7207
Title: *Youth and Love – I*] *Youth and Love*
Line
 2   parted.] parted:
 5   arise,] arise
 8   Odyssey] odyssey
 9   Kosmos] kosmos
11   open] onward
13   well, the cross,] weal, <come>the cross,
15   down] here

III *Youth and Love – II*
MSS: B7208, B6534, NLS 8842
{MSS of poems submitted by RLS for publication in the *Pall Mall Gazette* were kept together and eventually sold (Sotheby Catalogue, 24 July 1979, lots 286–90). NLS 8842 was one of them; it was published in the *Gazette*, 17 January 1895, and in the *Pall Mall Budget*, 24 January 1895; the other MSS were *ST* XVI, XVII, XLIV and XLV and *Auld Reekie* (above, p. 278).}
Title: *Youth and Love – II*] *Youth and Love* (B7208)
Number: In B7208 the two poems are written in reverse order from the copy-text; in NLS
          ST III has '<XIII>XIV' above the title and 'I' below it
Line
 2   for ever] forever (B7208, NLS)
 3   gardens golden] gardens, golden (B7208)
 6   down,] down (B7208)
 7   He to ... nobler fate] He, to ... nobler fate, (NLS)
                                ~ <godlier ~ >^nobler ~ ^ (B7208)
 8   Fares; and] <Passes>^Fares,^ and

10   Sings but a boyish stave and his face is gone.]
      <Passes and passes still in <<the wind and>>the dust and sun.>
      Sings <a heroic>^but a boyish^ ~ (B7208)
B7207, binding title 'Youth & love and other verses' continues the twenty-six lines of ST II
and III with four more four-line stanzas. McKay gives these sixteen lines a separate number,
B6534, and CP prints them as a separate poem on p. 67, but, as they seem to continue the
thought of ST III, they may be an unused part III of the Youth and Love unit:

'A little before me, and hark!
The dogs in the village bark.
And see, in the blank of the dark,
  The eye of a window shine!

There stands the inn, the small and rude,
In this earth's vast robber-wood
The inn with the beds and the food,
  The inn of the shining wine.

We do but bait on life's bare plain,
And through the new day's joy and pain
Reach to the baiting place again.
  O rest, for the night, be mine!

Rest for the night! For to love and rest,
To clasp the hands, to keep the nest,
Are only human at the best;
  To move and to suffer divine.'

IV 'In dreams, unhappy, I behold you stand'
MSS: B6406, B6407, B6408, B6409
Title: untitled] The Unforgotten – I (Thistle)
Number: IV] XVI (B6408)
Line
  1   In dreams, unhappy, I behold you stand]
      Unhappy, in the door I see you stand (B6406)
  2   As heretofore:] as heretofore, (B6406)
  3   tokens] token (B6406)
  4   Avail] Avails (B6406)
  9   He came and went. Perchance you wept a while]
      May came and went; you wept <a little while>^perchance a while^ (B6406)
      <May>^He^ ~ awhile (B6408) May came … You wept perchance ~ (B6409)
      He came, he went. ~ (Thistle)
 11   Ah me! but] <I trust; but><Remember>^Ah me, but^ (B6406)
                                          Ah, me! (B6408, B6409)
{B6406 continues after line 12 as follows:}
      <Perchance you waited, hoped, aspired, expected – pined
                    Perchance away;>

<The wound of his dishonour in his mind>
Bleeds to this day.
‹Forget! The wronged forget.
Forgets you and forgot you nevermore
Your hand and name,
Plucked at his heart>'

V 'She rested by the Broken Brook'
MSS: B6837, B6838
Title: untitled] *The Unforgotten* – II (*Thistle*)
Number: V] XX (B6838)
Line
1 Broken Brook] <b>^B^roken <b>^B^rook (B6837)
3 moved] <found> ^ ~ ^ (B6837)
4 Ah,] <And,>Ah! (B6837)
{In *EDIN* there is a space between stanzas after line 4; B6837 has two stanzas of eight lines each with an incomplete, trial 3rd stanza, mostly cancelled, ending in fragments; the following transcription of B6837 begins at line 5:}

'She came, she fared {"passed" B6838} like summer rains,
She went like summer dew:
The azure of her eyes remains
Eternal in my view.

<She went – I know>^I know it well,^ in other lands,
Embowered by fairer skies,
Her hands shall mix with other hands
Her eyes with other eyes.
<The glitter of the sunny rain,
The glint of summer dew
The lad that gazed and gazed again,
Will she remember too?>

<She went, the city called aloud,>
<To come, among the dirty crowd,>
She <went>vanished <and><but>in the sounding town,
<Will>Does she remember too?
Does she recall the eyes of brown,
As I recall the blue?'

5–8 {B6838 is identical with B6837 except for one word, 'passed', in line 5.}

VI 'The infinite shining heavens'
MSS: None found.

VII *Madrigal*
MSS: B6913, B6720, B6721

{B6913, despite its separate McKay no., is an early, untitled eleven-line draft of *ST* VII:}

'The stars of night no plainer shine
In wells and watery brooks
Then love appeared and called on mine
And melted in her looks.
The beacon-lamp that Hero set
No fairer shone on sea
No plainer called
        But was the call for me?
<Starshine>The stars at night no brighter burn
These brimming lustrous beauties turn
        But do they turn for me?'

B6720 is a thirty-three-line pencil draft:
Number: VII] XXI
Line {MS has no stanza breaks.}

1   Plain as the glistering planets shine] <No plainer <<glow>>^show^ the stars
                                above><The stars of> ^ ~ glistered ~ ^
2   cleaned] <swept><cleared> ^ ~ ^
3   Her love appeared, appealed for mine]
                        <Then love appeared – appealed for love> ^ ~ mine,^
        {*EDIN* and *Thistle* have no comma at the end of this line but all the MSS and *ST*
        (1896) do, so I have adopted it.}
4   wantoned] melted
7   Those … turned,] These … turned
9   beacon-lamp] beacon lamp
10   shone on] <over>^ ~ ^
11   plainlier summoned … wit,] <clearlier called on>^ ~ wit^
13   I thrilled to feel her influence near,] <As [?] bugles pealing near>^ ~ ^
14   I struck my flag at sight.] <As sudden drums at night.> ^ ~ ^
15   smote] struck
17–18   I ran as, at the cannon's roar,
                The troops the ramparts man –]
        <I ran, I waited not for more
                Her chattel, squire and man> ^ I ran, as at ~ ^
21   lo! that servant stands]<here your servant stands;><see the servant stand>^ ~ ^
22   men,] men.
23   And should you need] <Should you require>^Yet should you lack^
24   He bows and goes] <He bows and goes>^I can but go^
B6721, from *Verses* (B7065), is the latest version:
Number: VII] XXI
Title: untitled] *Madrigal*
Line
 1 glistering] glistered
 9 beacon-lamp] beacon lamp
19 yore] yore,
21 lo! that] lo! <you> that

{Since the title *Madrigal* was used in B7065 and the Gosse proofs, and restored by the editors of *Thistle* and *CP*, I have adopted it in this edition.}

VIII *Dark Women*
Letter: Fanny Stevenson to Colvin (quoted *CP*, p. 501): {The date of this letter is unrecorded but it must have been written during Colvin's preparation of *ST* for the press.} 'I have just received your letter asking about adding the poem addressed to me, "Dusky, trusty," etc. {XXVII} to the new edition. Do just what you think well to do. It is a very beautiful thing, and I do not think it would be bad taste to publish it … But there was another that Louis rather liked – I *think* it was called "In praise of dark women"; what do you think of adding that? I only suggest the looking at it.' {Colvin did add *My Wife* as XXVII but included only the 2nd and 3rd stanzas of *Dark Women* as VIII, suppressing the remainder. JAS printed four additional stanzas in her notes while holding her nose and commending Colvin's omission of them from his text (*CP*, pp. 503–4). The poem was first printed in a six-stanza version by Belle Strong (one of the dusky women celebrated along with her mother in the poem) in *R.L.S. Teuila* (1899).}
MSS: B6136, B6137, B6138, BRBML 903104–6 (Uncat.), Gosse (printed in *CP*, pp. 503–4); Silverado (Foot).
{B6136 is an early sixty-eight-line draft; B6137 is a thirty-four-line sketch of stanzas 7 and 8; B6138 is the version Belle Strong printed in *Teuila*, recorded in her Vailima journal known as *Grouse in the Gunroom*: I use this MS in the following collation as *Teuila* contains numerous errors; BRBML is a rough fragment; Gosse appears in *Biographical Notes* (1908), p. 124; in *The True Stevenson* (1925), Hellman printed a facsimile of Foot on pp. [224–6]. Since none of these MSS is suitable as a copy-text, I have resorted to conflation; a full collation follows:}
Title: *Dark Women* (Teuila); *To A Dusky Woman* (Foot); *Tiger Lilies* (written in pencil on B6136 but not by RLS): all other MSS untitled.
Line
1 cease from singing] <leave my station> ∧ ~ ∧ (B6136) ~ singing, (Gosse)
2 unsung,] unsung. (B6138, Foot)
3 women] the women (Foot) women, (Gosse)
4 I have loved … young;] <I have loved>∧I've loved∧ ~ (B6136)
                    I've loved ~ (Gosse) ~ young, (Foot) young. (B6138)
5 They shine] That shine (Foot, B6138) That shone (B6136)
8 dear] clear (Gosse)
9 you, let] you let (B6138)
10 belong:] belong. (*EDIN*)
13 For her … lustre] But for her … lustre, (B6138)
14 Whose favour still I wear,] <For her that I call fair>∧ ~ ∧ (B6136)
16 hair!] hair. (B6138)
17 highland rivers] <a highland river> ∧Highland rivers∧ (B6136)
                a highland river (B6138, Foot) Highland ~ (Gosse)
18 Careering,] <That's flowing,>∧ ~ ∧ (B6136) That's flowing, (B6138, Foot)
20 pool;] pool – (*EDIN*)
21 heather honey,] heather-honey, (*EDIN*)
22 honey bees,] honey-bees, (*EDIN*)
23 shoulder,] shoulder (B6138)

{Stanzas 4 and 5, lines 25–40, appear only in B6136:}
25   Dark as a wayside gypsy,] <She shall be black and tawny> ^ ~ ^
38   shall] <must>^ ~ ^
40   fight and die.] <combat>^ ~ ^
      {The following stanza in B6136 does not appear in any other version:}
      'Take, O tiger lilies
              O beautiful ones – my soul
      Love lives in your body
              As fire slumbers in coal.
      I have been young and am old,
      <I have gloried in love and strife – >
      <Now I am done with my days>
              And trodden various ways
      And the touch of a dusky woman
              Is the <true>^dear^ reward of life.'
      {The following fragment was cancelled in B6137:}
      'I knew the good and the evil,
              I count and I recall,
      And the touch of a dusky woman
              Is the dearest joy of all.'
41   There shines in her glowing favour] {alt.} 'In her face of yellow and azure' (B6136)
43   coal] <gold>^ ~ ^ (B6136) {Belle Strong has 'topaz' in Teuila.}
44   brook;] brook. (Foot) brook (B6138)
45   sunshine,] <sunlight>^ ~ ^ (Foot)
46   Or] And (Gosse, Foot)
49   old,] old; (Gosse) old (B6137)
50   And trodden various ways,] ~ ways (B6138)
      I have trodden various ways; (Gosse)
      <Now I am done with my days> ^ ~ ways ^ (B6137)
51   behold] <look back> ^ ~ ^ (B6137)
52   bygone days,] by-gone days; (Gosse) by gone days. (B6137)
      {This stanza fragment precedes the concluding lines in B6137:}
      '<The beat of my eager heart
              Burns to you true as before
      I follow you still as I followed>
      You are, as you were ever,
              In my days and lands,
      The joy of my hungry eyesight,
              The desire of my empty hands.'
58   goal; –] goal, (Gosse)
60   whole.] whole; (Gosse)
61   morning] morning, (B6137)
62   recall;] recall, (Gosse) recall (B6137)
63   dusky] <swarthy> ^ ~ ^ (Foot)
64   Outweighed] Outweighs (Gosse)
      {BRBML is a sketch from which some lines suggest a link with this poem:}
      'I found her on a mainland with the rivers and the breeze

I found her in a mountain like the spirit of the place;
Golden was her bosom as the humming honey bees,
And brown as heathen being was her sun-beloved face.'

IX 'Let Beauty awake in the morn from beautiful dreams'
MSS: None found.

X 'I know not how it is with you –'
MS: Pierpont Morgan MA500
Number: X] XV
{MS stanzas were numbered 1–3: RLS transposed and renumbered stanzas 2 and 3 to achieve
the printed order. Stanza numbers, not in *EDIN*, are included here.}
Line
10   symphony] <sympathy>^ ~ ^

XI 'I will make you brooches and toys for your delight'
Letter: RLS to Henley, 15 July 1894 (*LETBM*, Vol. VIII, p. 330): 'You and Meredith and
Yeats are the only people I would have singing, and not the present Meredith, but the singer
of *Love in a Valley*. Yeats I mention, though I may say I do not know his work; but all the
snatches that have come my way are very tuneful and genuine; and one piece, *The Lake Isle
of Innisfree*, has simply refused to leave my memory:
"And always, day and night, I hear lake water lapping with low sounds by the shore."
How good that spondee is! It is almost a discovery of modern prosody what a good effect is
to be got out of the English spondee.'
MSS: H2401, B6376, B6377, B6378
Magazine publication: *Pall Mall Gazette*, 3 January 1895; *Pall Mall Budget*, 10 January 1895;
no MS of this poem was in the 1979 Sotheby's sale (see above, p. 485).
The HL draft, scattered across four pages of notebook fragments from the South Seas period,
suggests that this version of the poem began in imitation of Yeats:

'<I will arise and go> where
Fair son of man
But if you come courting me
Green days in forests and blue days at sea
Bird song at morning & starshine at night
I will build a palace <on the shores>^in the field^ of time
<For I shall <<take>>^bear^ you <<farther>> and take and make you mine>
<Happy>Green days for us then that'll be years, and its there that you'll be mine,
When the green leaves rustle and the blue days shine.

I will <fashion>make you brooches and rings for your delight
Of bird-song at morning and starshine at night
And I will make a palace that's fit for you and me
Of green days in forests and blue days at sea.

And you shall have to drink in the <country><cabin where>autumn when we stay
<Of>The rare air of even, <and>the fair air of day;

<For><And><So>You shall make your diet <of better things than these>
^afar across the seas^
Of the good roots of digging and the rude fruits of trees
For the country <we shall live in>^where we're going^ is the land that has
The good fruits flourish and the fair air blows.

<And>For its you shall be the queen, and its I shall be the king,
Where the <full stream whispers>^white stream gushes^ and the <high>broom birds sing.
<For all that I am>And this shall be for music, when no one else is near –
The fine song for singing, the rare song to hear.
The song that I remember, and all the world forgets,
Of the brown plain that stretches, the red sun that sets.
<Red stars in houses and white stars on high>
<So <<say>>^bid^ farewell to <<chambers>>^cities^, and [?] your ways along
<Now say farewell to all, for its you have heard the song,>
<It's the fine song I'll sing you, the <<rare>>^strange^ song you'll hear>
The fine song for singing, the rare song to hear
The broad road that wanders, the bare feet that walk,
<When the white racing rivers and the [?] blow>
[several illegible fragments]
<And the great wheel of nature that turns all the time.>'

B6377 has three stanzas but, unlike the copy-text, these stanzas have six rather than four lines; B6378 is printer's copy from *Verses* (B7065); collation with the Yale MSS follows:
Number: XI] XVIII (B6378)
Line
    1   and toys] and <rings>^toys^ (B6377)
    2   bird-song] birdsong (B6378)
    3   palace fit for you and me] palace, fit for you and me, (B6377)
    {5–6}   <For> it's there that I'll be yours, <and> it's there that you'll be mine
             Where the green leaves rustle and the blue days shine. (B6377, B6378)
    5   will ... my kitchen, ... room,] shall ... <your>^my^ kitchen ... room (B6377)
    8   dewfall] dew-fall (B6377)
    {11–12} <For>It's you shall be the queen, <and>it's I shall be the king,
             When the full stream gushes and the brown birds sing. (B6377)
    11–12   That only I remember, that only you admire,
             Of the broad road that stretches and the roadside fire.]
             The song that I remember, <that>and all the world forgets,
             Of the brown plain that stretches, the red sun that sets, (B6377)
             {alt.} The broad road that wanders, the bare feet that go,
             Where the white rain kisses and the loud winds blow. (B6377)

XII *We Have Loved of Yore*
    (*To an air of Diabelli*)
MSS: B7098, B7101, BRBML Uncat. Proof (B7065)
{The following fragment at the beginning of B7098 may be the genesis of this poem:}

'Up the river where the berries hang in the island brakes
Up the still enchanted river
Where the ruby berries cluster islanded
Where the mill wheel hums, and sings the weir
Where the mill wheel shakes the lilies
Where berried and begarlanded the islands ...

Too late, your love is murdered,
Too late you see before you, the love that might have been
What was to be is finished, what is to be begun
The seal of the eternal proclaims your story done
Too late the fault repented, too late the evil seen
Too late the love that might have been.'

{B7098 continues in this loose, experimental fashion, with much repetition and revision, for some 150 lines; the following is a selective transcription, as was the *BBS* version (II, pp. 123–36) printed in *NP*, pp. 214–17:}

'Like the stream, golden the sky above
Bright were your eyes in the gray night
We have lived, my love, O, we have lived, my love.

Now along the silent river
Through the heaven's inverted image
Swiftly ran the shallop of our love
In the reedy mazes winds the river
See of old the lovers' shallop steer.

Berried brake and reedy island,
Heaven below and only heaven above,
Through the sky's inverted image
Swiftly swam the shallop of our love.

Days of April, airs of Eden
Call to mind how bright the minutes
When our boat drew homeward filled with flowers
O darling call them to mind, love the past my love.

Days of April, airs of Eden;
How the glory died through golden hours,
And the shining moon arising,
How the boat drew homeward filled with flowers!
Age and winter close us slowly in.
O half in vain they grow old
Now the halcyon days are over
Age and winter close us slowly round
And beside the winter fagot
Joan and Darby sit and doze and dream

> See the berries in the island brake
> Dream they hear the weir
> See the gliding shallop mar the stream
> Hark, in your dreams do you hear?
> Frost has bound our flowing river,
> Snow has whitened all our island brake.'

{The next fourteen lines closely approximate the 1st stanza of the copy-text, including indentation; variants occur as follows:}
Line
  2   below, and] below and
  3   azure] image
  4   Softly] Swiftly
  5   Bright] Dear
  8   Eden,] Eden:
 13   lived, my love –] lived my love,
 14   loved, my love.] lived my love.
> 'Hear the river ripple in the reeds
> Lo, in dreams they see their shallop
> Run the lilies down and drown the weeds
> Mid the sound of crackling fagots
> Happy past returns, today recedes.'

{The next fourteen lines approximate the 2nd stanza of the copy-text, although the indentation differs and the lines are not in the same order; variants occur as follows:}
Line
 16   brake,] brake;
 19   Still, in the river of dreams] Still in the hush of the past
 20   love –] love,
 21   oar!] oar.
 24   those … agèd] these … aged
 26   O my love!] my love:
{B7101 is a fair copy in file B6159, *Far Ballads and Songs of Travel*:}
Number: XII] <XVIII>^XIX^
Title: *We Have Loved of Yore (To an air of Diabelli)*] *An air* <of><after>*of Diabelli's*
Line
  2   Heaven … heaven] Heav'n … heav'n
  4   love.] love
 19   dreams] dreams,
 24   agèd] aged
{The uncatalogued, annotated proofsheet, page number 31 (in *Verses*, filed under B7065), has marginal instructions in RLS's hand to put the 1st stanza into the same format as the 2nd; there are revisions and variants as follows:}
Number/title: XII. *We Have Loved of Yore (To an air of Diabelli)*]
                    <XVIII>^XXII^ <To> *An Air of Diabelli's*
Line
  1   Berried] <Buried>^Berried^
  2   Heaven … heaven] Heav'n … heav'n

10 {Terminal comma appears in the MSS and *ST* (1896) but not in *EDIN* or *Thistle*; it has been adopted.}
19 ~~dreams~~] ~~dreams,~~
24 agèd] aged
26 O] O,
28 O,] <Oh,>^O,^

XIII ~~Ditty~~
  (*To an air from Bach*)
Date of composition: March 1876 (B6157 is so dated: *CP* states that the poem was written at Vailima (p. 505) but the version first published in *Thistle* was an extensive revision of the six-line fragment B6157, torn from Notebook A.155, and the early sixteen-line sketch in B8333 in the *Travels with a Donkey* notebook dating from 1879.
Text and MSS: the poem appears in the Gosse proofs of *EDIN* but was omitted by Colvin; the text followed here is that of the poem's first publication, in Scribner's *Thistle Edition* of 1895, p. 214. It also appeared on p. 9 of the Christmas 1895 number of *Black and White Magazine*. BRBML has five MSS: B6157, B6158, B6159, B8333, B7065 (uncatalogued proof). At Silverado there is an eight-line draft among the Foot MSS. B8333, untitled, seems the earliest version:

> 'When I shall be no more
> The cocks shall sing aloud in the morning gray,
>   In the morning gray,
> The jolly cocks shall sing
> And merry bugles ring,
> <But quiet in a shroud, I shall lie down,
> I shall not mind the day>
> But I'll be in my shroud
> In the underground.
> <Love nor hate nor sun.
> I shall not heed the bells
> Purple e'en or morning gray,
> I shall be below the sod
> While my fellows go abroad>
> <The rain is over and done
> I am aweary, dear, of love,
> Aweary of the sun.>I look below and look above
> On russet maiden, rustling dame,
> And love's so slow and <life>time so long,
> And hearts and eyes so blindly [?]
> I am half weary of my love
> And pray that life was done.'

{Foot is written in pencil:}
> 'The cock shall crow in the morning gray
> The bugles blow at the <dawn>break of day
> The cock shall crow, and the merry bugles blow
> And all the little brown birds <are singing in the spray>

^are quiring in the grass.^
Here thorn shall flower in the month of May
And my love shall go in her holiday array,
But I shall be in the kirkyard nigh
While all the little brown birds are <singing>quiring in the May.'

{B6159 is a fair copy for *Far Ballads and Songs of Travel*; it is arranged in fourteen rather than twelve lines as lines 5 and 10 in *Thistle* are each broken into two lines here:}
Title/number: XIII Ditty (To an air from Bach)]
                    <XVII>^XVIII^ *Ditty (To an air <after>^from^ Bach)*
Line
  4   At the break of day:] <In the golden day,>^At the break of day;^
  5   merry bugles ring,] <jolly>^merry^ bugles <sing><blow>^ring,^
{The uncatalogued, annotated proof page numbered 32 (in *Verses*, filed under B7065) has a fourteen-line version but RLS has indicated in the margin that he wants lines 5–6 and 12–13 to be combined, making it a twelve-line version as in *Thistle*. He has also written in 'Ditty' at the top of the untitled proof.}
Number: XIII] XIX
Line
  4   day:] day;
  5   and the merry] and merry
 10   array:] array;
 11   nigh] nigh,
{The only variant in the Gosse proofs is 'When' for 'While' in line 13.}

XIV *Mater Triumphans*
MSS: B6568, B6569
Magazine publication: *The New Review*, January 1895
{The first stanza in B6568 is quite different from *ST*:}

'Son of my woman's body
You go on the march of life,
To taste the colour of love
And the other side of life.
Eternal swing of the balance,
Eternal head and tail,
Eternally through the ages from the female and the male.'

{The rest of B6568 collates with *ST* as follows, although the lines are differently ordered in the MS and the text:}
Line
  5   toes, and] toes and
  6   gems and the tongue … speech;] gems, the tongue … speech.
  9   king, … priest,] King, … priest
 10   the breast.] <my>^the^ ~ ^
 11   rings,] rings.
 12   You, that … doors, shall …] You that … doors, you shall
B6569 is a twelve-line fair copy:

Title: *Mater Triumphans*] <*Mater Triumphans*>^ *Triumph*^
Line
1   you go, to] you go to
2   life –] life.
3   From out of the dainty the rude, the strong from out of the frail,]
    <Eternal swing of the balance, eternal head and tail><Out of the rude the dainty, out
    of the strong the frail>^ ~ ^
5   toes, and] toes and
10 nozzle] *EDIN* and *Thistle* have 'nozzle' but *ST* (1896) and B6568–9 have 'nuzzle', which
    I have adopted.}
11 bosom shall] bosom, shall
{'Kings', the final word in the poem, is capitalised in *EDIN*, *Thistle* and B6568 but not in *ST*
(1896) or B6569: I have adopted 'kings'.}

XV 'Bright is the ring of words'
MSS: B6051; B6052
{B6051 is a much-tattooed forty-one-line draft in pen and pencil filling a folio page in a
notebook called '*First Drafts of Poems*' (filed as B6022). One of the most fascinating of the
poet's MSS, it has drawn much comment: this notebook page is reproduced in facsimile in
Robert H. Taylor and Herman W. Liebert, *Authors at Work*, New York: The Grolier Club,
1957, No. 44; it is facsimiled, transcribed and analysed in P. J. Croft, *Autograph Poetry in the
English Language*, New York: McGraw-Hill, 1973, Vol. II, p. 145. What catches the eye first
is an ugly stain in the upper left corner, half an inch from the first word of text, evidently the
result of RLS squashing a tropical insect – he has identified the mark as 'a yellow beast's guts',
signing himself 'The Bard!' The MS deteriorates in clarity and effectiveness as the poet tries
to extend the first eight-line stanza with a series of quatrains, most of which were abandoned,
chips on the workshop floor, as he compacted more than thirty lines into the eight
comprising the 2nd stanza in *ST*. In an MS note inserted into B6022 at this point, Roger
Swearingen commented as follows:

> The first stanza came readily, was perhaps already composed in the poet's mind, the
> second less easily, with an alternative reading in pencil at the right; the third only with
> difficulty, perhaps because of the distraction of the insect whose demise he records.

Collation of the 1st stanza follows, then a transcription of the rest of B6051:
Title: {untitled}] *Songs*
Line
2   them,] them;
5   said –] said <;>^ – ^
6   carried –] carried <;>^ – ^
    'After the <man>^maker^ is laid
            In the grave of thistles,
    Still the lover <hums>^sings^
            And the ploughboy whistles:

    After the story is done
            And the field foughten

The charm {alt. "spell"} of the <spoken>^uttered^ word
        Is unforgotten:

<After>^Low as^ the <maker>^singer^ lies
        In the fair field of heather,
The <beautiful><wonderful><fair>lilt of songs
        Goes on forever.

Lasses and lads shall sing
        His carols together. {alt. "In the summer weather."}
Music and song <and>^shall^{alt. "forever"} sound
        In the April weather.

Low as the singer lies
        In the field of heather,
Songs of his fashion bring
        The swains together.

{alt. "She [?] to the wheel"} So to her singing wheel
        How the granddam chanted
So at <her>^the^ mother's knees,
        The father panted.

And <lo>when the west is red
        With the sunset embers,
The lover <lingers><courts>^searches^ & sings
        <And>The maid remembers.

<And>Song, <the><fair>bright <and>from of old,
        By years and <the>weather
Binds, with a chain of gold,
        <The>Ages together.'

{B6052 is a fair copy in Belle Strong's journal, *Grouse in the Gunroom*:}
Line
10   heather,] heather
12   together.] together,

XVI 'In the highlands, in the country places'
MSS: B6424, B6680, Princeton (Parrish), NLS 3791, NLS 7483
Magazine publication: *Pall Mall Gazette*, 21 December 1894; *Pall Mall Budget*, 27 December
1894; see note on *Youth and Love* II, p. 485.
{B6424 is an early sketch of forty-six lines:}

        'Near the murmuring river in the grasses
        Through green island meadows dreams and passes
        When the quiet evening music
        Broods and dies.

Let the "unco privileged" hear it
Hear and keep it holy, hear and near it
Let the enraptured spirit
Droop and die.

Mark the last faint thrill of sound expiring
Till we hear essential silence quiring
O'er entranced stream and
Dreaming hill.

In the highlands, in the country places,
Where the old plain men have rosy faces,
And the young fair lasses
‿   Quiet eyes.

Where essential silence cheers and blesses,
And forever in the hill recesses
Her more lovely music
Broods and dies.

For to you then only the flowers and grasses
<For only the silent are thine, the flowers and grasses:>
Only the mightier movement sounds and passes
<Rains and wind and>
<Life and death>
Only <the>winds and rivers <and>
Life and death.

<O<<then>> to dream, <<then>>O to arise and wander,
There, <<to hearken,>>and with delight <<then>> to take and render
 <<For>>Through a trance of silence
Quiet breath.>
<Only silence. O my soul to hear it,
Hear and keep it holy, hear and fear it.>

O to mount again where erst <we>^I^ haunted
Where the old red hills are bird-enchanted,
And the low green meadows
Flower bestarred.

And <the golden>^when^ even dies, the million-tinted,
<And when cottage windows forth have glinted,>
^And the night has come and planets glinted^
Lo, the valley hollow
Lamp bestarred!'

{B6680 has a draft of the first four lines:}

> 'In the highlands in the country places
> Where the sheep go bleating up the hills
> Where the old plain men have rosy faces
> <And>Where bare brown legs run rings & races.'

{Princeton is a similar jotting headed 'In the highlands':}

> 'In the highlands in the village places
> When the sheep go bleating up the hill
> Where the old plain men have rosy faces,
> <Sit and play><Sit and doze and dream>
>
> In the highlands in the country places
> Life is sweet and long, and death is short and still.'

{NLS 3791 is headed 'On the gorgeous hills of morning' and was transcribed in *BBS*, III, p. 135 (*NP*, pp. 188–9) without the editor noticing that the MS breaks off after thirteen lines; what follows then is an eleven-line fragment from *ST* XVI which Hellman tacks on the end of the quite unrelated verses that precede it. The first four lines of the fragment are the same as the *ST* text, then four lines are cancelled, followed by this passage:

> 'Light and heat begin, begin and strengthen,
> And the shadows turn and shrink and lengthen,
> <And>^As^ the great sun passes,
> In the skies.
>
> Life <and sleep> and death <with silent paces>
> <Pass and watch and mock>go by with heedful faces
> Mock with silent steps these empty places.'

{NLS 7483 is a fair copy in ink numbered VII, evidently copy-text for the *Pall Mall Gazette* printing, lot 286 (including a facsimile) in the Sotheby's sale of 1979 (see above, p. 485:}
Line
2   faces,] faces
3   maidens] <lasses>^ ~ ^
8   dies.] dies,
9   haunted;] haunted,
12 Bright with sward;] <Flower bestarred.>^ ~ ^
16 Lamp-bestarred!] <Flower bestarred!> ^ ~ ^
22 passes;] passes,
{In the first issue of *EDIN*, line 15 was omitted and line 16 ended with a comma: these errors were rectified by a cancel leaf and *erratum* note.}

XVII (*To the Tune of Wandering Willie*)
Place/date of composition: Tahiti, November 1888 (MS in *LETBM*, Vol. VI, No. 2122)
Letter and source: 1. RLS to Charles Baxter [8 or 9 November 1888] (*LETBM*, Vol. VI, p. 222): {Delayed in Tahiti while his chartered yacht *Casco* was being repaired, the poet sent a two-stanza version of this poem to Baxter inviting comparison with a variation by Robert Burns – 'Here awa', there awa' wandering, Willie.' – on this old Scottish song.} 'Our main-

mast is dry-rotten; and we are all to the devil. I shall lie in a debtors' jail. Never mind: Tautira is first chop. I am so besotted that I shall put on the back of this my attempt at words to Wandering Willie; if you can conceive at all the difficulty you will also conceive the vanity with which I regard any kind of a result; and whatever mine is like it has some sense and Burns's has none.'

2. During the voyage of the *Casco* in the South Pacific, RLS, writing the final chapters of *The Master of Ballantrae*, inserted some lines from this poem into Ch. IX: in this episode, the Master, having left the house of Durrisdeer behind him in a drenching mist, 'began first to whistle and then to sing the saddest of our country tunes, which sets folk weeping in a tavern, *Wandering Willie*. The set of words he used with it I have not heard elsewhere, and could never come by any copy; but some of them which were the most appropriate to our departure linger in my memory. One verse began –

> "Home was home then, my dear, full of kindly faces;
>> Home was home then, my dear, happy for the child."

And ended somewhat thus –

> "Now, when day dawns on the brow of the moorland,
>> Lone stands the house, and the chimney-stone is cold.
> Lone let it stand, now the folks are all departed,
>> The kind hearts, the true hearts, that loved the place of old."

I could never be a judge of the merit of these verses; they were so hallowed by the melancholy of the air, and were sung (or rather "soothed") to me by a master-singer at a time so fitting. He looked in my face when he had done, and saw that my eyes watered.'
MSS: B7088, B7089, B7090, *LETBM*, No. 2122
Magazine publication: *Scots Observer*, 19 January, 1889; *Pall Mall Gazette*, 17 December 1894; *Pall Mall Budget*, 20 December 1894. {The *Pall Mall* printings include all three stanzas at the head of an article on 'The Late Mr Stevenson', which begins: 'This poem, which is one of an unpublished series entrusted to us for publication by Mr R L Stevenson.' Clearly, this series of five poems (see above, p. 485) came with RLS's authority. The MS, with facsimile, was lot 287 in the Sotheby's sale of 24 July 1979; headed 'VIII' and subscribed 'Tautira', it is written in the hand of Isobel Strong.
B7089 was No. XIV in *Far Ballads and Songs of Travel* (filed under B6159) with 'Tautira' written at the bottom; B7090 is a proof page from *Verses*, filed under B7065: to the two stanzas printed on this page, RLS added the third in his own hand. B7089, 2122 and *Scots Observer* also consist of two stanzas only. Collation of these MSS follows:}
Title: (*To the Tune of Wandering Willie*)] *Wandering Willie* (B7088, B7089)
   To the Tune of Wandering Willie. (B7090) *The Wanderer* (*Scots Observer*)
Number: XVII] XIV (B7089) XXIII (B7090)
Line
  1 must] shall (2122)
  2 must.] must, (B7090)
  3 heather;] heather, (B7088)
  4 rain, and] rain and (B7088)
  5 roof-tree.] roof-tree; (B7088, B7089) roof-tree, (*Scots Observer*, 2122)
  6 door –] door. (all MSS)

8   old, you] old you (*Scots Observer*)
9   faces,] faces; (*Scots Observer*) faces: (2122)
11   moorland;] moorland, (2122)
13   Now, when] Now when (B7088, 2122)
14   house, and ... chimney-stone is cold.] house and ... chimney stone ~ (B7089, 2122) ~ chimney stone ~ (B7088) ~ cold; (*Scots Observer*)
15   stand, now the friends ... departed,] stand now the folks ~ (*Scots Observer*) ~ folks ... departed (B7088) ~ <folks>^friends^ ~ (B7089) ~ folks ~ (2122)
16   place] house (2122, *Scots Observer*)
20   hours;] hours: (B7090)
21   Fair the day] <The sun shall>^Fair the day^ (B7088)
22   shine] <stand>^ ~ ^ (B7088)
24   for ever] forever (*Thistle*)

XVIII *Winter*
Place/date of composition: Saranac Lake [?November] 1887 (*LETBM*, Vol. VI, No. 1936, n.2, p. 54, notes a reference in this letter to the fact that RLS had contributed this poem for the Christmas number of the *Court and Society Review*.)
Letter: RLS to his mother [18 March 1890] (*LETBM*, Vol. VI, No. 2218): {At the end of this letter RLS asked his mother, who tried to save all newspaper clippings and periodical pieces relative to her son, including the many poems he sent out to the press, to send copies of some of this printed poetry to Scribner's as copy-text for his projected volume of verse. The poems he asked her for were XVIII, XX, XXIX, XXX, XXXI, XXXIII and Dr T. G. Hake's poem addressed to him (B7233). The only MS extant for this poem, B7173, is in the hand of Margaret Stevenson and was sent as printer's copy for *Far Ballads and Songs of Travel*.}
MSS: B7173, uncatalogued proof (B7065)
First publication: *Court and Society Review*, 14 December 1887
Collation of all these MSS:
Number: XVIII] <XII>^XI^ (B7065) XIII (B7173)
Line
3   haws,] haws. (B7173) haws<.>^,^ (B7065)
4   window-pane] window pane (both MSS, *Court and Society*) {This reading has been adopted.}
5   draws.] chews. (B7173)
6   hill] hill<s> (B7065)
11   roses, lo, the flowers of fire!] roses, lo ~ (B7173) roses < – >^,^ ~ fire! < – > (B7065)
{Both ST and B7065 have 'Saranac Lake' below the text; B7173 and *Court and Society* do not.}

XIX 'The stormy evening closes now in vain'
MSS: None found.

XX *To Dr. Hake*
    (*On receiving a copy of verses*)
Place/date of composition: New York, September 1887 (MS sent in *LETBM*, Vol. VI, No. 1886)
Letter: RLS to Henley [c. 24 September 1887] (*LETBM*, Vol. VI, p. 11): {Hake had sent RLS

some verses to which he is here replying} 'Herewith verses for Dr Hake ... I hope you will like my answer to Hake, and specially that he will.'
MSS: B6996, B6997, uncatalogued proof (B7065)
{B6997, in the hand of Margaret Stevenson, was sent as printer's copy for *Far Ballads and Songs of Travel* (see notes to XVIII); the proof was for *Verses*. RLS thought at one point of including Hake's poem to him in *Far Ballads and Songs of Travel*.}
Title/number: XX. *To Dr Hake* (On receiving a copy of verses)]
        XI *To Thomas Gordon Hake* (B6997) <V>^X^ *To Dr Hake* (B7065)

Line
1   belovèd] beloved (B6997, B7065)
4   réveillé] reveillé (B6997, B7065)
4   Thus on my pipe I ... two;] ~ pipe, I ... two. (B6997) Thus, on my pipe, ~ (B7065)
5   but 'twas] but 't was (B7065)
6   art,] art; (B6997)
12 Heaven ... vain,] heaven ~ (B7065) ~ vain. (B6997)
13 For, lo! ... dale,] ~ dale (B6997) For lo! ~ (B7065)
{B7065 has 'New York' printed below the text.}

XXI *To* ——
Place/date of composition: Bournemouth, 1884–7 (McKay, Vol. VI, pp. 2530–1)
Letters: 1. RLS to Colvin, [?3 June 1887] (*LETBM*, Vol. V, pp. 418–19): {RLS had intended this tribute to 'the perfect friend' for *UW*.} 'I want to tell you also that I have suppressed your poem. I shall send it you for yourself, and I hope you will agree with me that it was not good enough in point of view of merit and a little too intimate as between you and me. I would not say less of you, my friend, but I scarce care to say so much in public while we live. A man may stand on his own head; it is not fair to set his friend on a pedestal.'

2. Colvin to Edmund Gosse (bound up with Gosse proofs), 14 November 1895: 'You ask to whom the piece "I knew thee strong and quiet etc." is addressed. It is an old thing of Bournemouth days to me, which I would not let him print in the first *Underwoods*. Of course it would be fatuous of me to print it at all if people knew: but 'Felix' is only a name used for me by the smallest circle of intimates (originally Slade (=Slade Professor), then Felix, the founder's name having been Felix Slade), and quite unknown outside. Do you agree with me in thinking the verses have too much beauty to be lost?' {Colvin was Slade Professor of Fine Arts, Cambridge, 1873–85. See Explanatory Note on this poem, p. 628.}
MSS: None found.
The Gosse proofs have variants as follows:
Line
2   endure,] endure:
7   child;] child,
{Line 22 has a comma after 'friend' in *EDIN. ST* (1896) has a semicolon. *Thistle* has a full stop. The sense calls for a semicolon, so I have adopted this punctuation.}

XXII 'The morning drum-call on my eager ear'
MS: H2404 (on p. 24 of Notebook A.270 is the following thirteen-line sketch:)

'But the long shadows on the path appear
And me I pause at whiles in what I do <as one should do>
And count the bell, and <trouble lest I><wonder not to>hear
My work untrimmed, the sunset gun too soon.

The morning drum call in my eager ear
Thrills unforgotten yet: the morning dew
Lies nearly all undried along my <path of life>^field of noon:^
<But are>At my delighted labour [the rest is indecipherable]'

{ST (1896) splits this poem into two three-line stanzas but I found no authority to do so.}

XXIII 'I have trod the upward and the downward slope'
MS: B6396: buried in this long draft of XXVI are these four lines which never appeared in
that poem but closely approximate this one; see below p. 507:

'Then trod the upward and the downward slope
Then knew all and now will know no more
Then hoped all and bid farewell to hope,
And I have lived and loved and closed the door.'

XXIV 'He hears with gladdened heart the thunder'
MSS: B6276, B6277, B6278
{B6276 is a cancelled eighteen-line version:}

'<He hearkens all to melt or harden>
He hears the children in the garden
        Sing, and the sexton delve the <tomb>^grave^
At dawn he hears the wood birds twitter
He sees the lights of cities glitter,
        And the <dusk>^shade^ of <thickets gloom>^forests wane.^

He knows the earth above and under
He hears with gladdened heart the thunder
        Peal, and loves the falling dew.
He sees the ship and longs to man it –
He sees, and longs to <seize>^touch,^ the planet –
        Sits and is content to view.

The mean may crouch, the proud may clamber,
He sits beside the dying ember,
        God for hope and man for friend:
He sits alone in the high chamber
Content to see, <proud>^glad^ to remember
        Expectant {alt. "Conscious"} of the certain end.'

{B6278, in the bound volume *Verses*, is identical with *ST* except for its number, XXVI;
B6277, found like the above version in the folio notebook '*First Drafts of Poems*', varies from
ST as follows:}

Line
5   beside the dying ember,] <aloof in the high chamber,>^ ~ ^
6   friend,] friend,
7   remember,] remember

XXV 'Farewell, fair day and fading light!'
MSS: B6213, B6214
{B6213 is an early, twenty-seven-line version, as follows:}
Title. [untitled]] *Pereant et imputantur*

'<Farewell, fair day. We meet again no more.>
<The glory reddens and the glow decays>
<Farewell, lo, the day departing, fading>
Farewell fair day <in the>^and^ falling light!
The clay-born here with upward eyes
<Sees the>^Marks the^ huge sun now downward soar.
Farewell we <two shall>^twain^ meet <again>^no more.^

Farewell, fair day. <Succour>The cock shall cry
<The night bird from the forest nigh> and flaming sun
He mourns another respite done,
Farewell fair day, so foully <used>^spent.^

Farewell fair day, if any god
At all consider this poor clod,
<Bear my repentance and lament>
<If in your circle>
Let him appoint
Another sun, another day,
<To misdirect and misapply>
<To misapply and cast away>
May rise: not this I
He who the fair occasion sent
Prepared and placed the impediment
<With heavy heart, with bursting sigh,
I see my last occasion die>
<The enlightened east awake these eyes>

Farewell. I watch, with bursting sigh
My late contemned occasion die;
Hope came at noon, with eve hope went:
Farewell fair day, so foully spent!'

{*Verso* on this MS is a draft of the 4th stanza, misidentified and given a separate number, B6508, by McKay:}

'<Let him the><Divinely let him vengeance take>
Let him diviner vengeance take
Give me to sleep, give me to wake,

<With the wild bugles of the break>
<Farewell fair day; <<that>>he from some new <<eastern>>shore>
Girded and shod; and true and gay
Do gladly in the returning day.'

{B6214 is a fair copy for *Verses* (B7065) which has the following variants:}
Line
  1   light!] light! –
  4   Farewell.] Farewell<!>^.^
  7   linger] loiter
13   {This cancelled line has no equivalent in *ST*:}
      <My loins are girt, my feet are shod>
{This poem is also known under the title *The Lost Occasion* (*Thistle*).}

XXVI *If this were Faith*
Date of composition: 1893 (Balfour)
MSS: B6395, B6396, Gosse proofs
{The first of these pencil MSS, both from the folio notebook 'First Drafts of Poems', is a
seminal sketch:}

      '<But we go down forever into the sea>
      I hark, and the ring of it all
      Rings in my ears a trumpet call;
      And I hear the sound of the whole world speak
      <In racket, explosion and shriek
      The driving thunder, the drowned>

      Wanted volunteers
      To do their best for two score years.

      If deep in my bosom the note rings clear,
      And I hear it <repeated>resound from far and near
      The note of the joy of girded men
      To go on forever and fail, and go on again;
      And to be mauled to the earth and arise.
      <And to <<gaze>>^face^ forever with steadfast warrior eyes,
      The enveloping ...>
      And fight for a word and a thing not seen with the eyes, not felt with hands'

{B6396 is a much-revised draft over two pages:]

      'God, if this were enough.
      That I ask no nut in the husk
      Nor dawn beyond the dusk,
      But see things bare to the buff.'
      {alt. beginning:} 'God, if this were enough
      That I see things bare to the buff
      And up to the <hips>^buttocks^ in mire,
      <And>That I ask nor hope nor hire,

Nut in the husk,
Nor dawn beyond the dusk:
Nor life beyond death,
God, if this were faith?'

{Six lines cancelled:} 'Taking life by the twist,
In its [?] up to the wrist
Feeling it hairy, rude,
Knowing it bloody and lewd,
And the day of the hero brief,
And long the day of the thief:'

'Having felt the wind in my face
<Blood>Spit, sorrow and disgrace,
<And the brutes>Having seen thine evil doom
<Everywhere under the sun>At Golgotha and Khartoum,
And the brutes, the work of thy hands
Fill<ing> with injustice lands
And stain with blood the sea:
If still in my veins, the glee

Of the black night and the sun,
And the lost battle, run;
<If still the glory of losing, dying, falling,><If, an adept,>
The iniquitous lists <still I>I still accept,
With joy <And joy to face>affront the old night
And joy to attack and be withstood
<For what I know not to be right>
<For what I could not think was right>
[line illegible]
To affront <And still to battle> and perish for a <dream><fancy>dream of good:
God if that were enough?
If, to feel in the <dank>ink of the slough
And the sink of the mire
Veins of glory and fire,'

{Here follows a variation on the four lines that comprise ST XXIII, lifted from this MS to become a separate poem; see above p. 504. The next six lines do not seem to be part of this poem either. It continues as follows:}

'Run through and transpierce and transpire
And a secret purpose of glory <and goodness> in every part
And <an>the answering glory of battle fill my heart,
To go on forever blindfold in thy beaten cause,
The air alive with talons, the mire with claws,
And the end be it wrong, be it right,
Submerged in <infinite>night
Only the prowess glorious, and the fight <golden the joy of the fight,>

If to go on forever and fail and go on again,
<Go on forever they>More to endure yet to
Know no more than the ruck of babbling men,
For a glorious star that shines and deathless
<And to know not><If this be faith><Help thou mine unbelief,>'

{In line 31 *EDIN* and *ST* (1896) have 'for ever'; *Thistle* and the MSS have 'forever' – I have adopted the latter reading.}

'Wanted volunteers
To do their best for twoscore years.
A ready soldier here I stand,
Primed for thy command
<But be my>with burnished sword.
If this be faith O Lord,
Help thou mine unbelief
And be my battle brief!'

{A version of these last eight lines in B6396 occurs at the end of the Gosse proofs, where it is blue-pencilled and ultimately omitted. In their printed form they read as follows:}

'Wanted Volunteers
To do their best for twoscore years!
A ready soldier here I stand,
Primed for thy command,
With burnished sword.
If this be faith, O Lord
Help thou mine unbelief
And be my battle brief.'

{Balfour, calling these lines 'Envoy to No. XXV {XXVI} of *Songs of Travel*', prints them in Vol. II, p. 173, as an epigraph to his Chapter XVI, 'The End – 1894'; there are variants from the Gosse proofs as follows:}

Line
3   soldier here] soldier, here
4   thy] Thy
6   Lord] Lord,
7   thou] Thou

XXVII *My Wife*
Letter: Colvin to Edmund Gosse, 14 November 1895 (bound up with the Gosse proofs): 'You made no remark on the one to his wife "Dusky, trusty, etc." which I wanted for its strong personal note, but which I feared might strike you as ill-written and even a little ridiculous in its first line.'
MSS: B6619, BRBML Uncat, Princeton (Parrish) CO171
{The uncatalogued MS at Yale is the earliest version, having thirty-two lines (with revision and repetition) to *ST*'s 15:}

'<Trusty, and dusky, and lively and true
Swart as the coals of the furnace are you.

Changing and glowing in love and in ire
As glow to the bellows, the coals of the fire.>

<True as the steel and straight as the blade
Your eager spirit is laid and made
Laid and made and hammered and forged.
In this small body God enclosed>

~~Trusty, dusky, vivid true~~
Swart as furnace coals are you.
Change and glow in love and ire
As to the bellows glows the fire.
And true as the steel, straight as the blade
Your eager <spirit>^soul^ was laid and made.

Trusty, dusky, vivid, true;
<Swart as the coals and bright as the fire>
^With eyes of gold and bramble dew – ^
Steel true and blade straight,
The Good Lord
Made my mate.
Honour, anger, valour, fire,
<With heart and hand that count true>
A love that life could never tire
A <little sheath>^small body,^ <a huge soul>
<Love that death could never stir>
Death quench nor evil stir
The mighty master
Gave to her.
Teacher, helper, comrade, bride,
A fellow-farer true and tried,
Heart-whole and soul-free,
My pitying father
Leavit to me.'

{B6619 is a fair copy written in Belle Strong's journal, *Grouse in the Gunroom:*}
Line 8 stir,] stir
{CO171 is also a fair copy with no variants from *ST* but its cancelled title, 'II. *The Mother'*
suggests that this poem may at one time have been part of RLS's series, *The Vailima Family.*
CP prints line 11 thus: 'Teacher, tender comrade, wife,'; JAS justified this emendation of the
text of both *EDIN* and *Thistle* by claiming to follow the Gosse proofs in omitting the comma
after 'tender' (p. 508). However, the comma is not omitted in these proofs and it is present
in all the MSS. In BRBML the word used in line 11 instead of 'tender' is 'helper', also a noun
and near-synonym. It could be argued as well that RLS uses 'tender' as a noun identifying his
wife in line 114 of *The Woodman* (XXXIX). Furthermore, eliminating the comma disrupts
the trochaic rhythm of the line. I have followed the MSS and proofs.}

XXVIII *To the Muse*
Place/date of publication: Apemama, 1889 (*LETBM*, Vol. VI, pp. 325ff.)
MSS: B7042; uncatalogued proof (B7065)
{B7042 was No. IV, then No. VI in *Far Ballads and Songs of Travel*; on the proof page the number has been altered from VI to XIII. B7042 is twenty continuous lines but RLS indicates in the margin how leading should break the poem into four-line stanzas, as was done on the proof and in *ST*; variants are as follows:}
Line
  7   long] long<,> (B7042)
10   fame] <man>^ ~ ^ (B7042)
12   pot:] pot; (B7065)
14   evensong] <even song>^ ~ ^ (B7065)
16   our] <one>^ ~ ^ (B7065)
17   heart!] heart, (B7042)

XXIX *To an Island Princess*
Place/date of composition: Tautira, Tahiti, 5 November 1888 (Scrapbook V, Monterey)
Letter and source: 1. Fanny Stevenson to Colvin, 4 December 1888 (*LETBM*, Vol. VI, pp. 226–7): 'I write you from fairyland, where we are living in a fairy-story, the guests of a beautiful brown princess. We came to stay a week, five weeks have passed, and we are still indefinite as to our time of leaving.'

2. Full accounts of this idyllic visit to Tahiti are given:(a) by Fanny in the rest of letter no. 2127 and in *The Cruise of the Janet Nichol* (1915, pp. 172–3); (b) by Balfour (II, pp. 72–6) and (c) in *LETBM*, Vol. VI, pp. 218–19. Fanny, who appealed to Princess Moë for help when RLS lay dangerously ill, believed that her hospitality and special Tahitian cooking saved his life. On her departure from Tautira for Papeete, RLS presented her with these verses. The footnotes to this poem and the next one seem to be Colvin's work.
MSS: B6990, B6991, Monterey
{B6990, an early version, was not checked. B6991, copied by the poet's mother from a TS in her Scrapbook (No. V, pp. 80–1, at Stevenson House, Monterey) and sent as copy for *Far Ballads and Songs of Travel*, is marked to be the first of the *Songs* in that collection. In the following collation, B6991 and Monterey are identical unless otherwise noted:}
Title: *To an Island Princess*] *To Princess Moë Tamatoa*
Line
  3   willed,] willed;
  6   laid] laid,
  7   sky] sky,
  8   Rain-deluged and wind-buffeted:] Rain deluged and wind buffeted: –
10   turned – Love's … lost,] turned: Love's ~ (B6991) turned: Love's … Lost (Monterey)
      {In MS there is a stanza break after this line, making the 2nd stanza twenty lines long as opposed to sixteen lines long in *EDIN*}
12   and, like one] and like one
13   eyes,] eyes
14   cries.] sighs. (B6991) cries. (Monterey)
16   forecast:] forecast;

26 Keep up] Make a
32 Fairyland.] fairyland. {also in line 36; Monterey has both spellings}
33 oo] oo, {This reading has been adopted.}
34 I lacked. For, Lady (as you know),] {In B6991 'For Lady (as you know)' appears as the
    next line, beginning a new verse paragraph.}
39 Fairy princess] fairy Princess (Monterey)
40 waited; soon] waited, soon
42 Gracious] Fair {The Gosse proofs and *Thistle* also have 'Fair'.}
43 Moe] Moe
{Monterey is subscribed, in the hand of Margaret Stevenson, 'Tautira – Tahiti Nov.5 1888'.}

XXX *To Kalakaua*
    (*With a present of a pearl*)
Place/date of composition: Honolulu, 3 February 1889
Letter and source: {Kalakaua, the last king of the Hawaiian Islands, enjoyed many festive
occasions with the RLS entourage while the *Casco* was moored near Waikiki.} 1. RLS to
Charles Baxter, 8 March 1889 (*LETBM*, Vol. VI, p. 264): 'Happy and Glorious, *Hawaii
Ponoi I Kou moi* (Native Hawaiians, dote upon your monarch!) – Hawaiian God Save the
King ... Kalakaua is a terrible companion; a bottle of fizz is like a glass of sherry to him;
he thinks nothing of five or six in an afternoon as a whet for dinner ... You should see a
photograph of our party after an afternoon with H.H.M.: my! What a crew!'

2. *LETBM*, Vol. VI, pp. 242–3: 'Despite the corruption and scandal that characterized his
regime, Kalakaua himself was a man of great personal charm and ability, deeply interested
in Hawaiian history and legend: RLS was later to describe him as an "amiable, far from
unaccomplished, but too convivial sovereign." ... The King visited the *Casco* on the afternoon of 1 February [1889]. He was given champagne, sherry and cake; RLS read *Ticonderoga*,
Captain Otis played the accordion, Belle danced and Lloyd sang *The Dollars of Peru* (a
poem written by RLS in Tahiti) {see above, p. 333}. Two days later Henry Poor gave a *luau*
or native feast at Manuia Lanai in honour of RLS, with Kalakaua and Princess Liliuokalani
as chief guests. Fanny presented the King with a golden pearl and RLS read a specially
written poem.'
MS: B7006 {Copied by Margaret Stevenson, this version was sent as copy for *Far Ballads and
Songs of Travel*, where it was placed as No. II among the *Songs*:}
Title: B7006, lacking the subtitle, is headed *To His Majesty King Kalakaua*; in *Thistle*, the
subtitle reads: 'With the gift of a pearl'.
Line
  2 fathers] Fathers
  3 winds] wind
  4 Below your palace in ... rides:] <Beneath>^Below^ your palace, in ... rides;
  5 seafarers,] sea-farers,
  6 merchants count] merchants, count
  7 thing,] thing
  8 precious since] precious, since
{B7006 is divided into units of four, four and six lines; *EDIN* is divided into eight- and six-
line units. The MS is signed as in *ST*.}

XXXI *To Princess Kaiulani*
Place/date of composition: Waikiki, 24 April 1889 (B8359 is so dated)
Letter: {'The Little Princess', as RLS called her, was heir to the Hawaiian throne: her father
was a Scot from Edinburgh living in Honolulu but her mother was sister to the King. The
poet often sat talking to the Princess under a giant banyan tree. He marked the occasion of
her departure for school in England with this poem:}
1. RLS to Will. Low [?20 May 1889] (*LETBM*, Vol. VI, p. 302): 'If you want to cease to be
a republican, see my little Kaiulani, as she goes through – … You will die a red: I wear the
colours of that little royal maiden.'
MSS: B7026, B8359 {Both are in the hand of Margaret Stevenson and include the prefatory
note. In the Gosse proofs the unsigned note follows the text; in *EDIN* and *ST* (1896) the
note is signed 'R.L.S.' and precedes the text. In *Thistle* the signed note follows the text.}
B7026 was sent as copy for *Far Ballads and Songs of Travel*:}
Line
  1   goes,] goes (both MSS)
  2   island] Island (B8359)
  5   Southern] southern (both MSS)
  6   gone,] gone (both MSS)
 10   day,] day (B7026)

XXXII *To Mother Maryanne*
Place/date of composition: Kalawao, 22 May 1889 (B3189 is so dated)
Letter: RLS to Colvin [early June 1889] (*LETBM*, Vol. VI, pp. 310–11): 'I am just home after
twelve days' journey to Molokai, seven of them at the leper settlement, where I can only say
that the sight of so much courage, cheerfulness and devotion, strung me too high to mind
the infinite pity and horror of the sights. I used to … go to the Sisters' Home which is a
miracle of neatness, play a game of croquet with seven leper girls (90° in the shade), get
a little old-maid meal served me by the Sisters and ride home again.' {When he was at
the home for leper girls, RLS handed this poem to the director, Mother Marianne Kopp
(1836–1918); see Jacks 1935: 100–7.} RLS consistently misspelled her first name.
MSS: B3189, B7019, uncatalogued proof (B7065)
{B3189 is a photostat of the original signed and dated MS given to Mother Marianne; it is
now in the archives of her order, the Franciscan Sisters, in Syracuse, New York. This MS is
facsimiled and transcribed in Jacks 1935: Ch. VII. B7019 is copy for *Far Ballads and Songs of
Travel*, in which collection it was No. IV. The proof was for *Verses*. Collation of these MSS
follows:}
Title/number: XXXII. *To Mother Maryanne*] <II><V>^IV^ ~ (B7019)
                    <IV>^I^ To Mother<Mary Anne>^Maryanne^ (B7065)
      Reverend Sister Maryanne: matron of the Bishop Home, Kalaupapa (B3189)
Line
  1   place,] place (B7019)
  3   sufferer … rod –] sufferers … rod, (B3189)
  5   he shrinks. But … gaze] and shrinks. But … look (B3189)
  6   pain!] pain! – (B3189)
  7   marks … mournful shores;] <sees>^marks^ ~ (B7019) ~ painful shores, (B3189)
Date/place at bottom: *Guest House, Kalawao, Molokai*.]

Robert Louis Stevenson/Kalawao. 22 May 1889 (B3189)
{B3189 is divided into two stanzas of four lines each; this division has been adopted.}

XXXIII *In Memoriam E.H.*
Place/date of composition: Honolulu, [?March] 1889 (*LETBM*, Vol. VI, No. 2145)
Letter: RLS to Henley [?March 1889] (*LETBM*, Vol. VI, p. 266): {E.H. was Emma Henley,
Henley's mother, who had died at sixty the previous October; widowed early and left
penniless, she had nevertheless raised six children.}'I was pained to see your mother had
gone, perhaps even more to observe how young she was; but she had a long day, and made a
gallant fight, and now inherits peace.'
MSS: B6418, uncatalogued proof (B7065)
First publication: *Scots Observer*, 11 May 1889
{B6418, in the hand of Margaret Stevenson, was sent as copy for *Far Ballads and Songs of
Travel*, in which collection it was No. XII. The proof was for *Verses*. Henley was at this time
Editor of the *Scots Observer*. Collation of these MSS follows:}
Number: XXXIII.] <IX.>^X.^ (B7065) XII. (B6418)
Line
 2   hair.] hair<,>^.^ (B7065)
 3   valour and ... renown,]valour, and ~ (B7065) ~ renown – (B6418, *Scots Observer*)
 4   Life, that] Life that (B6418)
 5   age.] age, (B7065)
 7   poorest part –] <purest part>^ ~ ^ (B7065) ~ part: (*Scots Observer*)
 9   frail,] frail; (B6418, *Scots Observer*)
 11 but, honoured] but honoured (all MSS, Gosse proofs, *Thistle*) {This reading has been
     adopted.}

XXXIV *To My Wife*
     (*A Fragment*)
Place/date of composition: on board the schooner *Equator*, 1889 (Balfour)
Letter: RLS to his mother, 1 December 1889 (*LETBM*, Vol. VI, pp. 332–4): 'We are drawing
(we fondly hope) to the close of another voyage like that from Tahiti to Hawaii: we sailed
from Butaritari on the 4th November, and since then have lain becalmed under cataracts of
rain, or kicked about in purposeless squalls. We were sixteen souls in this small schooner,
eleven in the cabin; our confinement and overcrowding in the wet weather was excessive;
we lost our foretopmast in a squall ... To ... the small, lamplighted, tossing cabin, nine feet
square, – add the incessant uproar of the tropic rain, the dripping leaks, the slush on the
floor, and the general sense that we were nowhere in particular and drifting anywhere at
large ... Fanny has stood the hardships of this rough cruise wonderfully; but I do not think I
could expose her to another of the same.'
MSS: B7022, B6213
{The first eighteen lines of B7022, an untitled fifty-two-line draft, are almost a fair copy:}
Line
 3   lane with] lane, with
 5   smoke, perchance] smoke perchance
 7   leads,] leads
 10 When] Where {This reading has been adopted.}
 11 vale] vale,

{B7022 continues as follows:}
'From the salt waste the <sterile>^unfruitful^ sun shall rise
Bake the bare deck and blind the unshielded eyes,
<And all the long day>The allotted hours aloft shall wheel in vain,
And in the unpregnant ocean plunge again.
The unceasing evil of calms,
Assault of squalls that mock the watchful guard
<That tear>And rend the <howling>^bursting^ canvas from the yard,
<The unceasing evil of calms you shall endure,>
<The unceasing>And senseless clamour of the calm <you mark>hear at night
<Still haunted>
<And in the stifling cabin, lend an ear,>
<Imprisoned, barely hear,>
<Awakes you><by>to the living light
<Starts you from>Shall mar your slumber; by the plunging light,
In the <sick->^wild^-swerving cabin, hour by hour,
<You hearken to the roaring of the rain>
<You hear the tropic avalanche of rain>
Hour after hour, poor soul, you must endure
To hear the tropic rain roar overhead,
And the <sails billow and the hulks clatter> and the seamen tread.
So much awhile you bear
<When you behold again>lustration of the rain'
{B6213 has a later draft of the last ten lines, unidentified as such by McKay:}
Line
20 Bathe] Bake {Both MSS read 'Bake', which I have adopted as both more sensible and
    more onomatopoetic than 'Bathe'.}
21 vain] vain,
23 squalls that ... guard,] squalls, that ... guard
24 pluck] <rend>^ ~ ^
25 And] Or
26 Must] <Shall>^ ~ ^
27 In beetle-haunted] In your beetle-haunted
{B6213 has one more legible line, 'And spread the greasy cards for solitaire'.}

XXXV *To My Old Familiars*
Place/date of composition: Apemama, 1889 (*LETBM*, Vol. VI, No. 2203)
Letter: RLS to Charles Baxter, [c. 5 February 1890, on board the ship *Lübeck*] (*LETBM*, Vol.
VI, pp. 358–60): 'Sad and fine were the old days: when I was away in Apemama, I wrote two
copies of verse about Edinburgh and the past, so ink black, so golden bright. I will send them,
if I can find them; for they will say something to you, and indeed one is more than half
addressed to you. This is it. {XXXV follows.} They're pretty second rate, but felt. I can't be
bothered to copy the other.' {The other poem about Edinburgh written at Apemama is
XXXVI, *The Tropics Vanish*.}
MSS: BRBML Box 370, B7020, *LETBM*, 2203
First publication: *The Antipodean, An Illustrated Annual*, No. II (November 1893)
370, an uncatalogued collection, includes Notebook *No. A.282, 'Verses and Essays'*,

containing many sketches relative to XXXIV–XXXVIII dating from c. 1889–90. With the bookplate of Belle Strong and her signed inscription, 'From the Library of Robert Louis Stevenson at Vailima', it contains twenty six pages, mostly in pencil. RLS must have carried this notebook with him on the *Equator* and drafted the various Apemama poems in it. On page 12 is this early draft:}

'Do you remember – can we e'er forget
How in the dire adversities {alt. "extremities"} of youth
We gloomed and shivered, sorrowed, sobbed and <laughed>feared?
In our wild climate, in the scowling town,
Do you remember how the winter went
The scolding of the winter wind, the missile rain
The rare and welcome silence of the snows,
<And everywhere the monster of the night>
<With lamps and rivers, and brothels and remorse>
<The laggard morn, low day and hasty eve>
The laggard morn, the haggard day, the night
The monstrous spell <Night and the spell> of the nocturnal town
The lamp, the river, the brothels, the remorse
<Marr'd with lamps, and brothels and remorse>
Do you remember? – ah could one forget!
The ever welcome <voice>^song^ of chanticleer
Heard in the rain, or swelling of the wind
Away goes darkness, by the wakeful sick
The siren song of poetry and hope
The dim, the golden glories of the dawn
Do you remember? Who would e'er forget.
Unhappy {alt."And lo, as"} in the palace <stairs>porch of life,
<At the palace doors of life, before the day>
<With night <mares>^hags^ and chimaeras in the rain>
We huddled with chimaeras all a cold
<Like privileged beggars at cathedral gates;>
How from within the music swelled and fell,
And through the breach of the revolving doors
What <sights>^dreams^ of splendour blinded us and fled: –
Those <primary>sorrowing notes of poetry and hope –
<The dim, the golden glories of the day,>
Do you remember? Who would e'er forget?

I have since then contended and rejoiced
<In many lands and chances,>
<And travelled in the isles of paradise.>
[line illegible]
And with new vigour pants to greet the dawn.
Or as to thwarted seamen all night long
Some cape repassing, by that cape repassed,
Alternately [?] and revealed,
The <glare of the> great city shows.'

{Collation of B7020 (copy for No. XII in *Verses*), 2203 and *Antipodean* with *ST*:}
Title/number: XXXV. To My Old Familiars] XII. <Ad Sodales>^*To my old familiars*^
(B7020) *To My Old Comrades* (2203)
Line
  1   forget? –] forget? (*Antipodean*)
  5   wind,] <rain,>^ ~ ^ (B7020)
  8   town,] town, – (*Antipodean*)
  9   – Ah,] – ah, (2203, *Antipodean*)
 13 Sing in … dawn, –] Sing, in … dawn: (All MSS)
 14 ardour, these … day:] ardour these … day. (2203, *Antipodean*) ~ day. (B7020)
       {Interpolated in 2203 by RLS: '(Here a squall sets all flying)'}
 16 hearkened] listed (2203)
 17 For lo! as in] For as in (2203) For lo, ~ (*Antipodean*)
 18 within –] within, (2203)
 19 hear! –] hear! (2203)
 20 doors] doors, (2203)
 22 rejoiced;] rejoiced; – (2203)
 24 entered, … beheld:] entered; … beheld. (*Antipodean*) entered; ~ (2203)
       'Kindlier it glows and brighter than we dreamed!' {Line 25 in 2203 and B7020 but
       omitted in *ST*.}
 27 Fall] Faint (2203)
 30 youth,] youth? (2203) {The letter MS lacks the next two lines, 32–3.}
 31 footsteps and that voice] footsteps, and the voice (B7020, 2203)
 32 {After 'and despair', in B7020 RLS inserted 'the miserably merry, the defiled Dis-
       honoured, undishonourable days?'.}
 33 So, as] So as (2203)
 35 perish,] vanish, (2203)
{'Apemama' appears below the text only in *ST*.}

XXXVI. 'The tropics vanish, and meseems that I'
Place/date of composition: Isle of Apemama, October 1889 (MS of poem enclosed with
LETBM, Vol. VI, No. 2205 is so dated)
Letters: 1. RLS to Henley [early February 1890] (*LETBM*, Vol. VI, 363–5): 'I had been
turning over in my head what I could do for the *Observer*, and it occurred to me that the
following, if good enough, was suitable; of course … I expect you to judge as a friend, and
suppress if it seem rot. What to call it – I know not – perhaps, A *Voice from Home*. {Here
follows this poem. At the end he wrote, then cancelled, 'I don't believe it's bad.'} I am in a
glow of ingenuous admiration myself, which I trust you may, with more philosophy, share;
anyway the piece is fitting in an Embro' publication … Remember me to my birth street;
I feel as if I could not bear to go there, or round the back way by the Cemetery, or up the
Broughton road; something would snap … almost nothing saddens me, but to recall such
places.'

2. RLS to Charles Baxter [c. 5 February 1890] (*LETBM*, Vol. VI, No. 2203) {See notes to
No. XXXV above.}
MSS: B7087; *LETBM*, No. 2205; uncat. proof B7065
First publication: *Scots Observer*, 5 April 1890

{B7087 was copy for *Far Ballads and Songs of Travel*; the proof was pulled for *Verses*.}
Title/number: {untitled} XXXVI.] VII (B7087) III. (B7065)

A Voice From Home (Scots Observer, 2205)

Line
1   vanish,] vanish; (2205, *Scots Observer*)
2   Halkerside, ... Allermuir,] ~ <Allermure,>^ ~ ^ (B7065)
                               <Halkersides, as from ... >^ ~ ^ (B7087)
3   dreaming gaze] dreaming, gaze (2205, *Scots Observer*)
4   Far set] Far-set (B2205, *Scots Observer*)
6   Cragged, spired, and] Cragg'd, spired and (B7087, B7065) ~ spired and (2205)
                               Cragg'd ~ (*Scots Observer*)
7   Beflagged ... seaward-drooping] Beflagg'd ... seaward drooping (B7065, B7087)
9   {Following this line there are these four lines (omitted in *ST*) in 2205, B7087, and *Scots
    Observer*; they are present in B7065 but have been cancelled:}
    'There, in the silence of remembered time
    Sounds yet the innocent laughter of a child,
    Sound yet the unresting footsteps of a youth,
    Now dead forever, and whose grave I am.'
12 house ... dead,] ~ dead <;>^,^ (B7065) <place>^house^ ~ (B7087)
13 word.] <speech.>^ ~ ^ (B7087)
14 survive;] survive: (All MSS) {This reading has been adopted.}
15 towers; the] towers, the (All MSS) {This reading has been adopted.}
17 here in] here, in (2205, *Scots Observer*)
22 child] child: (All MSS) {This reading has been adopted.}
23 In vain. The voice] <In vain the voice>^ ~ ^ (B7087, B7065)
25 retrace,] retrace. (*Scots Observer*)
26 And, all] And all (B7087, B7065, 2205) {This reading has been adopted.}
27 {JAS emended this line from MS, replacing 'denoted' with 'devoted' (*CP*, p. 512). I
    cannot construe any of these MSS to yield this reading, although in RLS's hand 'v' and
    'n' are similar; *LETBM* states that he 'may have written "devoted"' (Vol. VI, p. 364,
    n.4). I see no improvement in sense with 'devoted'.}
{All MSS have either 'Apemama' or 'Isle of Apemama' below the text.}

XXXVII *To S.C.*
Place/date of composition: Isle of Apemama, October 1889 (B7030 is so dated)
Letters: 1. RLS to Colvin [30 September 1889] (*LETBM*, Vol. VI, p. 329): 'I have been
thinking a great deal of you and the Monument {i.e. the British Museum, where Colvin lived
and worked} of late and even tried to get my thoughts into a poem, hitherto without success.
God knows how you are: I begin to weary dreadfully to see you.'

2. RLS to Colvin, 2 December 1889 (*LETBM*, Vol. VI, pp. 337–8): 'Now that my father is
done with his troubles, and 17 Heriot Row no more than a mere shell, you and that gaunt
old Monument in Bloomsbury are all that I have in view when I use the word home; some
passing thoughts there may be of the rooms at Skerryvore, and the blackbirds in the chine
on a May morning; but the essence is S.C. and the Museum ... I will copy for you here a copy
of verses made in Apemama.' {Here is enclosed the text of this poem.}
Magazine publication: *Longman's Magazine*, January 1895

MSS: BRBML Uncat. Box 370; B7029; B7030; *LETBM*, No. 2191; uncat. proof B7065
{370 includes Notebook A.282, which has sketches for this poem on pp. 1–3, 6–8, 13–14 and
19–21. B7029 is copy for *Far Ballads and Songs of Travel*. There is a facsimile and
transcription of the first page of B7030 in *BBS*, II, pp. 161–2. The proof is for *Verses*. The
following are selective transcriptions of some early drafts from Notebook. A.282, beginning
with an abandoned experiment using couplets:}

{Lines 1–7}   'I heard it waking, heard it half asleep
                <I heard> the <thrill> of the besieging sea
                Loud as a railway rolls
                Incessant the quaking ocean front,
                Billow on bursting billow, mile by mile,
                Beleaguer and beshadow all the isle.
                I heard the cock that tells the hours of night,
                Sing lusty shrill; <I heard> the <sudden>caroling flight
                I looked abroad upon our various land
                And saw the moon enlighten the white sand,
                The turning forms and shadows of the palm,
                And the huge clouds reel past the starry calm;
                Well, my friend, it has been so decreed
                That I should go wherever winds might lead.'

{Lines 1–16}   'Sleepless all night I lay, sleepless I heard
                The apocalyptic clamour of the sea
                Besieging our low island, as the winds
                Pass swinging in the top knots of the palms.
                <At times><I heard>the cock <I heard the hours of night>
                <I heard the cock tell forth the hours of night>
                I heard the cock that keeps the watch …

                As the unknown fowl of night, that carolling loud,
                Crosses our various land from sea to sea.
                At times below the wattled blinds I peeped
                And saw, in the palace precincts, where a fire
                Blazed single, in the wind, under the stars,
                Among the slumbering cabins. Thus I lay
                And other sleepless nights before my mind
                In long succession passed. Your house I saw,
                The many pillared and the well belov'd;
                <Your hearth that in the fog-embrumed air
                Sparkled for me like home; your welcome doors>
                That friendship ever opened.
                Eager as children come to spend the day
                To that dear door how oft <our way we took>
                We hasted; and how oft, ere yet we knocked,
                The eager hand of welcome clutched us in.'

{Lines 1–3}   'All night upon the mats sleepless I lay,
　　　　　　　　I heard the breath of the besieging sea
　　　　　　　　Beleaguer and becanopy the isle
　　　　　　　　With sound and fear of inroads; heard the wind
　　　　　　　　Fly crying, and convulse tumultuous palms.
　　　　　　　　Heard whiles the watcher with the scarlet comb
　　　　　　　　Sings lusty shrill; or that mysterious fowl
　　　　　　　　Of night and ocean, that carolling {alt. "out-croaking" B7030} loud
　　　　　　　　Crosses from sea to sea the various isle;
　　　　　　　　Whiles peeped abroad beneath the wattled blinds
　　　　　　　　Up-strutted, whence the brightness {alt. "effulgence" B7030} of the night
　　　　　　　　Leaked in and lit the cabin, scattering sleep:'

{Collation of all MSS:}
Title/number: XXXVII. *To S.C.*] I. *To Sidney Colvin* (B7030) <III>^V^ ~ (B7029)
　　　　　　　　　　　　　　　　　<V>^II^ ~ (B7065)

Line
2   far away] far-away (2191)
3   crying and] crying, and (2191)
4   I rose] Whiles rose (370)
5   palm;] palm: (B7029)
6   moon and wind and … vault;] moon, and wind, and … vault – (B7029)
　　　moon, and ~ vault, (370)
7   keenest] <nearest>^ ~ ^ (B7065)
　　　{2191 has no verse paragraph break after this line; all other MSS and ST do.}
8   king, my neighbour, with his host of wives,] King ~ (2191)
　　　king my neighbour <and host with all his wives>^with his host of wives^ (370)
9   palisade;] palisade: (2191) palisade (37)
10   Where single, … moon,] Where, single, … moon (370) Where, single, ~ (2191)
13   turned –] turned, (2191, B7029, B7065) turned: (370)
14   first, and] first and (370)
15   many-pillared] many pillared (370, B7029, B7065)
16   lighted; there again] lighted: ~ (370) ~ again, (B7029)
17   lay, and] lay and (2191, B7029)
19   Museum] museum (370, B7029, B7065)
20   more went by me;] more by me (B7029) < more by me>^ ~ ^ (B7065)
22   Again I longed for the returning morn,]
　　　Wearied again for the return of day, (370)
23   The awaking traffic, the bestirring birds,]
　　　And from the innumerable throng of birds (370)
　　　{Between lines 24 and 25 in 37) is inserted this line:}
　　　'And flight of inconsiderable wing'
26   A passing charm of beauty. Most of all,] ~ beauty: most of all, (2191)
　　　A changing wealth of beauty: most of all (370)
27   wearied, and] wearied and (370)
28   glad réveillé] morning planet (370) ~ reveillé (B7029, B7065)
29   Lo, now, when] Lo now when (370) Lo, now; when (2191)

31   glance, where by the pillared wall] ~ where, by the pillared wall, (370, 2191)
        glance where ~ (B7065, B7029)
32   Far-voyaging island gods, begrimed with smoke,]
        <<And where all grimy with <<the>>London <<soot>>^smoke^> (370)
        Far-voyaging, island gods, ~ (2191)
        <Rude>^Far-travelled^ island gods, (370)
33   Sit now unworshipped, the rude monument]
        <Sit sole memorial and dark monument> (370)
34   undivined:] undivined; (2191), undivined; – (370)
38   Incessant, of the breakers on the shore.] Incessant of the <surf about the isle>
                                        breakers <on the beach> round the isle. (370)
40–1   So far, so foreign, your divided friends
        Wander, estranged in body, not in mind.]
        <So far><As strange to their>So foreign to their [?], your friends
        Wander divided nor forget the past. (370) ~ estranged – in body ~ (2191)
{Below text:}
Apemama] Isle of Apemama (B7029) Isle of Apemama, October 1889 (B7030)

XXXVIII *The House of Tembinoka*
Place/date of composition: at sea on the *Equator*, November–December 1889 (*LETBM*, Vol.
VI, pp. 325–6)
Letters: {The Stevenson party spent two months on Apemama as the guests of the
formidable tyrant Tembinok' while the *Equator* went off on trading visits to other islands.}
1. RLS to Colvin [30 September 1889] (*LETBM*, Vol. VI, p. 329): 'The king is a great
character; a thorough tyrant, very much of a gentleman, a poet, a musician, a historian or
perhaps rather more a genealogist – it is strange to see him lying in his house among a lot of
wives (nominal wives) writing the History of Apemama in an account book.'

2. RLS to E. L. Burlingame [February 1890] (*LETBM*, Vol. VI, p. 365): 'The only thing I
have ready {for *Scribner's Magazine*} is the enclosed barbaric piece; as soon as I have arrived
in Sydney, I shall send you some photographs, a portrait of Tembinoka, perhaps a view of the
palace or of the "matted men" at their singing; also T's flag which my wife designed for him
… It will thus be a foretaste of my book of travels {never written, but see posthumous
collection *In the South Seas*}. I shall ask you … to make up a little tract of the verses and
illustrations of which you might send six copies to H.M. Tembinoka, King of Apemama.'
MSS: B6322; B6323; B6207; uncat. proof (B7065); H2401; Silverado Foot, MR.VII#3:A–11
First publication: *Scribner's Magazine*, July 1890, pp. 96–9
{Silverado has three sketches of the *Envoi*: two of them are on one page of MR.VII#3:}

        'King of the lions fell and the red hand
        <Like friends we part> We part like brothers; let us part like bards,
        If two should meet and part without one verse,
        Apollo well might wonder; he, the God,
        Far-darter, stronger than your Church, my land
        And little as you think it yours' {breaks off}

        '<But>^And^ our division fitly <celebrate>^solemnize^
        You in your tongue and measure, I in mine,

Our meeting and our parting to rehearse.
Shall you deliver, [?] and he, to his barbaric chorus,
And these, night after night, in the open hall of dance
Shall thirty matted men, to the clapped hand
Intone and bray and bark. Woe with the day!
Paper and ink alone shall honour mine.'

{There is also a sketch for the *Envoi* among the Foot MSS:}

'Unlike our strains, and yet the theme is one
Unlike the strains, and how unlike their fate!
You to the blinding palace yard shall call
<The captain of your men of song> ^The prefect of your singers; to him^
<To a trained man, your valedictory <<verse-strains>>verse>
<Shall you>Deliver; and he next, his part fulfilled,
<To that barbaric chorus hand them on>
To his other island chorus hand your <verses>^measures^ on
<Wed with unblended song>^Wed now with harmony;^ so them, at last'
{The last four lines, 12–15, are identical with *ST* except that in line 14
'Unfortunate!' replaces the cancelled reading 'Woe with the day!' and in line 15
'print' replaces the cancelled reading 'ink'.}

{H2401, a G. S. Hellman confection of six notebook pages from the South Seas period, has
several sketches for XXXVIII, including one for Part I; fragmentary drafts of this portion are
also among the Foot MSS. and at BRBML (B6207):}

'Seed of the shark, her valour first I sing
Who from the shore and puny homes of men
Set <her to>seaward, breasting the <cold waves>^lone deep^ <and met>
That monster <or so they tell>
So they relate; and from that sea-embrace
<Mothered a stronger race and thee, O king>
Conceived the virtues of a stronger race.'

(Foot)

'<Seed>^Bride^ of the shark, her valour first I sing,
<That made thy house, a fit house for a king>
^That on the lone seas quickened with a King.^
<She>Who, from the shore and puny homes of men,
<Filled with strange fire and of undaunted [word omitted]
<Swam unaccompanied <<out>>^forth^<<beyond>>^and past^ the ken
<<Of the>>To her strange tryst with that sea denizen.>'

(B6207) {not noted by McKay}

'The simple sea without an isle or sail
She saw and scanned its face without avail
Sole, <in the heaven> overhead, the unsparing sun was reared
When the deep bubbled and the brute appeared.
<She, not the less, strong in the decree of Fate>
But strong the while in the decrees of Fate
Strong her resolve to face the appointed mate

                    <And men relate>
                    She bared her bosom and received the mate.'

                                          {Lines I 13–14 identical with ST} (Foot)

{There are drafts for Part II at Silverado and HL:}

                    '<Her first, my song shall celebrate
                    Ancestral mother of the state>
                    Her late descendant next I praise
                    Survivor of a thousand frays
                    <Who after growing old in fields of war
                    Displayed a breast without a scar
                    He, when after years of <wicked>war
                    <Death found him, at his hour to die>
                    Death found immaculate of a scar
                    <Bearing his silver crest on high
                    Light of foot and bright of eye>
                    And his followers in the fray
                    Heard him laughing as he smote
                    Blows rained upon his armour coat.
                    Softly the king sat on the throne
                    Who ruled the synod, scorned the throng
                    Led and was trusted by the strong,
                    And when spears were in the wood,
                    Like to a tower of vantage stood.'

                                                  (Foot)

                    'Him next I praise
                    Untouched survivor of a thousand frays
                    Who spoke and led the synod, and who stood
                    Undaunted when the spears were in the wood.
                    Him after seventy years pursuit
                    Still bright of eye, still light of foot,
                    Death, the quarry to pursue,
                    The hunter struck and overthrew.'

                                                  (H2401)

{Fragmentary drafts of Part III exist at Silverado and HL:}

                    'Next the brothers twain I sing
                    One the captain, one the king
                    The greater in the lesser place.'

                                                  (Foot)

                    'The brothers next, the songful and the strong
                    Twin tamers of the [line incomplete]
                    Twin founders of the throne of these [?] isles'

                                                  (H2401)

{This draft at HL anticipates parts IV and V:}

                    'Him last, the King and poet, strong to rule
                    Courteous by race and wise without a school

Who with fell hand laid all opposers low
Yet grieved and wept to see the strangers go.
‹I Ihm better days I wish, and nobler songs›
Him, at his books or cards, at work or sport,
May the cool wind across the palace court
Forever fan; and from <the sighs of village men>^high and swelling seas^
Forever the loud song divert his ear.'

{The other BR.BML MSS and the Scribner's printing collate with ST as follows}
Number: XXXVIII.] <VIII>^IV^ (B7065)
Subtitle: *Envoi*] Envoy (B7065, *Scrib.*) {This section is in italics in *ST* only.}
Line
3, 11   {JAS silently emends 'now' in line 3 to 'new' but I see no authority for this.
         In line 11 she silently emends 'them' to 'then', also without authority:
         'them' clearly refers back to 'measures'.}
8   listening] listing (*Scrib.*)
32   And, men] And men (*Scrib.*, B7065)
51   state,] state; (*Scrib.*)
61   circumstance:] circumstance; (*Scrib.*)
67   untrodden] untrod (*Scrib.*, B7065)
69   constrain,] constrain (*Scrib.*, B7065)
72   head] head, (*Scrib.*)
73   charmed, and] charmed and (*Scrib.*)
80   Tembinok'] Tembinok<,>^'^ (B7065)
83   cocoa-islands] coco-islands (*Scrib.*) <coco-islands>^ ~ ^ (B7065)
{All MSS have variations below the text on 'Schooner *Equator*, at Sea'.}

XXXIX *The Woodman*
Place/date of composition: Vailima, November 1890 (*LETBM*, Vol. VII, No. 2266)
Letter: RLS to Colvin, 2 November 1890 (*LETBM*, Vol. VII, pp. 19, *passim*): 'This is a hard
and interesting and beautiful life that we lead now: our place is in a deep cleft of Vaea
Mountain, some six hundred feet above the sea, embowered in forest, which is our strangling
enemy and which we combat with axes and dollars. I went crazy over outdoor work, and had
at last to confine myself to the house, or literature must have gone by the board. *Nothing* is
so interesting as weeding, clearing and pathmaking ... .Knife in hand, as long as my
endurance lasted I was to cut a path in the congested bush. At first it went ill with me; I got
badly stung as high as the elbows by the stinging plant; I was nearly hung in a tough liana –
a rotten trunk giving way under my feet ... The saplings struggled, and came up with that
sob of death that one gets to know so well; great, soft, sappy trees fell at a lick of the cutlass;
little tough switches laughed at and dared my best endeavour ... Right in the wild lime
hedge which cuts athwart us just homeward of the garden, I found a great bed of *tuitui* –
sensitive plant – our deadliest enemy. A fool brought it to this island in a pot, and used to
lecture and sentimentalise over the tender thing. The tender thing has now taken charge of
this island, and men fight it, with torn hands, for bread and life. A singular insidious thing,
shrinking and biting like a weasel; clutching by its roots as a limpet clutches to a rock. As I
fought him, I bettered some verses in my poem, *The Woodman* ... My long silent contests in
the forest have had a strange effect on me. The unconcealed vitality of these vegetables,

their exuberant number and strength, the attempts – I can use no other word – of lianas to enwrap and capture the intruder, … the whole silent battle, murder and slow death of the contending forest – weighs upon the imagination. My poem *The Woodman* stands; but I have taken refuge in a new story, which just shot through me like a bullet in one of my moments of awe, alone in that tragic jungle: *The High Woods of Ulufanua* {*The Beach of Falesá*}.'

MSS: B7179, B7180, B7181, BRBML uncat. Box 370

First publication: *The New Review*, January 1895

{B7179, on four pages of the notebook called *First Drafts of Poems*, lacks the last seventy-two lines:}

Line

1   bird] bird,

2   heard,] heard;

3   dress –] dress,

5   From the island summit to the seas,]
        <Down all the slope of the huge hill>^ ~ seas^

6   and trees] and <still> trees

7   Groped upward] <Trees sprouted><Pushed upward>^ ~ ^

12   a sea,] the sea

{14–17 in B7179:}

       'Late from this scene my labourer fled
       Fear-footed, with averted head
       <Some presence, what he could not tell,>
       ^From something, what he scarce could tell^
       Of life or not, <of heaven or hell>^but something fell^'

19   trod,] trod.

20–1 And triumphed when he turned to flee.
       How different fell the lines with me!]
       How different was the chance for me
       Who only longed to hear and see,

23   shade –] shade<s>;

24   cold,] cold

{This block in B7179 corresponds to lines 26–33; the last nine lines are published only in *BBS*, II, pp. 162–3:}

       'In vain. The rooted multitude
       All dumb and green <about>^around^ me stood
       <And tranquil>^Impassive^ as departed kings
       The stupid fair and sturdy things –
       My troubled heart, how still they seemed! –
       Nodded and brooded, bloomed and dreamed.
       <No other art it seemed>^And sure no other art^ they knew
       Than clutch the earth and seek the blue.
       Daily to spread a greener hood,
       Drink deep of air and rain, and brood
       <In all their> On timber navels. I could <trace>^see^
       No sting to their vitality,
       <No glory> of the wealth and race,
       No pang <to fire the> to set a price on life,

No wink before the falling knife –
No empty tombs, no broken rules,
In that green paradise of fools.'

{In ST there is a stanza break between lines 33 and 34.}
35   (the only beast)] the only beast
36   beast's work, killing;] <beasts'> hunters' work, killing –
39   sheaves;] sheaves:
41   path,] path:
42   that, later on,] that later on,
44   bear] smile
45   Here and there,] All the while,

{This block in B7179 corresponds to lines 46–60:}
  'I plucked the root that loves to live,
  The toothed and killing sensitive.
  I saw it shrink, I felt it bite.
  Straight were my eyeballs touched with sight.
  I saw the wood for what it was: –
  The lost and the victorious cause: –
  The deadly battle pitched in line,
  Where silent weapons cross and shine: –
  Silent defeat, silent assault:
  A battle and a burial vault.'
64   reluctant] affrighted
65   There the green murderer throve and spread,]
  <And the green murderer spreading strife>^ ~ <fed>spread^
66   Upon his smothering victims fed,] <Fed slow upon a shuddering life –>
        ^ ~ <shuddering>strangling victim fed
67   And wantoned on his climbing coil.] <Sang merry by his climbing coil.>^ ~ ^
68   roots] <branches>^ ~ ^
72   dead:] dead.
{Trial fragments from B7179:}
  'Not as when men to battle go
  And the reviving bugles blow,'

  'Behind my warrior saplings, I
  A more insidious foe could spy,' {Cf. Letter 2266, p. 25}

{B7180 is a fragment beginning at line 90:}
91   And all] And <through> all
92   Ring with] Ring<s> <round> with
  {The line here in B7180 is not in ST:}
  'So unremitting, so ingrained,'
93   perceive.] perceive;
94   Crowds perish,] <They>^Crowds^ perish;
95   A few!] the few

97   scanty] paltry
100   – See, … bridge] See, … bridge,
104   unbrotherly] unpaternal
114   the tender, kind, and gay,] the tender <bland>^kind^ and gay
115   the spud] her spud,
118   See!] See,

{The following is a collation of *ST* with B7181, 370 and the magazine printing, which deserves attention as copy for it was sent by RLS to Henley, editor of *The New Review*:}
Number: XXXIX.] VII. (B7181)
Line
    2   was heard,] ~ heard (*New Review*) were ~ (370, *Thistle*)
    3   dress –] dress, (370)
    4   silentness.] <silences.>^ ~ ^ (B7181)
    9   multitude,] multitude (370)
    11   stood:] stood, (*New Review*)
    12   sea,] sea (B7181, 370)
    15   Late from this scene my labourer fled,]
            <Fear-footed, with averted head>^ ~ fled^ (370)
    19   trod,] trod (370)
    21   How different fell the lines with me!]
            <Who> How different <was>^fell^ the <choice>^lines^ with me, (370)
    22   Whose eye explored the dim arcade] ~ arcade, (*New Review*)
            <Who only longed to hear and see>^ ~ ^ (370)
    23   shade –] shade. (370)
    25   old:] old! (370)
    26   Vainly. The fair and stately things,]
            In vain. <The rooted multitude>^These ~ things^ (370)
    29   And dumb. The rooted multitude]
            <And in the dumbness of the wood>^<All>^And^ ~ ^ (370)
    31   Unmeaning, undivined.] Unmeaning; <and for sure> undivined. (370)
    32   hope, they] hope they (*New Review*)
            {Stanza break between lines 33 and 34 in *ST* and *Thistle* and in all MSS: not observed in B7179, *ST* 1896 or *CP*.}
    34   'Mid] Mid (370, *New Review*)
    35   I (the only beast)] I, the only beast, (370)
    36   work, killing; hewed] work killing – hewed (370)
    39   sheaves;] sheaves: (B7181) sheaves (370)
    40   math] math – (*New Review*)
    41   path,] path: (*New Review*)
    42   Golgotha that, later on,] Golgotha<,> ~ (B7181) ~ that later on (370)
                                Golgotha, that ~ (*New Review*)
    43   watered, and suns shone,] watered and suns shone (370)
    44   place, should bear] place should <smile>^bear^ (370)
    45   Here and there,] Once in a while {'Here and there' appears in the margin} (370)
    46   by the green hair] <a few><by its>^ ~ ^ (370)
    46–7   I spied and plucked by the green hair
            A foe more resolute to live,]

Betwixt my stalwart saplings, I
A more insidious foe <would>^might^spy:
The plant that lives to stay and hive, (370)

47   live,] live – (*New Review*)
48   sensitive.] sensitive (B7181)
50   He ... his ... back;] It ... its ... back, (370) ~ back, (*New Review*)
51   And ... his ... strand,] Or ... <its>^his^ ~ (370) And, ~(*New Review*)
                                          ·· strand (B7181)
53   him ... him bite;] <it>^him^ ... <it>^him^ bite: (370) ~ bite, (*New Review*)
54   And straight my eyes were ... sight.] Straight were my eyeballs ... sight (370)
55   was:] was – (*New Review*)
56   cause,] cause; (*New Review*)
58   Saw silent ... shine:] The silent ~ (370, B7181) ~ shine; (*New Review*)
59   assault,] assault – (*New Review*)
60   burial] final (370)
61   mud] mud, (*New Review*)
64   reluctant ... in:] <reluctant>^affrighted^ ... in. (370) ~ in; (*New Review*)
66   smothering victims] throtling victim (370)
69   frightened demons:] ~ demons; (*New Review*) frighted ~ (B7181, 370)
71   overhead] overhead, (370)
72   dead:] dead; (*New Review*)
73   silvan] sylvan (*ST*, 1896)
74   yield:] yield; (370, *New Review*)
        {inserted after this line in 370 but cancelled:}
        'Not as when men to battle go,
        And the reviving bugles blow: –'
77   as in ... ring] ~ ring, (*New Review*) as, in (370)
78   Two chartered wrestlers strain and cling,]
        <The>^Two^ noted ~ <swing>^cling;^ (370) ~ cling; (*New Review*)
79–80   Dumb as by yellow Hooghly's side
        The suffocating captives died:]
        <Strove, struggled, stumbled <<strangled>> fell and died>
        <The suffocating mob>
        <The murdered <<of the dungeon>>struggled, thronged and died>
        <The expiring rack of wretches shut
        In the black hole of Calicut: – >
        <In silent battle, dumb defeat,> (370)
79   <Silent>^Dumb,^ (370)
81   So hushed ... goes] <All still>^ ~ goes,^ (370)
82   Unceasing; and ... foes] <So>Incessant and ... foes, (370) <Incessant>^ ~ ^
        (7181)
84   {stanza break indicated here: 370, B7181.}
85   God,] God. (370)
86   Here too] Here, too (*New Review*)
88   earth, thy threshing-floor!] ~ <winnowing>^threshing^ floor. (370)
                                    earth thy ~ (*New Review*) ~ threshing floor! (B7181)
        {After line 89, 370 breaks off, with this fragment:}

'Shall then thy gentle service cease
My master? And the word of peace
Inefficacious fall? And good
Be exiled? In the deadly wood
The egoist tree fights for his hand …'
94   perish,] perish, – (*New Review*)
98   Wilderness?] wilderness? (*New Review*) Wilderness? – (B7181)
99   ridge?] ridge? – (*New Review*)
100   – See,] See, (*New Review*)
107   sound.] sound; (*New Review*) sound: (B7181)
114   wife, the … gay,] wife – the … gay – (*New Review*)

XL *Tropic Rain*
Date/place of composition: Vailima, 1890 (Balfour)
Letter: RLS to Colvin, 24 December 1890 (*LETBM*, Vol. VII, p. 59): 'Yesterday, who could write? … the rain descending in white crystal rods and playing hell's tattoo, like a *tutti* of battering rams, on our sheet iron roof; the wind passing high overhead with a strange dumb wuther, or striking us full, so that all the huge trees in the paddock cried aloud, and wrung their hands, and brandished their vast arms. The horses stood in the shed like things stupid. The sea and the flagship lying in the jaws of the bay vanished in sheer rain. All day it lasted … I have always feared the sound of wind beyond everything: in my hell it would always blow a gale.' {For RLS's reactions to storms cf. *UW* 2. XIII, *Late in the Nicht*, and the notes on *Windy Nights*.}
MSS: B7064, B7065, B7066
{B7064 is a thirty-one-line version in the notebook, *First Drafts of Poems*:}
'The murk of the night was solid; a trowel had plastered it on;
Blue as the summer heaven, the levin glanced and was gone.
As the single pang of the blow, when the metal is mingled well,
Rings <live>, and lives and resounds in all the bounds of the bell,
So the thunder above spoke with a single tongue –
So in the <guts> heart of the mountain the sound of it rumbled and <clung.>^rung.^
<Long was the storm>So thundered and strove – till lo! a jubilant river of rain
<Suddenly stunned the storm, and the mountains answered again>
<Suddenly pealed and fell, with a sound that beat on the ear>
<The innocent joys of bathers, the innermost pangs of fear>
And pleased as a girl of the islands stands, with streaming hair,
By the well known pool of the river, when all of the village is there,
And laughs aloud to her <virgin> mates, and shivers and plunges deep:
The virgin spirit of rain laughed and leaned to her leap.
So – spirit of rain – for a moment I saw you attired
<In freshness and mirth, and my heart and the eyes of my heart admired>
And loud as the maddened <cataract>^river^ raves in the cloven glen,
Spirit of rain! You bellowed and fell on the houses of men.
And the houses shook and the hearts of men were amazed as you fell.
You struck, and my cabin quailed; the roof of it roared like a bell,
You spoke, and at once the mountain shouted and shook with brooks.

You ceased, and the day <came over the hills>returned, rosy, with <modest>^virgin^
looks. {alt. "hills."}
<And behold in the forge of the watcher, the sedulous smith of books,
The fire sprang in the ash and the metal rang as I heard,
And rhyme rallied to rhyme, and word was wedded to word.>
And I wrote that terror and beauty were only one, not two'

{The rest of the MS is identical with *ST*, as is B7066, a fair copy in the hand of Belle Strong. Also present on this MS are the number XXXI and the following note below the text, both in the hand of RLS: 'To S.C., Is it worth a note that I had written this ere I saw Henley's poem, which has identical words?' B7065 is copy for *Verses*, collated below with *ST*:}
Number: XL.] VI
Line
  5   Sudden] <And> ~
  6   angel-spirit] angel spirit
10   bell,] bell.
15   all the] <the>^ ~ ^
16   rock, … fair.] rock – fair<:>^.^
{RLS has indicated stanza breaks after the following lines: 4, 9, 12, 16; *ST* has stanza breaks after lines 4 and 12. B7065 has been followed.}

XLI *An End of Travel*
Place of composition: Vailima
MSS: B6189, B6190, NLS3791
{B6189 is in fact two sketches for this poem in the notebook, *First Drafts of Poems*:}

    '<This be my enduring balm, wherein>
    Let now <my>^your^ soul more constantly embrace in this substantial world
    Some anchor strike; be now <your>^the^ body moored
    Or as the kite, migrant in windy heaven,
    <Where the moon> and from this world, wherein your horse
    Conveys you dreaming; when the time arrives
    <The latest helpers bear your body dead:>
    And the last helpers – where your horse today
    Conveyed you dreaming – bear your body dead.'

    'Let now your soul in this substantial world
    Some anchor strike. Be here the body moored.
    Be this green scene immutably from now
    The picture in your eye; <till all go and> Let in your ear,
    The neighbouring valley falls <And the near streams> and the far surf,
    Scarce audible, forevermore contend
    <And mingle, and the unheeded world go by>
    The unheeded stream of the' {A line here indicates that RLS meant to conclude this draft with the last two lines of the draft above.}

{B6190, copy for *Verses*, and NLS are collated with *ST* as follows:}

Title/number: XLI. *An End of Travel*] III. {untitled} (B6190)

{untitled, unnumbered} (NLS)

Line

2   strike.] take. (NLS)

5   blind –] blind, – (NLS)

6–7   helpers, where your horse today

         Conveyed you dreaming,]

         Helpers (where your horse today

         Conveyed you dreaming) (B6190)

XLII 'We uncommiserate pass into the night'

MSS: B7104; Pierpont Morgan MA4500

     {MA4500 is a fair copy identical with the copy-text; B7104 is a sketch, as follows:}

'<Lo, one by one, we go>^We uncommiserate^ pass into the night

From the loud banquet; and departing leave –

A tremor in men's memories, faint and sweet

And frail as <is the voice of violins><as violin's>music

So we <depart> vanish in oblivion progressive; <our voices die to silence>

                                    and <our traits> <face> features of our face

Grow dim in the inward mirror of the mind.

<Oblivion on the music of our voice

Consuming feeds, and the>

<Tones of our nice speech, the image of our life>

^The tones of the voice, the touch of the loved hand^

Perish, and vanish, one by one, from earth:

<Last in the lighted hall mid the new youth

One inconspicuous image lingers in the crowd>

Meanwhile in the hall of song, the multitude

Applauds the new performer. Only a while

Some lone survivor <calls our image of youth><sitting with the new>

                                    lingers in the crowd,

And smiles and to his ancient <heart>^eyes^ recalls

<One transient image>

The long-forgotten. Ere the morrow die

He too <the straggler>^returning^ through the curtain comes

<He><By the low stage door and the new play goes on.>

<But we <<the generation>>^that lived and^ sang in the sad past

And <all is at an end> ^the new age forgets us,^ and goes on.'

XLIII *The Last Sight*

Place/date of composition: Edinburgh, 1887 (Thomas Stevenson, the poet's father, died at his home on 8 May 1887.)

Letters: 1. RLS to Colvin [late May 1887] (*LETBM*, Vol. V, p. 411): 'About the death, I have long hesitated, I was long before I could tell my mind; and now I know it and can but say that I am glad. If we could have had my father, that would have been a different thing. But to keep that changeling – suffering changeling – any longer, could better none and nothing. Now he rests; it is more significant, it is more like himself; he will begin to return to us in the course of time as he was and as we loved him. My favourite words in literature, my favourite scene – "O let him pass," – Kent and Lear – was played for me here in the first moment of my return. I believe Shakespeare saw it with his own father. I had no words; but it was shocking to see. He died on his feet, you know; was on his feet the last day, knowing nobody – still he would be up. '

2. RLS to Adelaide Boodle, 14 July 1894 (*LETBM*, Vol. VIII, p. 327): 'You remember perhaps, when my father died, you told me those ugly images of sickness, decline and impaired reason, which then haunted me day and night, would pass away and be succeeded by things more happily characteristic. I have found it so; he now haunts me, strangely enough, in two guises: as a man of fifty, lying on a hillside and carving mottoes on a stick, strong and well – and as a younger man running down the sands into the sea near North Berwick, myself – *aetat.* eleven – somewhat horrified at finding him so beautiful when stripped!'

MSS: B6493, B6281, B6282

{The last two MSS contain pencil sketches for a poem on RLS's father; about twenty-five lines long, it begins, 'He was a man as debonair to view'. It remained unfinished and unpublished until he sent the last six lines to Colvin as part of *ST*. Colvin set it up in type along with the other verses but suppressed it. It was first published in *Thistle*, Vol. XVI, p. 261, the text which is followed here. Edmund Gosse published a bowdlerised version in his *Biographical Notes* (1908), omitting the words, 'sate attired / A something in his likeness'. B6493 is copy for *Verses*, in which collection it was to have been No. XV. I did not examine B6281 and B6282. B6493 collates with *Thistle* as follows:}

Line

1   lofty] <left>^ ~ ^
3   trump to honest laughter,] <the honest trump to laughter,>^ ~ ^
4   look up, it] look up it

XLIV 'Sing me a song of a lad that is gone'

Date of composition: 1887 (Balfour)

Source: 'The writing of *Over the Sea to Skye* grew out of a visit from one of the last of the old school of Scots Gentlewomen, Miss Ferrier, a granddaughter of Professor Wilson (Christopher North). Her singing was a great delight to my husband, who would beg for song after song, especially the Jacobite airs, which had always to be repeated several times. The words to one of these seemed unworthy, so he made a new set of verses more in harmony with the plaintive tune.'

   Fanny Stevenson, Prefatory Note to *Underwoods*, VAIL, Vol. 8, p. 89

MS: Uncat. proof (B7065)

First publication: *Pall Mall Gazette*, 31 December 1894; *Pall Mall Budget*, 3 January 1895. {No MS of this poem was included in the Sotheby's sale of 1979 (see above, p. 485).}

Title/number: XLIV. {untitled}] <XV>^XXIV^ *Over the Sea to Skye* (B7065)

                    Over the Sea to Skye (*Pall Mall*)

Line

5   Rum] Egg (both MSS)
6   Eigg ... bow;] Rum ... bow: (both MSS)

XLV *To S. R. Crockett*

(*On receiving a Dedication*)

Place/date of composition: Vailima, c. 15 August 1893 (*LETBM*, Vol. VIII, No. 2622 is so dated)

Letters: {Crockett had dedicated his *The Stickit Minister and Some Common Men* as follows: 'To / Robert Louis Stevenson / of Scotland and Samoa, / I dedicate these stories / of that grey Galloway land, / where, about the graves of the martyrs, / the whaups are crying – / his heart has not forgotten how.' In later editions of his story collection, Crockett included XLV as a prefatory poem, altering the final words of his dedication to echo line 4, 'his heart remembers how'. RLS enclosed the poem with his letter to Crockett of 15 August 1893. See Explanatory Note on this poem, pp. 628–9} 1. RLS to Crockett [c. 15 August 1893] (*LETBM*, Vol. VIII, pp. 152–4): 'Thank you from my heart, and see, with what dull pedantry I have been tempted to extend your beautiful phrase of prose into three indifferent stanzas.'

2. RLS to Colvin, 4 September (*LETBM*, Vol. VIII, p. 159): 'And then you could actually see Vailima, which I *would* like you to, for it's beautiful and my home and tomb that is to be; though it's a wrench not to be planted in Scotland – that I can never deny – if I could only be buried in the hills, under the heather and a table tombstone like the martyrs, where the whaups and plovers are crying! Did you see a little man who wrote *The Stickit Minister*, and dedicated it to me, in words that brought the tears to my eyes every time I looked at them. "Where about the graves of the martyrs the whaups are crying. *His* heart remembers how." Ah, by God, it does! Singular that I should fulfill the Scots Destiny throughout, and live a voluntary exile, and have my head filled with the blessed, beastly place all the time!'

3. RLS to Lord Roseberry, 5 December 1893 (*LETBM*, Vol. VIII, pp. 193–4): 'My father is dead; many of my friends are "lapped in lead"; and to return {to Scotland} would be to me superlatively painful. Only I wish I could be buried there – among the hills, say on the head of Allermuir – with a table tombstone like a Cameronian.'

MSS: Letter No. 2622; NLS 7482; 8th edition of *The Stickit Minister* (1894) – this limited issue includes a facsimile of the MS enclosed with Letter 2622, a printed transcription of it and Crockett's altered dedication to RLS.

First publication: *Pall Mall Gazette*, 12 December 1894

{NLS is printer's copy for *Pall Mall*; 2622 and the Crockett facsimile are identical; NLS was in the Sotheby's sale of 1979.}

Title/number: XLV. *To S. R. Crockett*

(*On receiving a Dedication*)] {untitled, unnumbered} (2622)

Home Thoughts From Samoa (*Pall Mall*) <XVIII>^XV^ {untitled} (NLS)

~ *On Receiving A Dedication* (Gosse proofs)

Line

1 flying,] flying – (2622)

5 Grey recumbent] Grey, recumbent (2622)

6 Standing-stones … vacant wine-red] Standing Stones (2622, NLS) {The reading, 'Standing Stones', has been adopted.} vacant, wine-red (2622)

7 homes of the silent] howes ~ (NLS, 2622) {This reading has been adopted.}
                          ~ <dead and silent>^silent^ (Crockett: MS facsimile)

8 pure:] pure! (2622) pure<!> [?^ – ^] (NLS) {Neither a colon nor a dash is required here, unless one considers the second stanza vocative rather than evocative, so I have

adopted the reading found in all the extant MSS, 'pure!'; although the exclamation mark seems to have been cancelled in NLS, it is unclear whether the line through the bottom of it is a dash replacing it or just part of the cancellation; no other replacement punctuation is evident on this MS. The exclamation mark has the further effect of paralleling the final line of the first stanza.}

10   home! ... call;] ~ call – (2622) Home! ... call. (NLS)
11   peewees] pee-wees (2622)
{Below text} *Vailima.*] {only in *ST*}

XLVI   *Evensong*
Place of Composition: Vailima
MSS: B6200, B6201, B6202
{The first two versions are in the notebook, *First Drafts of Poems*: the last seven lines, printed as a third stanza in *BBS*, II, p. 168 and in *CP*, p. 519, because Hellman thought they continued the fifteen lines comprising XLVI, seem utterly unconnected with this poem, being one of RLS's martial effusions. B6202 is copy for *Verses*.}
Title/number: XLVI. *Evensong*.] *Even Song* (B6200, B6201) IX. ~ (B6202)
Line
4   spread:] spread; (B6200)
5   overhead,] overhead (B6201)
8   Thy] thy (B6202)
9   from the embalmèd land] from <off> the <hot><scented> (B6200)
10   Blows ... shore,] Draws ~ (B6200) ~ shore (B6201, B6202)
13   Lord – I understand.] <lord,>^Lord – ^ <and>^I^ understand<:>^.^
14–15 The night at Thy command
         Comes. I will eat and sleep and will not question more.]
         <Sleep is at hand>The night <comes> at thy command,
         Comes;<and><I lay me down and will not wonder> more. I will eat and sleep,
         <nor question more> and will not question more. (B6200)
15   sleep and] sleep, and (B6201)
{Below text, *Vailima*}] Only in B6202

{Hellman's 'additional second stanza' is as follows:}
'So in the furthest camp of man –
         Where he deems himself alone,
Left without sign or plan,
         At random in a desert thrown –
For ears that hear, for running feet,
There daily is the tattoo beat,
         There the réveillé blown.'

The Private Printings of S. L. Osbourne & Co.

History of Composition and Publication

The publisher is of course RLS and his stepson Lloyd, who issued printed items between 1880 and 1882 from San Francisco, Silverado, Davos-Platz, Edinburgh and Kingussie. Assessing this aspect of RLS's poetic activity requires a perspective which can balance high-spirited schoolboy playfulness with underlying moral and aesthetic seriousness. When Colvin refused to include *Moral Emblems* in *EDIN*, the poet was indignant, telling him flatly that he was wrong:

> They're a lark, they will occupy but a few pages of the Edition, they are known to be mine, they have something of the currency of a temporary classic – for instance, what quotation do you see more commonly than 'he will regret it when he's dead'? [see above, p. 208]; and considering all this to leave them them out would appear to me only the wisdom of the ostrich. (*LETBM*, Vol. VIII, p. 383)

In 1880, Sam Osbourne (as Lloyd was then called) acquired a printing press while attending school in California. Not a toy but a real platen press, it was nevertheless simple enough for a child to operate, with automatic inking. His new stepfather took an immediate interest in *The Daily Surprise*, the newspaper that the eleven-year-old boy was writing and printing. On 6 March that year the first verse of RLS's poem *Not I*, written especially for the young printer, appeared in *The Surprise*, a semi-monthly periodical that Sam was selling for 25 cents per month. When on 4 November he accompanied his mother and stepfather to the Belvedere Hotel in Davos-Platz, the printing press went with him and *The Surprise* was succeeded by *The Davos News*, offered for 5 centimes per issue. The boy earned pocket money printing menus for the hotel, programmes for recitals and lottery tickets for a local bazaar. In Osbourne's Preface to his 1921 edition of *Moral Emblems*, he recorded his anxieties over how much he was costing his parents, all too conscious that Fanny was still dependent on her father Sam and RLS depended on his own father for periodic bail-outs. For RLS, what had begun as a game to amuse a child became an opportunity for a frustrated graphic artist (his notebooks abound in drawings) to experiment with woodcuts and verses to match: *A Martial Elegy For Some Lead Soldiers*, the first of the Davos-Platz pamphlets containing poetry by RLS, was produced late in November of 1880, followed next year by *Not I, and other Poems*, issued in October. In March of 1882 RLS was sending proofs of his wood engravings for *Moral Emblems* to amuse his family and friends; to his parents he said,

> Inclosed are two woodcuts of my cutting: they are moral emblems; one represents 'anger' the other 'pride scorning poverty'. They will appear among others, all accompanied by verses in my new work published by S.L. Osbourne. If my father does not enjoy these, he is no true man. (*LETBM*, Vol. III, p. 299)

By April a second series of *Moral Emblems* was in the press.

Shortly after the Stevensons left Switzerland for Scotland in the spring of 1882, the small press broke down, but the intrepid printer and his author managed to execute their most ambitious scheme to date, a miscellany of illustrated verses called *The Graver and the Pen*, by gaining access to a printing press at Kingussie. *Moral Tales* was the next project of Osbourne & Co. *The Builder's Doom*, begun in March 1870 as *The Deacon's Crescent*, was now revised. *Robin and Ben* and *The Perfect Cure* were written in 1881–2; woodcuts were made for *Robin and Ben* but none of this verse ever got beyond fair copy and typescript in RLS's lifetime. Even though her husband and son had been eager to publish these productions, Fanny opposed it; just after RLS's death, she wrote to Fanny Sitwell, later Lady Colvin, as follows

> Please tell him [Colvin] I absolutely forbid the *Moral Emblems* from going into the Collected Edition. It is not fit nor dignified that they should. Never mind what anyone else says: I have the first right and I say that *they shall not* go in. (December 1894: McKay, Vol. III, B3741)

However, Colvin belatedly acceded to the late author's wishes rather than to those of his wife, including two of the unpublished *Moral Tales* along with facsimiles of the major Osbourne & Co. pamphlets in the Appendix to *EDIN*, Vol. XXVIII (1898). In the following year, this material, augmented by facsimiles of some MSS of *Moral Tales*, was republished by Chatto and Windus in a limited issue of 350 copies called *A Stevenson Medley*. Less complete and exact reproductions appeared in the Swanston Edition, *VAIL* and *TUS*.

Copy-texts chosen are the first editions of each pamphlet or, when the poem is unpublished, the MS. It has been thought pedantic to reproduce every crudity of Lloyd Osbourne's typesetting. Details of MSS and printed texts will be given below in the Textual Notes on Individual Poems; variants are given selectively. Full bibliographical descriptions will be found in McKay, Vols I and VI, Prideaux and Livingston (1917) and Thomas J. Wise's *A Catalogue of the Ashley Library*, Vols IX and X (1922–36). The fullest study of this matter is James D. Hart's *The Private Press Ventures of Samuel Lloyd Osbourne and R.L.S.* (The Book Club of San Francisco, 1966), which also offers removable facsimiles. At BRBML there is a sort of scrapbook, an oversize folio volume containing what must be every scrap of Davos-Platz ephemera. Titled *DAVOS-PLATZ 1881–82* and shelf-marked Iip / St48 / C881, it contains 'a collection of woodcuts, proofs, original drawings, manuscripts, advertisements etc. executed by [RLS and Lloyd] at Davos-Platz during the winter of 1881–2' (from the title-page). The Boston Public Library has eighteen wood blocks from which the *Moral Emblems* were printed: the call number for these is G.Cab.3.128. On 3 November 1921, Chatto and Windus and Scribner's published an edition of *Moral Emblems and Other Poems* including reproductions of the woodcuts with a preface by Lloyd Osbourne.

Textual Notes on Individual Poems

A Martial Elegy for Some Lead Soldiers
Place/date of composition: Davos, November 1880 (*LETBM*, Vol. III, No. 745)
Letter: Fanny Stevenson to Margaret Stevenson, 21 November 1880 (*LETBM*, Vol. III, p. 122): 'If the press comes in time, Sam will set up and print a poem by Louis, (not yet written) and sell it for the ladies' Church Bazaar.' {Lloyd wrote to Mrs Stevenson a week later to say that his repaired press had arrived and that he had printed twenty-four copies of this poem, the first fruit of the Davos Press.}
Printed text: 'A *Martial Elegy for some lead Soldiers*' / [rule] / [followed by 18 lines of verse]

[Below text:] 'Price 1 penny.(1ˢᵗ Edition.)' Twelvemo leaflet. *Verso* blank. Wove paper. On Edmund Gosse's presentation copy RLS wrote these lines:

> The verse is mine; the printing done by Sam
> > The Boss of printing Bosses;
> This copy, of the first edition last,
> > I testify is Gosse's.

> > > > > R.L.S.

{There is a facsimile of the Gosse inscription in Hart 1966b: 20. In the *Davos-Platz 1881–2* folio at BRBML, this leaflet is mounted on a page with a printed map depicting the imaginary country where RLS and Lloyd staged one of their elaborate campaigns with lead soldiers; also on this page is a crude woodcut vignette of the head in profile of a lead soldier, presumably one of the casualties lamented in this poem.}
MSS: B6561, B6562 {B6561 is No. II in 'Pieces in English', in the dismembered Notebook A.155; B6562 is written in Notebook 'H'.}
Title: *A Martial Elegy For Some Lead Soldiers*]
> II. *A Martial Elegy on some lead soldiers.*
> > (*sold for one penny*). (B6561)

Line
1   For certain soldiers lately dead] <For certain heroes dead>^ ~ ^ (B6562)
4   appalled;] appalled. (B6562)
6   them steadfast] them, steadfast (B6562)
7   foe,] foe (B6562)
10 Pea-cannon's] Pea-Cannon's (B6561) peacannon's (B6562)
11 O not for them the tears we shed,] O! not for them, the tear we shed, (B6561)
12 lead;] lead, (B6562)
13 their sleep they take,] <they take their sleep>^ ~ take^ (B6562)
14 We mourn for their dear Captain's sake,] ~ captain's sake. – (B6561)
    <For their dear general we weep – >^ ~ captain's sake – ^ (B6562)
16 heart,] heart; (B6562)
18 more!] more. (B6561)

Not I, and Other Poems

Date of composition: February 1880 (*LETBM*, Vol. III, No. 691)
Letters: 1. RLS to Lloyd Osbourne, [?February 1880] (*LETBM*, Vol. III, pp. 67–8): 'If the enclosed should be found suitable for the pages of your esteemed periodical, you will oblige me by giving it an early insertion.' {Copied in the margin is a three-stanza version of *Not I*; the first verse was published in *The Surprise* on 6 March (facsimile in Hart 1966b: 10). The complete version including the 'other poems' appeared in the Davos Press pamphlet of 1881.}

2. Lloyd Osbourne to Margaret Stevenson, 24 October 1881 (McKay, Vol. VI, B8268): 'Today I have finished *Not I* much to my delight.'
Printed Text: 'NOT I, / And Other POEMS, / BY / Robert Louis Stevenson, / Author of / *The Blue Scalper, Travels* / *with a Donkey* etc. / Price 6d.' *Verso* of title-page is the following: 'Dedicated to / Messrs. R. & R. Clark / by / *S.L. Osbourne* / Davos / 1881' At foot of p. 8 is

the colophon: 'Begun Feb. ended Oct.1881.' Twenty-fourmo pamphlet, sewed, without wrappers. Wove paper, leaves trimmed. 1 signature, pp. [1 – 3] 5 – 8. 50 copies printed. MSS: B6635 (text of poem in Letter 1); B6636

{B6636 is a draft on p. 55 of Notebook 'C' of the dedication, but in the hand of RLS: 'Dedicated to Messrs. R. & R. Clark, printers, without permission, by S. L. Osbourne, Davos, 1881.' B6635 has three numbered eight-line stanzas, all lines aligned left; the copy-text has four unnumbered four-line stanzas with lines 8, 12 and 16 indented:

Title: *Not I.*] *Not I!*

Line

 2 pot,] pot.

10 Scott,] Scott.

13 laugh,] fight,

15 Some like chaff;] Sam likes to write;

{B6635 has a third stanza not in the copy-text:}

> 'Now, there's enough;
> Clear without a blot.
> Some may like the stuff;
> Some not.
> Some will say "Encore!"
> And Some "O fie!"
> Some would do some more;
> Not I!
>   R.L.S.'

{No MS was found for the 'Other Poems'.}

Moral Emblems

Date of composition: March–April 1882 (*LETBM*, Vol. III, Nos 929–33)

Letter: RLS to Alexander Ireland [late March 1882] (*LETBM*, Vol. III, p. 303): {He included some proofs of *Moral Emblems*.} 'I enclose a good joke – at least, I think so – my first efforts at wood-engraving printed by my stepson, a boy of thirteen. I will put in also one of my later attempts. I have been nine days at the art – observe my progress.'

Printed text: twenty-fourmo pamphlet, unbound, laid paper. One signature: six leaves, sewn through the middle, no pagination, no numbering of verses. There are five emblems, each consisting of a poem with an illustration. A wood engraving occupies the *verso*, and verses the *recto* of each leaf; page [1] is the title-page and page [12] is an advertisement of '*Works recently issued by / Samuel Osbourne & Co. / Davos*.

MSS: None found.

A second series of *Moral Emblems* containing five more woodcuts with accompanying verses by RLS was announced by S. L. Osbourne & Co. in a printed advertisement on the back of a Davos concert programme dated 4 April 1882. They have the same format and collation as the first series except that wove paper was used.

MS: *Lord Nelson and the Tar* (NLS Notebook 'T', MS 19637, f.2). {These lines were first published as one of the *Moral Tales* on p. 449 of the revised edition of *CP* (1971). JAS took her text from a copy made by Graham Balfour that she found among the Balfour Papers in NLS. Since then NLS acquired Notebook 'T': the sixteen-line draft therein, selected as copy-text, collates with the *CP* text as follows:}

Line
6   a-bobbin',] a bobbin;
7–8   [2 lines cancelled, illegible]
9   rear admiral] your Admiral
13   <*Thus*> ^*Hence*^ ... *vanity*,] ~ vanity
13–14   {In italics in NLS}
{This short piece with its accompanying woodcut is not a tale; it has been placed at the end of the *Moral Emblems*. There is a copy of the woodcut at BRBML.}

The Graver and the Pen

Date of composition: August 1882 (*LETBM*, Vol. III, No. 978, n.4)
Printed text: 'THE / GRAVER & THE PEN, / or / Scenes from Nature with / Appropriate Verses / by / ROBERT LOUIS STEVENSON / author of / 'The New Arabian Nights', 'Moral Emblems', / 'Not I', / 'Treasure Island', etc. / *Illustrated*. / Edinburgh / *S.L. Osbourne & Company* / No.17 HERIOT ROW. / [It was only by the kindness of Mr. CRERAR of Kingussie / that we are able to issue this little work – having allow– / ed us to print with his own press when ours was broken.]'
Sixteenmo pamphlet bound in French-grey paper wrappers with lettering in red on upper cover: *The / Graver & The Pen.* / Wove paper. Edges uncut. One signature: twelve leaves, sewn through the middle with red thread, no pagination, no numbering of verses. There is a title-page with *verso* blank, a proem and five poems and five full-page wood engravings with *verso* blank; p. [24] is blank.
MSS: None found.
CP reproduced the text of the first edition, with some changes. JAS omitted the full stop after each title. On p. 428 she indented every other line of *The Precarious Mill* whereas the copy-text is aligned left throughout. In *The Disputatious Pines*, lines 5, 8 and 10, she corrected errors in the positioning of quotation marks and added a comma after 'tree' in line 7. In line 16 she changed 'martens' to 'martins', presumably correcting a reference to mammals where one to birds seems to have been intended: this emendation I have not followed, as either spelling is acceptable in reference to birds. I have not changed the RLS readings and format except to correct misspellings. He refused Colvin's request that he correct and improve these collaborations with Lloyd for *EDIN* (see *LETBM*, Vol. VIII, p. 308). Finally, I do not follow JAS in eliminating a space and a rule separating the last six lines of *The Foolhardy Geographer* from the rest of the poem: these were appended as an afterthought – the 'blemish in the cut' is a scratch on the block caused when RLS jabbed the graver into his thumb.

Moral Tales

Date of composition: 1882 (*LETBM*, Vol. IV, p. 29, n.1)
Source: In his Preface to the Chatto & Windus / Scribner's 1921 *Moral Emblems and Other Poems*, Lloyd Osbourne wrote, 'The Pirate and the Apothecary* was projected; three superb illustrations were engraved for it; yet it never saw more light than the typewriter afforded. *The Builder's Doom* has remained in manuscript until the present time.' {Osbourne failed to note that both these tales appeared in *EDIN*.}
Printed text: Copy-text is the First Edition, *EDIN*, Vol. XXVIII, Appendix (1898):

Collation: Pp. ii +20. Half-title, *MORAL TALES* [i, ii], *verso* blank; 'Rob and Ben / or / The PIRATE and the APOTHECARY. / Scene the First.' pp. [1,2], *verso* blank; '[title repeated] Scene the Second.' pp. [3,4], *verso* blank; '[title repeated] Scene the Third.' pp. [5,6], *verso* blank. Text of *Robin and Ben*, pp. 7–13; p. 14 blank. Text of *The Builder's Doom*, pp. 15–20. The three 'Scenes' are illustrative woodcuts worked off by RLS; the text of the poems was set up by Colvin from MS.

MSS for all *Moral Tales*: B6796 (*Robin and Ben*); B6591 (Contents list, *A Perfect Cure*); B8352 (*Robin and Ben*); B6713 (*The Perfect Cure*); B6056 (*The Builder's Doom*); B6057 (*The Builder's Doom*); BRBML Uncat. MS 649, Box 370 (*The Builder's Doom, The Perfect Cure*); NYPL, Berg Collection (*Robin and Ben*)

{B6796 is the fullest MS, 6pp. in a morocco slipcase lettered on the spine, *Robin / and Ben / and / The / Builders / Doom / ;* the following variants are from this MS unless they are noted to be from NYPL or B8352, a few lines written on the back of a crude drawing by RLS for *Robin and Ben*. Colvin's text matches none of these MSS exactly: it may be that he set up the two tales from an untraced MS, pp. 9–17 of a notebook, described in the Catalogue of the Strong Sale, II, No.382.}

I *Robin and Ben: Or, the Pirate and the Apothecary*
Line
13   grew;] grew. (B6796, NYPL) {This reading has been adopted.}
14   through] through, {This reading has been adopted.}
15   inconsiderate, and] inconsiderate and (B6796, NYPL) {This reading has been adopted.}
17   soul,] soul. (B6796, NYPL) {This reading has been adopted.}
19   choir,] choir {This reading has been adopted.}
20   passing Squire.] village squire.
30   seas.] seas!
36–7   {*EDIN* has two lines here not in MS:}
        'Opened his eyes and held his breath,
        And flattered to the point of death;'
41–6   {*EDIN* has six lines here not in MS:}
        'So Ben, while Robin chose to roam,
        A rising chemist was at home,
        Tended his shop with learnèd air {*EDIN* has "learnéd"}
        Watered his drugs and oiled his hair,
        And gave advice to the unwary,
        Like any sleek apothecary.'
        {MS has the following instead of the above lines:}
        'Now fired with an esurient flame,
        A rising chemist Ben became;
        [cancelled line, illegible]
        Watered his drugs and oiled his hair
        And donned the consultative air;
        And soon, succeeding to his master,
        Became the lord of pill and plaster.'
42   was] <was>^dwelt^ (B8352)
45   unwary,] unwary (NYPL)

46   sleek] bold (NYPL)
47   Meanwhile upon … afar] Meanwhile, upon … afar,
48   war,] war
57   law,] law;
58   awe.] awe,
61   from years of anxious toil,] fatigued of fame and toil,
63   affairs,] affairs {This reading has been adopted.}
71   good,] good (B6796, B8352)
72   Once more] <On this occasion>^Once in a while^ (B8352)
74   go.] go! (B6796, B8352)
77   A certain] A kind of (B8352)
90   revelations.] revelations!
97–8   And Robin, like a boastful sailor,
        Despised the other for a tailor.]
        And with deep-sea superiority
        Robin contested the priority.
99   envy, see] envy see
101   big, and brown] big and brown
105   head:] head.
106   bread.] bread;
108   either how … eaten.] eitherhow … eaten; {The reading 'eaten;' has been adopted.}
110   small-ly.] smally. (B6796, NYPL)
121   tremens,] tremens – (B6796, NYPL)
124   Trevanion] Trevanion, (B6796, NYPL)
125–6   {in parentheses}] {not in parentheses}
126   Heaven] Lord {This reading has been adopted.}
141   Robin –] Robin,
144   Still worked and hankered after gain.] Pursued the single end of gain.
149   right and wrong:] Right and Wrong:
155   master] master,
156   softer] safer
170   abhorred] abhorrèd
176   you, I settle] you I settle
177   cutlass,] cutlass;

II *The Builder's Doom*

Date of composition: March 1870 (*LETBM*, Vol. I, p. 193, n.1)

Letter: RLS to Bob Stevenson, 29 March 1870 (*LETBM*, Vol. I, p. 193): 'Yesterday, I was in high spirits writing *Deacon Thin*;' {a note at the foot of the enclosed MS of the poem, quoted in Sotheby Catalogue 27 July 1917, states: 'No captious critics: the irregularity of rhythm is intentional: Deacon Thin is an historical character … The paragraph in the story relating to the fall of number one, I may remark, has been considered like Shelley, in its intensity and vividness; but Shelley wanted realism.'

MSS: {Obviously this poem does not date from the Davos period, as was previously thought, but was begun c. March 1870, when RLS enclosed it in the letter to Bob: this may have been the MS of *The Deacon's Crescent* described in Sotheby's Catalogue as longer than the published version and differing from it nearly all the way through. This MS was not found but there are several sketches extant: B6796 (174 lines), 649 (160 lines) and B6056–7 (fragmentary). There seems to be a draft of some lines in NLS Notebook 'T', but I have not seen it. Clearly RLS revisited the poem in the 1880s after the plan for *Moral Tales* was drawn up. *EDIN*, not set up exclusively from any one of these MSS, has 156 lines. Variants below are from B6796 unless otherwise noted:}

Line

8	rang;] rang. (B6796, 649)
10	way.] way:
19	glance] glance,
27	builder] Builder (B6796, 649)
33	emperors] Caesars
34	for different reasons –] for <different>^various^ reasons: (B6796) ~ reasons; (649)
35	pride –] pride, (B6796, 649)
53	die:] die;
54	*emptor!*] emptor: (B6796), emptor; (649)
56	{CP, following the 1921 Chatto/Scribner's edition of *Moral Emblems and Other Poems*, replaces 'Troy' with 'Thebes' to conform to the Greek myth that Amphion, son of Zeus, fortified Thebes, not Troy, by using his magic lyre. But this emendation ignores RLS's marginal note on this line in B6796 declining to accept this correction (JAS also misquotes the note): 'I am informed that there is here some error; but I have a kindness for the line, and I would rather do injustice to Amphion than to my own poetical talents.' In B6056, the following alternate lines for 55–60 appear in the margin: } 'As to the fiddle Amphion Rise up some unauthentic Zion So to our Thin's astute financing The swelling crescent kept advancing;'
60	{At this line in 649 there is an arrow directing attention to the *verso* of this MS, where the following trial fragments are found:} 'And still the creeds waxed and waned But Thin's construction still remained' 'It met the eye; and yet awhile It bore the foot'
61	When first the brazen bells of churches] <When went the ecclesiastic clapper> (B6056)
66	Before the roof was rattled on:] Before the roofs <had been clapped>^were rattled^ on (B6056)
67	And when the fourth was there,] <And standing><When>And when the fourth <Sunday came>was there, (B6056)
69	courses,] courses. (649)
71	sinewed;] sinewed, (B6796, 649, B6036) {This reading has been adopted.}
73–6	Thrones rose and fell; and still the crescent, Unsanative and now senescent, A plastered skeleton of lath, Looked forward to a day of wrath.]

Thrones rose and fell; creeds waxed and waned;
But Thin's construction still remained.
Unsanative and now senescent,
It seemed – and yet was not – a crescent. (B6796)
<The rooms in case the rats invaded
Were wainscoted and barricaded> (B6056)

75–6   Smiled with a bow of painted lath
Above the causeway and the path. (B6056)
76   <Still waved the tempest's idle wrath.>
<Nodded and muttered tales of wrath> ^ ~ ^ (649)
79   And, like] And like (B6796, 649) {This reading has been adopted.}
79ff.   'And like Dodona's <wood oracular>^talking oak^
<Talked>Of oracles <in the vernacular> and judgements spoke
When <By the chaste piano fluttered> to the music fingered well
<light upon the parlour floor>
The feet of children lightly <pattered> fell,
The <father>^sire^ who dozed by the decanters
Started and dreamed of misadventures.
At last, the fiftieth year completed,
The owner judged it should be feted;
And summoned friends to number three
To <celebrate that> toast the Crescent's jubilee.
<Chief of the guests was Deacon Thin>
The night was wild with wind and rain;
The wading moon was on the wane,
The lamps winked over all the city.
And the wind <chaunted> sang a sailor's ditty:
The lone policeman in the street,
With shining cape, with shaken feet,
Paused in his dim perambulations
To watch the festive preparations:' (B6056)
80   Of oracles and judgments spoke.] It muttered mysteries when it spoke.
84   started, and] started and (B6796, 649, B6056) {This reading has been adopted.}
85   dust;] dust,
90   Until, when seventy]<Till><And><1870>Until when seventy (649)
93   charging rack] <wading moon>^ ~ ^ (B6056)
96   And the lamps winked through all the city.]
<The lamps winked and the rainpools quivered.> (B6056)
97   house, where] house where (B6796, 649) {This reading has been adopted.}
98   feeders, grossly] feeders grossly
{Alt. for lines 99–100:} 'Whence could be heard the cork a-popping,
The <vague>^loud^ guffaw the talk out-topping' (B6056)
99   hum and rattle,] ~ rattle (B6796) hum, and rattle (649) {'rattle' has been adopted.}
100   battle.] battle – (B6796, 649) {This reading has been adopted.}
101   As still] <While>^ ~ ^ (649)
102   lingered;] lingered. (B6796) lingered – (649)
103   While far the infernal tempest sped,]

While far <ahead the hurricane>^ ~ ^ (B6056)
107   within, a hush! the host] within a hush! The host
107ff. [In B6056 there is the following draft:]
'Lo from within a pause! The host
<Stands><Gets to his feet>Arises to propose a toast;
The toast is drunk, the glasses dry;
The Deacon rises to reply.
"The compliment," he says, "is one
Due to all work sincerely done;
<I now am no longer young; my>
Here in this house which once I built
Painted and papered, carved and gilt;
And out of which, to my content,
I netted seventy five per cent,
Here in this <house>group of honoured neighbours,
I reap the credit of my labours.
<There now is something>
<These were the good old days>
Something, as I am made afraid
Is rotten in the building trade.
Shoddy, alas! begins to enter
In the scheme of my venture;
A thrift of bricks, a greed of guilders,
<Mark>Characterise the modern builders:
<Had this, where now we taste our toddy>"'
110   reply!] reply.
111   Here in] Here, in
114   seventy-five per cent.;] sixty three per cent – (B6796) ~ cent; (649)
115   Here at] Here, at
119   builder] Builder
120   He watched … brick] He <saw>^watched^ … nail
122   {After this line in B6796 come six lines not in *EDIN*; there is also a variation on them in 649:}
'It was the year (I mind it well)
When two of Thomson's houses fell,
<When I, then young and full of ardour>
<When I, my ships unfurling sail on sail,>
And I, though now so much looked up to,
Was one whom few took off their cap to.
<Till from the backmost ranks I burst,
Boldly to struggle>
My business, relatively small,
Strained my exiguous capital.
<Some men would thus have slumbered; I>
<Till in that year, with borrowed cash,
And careless of affluence or kisses
Poured forth my soul in edifices.>

123–4   These were the days, our provost knows,
         When forty streets and crescents rose,]
         Since then how changed! Before my eyes
         Did forty squares and crescents rise,
129   quarter;] quarter, (B6796), quarter – (649)
130   I leave] <And left> ^ ~ ^ (649)
131   actor –] actor
132   And am this city's] <I am the city's>^ ~ ^ (649)
         {Two lines not in *EDIN* come here in B6796; in 649 they are *verso* on the MS}
         'If I have risen, my trade, alas!
         Descends toward the nether pass.'
133–4   Since then, alas! both thing and name,
         Shoddy across the ocean came –]
         Shoddy or Jerry – what's a name? –
         Across the western ocean came – (B6796, 649) {alt.}
137–40   Had this good house, in frame or fixture,
         Been tempered by the least admixture
         Of that discreditable shoddy,
         Should we today compound our toddy,]
         Had this good house where now we dine
         Been planned by other hands than mine,
         Should we, today, compound our toddy,
         A safe and a most smiling body, (B6796, 649) {alt.}
139   discreditable] <abominable> ^ ~ ^ (B6056)
141   Or gaily marry song and laughter] <Or>^And^ ~ ^ (649)
         <Or spread>And gaily marry <talk>^song^ and laughter, (B6056)
142   Below … rafter?] Beneath … rafter<s>? (B6056)
145   house … fated,] hour … fated. (B6796, 649) {The reading 'hour' was adopted.}
146   The rotten structure crepitated!]
         The <avenging>^rotten^ structure <loudly> crepitated! (B6056)
147ff.   <Instant, the speech was stilled, the guests fled
         The Deacon paled and
         And crepitating, ran together
         In one wild whirl of wind and weather,> (B6056)
150   avalanche,] avalanche – (B6796) avalanche; (B6056)
151   Story on story, floor on floor,]
         <Top, sides and bottoms, front and back> (B6056)
153   Dead weight] Deadweight
154   cataclysm] helluo (B6796, 649, B6056)
         {After this line in B6796 come four lines not in *EDIN*:}
         'His structure on the Deacon's crown
         Came from above redoubling down
         And Hell – the empire of Astarte,
         Gaped and engulphed that dinner party!'
         {Two other alt. versions appear in 649:}
         'Thunder and ruin, death and flame
         There from above redoubling came

<The planets waked, appalled spectators>
And Hell – the empire of Astarte
Gaped and engulphed that dinner party!'
'A helluo of lath and plaster
Swooped like an eagle on the eaters;
And from the eyes of the spectators,
The pale policeman and Astarte
Had straight engulphed that dinner party!'
{On 649 there is an x against 'helluo' and a line verso to 'cataclysm', this not being obviously in RLS's hand: perhaps Colvin as editor replaced this archaic word.}

155   sinner –] sinner: (B6796), sinner. (649)
          {This line is italicised in *EDIN* but not in either MS.}
156   builders] Builders

III *A Perfect Cure: Or, the Man of Habit*
In B6591 there is a contents list for *Moral Tales*; besides the two published in *EDIN*, this list includes this unpublished poem and *The Expressman's Tragedy*, which evidently exists only as a title. In the same file, numbered B6713, is a 34-line MS fragment of *The Perfect Cure*. BRBML has acquired a complete MS, filed with other uncatalogued materials in Box 370: this very rough version, its revisions and deletions unrecorded here, served as copy-text.

Selected Poems

Songs and Little Odes

This title appears, sometimes reversed as *Little Odes and Songs*, among the ruins of RLS's notebooks torn up by Hellman. One of the few entries in RLS's hand left in the dismembered Notebook A.155 '*Book full of poems*' (BRBML) is a title-page for this unit bearing a Latin epigraph from George Buchanan's *Opera Omnia*. Folder B6149 contains fourteen poems numbered I–XV (there is no VII) written in ink on fourteen pages with the title *Songs*; these were among the eighty-three titles listed by Hellman as the contents of A.155. Most of these poems have been dated by RLS between 1870 and 1872, often with a place specified, and designated part of a 'Cyclus' which never progressed beyond these seven leaves torn from a notebook. A process of evaluation, selection and ordering preparatory to publication took place as RLS arranged his MS verses into units by numbering them, cancelling stanzas and entire poems and using a mixture of French and English to indicate his judgements in margins, e.g. 'atroce', 'pas mal', 'bon' or 'bah!' *UW* was assembled in this way. The *Songs* unit seems to have been intended, by a young poet under the influence of Tennyson and Rossetti, as a lyric sequence beginning with passionate love; however, desire is thwarted, despair is experienced but consolation is achieved through, variously, elegiac regret, aesthetic sublimation and martial heroics. The young lady who inspired this sequence during 1870–1, named in Song III as Jeanie or Jenny, has not been clearly identified, not even by the poet, who usually lost no opportunity to show his heart to his friends. His biographers agree that she was probably a respectable Edinburgh girl from a family somewhat friendly with the Stevensons: in a letter of 16 June 1870 to Bob Stevenson, RLS coyly refuses to name the lady who may be the 'Jenny' of *Songs*:

> I have been … very much hit with a certain damsel who shall be nameless during the last month or so. This last obstacle is now removed, as the lady in question has been withdrawn to the paternal province. (*LETBM*, Vol. I, p. 194)

This young woman is no doubt the same 'lady with whom my heart was at that time somewhat engaged, and who did all that in her lay to break it ('A College Magazine', *EDIN*, Vol. I, pp. 132–3). J. C. Furnas and Frank McLynn both speculate that this damsel was 'almost certainly' the girl of Song XI with whom RLS went skating at Duddingston Loch (Furnas 1951: 48; McLynn 1993: 53).

There are other BRBML MSS of *Songs* showing that RLS prepared an earlier version of the cycle in which contents and order differ from B6149, the *Songs* folder which I have taken as copy-text; some of these earlier readings are noted below. Since the MSS from the *Songs* folder each have their own McKay number, I have marked them with an asterisk; all copy-texts in the *Selected Poems* section will be similarly identified.

Little Odes is the title of another unit projected and partly assembled in a notebook during

1870–2 (file B7032). For it there is no unitary copy-text. The disbound leaves all have separate McKay numbers, some poems existing in more than one version, but I have reconstructed this incomplete sequence to consist of six poems: originally it was to include at least eight, but No. VII, *To Minnie*, was published as *UW* VIII and No. VIII, *To Walt Whitman*, breaks off after only two lines: possibly it was continued in the notebook but lost as a result of mutilation. All texts derive from MSS: the *NP* printings are less reliable than those of *CP*, needing such frequent correction from MS that I have generally not recorded their variants. On occasion, however, an *NP* poem may have been set up from an untraced MS or may offer a superior reading.

Songs

Song I 'Lo! in thine honest eyes I read'
Place/date of composition: ?Edinburgh, 'October 1870'
MS: B6538*
Printed text: *NP*, 84

Song II *The Blackbird*
Place/date of composition: Edinburgh, 'February 1871' (B6605); 'Spring 1871, Botanical gardens' (B6604)
MSS: B6604, B6605*
Printed text: *NP*, 85
Line
2   My heart drinks in the song:] My heart<is stirred in song> ^ ~ ^ (B6605)

Song III 'I dreamed of forest alleys fair'
Date of composition: 'February to October 1871'
MSS: B6336–40, B6822–3, B6149 (copy-texts are B6340*, B6823* and B6149*)
Printed texts: *CP*, p. 59 (Part 6); p. 60 (Part 3); *NP*, pp. 86–7 (Parts 1–4); pp. 94–5 (Part 5) and p. 100 (Part 6)
Line
4   Jenny] <Jeanie>^Jenny^ B6340 {also in line 8}
20   {B6336 has eight more lines, cancelled, as follows:}
    'O do not let me sleep, kind God,
          Or let me dream of her;
    For she is white as the great white moon
          Behind the sable fir.
    The thoughts of her are more than trees,
          And more than moonshine stir –
    O do not let me slumber
          Or let me dream of her.'
    {At bottom RLS has written, 'Swanston March or April 1871'}
    {On B6340, evidently designating the first nine stanzas of Song III, RLS wrote 'stet'. On B6339 (Part 4), RLS wrote 'June 1871, Princes Street Gardens'. He dated B6822 (Part 5) 'Sept. 1871'.}
58   words] <eyes>^ ~ ^ (B6822)
71   I speak the truth] <And yet old love> {abandoned trial} (B6149)

74   trifles,] <songs,>^ ~ ^ (B6149)
75   with] <in>^ ~ ^ (B6149)
78   due] <ripe>^ ~ ^ (B6149)
81   road forks,] <roads fork>^ ~ ^ (B6149)
     {At bottom of B6149, RLS wrote 'Edinburgh Feby to October 1871'}

Song IV *Dawn*
Place/date of composition: 'August 1871, Swanston'
MSS: B5931, B5932*
Printed text: *NP*, 103–4
{On B5931 RLS wrote 'Bon' and on B5932 'stet'}

Song V *After Reading 'Antony and Cleopatra'*
Place/date of composition: 'Sept. 1871, Nairn'
MSS: B5948, B5949*
Printed text: *CP*, 60–1; *NP*, 102
   3   thorough] {*CP* and *NP* both read 'throughout' but RLS wrote 'thorough' in both MSS
         (cf. Marvell's 'thorough the iron gates of life'}
  5, 7 sea's roar] <sea-roar>^ ~ ^ (B5949) {*CP* follows B5948's 'sea-roar'.}
         {At bottom of B5948 RLS wrote 'Pas mal'.}

Song VI 'I know not how, but as I count'
Place of composition: 'Edinburgh' {n.d.}
MS: B6351*
Printed text: *NP*, 104

Song VII *Spring Song*
Place of composition: 'Edinburgh' {n.d.}
MSS: B6910, B6911*, Edinburgh Writers' Museum LSH 137/91
Printed text: *CP*, 61; *NP*, 105
Line
   4   leafless] <lifeless>^ ~ ^ (B6910)
  11   Spring,] <s>^S^pring, (B6910)
         {RLS wrote in the margins of B6910 'Cyclus', 'Bon', 'Road behind C ... 's gymnase' and
         'first conceived out hunting, however'. LSH 137/91 places this poem in a series therein
         titled *Schumann's 'Frölicher Landmann'*; this series consists of the poem beginning
         'Come, here is adieu to the city' (see above p. 315 as No. I, this poem, untitled, as No.
         II and a blank space after No. III, all on 2 pp. numbered 19 and 20.}

Song VIII 'The summer sun shone round me'
Place of composition: 'Edinburgh' {n.d.} (B6942)
MSS: B6942*, B6151 (Notebook No. 59), Silverado (Foot)
Printed text: *NP*, 106
{Foot is later than B6942, a fair copy in ink; B6151 is a draft of lines 5–8.}

Song IX 'You looked so tempting in the pew'
Place of composition: 'Edinburgh' {n.d.}

MSS: B7198, B7199*
Printed text: *NP*, 106
{At bottom RLS wrote 'Et bon'.}

Song X *Love's Vicissitudes*
Place/date of composition: 'Edinburgh, the same summer'
MSS: B6549, B6550* (*BBS*, I facs. between pp. 76–7)
Printed text: *CP*, 61 2; *NP*, 107
Title: *Love's Vicissitudes*] {untitled} (B6549)
Line
  5   travel,] travel – (B6549)
  13   Until in] Until, in (B6549)
  15   Indiff'rence] Indiff'rence, (B6549)
  16   Free stepping straight] Free-stepping, straight (B6549)
  17   lamenting,] lamenting – (B6549)
{At bottom of B6549 RLS wrote 'Cyclus' and 'Bon'.}

Song XI *Duddingston*
Place/date of composition: 'Autumn '71' (B6171); 'Edinburgh' (B5972)
Letter: RLS to Fanny Sitwell, [21–2 December 1874] (*LETBM*, Vol. II, pp. 91–2):
'Duddingston, our big loch, is bearing; and I wish you could have seen it this afternoon,
covered with people, in thin driving snow flurries, the big hill grim and white and alpine
overhead in the thick air, and the road up the gorge, as it were into the heart of it, dotted
black with traffic … I … skated all afternoon. If you had seen the moon rising, a perfect
sphere of smoky gold, in the dark air above the trees, and the white loch thick with skaters,
and the great hill, snow-sprinkled, overhead! It was a sight for a king.'
MSS: B6170; B6171*; B5972*; Notebook No. 59 has on pages 11–12 rough drafts of all
seven stanzas which are given four McKay numbers: B6536, B6792, B6796, B6160
Printed text: *CP*, 62–3 (Parts 1, 2); *NP*, 109–10 (Parts 1, 2), *NP*, 114 (Part 3)
Line
  7   stars] {*NP* has 'stones' but the following trial for stanza 2 in B6976 shows that RLS wrote
       'stars':}
       'A nearer touch of sympathy
       Shot though thro' each essence
       I think the very stars are glad
       To feel each others presence'
  14   you were here,] <thou wert here,> ^ ~ ^ (B6170)
       {At bottom of B6170 RLS wrote 'Bon'.}
       {Alt. lines for 15–16 in B6792:}
       'The ringing ice was smooth as air,
       The red sun fired the reeds.'
  21   way] course (B6792)
  23   shifting] rapid (B6792)
  24   level] open (B6792)
       {Cancelled lines at this point in B6792:}
       'The sharp air stung – your fingers burned
       The whole ice hissed and ran'

34   Blame not that I sought such aid] <Do not blame the doubtful aid> (B5972)
35   To cure regret:] <To help forget:> ^ ~ ^ (B5972)
44   smile, then,] smile, <dear,>^then,^ (B5972)
47   a jest and – yet] <a jest; – and yet>^ ~ ^ (B5972)

Song XII *Prelude*
Place/date of composition: 'Edinburgh, Spring '71'
MSS: B6741*, Silverado (Foot)
Printed text: *NP*, 100–1
{RLS wrote 'stet' and, across the top, 'When first I began to take an interest in the poor and the sorrowful.' This poem was at one time placed first in a unit dating c. 1871 to be called *Recruiting Songs*: the title-page and twelve poems following are among the Foot MSS at Silverado. Striking a brassy, militant note often found in early RLS poems, the compilation introduced by *Prelude* had the following title-page dedication: 'Ad Dilectos Tres Amicos / Stevenson / Wilson / Baxter / et / Hanc Fere Puerilium Nugarum Fas: / Ciculum / DEDICAVIT / Auctor;' this was followed by the same Latin epigraph from George Buchanan used on a MS title-page for *Little Odes and Songs*. *Recruiting Songs* was to include the following: *Prelude*; 'The old world moans and tosses' (*NP*, 97); 'The whole day thro', in contempt and pity' (*NP*, 98); 'The old Chimaeras, old receipts' (above, p. 312); 'Here he comes big with Statistics' (above, p. 301); 'All influences were in vain' (*NP*, 95); 'The moon is sinking – the tempestuous weather' (*NP*, 107); *The Vanquished Knight* (like *Prelude*, moved to *Songs*); 'Link your arm in mine, my lad' (*NP*, 120); and *Epistle to Charles Baxter* (see above, p. 287), the last six stanzas of which were titled *Sigh for the South* and moved to *Little Odes*. Few of these attempts survived RLS's second thoughts, drawing such marginal comments as 'Atroce', 'Bien mal', 'Intolerable', 'Bah!' and 'Bully for you, L. Stevenson'. Indeed, most of these efforts are vigorously cancelled and the entire project abandoned. G. S. Hellman made a fool of himself, not only by publishing these weak lines but also by, at times, incorporating RLS's scornful comments in the margins as part of the poetry (see *NP*, p. 107, bottom).}
Line
15   But whenever] <And when>^ ~ ^ (Foot)

Song XIII *The Vanquished Knight*
Place/date of composition: 'Edinburgh, Spring '71' (B7083)
MSS: B7083*, Silverado (Foot)
Printed text: *NP*, 101

Song XIV 'Away with funeral music – set'
Place/date of composition: 'Boulogne, Autumn '72'
MS: B5999*
Printed text: *NP*, 110

Little Odes

Ode I *To Sydney*
Place/date of composition: 'Edinburgh, Spring '72'
MSS: B7031, B7032*

Printed text: CP, 72–4; NP, 111–12
Title: *To Sydney*] *Epistle to Robert Alan Stevenson* (B7031)
Line
33 Horror of famine, fire and steel]
    <The roar as powerful <<nations>>^monarchs^ reel> ^ ~ ^ (B7032)
34 When] <And>^ ~ ^ (B7032)
36 I mark] <And>^I^ mark (B7032)

Ode II *To —*
Date of composition: 'Dec. 1870'
MS: B6980*
Printed text: NP, 85

Ode III 'The relic taken, what avails the shrine?'
Place/date of composition: 'Swanston, July 1871' (B6786)
MSS: B6786*, Silverado (Foot)
Printed text: CP, 63–4; NP, 103
Line
 3–4 Art thou not less than that?
        Still warm, a vacant nest where love once sat.]
          <Is not thy life left bare
        Of all that made it reverend and fair?> ^ ~ ^ (Foot)
 8   weather-gleam] <weathergaw>^weather-gleam^ (B6786) weathergaw (Foot)
{RLS wrote 'Pas mal' in the margin.}

Ode IV *To Marcus*
Place/date of composition: 'Edinburgh, Feby 1872'
MSS: B6664*, Silverado (Foot)
Printed text: CP, 68–71
{CP prints this poem as stanzas 10–15 of *Epistle to Charles Baxter*; 'Marcus' is a pseudonym
for Baxter.

Ode V *Consolation*
Place/date of composition: 'Swanston, July 1872' (B6243)
MSS: B6242, B6243*, Princeton (Parrish CO171)
First publication: *R.L.S. Teuila* (1899), pp. 62–4, there dated 'June 27, 1872'
Printed text: CP, 71–2; NP, 87–8
{This poem has been given many titles. In B6664, JAS misread the last line of Ode IV,
'Toward the South' (appearing isolated at the top of p. 7 in that MS), as the title for Ode V
(B6243), noting that in B6242 it was changed to *Consolation* (CP, p. 458). But there is also
a pencil heading on that MS, 'Inscribed to Sydney' (i.e. Bob Stevenson). CO171 is untitled.
McKay titles both BRBML MSS 'A Fragment In Memoriam' (Vol. V, p. 1797), presumably
because the poem had appeared under this title in *Teuila*. In his *Biographical Notes* (1908),
Gosse prints it as *To A Mourner* and misinforms the reader both that it is unpublished
and that it was written when RLS gave up engineering for legal studies. NP calls it *Verses
Written in 1872*, presumably because it was published under this title in *Scribner's Magazine*
for December 1902. Finally, it appeared in *Current Opinion* in 1921 as *Resurgence*.}

Line

18   nearer to the end;] <hidden by a bend;>^ ~ ^ (CO171)

26–8   And strains his eyes to search his wake,
        Or whistling, as he sees you through the brake,
        Waits on a stile.]
        <And loitering so, in heath and brake,
        <<Casts>>With many an eager <<look>> glances along his wake,
                For you the while.>
        <Or><And having seen you><With eager eyes that search his wake;>
        <o'er>^through^ the brake ^ ~ ^ (CO171)

26   eyes to search] <eyes along>^ ~ ^ (B6242)

Ode VI 'This gloomy northern day'
Place/date of composition: 'Edinburgh, October 1872'
MS: B6971*
Printed text: NP, 116–17
{Ode VIII, To Walt Whitman, breaks off after these two lines:}
'Prophet-poet, who revealed
        All my better hopes to me,'
Whitman was a potent influence on RLS at this time; he eventually published an article,
'The Gospel According to Walt Whitman', in New Quarterly Magazine, London, October
1878; repr. Familiar Studies of Men and Books (1882). The next group, Poems (1869–70),
illustrates this influence intermingled with those of Arnold, Baudelaire and Swinburne.}

Poems (1869–70)

At BRBML there is another unit apparently intended for publication, an uncatalogued
folder in Box 370 marked 'POEMS', dated 1870 and accompanied by the following contents
list: I. The Lightkeeper II. The Daughter of Herodias III. The Cruel Mistress IV. Storm V.
Madame from Paris VI. Stormy Nights VII. Song at Dawn VIII. The town-confessor. The folder
contains seven poems written on sixteen pages (there is no No. V); the MS of No. VIII has
no title and was eventually published in VAIL, Vol. VIII with Nos II, III, IV, VI and VII
above. No. I was first published in EDIN, Vol. XXVIII. The rugged northern maritime
setting for many of these poems no doubt derives from RLS's trips as apprentice engineer to
lighthouse sites near Fife, Anstruther, Wick and Earraid during 1868–70. See also Sonnets
Nos 1–3 and Explanatory Note on them, p. 629.

I The Light-keeper
Date of composition: Part I 'May 1869' (B6520 is so dated); Part II 1870 (so dated in EDIN)
MSS: B6520, BRBML Box 370
Printed text: EDIN*, Vol. XXVIII, 5–7; CP, 79–81
{B6520 has Part I only; 370 has Part II only. Copy-text is EDIN.}
Line

11   The clear bell chimes: the clockworks strain:]
        <The grinding pulleys creak and strain:> ^ ~ strain:^ (B6520)

19   charm] <force>^ ~ ^ (B6520)

30   {After this line in B6520 there is a cancelled stanza, as follows:}

'The morning mist lies leaden pale
About the western brow of sea:
The glassy swell appears to fail
That heaves as gently as may be
And, washing round the scattered reef,
Scarce stirs the sea-weed's oily leaf;
And now my task is nearly done;
For, set against the brightening sky,
The lights burn yellow wan; and I
Can see the shoulder of the sun.'

38 With] <Wan> ^ ~ ^ (B6520)
46, 62 {EDIN has both 'light-keeper' and 'Light-Keeper'; 370 has ' lightkeeper'; 'light-keeper' has been adopted.}
59 {CP omits the word 'all' from this line.}
65 him;] him. 370 {This reading has been adopted.}
68 him;] him. 370 {This reading has been adopted.}

II *The Daughter of Herodias*

Date of composition: 1870 {For Nos II–VIII in the 370 'Poems' folder this date
seems valid; other MSS were not found for any of them except *Song at Dawn*. 370 is copy-text for Nos II–VII.}
Printed text: Nos II–VIII in the 370 'Poems' folder were first printed in VAIL (1922).

V *Stormy Nights*

Line
33 itching <secrecy>^mystery^ <for>^to^
60 <untried>^feverish^
67 <his>^my^
71 <Spoke into him> Plunged like a dagger <in his>
74 <olives>^statues^
78 <men's> ^inordinate^

VI *Song at Dawn*

MSS: 370*, H2406 (Notebook A.259 '*Kept as a student in Edinburgh*')
2406 has variants, cancelled, for lines 5ff.:

'It leaps forth free and rapid
With firm keen margin like a knife; …
Here wakening cocks in distant farms, and there
Stealthily flooding over smokeless towns,
Towns of still blinded streets and silent steeples.
The cocks crow gladly at the upland farms.
The sick man's soul is satisfied;
The watch treads brisker on the deck;
And what to us too, with its healing hands,
Brings the cool morning?
What to us, the wakeful?'

Line
 1   dawn] silent dawn (2406) {This reading has been adopted.}
 6   <Drifting>^Driving^ (370)
20   rise] linger (2406) {This reading has been adopted.}
21   {cancelled after this line in 2406:}<Spreading and beautifying>
33   {These lines following line 33 in 2406 have been adopted:}
     'Get back to bed,
     Girl with the lace-bosomed shift,
     O leaning, dreaming girl, I too grow cold,
     I do the same.'

VII 'My brain swims empty and light'
{Since this poem is numbered VIII in the 370 sequence, it seems reasonable to assume that
it was once titled *The town-confessor*.}

Sonnets and Rondeaux

An RLS folio containing six MS sonnets was lot 323 in the 1915 Strong Sale, having on its
last page the following lines:

> Those are very clever men
> Who can write with current pen
> Those fourteen convoluted lines,
> That experts call a sonnet.
>   (B7043)

This folio became B7043, now at BRBML. Another folder at Yale, B6633, has eight sonnets
dating from 1870 to 1872: G. S. Hellman printed them in *BBS*, II, arguing unconvincingly
(pp. 101–6) that the contents of B6633 form a consecutive sonnet sequence with narrative
and thematic lines. Although they are numbered 1–8 on notebook pages 26–31, with each
sonnet dated below the text, I can find no sequential unity, but perhaps RLS was trying to
ready a group of his sonnets for publication. Two from B7043 are also included in the series
of eight for an overall total of twelve. The six from B7043 first appeared in print in the
'Sonnets and The Light-keeper' section of *VAIL*, Vol. XXVI (1923).
    RLS, who liked intricate verse forms, wrote sonnets from boyhood to at least 1886, when
he sent two of them to William Sharp after reading Sharp's anthology, *Sonnets of this
Century*, with the following comment:

> The form of my so-called sonnets will cause you as much agony as it causes me
> little. I am base enough to think the main point of a sonnet is the disjunction of
> thought coinciding with the end of the octave; and when a lesser disjunction
> marks the quatrains and sestets I call it an ideal sonnet. (*LETBM*, Vol. V, p. 192)

Copy-texts for the sonnets selected for this edition are derived from MSS.

Sonnets

Sonnet 1 'The roadside lined with ragweed, the sharp hills'
Place/date of composition: '15 August 1870. Ross of Mull.' {For the remote northern setting

of the first three sonnets, see Explanatory Note on them, p. 629. A signed note in folder B7043 by E. J. Beinecke suggests that RLS's dating of these sonnets was done many years after these fair copies were made.}
MS: B6794* (in folder B7043)
Printed text: CP, p. 78; NP, p. 202
Line
5   <keen grey>^northern^

Sonnet 2 *Lines to be Sent with the Present of a Sketch Book*
Place/date of composition: 'Earraid 1870' (both MSS)
MSS: B6525* (in folder B7043), B6526 (in folder B6633: there is a facsimile of the first six lines in *BBS*, II, pp. 106–7)
Printed text: *NP*, 203–4
Line
1   wax like] <become>^ ~ ^ (B6525)
2   brim,] brim (B6526)
3   tarn that eager curlews] <loch>^tarn^ ~ (B6525) tarn, that wailing curlews (B6526)
4   Glassing {In his TS of the sonnet in folder B7043) E. J. Beinecke reads this word as 'Sloping' but both MSS, *NP* and *VAIL* have 'glassing', an archaic word meaning 'reflecting'.}
6   of noon] with noon (B6526)
7   laid,] laid (B6526)
9   leaves, once] leaves once (B6526)
10 ruined, and] ruined and (B6526)

Sonnet 3 'I have a hoard of treasure in my breast'
Place/date of composition: 'Earraid 1870' (B6346)
MSS: B6346 (in folder B7043), B6347* (in folder B6633)
Printed text: *NP*, 204
Line
1   in] <laid> in (B6346)
3   garnered] <treasured>^cherished^ (B6346)
4   sorrow for a zest,] sadness ~ (B6346) {This reading has been adopted. *NP*, *VAIL* read 'jest' for 'zest'.}
7   That like a new evangel, more and more]
    That, like our own evangel, at the core (B6346) ~ <at the core> ^ ~ ^ (B6347) {*NP*, *VAIL* end the line with 'at the door'.}
8   Supports] Beckons (B6346)
10 joy or … tell?] joy and … tell (B6346)
12 That we shall … fears] Nature shall … fears, (B6346)

Sonnet 4 'Not undelightful, friend, our rustic ease'
Place/date of composition: 'Between B.[ridge] of Allan & Dunblane 1872' (B6638) {This Horatian *locus amoenus* is the Stevenson country cottage at Swanston in the Pentlands, also celebrated in Scots in *Ille Terrarum* (*UW* Book 2. II). See Explanatory Note on *Ille Terrarum*, p. 625.}
MSS: B6637 (pp. 16v., 17 of Notebook 'P'); B6638* (in folder B6633)

Printed text: *CP*, 78; *NP*, 205
Line

1–2	Not undelightful, friend, our rustic ease
	To grateful hearts; for by especial hap]
	<To no unloved or undelightful seat
	I ask your stay. For by especial hap> ^ ~ hap,^ (B6637)
3	lap] lap, (B6637)
4	trees] trees, (B6637)
5	cottage – nor] cottage; nor (B6637)
6	rose-carpeted] ~ rose carpeted (B6637)
7	sprung,] sprung (B6637)
9	Spring,] spring, (B6637) <s>^S^pring (B6638)
11	Where, … remote, unseen,] Where … remote unseen, (B6637)
12	trees it] trees, it (Both MSS)
14	coolly buried, to] coolly-buried, to (B6637) {I have deleted the comma.}
9–14	{B6637 has two drafts of the sestet:}

'Far from the stir of town, among the ways
Of <the><all>deep-rutted <of> unchanging country folk,
By its own group of hill tops only seen,
From its tall trees it breathes a slender smoke
<All day><Not> To Heav'n, and in the <sleep>noon of sultry <days>day
Stands coolly-buried, to the neck in green.'

'Thither in early spring, unharnessed folk,
We and the swallows <make>^take^ our easy way,
Where, by the sun-clear hill tops only seen,
We join the pairing swallows, glad to stay
Where bosomed in the hills, remote, unseen' [breaks off]

Sonnet 5 'As in the hostel by the bridge, I sate'
Place/date of composition: 'Dunblane 1872' (B5978)
MSS: B5977 (pp. 17*v*., 18 of Notebook 'P'), B5978* (in folder B6633)
Printed text: *NP*, 205
{In B5977 there are two drafts of the octave, as follows:}

'In the small hostel by the bridge, I sate
Unthinking, all the idle afternoon
To the thin river's melancholy croon
Hearkening as in a dream, till, calm, sedate,
The counterfeit of her that was my fate
<And blighted it, went slowly up the street>
<Went loitering> Passed slowly up the vacant village street,
The still small sound of her most dainty feet
Knocking at memory's door.'

'As in the hostel by the bridge, I sate
Free from all care, in complete

(Cased in new armour fondly deemed complete)
And (O strange chance, more sorrowful than sweet)
‹Perfect resemblance, her true counterfeit›
The <breathing counterfeit> counterfeit of her that was my fate,
Dressed in like vesture, graceful and sedate,
Went quietly up the vacant village street,
The still small sound of her most dainty feet
<Wounding><Paining me step by step><Did pain me to the echo>
Shook, like a trumpet blast, my soul's estate.'

Line

9 revolt ran riot through my brain;] <revolt awoke>
<revolt; a rout in all my being bred;> ^ ~ in my brain^ (B5977)

10 And all night long thereafter, hour by hour,] <Thereafter I was not alone>
<Thereafter all the night> ^ ~ ^ (B5977)

12 Went proudly; and old hopes broke loose again,]
Went proudly, and old hopes <with downcast head
And shameful faces
Followed the car; and with> broke loose again, (B5977)
{I have inserted a comma after 'hopes' and deleted the comma after 'again'.}

13 From the restraint of wisely temperate power,]
<Clad in the semblance of some vital power,> ^ ~ ^ (B5977)

Sonnet 6 'As Daniel, bird-alone, in that far land'
Place/date of composition: 'Above Dunblane, by the riverside 1872' (B5976)
Letter: RLS to Charles Baxter, 9 April 1872 (*LETBM*, Vol. I, p. 225): 'I send here the
competition sonnet to the L.J.R.; you will soon get one from Bob, and will please consider
yourself as Judge and lawgiver over us in this matter.' {The L.J.R., a secret society and
discussion club devoted to Liberty, Justice and Reverence, comprised RLS, Baxter, Bob
Stevenson, Walter Ferrier and two others; anti-clerical and anti-establishment, it met
regularly in a pub.}
MSS: B5975 (on p. 18 of Notebook 'P'); B5976* (in folder B6633); *LETBM*, Vol. I, No. 98
(B2646)
Printed text: CP, 79; NP, 206
Title: {untitled}] *To the Members of the L.J.R.* (98)
Line
{B5975 has a false start, as follows:}
   <To whom shall I compare, light-hearted crew,
   Your name and [?]
   The idle graceful>

1 bird-alone] burd-alone (B5975) {This latter reading, adopted by CP, seems a conflation
since the Scottish phrase, used in *UW* Book II. X, is 'burd-alane'.}

2 fervent … eyes] fervid … eyes, (98) fervid ~ (B2646) {i.e. the MS of the sonnet
enclosed with the Baxter letter does not have the comma placed at the end of line 2 in
LETBM.}
Kneeling in fervent prayer with heart-sick eyes] ~ prayer, with ~ (98)
<Kneeling in prayer with heart-sick eager eyes> ^ ~ ^ (B5975)

3 Turned through the casement toward the westering skies;]

<At the oped casement toward <<his native skies,>>the westering skies,> ^ ~ skies,^
(B5975)
4   Or as untamed Elijah,] <As> Elijah in rough mantle, (B5975)
5   or that band] as the band (B5975)
6   sanctities,] sanctities (B5975) {This reading has been adopted.}
7   Who, in all times, when persecutions rise] That in all <seasons when doubt><times of>
     <times when> That <still> in all times, ~ (B5975)
8   Cherish … hand;] <Keep>^Cherish^ … hands; (B5975)
10   O turned to friendly arts with all your will,]
     <That follow joy with all your store of skill,> ^ ~ skill,^ (98)
     <Bent to slight arts with all your store of skill,>
     Turned to <light> friendly arts with all your skill, (B5975) ~ <skill,>^will^ (B5976)
12   One rood of Holy-land in this bleak earth] ~ Holy-ground ~ (98)
     <To mirth and Bacchus and the> Holy land (B5975)
13   (an homage surely due!)] (as surely is most due) (B5975)

Sonnet 7 (double) 'I am like one that for long days had sate'
Place/date of composition: London, '16 June 1874' (B6328)
MS: B6328*
Printed text: CP, 77; NP, 131
Line
 7   ship … mast] {I have followed CP in placing commas after these words.}
21   spread] <stretched> ^ ~ ^ (B6328)

Sonnet 8 (double) *Music at the Villa Marina*
Place/date of composition: Mentone, France, 'Spring 74' (B6598) {The music was the piano-
playing of Mme Zassetsky; see the Explanatory Note on this poem, p. 629.}
MS: B6598* (BBS, I, has a facsimile of the first twenty-four lines of this MS at pp. 126–7.)
Printed text: NP, 127–8
Line
11   night,] night. NP {This reading has been adopted.}
23   heart-strings] <heart-chains>^ ~ ^ (B6598)

Sonnet 9 'Fear not, dear friend, but freely live your days'
Place/date of composition: London, Euston Station, autumn 1874 (B6218, B6629)
Letter: RLS to Fanny Sitwell, 18 August 1874 (LETBM, Vol. II, p. 40:) {The poet's
infatuation with Mrs Sitwell had reached crisis proportions that summer, culminating in
what Furnas calls an 'explosion' and ending in the desolation expressed in Sonnet 7 (1951:
94–8). In the following letter and this sonnet written soon after, he assures her that his
passions are now under control and her untouchable status as *dame lointaine* has been
restored. See 'If I had wings, my lady, like a dove' (p. 320 above) for another love poem of
this period addressed to Mrs Sitwell and the Explanatory Note on To F.J.S., p. 624.} 'First …
I wish to return you thanks for the life that you gave to me; I may surely speak and think of
you as of a parent, for you were the mother of my soul as surely as another was the mother of
my body. I bless you now, and shall always bless you, for the great joy that you brought into
my existence.
     Second, I want you to know that I shall never doubt or question you. How should I dare?

I believe in you, as others believe in the Bible.

Third, I want you to face up to life as selfishly as you can. O try to get some good, some pleasure out of it, remember what I want is that you should be happy.

Fourth, Have no fear for me; I am stronger and I am so content with my life that I feel as if interests could never fail me.'

MSS: B6217, B6218*

Printed text: *NP*, 128–9

{Subscribed on B6218: 'Autumn 74 Hotel smoking room. – *ex perturbato corde*.' The poem is on stationery of the Euston and Victoria Hotels, Euston Station.}

Sonnet 10 *The Touch of Life*

Place/date of composition: Bournemouth, February 1886 (*LETBM*, Vol. V, No. 1535)

Letters: 1. RLS to William Sharp [early February 1886] (*LETBM*, Vol. V, pp. 191–3): {Sharp had sent RLS a presentation copy of his anthology, *Sonnets of this Century*, published the previous month. It inspired him to write *The Touch of Life* and *The Arabesque* and send them to Sharp with this letter; perhaps the fact that the book was dedicated to Rossetti led RLS to parody the Rossettian sonnet style of *The House of Life* (1881).} 'Having at last taken an opportunity to read your pleasant volume, it has had an effect upon me much to be regretted and you will find the consequences in verse. I had not written a serious sonnet since boyhood, when I used to imitate Milton and Wordsworth with surprising results.' {RLS notes that the cross rhyme 'tears' – 'fear' (in lines 4 and 9 of *The Touch of Life*) 'is … a vile flaw'.}

2. RLS to William Sharp [?mid-February 1886] (*LETBM*, Vol. V, pp. 200–1): {Sharp had offered to include RLS's sonnets in subsequent editions of his book: while he demurs in this letter, he must have accepted later as the sonnets do appear in the large paper *de luxe* issue of 1886, *The Touch of Life* on p. 208 and *The Arabesque* among the notes on p. 321.} 'It is very good of you, and I should like to be in one of your pleasant and just notes; but the impulse was one of pure imitation and is not like to return, or if it did, to be much blessed. I have done so many things and cultivated so many fields in literature, that I think I shall let the "scanty plot" lie fallow … I think *The Touch of Life* is the best of my muff-shots; but the other {*The Arabesque*} was the best idea. The fun of the sonnet to me is to find a subject; the workmanship rebuts me.'

MSS: *LETBM*, Vol. V, No. 1535; BRBML Uncat. MS No. 19950701-il* {This latter MS has the enclosed sonnets sent with 1535 to Sharp and is used as copy-text here.}

Printed text: Sharp, pp. 208, 321; *CP*, 459–60

Line 9   fear:] fear; (1535)

Sonnet 11 *The Arabesque (Complaint of an Artist)*

Place/date of composition, letters, MSS: see notes for Sonnet 10 above. This sonnet is mentioned but not printed in *CP*.

Line

3   wind-swept] wind-spent (Sharp)

10   o'erscrawled] o'er scrawled (1535)

Rondeaux

Like the sonnet, the rondeau is a short poem of fixed form. Usually it consists of thirteen lines on two rhymes; the rondel has fourteen lines. With both, the initial couplet is repeated in the middle and at the end, the second line of the couplet sometimes being omitted at the end. RLS's models included Charles d'Orléans, Villon and Banville.

Rondeau 1 *Nous n'irons plus au bois*
Place/date of composition: Château Renard, Loiret, France, late August 1875 (*LETBM*, Vol. II, No. 415)
Letter: RLS to Fanny Sitwell [late August 1875] (*LETBM*, Vol. II, pp. 158–9): 'I send you here two Rondeaux; I don't suppose they will amuse anybody but me; but this measure, short and yet intricate, is just what I desire; and I have had some good times walking along the glaring roads, or down the poplar alley of the great canal, fitting my own humour to this old verse.' {RLS was on a walking tour in the Loing Valley of France with Sir Walter Simpson, described in 'An Epilogue to *An Inland Voyage*', where he says that he 'carried in his knapsack the works of Charles of Orleans and employed some of the hours of travel in the concoction of English roundels. In this path, he must thus have preceded Mr Lang, Mr Dobson, Mr Henley and all contemporary roundeleers'. In the 1870s there was much interest in the revival and imitation of the traditional French forms of rondeaux, ballades and triolets. This rondeau is a paraphrase of Banville's poem, *Nous n'irons plus aux bois*, which was itself derived from an old French nursery rhyme. Housman, who may have seen this poem in Colvin's 1899 edition of RLS's *Letters*, introduced his *Last Poems* with lines beginning 'We'll to the woods no more'.}
MSS: B6643; *LETBM*, Vol. II, No. 415* (B3275)
First publication: Colvin 1899: Vol. I, pp. 105–6
Printed text: *CP*, 90; *NP*, 145
{I have selected 415, which is identical with B3275, as copy-text for both rondeaux in this letter; B6643 is a rough draft, as follows:}

> 'Go to the woods no more
> <Sit at home by>But stay beside the fire
> Sweetheart when the heart is bare
> To weep for old desire
> And things that were before.
> The woods are spoiled and hoar
> The ways are full of mire
> Go to the woods no more
> Sit at home by the fire
> <The wind pipes at the door
> And silent is the lyre
> As these things were before>
> We loved in days of yore
> Love laughter & the lyre
> Ah God but death is dire
> And death is at the door
> We'll walk the woods no more.'

Rondeau 2 'Far have you come my lady from the town'
For place/date of composition, letters and copy-text see notes to Rondeau 1 above.
MSS: *LETBM*, Vol. II, No. 415* (B3275); B6210 (first four lines only)

First publication: Colvin 1899: Vol. I, p. 105
Printed text: *NP*, 144

Rondeau 3 'Since I am sworn to live my life'
Place/date of composition: France, autumn 1875 {B6210, a portion of Rondeau 2, is written
on this MS, so presumably both poems were written at about the same time; McKay dates
this poem 1875 (Vol. V, p. 1971)}.
MSS: B6848, B6849
Printed text: *NP*, 145; Balfour 1901: I, 131* (selected as copy-text)
{B6848 is an early pencil draft, as follows:}

> 'I make the choice to live my life
> Not to seek a quiet heart
> I cannot bear to sit apart
> But bear a banner in the strife.
> Some can take quiet thought to wife
> I am all day at tierce and carte
> I cry all day in pleasure's mart
> I make the choice to live my life
> While others seek a quiet heart
> Wherever keen delights are rife
> I go head-first
> Boldly I go into the mart
> I have no compromising art
> But simply face the lurking knife
> I make the choice to live my life
> I light my pipe with wisdom's chart
> I dare misfortune to the knife
> Scorn wisdom stretching out a chart
> And Prudence bawling in the mart
> And follow after fortune's pipe.'

{Balfour collates with B6849 as follows:}
Line
  1 life] life,
  5 wife,] wife.
10 Wisdom ... chart,] wisdom ... chart
11 Prudence brawling] prudence bawling
12 Misfortune ... knife,] misfortune ... knife;

Rondeau 4 'In Autumn when the woods are red'
Date of composition: 1875–6 (CP, 464)
MS: B6405*
Printed text: CP, 90; NP, 139
11–12 {Two lines deleted in MS, as follows:}
       '<Tho gone are all the joys that led
       The waning of the year,>
11   For] <Yet>^ ~ ^

13   dead,] <spred><fled>^ ~ ^
14   {Both CP and NP repeat line 2 to make line 14: there is no MS authority for this,
        nor was it the usual practice of RLS to do so – his rondeaux are normally thirteen
        lines long; McKay notes this discrepancy between the MS and printed versions
        (Vol. V, p. 1842).}

Rondeau 5 *Of his Pitiable Transformation*
Date of composition: 1876 (see note below)
MS: None found.
First publication: *Longman's Magazine*, April 1888, p. 677*
Printed text: NP, 148
{In his introduction to his *Longman's* 'causerie', 'At The Sign of the Ship', Andrew Lang
states that he is printing this poem without permission as the author is presently in Saranac
Lake, where he spent the winter of 1887–8:} 'The following rondel was given, twelve years
ago, to a friend of mine, by another friend of mine. He is so far away, and it is such a very
little poem, that I venture to print it without telegraphing to the Adirondacks for
permission. Presumably, the author's hand will be easily recognised, and I presume that,
twelve years ago, the sage who laments his youth was just twenty-five. And as to his hair
being "grey", it is not even "brindled".' See above, UW XIV. Possibly the title was supplied
by Lang.}

Poems (1879–80)

The selections which follow are all taken from two folders at BRBML, B6372 and B6705.
While not organised into units by RLS, this verse was evidently written in notebooks during
1879–80. B6372 appears to be another disbound/rebound confection from G. S. Hellman:
some numbered leaves taken from Notebook A.155 have been bound together in full
morocco and given the title 'Fourteen Poems including / some Written in America / The
Original Manuscripts', accompanied by Hellman's notes, an etching of RLS, etc. B6705
contains thirteen poems on pages numbered 59–72 also torn from this notebook which
originally contained eighty-three poems: the eight included in this section were numbers 49,
43, 46, 45, 60, 50, 51 and 52.
     This was a heroic period for RLS, when he left family and friends to undertake solitary,
arduous crossings of the Atlantic and the vast wilderness of America, risking everything to
make Fanny Osbourne his bride and bring her back home. Some of his best poetry, such as
Requiem, was written during this time. The following selection emphasises the journey to
California and back.

I 'Know you the river near to Grez'
Place/date of composition: 'S[an] F[rancisco] [18]79 Dec[ember]' (B6482 so dated); RLS and
Fanny met for the first time in the autumn of 1876 'at the river near to Grez'.
MS: B6482* (in folder B6705)
Printed text: NP, 159
Line
  5   snowy] <reedy>^ ~ ^
  9   To present on from past.] <From present on to past.>^ ~ ^
       {Stanza 3, cancelled in MS, was omitted in NP; there is a marginal version:}

'Through all her deeps, in summer time
   The sun parades his light;
She moves, as in a foreign clime,
   By willow, lily, fish and slime,
Yet issues clear and bright
   <Below the town of Grez.>Beside the bridge at Grez.'

II 'The wind blew shrill and smart'
Date of composition: 1879 (BBS, I, 165–6)
MSS: B7167, B7168* (in folder B6372)
Printed text: NP, 151–2
{B7167 lacks the first four lines; B7168 is the copy-text: the two are collated below:}
Line
  8 It is time to stir the feet;]
      <Who can><Can you reef and band a sheet>^ ~ feet.^
  9 row!] row
 11 wine,] wine
 12 And its drain … go!] <To>And drain … go.
 13 my lads, we sail;] my <boys,>^lads,^ … sail,
 14 gale] gale,
 17 In the tempest and the squall,]
      <In the tempest> And the Lord High Admiral,
 18 And the ruler … wide!] And ruler … wide.

III. 'The cock's clear voice into the clearer air'
Place/date of composition: 'Train August 79' (B6104)
Letter and source: RLS to Edmund Gosse [8 October 1879] (LETBM, Vol. III, p. 16): 'There is a wonderful callousness in human nature, which enables us to live. I had no feeling one way or the other, from New York to California, until, at Dutch Flat, a mining camp in the Sierra, I heard a cock crowing with a home voice; and then I fell to hope and regret both in the same moment.'
{Cf. the penultimate paragraph of Across the Plains (1879)}: 'At every turn we could see farther into the land and our own happy futures. At every town the cocks were tossing their clear notes into the golden air, and crowing for the new day and the new country. For this was indeed our destination; this was "the good country" we had been going to so long.'}
MS: B6104* (in folder B6372)
Printed text: NP, 153–4

IV 'Of where or how, I nothing know'
Place/date of composition: 'Train Aug[ust] [18]79' (B6951)
Letter and source: 1. RLS to Colvin [20 August 1879] (LETBM, Vol. III, pp. 7–9): 'I am in the cars between Pittsburgh and Chicago, just now bowling through Ohio … I reached N.Y. Sunday night; and by five o'clock Monday was under way for the west. It is now about ten on Wednesday morning, so I have already been about forty hours in the cars. It is impossible to lie down in them which must end by being very wearying … I had no idea how easy it was to commit suicide. There seems nothing left of me; I died a while ago; I do not know who it is that is travelling.' {Here the poem is inserted; later, he ends the letter in a quite different

mood:} 'No man is any use until he has dared everything; I feel just now as if I had, and so might become a man. "If ye have faith like a grain of mustard seed." That is so true! Just now I have faith as big as a cigar case, I will not say die and do not fear man or fortune.'

2. {From *Across the Plains* (1879); published as the second part of *An Amateur Emigrant* in 1892:} 'Our American sunrise had ushered in a noble summer's day ... I stood on the platform by the hour ... And when I had asked the name of a river from the brakesman, and heard that it was called the Susquehanna, the beauty of the name seemed to be part and parcel of the beauty of the land. As when Adam with divine fitness named the creatures, so this word Susquehanna was at once accepted by the fancy. That was the name, as no other could be, for that shining river and desirable valley.'
MSS: B6951* (in folder B6372); *LETBM*, Vol. III, No. 645
First publication: Colvin 1899: Vol. I, 145
Printed text: CP, 100–1; NP, 155–6
{Copy-text is B6951, which is later than 645; collations follow:}
Title: {untitled}] *The Susquehanna and the Delaware* (Pentland Edition)
               The Susquehanna and the Delaware / To Sidney Colvin (NP)
Line
   1   know,] know;
   2   And why I do not care.] And why, I do not care;
   3   Enough if even so,] Enough if, even so,
   4   mind can go] mind, can go
   5   fair] fair, {This reading has been adopted.}
  10   before,] before;
  11   Or breathed perchance too deep] And drunk too deep perchance
  14   East ... declare;] east ... declare,
  15   East] east
  16   Outward and upward bound; and still shall roll,]
         And still aspire to rise above the whole,
  17   live, as ... despair] live as ... despair,
  20   air,] air;
  22   superber spirit boldlier sing,] enfranchised spirit loudlier sing
         ~ <loudlier>^boldlier^ sing, (B6951) {CP emends 'superber' to 'superior' and adopts 'loudlier'.}
  23   now I wear,] I now wear

V 'It's forth across the roaring foam, and on towards the west'
Place/date of composition: Pitlochry, July 1881 {Obviously this poem draws on his 1879-80 sojourn in San Francisco and Oakland, but, as 'Kinnaird' is written at the bottom left of B6471, it must have been completed in Scotland in July 1881 when RLS wrote Letter No. 827 from Kinnaird Cottage, Pitlochry, to Virgil Williams, who had befriended him in California; several phrases in the letter occur also in the poem.}
Letter: RLS to Virgil Williams [c. 11 July 1881] (*LETBM*, Vol. III, p. 211): 'It seems to me, on a retrospect, that at every stage of my life's journey, God must [have] arisen before the day and gone before me on my path, raising me up friends. But if there was ever a place where I most needed them it was San Francisco; for there I was sick, sad and poor; and if ever I found friends equal to my need it was in you and your wife, whose house was made a home to me

in the worst hours of my life. No one but myself can ever know how much I suffered; and so none can tell how opportune were the confidence, the welcome and the unwearying, invariable friendship, that I had from you and Mrs Williams. This is not a thing that can be told. But in that (to me) dreary city, the one spot I shall be pleased to see once more, is the house you were then living in.'

MSS: B6471* (in folder B6705), B6473

Printed text: *NP*, 160

{B6471, the copy-text, is headed 'D.N.W. & V.W.'; the initials stand for Dora and Virgil Williams, the 'friends' referred to in line 12. B6473 is a rough, fragmentary sketch across pp. 46, 48 and 49 of Notebook 'C' (1880–2), ultimately identified by McKay as a draft for part of this poem in Vol. VI: it reads as follows:}

{Stanza 2}

'<I have been>Its there that I was sick and sad, alone and poor and cold,
In your <unlucky>distressful city <by the sea><where they ship> beside the gates of gold
<O you know the golden>Where falls the fog at eventide and blows the breeze at morn,
Where all the <great> deep-sea galleons ride that come to bring the corn.

{Stanza 1}

Its far and some to travel there,
The days [?] will arise to set in other seas,
A man must <travel> journey many a day and night of little rest
From where the dogs of Scotland call the sheep into the fold.
The world, they say's a little place, and growing smaller still,
{Here follows the first stanza as it appears in *NP*.}

{Stanza 3}

<To God<<perhaps>>above my <<spirit>>heart turned, to God my prayer arose.
But God who>
<For none was there to know my face & none was there to greet>
In all that strange unholy place no friendly face I found.
For none was there to grasp my hand
<as for the tribes>as through the sands

{Trial fragments for stanzas 3, 4}

God the unflagging God, that still
In all my journeyings
Rose with me ere the sun was up,
Was on the topmost hill
And walked ahead of me till the day was done
He, oft-remembered, oft-forgot
Himself remembered still
I lay and slept
Before the morning, God arose
While still I slept, my path he chose
I lay meanwhile behind my [word(s) omitted]
And planned the coming day
Prepared my <friends and foes>friends, restrained my foes
<He sped along the way>

And watered all my way
He set the stars aside
Afar before me forth he went.'
{Collation of B6471 with B6473:}
Line
13   I have been near, I have been far, my back's been at the wall]
       To all the earth's remotest ends, and forth beyond the grave,
14   aye ... guide] <still>^aye^ ... <steer>^guide^
15   The love of God, the help of man, they both shall make me bold]
       And helped of God, and helped of friends
16   of darkness ... Gates of Gold.] of <hell>darkness ... gates of gold.

VI 'What man may learn, what man may do'
Place/date of composition: Monterey, 13 November 1879 {It seems to be a birthday poem:
line 4 states that the poet is 29 and a marginal comment on B7136 reads 'This was a birthday
indeed.' RLS turned 29 in California on 13 November 1879 amid dreadful crises: his health
was extremely bad, his future with Fanny was looking quite uncertain, he was out of money,
and his parents were making hysterical demands that he return home at once or be guilty
of murdering them. This poetic attempt at philosophical calm is paralleled in his letter of
15 November to Gosse (LETBM, Vol. III, No. 663). Around this time he also wrote the first
version of Requiem, No. 47 in the same notebook (see above, pp. 413–16).}
MS: B7136* (in folder B6705)
Printed text: NP, 155
Line
 3   skipper-like,] <captain-like>^ ~ ^
 4   years:] years<,>^:^
 5   forgot] forgot<,>
 9   check] <hold>^ ~ ^
11   act] <do>^ ~ ^
{Stanza 3 is cancelled in B7136, but there is a 'stet' beside it which may refer only to it or to
the poem as revised.}

VII The Piper: 'Inveni portum'
Place/date of composition: 'San Francisco [18]80' (so dated on B6717)
MS: B6717* (in B6705)
Printed text: NP, 165–6
Line
 2   You that rouse the heart to wander] <You that stir the heart to travel>^ ~ ^
 5   piping, on] piping on (NP) {This reading has been adopted.}
 9   sound] <blow>^ ~ ^

VIII 'Small is the trust when love is green'
Place/date of composition: 'S[an F[rancisco Jan[uary] 1880' (B6869 is so dated)
MS: B6869* (in folder B6705)
Printed text: NP, 158–9
Line
19   to hold] <that holds>^ ~ ^

20   helping] <helpful>^ ~ ^
23   And, with … will, to] <And with … will to>^ ~ ^

More Pieces in Scots

RLS made fair copies of fifteen of his Scots poems in a notebook, titling the selection *Pieces in Lallan* (see above, pp. 395–6). In 1887 he printed eleven of these in *UW* Book II – *in Scots*. The other four are printed here from MSS torn from the dismembered *Lallan* notebook: two of them are at BRBML, the other two at the Writers' Museum, Edinburgh. In this section variants are given selectively.

I *To the Commissioners of Northern Lights, with a Paper*
Place/date of composition: 'Swanston. 1871' (B7038) {The 'Paper' of the title was *On a New Form of Intermittent Light for Lighthouses*, which won a silver medal after it was read in March 1871 to the Royal Scottish Society of Arts. However, it and this poem were RLS's farewell to civil engineering.}
MSS: B7037, B7038* {The earlier MS is a draft in Notebook No. 60, collated below with the copy-text from the *Lallan* notebook, B7038.}
Printed text: CP, 101–2; NP, 101–2
Title: {Above the title in B7038 is *Pieces in Lallan*: this was the first poem in the torn-up
        notebook. B7037 is untitled.}
Line
 6   Before] Afore
11   I'll service wi'] I'll serve, sirs, wi'
14   Cam' … to] Came … toward
16   Straucht took the rue,] Straight took the grue,
19   I kent on cape and isle,] I kent, on cape an' head,
20   ilka] every
22   As sune's I saw,] And [?eke] at you
24   Gaed straucht awa.] My stake withdrew.
25   I now] I do
26   I'll cairry] to carry
27   sall] shall
28   An' – wha can tell? –] An wha can tell
29   Some ither day] Some ither I may
30   O' you mysel'.] O' you, my sel.

II *To Mesdames Zassetsky and Garschine*
Place/date of composition: 'Mentone Feb. 1874' (both MSS) {See Explanatory Note on
Music at the Villa Marina, p. 629.}
MSS: B7013, B7014* (in folder 7038)
Printed text: CP, 102–3; NP, 126–7
Title: *To Mesdames …*] *To Madame … Madame* (B7013)
Line
 4   Where a' … gang –] We a' … gang, (B7013)
 9   couthy] cosy (B7013)
15   Kirk an' State,] {Both MSS: CP and NP have 'kirk'.}

28   My] Ma (B7013) <Ma>^My^ (B7014)
30   lee.] lee! (B7013)

III *To Charles Baxter*
Place/date of composition: 'Edinburgh: October 1875' (MS LSH 136/91 is so dated)
MS: Edinburgh Writers' Museum LSH 136/91*
Printed text: *CP*, 104–5; *NP*, 223–5
{This poem was first published (Colvin 1899: Vol. I, 109–10) as a 'verse epistle' to Baxter
dated Edinburgh, October 1875. But there is no letter of that date in *LETBM*, nor any
mention made of this poem in that edition, although it was included in the Baxter–RLS
letters (Ferguson and Waingrow: 1956). CP set up from LSH 136/91, notebook pages 6–12
from *Pieces in Lallan* which serve as copy-text for this and the next epistle to Baxter. *NP* set
up from Colvin's *Letters*.}
Line
11   scowtherin<g>^'^
35   whether <o'> Christian ^ghaists^ or Turk
37   <twa>^three^
51   <gate>^road^

IV *To the same, on the death of their common*
     friend, Mr John Adam, Clerk of Court.
Place/date of composition and MS: same as previous poem
Letter: RLS to Charles Baxter, 11 December 1873 (*LETBM*, Vol. I, p. 397): 'Is there
anything new about Johnny Adam? Dear man! How my heart would melt within me and the
tears of patriotism spring to my eyes, if I could but see him reel towards me, in his dress clo'
like a moon at midday and smiling his vulgar, Scotch grin from ear to ear!'
Printed text: *CP*, 106–8; *NP*, 135–8
{JAS draws attention to the unreliability of the *NP* text for this poem in *CP*, 43.}
Line
11   <He was> ^Bein'^
43   <Like> ^The^

V *Song*
Date of composition: 1872 (*recto* of B6861 is so dated)
MS: B6861*
Printed text: *NP*, 131–2
Hellman dates this poem 1874 (*BBS*, III, 76–7) but gives no source; written on the *verso* of
the ode *To Sydney*, which is dated 1872, it more likely belongs to that year. Hellman omitted
the MS title *Song* and in line 20 printed 'roarin' instead of 'ravin'.

VI *Auld Reekie*
Place/date of publication: Samoan period, 1890–4
MSS: B5994–6 (Notebook No. 53), BRBML Uncat. No. 940902-j; NLS 3793*
First publication: *Pall Mall Gazette*, 21 January 1895; *Pall Mall Budget*, 24 January 1895. The
MS used for these printings was Lot 289 in the 1979 Sotheby's sale, then NLS 3793 (see
above p. 485). It first appeared in book form as one of the 'Additional Poems' in Vol. XIII,
p. 315 of the Pentland Edition (1907), collected under this title by Gosse together with

poems from the Colvin *Letters*, Balfour's *Life* and periodicals.
Printed text: *NP*, 254
{None of the various drafts in Notebook 53 is finished, but some phrases ('O my gusty
mither') and lines are recognisably part of this poem in process, e.g.:}

> 'Nae mair for me, at evenfa'
> Your lights sall glint'
>
> 'Hie owre the windy Firth she stands ...
> Over kirk and market, field and shaw
> Loud shall your bonnie bugles craw
> But nae mair for me'
>
> 'Hie is your seat and proud your stan'
> <To east and west on ilka han'>
> Braid in your glisk on sea an lan'
> Meadow and muir,'

(B5995)

> 'Though far ayont the muckle sea,
> In kintries, unco lands I be
> An' far from Kirk and Tron,
> O still the tear sall wut my e'e ...'

(B5996)

{940902-j and 3793 (copy-text) are fair copies with no variants:}
Line
  7   whaur] where (*Pall Mall*)
  9   frae] fraw (*Pall Mall*)
 10 still, ayont] still ayont (*Pall Mall*)

VII *To C. W. Stoddard*
Place/date of composition: Oakland, spring 1880 (*LETBM*, Vol. III, No. 757)
Letter: RLS to C. W. Stoddard [December 1880] (*LETBM*, Vol. III, pp. 138–9): 'Let me copy
... some broad Scotch I wrote for you when I was ill last spring in Oakland. It is no muckle
worth; but ye shouldna look a gien horse in the moo'.' {See Explanatory Note on Stoddard,
p. 630.}
MS: *LETBM*, No. 757 (B6993*)
First publication: Stoddard (1903), *Exits and Entrances*, Boston

VIII 'When I was young and drouthy'
Place/date of composition: Hyères [c. 1 May 1883] (*LETBM*, Vol. IV, No. 1094)
MS: *LETBM*, No. 1094 (B2754*)
Like the next poem, this was written to Baxter (Thomson) by RLS in his *persona* of Johnson:
the two friends often wrote and spoke to each other in their invented, interchangeable
characters of two bibulous Scotsmen (see Explanatory Note on *The Scotsman's Return from
Abroad*, p. 626).

IX 'O dinnae mind the drams ye drink'
Place/date of composition: Hyères [20 May 1883] (*LETBM*, Vol. IV, No. 1106)
Letter: RLS to Charles Baxter [20 May 1883] (*LETBM*, Vol. IV, pp. 126–7): 'Enclosed, please find a recipse for that twenty pound ye sent me. I'll sune have a hunner o' my ain; it'll no last very long but the Lord'll can Provide.' {Poem follows here. See note to previous poem.}
MS: *LETBM*, No. 1106 (B2753*)

X *Athole Brose*
Date of composition: ?1888–94 (Swearingen 1980: 200)
MS: Not found.
Printed text: *CP*, 357*; *VAIL*, Vol. XXVI, 'Stevenson's Companion to the Cook Book: Adorned with a Century of Authentic Anecdotes', pp. 187–8.
{This poem appears in Anecdote III (about Robert Burns) in a series of humorous sham anecdotes and imaginary letters begun aboard the yacht *Casco* in June 1888 but continued at Vailima.}

> On the way, Burns and Nichol were overtaken by a storm of rain, took refuge in a wayside inn beside the Blair, and passed some hours of the afternoon in drinking Athol Brose. It was the first time the poet had tasted the confection; he enquired exactly as to its constituents and going to the window, looked out with an abstracted countenance into the falling rain … In less than twenty minutes, the poet returned to the table, called for pen and ink, and wrote the following ingenious trifle.

{Here follows the poem. JAS, whose text I have followed, has this note on p. 550:

> In 1950 I made some emendations to the text of the Vailima Edition, and printed 'reek' for Vailima 'reck' (line 5), 'Killiecrankie' for 'Killicrankie' (line 8), 'neist' for 'neiest' (line 15). I have now emended the Vailima 'Rye'' (lines 3, 11) to 'kye' (cows). (Stevenson's 'k', lower or upper case, is very like 'R' …)
> In Chapter 25 of *Kidnapped*, Stevenson describes the constituents of Athole Brose: 'old whisky, strained honey, and sweet cream, slowly beaten together in the right order and proportion'. So in the still, the bee-skeps and the kye of the poem he is celebrating the source of the three ingredients. Nor would a Scottish poet associate 'Rye' with whisky, though American editors might.}

XI *Impromptu Verses Presented to Girolamo, Count Nerli*
Place/date of composition: 'Vailima, Samoa. Sept. 1892' (B6155 is so dated)
MS: B6155* (facsimile in *The Cosmopolitan*, New York, July 1895)
{Margaret Stevenson records in her Diary that RLS sat for the Italian painter Count Nerli ten times between 15 September and 3 October. The results were a portrait that, some say, RLS thought the best likeness ever done of him (although he did not purchase it), and this poem was written impromptu and presented when Nerli finished the picture. See Frontispiece and Explanatory Note on Nerli and this picture, p. 630.}

The Vailima Family

The following proposal to Baxter, made New Year's Day 1894, sheds light on the question of why none of these poems appeared in either *ST* or *EDIN*:

If I were to get printed off a very few poems which are somewhat too intimate for the public, could you get them run up in some luxurious manner so that blame fools might be induced to buy them in just a sufficient quantity to pay expenses and the thing remain still in a manner private? We could supply photographs for illustrations, and the poems are of Vailima and the family. I should much like to get this done as a surprise for Fanny. (*LETBM*, Vol. VIII, p. 227)

This privately printed collection appeared five years later, edited not by RLS but by his stepdaughter, Belle Strong. Entitled *R.L.S. / Teuila / Being fugitive verses and lines / by Robert Louis Stevenson / now first collected* (1899), it contained more scraps and versicles than the poet probably would have sanctioned, but it did surely bring together most of the poetry RLS had in mind when he wrote to Baxter on 1 January 1894. Belle was familiar with this verse because she often served the poet as amanuensis during the Vailima years; indeed, she had much of it written down in her own journal, known *en famille* as *Grouse in the Gunroom*, B7371 at BRBML. Also at Yale is the notebook labelled *First Drafts of Poems* (file B6022), which has experimental versions of the material that JAS grouped together as *The Family* in *CP*, 1950; there are also fair copies of these poems at BRBML. RLS began writing them in January 1893, the beginning of the third year at Vailima, after the large addition to the house had been completed. He wrote to his mother at that time:

Altogether this new house has supplied a felt want; and now that it is paid for I can be vain about it with a clear conscience. It and its inhabitants have been made the subject of some bee-*ea*utiful poetry which (if you are good) you may someday be privileged to see. You are in it! {See No. VI in this series} (*LETBM*, Vol. VIII, p. 15)

I *Mother and Daughter*
Place/date of composition: Vailima, January 1893 (*LETBM*, Vol. VIII, p. 15, n.3)
Letter and source: 1. Belle Strong noted in her journal for 22 January that 'today he [RLS] read us some beautiful verses about Aolele [one of Fanny's Samoan names] and me' (Osbourne and Strong 1902: 27).

2. RLS to J. M. Barrie, 2 or 3 April 1893 (*LETBM*, Vol. VIII, pp. 44–8): 'Here follows a catalogue of my menagerie:' {In this long letter he provides Barrie with prose sketches of the Vailima household under the following headings: 'R.L.S. / The Tame Celebrity. / Native name, *Tusi Tala* / ; Fanny V. de G. Stevenson. / The Weird Woman. / Native name, *Tamaitai* / ; Isobel Stewart Strong. / Your humble servant the Amanuensis. / Native name, *Teuila* / Lloyd Osbourne. / The Boy. / Native name, *Loia*.'}
MSS: B6593–6; copy-text is B6595*
Printed text: *Teuila* 5–7; *Memories of Vailima*, pp. 17–19; *CP*, 311–12; *NP*, 206–7
{As there is a prodigious quantity of MS for this and the other *Vailima Family* poems, variants will be given selectively. The following trial fragments for lines 9–29 occur in B6593 (in B6022):}

> 'The one, her curls of grizzle and gold,
> Wanders, as a truant girl,
> One, her crop-halo, stained with sun,
> Rough as a thicket wears,
> Wild as a child of wood and wold'

> 'Alike, my pair are marked, defined
> From European womankind
> By something simple, straight and free
> Learned here in our part savage state'

> 'Lo, either body turns and sways
> Forgets the long-discarded stays
> And fashioned like to goddesses …'

> 'Yet lest my eye should pause in doubt,
> One's nose turns down and one's turns out.'

{The following trial fragment occurs in B6594:}

> 'Alike the steps on stair, in bower
> Alike the heads poised like a flower,
> The inimitable arms, the lines
> Initimably feminine
> Of tender limbs.'

{B6595, a fair copy, is the copy-text; B6596, in Belle's journal, is the source for her printed versions; B6594 had a different title, one adapted from Horace:}
The Family / I /*Mother and Daughter*] II *Mater Pulchra nec filia pulchrior.* (B6594)
{*Memories of Vailima* varies from the copy-text in lines 11–12:}
the plain mind … naked foot,] wider mind … little foot,

II *The Daughter* / *Teuila* – her native name – The Adorner
Place/date of composition: Vailima, January 1893 (see notes to I *Mother and Daughter*)
Letters: 1. RLS to Colvin, 8 October 1892 (*LETBM*, Vol. VII, p. 388): 'Belle had that day been the almoner in a semi-comic distribution of wedding rings and and thimbles (bought cheap at an auction) to the whole plantation company, fitting a ring on every man's finger, and a ring and a thimble on both the women's. This was very much in character with her native name *Teuila*, the adorner of the ugly.'

2. RLS to J. M. Barrie (see notes to I *Mother and Daughter*): 'Rich dark colour; taken in Sydney for an islander. Eyes enormous and particoloured, one three-fifths brown the other two-fifths golden … Doesn't go in for intellect – still less for culture … thing she likes best in the world, dress for herself and others – rather adornment. Will arrange your hair and stick flowers about you till you curse. Meaning of her native name, The Adorner of the Ugly … Manages the house and the house boys who are very fond of her. An unaffected Pagan, and worships an idol with lights and flowers.'
MSS: B6139–41, B5944–6, copy-text is B6040*
Printed text: *Teuila*, 8–12; *Memories of Vailima*, pp. 19–22; *CP*, 313–14; *NP*, 208–11
{B5944–5 are two consecutive pages in B6022 comprising fragmentary trials for lines 34ff., sixteen lines from which were printed in *NP* as a separate poem (pp. 210–11). Many trials were made for lines 51–3 in both B5944 and B6139: RLS recycled these verses about particoloured eyes into an unhappily ranting ballad spoken by one Jock o' Hazeldean (B7033–4), which he wisely abandoned. Belle, however, printed it as one of two poems

called *To Teuila* in *Teuila* (pp. 23–4). B6141 is written in *Grouse in the Gunroom*. Excerpts from B5944–5 follow:}

'The Adorner of the Uncomely. Well
The title fits and pictures Belle.
Now with a gibe and now with tears she <rules> …
                    Those she commands
When satire fails her, with an April burst
Of girlish weeping, her half-savage, nude
Gigantic servants …
I hear her voice
Rating her laggard giants; or when all
Fails her, amidst her laggard giants, sits
Weeping, and their hurt hearts relent.'

                    'There
Amidst whose tall battalions goes
<Pigmy and dimpled person goes, nought great therein but hair and eyes>
Her pretty person out and in
All day with an endearing din,
Of censure and encouragement
And when all else is tried in vain
See her sit down and weep again.
She weeps to conquer;
She varies on her grenadiers
From satire up to girlish tears!
Or rather to behold her when
She plies for me the unresting pen;
And when the loud assault of squalls
Resounds upon the roof and walls,
And the low thunder growls, and I
Raise my dictating voice on high.'

{B6040 is collated selectively with the other MSS and printed sources:}
Subtitle: HER NATIVE NAME – THE ADORNER] HER NATIVE NAME THE DECORATOR (*Memories*)
Line
10 {Here in B6139 this couplet is inserted but cancelled:}
    'Who brightens, lives, and finds her books
    And melody in human looks'
20 {Here in B6139 this couplet is inserted but cancelled:}
    'Her sit, scarce browner than herself,
    Smoothing her dress and pillaging her shelf.'
23 tender] bended (*Memories*)
29 draw] dress (*Memories*)
32 pigmy,] graceful (*Memories*, CP, 1950 {in 1971 JAS adopted 'pigmy'})
42 hang on] obey (*Memories*)
45 pay her in her girded] <serve>^pay^ ~ (B6139)

do her in her kilted (*Memories*, CP, 1950 {in 1971 JAS changed 'kilted' to 'girded'})
49   And while her crimson blood peeps out,]
      While through the brown the blood breaks out (B5944)

III 'About my fields, in the broad sun'
Place/date of composition: Vailima,1892–3 (*LETBM*, Nos 2469, 2531)
Letter: RLS to Ida Taylor, 7 October 1892 (*LETBM*, Vol. VII, p. 395): 'Nor is Fanny any less
active. Ill or well, rain or shine, a little blue indefatigable figure is to be observed howking
about {Scots. "digging"} certain patches of garden. She comes in heated and bemired up to
the eyebrows, late for every meal. She has reached a sort of tragic placidity. Whenever she
plants anything new the boys weed it up. Whenever she tries to keep anything for seed the
house boys throw it away. And she has reached that pitch of a kind of noble dejection that
she would almost say she did not mind.'
MS: B5930* (in B6022)
Printed text: CP, 315; NP, 209–10

IV 'Tall as a guardsman'
Place/date of composition: Vailima, January 1893 (*LETBM*, Vol. VIII, No. 2531)
MSS: B6882–4, B6884 is in *Grouse in the Gunroom*
Printed text: *Teuila*, 13–14; CP, 315–16; NP, 210
{B6883* (in B6022) is the copy-text: it collates with the other MSS as follows:}
Title: {*The Son* only appears in B6884 and *Teuila*}
Line
  1   east] East (B6884)
  4   boys escaped from school) with song]<children done with>boys escaped <out of>from
        school, with <jest>song (B6882)
  6   Part we deride the child, part dread the antique!] ~ child – part ~ (B6882)
        Part dread the uncle, part deride the child. (B6882) {in the margin}
  7   among the dew] in the strong dew, (B6882)
  9   kilts; and their swift eyes] kilts – and their <dark>^swift^ eyes (B6882)
 13   Now ministers alarm,] Now <scatters terror and> ^ ~ ^ (B6882)
 14   chord – now tweaks] triad – now upbraids (B6882)

V 'What glory for a boy of ten'
Place/date of composition: Vailima, 1892–3 (*LETBM*, Vols. VII, VIII, Nos 2443, 2531)
Letter: RLS to Colvin [12 August 1892] (*LETBM*, Vol. VII, p. 346): 'This morning the
overseer – the new overseer Mr Austin Strong – went down in charge of the pack-horses and
a squad of men, himself riding a white horse with extreme dignity and what seemed to
onlookers a perhaps theatrical air of command [also hand on hip in elaborate imitation
of Louis. *Belle*]. He returned triumphantly, all his commissions apparently executed with
success.'
MS: B7134*
Printed text: CP, 316; NP, 211
{The MS, titled *He*, runs forty lines in the notebook (B6022), comprising three separate
drafts; interspersed with *He* is a draft for *The Snoring Conch* (B6872), another Vailima poem
about Belle's son Austin which was never completed or printed. The final version, in which
the title is dropped, serves as copy-text. Some trial fragments follow:}

'Breeches unbuttoned at the knee,
Bare shanked and footed, ragged, brown,
Treads now the planked verandah down
Our overseer, capped and whipped;
Is once by an anxious mother clipped,
Head to her bosom; flings her by, –
<And straightway to his charger climbs
Being concerned with graver things.>
                    And with heed
Climbs to his disproportioned steed.
Lord, what a [blank space left] for a boy of ten!
Mounted himself, he shall three <stalwart>monstrous men
And two more monstrous cart horses command
<And planting gallantly his hand>And chivalrously planting hand
On hip <assumes his uncle's> (a borrowed attitude)
<And freely>Valiantly rides into the wood.
Our overseer aged ten
Or one year over, leads his men
And [?] pack train thus; and these
Three labourers tattooed to the knees
And each three times his bulk, and three …' [breaks off]

VI *'The old lady (so they say) but I'*
Place/date of composition: Vailima, January 1893 (*LETBM*, Vol. VIII, No. 2531)
MS: B6673*
Printed text: *CP*, 316; *NP*, 211–12
{There are forty-nine lines of verse covered under this one McKay number, most of which have no connection with these ten lines referring to the poet's mother. Both *CP* and *NP* add ten lines at the end, which I have omitted; I have also restored several readings from the MS that they altered or ignored. There are two variants in the MS, as follows:}
Line
1   (so they say) but I] ah but rather I {alt.}
8   Thus calling] <to summon>^ ~ ^

VII *Tusitala*
Place/date of composition: Vailima, January 1893 (so dated in *Teuila*)
Letters: 1. RLS to George Meredith, 5 September 1893 (*LETBM*, Vol. VIII, p. 163): 'I am now living patriarchally in this place 600 feet above the sea on the shoulder of a mountain of 1500 [feet]. Behind me, the unbroken bush slopes up to the backbone of the island (3 to 4000) without a house, with no inhabitants save a few runaway black boys, wild pigs and cattle, and wild doves and flying-foxes, and many particoloured birds, and many black, and many white: a very eerie, dim, strange place and hard to travel. I am the head of a household of five whites, and of twelve Samoans, to all of whom I am the chief and father; my cook comes to me and asks leave to marry – and his mother a fine old chief woman, who has never lived here, does the same. You may be sure I granted the petition.'

2. RLS to W. H. Triggs, 6 December 1893 (*LETBM*, Vol. VIII, pp. 200, 203–4): 'Of course

no Samoan works except for his family. The chief is the master; to serve another clan may be possible for a short time, and to get money for a specific purpose. Accordingly in order to insure [ensure] permanent service in Samoa I have tried to play the native chief with necessary European variations. Just now it looks as if I was succeeding. Our last triumph was at the annual missionary feast. Up to now our boys had always gone home and marched into the show with their own individual villages. This time of their own accord they marched in a body by themselves into the meeting clad in the Vailima uniform, and on their entrance were saluted as 'Tama ona' which may be literally translated into Scotch 'MacRichies' (children of the rich man) ... When I say 'boys' I mean men ... I rise at six, write till twelve, lunch then, and either write or read again, or walk or ride, or receive an occasional guest, or if my company are Samoans, I may sit down to a solemn *ava* drinking, with the correct libations and salutations – this is a thing in which I consider myself a past master, and there are perhaps not twenty whites in the world who could say so much. At six I dine, on fish and claret, and go to bed at eight.'

MSS: B6565–7; B6567 is in Belle's journal; copy-text is B6566*
Printed text: *Teuila*, 15–19; CP, 317–18; NP, 212–13
{B6565 (in B6022) is a 69-line draft with a false start and a cancelled passage following line 44; here is the false start:}

> 'Here all day long the trade winds ...
> Thrice fortunate, who lately wrote
> A while with an inky table
> <Meanwhile apart> I meanwhile <now> in the populous house apart
> Sit; snugly chambered and my silent art
> <Ply unremitting>'

{The six lines cancelled at the end of B6565 appear in a less rough version, but still cancelled, in B6566, as follows:}

> 'Or stranger still; can the wisest understand
> That here, with him, a well-descended race,
> We linger and labour in this rustic place?
> <And still our valued lives and spirits risk>
> <Or risk our souls in this foolhardy way>
> <Among uncounted bogies?><Among his neighbour ghosts?>
> That still, in dread and peril, we support
> The neighbourhood of bogies? And, as at a court,
> One village – and two family-chiefs – attend
> About his pots and pans and garden end?'

{B6566, the copy-text, is collated below with the other MSS. The nine MS lines tacked on to the end of this poem in NP and CP 1950 (not the cancelled lines in B6565–6 quoted above but verses on Scotland unconnected with *Tusitala*) have been omitted; I have also restored several MS readings altered or ignored in NP and CP.}

Title: VII. *Tusitala*] VII. <Aladdin>^ ~ ^ (B6566) {untitled} (B6565)
        THE MASTER OF THE HOUSE / Tusitala (*Teuila*)

Line
6   westward peak] westering hill (B6565)
15   Before the earliest] <Bothers him still><Wakes him before the> ^ ~ ^ (B6565)

22 in the wild-wood glade: he still,] <to the world; why must he still,> in the forest glade: he still (B6565)
23 Unthinkable ... dawn and dark,] <Inscrutable> ^ ~ ^   from the rising dark (B6565)
{Trial fragment for lines 21–3 in B6565:}
'<Far>Adown the hill to the blue sea thy gaze,
Far distant whispers catch
Behold the bright true beacon in the wood,
Unthinkable Aladdin! They conclude'
36 Here too, no doubt,] <With devils all around>
                      <Here beyond><Doubtless>Here, too, beyond doubt, (B6565)
37 brawls] <threads> ^ ~ ^ (B6565)
38 crawfish. These be] <prawns.> ^ ~ ^ These <are> ^ ~ ^ (B6565)
39 understood?] understood<?>^ : ^ (B6565)
42 compeers, in the mountain dwells?] chiefs here in the forest dwells, (B6565)
44 Apart from] <Far from all> ^ ~ ^ (B6565)

VIII 'These rings, O my beloved pair'
Place/date of composition: Sydney, March 1893 (B7085 is so dated)
Source: in her journal for 3 March 1893 Belle Strong recorded: 'He [RLS] has had three topaz rings made, for topaz is the stone of his birth month, November. Inside two of them are his initials, and these he has presented, with a memorial poem, to my mother and myself. On his own we engraved the first letters of our names' (Osbourne and Strong 1902: 31).
MSS: B7084–5, B7085* is the copy-text
Printed text: *Teuila*, 25–6; *Memories of Vailima*, pp. 31–2; *CP*, 319; *NP*, 214
{first and second drafts are in B7084, as follows:}
> 'Our tender confraternity
> Is triple and the rings are three
> Let – when at morning <first you> as ye rise
> Lo <when from sleep my lovers arise>the golden topaz takes your eyes
> <Daughter and wife> To each her emblem whisper sure
> That love was <up> awake an hour before:
> Ah yes! An hour [?] before you woke.'

{The second draft switches to quatrains, the first of which is identical to copy-text B7085: the rest follows:}
> 'Whether you walk, whether you sleep,
> That finger on your pulse I keep,
> And near or far, faithful and fond,
> Still hold you by that slender bond.
>
> First in the morn, before you rise
> Your rings are swift to woo your eyes.
>
> Be sure that [?] before you wake
> Low to my heart my emblem spake; –
> And sure, as men renew an oath
> *It* I have kissed, and blessed you both.'

Occasional Verse

Epistles and Verses Addressed to Friends and Family

I *To Charles Baxter*
(a) *Epistle to Charles Baxter*: 'Reaped grain should fill the reaper's grange.'
Place/date of composition: 'Edinburgh. Feby 1872.' (Silverado MS so dated)
MS: Silverado (Foot*)
First publication: *CP*, 68–71
{This was to have been included as one of the projected *Recruiting Songs*, dedicated on an
MS title-page to *Tres Amicos Stevenson Wilson et Baxter* (see above, p. 550). *CP* prints it as a
poem of fifteen stanzas but RLS divided it at the end of stanza 9 (there is a rule at this point
in the MS) and moved the six stanzas beginning 'O South, South, South!' to his *Little Odes*
collection. I have made minor corrections to the *CP* text from MS.}

(b) 'Blame me not that this epistle'
Place/date of composition: 'Boulogne Sur Mer / Wednesday 3ʳᵈ or 4ᵗʰ September / 1872'
(actually the 4th – *LETBM*, No. 111 is so dated)
MSS: BL Ashley* (Catalogue Vol. VII, p. 10); *LETBM*, Vol. I, No. 111
First publication: T. J. Wise, *Familiar Epistle in Prose and Verse*, privately printed, London,
1896.
Printed text: Colvin 1911: Vol. I, 53–6; *CP*, 330–2; *NP*, 232–3
{Bibliophile, pirate and forger Thomas J. Wise received the MS of this verse epistle to Baxter
from his friend Clement Shorter and printed it without authority; Baxter and Colvin
considered legal action against him.}

(c) *To Charles Baxter*: 'The wind is without there'
Place/date of composition: 'Malvern. January 1873' (B7170 is so dated)
Letter: RLS to Baxter, 16 January 1873 (*LETBM*, Vol. I, pp. 270–1): 'Without, it rains –
within, muddle o' the brains … I feel as if I could write poetry today: probably shall, before
night.' {*LETBM* speculates in n.6 that, since both MS and letter are dated in January 1873
from Malvern, both were sent together, suggesting further that this mailing also included the
poem *Ne Sit Ancillae Tibi Amor Pudori*, addressed to a 'graceful housemaid' at the Imperial
Hotel, Great Malvern, where he was staying with his mother (see above, p. 314 and notes).
However, even though the two poems are written on pages from the same notebook
(A.155), B6624, the 'housemaid' poem MS is dated 1872.}
MS: B7170*
Printed text: *NP*, 121–2
{Copy-text is the MS, which was revised as follows:}
Line
17   <future>Future
30   <And my plans be all shattered in strife,><if God should>
        ^And if fortune go cross to my plan,^
32   <life.> ^man.^

II *To W. E. Henley*: 'The Gods are dead'
Place/date of composition: [?Paris] July 1877 (*LETBM*, Vol. II, No. 475)
Letter: RLS to Henley [July 1877] (*LETBM*, Vol. II, p. 214): {This letter consists of this

untitled poem plus the following: 'There! You see I'm not dead. I'm all right, and quite the poet.'}
MSS: NLS* 9821 f.13r; LETBM, No. 475
Printed text: CP, 358
{First published from the poet's MS by JAS in 1971, this poem is identified in her note as a rondeau. Accordingly, she (followed by LETBM) restored the penultimate line (cancelled by the poet) as follows: 'The fair, the brave, the liberal-conceited'. However, NLS is otherwise a fair copy, the cancellation is unambiguous and the rondeau form only loosely adhered to (cf. XX 'My wife and I, in our romantic cot', above p. 328) so I have followed the MS strictly. There are no other variants. For Henley's printings of this poem see Explanatory Note on it, p. 630.}

III *To Horatio F. Brown*
Place/date of composition: Davos, March–April 1881 (*LETBM*, Vol. III, No. 784)
Letter: RLS to H. F. Brown [c. 1 April 1881] (*LETBM*, Vol. III, pp. 165–6): 'Please, my dear Brown, forgive my horrid delay.' {This letter contained the untitled poem, although *LETBM* set up from Colvin's text rather than from MS. When he printed it in his 1899 Letters, Colvin prefixed this note: ' The following experiment in English alcaics was suggested by conversations with Mr Brown and J[ohn] A[ddington] Symonds on metrical forms, followed by the despatch of some translations from old Venetian boat-songs by the former after his return to Venice' (Vol. I, p. 200).}
MSS: B5950*, B6049, B7192, B6923, B7205, B6484
Printed text: Colvin 1899: Vol. I, 200–1; CP, 287–8; NP, 228
{These twenty-eight lines of Horatian alcaics in English cost RLS dearly: he wrote nearly 300 lines, scattered across sixteen pages of Notebook 'C' (pp. 16–17, 22–6, 27–35, assigned several McKay numbers but all part of this one verse epistle) before arriving at the finished text on two notebook pages in B5950, the copy-text. To achieve his neo-classical effect, he used a dactylic metre to write stanzas consisting of two eleven-syllable lines, one line of nine syllables followed by a final line of ten syllables. The 'horrid delay' spoken of in the letter was the time elapsed between receiving the book from Brown and responding to him in this intricate, difficult verse form. At first he tried his usual octosyllabic idiom:}

> 'Friend I received the book, and read
> Into the starry night I read
> <And saw as down a watershed>
> These brave old student songs.'
>
> ('C', p. 16)

> '<Such the gospel I adore
> Buried I thought for evermore
> Or grasped a moment at the tavern door>
> To walk about both late and soon
> Before the dawn, behind the moon
> And chanting at the tavern door … '

{Further drafts follow:}

> 'The grand old monumental tongue
> More, somehow, like a dancing bear

But gladly, to a gladsome air,
<Chirruping latin> Trips in a little, plaintive, rhythmic dance,
By tavern doors, when May was fair
The latin changing to Romance'

'And from the Adriatic sea
A little book, your gift to me!
There the old monumental tongue
Tripped to new dialects of the young;
The young that were, long laid below,
Young once afterward years ago.
There by the hills of trilling birds
Were lifted monolithic words
And Augustine and Tacitus
Sing from the alehouse down to us.'

'In vain the music I woo
            For still the muse refuses,
As I, to tell you true,
            Still find it with the muses'

                                                                ('C', pp. 22–3)

{Then he started trying to write English verse as though it were Latin verse:}

'<Loud old> Great-heart ancient boys by ale-house doors in the evening,
Sang to the moon as she rose
Sang these songs you send me a thousand years ago.'

                                                                ('C', p. 23)

'Friend, days elapse and cross taciturnity
Still chains my muse; my pusillanimity
Still keeps the muse in egregious incompetence
      Still keeps my muse tongue-tied …
Friend, days elapse and pusillanimity
Lies dead-alive on body and phantasy
      Lead-heavy, soul-slain, rhyme-denying
Warm-defying and dull decadence
Days pass and still egregious incompetence
Weighs down my muse, unskilled with distempering
Dreams …'

                                                                ('C', p. 24)

'Brave old bearded lads by the alehouse doors at night
Sang these songs you send me years and years ago.
Time, old time the artist, who maketh man's delight
The muse that will not and the heart that will.
How shall we do?
Write, in god's name; indifferent, well or ill:

Write still.
The book you sent me, I acknowledge. I commend it freely;
It is a pearl . . . .'

('C', p. 25)

{A leaf was torn from the notebook, as recorded in ink on p. 26: 'pp. 27, 28 *Lads of Yore &
Lasses* taken to S.C. [Sidney Colvin] 8 Nov.95'; it is now filed as B6484.}

'If you only knew the vast amount of verses
    I have since deserted indeterminate
If you only knew how long, with sanguinary curses
    Since the book arrived, to answer I have sate,
Brown, I must believe, although your heart were harder
Than the grinding stones that circle in the mill,
You would scorn to hate a man whose scanty larder,
Not his faulty will, has made that answer late.'

('C', p. 28)

{JAS capitalised 'ocean' in line 20 but her version is otherwise identical with the copy-text,
B5950.}

IV *To Mrs MacMorland*
Place/date of composition: 'Feb.2ⁿᵈ 1881 at Davos-Platz' (LSH 348/91 is so dated)
MSS: Edinburgh Writers' Museum LSH 348/91*, B7017
Printed text: CP, 301–2; NP, 169–70
{LSH 348/91, the later of the two MSS, is the copy-text: collation follows:}
Line
  2   accords – :] accords –
  5   crew we dwell,] crew, we dwell
  9   plain] plains
16   eyes!] eyes.
21   life] life,
28   war:] war.
29   love] love, {This reading has been adopted.}
{During February–March 1881 RLS published five articles in the *Pall Mall Gazette* on the
Swiss Alps (Swearingen 1980: 58).}

V *To A. G. Dew-Smith*: In return for a box of cigarettes
Place/date of composition: Davos [November 1880] (*LETBM*, Vol. III, No. 739)
{This letter was sent as a purely verse epistle.}
MS: B6194*
First publication: Colvin 1899: Vol. I, 185–7: {The two final stanzas are omitted and in line
32 'God help me,' is replaced by 'I vow that'.}
Printed text: NP, 166–8 (Colvin's text) {In 1950 the entire poem appeared in CP, 341–3:
JAS did not undo Colvin's bowdlerisation in line 32 but *LETBM* did. See Explanatory Note
on this poem, pp. 630–1.}

VI *To Frederick Locker-Lampson*
Place/date of composition: Bournemouth, 4 September 1886 (*LETBM*, Vol. V, No. 1692)
Letter: RLS to Frederick Locker-Lampson, 4 September 1886 (*LETBM*, Vol. V, pp. 312–13):
{The letter consists entirely of this untitled poem with salutation and signature. Locker, author of elegant lyrics, collector and anthologist specialising in *vers de société*, had asked through Andrew Lang for 'a scrap of verse, in your fist, published or not' (n.1, p. 312). These lines were first published as the introductory poem to Locker's *Rowfant Rhymes*, an edition limited to 127 copies published in 1895 by the Rowfant Club, Cleveland.}
MS: Rowfant Club (not seen); *LETBM*, Vol. V, No. 1692*
Printed text: Colvin 1899: Vol. II, 43; *CP*, 309–10; *NP*, 226
{1692 is copy-text as it was set up from MS; *CP* and *NP* set up from Colvin as they all have twelve identical variants from 1692.}

VII *To Master Andrew Lang: On his re-Editing of* Cupid and Psyche.
Date of composition: 1887
MS: Not found.
Printed text: *CP*, 310–11; *NP*, 221
{This brief epistle was first printed in 1887 in a very few copies of the large paper edition of Lang's *Cupid and Psyche* edition; according to RLS's bibliographers, the lines 'were rigidly suppressed before the book was published ... and ... have not ... been reprinted'. Lang responded in a dedication to his edition of Robert Kirk's *The Secret Commonwealth of Elves, Fauns & Fairies* (1893) as follows:

> O LOUIS! you that like them maist,
> Ye're far frae kelpie, wraith, and ghaist,
> And fairy dames, no unco chaste,
>   And haunted cell.
> Amang a heathen clan ye're placed,
>   That kens na hell!
>   (Prideaux and Livingston 1917: 158)

{This very rare item is described and facsimiled (opposite p. 430) as No. 837* in McKay, Vol. II. Using this facsimile as copy-text, I have corrected errors in the other printed versions, e.g. *CP* omits line 5 and *NP* reads in lines 12–13 'Death,/ the unforgettable shepherd,'.}

VIII *To Harriet Baker*
Place/date of composition: Vailima, December 1893 (*LETBM*, Vol. VIII, No. 2661)
Letter: RLS to Harriet Baker [?5 December 1893] (*LETBM*, Vol. VIII, pp. 195–6): 'This Braille writing is a kind of consecration, and I would like if I could to have your copy perfect ... You say, dear madam, you are good enough to say, it is "a keen pleasure" to you to bring my book within the reach of the blind. Conceive then what it is to me!' {Here the untitled poem is inserted to conclude the letter; Mrs Arthur Baker was a Braille writer preparing *Kidnapped* and *Catriona*.}
MS: *LETBM*, Vol. VIII, No. 2661*
Printed text: Colvin 1899: Vol. II, 315; *NP*, 254–5
{Although the poem appeared in both printings with the title, *The Consecration of Braille / To Mrs A. Baker* there is no MS authority for this or any title. The only variant between the copy-text 2661, set up from a facsimiled MS, and the printed versions, is in lines 5–6:}

'lend your hand – I bring
My sheaf for you to bind –]
lend your hand, I bring
My sheaf for you to bind,'

Dedications and Presentations

1 *To the Hesitating Purchaser*: Prefatory verses to *Treasure Island*
Place/date of composition: Hyères, 1883
MS: B7060
Printed text: *Treasure Island* (1883) – facing Contents page; CP, 321–2
{The MS is a rough 35-line draft on pp. 8–9 of Notebook A.269 (1880–3), revised to the point where it accords closely with the published version in the novel. I give a selective reconstruction of the early draft below. The variants in B7060 have been fully recorded by Wendy R. Katz in her edition of *Treasure Island** (Edinburgh University Press, 1998, p. 244), which is copy-text for these lines.}

'<If Pirates and if hidden gold
        Now please as once they pleased of old>
If Schooners, Islands and Maroons
        And Buccaneers and Buried Gold,
And Torches red and rising moons,
        <And the young Hero fair and bold,
        In his adventures manifold
No more, O reader, please no more
        As me they pleased of old,
Then reader pass my volume o'er.>
<If the old tales, in short, retold
        With all the <<classic>>cut-and-dry array>
If all {continues exactly as in printed text lines 5–9}
        If all the boys on <better things>solid food
Have set their <spirits>fancies and forgot
        Kingston and Ballantyne the good
And Cooper of the sea and wood,
        So be it also, and may I
And my late-born piratic band
        Unread beside the ancients lie.

{Another draft of lines 10–16 follows:}

If <stronger diet youth shall crave>
<A stronger meal, and have forgot><Their ancient appetites>
                <wiser>studious youth no longer crave,
Their ancient appetites forgot,
        Kingston and Ballantyne the brave
Far Cooper of the wood and wave; –
        So be it also, and may I
And all my pirates share the grave
        Where these and their creations lie.'

{In line 9 CP omits the initial dash in the first edition of *Treasure Island* (Katz, p. 7).}

II *To Mr and Mrs Robert A. Robertson*: Presentation inscription in a copy of CGV
Place/date of composition: Bournemouth, 'April 3 1885' (the verses are so dated)
Letter: RLS to R. A. Robertson, 22 October 1885 (*LETBM*, Vol. V, p. 137): 'I find … I have
never sent you a copy of my book, in which your child's name was written, and to which I
have added a few lines to yourself and Mrs Robertson. I hope you will excuse this delay and
take the verses as they were intended.'
MS: Silverado (Foot)
Printed text: Masson* 1923: 276; *NP*, 178
{The copy of CGV sent with this letter had been inscribed 'To the author's Robertson
godchild with all good wishes March, 1885' but the wrong book was sent in March. RLS
added the verses after the little boy's death, which RLS must have heard about on or about
3 April 1885. Robertson was an Edinburgh solicitor and family friend who had asked RLS
to be godfather to his son James. G. S. Hellman misidentified the intended recipient as
Nelly Sanchez. The Silverado MS is identical with *NP*; they vary as follows from the MS
inscription as transcribed from the book in Masson:}
Line
  4   Farewell.] farewell.
  6   keep] be
  7   children;] children,

III *To H. C. Bunner*: Presentation verses with a copy of CGV
Place/date of composition:'Skerryvore/Bournemouth/Oct. 21 1885' (B7003 is so dated)
Letter: RLS to Will. Low [22 October 1885] (*LETBM*, Vol. V, p. 136): 'I will send you (with
this) a copy of the English edition of the *Child's Garden*. I have heard there is some vile rule
of the post office in the States against inscriptions; so I send herewith a piece of doggerel
which Mr Bunner may, if he thinks fit, copy on the fly-leaf.' {Enclosing these verses, 'You
know the way to Arcady', with a presentation copy was RLS's acknowledgement of Bunner's
book *Airs from Arcady and Elsewhere* (1884), sent with a request for a copy of the English
edition of CGV.}
MS: B7003*
Printed text: *Scribner's Magazine*, New York, December 1909; CP, 325–6
{CP deviates from the MS and *Scribner's* at the end of line 10, where a colon is replaced with
a semicolon.}

IV *To Virgil and Dora Williams*: Presentation inscription in a copy of *The Silverado Squatters*
(1883)
Place/date of composition: Hyères, 1883 (B7050 is so dated)
Letter: RLS to Henley [April 1882] (*LETBM*, Vol. III, p. 321) {RLS is explaining why he
wants to dedicate *The Silverado Squatters* to the Williamses, who had befriended him in San
Francisco (see above, pp. 564–5:} 'You know they were the parties who stuck up for us about
our marriage, and Mrs W was my guardian angel, and our Best Man and Bride's Maid rolled
in one.'
MS: B7050*
Printed text: *The Lark*, San Francisco, June 1895; Osbourne 1911: 81; *NP*, 252; CP, 323
{B7050, a photostat of this signed inscription written at Hyères on the half-title of a first

edition of *The Silverado Squatters*, is the copy-text. In all the printed versions (except Osbourne's) until *CP* 1971, line 3, 'Or – shall we say? Defaced by Joseph's art.', was omitted; Joe Strong, Belle's husband, had designed the frontispiece for the book.}

VI *To Nelly Van de Grift Sanchez*: Presentation verses with a copy of *Prince Otto*
Date of composition: 1885
MS: Silverado (Foot*)
Printed text: *CP*, 324–5; *NP*, 179–80

VII *To Katharine de Mattos: Ave!*
Place/date of composition: Bournemouth, 19 May 1885 (Colvin's Galleys, Silverado)
Letter: RLS to Katharine de Mattos, 1 January 1886 (*LETBM*, Vol. V, p. 168): 'Here, on a very little book [*The Strange Case of Dr Jekyll and Mr Hyde*] and accompanied with your lame verses, I have put your name. Our kindness is now getting well on in years; it must be nearly of age; and it gets more valuable to me with every time I see you. It is not possible to express any sentiment, and it is not necessary to try at least between us. You know very well that I love you dearly, and that I always will. I only wish the verse were better, but at least you like the story; and it is sent to you by the one that loves you – Jekyll and not Hyde.'
MSS: B7007, Silverado (Colvin's Galleys*)
Printed text: Colvin 1899: Vol. II, 6; *CP*, 326; *The Strange Case of Dr Jekyll and Mr Hyde* (1886) – 2nd stanza. {Colvin, by printing this poem as though it were part of the text of the letter, misleads the reader into thinking that RLS enclosed it with his letter of 1 January to his cousin Katharine. In the galley proofs of his *Letters* (now at Silverado), these verses are dated 19 May 1885 and were evidently written for the wedding anniversary dinner on that date (cf. *LETBM*, Vol. V, No. 1433). What actually got sent to Katharine on New Year's Day 1886 was an inscribed presentation copy of *Jekyll and Hyde* with the second stanza of this poem as part of the printed dedication to her. The title *Ave!* appears only in the Colvin printings and not in B7007 or the printed dedication; doubtless it was part of an untraced MS presented to Katharine as one of the guests at RLS and Fanny's wedding anniversary. Colvin's galley setting serves as copy-text except for line 5, which varied in MS and print as follows:}
'We cannae break the bonds' (Colvin)
'<We cannae> ^It's ill to ^ break the bonds' (B7007, CP)
'It's ill to loose the bands' (*The Strange Case of Dr Jekyll and Mr Hyde*)
{I have adopted the revised MS reading from B7007. The other variants from *Jekyll and Hyde* are as follows:}
Line
  5   bind,] bind;
  6   Still we'll be ... wind;] Still will we be ... wind.
  7   O, it's] O it's
  8   countrie!] countrie.

VIII *To Fanny Stevenson*
(a) Verse for her birthday (1887)
Place/date of composition: Bournemouth, 10 March 1887
MS: NLS 3770*
Printed text: *CP*, 534n.

{RLS often presented a birthday verse to Fanny. This MS of the one for 1887 came from Lloyd Osbourne's collection.}

(b) *'To The Stormy Petrel:'*
Place/date of composition: Vailima, '10 March 1894' (B7045 is so dated)
Sources: {Belle Strong wrote the following in her journal for 10 March 1894:} 'Today is my mother's birthday, and she says the best of her presents is the piece of paper she found pinned on her mosquito-netting in the morning. It was signed 'RLS' and addressed 'To the Stormy Petrel' (Osbourne and Strong 1902: 73–4).
MSS: B7044, B7045*, B7046
Printed text: Osbourne and Strong 1902: 73–4; *CP*, 320; *NP*, 221
{B7044 is a draft in Notebook 'M' with a false start, as follows:}

> 'To the stormy petrel: Or of sea or land,
> <You> Ill fortune calls you here, and so today,
> When the drums of war reverberate in the land,'

{B7045, the copy-text, may be the original 'piece of paper' presented to Fanny: it is dated and signed, 'Robert Louis Stevenson / to / Mrs F v de G S '. The poem and date may be in the hand of Belle Strong, the signature is by RLS and Fanny's initials are apparently in her own hand. B7046 is Belle's transcription in *Grouse in the Gunroom*. Selective collation of these MSS follows:}
Title: {Precisely speaking, there is neither title nor subtitle: 'To The Stormy Petrel:' unitalicised, without caps in B7044 but with them in B7045–6, seems to be the first half of line 1; 'Ever perilous', dropped down one space, is the second half.}
Line
5   blacked,] blacked; B7044
10–11   Yet amid turmoil keep for me, my dear,
         The kind domestic faggot. Let the hearth]
         <Yet amid war, do not forget. Some price>
         Yet, amid turmoil, keep for me, my dear
         Some kind domestic faggot; let the hearth (B7044)
12   Shine ever as (I praise my honest gods)]
         Shine ever, as I praise the kindly gods (B7044)
13   tempest it] tempest, it (B7044)

(c) *To My Wife*: Dedication for *Weir of Hermiston* (1896)
Place/date of composition: Vailima, May 1894 (*LETBM*, Vol. VIII, No. 2734)
Letter and sources: 1. RLS to Charles Baxter [18 May 1894] (*LETBM*, Vol. VIII, p. 291): 'I send now with some blanks which I may perhaps fill up ere the mail goes, a dedication [for *EDIN*] to my wife. It was not intended for the E.E. but for *The Justice-Clerk* when it should be finished, which accounts for the blanks. "To my wife / I dedicate / This Edinburgh Edition of my works."' {Here follows the thirteen-line poem. Below it RLS wrote, then deleted, the following: 'Well, I shall see about this before the mail goes. It don't seem the right thing for the purpose somehow.' Colvin was opposed to publishing the poem as part of the general dedication. RLS did finally dedicate *EDIN* to Fanny, but *The Justice-Clerk*, when posthumously published in 1896 as *Weir of Hermiston*, was also dedicated to Fanny with a later version of these lines. She discovered and sent them to Colvin in a letter of 17 July 1895

with these instructions: 'In looking over further papers to give Mr Balfour to carry to you, I found the dedication to me as Louis first [wrote] it for *Hermiston*. Please put it in as he meant it to be. He pinned it to my bed curtains when I was asleep' (*CP*, 530).}

MSS: Pierpont Morgan MA 1419; *LETBM*, No. 2734 (B2883), B7112–14
Printed text: *Weir of Hermiston* (1896); *CP*, 326; *NP*, 222
{The complex history of the publication of *Weir of Hermiston* is fully given by Catherine Kerrigan in her edition of the novel (1995: 159–61); she deals with MSS and variants concerning the Dedication on pp. 157–9 and 165. Professor Kerrigan notes that the first edition in book form appeared on 20 May 1896, published simultaneously by Chatto and Windus in London and Scribner's in New York. Copy-text for these verses is p. 4 of her edition.*

MA 1419 and 2734 are early drafts of 14 and 13 lines respectively; *NP* is set up, blunderingly, from MA 1419. B7112 is a photostat of MA 1419. B7113 comprises two identical copies made by Belle Strong in *Grouse in the Gunroom*. B7114, the latest MS, is twelve lines. Collation follows:}

Title: *To My Wife*] untitled (MA 1419, 2734)
　　　The Justice-Clerk – ~ . (B7113) *The Justice-Clerk* / ~ . (B7114)

Line
　1　{MA 1419 has these lines before line 1:}
　　　'The indefeasible impulse of my blood
　　　Summoned me sleeping in this isle; and I'
　　　{*NP* reads 'indefensible' in the first line and 'surround' in the second.}
　　　I saw rain falling and the rainbow drawn] Behold ~ (MA 1419)
　　　Behold ~ dawn (*NP*) I see <a> ~(2734)
　2　Lammermuir. Hearkening I heard] <Allermuir;>^Lammermuir;^ hearkening, I hear
　　　　　　　　　　　　　　　　　(2734)
　　　Lammermuir; and hearkening heard again, (MA 1419)
　4　wind. And here afar,] wind. So this I wrote (MA 1419)
　　　wind; and looking back (2734) ~ and hereafar (B7113)
　5　Intent on my own *race* and place, I wrote.]
　　　Of my own race and place: which being done,
　　　{No space between this line and the next} (MA 1419) ~ race ~ (first English edition)
　　　Upon so much already endured and done
　　　<First>From then <and then> to now – reverent, I bow the head! (2734)
　6　writing: thine it is.] writing. Thine ~ (MA 1419) writing; thine ~ (2734)
　7　blew] breathed (MA 1419)
　9　censure –] counsel (2734)
　10　now, in … good,] here in … well, (MA 1419) now in ~ (B7113)
　　　　　　　　　　　　　　　　　　<here,>^now,^ ~ (B7114)
　12　thine.] thine! (All MSS) {This reading has been adopted.}

VIII *Dedication*: 'To friends at home'
Date of composition: Samoan period
MS: B7001*
Printed text: *NP*, 187 {Possibly this is a trial dedication for *ST*.}

X 'Much of my soul': MS initialled inscription on a card in the Hutchinson copy of RLS's

Memories and Portraits (1887), at Princeton (Wainwright 1971: 24,102)
Place/date of composition: 'Vailima / November 5 1893' (the card is so dated)
Printed text: *Teuila*, p. 51; Osbourne and Strong 1902: 63

Stephen Donovan was kind enough to bring to the editor's attention a virtually unknown printing of a hitherto unpublished MS of presentation verses by RLS. Unfortunately the three-stanza poem arrived too late for inclusion in the text but appears below. Addressed to an eight-year-old American girl named Mary Johnson, it is signed and dated 'Mentone January 13th 1874'. The poet's delight in the graceful play of Mary and the other children at the French resort where he was staying is recorded in *LETBM*, Vol. 1, Nos 202–4. In No. 210 to Fanny Sitwell, dated the same day as the poem, he explains that he has presented the girl with a gift of doll's accessories 'with some verses telling how happy children made every one near them happy also' (p. 437); these verses were completed by a prose note:

> To Mary Johnson
> Children happy all day through
> Can make others happy too.
> So, dear child, the sight of you.
> Makes me glad whate'er you do.
>
> Keep these lines and some fine day
> Dear, when you are far away,
> Older, taller, strong and well,
> Grown a stately demoiselle,
> It may make you glad to know
> You gave pleasure long ago.
>
> It may make you glad to see
> How your childhood, fair and free,
> Here, beside the southern sea,
> Was a pure delight to me.

And, in the meantime, play with your toys and the ugly little dog, and do not trouble your little head about the meaning of my bad verses. You will be ill someday like me, and then you will know all that they mean, and you will be glad to see them.

(Published in *The South African Magazine*, I, No. 6, Capetown, October 1906, 733–7.)

Epigrams and Satire

I 'Here he comes big with Statistics'
Place/date of composition: Edinburgh, 1871 (This poem was No. 5 among *Recruiting Songs*: see above, p. 550)
MS: Silverado (Foot)*
Printed text: CP, 329; NP, 132
{This seems to be a lampoon on one of RLS's professors. Copy-text is the MS, which varies from the printed versions only in the first line:}
comes big with Statistics,] comes, big with statistics, (NP) comes, big ~ (CP)
{Below the text RLS pencilled 'Pas mal, je crois'.}

II 'Browning made the verses'
Place/date of composition: Edinburgh, 1875–6 (*LETBM*, Vol. II, No. 427)
Letter: RLS to Fanny Sitwell [?6 December 1875] (*LETBM*, Vol. II, p. 169). 'I have done rather an amusing paragraph or two for *Vanity Fair* on the *Inn Album*. I have slated R.B. pretty handsomely.' {RLS's unsigned review of Browning's *Inn Album* appeared 11 December 1875.}
MS: B6601*
Printed text: Shorter 1915: [9]; *CP*, 335 {Copy-text is B6601, a photograph of Browning: the poem is written on the back. Shorter's text was set up from a notebook labelled 'Notes on Law while a student at Edinburgh', No. 307 in the Strong Sale; it varies from the copy-text as follows:}
Line
  1   made the verses,] makes the verses;
  3   all –] all:
  5   his] the
  6   deil] Deil
  7   Browning's verse,] Browning,

III 'I had companions, I had friends'
Place/date of composition: Hyères [May 1884] (*LETBM*, Vol. IV, No. 1269)
MS: *LETBM*, Vol. IV, p. 287
Printed text: *CP*, 350; Colvin 1911
{*CP* gives a four-line version. RLS is complaining to Henley that his friends were not writing to him while he recuperated from acute illness.}

IV *Epitaph*
MS: NLS 3791*
Printed text: *CP*, 354; *NP*, 104
{3791, the copy-text, differs from *CP* and *NP* in line 1, which ends with a semicolon.}

V *Epigrams from Notebooks*
MSS: (a) H2404 (Notebook 'A.270'); (b) B6452 (Notebook 'F'); (c) H2406 (Notebook 'A')

VI 'O Pilot 'tis a fearful night'
Place/date of composition: South Seas, 1888–90
MS: H2458*
Printed text: Hellman 1925: 209
{On a page torn from a notebook dating from the South Seas cruising when RLS was writing *BAL* and *ST*.}

VII 'Awhile you have paused'
Place/date of composition: Samoan period
MS: B6000
{This epigram was written on the back end-papers of Notebook B6022, 'First Drafts of Poems'.}

VIII 'Let no sour looks degrade my burial day'
Place/date of composition: Samoan period
MS: B6511
{This epigram was written in Notebook B6022, 'First Drafts of Poems.'}

IX 'I, whom Apollo sometime visited'
Place/date of composition: Vailima, 1891–4 (CP, 534)
MSS: B6373–5; NLS 3791*
Printed text: CP, 320; NP, 187
{B6373–4 are from B6022, 'First Drafts of Poems'; B6375 is fair copy for the projected collection Verses (B7065). 3791 is copy-text. B6373 is an early draft as follows:}

Enough if in the vale of shady falls
The muse relenting blessed or seemed to bless,
Enough if in my [?room] to the talking fire
                                   Apollo visited
Or seemed to visit. <Ah what matters then>
With these gracious guests
Or demons of little divinity
Awhile in life I talked, <awhile was> fulfilled
Then in my heart the [?]
Immeasurable sands of centuries
Drink up the blanching ink, and the loud sound
Of generations <tread>^beat^ the music down.'

{Collation of the other MSS and printed sources follows:}
Line
  3   Do slumber wholly;] Do wholly slumber, (B6374)
  4   changes,] <progress> ^ ~ ^ (B6374)
  6   or the loud] <nor> or the <living> loud (B6374) and ~ (B6375)

X Casparides
Place/date of composition: Davos, April 1881 (LETBM, Vol. III, No. 788)
MSS: B6414–17, B6417* {This hitherto-unpublished series of mock-heroic lampoons against the frauds perpetrated against RLS by two Davos tradesmen, Jacob Casparis and Sigrist Maler, was mailed to Colvin 19 April 1881; the conclusion, Exegi Monumentum (after Horace, Exegi Monumentum Aere Perennius: 'I have erected a monument more lasting than bronze.' attempts a comic apotheosis in the manner of Pope. These four MSS range from rough draft to fair copy, showing that RLS worked hard at these lampoons. He told Gosse he hoped to publish them in Cornhill Magazine or Quarterly Review but they were never printed or even typed (LETBM, Vol. III, No. 792). They went with him to Samoa, where he wrote on the back of B6415, 'Unique copy. / To be returned under / pain of the Extreme Taboo.' During the Winter of 1881 at Davos, RLS experimented widely with satirical verse. W. H. Mallock was the target of six lampoons (see UW XXX) and the Edinburgh wine and spirit merchant Thomas Brash inspired the mock-heroic sonnet sequence and Pindaric ode which follow Casparides. There are two variants:}
Line
  20   by one and all!] from cot and hall! (B6417)

137–40 <Forevermore: since surly time
My rage shall not forget, your ryhme,
Till all the parted ages meet
Shall still remember, still repeat.> (B6416)

XI *Brasheana*: A sequence of sonnets dedicated to Charles Baxter
Place/date of composition: mostly Davos, 1882–3
Letters: 1. RLS to Charles Baxter, 15 December 1881 (*LETBM*, Vol. III, pp. 263–4): 'Ah! What would I not give to steal this evening with you through the big, echoing, college archway, and away south under the street lamps, and to dear Brash's, now defunct! But the old time is dead also; never, never, to revive. It was a sad time too, but so gay and so hopeful, and we had such sport with all our low spirits, and all our distresses, that it looks like a lamplit, vicious fairy land behind me. O for ten Edinburgh minutes – sixpence between us, and the ever glorious Lothian Road ... Do you remember Brash? The L.J.R.? ... the compass near the sign of the Twinkling Eye? The night I lay on the pavement in misery?

        I swear it by the eternal sky
        Johnson – nor Thomson – ne'er shall die!
Yet I fancy they are dead too; dead like Brash.'
{Thomas Brash was a surly wine and spirit merchant in Clerk Street who died in 1873; with Letter 2 below, RLS enclosed four 'Sonnets dedicated to Charles Baxter' – Nos 1, 3, 4 and 6 in the sequence here printed.}

2. RLS to Charles Baxter [late March 1882] (*LETBM*, Vol. III, pp. 303–5): 'No sooner yours came than down I sat and penned the enclosed. I could go on a while longer, but these shall go. I think No. 4 very fine; I dote on the last line of No. 2; I like the simile at the beginning of No. 1; and the sestett of No. 3 is just. If you like 'em, I'll do more ... I don't actually remember if T.B.'s counter was zinc. I now believe it was wood; but the licence, at least, is fair.'

3. RLS to Charles Baxter [?April 1882] (*LETBM*, Vol. III, Nos 948–9, pp. 317–20): 'I've been ill and here is the result. I don't know about order. You'll have to see. I forget about the others. Here is a hypothetical order ... Of course, you edit and have my leave to reject any piece unworthy of his memory. A cut is under way.' {With these letters RLS enclosed a further seven sonnets; the order he suggested has been followed in this edition, where the sonnet sequence has been printed for the first time as the poet arranged it. He and Baxter planned to issue *Brasheana* as a pamphlet of fifteen to twenty sonnets: by December 1882 RLS was correcting proofs of Nos 1 and 3 that Baxter had set up in type as a four-page folder (*LETBM*, Vol. IV, No. 1025); on 12 January 1883 the poet acknowledged receipt of a second state of these proofs in Letter 4 below, a Thomson–Johnson epistle, but the projected *de luxe* pamphlet never materialised, surviving only as a unique copy of these Baxter proofs at Harvard.}

4. RLS to Charles Baxter (*LETBM*, Vol. IV, p. 51): 'Ye crack o' Maecenas; he's naebody by you! He gied the lad, Horace, a rax forrit by all accounts; but damn! he never gied him proofs like yon. Horace may hae been a better hand at the clink than Stevison, – mind, I'm no sayin' 't – but onyway he was never sae weel prentit. Damned, but it's bony! Hoo mony pages will there be, think ye? Stevison maun hae sent ye the feck o' twenty sangs – fifteen I'se

warrant. Weel, that'll can make thretty pages, gin ye were to prent on ae side only, whilk wad be perhaps what a man o' your *great* idees would be ettlin' at, man Johnson. Then there wad be the Pre-face, an' prose ye ken prents oot langer than po'try at the hinder end, for ye hae to say things in't. An' then there'll be a title page and a dedication and a index wi' the first lines like, and the deil an' a'. Man, it'll be grand. Nae copies to be given to the Liberys!'

MSS and proofs: Notebook 'A.269'(BRBML); B6024–48; B2615; Harvard proofs 10.13.10–11. {Several of the McKay items are fragments or pencil drafts in 'A.269', a notebook dating from the Davos period: one fourteen-line draft that RLS never copied to Baxter is printed below; B2615 is a proof copy of Sonnet 1 with corrections by RLS that were not adopted in any printed version; copy text is MS.}

Printed text: Sonnet 1 was first published in the *Outlook* for 26 February 1898 under the heading, 'A *Literary Enigma*': readers were invited to guess the identity of the poet (see Prideaux and Livingston 1917: 146). Five sonnets (nos 1, 3, 4, 6 and 10) were facsimiled and transcribed in the Widener Catalogue (Rosenbach 1913: 223–8); these were reprinted in *CP*, pp. 338–40. All eleven completed sonnets (i.e. fair copies on separate pages headed '*Brasheana*') were published for the first time as a unit in *LETBM*, but the order followed was that in which they were sent in letters to Baxter rather than the poet's hypothetical order suggested in Letter No. 948. On the back of the Harvard proofs of Nos 1 and 3, Baxter has written, 'Words by Stevenson, printing paid by me. Imitation from quarto Subscription Edition (original) of Gay's Poems. C.B.'

Drafts and variants:

{The following sonnet seems intended as an alternative to No. 11.}

> 'Fear not at all, for we have won the crown
> Safe in the port, our sea-tost pinnace lays
> And our two names shall arm in arm go down
> Stair after stair, year after year, until
> The latest born of man shall sound our praise;
> And we, and Brash, and that illustrious town
> That bore us all, and ever upon her hill
> Sits dominant in that eternal haze.
>
> And still beholds the sea, and still beholds
> The green and golden Lothians, shall outlast
> Time, and all weather with its heats and colds,
> Day and the dayspring, eve and evensong,
> Shall still to history and the muse belong,
> And all's done and what is future past.'
>
> (pp. 6, 8, Notebook 'A.269', B6042–3)

Title: {RLS used 'Brasheana' and 'Brasheanna' interchangeably while Baxter sometimes used 'Brashiana': 'ana' has been adopted as a suffix denoting a collection of material on a single subject.}

Sonnet 1

Line

8   hatcd] <hatcd>^fatcd^ (B2615)
13   wrath upon] <wrath upon>^anger on^ (B2615)

Sonnet 5: {On B6029 RLS subscribed this note:}
    'I own I think this one very fine.'
  Line 5 O not,] Or not, (*LETBM*)
Sonnet 10:
  Line 1 Goodness] To Goodness (*CP, LETBM*)
          {This misreading originated in the Harvard proofs: RLS wrote 'Tr' in the margin
          against this line indicating his wish that 'Goodness' be transposed with 'Great-
          ness': the printer misread it as 'To'.}

XII *Ode by Ben Jonson, Edgar Allan Poe, and a Bungler*
Date of composition: [March 1882] (*LETBM*, Vol. III, No. 926)
Letters: {See Letters and notes for No. XI above; the final fourteen lines of this ode modulate
into a 'Brasheanum' sonnet.}
MS: Enclosed with *LETBM*, Vol. III, No. 926*
Printed text: Ferguson and Waingrow 1956: 96–7.

Miscellaneous Verse

I 'The old Chimaeras, old receipts'
Place/date of composition: Edinburgh, spring 1871 (B6671 is so dated)
MSS: B6670, B6671*
Printed text: *NP*, 98–9
{B6670 is a fragmentary pencil draft on pp. 6–7 of the Academic Exercise Book (B6070),
a notebook containing mostly lecture notes on Public and Civil Law taken between
3 November 1871 and 20 March 1872 (see Appendix One, p. 609). The careful tran-
scription of B6671 on pp. 17–18 of what must have been a notebook of fair copies indicates
that RLS thought enough of these lines to give them some polish; the MS is subscribed 'Edin
Spring 71'. The following fragments are excerpted from B6670:}

> 'These myths and all their brood made eyes
> They winked and beckoned me
> But I was strong and chaste, and laughed …'
>
> 'I left my early garden,
> To seek a better land'
>
> 'All through the sultry day I chased
>   A hundred phantom hopes
> A hundred dreams enticed – I grasped
>   I followed down the slopes.'
>
> 'All through the sultry sweltering day,
>   The sweat ran down my brow.
> Where all mankind was beat before
>   Lo! I should conquer now.'
>
> 'But now full weary, I go home
>   In the tranquil eventide,

And the risen moon shall see me sit
By my old master's side.'

II 'I look across the ocean'
Place/date of composition: Edinburgh, 1871–2 (B6070 is so dated)
MS: B6354* (written on p. 10 of the Academic Exercise Book, B6070)
Printed text: CP, 484; NP, 218
{JAS prints these unfinished lines in her notes to UW XXIX, *In the States*, speculating that they were written at the same time; however, their presence in this notebook indicates that RLS's fascination with America and its destiny had commenced at least seven years before he went there.}

III 'My summer health is gone away'
Place/date of composition: ?Paris, September 1872 (MS *verso* of B6618 is so dated)
MS: B6618* {McKay labels this MS 'Tentative verses by Stevenson in an unknown hand' but the dated lines *verso* (B6145) are certainly his.}
Unpublished

IV *Ne Sit Ancillae Tibi Amor Pudori*
Date of composition: 1872 (B6624 is so dated)
Letter: {Despite the date of 1872 on B6624, *LETBM* speculates that these verses were 'addressed to a graceful housemaid' at the Imperial Hotel, Great Malvern, where RLS was staying with his mother in January 1873; his letter to Baxter dated the 16th contains the line from Horace (*Odes* II.iv.i) used as title for the poem – it means 'You need not be ashamed of your love for a servant lass' (see notes on the *Epistle to Charles Baxter*, p. 578 above, and *LETBM*, Vol. I, p. 271, n.6). Copy-text B6624, one of the fair copies torn from disbound Notebook A.155, may have been misdated 1872 from memory; B6623, lacking any reliable date, is more likely to have been written at the time. I am indebted to Ernest Mehew for the suggestion that the phrase 'shy imperial air' in line 18 could be a cryptic reference to the fact the housemaid in question was an employee of the Imperial Hotel. G. S. Hellman misdates this poem from the Hyères period, proceeding then to identify the 'graceful housemaid' as Valentine Roch, the Stevensons' Swiss maid with whom Hellman claims RLS had an affair, a canard repeated by biographers McLynn and Callow (Hellman 1925: 114–15).}
MSS: B6623, B6624*
Printed text: CP, 332–3; NP, 195–6
{JAS conflated these MSS to arrive at her text. B6623 is an untitled early draft in pencil, longer than B6624, the copy-text, which is divided into three stanzas of eight lines; CP has six stanzas of four lines. NP is set up from B6624. Collation follows:}
Line
  4   waist<!> ^.^ (B6624)
  5   I hear too … go,] I know too … go (B6623)
13   Is set … art,] <Is worn> ^You set^ … art (B6623)
14   Is] And (B6623)
18   I love your shy imperial air,] <With honey eyes and chestnut hair,>^ ~ shy, ~ ^ (B6623)
19   stair,] stair (B6623)
[21] <In narrow doors I take my stand> (B6623)
22   stand,] stand (B6623)

{Additional or alternate stanza in B6623:}
'<It does seem hard>
This world you know's a surly brute
For, just one innocent salute,
And I should lose my good repute
        And you would lose your place.'

V *Schumann's 'Frölicher Landmann'*
Place/date of composition: Edinburgh, ? 1872 (*LETBM*, Vol. I, p. 264)
MSS: Edinburgh Writers' Museum LSH 137/91*, B6108
Printed text: *NP*, 195 (set up from B6108)
{These twenty lines are headed 'I' and followed by twelve cancelled lines headed 'II' with
a 'III' after them, so it appears that this is the first poem in a projected cycle based on
Schumann's music; the cancelled lines turn up as *Spring Song*, No. VII in *Songs* (p. 243).
B6108 lacks the title and has two eight-line stanzas; the copy-text has five stanzas of four
lines each. LSH 137/91 collates with B6108 as follows:}
Line
  2   again!] again.
  4   {MS has an additional stanza here:}
  8   tumbled … me] timbered … me,
  9   hough,] bough;
10   away … furrow] again … fallows,
11   his] the
14   time] time,
18   spring,] Spring
19   weeping] reaping,

VI *'Inscription for the Tankard of a Society Now Dissolved'*
Place/date of composition: 'Edin. Spring 73.' (B6455 is so dated)
MSS: B6453–6, B6455*
Unpublished
{The Society was the L.J.R., formed by RLS, Charles Baxter, Bob Stevenson and others;
the initials stood for Liberty, Justice and Reverence (see notes on Sonnet 6, above pp.
557–8). This Society was effectively dissolved by Thomas Stevenson, who discovered a copy
of its Constitution, drawn up by Louis and Bob, which he declared to be blasphemous. He
blamed these bad companions, especially his nephew Bob, for corrupting his son (Bathurst
1999: 232). B6453–4 are drafts in Notebook 57. B6455 is the copy-text. At the end of B6456
is written (not in RLS's hand): 'Lines written to be engraved on the Drinking Tankard of the
L.J.R. by R. L. Stevenson – C. Baxter.'}

VII A *Valentine's Song*
Place/date of composition: 'Edin. Feb 73' (B7082 is so dated)
MSS: 'The Geometry Notebook', Haverford College; B7082*
Printed text: *NP*, 122–4
{Copy-text is B7082, from which several errors in *NP* have been corrected. Haverford has
an earlier, much-revised draft on pp. 14–19 of this school notebook which is followed on
pp. 20–5 by a sketch of the poem following below, No. VIII. These rambling experiments

belong to RLS's adolescent student period (1867–71). The Valentine poem seems to have begun as a ritual anticipation of spring:

> 'With hopeful faces, now we sight
> (A month or so in front) the sun
> In the next springtime shining bright,
> And know the year is rebegun.
> So come and snap the castanettes
> And gaily lead the dance adown,
> Away with reasons!' (Haverford, p. 14)

The young poet soon turns to a lively rebellion against the ruling conventions of middle-class Edinburgh society, but finds that the form he has chosen, with its repeated phrases and uneven line length, is unwieldy. The poem was revised and shortened in B7082 but ultimately cancelled there.}

VIII 'Hail! childish slaves of social rules'
Place/date of composition: 'Edin. Spring 73' (B6268 is so dated)
MSS: 'The Geometry Notebook', Haverford College, B6268*
Printed text: *NP*, 124–5
{The copy-text is B6268, from which several errors in *NP* have been corrected. See notes on No. VII above. Haverford is a rough draft on pp. 20–5 which continues the rebellious themes of *A Valentine's Song* but in a more regular form. The nucleus of this poem appears in four lines at the top of p. 20:}

> 'An old fight stands between the two
>   The lowly and the haughty varlets
> I know not how you judge it – you.
>   I'm for the Publicans and Harlots.'

{Another trial opening is the following:}

> 'I see you ofttimes broken down
>   With fancied burthens – (O poor sinner,
> You ought to call on Mrs Brown,
>   You really must ask Jones to dinner.)'

{This is a trial for stanza 6:}

> 'A lie is still a lie, I hold,
>   And hate the world that taught me lying
> The world that lies in life for gold
>   And lies too when it lies a-dying.
> And I intend to lie no more
>   But lead my own preferred existence,
> You dare not slake your hate in gore
>   So vainly scorn me from a distance.' (Haverford)

IX 'If I had wings, my lady, like a dove'
Place/date of composition: Edinburgh, November 1874 (*LETBM*, Vol. II, No. 331)

MSS: B6386*; *LETBM*, Vol. II, No. 331
Printed text: *NP*, 143–4 (set up from B6386)
{This is another outpouring of the poet's barely sublimated sexual passion for Mrs Sitwell, enclosed in one of a series of long swooning letters to her; see notes on Sonnet 9, above, pp. 558–9. The earlier version (B6386) was diluted somewhat before he mailed it to her. In 331 the first and third stanzas were omitted, eliminating the reference to kissing breasts, and stanza 4 became stanza 2 in the letter; variants between these versions follow:}
Line
  8 ~~be gone] begone~~
  9 disparting] division
 16 love;] love
 24 breath,] breath;
{331 adds a final stanza as follows:}
> 'You ask who then, my lady, is my love?
>   Who then is this I love so well?
> When I have wings, my lady, like a dove,
>   I shall fly southward first to you and tell
> This that you ask, my lady and my love.'

X 'Death, to the dead for evermore'
Date of composition: '[18]75' (B6148 is so dated)
MSS: B6148*, Silverado (Foot), H2399
Printed text: *CP*, 94; *NP*, 135
{Foot is an early draft of the first two stanzas; H2399 is also a two-stanza draft in which 1 follows 3; B6148, No. 57 in disbound Notebook A.155, is the copy-text. The first stanza of Foot is as follows:}

> 'Death
> Like a kind host comes smiling to the door
> The young to greet
> And comfortably welcomes weary feet.
> \<For here, he says, are quietness and cool sleep\>
> Smiling he lands them on the shore
> Where neither piping bird nor peeping dawn
> Disturb \<the silence and the dark\> the eternal sleep
> But \<thousand fathoms deep\>
> \<Your\> Our dreamless rest forevermore \<you\> we keep'

{Collation of all other MS sources follows:}
Line
  1 to the dead for evermore] to the dead, for evermore, (H2399)
  2 the last, the best of friends –] the first and best of friends, (H2399)
  3 mortal journey ends] lifelong journey ends, (H2399)
  4 Death, like a] \<Kind like a\>\<Death like a\> ^ ~ ^ (B6148) Like a kind (H2399)
  5 Smiling, he greets us,] Smiling he lands \<thereon\> us (H2399)
 10 For as ... windows] For, as ... windows, (Foot)
 11 \<When high the night in wassail runs\> (Foot)
 15 evenly; and lo!] evenly. And lo! (Foot)

17   Death] death (Foot) <death>^ ~ ^ (B6148)
19   sunshine;] sunshine, (H2399)
20   Weary of utterance, seeing all is said;]
     Weary of <pleasing and the voice of reeds> ^ ~ said.^ (Foot)
21   Soon, racked by hopes and fears,] <And> Soon that <all pondering, all contriving
     head> racked <overlong> with hopes and fears (Foot)
24   dead;] dead (Foot)

XI 'I have a friend; I have a story'
Date of composition: ?1876 (B6345 is in Notebook 'F', containing MS of *An Inland Voyage*
written in that year)
MS: B6345*
Printed text: *NP*, 119–20
{Perhaps inspired by the famous phrase of Catullus, *odi et amo*, 'I hate and I love.'}

XII *Poem for a Class Reunion*
Place/date of composition: Edinburgh, January 1875 (*LETBM*, Vol. II, No. 354)
Letter: RLS to Frances Sitwell [16 January 1875] (*LETBM*, Vol. II, pp. 108–9): 'I was at the
annual dinner of my old Academy schoolfellows last night. We sat down ten, out of seventy-
two! The others are scattered all over the face of the earth; some in San Francisco, some in
New Zealand, some in India, one in the backwoods – it gave one a wide look over the world,
to hear them talk so. I read them some verses. It is great fun; I always read verses, and in the
vinous enthusiasm of the moment they always propose to have them printed; *ce qui n'arrive
jamais, du reste*: in the morning, they are more calm.'
MS: B6726*
Printed text: *CP*, 333; *NP*, 140–1
Variants:
Line
     <Nor hear prayers in the hall in great state> {trial line for the fifth stanza}
41   peeries for luck,] {*NP* reading is one of Hellman's howlers:} pennies for lunch
45   But still for the sake of the past,] <But we who were early together,> ^ ~ ^
{Cf. *UW* Book II, No. X, the following poem and Explanatory Note on these ceremonial
performances, p. 626.}

XIII *To the Thompson Class Dinner Club from their Stammering Laureate*
Place/date of composition: Hyères, December 1883 (*LETBM*, Vol. IV, No. 1202)
Letter: RLS to John Wilson Brodie, 20 December 1883 (*LETBM*, Vol. IV, pp. 221–4): 'You
will think me a most truculent ogre and unlicked bear to have been so long of answering;
but I did not wish to write at all till I had strung some doggerel, and this, overpressed as I was
with work and a good deal out of sorts, I found no easy job. However – now the deed is done,
and I enclose some seasonable but most halting stanzas. I shall say better in prose how very
heartily I wish to you and all my old schoolfellows, the wale of good living and good luck.
Salute them from the exile …'
MSS: B7047; *LETBM*, No. 1202*
Printed text: these verses were first published by Constable in a privately printed octavo
leaflet of four pages, signed 'For Christmas 1883 R.L.S.'; there are copies at BRBML, Harvard
and Monterey. The poem was reprinted in the Widener Catalogue (Rosenbach 1913: 73–6).

Letter 1202, including the verses, was published in the *Edinburgh Academy Chronicle* for
March 1895.
{B7047 in Notebook 'M' is a tortured preliminary sketch of some thirty-two lines; with
revision it became the final twenty-eight lines of the printed poem. It begins as follows:}

> 'Dux and boobies, fill your glasses,
> And with beaming eye,
> To your friends and fellow asses,
> Drain the goblets dry.'

XIV *Praise and Prayer*

Place/date of composition: Monastier, France, September 1878 (B6735)
MSS: B6735*, HM2408
Printed text: first published, with a facsimile of the MS, in *Scribner's Magazine* for January
1922, in W. H. Arnold's article, 'My Stevensons', then reprinted in Arnold 1923: 287; CP,
98
{This poem was at one time written in Notebook 'G', the Cevennes Journal (HM2408),
which contains the MS of *Travels with a Donkey*. It is dated from Monastier in central France,
where RLS was staying before buying his donkey and commencing his tour. As noted above
on pp. 398–9, this and the poem following, *John Cavalier*, were torn from Notebook 'G' and
sold as separate items in the Arnold Sale of 1924: no suspicion attaches to G. S. Hellman
for this act of vandalism. There is a facsimile of B6735 in the Berg Collection, NYPL.

XV *John Cavalier*

Place/date of composition: Cevennes, 1878 (MS was in Notebook 'G')
MSS: B6087, HM2408
Printed text: *Scribner's Magazine*, then Arnold* 1923: 285–6 (as with No. XIV above); CP,
98–9 {B6087 is a very rough pencil draft of some nineteen lines in Notebook 'F', cancelled.
The more finished 34-line MS from which Arnold made his transcription was torn from
Notebook 'G' before it was purchased by HL to become HM2408 (see note on No. XIV
above). Since this MS is untraced, I have adopted Arnold's printed version of it as copy-text.
See the Explanatory Note on this poem, p. 631. In B6087 RLS tried doubling up short lines
to make sixteeners, no doubt striving for a martial effect, but he abandoned the experiment.
A selective transcription of this MS follows:

> 'These are your hills, John Cavalier
> That right and left and far and near
> With many a [ ] deep ravine
> Stretch round me
> Much would I give
> In some ravine, if I could spy
> The brave battalions marching by
> And <I do wish> on the wind, that I <could> might hear,
> Your drums and bugles, Cavalier
> Long time, where'er you went,
> Loud music its attendance leant;
> <The flags>You shook the earth with martial tread;

The ensigns fluttered at your head
In Spain or France, Velay or Kent,
The music sounded as you went.
A shepherd of the upland hills
French lad, you listened to the rills
<And oft among your [ ]rocks,>
And heard the bleating of the flocks
Alone, among the topmost rocks.
Then, bold marshalls doffed the hat to you
God whispered counsels in your ear
To guide your sallies, Cavalier
<Long>Where are the flags, and where the stars
The thrilling uproar of the wars
The bow, the clarion and the spear –
Where are they now, John Cavalier?
All is returned to where it was.'

XVI *The Iron Steed*
Place/date of composition: Paris, 12 May 1881 (the MS in Notebook 'C' is so dated)
MSS: B6459, B6466, B6921 in B6049, Notebook 'C'; facsimile on plate 41 of Flower and Munby* (eds) (1938), *English Poetical Autographs*, London: Cassell – MS otherwise untraced.
Printed text: CP, 100, set up from facsimile and transcription in Flower and Munby.
{On the inside front cover of Notebook 'C' RLS indexed a two-page unit (pp. 40–1) as follows: 'A Dream May 1281 and verses on it p. 40.' It begins with six lines of prose (B6466) describing a phenomenon of mountain railroad tracks in which 'the locomotive engines hear each other's screams across the night and tremble like wild animals. Read in a dream Thursday May 12/81.' Then follow twenty-nine lines of rough verse, (McKay Nos B6921 and 6459): some lines are cancelled and/or illegible, others are identical with those in Flower and Munby though differently ordered and with much repetition. These two pages were facsimiled and transcribed by W. P. Trent (1921), *Stevenson's Workshop*, Boston Biblio-phile Society, pp. 52ff. A selective transcription of the verse from Notebook 'C' follows:

'The still air sharpened to a blast
The canyon [?] as we past;
With roar and rattle, scream and clang
The many-antred mountain rang
And plunging from the light of day
The many-antred mountain <heard the cry> rang
And shook through all her pillars, but that steed …'

(B6921)

'<In our black stable, fed with fire>
In our black stable near the sea
Five and twenty strong are we
Five and twenty stalls you see.'

'<And silent heard, as in a dream><We slept, and while we slept we heard>
Iron chimaeras fed with fire
Earth's oldest veins our dam and sire
Inactive we, steeds of the day,
And shakers of the mountains, lay
And trembled, as we slept, to hear …'

'<Day broke, the riders>Morn came at last; the <roaring coal> morning star
Burned in the amber heavens afar:
Dew and the early day …'

(B6459)

XVII 'Here you rest among the valleys, maiden known to but a few'
Place/date of composition: ?Swanston, 'Feb 79' (B6316 is so dated)
Letter: RLS to Fanny Sitwell [early March 1879] (*LETBM*, Vol. II, pp. 304–5): 'On the back, the desired poem; for I believe it is one, though small.'
MSS: *LETBM*, 602; B6316*
Printed text: first printed (privately) in 1898 in *Three Short Poems* (Prideaux and Livingston 1917: 104–5); CP, 92; NP, 234–5
{Copy-text is B6316, which is identical to 602. This MS was No. 41 in the disbound notebook A.155 and was facsimiled in *BBS*, I, facing p. 40.

XVIII *On Some Ghastly Companions at a Spa*
Place/date of composition: Strathpeffer, August 1880 (*LETBM*, Vol. III, No. 714)
Letter: RLS to Charles Baxter [?26 August 1880] (*LETBM*, Vol. III, pp. 95–6): 'This is a beastlyish place, near delightful places, but inhabited alas! by a wholly bestial crowd.' {This is the 'dreary hydropathic' referred to by Fanny where the elder and younger Stevensons were holidaying after the newlyweds had returned from America; to amuse his father, who used the word 'ogre' to describe hotel guests he did not care for, RLS read this poem and UW Book II, XII, *The Scotsman's Return From Abroad* (see above, p. 446).}
MSS: *LETBM*, No. 714; B6681*
Printed text: first published in Colvin 1911; CP, 337–8
Variants: Colvin misread 'ghastly' as 'ghostly', an error in which he was followed by McKay. CP and 714 vary from B6681 as follows:
Line
3   soul] soul, (714)
4   ogres] Ogres (714, CP (also lines 10, 17 in CP))
7   feet] feet, (714)
9   done,] done – (714)
10 one.] one: (714)
13 list] lisp (CP)
16 Blasted Eye!] blasted eye! (714, CP)
17 Detested] Detected (714)
18 night!] night. (714)
21 dream.] dream (714)
23 As, by some] Or, as by (714)
28 ogres,] ogres – (714)

XIX 'Since years ago for evermore'
Place/date of composition: ?Hyères, 1883–4 (These may be some of the recently composed verses referred to by RLS in *LETBM*, Vol. IV, No. 1246 to Henley from Hyères, April 1884)
MSS: B6851–3, B6853*
Printed text: *CP*, 303–4; *NP*, 176
{An early version of this poem is B6852, a draft of sixty-five lines. B6853 is No. 19 in the 'Pieces in English' group torn out of Notebook A.155: it is identical to *CP*. B6852 begins as follows:}

> 'Since long ago for evermore
> My cedar <ship>^ark^ I drew to shore,
> And my neglected haversack
> Slipped down behind the cupboard back
> Since road and river now alike
> Deny me;
> Now I <share>^divide^ a sluggish life
> Betwixt my <inkpen><writing><garden>^verses^ and my wife.'

{B6852 continues after line 12 as follows:}

> 'And posting in by vale and hill
> The names of cities visit still
> Across the green page, and sail
> The names of rivers; still I scale
> Untenantable mountains
> Or linger in the hazel copse.'

XX 'My wife and I, in our romantic cot'
Place/date of composition: Hyères, 1883–4 (Colvin 1921: 135–6)
MSS: B6620–1; Princeton (Gerstley*)
Printed text: first published in Colvin 1921: 136; *CP*, 344–5; *NP*, 157
{B6620 is a TS made by Colvin of B6621, an early draft written on p. 29 of Notebook 'A.269'; *CP* is set up from B6621 as facsimiled in *BBS*, III, opp. p. 118. Gerstley was cut into three pieces, each one containing a stanza (of five, four and six lines), then pasted to a hand-lettered quote from Romans XII.18, written in a red and black Gothic script over a floral design, as follows: 'If it be possible, as much as lieth in you, live peaceably with all men.' (Wainwright 1971: No. 27, p. 102). The whole has been framed and glazed; according to Belle Strong, it was in the Stevenson home in Edinburgh, then at Vailima. Copy-text is this later, framed, MS. Collation, which does not include the careless *NP* transcription of B6621, follows:}
Line
       {after line 2} <Behold the evening and morning go> (B6621)
       {after line 3} <And what we have we like extremely well,
                   And what we can't obtain> (B6621)
4   the things] <the>what things (B6621)
7   pledge … yacht:] stake … yacht; (B6621) ~ yacht; (Colvin)
8   Which shall be first remembered, who can tell –]
       <Give us an inch and we'll demand an ell> ^ ~ tell,^ (B6621)

9   or] <and> ^ ~ ^ (B6621)
10 plot] plot, (CP)
11 spot,] spot (B6621)
    {after line 11} <both repel / Their partners' aspirations> <deride as well>
                    <And both the other's><Each on his own> (B6621)
13 hotel] hotel, (Colvin, CP)
14 That portly ... lot] Where <all our>^portly^ ~ (B6621) ~ our lot – (Colvin)
15 Of wife] My wife (Colvin)

XXI 'At morning on the garden seat'
Place/date of composition: Hyères, 1883–4
MSS: B7074, B5988* (facsimiled in *BBS*, III, opp. p. 110), Notebook A.269 (BRBML)
Printed text: CP, 345
{This appears to have begun as a CGV poem. B7074 is a three-line sketch on p. 63 of
Notebook 'C' among many drafts of children's poems. But it became, like the previous poem,
an expression of Hyères euphoria:}

> '<Up in the morn, when children>
> Up in the morn when I arise
> I dearly love to drink and eat,'

{These lines appear in two other MSS, B5988 in Notebook 'A269' and in another passage
on p. 23 of that Notebook not listed in McKay. CP prints B5988 from the *BBS* facsimile in
the 'Light Verse' section, there dating it Hyères, 1883–4. This version on p. 23 of Notebook
'A269' seems to predate B5988:}

> 'Up in the morn when I arise
>   I dearly love to <eat and> drink and eat
> At even when the sunset dies
>   Once more I take my meat.
> <Larks that carol and skies that shine,>
>   And dew that decks the grass,
> Victuals and drink are dear to me
>   At even, under golden skies,
> I by the flagon take my seat,
>   <At morn> It is my earnest enterprise
> To get my daily ... [breaks off]'

{Collation of CP with B5988 follows:}
Line
6   their possets] <a posset> ^ ~ ^
7   round,] round <again,>
     {after line 11} <The dew and <<birds>>perfumes all declare
                     It is the time to banish care.>
13–14 {these lines marked for indentation: not done in CP}

XXII *To Time*
Place/date of composition: Hyères, 1883–4 (MS written in H2404)
MSS: B7049, H2404

Printed text and first publication: CP, 346–7*
{B7049 is a nine-line pencil fragment; H2404 is a sprawling draft over leaves 6v.–8r. in a notebook from the Hyères period labelled, 'Notebook kept during a severe illness, while not allowed to speak'; the MS used as copy-text in CP is untraced but was clearly more finished than the others. The earliest sketch, a fragment, seems to be a protest against the practice of clearcutting:}

> 'Then, O baldheaded godhead, hear:
> Nor drive then forth the dappled deer
> O cleaver of the crowded woods
> From their subverted solitudes
> Nor plot with thy rough-handed aides
> The fall of forest colonnades.
> Strip then no longer, patch by patch,
> The [?] inhospitable thatch;
> Nor glory to lay desolate
> The wounded glen ... [breaks off]' (H2404)

{The following is a selective collation between the copy-text, CP, and H2404:}
Line
1   {alt. in 2404} Time, if before your temple dark and old
5   cleaver of the crowded woods,] <hater>^cleaver^ of the tangled <groves>^woods^
6–7   That drivest from green solitudes
          The sylvan deer; and dost conspire,]
          That <drivest>like a hunter from green solitudes
          Drivest the sylvan deer; <that>^ ~ ^
8   Or for the shipyard or the fire,] <For the loud shipyard and the
                                  <<spluttering>>whispering fire,>^ ~ ^
9   colonnades;] <porticos;>^ ~ ^
10   O Time, that lovest in the glades] <Time the unevener><untunes the modest><Now lover of the open glades><That in the densest><To the axe's din>^ ~ ^
11   cheer the ringing area's din] <hear>^cheer^ the ringing axe's din {This reading has been adopted.}
12   And let ... sunshine in:] Lets ... sunlight in
13   Think but once more, nor let this be,] <Nor suffer this, O Time, to be,>
16   Lie both] Both be
      {H2404 continues as follows:}
      'If Jove's ambrosial curls, alack!
      Fall not properly adown thy back
      Let me confront a searching look [breaks off]'

XXIII 'God gave to me a child in part'
Place/date of composition: [?Hyères, 1883] (LETBM, Vol. IV, No. 1208)
Letter: RLS to Sir Walter Simpson, [?31 December 1883] (LETBM, Vol. IV, p. 228): 'I must tell you a joke. A month or two ago, there was an alarm: it looked like family. Prostration: I saw myself financially ruined, I saw the child born sickly etc. Then, said I, I must look this thing on the good side; proceeded to do so studiously; and with such a result that when the alarm passed off – I was inconsolable!' {Whether the 'alarm' was a false one or Fanny, who

was then 44, miscarried, there is no record of RLS's frustrated paternal emotions outside of this letter and these MS lines, and no evidence that the lines were written when the letter was. However, Furnas demonstrated that the various allegations about illegitimate children sired by RLS are all most dubious. Linking the letter with these verses is the simplest and soundest way of explaining what must otherwise be a literary conceit, after the manner of Burns' poem addressed to his illegitimate daughter or Rossetti's *House of Life* sonnet, 'Stillborn Love' (Furnas 1951: 463–4; cf. McLynn 1993: 229).}

MSS: B6257, B6258*

Printed text: *NP*, 193–4

{B6258 was No. 56 in disbound Notebook A.155; B6257 is a 56-line draft from which some excerpts follow:}

> '<If love, if longing><I saw thee not, my child: a father's>
> Where mayst thou go, unborn, unknown,
> Where disavowed, unmothered and alone,
> O unborn child, you stray,
> A father's longing follows.'
>
> 'Perhaps at last
> That child a living glance may cast
> From that far ocean of the blue
> On the poor father who now alone, …'

{These trial lines come after the copy-text's final line (16) in the longer, draft version of the poem in B6257: they may be part of other sketches:}

> 'Where art thou gone? And where is she?
> Alas! She too has left me, O my child,
> As you I left, …
>
> 'When they told me you were dead
> Forgive me, bright and laughing lad
> Forgive me if my soul was glad.'

Variants:

Line
8   Nor knew the kindly feel of home.] <No blink of life you knew,> ^ ~ ^ (B6258)
9   My voice may reach you, O my dear –]
    <Where'er, my child, where'er you are,><In what> <O let my voice> ^ ~ ^ (B6258)

XXIV 'Now bare to the beholder's eye'
Place/date of composition: Hyères, April 1884 (*LETBM*, Vol. IV, No. 1250)
Letter: {No. 1250 to Bob Stevenson, confessing the poet's fondness for female underclothes, and Henley's comments on this issue, are quoted above on p. 400 in connection with the closing lines of UW III, *The Canoe Speaks*. G. S. Hellman's idea that this poem is a suppressed continuation of the unfinished *The Canoe Speaks* (BBS, II, p. 90) is unconvincing: as No. 21 of 'Pieces in English' in disbound Notebook A.155, it precedes *The Canoe Speaks* and is clearly written out as a separate poem. Tone and time of day differ as well: only one girl has undressed and it is evening.}

MS: B6645*
Printed text: *CP*, 305–6; *NP*, 197–8
Variants:
Line
9   looker] lover {I disagree with *CP* and *NP* on this reading.}
28   Through … through] <By> … <by> ^ ~ ^ (B6645)

XXV *Verses on Bogue* [RLS's dog]
1, 2
Place/date of composition: Hyères, 1883–4
Source: {Bogue, a.k.a Wogg or Woggs, was a Skye terrier given to the Stevensons on their
return from America by Walter Simpson; on his visit to Hyères, Colvin noted that the
constant bad behaviour of 'the most engaging, petted, ill-conducted and cajoling little
thorough-bred rascal of his race, was turned by Stevenson into a matter of abounding delight
or diversion' (1921: 137).
MS: H2407 (Notebook 'D' pp. 66, 28: No. 1, sketched here among many CGV poems, may
have been intended as one.)
Unpublished

3. *To A Warrior Dead*
Date/place of composition: Bournemouth, 1886 (A battler to the end, Bogue died after a
dogfight at Skerryvore, still bandaged from injuries sustained in an earlier mismatch with a
much larger dog. This formally finished MS gives credence to the rumour that RLS intended
that his tribute be published, perhaps in *UW*.)
MS: MA1451, Pierpont Morgan Library
Unpublished

XXVI 'Ye chimney pots of London'
Place/date of publication: Samoan period, 1890–4 (Notebook 53 contains drafts of *Auld
Reekie*, written at this time, and other verses expressive of longing for the Scotland of his
boyhood. In letters of this period to Colvin and others who deplored his refusal to return to
the 'civilised' world of London, RLS sometimes contrasted the pristine Samoan environ-
ment with teeming, polluted London.)
MS: B7190 (Notebook 53)
Unpublished

XXVII *The Far Farers*
Place/date of composition: ?San Francisco, 1888 (on 28 June of this year the *Casco*, with
RLS, Fanny, Lloyd and Aunt Maggie aboard, sailed for the South Seas: Louis was never to
return.)
MS: B6215*
Printed text: *NP*, 187–8
Variants:
Line
10   <loved>^loud^ (B6215) loved (*NP*)
12   {B6215 offers three alternates for the initial word of this line: 'Sail' 'Return'
                              'Come'; *NP* has 'Return'}

XXVIII *The Fine Pacific Islands*
　(*Heard in a Public-house at Rotherhithe*)
Place/date of composition: Tahiti, August 1888 (*Longman's Magazine*)
Source: Andrew Lang's introduction to the poem as first published in his causerie, 'At the
Sign of the Ship', *Longman's Magazine*, January 1889: 'The next sea-song came to us from the
sea in an envelope with the postmark, "Taiohae Taiti, 21 Août, '88." The handwriting of
the address appears to be that of the redoubted Viking who sailed in John Silver's crew, who
winged *The Black Arrow*, and who wandered in the heather with Alan Breck. *Aut Robertus
Ludovicus aut Diabolus* sent the song, I presume, but whether he really heard it sung at
Rotherhithe, or whether he is the builder of the lofty rhyme, is between himself and his
conscience.'
{Lloyd performed this poem as a song the following February at a party in Honolulu hosted
by the Hawaiian King Kalakaua (see above, p. 511).}
MS: H2416
Printed text: *Longman's Magazine**; *R.L.S. Teuila* (1899); CP, 355–6
{Lang's MS is untraced; H2416 is a TS with inked corrections not in RLS's hand: its variants
are as follows:}
Line
　1　Yellowboy] Yellow-boy
　7　Hislands] hislands {so throughout}
　8　Peru:] Peru. {so throughout}
　10　Peru!] Peru. {so throughout}
　12　Mast'eaded] Mastheaded
　21　up,] up
　26　anew] anew,

XXIX 'As with heaped bees at hiving time'
Place/date of composition: ?Samoan period, 1891–4 (CP, p. 534)
MS: NLS 7482*
Printed text: CP, 321; NP, 189
{Both printed versions have been set up from the MS, a copy-text difficult to read.
The first four lines of 7482 are alternates for lines 9–12, written in the third rather than the
first person. MS variants follow:}
Line
10　twisting] {alt.} twisted
12　death pursuing it.] {alt.} <and death following>^ ~ ^

XXX *Early in the Evening*
Place/date of composition: Vailima, 1893 (*LETBM*, Vol. VIII, No. 2530: RLS sent the poem
with this letter of [30 January] 1893 to Burlingame for publication in *Scribner's Magazine*.)
MSS: B6175, B6176*: JAS reports a facsimiled MS in NYPL but that was not found.
First publication: *Scribner's Magazine*, Vol. XIII, May 1893
Printed text: CP, 319–20 (first publication of the complete poem in book form); Balfour
1901: I, 82 (lines 1–4), II, 173 (lines 13–16); NP, 219 (reprint of Balfour excerpts)
{B6175 is in B6022, 'First Drafts of Poems'; B6176, the copy-text, is fair copy for *Verses*
(B7165), so at one time this poem was to have been included in *UW* Book III. Collation of
these sources follows:}

Title: *Early in the Evening*] {untitled} B6175, *Early in the Spring* (*Scribner's*) *Song* (NP)

Line
1   foot ... foot] foot, ... foot, (Balfour)
2   spread,] spread: (*Scribner's*) (also line 6)
3   morning –] morning, (Balfour)
4   hope is on ahead.] hope's on ahead (B6175)
7   evening –] evening, (*Scribner's*)
9   life,] life – (B6175, *Scribner's*)
10 said,] said – (*Scribner's*)
14 red,] red – (B6175)

XXXI *Student Song*
First publication: *Scribner's Magazine*, Vol. LV, January 1914 (copyright 1913)
Printed text: NP, 255–6

Appendices

Appendix One: Stevenson's Notebooks and Copybooks

It is now difficult to know how many notebooks RLS used and whether or not they contained poetry since many of them were mutilated by G. S. Hellman and others, who sold the disbound leaves separately or distributed them, extravagantly packaged and priced, as 'collector's items'. There were at least forty-nine intact notebooks in the three-day Strong Sale at the Anderson Galleries, New York City, 1914–16. No fewer than twenty more were extant at that time in various public and private collections; most of them had been in Fanny's possession until her death in 1914. Fourteen of them are known by a single letter: A, C, D, F, G, H, I, M, P, Q, S, T, U and V; twelve are identified by a number, nos 51–62. Others have more complicated labels: 'Academic Exercise Book' (B6070); A.269, 'Verses used and incomplete' (B6050); 'First Drafts of Poems' (B6022); A.154, 'Book Poems and Essay' (B6123); 'Copy Book Containing Autograph Poems' (B6647); A.259 (H2406). As for the disbound notebooks, it is easier to determine that certain bound units existed than to reconstruct exactly what was in them. We know that RLS copied fifteen 'Pieces in Lallan' in one notebook (the contents list survives) and that *Songs* and *Little Odes* were once fair copies on consecutively numbered notebook pages (see above, pp. 395–6). There was a notebook section containing poems written in America during 1879–80 (B6705), another notebook with poems written in the South Seas (H2401) and ones called 'Public Law' and 'The Geometry Notebook' (still intact), in which the daydreaming student scribbled verses while attending lectures. BRBML has the covers and a few surviving pages from four disbound copybooks, as follows: A.264A 'Early Notes'; 'Early Verses 1872 etc.'; A.267 'Essays and Verses'; A.155 'Book full of poems'. Not all of these titles were assigned by RLS. We have some information about the contents of these volumes since G. S. Hellman thoughtfully inserted into these remains handwritten lists of the poems on the pages that he had torn out of them. McKay's Catalogue includes many details enabling us to reconstruct dismembered notebooks. For instance, we know that 'Early Verses 1872 etc.' included *Recruiting Songs* and a version of *Schumann's 'Frölicher Landmann'*. A.267 contained several ST titles. A.155 was annotated by Hellman as 'Original MSS of 83 Poems', which he listed with titles, numbers and notebook page numbers before he fabricated some eighteen 'volumes' from them: most of these have now found their way into BRBML.

Many of these notebooks provide a context, a frame for the verse they contain. Because RLS used them for shopping lists, scores of card games, homework assignments, drafts of letters and all sorts of mundane data, we can date some poems in them, or at least situate them in relation to people, places and events in the poet's life. We can also watch the poet working at his craft, over a period of time, at one poem or a series of them, experimenting, revising, discarding, condensing. He may start with a prose sketch, or 'cartoon', which he then converts to verse, or he may switch from blank verse to octosyllabics when the former isn't working. Some notebooks are journals containing the raw material for a collection: Notebook F (B6452) was the source of *An Inland Voyage* and some *UW* poems; Notebooks C (B6049) and D (H2407) contain between them drafts and contents lists for nearly all the poems in *PW* and *CGV*. If we can follow the convolutions and sudden leaps, we can gain insight into how this collection developed. RLS will leave one poem to begin another with no more than a space or a line between them; sometimes a poem is taken up again several pages later with a sketch for a prose story interposed. McKay's compilation of detail about the BRBML notebooks for his Catalogue, in which he assigns a number to each discrete unit of MS, often leads him to identify several units within the space of one page. This procedure at times prevents him from identifying groups of poems, and from recognising certain verse passages as continuations of other ones (see notes on *UW* XXVII and on *Epistle to Horatio F. Brown*).

To appreciate the interest and value of these notebooks, one should take a close look at them. The best-known one is C: it is available for examination, having been microfilmed complete (No. 870 at BRBML), reproduced on copyflo and extensively facsimiled in W. P. Trent's *Stevenson's Workshop*. Dating from 1880 to 1882, it contains most of the early poems written for *CGV*. Its eighty-eight numbered pages include thirty-eight poems with separate McKay numbers. Pages 54–65 have most of the *CGV* drafts. Experiments for the Brown epistle are spread across pp. 16–17 and 22–35, 293 lines that became 28. On p. 40 he wrote a prose account of a dream, then made it into a poem called *The Iron Steed* (see above, p. 600). In another section he has rattled off lines addressed to fellow-sufferers at the Alpine health resort at Davos, e.g.

> Talkers you'll find, all sorts, discreet and witty
> As Mrs Bradshaw Smith and me and Clitty
> So, undisturbed, we look and nod, read books,
> Or treat the scenery to adoring looks. (p. 8)

The 'Academic Exercise Book' (B6070) dates c. 1871–2. It has fifteen poems on eighteen leaves, all in pencil, mixed up with lecture notes on public and civil law, caricatures of the professors, memories of his trip to Italy and sketches towards short stories. On p. 15 the young poet essays the decadent idiom, scribbling twenty lines about spleen, 'maladie du siècle' and the like in the best manner of Baudelaire and Swinburne. Long, ranting drafts of socio-political protest, 'All influences were in vain' (*NP*, 95–6) and 'The old Chimaeras, old receipts' (below, p. 312) take up many pages. There are examples of RLS trying to torture prose into verse: one follows:
'O Italy I remember the boy who sang the proscribed song on the step of the [illeg.]. He sang it as blackbirds twitter. From a gracious, childish impulse ...'

> O Italy, as I look back
> At my [illeg.] stay with thee,
> It seems thy children twittered,
> He sang as blackbirds twitter
> Or sparrows take the wing
> And he sang a song of freedom
> From mere desire to sing!
> He set himself in danger
> A gracious childish impulse,
> A beautiful caprice

Nothing came of this attempt, which was abandoned. However, the textual notes above show that some of RLS's best poems began this way. A few prose phrases, like musical motifs, get worked up into a few stanzas, often with many clichés and overall banality of diction. With his best poems, the chaff is winnowed: the diction is sharpened, the structure is clarified and tightened, the rhymes purged of crudities, and the clichés and redundancies are eliminated.

Appendix Two:
Principal Editions of Stevenson's Poems and *Works* Including Poems

EDINBURGH EDITION. London: Chatto and Windus *et al.*, 1894–8. 28 vols; vol. XIV has the poems; Vol. XXVIII, *Appendix*, has miscellaneous poems including facsimiles of *Moral Emblems* and the woodcuts for *Robin and Ben*.

THISTLE EDITION. New York: Scribner's, 1895–1912. 27 vols. Vol. XVI has the poems; facsimiles of *Moral Emblems* etc. are included with this set.

POEMS AND BALLADS. New York: Scribner's, 1896. First separate collected edition; text is that of vol. XVI of *Thistle*.

R.L.S. TEUILA. Printed for private circulation by Mrs Isobel Strong, 1899. Contents listed in McKay, Vol. II, p. 307.

BIOGRAPHICAL EDITION. New York: Scribner's, 1905. 31 vols. Preface to most volumes by Fanny Stevenson.

POEMS. London: Chatto and Windus, 1908.

MANHATTAN EDITION. New York: Bigelow, Smith, 1906. 10 vols. Vol. 8 has the poems and an essay on them by Edmund Gosse.

HOUSEHOLD EDITION. New York: Lamb, 1906. 10 vols. The Casco and Marquesan Editions were produced by the Davos Press from these plates.

PENTLAND EDITION. London: Cassell *et al.*, 1906–7. 20 vols. Vol. XIII has the poems published in RLS's lifetime plus 20 pages of 'Additional Poems' selected by Gosse from periodicals, letters, books and MSS; some early poems and Davos Press printings are included in Vol. XX. Edited with an introduction and notes by Gosse.

SWANSTON EDITION. London: Chatto and Windus *et al.*, 1911–12. 25 vols. Edited with an introduction by Andrew Lang. The poems are in Vol. I.

NEW CENTURY LIBRARY EDITION. New York: Nelson, 1912. 6 vols; vol. VI has CGV and *UW*.

POEMS BY RLS, HITHERTO UNPUBLISHED. Boston: The Bibliophile Society, 1916. 2 vols. Printed for Members Only. Edited with an introduction and notes by George S. Hellman.

NEW POEMS AND VARIANT READINGS. London: Chatto and Windus, 1918. Foreword by Lloyd Osbourne. Contains poems from the two *BBS* vols.

MORAL EMBLEMS AND OTHER POEMS. London: Chatto and Windus, 1921. Introduction by Lloyd Osbourne.

POEMS BY ROBERT LOUIS STEVENSON, HITHERTO UNPUBLISHED. Boston: The Bibliophile Society, 1921. Printed for Members Only. Edited with an introduction and notes by George S. Hellman and William P. Trent.

VAILIMA EDITION. London and New York: Heinemann/Scribner's, 1922–3. 26 vols; vol. VIII has the poems including 'New Poems'; vol. XXV has 'Moral Emblems and other Poems' and vol. XXVI has 'Sonnets and the Light-Keeper' plus 'Additional Poems'. *Vailima* contains all the poems published in the three *BBS* vols, the 'Additional Poems' from *Pentland* and several selections previously unpublished. Edited by Will D. Howe and Lloyd Osbourne with prefatory material by Fanny Stevenson published in earlier Scribner's collections..

COMPLETE POEMS OF ROBERT LOUIS STEVENSON. New York: Scribner's, 1923. Contains all poems from *Vailima* plus some hitherto unpublished and reprints, for the first and only time, a number of poems from *Teuila*.

TUSITALA EDITION. London: Heinemann *et al.*, 1923–4. 35 vols. Poems are found in vols XXII and XXIII, the latter vol. containing, under 'New Poems', almost everything printed in any of the previous editions listed here; it does not include poems from *Tenila* or those published for the first time by W. H. Arnold. Prefatory material by Fanny Stevenson is reprinted for the first time in England from the Biographical Edition. Introductions by Lloyd Osbourne.

SKERRYVORE EDITION. London: Heinemann, 1924–6. 30 vols. A Library Edition of Tusitala.

SOUTH SEAS EDITION. New York: Scribner's, 1925. 32 vols. Edited by Lloyd Osbourne with material by Fanny Stevenson and Sidney Colvin. This is the US equivalent of Tusitala.

COLLECTED POEMS. London: Rupert Hart-Davis, 1950. Edited with an introduction and notes by Janet Adam Smith. Second Edition 1971. American Edition issued in 1971 by The Viking Press.

Appendix Three: Repositories Holding Poetry MSS

1. BEINECKE RARE BOOK AND MANUSCRIPT LIBRARY, YALE UNIVERSITY, CT. This is the largest and most complete collection of RLS books and MSS. The collection was formed by E. J. Beinecke, for whom this library is named, but it has been and continues to be augmented by gifts and purchases. The picture archive contains thousands of photographs of RLS with family and friends, and a group of original illustrations for CGV by many artists. The collection is exhaustively described by George L. McKay in his six-volume *The Stevenson Library of E. J. Beinecke* (New Haven, Yale University Press, 1951–64). This catalogue is being revised and supplemented by the Beinecke's Stevenson expert, Vincent Giroud.

2. THE HUNTINGTON LIBRARY, ART COLLECTIONS AND BOTANICAL GARDENS, SAN MARINO, CA. This collection holds MSS of thirty-two poems and several notebooks and fragments, including the very important Notebook D and the Cevennes Journal.

3. WIDENER COLLECTION, HOUGHTON LIBRARY, HARVARD, CAMBRIDGE, MA. Poetry holdings here are described by A. S. W. Rosenbach in *A Catalogue of Books and Manuscripts of Robert Louis Stevenson in the Library of the Late Harry Elkins Widener* (Philadelphia, 1913).

4. BERG COLLECTION, NEW YORK PUBLIC LIBRARY, NEW YORK, NY. There are MSS of ten poems here. The library also has rare privately printed materials, facsimiles of MSS and early editions of poetry volumes, some with variant bindings.

5. PIERPONT MORGAN LIBRARY, NEW YORK, NY. Here may be seen among several MSS three important ones: *Weir of Hermiston* includes the dedicatory verses to Fanny; signed and dated, there is the original MS of the ballad *The Feast of Famine*; there is also a MS of *To A Warrior Dead*, RLS's elegy for his dog Bogue, published for the first time in this edition.

6. FIRESTONE LIBRARY, PRINCETON UNIVERSITY, PRINCETON, NJ. There are eight poetry MSS in the Gerstley and Parrish Collections, a framed MS with hand-lettering that hung on the wall at Vailima and documents relating to publication, especially of ST, in the Scribner Archive. Princeton's RLS holdings have been described by Alexander Wainwright in *Robert Louis Stevenson: A Catalogue* (Princeton, 1971).

7. THE SILVERADO MUSEUM AND VAILIMA FOUNDATION, ST HELENA, CA. In recent years this ambitious library acquired much MS material, including the collection of Isaac Foot. There are MSS of thirty-eight poems and verse fragments here, notebooks and notebook pages, rare early editions and wonderful memorabilia, including RLS's lead soldiers.

8. STEVENSON HOUSE STATE HISTORICAL MONUMENT, MONTEREY, CA. RLS lived here from September to December 1879, waiting on Fanny's divorce. The library has most of the Scrapbooks of Margaret Stevenson, the poet's mother, who saved every piece by or about him that appeared in newspapers or periodicals. In the Scrapbooks are several printed poems not published in book form and MS poetry in the hand of Graham Balfour. Two Scrapbooks not at Monterey are among the small collection of Stevenson memorabilia at Saranac Lake, NY.

9. NATIONAL LIBRARY OF SCOTLAND, GEORGE IV BRIDGE, EDINBURGH. MSS of more than twenty poems are held here, some in Notebook T, along with

the Balfour papers containing several poems copied in Graham Balfour's hand from documents he brought from Vailima for use in his biography.

10. THE WRITERS' MUSEUM, EDINBURGH. Formerly known as the Lady Stair's House Museum, this library has MSS of five poems and extensive memorabilia including the printing press on which RLS and Lloyd produced *Moral Emblems*, and a version of the Nerli painting on which RLS wrote impromptu verses in Scots for the artist.

11. THE BRITISH LIBRARY, LONDON. In the Ashley Collection there is a complete MS of the ballad *Ticonderoga* and other items from Thomas J. Wise's Stevenson collection including the MS of his privately printed *A Familiar Epistle in Prose and Verse* and several rare editions of poems, all fully described in Wise's *Catalogue of the Ashley Library* (London, 1922–36).

12. ROSENBACH FOUNDATION MUSEUM, PHILADELPHIA, PA. There is an MS of *Ticonderoga* here earlier than the one in the British Library.

13. HAVERFORD COLLEGE, HAVERFORD, PA. The library has 'The Geometry Notebook', one of the most interesting of the surviving copybooks from RLS's student days; many of the pages are filled with verse.

This list is not intended to be complete; there are RLS MSS in such libraries as Stirling (University of London), Boston Public, Temple University, Alderman in Charlottesville, SC, and doubtless many more that I have not found.

Glossary of Scots Words

This glossary has been compiled by reference to *Chambers Scots Dialect Dictionary*, the *Concise Scots Dictionary*, *Dictionary of the Older Scottish Tongue* and the *Scottish National Dictionary*.

A

a' all
abüne above
ae/ane one
a-glee obliquely
ahint behind
aiblins possibly, perhaps
aince once
air' early
airn iron
ait oat, flute (of oat-straw)
ajee off to one side
amang among
astony astonishment
a'thegither altogether
auld-farrand old-fashioned
awa away
ay (-e) yes; always
ayont beyond

B

bairn child
ballants ballads, songs
bauld bold
beek bask
bee-skeps beehives
ben towards the inner part
bethankit God be thanked
bewast on the west side of
bicker oor feet rush
bield shelter
bien in good condition
bigg build nests

billy comrade
birks birches
birling whirling around
birstle warm oneself
bittock small bit
blad (blaud) beat down
blaff blast
blate diffident
bluid blood
bogle ghost
boll o'bear large measure of whisky
brae a steep slope of ground
brander grill
brangled shaking
braw good, well, fine
bree forehead, brow
brig bridge
buckie an obstinate person
burd-alane all alone (as the only child in a family)
burke destroy
burn stream, brook
busk dress in
buss thicket, bush
but and ben backwards and forwards ('but' is the outer and 'ben' the inner room of a two-roomed cottage)
byke beehive

C

ca' (caw) call, drive
cairn pile of stones (often marks a grave)
callant youth

caller fresh
cangle dispute
canna(-e) cannot
canny(ie) careful, shrewd, good
canty(ie) happy, cheerful
chap blow, stroke
chucky-stane pebble
clackan wooden hand-bat, racquet
claes clothes
cla(m)njamfry a rabble; a crowd; clutter up
clart muck; muddy
clavers idle talk, gossip
cleg horsefly
cleik link arms with
clerkit (clarkit) wrote
cock make a threatening gesture, or
   display ostentatiously
coft bought
collieshangie turmoil, uproar
cosh snug
couthy comfortable
cowpit ruined
crack chat, gossip
crouse cheerful
crowdie porridge
cuddy donkey
cuist cast, throw

D

danders cinders
daunder (dander) saunter, stroll
deevil/deil devil
deid dead
denty(ie) dainty
devel strike violently
ding, dung strike hard
dink dainty
dinled thundered
dirl spin, rattle
dod euphemism for God
doddered shaking
doer a factor, law agent, one entrusted
   with another's affairs
donnered stunned, stupid, dull
douce-stappin sedately walking
dour sullen, hard
dowie dismal

dozened dazed, stupified
draigled bedraggled
dram a small drink (usually of whisky)
dreid dread
droukin' drenching
drouthy given to drink
drucken drunken
dule sorrowful
dunt (dunting) knocking

E

eident diligent
Embro Edinburgh
ettle aim

F

fair'n food
fash injure, trouble oneself
fashious troublesome
fecht struggle against misfortune
feck a great quantity
fegs! faith!
ferlie a marvel
fisslin' fussing
flegs flies
fleyed excited
forjaskit exhausted
füsh'n energy
fyke fidget, fuss
fyle soil, defile

G

gaby (gabies) chatterbox
gae go
gaed went
gait (gate) manner, way
gane gone
gang go
gangrel vagabond, vagrant
gar cause to happen
gash respectable
gate path
tak the gate to set off
gaucy stately
gesterin swaggering

gey an' very
gie give
girr gird
glander glandular swelling in a horse
glaur mud, slime
gleg quickly; quick (adj.)
as glegs a gled as keen as a hawk
gliff glance
glisk glance
gloaming twilight
goavin wandering aimlessly
goo disagreeable taste
gowden golden
gowsty gusty, wild, stormy
grieve land-steward
ta'en the grue fed up
guid good
gutsy gluttonous

H

ha(-e) have
haar fog, mist
hairst harvest
hale whole
hame home
hanna(-e) have not
hantle a great deal
hash a mess
hasna(-e) has not
heed/heid head
hinderlands buttocks, behind
hingin' hovering
hinney/hinny honey
hirplin' limping
hirsle scramble
hirstle harass, push, bustle
hizzie hussy, frivolous girl, wench
hoast cough
hosen stockings
hotchin' moving rapidly
howdie midwife
howe hollow
hurdies hips, backside

I

ilka each, every

J

jaw torrent
jo (joe) sweetheart
jow ring a bell

K

keek glance
kerlie fellow
kilted/kiltit tucked-up (skirts)
kintry country
kirk church
kist o' whustles church organ
kittle puzzling
kye cattle

L

laigh low
Lallan the language of the Lowlands as
    distinct from the Gaelic spoken in the
    Highlands
land'art from the country
lane/my lane alone; by myself
lave rest, remainder
laverock skylark
law hill
leal just
lear knowledge, knowledgeable
lee-lang entire
leuch laugh
lift sky, heaven
limmer rascal
link scamper, trip, go briskly
linking arm in arm
lintie linnet
loan green pasture
lowse/lowsent unsteady

M

mair more
mane moan, lament
maun must
mauna(-e) must not
mavis song-thrush
mear mare
micht might
mirk dark
mishanters misfortune

muckle   great, big, much
muir   moor
mutch   close-fitting cap worn by married
   women

N

na(-e)   no
neist   next
neuk   corner, nook
neukit   cantankerous
weel neukit   securely ensconced in a corner
nirly   pinching cold
noo   now

O

orra   of no account
ower   over, too much, excessively
owercome   familiar
owre   over

P

paction   bargain
paidle   paddle, dabble
paiks   punishment
pat   pot
pawkier   wilier
peeries   marbles
pentit   painted
Peter Dick   a rhythmic pattern: two or
   three short beats, then one long
peyink   neat and trim in appearance
pickle   small amount
pinge   whimper
pitaty-par'n'   potato peel
pit-mirk   intense blackness of sky, dark as a
   pit
plat   garden plot
pliskie   practical joke
plowter   fumble about
pockmantie   travelling bag, portmanteau
poind/p'ind   seize goods
poke   pouch
pouch   pocket
pow   head
powrin'   pouring
prec(z)entor   in Presbyterian church, leads
   the singing

preen   pin
puir   poor
puss   hare

Q

quaere   question

R

ram-stam   unrestrained
rankit   strong
ravin'   talking volubly, nonsensically
rax   stretch, strain, help oneself to
reaming   churning, boiling
reek   smoke
reist   balk
ripin'   searching
roosty   raucous
rouch   rough
rowpit   sold at auction
rowstin   shout, roar
rowth/routh   abundance
take the rue   repent
rumbled   wrinkled
rumlin   rumbled
rummer   toddy-tumbler
ryve   rip

S

sae   so
sair   sore, sorely
sall sair   shall serve
sappy   fervid; over-sweet
sax   six
scaddit   scalded
scart   scratch
scaur   a steep hill
scowtherin'   blowing, hither and thither
scrog   gnarled stump
sculdiddry   fornication, obscenity
scunnered   shuddered
sea-gleds   gulls
shauchlin   shuffling, feeble
shilfa   chaffinch
shintie   golf-club
shouther   shoulder
shüit   suit
sicker   secure

siller silver

sindry asunder

sinsyne since then, from that time

skelloch screech

skelp slap

skink gruel, wishy-washy drink

skirling screaming, shrieking

slee sly

slocken quench

smoor smother

sneckdraw deceitful person

snell severe

snowkit sniffed

sonsie attractive

soo sow, pig

soopit swept

sooth hum, croon; wise saying (n.)

soundin' box a canopy over a pulpit to amplify the preacher's voice

souple skilful

southernwood medicinal plant

spang spring, stride, sudden leap

speir ask

spunk spirit

stacher stagger

staw satiate, disgust

stawsome disgusting

steer stir

steigh steep

steik (steek) shut

stench staunch

stend rush to

stirk stupid, oafish person

stogt saunter

stookit stooked: sheaves of corn cut into stooks (shocks) to dry

stot stupid, clumsy person

stow commotion

suld should

sweir reluctant

syndit washed off, rinsed

syne since, then

T

tae to, two

tautit unkempt, disorderly

tent neat in appearance

tenter portable shelter

theek protective covering of foliage

thocht thought

thole suffer

thrang crowded

thrapple throat

thrawn cross-grained, twisted, crooked

throu'ther mixed up together

tint perished, lost

tirl beat (a drum)

toon town

tosh well-turned out

trystit met

twine part

tyke dog

U

unco strange, uncanny

W

wab web

wae (waefü') sad, woeful

Waesucks Alas

wale select, choose, distribute

walie the best, fine, strong

wamble wobble

wanchancy unlucky

warstle wrestle

wauf good-for-nothing

waukrif' vigilant

waur worse

wean child

wear spend

weeg wig

weird destiny, fate, curse

wersh tasteless

wha/whae who, whom

whammle upset

whang clobber

whaup curlew

whaur where

wheen a good few

wheepit whipped

whiles sometimes

whin furze, or gorse

whinny overgrown with furze

wouldna(-e) would not
Wullywauchts hearty swigs
wund wind
wyled beguiled

Y

yammer (of a bird) utter repeated cries, chatter

yammerin' pain incessant, gnawing

yett gate
yin one
yince once
yirk perform in a lively way
yokes on starts a quarrel with
yon that one
'yont beyond
yowd wild
yowes ewes

Explanatory Notes

The following notes do not identify all the parallel passages, echoes and literary allusions which abound in RLS's poems. Specific reference to the circumstances in which poems were written will be found in the Textual Notes above; there, too, cross-references are made between the poems and other writings, especially RLS's letters. The numbers preceeding the notes are page references.

p. 23 *Alison Cunningham* (1822–1913): 'Cummy', daughter of a weaver of Torryburn, Fife, joined the Stevenson household as RLS's nurse when he was eighteen months old. They became devoted to each other, exchanging affectionate correspondence all their lives. The twin passions of thwarted motherhood and fanatical Calvinist piety made her influence on RLS enormous.

p. 28 *palanquin*: a boxlike litter for one person borne by means of poles resting on the shoulders of several bearers.

p. 61 *Willie and Henrietta*: These Balfour cousins (surnamed Traquair) were among RLS's favourite playmates: it is they who are remembered in CGV VII, *Pirate Story*. Together with other cousins, children of Margaret Stevenson's brothers who worked in India, they were often to be found at Colinton Manse, the home of their grandfather, the Rev. Lewis Balfour. Here they were looked after by his unmarried daughter, Jane Balfour (see next note). Fanny Stevenson speaks of Henrietta in her *Prefatory Note* to CGV: '[RLS] was especially happy in the companionship of two of his Edinburgh cousins, – Willie and Henrietta Traquair. As a little girl Henrietta already showed the characteristics that were her charm in womanhood. Never quarrelsome, and always cheerfully willing to take a secondary place, she nevertheless made her individuality felt, and threw a romantic glamour over every part she assumed. Even the wicked ogre, or giant, she endowed with unexpected attributes of generosity, and her impersonation of a chivalrous knight was ideal. When I last saw Henrietta, a few years ago, we both knew that she had but a little while to live, but the undaunted light in her eyes seemed to say: –

> "Must we to bed, indeed? Well then
> Let us arise and go like men."'
> (*VAIL*, Vol. VIII, p. 7)

p. 62 *Auntie*: Miss Jane Whyte Balfour (1816–1907), of Colinton Manse, is also remembered in CGV XV, *Auntie's Skirts*. For a full account by the poet of his childhood and the central role Aunt Jane played in it, see Balfour's Chapter III, 'Infancy and Childhood', which quotes extensively from the poet's 'Reminiscences of Colinton Manse' (1901: 34–61); see also his 1880 'Memoirs of Himself' which contains the following passage: 'There were thirteen of the Balfours, as (oddly enough) there were of the Stevensons also; and the children of the family came home to her to be nursed, to be educated, to be mothered, from the infanticidal climate of India. There must sometimes have been half a score of us children about the Manse; and all were born a second time from Aunt Jane's tenderness' (*VAIL*, Vol. XXVI, p. 214).

Minnie: This Balfour cousin, Cecilia Henrietta Balfour Buckland, had one of the *Little Odes* addressed to her: it was later included in *UW* as No. VIII. Although this poem is addressed to her 'in distant India', she was one of the children who came home to Colinton Manse, the 'old manse' of line 22 with its exotic curios treasured by RLS's grandfather Lewis Balfour. See 'The Manse' in *Memories and Portraits*, *EDIN*, Vol. I, pp. 155–7.

Sebastopol: a bloody battle was fought during the Crimean War over this city on the Black Sea, won by the British and their allies in September 1855; RLS was greatly agitated by this conflict, praying nightly for the British soldiers.

The nursery rhyme alluded to in this poem runs as follows:

> How far is it to Babylon?
> Three score miles and ten.
> Can I get there by candle-light?
> Yes, and back again!

p. 64　*My Name-child*: Louis Sanchez, named for the poet, was his nephew, son of Fanny's sister Nellie Sanchez. RLS was befriended by Nellie in California while he was extremely ill. He addressed *UW* X to Nellie and dedicated *Prince Otto* to her in 1885 (see above, p. 299).

p. 78　*K. de M.*: Mrs Katharine de Mattos (1851–1939), sister of RLS's cousin and childhood playmate Bob Stevenson, was an intimate friend; *UW* XIX is also addressed to her, as are the lines originally titled *Ave*, which, in a shorter version, became the published dedication of *The Strange Case of Dr Jekyll and Mr Hyde* (see above, p. 300). The 'Nixie Affair', in which W. E. Henley accused Fanny of plagiarising one of Katharine's short stories, destroyed the friendship between Katharine and RLS.

pp. 79–80　*Will. H. and Berthe Low*: American artist (1853–1932) and his wife who became friendly with Bob Stevenson (a fellow art student), RLS and Fanny in France during the 1870s: Low studied there, 1872–7, recording his experiences in *A Chronicle of Friendships* (1908). Widely known as illustrator for the *de luxe* editions of Keats' *Lamia* and *Sonnets*, he also wrote art criticism and was a founding member of the Society of American Artists.

p. 81　*H. F. Brown*: Horatio Forbes Brown (1854–1926). During the long winters at Davos, RLS delighted in the company of Brown and John Addington Symonds, both erudite and enthusiastic students of classical, especially Latin, poetry. See also the verse epistle written to him in alcaics *To Horatio F. Brown* (above, p. 292). A Highland Scot who took up residence in Venice, he became a historian of that city, publishing *Life on the Lagoons*, the book RLS is praising in *UW* XIII, in 1884. In a passage on the gondola (p. 103), Brown describes 'the *felse*, or little house, in which the passenger sits, secure from rain or wind'.
cis-Elysian: this side of the Elysian fields

Alma Genetrix: one of the names of Venus

Friulan: a reference to Friuli-Venezia Giulia, a north-eastern Italian region at one time controlled by Venice.

Paron Piero: Captain of the *Beppi*, a trading ship that sailed between Venice and the coast; in *Life on the Lagoons* (p. 354), Brown celebrates one journey when he was on board during which the staple diet was *castradina* (smoked mutton ham) with *polenta* [see copy p. 854].

p. 82   *sanhedrin*: RLS wrote 'sanhedrim', a common misspelling: it was the supreme Jewish court of justice in ancient Jerusalem, responsible for the trial of Christ.

pp. 82–3   R.A.M.S.: Robert Alan Mowbray Stevenson (1847–1900) was one of the most important figures in RLS's childhood and early life. High-spirited and imaginative like the poet, he shared fantasy play-worlds and the literature of romance with his lonely invalid cousin. Later, he supported RLS in his rebellion against bourgeois Edinburgh and strict religious codes, encouraging him to defy his father and become a writer. Bob was himself a painter, philosopher and art critic who introduced RLS to a diverse artistic community in Paris and Fontainebleau. The title means, 'And you have lived in Arcadia.'

The Blatant Beast: a monster in Spenser, *The Fairy Queene*, VI, xii.

Roland: hero of the French epic, *Chanson de Roland*

Achilles: hero of Homer's *Iliad*

Afreet: a demon of Islamic myth

Tristram, Bedevere: knights in Malory's *Morte d'Arthur*

Samarcand: storied city in Uzbekistan

Chiron: wise centaur, famous as the teacher of heroes, especially Achilles

Pelethronian antre: Pelethronium was a mountainous district in Thessaly which included Mt Pelion, Chiron's home; an antre is a cave

p. 84   *W. E. Henley* (1849–1903): poet, editor and literary journalist, a member of RLS's inner circle of friends. Despite severe physical afflictions, Henley was a robust and aggressive man who inspired the sometimes diffident RLS to do and dare in the literary world. He was the model for Long John Silver in *Treasure Island*.

p. 85   *while that Consuelo sung*: Consuelo was the young heroine who sang in Venice in George Sand's novel of that name (1842–3), which RLS read at Mentone; the mirror was Venetian.

p. 86   *To F.J.S.*: the cancelled MS working title for this poem was *To Claire* (p. 413). Hellman and other biographers (such as J. A. Steuart), out to debunk eminent Victorians, constructed a myth around 'Claire', a beautiful Scots girl with whom the poet became hopelessly infatuated and entangled: she was, variously, blonde or swarthy, a blacksmith's daughter or a prostitute. Their standards of research and evidence being as low as they were, they never noticed that 'Claire' was nothing more than the first of the poet's many romantic names for Fanny Sitwell (others were Consuelo, Amalia, Madonna and Mother). J. C. Furnas explained in detail how he discovered and exposed the truth about the 'Claire' fallacy but this has not entirely destroyed its influence (1951: 457–63).

p. 95   *A Portrait*: W. H. Mallock (1849–1923): author of *The New Republic* (1877) and *Is*

Life Worth Living? (1879), satirical attacks on those who undermine traditional religious values. RLS and his friends regarded Mallock as a dilettante.

p. 96   *Skerryvore*: the masterpiece of RLS's uncle Alan Stevenson, built 1841–3: 'From a distance it looks like the last surviving remnant of a petrified forest. Skerryvore has been described as the most beautiful lighthouse in the world. It is twelve miles from the nearest land and was built to be avoided' (Bathurst 1999: 142).

p. 99   *In Scots*: Nos I–III, V, VII–VIII, X–XI and XIII–XV (and Nos I–IV in the *More Pieces in Scots*) are written in 'Standard Habbie' or the 'Burns stanza', although it is a troubadour measure dating from the fifteenth century. Sir Robert Sempill's *Epitaph of Habbie Simson, Piper of Kilbarchan* (early seventeenth century) is the poem after which the genre is named. Not only Burns but also Ramsay and Fergusson established it as the quintessentially Scottish measure.

p. 100   *Tantallon*: a splendid ruined castle a few miles along the coast from North Berwick.

p. 101   *Ille Terrarum*: this title is taken from Horace, *Odes*, 2.6 13–14: 'Ille terrarum mihi praeter omnes angulus ridet.' It means 'More than any other [place] that corner of the earth has a smile for me.' RLS retreated to Dunblane in poor health after his law classes ended in April 1872; he wrote some sonnets here (e.g. nos 4–6 on pp. 262–3 dated at Dunblane and Bridge of Allan, 'one of my favourite places in the world, ... a meadow and bank at a corner on the river ... connected in my mind inseparably with Virgil's *Eclogues*' (*LETBM*, Vol. I, p. 222).

p. 103   *the law*: North Berwick Law, the 613-ft hill to the south of the village which was a favourite holiday place in RLS's boyhood. Davie and Cherlie were his cousins David and Charles Stevenson.

pp. 104–7   *A Lowden Sabbath Morn*: RLS's cousin Charles Stevenson recorded in his reminiscences that the church was the old parish church of North Berwick and that the two ministers were Peter MacMorland (1810–81; minister: 1865–73) and George Washington Sprott (1829–1909; minister: 1873–1909). This poem was recently printed on p. 97 of *Bright Lights: The Stevenson Engineers 1752–1971* by Jean Leslie and Roland Paxton (Edinburgh: 1999).
An' in their restin' graves (second last line): a favourite quotation from Patrick Walker, whose account of the Martyrs who 'went to their resting Graves' is quoted in the 'Greyfriars' section of *Edinburgh: Picturesque Notes*; Walker (1666?–1745?), who wrote on Presbyterianism and the Covenanters, was the author of *Six Saints of the Covenant*, ed. D. Hay Fleming (1901).

p. 108   *The Spaewife*: Fanny Stevenson writes: 'The *Spae Wife* may have been due to unconscious memory. In the Scotland of my husband's childhood, nurses sometimes crooned to their charges ancient airs whose origin is forgotten, and whose words were long ago lost. A Scotsman, Mr George St J. Bremner, of San Francisco, has kindly written out one that perfectly corresponds with the peculiar movement of the poem. He says: "This melody, I firmly believe, must have been running through Mr Stevenson's head when he wrote the *Spae Wife*. If ever words and music were especially adapted to each other, certainly this melody and the song fit each other like hand and glove. The upward cadence of the first three lines, suiting so exactly with the interrogative character of the words, and the coarse downward cadence of the last, suiting so exactly with the noncommittal answer of the "Spae Wife", leave no room for doubt that a reminiscence of one of "Cummy's" lilts was haunting him at the time"' (*Prefatory Note, VAIL*, Vol. VIII, p. 90).

p. 112   *Their Laureate to an Academy Class Dinner Club*: RLS wrote several of these ceremonial pieces: two others are printed above, pp. 321–4. 'Dux and booby' are, respectively, the brightest and dimmest students in the class:

> 'The Thompson Class Club' was composed of the old pupils of the Edinburgh Academy who belonged to the class of Mr D'Arcy Wentworth Thompson. This school followed the old Scots system under which a master every year began with a junior class, and carried it through the school. Every fourth year the master took up the lowest class, teaching it concurrently with a higher one. Every boy thus had the same class master through the whole of his school career, and the class was called after the master. RLS joined Mr Thompson's class in 1861, and left the Academy in 1863. It was the custom to form a sort of club of the old members of the class, who dined together once a year, and in his capacity of elected laureate of the 'Thompson Class Club' RLS contributed [these verses]. (Prideaux and Livingston 1917: 147–8)

pp. 113–15   *Embro Hie Kirk*: St Giles' Cathedral in Edinburgh: restoration was in progress from 1872; the church re-opened 23 May 1883. James Begg (b.1808), the Free Church minister referred to, died in September 1883, so the poem was presumably written before then, although that makes it difficult to understand RLS's assertion (written in his mother's copy of *UW*) that the poem was written in Edinburgh, since he spent 1883 in France. In a footnote to this poem in *EDIN*, Colvin identifies Begg and Niven as 'two Scotsmen celebrated for their pronounced Presbyterian orthodoxy'. Begg was a vehement anti-Catholic: he denounced hymn-singing and instrumental music in public worship as popery. The Very Rev. T. B. W. Niven (1834–1914) preached and wrote against the Church of Rome, the union of the Free and United Presbyterian Churches and the use of organ music in services of worship.

pp. 115–18   *The Scotsman's Return from Abroad*: Thomson and Johnson are inter-changeable *personae* created by RLS and Baxter for use in correspondence and conversation. They seem to be middle-aged church elders who are nevertheless dissolute and disreputable hypocrites. *Cocklerye*: a hill near Bathgate, where RLS had stayed with the Baxter family in July 1879 *Smith of Aiberdeen*: William Robertson Smith (1846–94), Scottish theologian whose advanced views on the Bible caused bitter controversy, resulting finally in his dismissal from his post as Professor of Hebrew at the Free Church College in Aberdeen.
the bonny U.P. Kirks: the United Presbyterian Church was formed in 1847 by a union of various bodies which had seceded from the Church of Scotland in the eighteenth century; in its turn it united with the Free Church in 1900 to form the United Free Church.

pp. 121–2   *To Doctor John Brown*: John Brown (1810–82), Scottish physician, surgeon and author. *Rab and his Friends* (1859) deals with the nature and ways of dogs, a favourite RLS topic.

Niel: Niel Gow was a famous Scottish fiddler who flourished in Atholl at the end of the eighteenth century; his 'laments' are heard wherever country fiddle music is played.

p. 127   *Dedication*: shortly after their arrival in Tautira, Tahiti, the Stevensons were staying in the house of the tribal sub-chief Ori a Ori as his guests. Fanny Stevenson writes:

> Ori is the very finest specimen of a native we have seen yet; he is several inches over six feet, of perfect although almost gigantic proportions, and looks more like a Roman Emperor in bronze than words can express. One day, when Moë gave a feast, it being the correct thing to do, we all wore wreaths of golden yellow leaves on our heads; when Ori walked in and sat down at the table, as with one voice we all cried out in admiration. His manners and I might say his habit of thought are English. In some ways, he is so like a Colonel of the Guards that we often call him the Colonel. It was either the day before, or the morning of our public feast that Louis asked the Princess if she thought Ori would accept his name. She was sure of it, and much pleased at the idea. I wish you could have seen Louis, blushing like a schoolgirl, when Ori came in, and the brotherhood was offered. So now if you please, Louis is no more Louis, having given that name away in the Tahitian form of Rui, but is known as *Terii-Tera* (pronounced Tereeterah) that being Ori's Christian name. 'Ori of Ori' is his clan name. (*LETBM*, Vol. VI, pp. 228–9).

pp. 152–8   *Ticonderoga*: In the Iroquois language the name of this village at the south end of Lake Champlain means 'between two waters'. In 1759 Fort Ticonderoga was captured from the French and their Indian allies by the British, but this narrative concludes with an unsuccessful attack in 1858. RLS's note (above, p. 166) attempts to decide a controversy over historical fact in favour of 'the muse', or poetic licence. In *The Athenaeum* for December 1887 (Nos 3137–40), Lord Archibald Campbell had claimed that RLS had unfairly appropriated the true story of his kinsman, Major Duncan Campbell, who had died in the raid of July 1858: he was later supported in this claim by Andrew Lang in Vol. I of the Swanston Edition of RLS's *Works*. H. Buxton Forman wrote in support of RLS and Alfred Nutt, on the grounds that it is foolish to argue about the historicity of details in myth and legend.

Fanny Stevenson describes the circumstances in which this poem was written immediately after the death of the poet's father in May 1887:

During the gloomy days that followed, my husband, who occupied the rooms that had been set apart for him in his boyhood, with the many evidences of his father's affection surrounding him on every side, – the books on the shelves, the childish toys still sacredly cherished, – found that he must turn his thoughts into other channels, or he would be unable to fulfill the duties that now devolved upon him. He resolutely sat himself at his desk and wrote *The Ballad of Ticonderoga*, the theme of which had already been discussed with his father before that fine intellect had become obscured by the clouds that settled round his last days. (*Prefatory Note*, VAIL, Vol. VIII, pp. 85–6).

pp. 173–4   *Cytherea*: one of the names of Venus
Hero: a beautiful priestess of Venus: her lover Leander would swim across the Hellespont to be with her, guided by a lamp she lit for him.
Eli: RLS is in error here: in Samuel I 3: 1–10, it is the boy Samuel who runs willingly to the 98-year-old priest Eli.

p. 177   *Joan and Darby*: the archetypal husband and wife who are deeply attached to each other, usually imagined as in advanced years and humble circumstances.

p. 178   *Mater Triumphans*: the mother triumphant.

p. 181   *Dr Hake*: Thomas Gordon Hake (1809–95) was one of Dante Gabriel Rossetti's physicians and a member of his literary circle, author of several volumes of poetry.

pp. 181–2   *To –*: The 'Felix' to whom this poem is addressed is Sidney Colvin (1845–1927), principal mentor and trusted confidant of RLS, editor of his letters and *EDIN* but also a much-loved friend. He and Fanny Sitwell (later Lady Colvin) encouraged and guided the young writer through much emotional turbulence. During the South Seas period (1888–94), Colvin fussed, from what RLS scornfully described as a 'Cockney' perspective, over what he saw as RLS's breaches of Victorian decorum in matters of race, sex and politics, but this poem expresses the depth of the writer's respect and love for him. *ST* XXXVII is also addressed to Colvin. 'Felix' means 'fortunate' but it has other connotations: see above, p. 503.

p. 184   *Khartoum*: RLS was outraged by what he considered to be bungling by the British government which had led to the death of the gallant General Gordon while defending this city, capital of the Sudan, against the forces of the Mahdi.

p. 191   *the sunny frontage of a hill,/ Hard by the house of kings*: Calton Hill and the nearby Palace of Holyrood; *this grated cell* is the Stevenson family tomb in the New Calton Burial Ground where the *artificers*, the 'lighthouse Stevensons', rest in a small building containing a bust of RLS's grandfather, Robert Stevenson.

p. 192   *island gods*: 'the two colossal images from Easter Island which used to stand under the portico' of the British Museum' (Colvin 1899: II, 165).

p. 193   *Childeric*: a legendary Germanic warrior of the Dark Ages, Conqueror of Visigoths, Saxons and other barbarians.

pp. 195–8   *The Woodman*: this poem is and is not Marvellian. There are echoes of *To his Coy Mistress* in lines 91–2 and 106, and of *The Bermudas* and *The Garden*; however, RLS is not, in this garden, escaping the oppressive realities of ordinary life but confronting them – his 'green thought' is one of horror.
yellow Hooghly's side: these two lines refer to the infamous Black Hole of Calcutta, as an earlier draft of the poem makes clear (see Textual Notes, p. 527): in 1756, 100–200 British prisoners were herded into a small room where more than half of them suffocated during a hot, airless night. The British perceived this event as an atrocity requiring vengeance. The Hooghly river flows through Calcutta.
Delhi ridge: site of a battle during the Indian Mutiny of 1857.

p. 201   *the graves of the martyrs*: S. R. Crockett (1860–1914) was a Scottish minister, journalist and novelist. In his last years, RLS's thoughts ran much on the Covenanters and their heirs, the subject of his unfinished novel *Heathercat*. *Weir of Hermiston*, also unfinished but widely regarded as his finest novel, engaged most of his literary energies towards the end.

Although it is set in 1813, the historical context for this powerful tale is the struggle of the Presbyterian Scots who opposed attempts by Charles I and II to control Scottish civil and religious institutions. The Covenanters in whom RLS was most interested were the 'martyrs', the extremists who refused to accept the religious settlement imposed in 1662 by Charles II. Savage government repression culminated in the 'Killing Times', a frenzy of slaughter in which, over a short period of months in 1685, almost a hundred radical Cameronians were summarily executed on the barren landscapes evoked in this poem. At sixteen, RLS wrote a pamphlet on the Rullion Green martyrs killed earlier, during the Pentland Rising of 1669.

pp. 208ff.   *Moral Emblems*: Lloyd Osbourne writes: 'Thus *Moral Emblems* came out; ninety copies, price sixpence. Its reception might almost be called sensational. Wealthy people in the Hotel Belvedere bought as many as three copies apiece. Friends in England wrote back for more. Meanwhile the splendid artist [RLS] was assiduously busy. He worked like a beaver, saying that it was the best relaxation he had ever found. The little boy [Lloyd] once overheard him confiding to a visitor: "I cannot tell you what a Godsend these silly blocks have been to me. When I can write no more, and read no more, and think no more, I can pass whole hours in blissful contentment"' (*Preface* to *Moral Emblems* (1921), London: Chatto and Windus, pp. xiii–xiv).

p. 233   *Siloam did not choose a sinner –* : An illustration by Christ in Luke 13: 4: 'or those eighteen, upon whom the tower in Siloam fell, and slew them, think ye that they were sinners above all men that dwelt in Jerusalem?'

p. 250   *Mange-Olive*: a dove-like bird, also called an oyster catcher.

p. 255   *Obermann*: fictional creation of French novelist Étienne de Sénancour (1770–1846), this melancholy ascetic retreated to the Swiss Alps to escape the pain inflicted on his sensitive soul by an uncaring world; thus, he is the opposite of Shakespeare's urbane and sensual Falstaff.

p. 261   Sonnets 1–3: during vacations, RLS's father sent him for experience to the firm's lighthouses-in-progress in the Hebrides and Orkneys. In 1870 he spent several weeks on Earraid, an islet connected to the Ross of Mull by a tide-washed spit of sand. There, a shore station was established to commence the building of one of the greatest Stevenson lighthouses, Dhu Heartach. See RLS's 'Memoirs of an Islet' (*EDIN*, Vol. I, pp. 164–70); 'The Education of an Engineer' (*EDIN*, Vol. I, pp. 306–16) and 'On the Enjoyment of Unpleasant Places' (*EDIN*, Vol. XXI, pp. 134–42).

p. 262   *O matre pulchra filia pulchrior*: Horace, *Odes*, 1.16 1, meaning 'O daughter more beautiful than her beautiful mother'.

p. 264   *Music at the Villa Marina*: This villa in Mentone, a resort in the south of France where RLS had been sent in 1873–4 for his health, was the residence of two Russian sisters, Mme. Sophie Garschine and Mme Nadia Zassetsky. Colvin reports that RLS became 'quickly and warmly attached' to these 'brilliantly accomplished and cultivated women', the former being 'an exquisite musician' (1921: 113–14). The poet addressed verses in Scots to them (above, p. 273).

p. 276   *Like Peden, followin' the Law*: Alexander Peden (1626–86), rebel Covenanter prophet who preached at conventicles; Patrick Walker wrote his biography.
writer lads: Writers to the Signet, Scottish solicitors (Baxter was a WS).

p. 278   *Charles Warren Stoddard*: American journalist and poet (1843–1909). Author of *Summer Cruising in the South Seas* (1874), he was admired as one of the few writers to have captured successfully the spirit of the South Seas. He approached RLS in search of his autograph.
Ne sutor ultra crepidam: 'Let the cobbler stick to his last' (Pliny).

p. 281   *Girolamo, Count Nerli*: Marchese Girolamo Ballati Nerli (1860–1926) was a painter active in Australia and New Zealand from 1886, doing portraits and landscapes in a fluid, impressionistic manner. In 1892 he visited Samoa, there completing several portraits of RLS in various media. The oil painting in the National Portrait Gallery of Scotland is now thought to be the original; a later version was sold to BRBML along with a MS of these verses. A pastel study at Princeton serves as frontispiece to *LETBM*, Vol. VII. See Mehew 1997: 500.

p. 286   *Napier*: John Napier (1550–1617) was a brilliant Scots mathematician, inventor and zealous Protestant sympathiser who lived at Merchiston Castle near Edinburgh.

p. 289   *Pereunt et imputantur*: one of RLS's favourite phrases from Martial; it occurs in this passage from *Epigrams*, V, 20: 'Bonosque/ Soles effugere atque abire sentit,/ Qui nobis pereunt et imputantur.' It means: 'And he feels the good days are flitting and passing away, our days that perish and are scored to our account.'

p. 291   *To W. E. Henley*: After RLS sent the poem to Henley, he rearranged and partly rewrote it. It was published without signature in *London* (of which Henley was editor) on 28 July 1877. Ten years later Henley allowed Gleeson White to print a number of his unsigned poems from *London* in *Ballads and Rondeaus*, acknowledging them as his. Henley eventually included this poem as his in *The Song of the Sword* (1892).
Lemprière: John Lemprière (d.1824) was a scholar whose *Biblioteca Classica* (1788) was for long the standard reference work on ancient gods.

p. 293   *Im Schnee der Alpen*: A line from Beethoven's *Adelaide*, an RLS favourite; he quotes it again in his *Pall Mall Gazette* essay, 'Alpine Diversions'.

A. G. Dew-Smith (1848–1903): An elegant gentleman of refined tastes, Dew, as his friends called him, delighted RLS with his conversation and appearance in the dreary environment of Davos-Platz. Colvin describes him as follows: 'tall, with finely cut features, black silky hair and neatly pointed beard, and withal a peculiarly soft and silken, deliberate manner of speech ... some dozen years later we found his outward looks and bearing, and particularly his characteristic turns of speech, with something of dangerous power which his presence suggested as lying behind so much polished blandness, evoked and idealised by Stevenson in his creation of the personage of Attwater in that grimmest of island stories, *The Ebb Tide*' (1921: 126–7). Colvin also annotates *dancing and deray* (line 3): '"The whole front of the house was lighted, and there were pipes and fiddles, and as much dancing and deray within as used to be in Sir Robert's house at Pace and Yule, and such high seasons." – See "Wandering Willie's Tale" in *Redgauntlet*, borrowed perhaps from *Christis Kirk on the Green* [anonymous sixteenth century Scots poem]' (1899: Vol. I, 184).

p. 294   *A river*: the Landwasser, no doubt the one RLS described in this passage from one of his *Pall Mall Gazette* Alpine pieces: 'a certain furious river runs curving down the valley, its pace never varies, it has not a pool for as far as you can follow it; and its unchanging senseless hurry is strangely tedious to witness. It is a river that a man could grow to hate' ('Health and Mountains', 17 February 1881).

p. 295   *sterling*: a series of piles defending the pier of a bridge (architectural term).

p. 297   *Kingston*: William H. Kingston (1814–80) was a well-travelled English author of adventure books for boys.

Ballantyne: Robert M. Ballantyne (1825–94), Scottish author of adventure stories for boys, wrote *Coral Island* in 1858: this novel features a fifteen-year-old boy who, like Jim Hawkins in *Treasure Island*, is captured by pirates.

Cooper of the wood and wave: James Fenimore Cooper (1789–1851), American author who went to sea for five years before turning to fiction; besides the famous *Leather-Stocking Tales*, he also wrote numerous sea stories.

p. 325   *John Cavalier*: Jean Cavalier (1681–1740) led the Protestants of the Cevennes, the Camisards, in their stand against the French king. RLS was fascinated by this baker's apprentice who, without military training but with a genius for war, was chosen brigadier of the Camisards at age seventeen. But he was no Joan of Arc: he abruptly left the cause and died, at fifty-five, the English governor of Jersey. MS B7095 (in Notebook C) is RLS's unpublished sketch towards a study of him; it contains the following: 'His was a mouth by which the spirit of God delighted to deliver oracles for the guidance of his people ... it was reserved for John Cavalier to fight in the open field and under the ramparts of cities, as upon a public stage. His, too, after all these futures and promises, was the staggering defection that concluded all. What ... the armies of the great Louis had fought against ... for two years, Cavalier's almost simple treachery brought to the ground in a few months. From the day of his seduction, the Camisaderie was more than doomed; to all intents and purposes, it was already at an end.'

Principal Sources

Anderson Auction Co. (1914–16), *Catalogues of the Isobel Strong Sales Parts I–III*, New York: The Anderson Galleries.

Arnold, W. H. (1923), *Ventures in Book Collecting*, New York: Scribner's.

Balfour, Graham (1901), *The Life of Robert Louis Stevenson*, 2 vols, New York: Scribner's.

Barker, Nicolas, and John Collins (1983), *A Sequel to 'An Enquiry': The Forgeries of H. Buxton Forman and T. J. Wise Re-Examined*, London: Scolar Press.

Bathurst, Bella (1999), *The Lighthouse Stevensons*, New York: HarperCollins.

Booth, Bradford A., and Ernest Mehew (eds) (1994–5), *The Letters of Robert Louis Stevenson*, 8 vols, New Haven and London: Yale University Press; Mehew's one-volume *Selected Letters* (1997) has additions and corrections.

Calder, Jenni (1980), *Robert Louis Stevenson: A Life Study*, New York: Oxford University Press.

Calder, Jenni (ed.) (1981), *Stevenson and Victorian Scotland*, Edinburgh: Edinburgh University Press.

Colvin, Sidney (1921), *Memories and Notes of Persons and Places*, New York: Scribner's.

Colvin, Sidney (ed.) (1899), *The Letters of Robert Louis Stevenson*, 2 vols, London: Methuen; new edition in 4 vols, 1911.

Craig, Cairns (ed.) (1987–8), *The History of Scottish Literature*, 4 vols, Aberdeen: Aberdeen University Press.

Daiches, David (1947), *Robert Louis Stevenson: A Revaluation*, Glasgow: MacLellan.

Daiches, David (1981), 'Stevenson and Scotland', in Jenni Calder (ed.), *Stevenson and Victorian Scotland*, Edinburgh: Edinburgh University Press, pp. 11–32.

Dalglish, Doris (1937), *Presbyterian Pirate: A Portrait of Stevenson*, London: Oxford University Press.

Dowling, Linda (1986), *Language and Decadence in the Victorian Fin de Siècle*, Princeton, NJ, and Guildford, Surrey: Princeton University Press.

Ferguson, DeLancey, and Marshall Waingrow (eds) (1956), *RLS: Stevenson's Letters to Charles Baxter*, New Haven, CT: Yale University Press.

Furnas, J. C. (1951), *Voyage to Windward: The Life of Robert Louis Stevenson*, New York: Sloane.

Garrod, H. W. (1929), 'The Poetry of R. L. Stevenson', in *The Profession of Poetry*, Oxford: The Clarendon Press.

Garrod, H. W. (1948), 'The Poetry of R. L. Stevenson', in *Essays Mainly on the Nineteenth Century*, London: Oxford University Press.

Golding, Gordon (ed.) (1978), *The Cevennes Journal: Notes on a Journey Through the French Highlands*, Edinburgh: Mainstream.

Gosse, Edmund (1908), *Biographical Notes on the Writings of Robert Louis Stevenson*, London:

privately printed; consists of Gosse's commentaries in the Pentland Edition of RLS's *Works*, which he edited in 1906–7.

Hammerton, J. A. (1903), *Stevensoniana*, London: Richards.

Hart, James D. (ed.) (1966a), *From Scotland to Silverado*, Cambridge, MA: Belknap Press of Harvard University Press.

Hart, James D. (1966b), *The Private Press Ventures of Samuel Lloyd Osbourne and R.L.S.*, San Francisco: The Book Club of California.

Hellman, George S. (1925), *The True Stevenson*, Boston: Little, Brown.

Jacks, L. V. (1935), *Mother Marianne of Molokai*, New York: Macmillan.

Katz, Wendy R. (ed.) (1998), *Treasure Island*, Edinburgh: Edinburgh University Press.

Kerrigan, Catherine (ed.) (1995), *Weir of Hermiston*, Edinburgh: Edinburgh University Press.

Kinsley, James (ed.) (1955), *Scottish Poetry: A Critical Survey*, London: Cassell.

Knight, Alanna (1985), *A Robert Louis Stevenson Treasury*, New York: St Martin's Press.

Lewis, Roger C. (1995), *Thomas J. Wise and the Trial Book Fallacy*, Aldershot: Scolar Press.

McClure, J. Derrick (2000), *Language, Poetry and Nationhood: Scots as a Poetic Language from 1878 to the Present*, East Lothian: Tuckwell.

McGaw, Sister Martha Mary (1950), *Stevenson in Hawaii*, Honolulu: Hawaii University Press.

McKay, George L., compiler (1951–64), *A Stevenson Library: Catalogue of a Collection of Writings by and about RLS Formed by Edwin J. Beinecke*, New Haven, CT: Yale University Library.

McLynn, Frank (1993), *Robert Louis Stevenson*, New York: Random House.

Maixner, Paul (ed.) (1981), *Robert Louis Stevenson: The Critical Heritage*, London: Routledge and Kegan Paul.

Masson, Rosalie (ed.) (1923), *I Can Remember Robert Louis Stevenson*, New York: Stokes.

Menikoff, Barry (1984), *Robert Louis Stevenson and 'The Beach of Falesá'*, Stanford, CA: Stanford University Press.

Milton, Colin (1988), 'Modern Poetry in Scots Before MacDiarmid', in Cairns Craig (ed.), *The History of Scottish Literature*, Aberdeen: Aberdeen University Press, vol. 4, pp. 11–36.

Neider, Charles (ed.) (1956), *Our Samoan Adventure: Fanny and Robert Louis Stevenson*, London: Weidenfeld and Nicolson.

Osbourne, Katherine (1911), *Robert Louis Stevenson in California*, Chicago: McClurg.

Osbourne, Lloyd, and Isobel Strong (eds) (1902), *Memories of Vailima*, New York: Scribner's.

Prideaux, W. F. and Mrs Luther Livingston (1917), *A Bibliography of the Works of Robert Louis Stevenson*, London: Hollings.

Rosenbach, A. S. W., compiler (1913), *A Catalogue of the Books and Manuscripts of Robert Louis Stevenson in the Library of the Late H. E. Widener*, Philadelphia.

Sanchez, Nellie (1920), *The Life of Mrs Robert Louis Stevenson*, London: Chatto and Windus.

Saposnik, Irving S. (1974), *Robert Louis Stevenson*, New York: Twayne.

Scally, John (1998), 'Robert Louis Stevenson: Unravelled Travel', *Scottish Book Collector*, 5: 12, 26–7.

Sharp, William (1886), *Sonnets of This Century*, London: Walter Scott.

Shorter, Clement (1915), *Poetical Fragments by Robert Louis Stevenson*, London: privately printed.

Smith, Janet Adam (ed.) (1950), *Robert Louis Stevenson: Collected Poems*, London: Rupert Hart-Davis; second edition 1971.

Swearingen, Roger (1980), *The Prose Writings of Robert Louis Stevenson: A Guide*, Hamden, CT: The Shoe String Press (Archon).

Swinnerton, Frank (1914), *Robert Louis Stevenson: A Critical Study*, London: Martin Secker (repr. Port Washington, NY: Kennikat Press).

Trent, W. P. (1921), *Stevenson's Workshop*, Boston: Boston Bibliophile Society.

Wainwright, Alexander D., compiler (1971), *Robert Louis Stevenson: A Catalogue*, Princeton, NJ: Princeton University Library.

White, Gleeson (1892), *Letters to Eminent Hands*, Derby: Frank Murray.

Wise, Thomas J., compiler (1922–36), *A Catalogue of the Ashley Library*, 11 vols, London: Printed for Private Circulation (repr. London: Dawson's).

Wittig, Kurt (1958), *The Scottish Tradition in Literature*, Edinburgh: Oliver and Boyd.

Index of First Lines

General Index

THE CENTENARY EDITION OF ROBERT LOUIS STEVENSON

Over a century after his death, Robert Louis Stevenson remains an internationally popular writer. This edition of his selected works aims to give scholars, students and general readers authoritative texts with full introductions, textual and explanatory notes, and editorial commentary. For the first time Stevenson's original texts are available in a modern format, without the errors and misreadings of the first editions.

'The editors' claim that for accuracy, authority and authenticity, the Edition improves on all previous editions is well supported. The commentary and notes, explanatory and textual, lead the reader through the various stages of the work from its conception in RLS's mind up to its production in manuscript and printed form. The text itself is free from editorial signals and can be read for pure pleasure. Further instalments will be eagerly awaited.'

Books in Scotland

Strange Case of Dr Jekyll and Mr Hyde
Robert Louis Stevenson
Edited by Richard Dury

Edinburgh University Press is delighted to announce a new scholarly edition of Robert Louis Stevenson's popular novel, *Strange Case of Dr Jekyll and Mr Hyde.*

This story of a double-life in which the protagonist by day worked as a respectable doctor and by night roamed the back alleys of old-town London, was first published as a 'shilling shocker' in 1886 and became an instant classic. In the first six months of publication 40,000 copies were sold, and it remains one of the best tales ever written about the divided self.

Despite there being numerous paperback editions of this novel in print, this will be the only scholarly edition available.

Additional features include:

* Two pre-publication drafts of the novel to appear in an appendix
* Detailed information about the novel's production and reception

About the Author

Richard Dury is Associate Professor at the University of Brescia, Italy. He is editor of *The Annotated Dr Jekyll and Mr Hyde* (Guerini, 1993), and author of *English Alliterative Phrases* (Stefanoni, 1996) and *History of the English Language* (CELSB, 1996).

June 2004   256pp   Hardback   0 7486 1518 0   £30.00

Order from Marston Book Services, PO Box 269, Abingdon, Oxon OX14 4YN
Tel 01235 465500 • Fax 01235 465555 • E: direct.order@marston.co.uk
Visit our website www.eup.ed.ac.uk

R L Stevenson on Fiction
An Anthology of Literary and Critical Essays
Glenda Norquay

A fascinating range of Robert Louis Stevenson's essays on fiction. Better known now for the fiction he wrote himself than for his essays on the subject, this material nevertheless provides an illuminating insight to the thoughts on the craft of writing from one of Scotland's most famous literary figures. Such writings have hitherto been scattered throughout editions of his collected works; here they are brought together in a new and enlightening conjunction.

Essays selected include 'A Humble Remonstrance', 'A Gossip on Romance', 'Books which have Influenced Me', 'A Chapter on Dreams' and 'Popular Authors'. They reveal Stevenson's fascination with the process of creativity and the imagination, his interventions in contemporary debates over realism, his exploration of literary hierarchies, his theories of narrative desire, and the pleasures and influences he derived from his own reading.

Glenda Norquay introduces this collection with a fascinating and broad-ranging discussion of Stevenson's essay writing. Each essay is also introduced by a brief preface and the highly specific references within the essays are backed up with explanatory notes, making the Anthology accessible to a wide readership.

'It is Norquay's alertness to the complexities of Stevenson's discursive writing that situates this edition high and above what might otherwise have been a mere compilation… Norquay's editorial management, with its unrelenting attention to detail and studious clarity, benefits this edition tremendously. The format of this book is particularly effective. Each essay is preceded by a short preface giving details of production, publication and reception. Likewise, the essays have been annotated with exceptional thoroughness… rarely in recent times has Stevenson's work been handled so rigorously.'
Scottish Literary Journal

'The volume does valuable service by bringing together essays that have until now been available only in various editions of Stevenson's collected works. Norquay's well-written introduction to Stevenson's essay-writing is one of the book's attractions… This book is of interest both to scholars and to ordinary readers wishing to go beyond Stevenson's novels and poems.'
The Year's Work in English Studies

June 1999 224pp Paperback 0 7486 07773 £14.00

***Order from* Marston Book Services, PO Box 269, Abingdon, Oxon OX14 4YN**
Tel 01235 465500 • Fax 01235 465555 • E: direct.order@marston.co.uk
Visit our website www.eup.ed.ac.uk

All details correct at time of printing but subject to change without notice

The Edinburgh Edition of the Waverley Novels
Editor-in-Chief: David Hewitt, University of Aberdeen

At last – a complete, critically edited edition of the Waverley Novels as Scott originally wrote them!

The first of Scott's Waverley novels burst upon an astonished world in 1814. Its publication marked the emergence of the modern novel in the western world, influencing all the great nineteenth-century writers. This handsome new edition of Sir Walter Scott's novels captures the original power and freshness of his best-loved novels.

Find Out What Scott *Really* Wrote

Going back to the original manuscripts, a team of scholars has uncovered what Scott originally wrote and intended his public to read before errors, misreadings and expurgations crept in during production. The *Edinburgh Edition* offers you

- A clean, corrected text
- Textual histories
- Explanatory notes
- Verbal changes from the first-edition text
- Full glossaries

A Legend of the Wars of Montrose	Hb	0 7486 0572 X	£40.00
Anne of Geierstein	Hb	0 7486 0586 X	£40.00
Chronicles of the Canongate	Hb	0 7486 0584 3	£40.00
Guy Mannering	Hb	0 7486 0568 1	£40.00
Ivanhoe	Hb	0 7486 0573 8	£40.00
Kenilworth	Hb	0 7486 0437 5	£40.00
Quentin Durward	Hb	0 7486 0579 7	£40.00
Redgauntlet	Hb	0 7486 0580 0	£40.00
Rob Roy	Hb	0 7486 0569 X	£40.00
Saint Ronan's Well	Hb	0 7486 0535 5	£40.00
The Abbot	Hb	0 7486 0575 4	£40.00
The Antiquary	Hb	0 7486 0537 1	£40.00
The Black Dwarf	Hb	0 7486 0451 0	£40.00
The Bride of Lammermoor	Hb	0 7486 0571 1	£40.00
The Fair Maid of Perth	Hb	0 7486 0585 1	£40.00
The Heart of Mid-Lothian	Hb	0 7486 0570 3	£40.00
The Monastery	Hb	0 7486 0574 6	£40.00
The Pirate	Hb	0 7486 0576 2	£40.00
The Tale of Old Mortality	Hb	0 7486 0443 X	£40.00
Woodstock	Hb	0 7486 0583 5	£40.00

Order from Marston Book Services, PO Box 269, Abingdon, Oxon OX14 4YN
Tel 01235 465500 • Fax 01235 465555 • E: direct.order@marston.co.uk
Visit our website www.eup.ed.ac.uk

All details correct at time of printing but subject to change without notice

Related Reading from Edinburgh University Press

The Stirling/South Carolina Research Edition of the Collected Works of James Hogg

General Editors: Douglas S Mack, Professor of English at the University of Stirling and Gillian Hughes, James Hogg Research Fellow at the University of Stirling

After a hundred years of relative obscurity, James Hogg (1770-1835) now ranks alongside Scott and Stevenson as one of Scotland's leading writers. Highly regarded in his own lifetime, Hogg's reputation suffered as a result of bowdlerised posthumous editions of his work. Edinburgh University Press is proud to present the first modern authentic edition of Hogg's work, uncovering the full extent of his literary talents. Full introductions, explanatory notes and editorial comment accompany each text, making this collected edition the standard work on one of Scotland's leading nineteenth-century writers.

'These volumes are beautifully produced ... each comes with an introduction, notes and a glossary... It is hard to see how they could be bettered ... It is wonderful that at last we are going to have a collected edition of this important author without bowdlerization or linguistic interference.'
Studies of Scottish Literature

A Queer Book	Hb	0 7486 0506 1	£40.00
Altrive Tales	Hb	0 7486 1893 7	£40.00
Anecdotes of Scott	Hb	0 7486 0933 4	£40.00
Contributions to Literary Annuals	Hb	0 7486 1527 X	£40.00
Jacobite Relics Volume I	Hb	0 7486 1592 X	£60.00
Jacobite Relics Volume II	Hb	0 7486 1591 1	£60.00
Lay Sermons	Hb	0 7486 0746 3	£40.00
Mador of the Moor	Hb	0 7486 1807 4	£40.00
Queen Hynde	Hb	0 7486 0934 2	£40.00
Tales of the Wars of Montrose	Hb	0 7486 0635 1	£40.00
Tales of the Wars of Montrose	Pb	0 7486 6318 5	£8.99
The Private Memoirs and Confessions of a Justified Sinner	Hb	0 7486 1414 1	£40.00
The Private Memoirs and Confessions of a Justified Sinner	Pb	0 7486 6315 0	£8.99
The Queen's Wake	Hb	0 7486 1617 9	£40.00
The Shepherd's Calendar	Hb	0 7486 0474 X	£40.00
The Shepherd's Calendar	Pb	0 7486 6316 9	£8.99
The Spy	Hb	0 7486 1417 6	£70.00
The Three Perils of Woman	Hb	0 7486 0477 4	£40.00
The Three Perils of Woman	Pb	0 7486 6317 7	£9.99
Winter Evening Tales	Hb	0 7486 1556 3	£40.00

Order from Marston Book Services, PO Box 269, Abingdon, Oxon OX14 4YN
Tel 01235 465500 • Fax 01235 465555 • E: direct.order@marston.co.uk
Visit our website www.eup.ed.ac.uk

All details correct at time of printing but subject to change without notice